Foundations of Sensation and Perception

Third Edition

George Mather

 Routledge
Taylor & Francis Group

LONDON AND NEW YORK

Third edition published 2016
by Routledge
2 Park Square, Milton Park, Abingdon, Oxon, OX14 4RN

and by Routledge
711 Third Avenue, New York, NY 10017

Routledge is an imprint of the Taylor & Francis Group, an informa business

First edition published by Psychology Press 2006.
Second edition published by Psychology Press 2009.

British Library Cataloguing in Publication Data
A catalogue record for this book is available from the British Library

ﺗ07580187
Library of Congress Cataloging-in-Publication Data
Mather, George.
    Foundations of sensation and perception / George Mather. — Third edition.
        pages cm
    Includes bibliographical references and index.
    ISBN 978-1-84872-343-6 (hb) — ISBN 978-1-84872-344-3 (soft cover)
    1. Perception.   2. Senses and sensation.   I. Title.
    BF311.M4255 2016
    153.7—dc23
    2015016124

ISBN: 978-1-84872-343-6 (hbk)
ISBN: 978-1-84872-344-3 (pbk)
ISBN: 978-1-31567-223-6 (ebk)

Typeset in Times New Roman
by Apex CoVantage, LLC

Printed by Bell and Bain Ltd, Glasgow

MIX
Paper from
responsible sources
FSC® C007785

Contents

Preface to the third edition

The third edition has given me the opportunity to update the text and to incorporate the many helpful comments I received on the second edition. I hope that the changes significantly improve the book as a resource for students of sensation and perception.

As in previous editions, the book starts with the so-called minor senses and then moves on to hearing and vision, before dealing with several topics that span the senses: multisensory processing, attention, and individual differences. However I've made two changes to the sequence of chapters in the text. The chapter on color vision has moved from Chapter 12 to Chapter 8 so that rather than following on from motion perception, it now follows on more coherently from the material on visual physiology in Chapter 7. Also there is a new chapter (14) on attention and perception, which replaces and significantly expands the material on attention which was covered in the tutorial section of Chapter 13. In addition, three other chapters have been restructured, with new and/or reordered chapter sections to add material and improve the flow of the discussion: Chapter 1 (introduction), Chapter 11 (depth perception), and Chapter 12 (motion perception).

In this third edition I have tried to stay true to the aims I had in mind when writing the first and second editions. When reading other textbooks I was often less than satisfied with assertions about specific aspects of sensation and perception which were made without reference to a source, a primary reference which the reader could consult for confirmation and for more detail. So, by the second edition the text included over 600 references and I have added a further 200 references in this edition. I certainly would not expect any one reader to consult a significant proportion of these references but they are there to give the reader the option to do so as and when they need more detail and a primary source.

Another aim I had in mind was to introduce areas of the subject which are not normally covered in student texts, yet which are crucial for anyone wishing to understand or conduct research. Lack of knowledge in these areas can lead to misunderstandings and misconceptions becoming entrenched. Some of the tutorials are intended to fill this gap. For example, there are introductory tutorials in the hearing and vision chapters on the basic principles of Fourier analysis. This mathematical technique is fundamental in many areas of science and engineering, but textbook coverage of it usually assumes a high degree of mathematical competence. The Fourier tutorials assume relatively little formal training in math. Similarly there are non-technical tutorials on optics, light measurement, and Bayesian inference which are not in themselves essential for understanding the text but become much more important when one wishes to understand some of the details of research studies. Apart from these more technical topics, other tutorials discuss areas which tend not to be covered in student texts because they are slightly outside of the mainstream or are more controversial. Examples include music perception, consciousness, and individual differences in artists.

I am indebted to all of the reviewers who provided such detailed and helpful comments on the second edition, which I have tried to incorporate in the third edition. I am also grateful to the editorial and production team at Psychology Press, who have done an excellent job as usual. Though the fault for any remaining errors and problems with readability and intelligibility is entirely my own.

Finally, I would like to dedicate the book to Anne, whose patience and support were so important during the production of all three editions.

The companion website

Web-based supplementary materials to accompany *Foundations of Sensation and Perception, Third Edition*

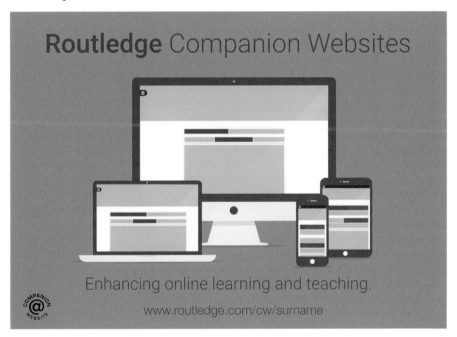

The companion website offers an array of supplementary materials for students and instructors.

Student Resources include:

- Animations and simulations of key perceptual phenomena
- Chapter summaries
- Multiple-choice and gap-fill quizzes
- Flash cards to test definitions of key terms.
- A comprehensive chapter-by-chapter glossary of key terms used in the book.

Access to the Student Resources is freely available and free-of-charge.

Instructor Resources include:

* A testbank of multiple-choice questions.
* A set of short-answer questions per chapter to stimulate discussion
* The figures from the book.

Access to the Instructor Resources is restricted to instructors only by password protection. These resources are free of charge to qualifying adopters.

Please visit www.routledge.com/cw/mather

General principles

1

Contents

INTRODUCTION

From a subjective standpoint, there seems to be little to explain about perception. Our perception of the world is direct, immediate, and effortless, and there is no hint of any intervening operations taking place in the brain. The apparent simplicity of perception is reinforced by the fact that our perceptions are almost always accurate. We rarely make mistakes when identifying people by their face or voice, or in judging how hot a cup of tea is, or in navigating a flight of steps. Moreover, our own perceptions nearly always agree with those of other people. Sounds, sights, and smells seem to be "out there" in the world, not constructed in our head.

Despite appearances to the contrary, our perceptual world is constructed in the brain by a huge mass of neurons performing complex, but hidden, operations. Three observations hint at the complexity of the brain processes involved in perception. First, a large proportion of the brain's most highly developed structure, the cerebral cortex, is devoted entirely to perception. Vision alone consumes over half of the neurons in the cortex. Second, despite the complexity and power of modern computer

KEY TERM

Prosopagnosia
A clinical condition resulting from brain damage, in which a patient is unable to recognize familiar faces.

technology, computer scientists have not yet succeeded in building general-purpose systems with the perceptual proficiency of even an infant. Relatively confined problems, such as detecting abnormalities in medical images, identifying a face or a voice, or guiding an autonomous vehicle, have proven to be formidable problems to solve by computer (see Huang, 2005). Third, as a result of brain damage through injury or disease, a small number of unfortunate individuals suffer deficits in their perceptual capabilities. These deficits can be very specific and debilitating, but also dramatic and perplexing to other people. It seems difficult to believe that someone can fail to recognize their own face reflected in a mirror (**prosopagnosia**), or cannot judge the position of their limbs without looking directly at them. Such people remind us of the sophisticated brain processes serving perceptual abilities that most of us take for granted.

Spectator sports provide a very clear example of the reliability, and occasional fallibility, of the information extracted by our perceptual systems. Everyone involved—participants, referees/umpires, and spectators—must make perceptual judgments in order to interpret events on the sports field, and to decide what should happen next. Did the tennis ball bounce out of court? Did the football cross the goal line and enter the goal? All those involved nearly always agree on what happened, because their perceptual systems arrive at the same decisions. Sporting activities would not be viable either for participants or for spectators without reliable perceptual systems. Certain critical judgments do require special skills and observation conditions. For instance, net-cord judges were once used in professional tennis tournaments to decide whether the ball delivered by the serving player had struck the top edge of the net (the net-cord) on its way across the court. They relied on a combination of three senses—sight (deflection of the ball in flight), sound (the impact of the ball on the net), and touch (vibration of the net). As a result, the net-cord judge could detect the slightest of contacts between ball and net that were missed by most or all of the spectators. Professional courts now use an electronic net-cord sensor rather than a human observer; the sensor picks up the tiny vibrations caused by the ball (the first version of the sensor, introduced in the 1970s was the pick-up from an electric guitar).

? Think of other reasons for disagreements between spectators about the same sporting incident.

Perceptual judgments are not infallible, as demonstrated by the disagreements between participants or observers that can and do arise in many sports. Such disagreements can offer hints about the nature of the underlying perceptual processes (as well as providing additional entertainment; see Figure 1.1). Common sources of disagreement involve decisions about whether a ball crossed a line on the sports field, such as whether a tennis ball bounced inside a court line. Participants often reach contradictory decisions in "close" calls. This disagreement is not simply a reflection of differences in skill or concentration level, or gamesmanship, but a natural consequence of the inherent variability in our perceptual decisions. In optimal conditions, perceptual responses are highly reliable, both within and between observers. When a ball bounces some distance to one side of a line, there is no disagreement as to where it bounced. However,

FIGURE 1.1
Fine sensory discriminations during sporting activities probe the limits of our perceptual abilities. Disagreements can arise from the inherent variability of sensory signals. Copyright © Brian Snyder/Reuters/Corbis.

psychophysical research has taught us that in marginal conditions when stimuli are very close together or indistinct, perceptual responses are probabilistic. When a ball bounces slightly to the left of a line, the response of the perceptual system itself will sometimes lead to a "left" response, and other times lead to a "right" response. As a result, different observers are likely to disagree a certain proportion of the time. Perceptual research aims to estimate the precise degree of uncertainty attached to perceptual judgments, and to identify its likely causes (see Mather, 2008).

SENSATION, PERCEPTION, AND SENSORY MODALITY

Sensations are simple conscious experiences generated by stimulation of a sense organ such as the eye: Your awareness of the brightness of a camera flash, or the sourness of a lemon, or the sharpness of a pinprick are all sensations. Perceptions are complex, meaningful experiences of objects and events. Sensations are immediate and automatic, whereas perceptions can take time to reach a stable state, and may require effort. For instance, at one of the sports events described earlier you may sense the green color of the grass, or the loudness of the public address system, but you perceive the identities of the players on the court or pitch, and the way their actions are interconnected.

Philosophers and psychologists call simple sensations **qualia** because they relate to the qualities of conscious experiences. By their very nature, qualia are private, and accessible only to the person who has them. Most researchers believe that qualia map onto specific brain states or functions of brain states. For example, there is a specific brain state associated with the sensation of the color red. If your sensation of color changed to, say, green, there would be a corresponding change in brain state. The assumed link between sensations and brain states lies at the very foundation of modern theories of perception, as will become clear below. However, an "explanatory gap" (Levine, 1983, 1999) remains between the physical world (brain states) and the mental world (sensations). No one has been able to explain precisely how the qualitative nature of sensation can be explained by reference to neural activity.

Qualia divide up the sensory world into qualitatively different modes of sensation, also known as **sensory modalities**. The sensations evoked by light, for example, are qualitatively different from those evoked by sounds, touches, or smells. There is no possibility of us confusing a visual sensation with an auditory one, but it is possible to confuse one auditory sensation with another (for instance, within limits you cannot discriminate between two sounds of different intensities). One of the most fundamental questions one can ask about sensation is: "How many different sensory modalities do we have?" The answer is important because it determines the divisions which perceptual science should respect when seeking explanations. For instance, we cannot investigate how the different senses interact (as we do later in the book) without first distinguishing between them as separate modalities.

Since the time of Aristotle, common sense has divided the sensory world into five modalities—seeing (vision), hearing (audition), touch (somatosensation), smell (olfaction), and taste (gustation)—on the basis of visible sense organs (eye, ear, skin,

KEY TERMS

Psychophysics
The scientific study of the relationship between physical stimulation and perceptual experience.

Qualia
Primitive mental states, such as sensory impressions induced by stimulation of a sense organ (e.g., loudness, brightness, heat).

Sensory modality
A mode of sensation that is qualitatively different from other modes, so its sensations cannot be confused with those of other modalities; for example, the experience of seeing is qualitatively different from that of hearing or touching.

nose, tongue). However we must consider another four candidate modalities for this list, none of which have visible sense organs. The sense of balance (vestibular sense) is now recognized as a distinct modality, for reasons that will become clear below, and three more modalities relate to sensory awareness of the body: The sense of body position (proprioception), the sense of body motion (kinesthesis), and the sense of pain (nociception).

The criteria for distinguishing between the different sensory modalities are summarized in Table 1.1. Seeing, hearing, and balance are easy to distinguish in physical terms, because they detect different forms of energy (electromagnetic radiation, air pressure waves, and motive force, respectively). Although smell and taste both detect chemical contact, they qualify as different modalities in the sense that they have different neural pathways. Touch, body position, and body motion do not really qualify as distinct modalities because they share a neural pathway and cortical destination. The status of pain as a distinct sensory modality is not clear-cut because it does have separate receptors and pathways but it shares the same cortical destination as the other body senses. Overall we can enumerate seven major sensory modalities, which are listed in Table 1.1 according to their scientific name: Audition (hearing), gustation (taste), nociception (pain), olfaction (smell), somatosensation (touch), the vestibular sense (balance), and vision (seeing). Nociception, somatosensation, and the vestibular sense will be discussed together in Chapter 3 as "the body senses."

All the senses require receptor cells which convert energy from the outside world (light, sound, and so on) into electrical nerve impulses. As the third column of Table 1.1 shows, there are just four basic types of receptor, though the number of receptor cells varies markedly between the modalities. Audition is based on surprisingly few receptors (about three and a half thousand in each ear), in contrast to the 125 million photoreceptors in each eye. Later chapters will consider what information is carried in the receptor signals, and how the brain interprets them.

Receptor signals are carried to the brain along a number of different pathways, with signals in each modality arriving at a specific area of the **cerebral cortex**. The cortex is a crumpled sheet of cells 2.5 mm thick and 1000 cm² in surface area (Braitenberg & Schuz, 1991). It contains approximately 20,000,000,000 cells. Figure 1.2 (top) shows a drawing of the human brain, identifying the receiving areas for different pathways. In the early 1900s the German anatomist Korbinian Brodmann distinguished over 50 different areas of the cerebral cortex, numbering them from BA1 to BA52. His numbering system has become the standard way of referencing the cortex. Table 1.1 shows the Brodmann cortical area (and Brodmann number) which receives incoming fibers from the nerves in each sensory pathway. It is important to note that Table 1.1 and Figure 1.2 indicate only the cortical *receiving* areas. Many other cortical areas are also devoted to the senses, by virtue of connections between cortical cells. There are interesting species differences in the total extent of cortical surface devoted to different senses. In primates, including humans, the visual cortex is the largest sensory area in the brain. Figure 1.2 (bottom) shows the relative area of cortex devoted to vision, hearing, and touch in two other species as well as in primates. Auditory cortex is dominant in bats, and somatosensory cortex is dominant in moles. The relative area of cortex devoted to different senses is indicative of their relative importance to the survival of each animal.

The right-hand column of Table 1.1 lists the most important functions served by the sensory systems, in terms of the computations they perform. The concept of computation will be discussed later in the chapter.

KEY TERM

Cerebral cortex
The outer layer of the human brain; approximately 2.5 mm thick, it contains the millions of neurons thought to underlie conscious perceptual experience.

? *Think of other reasons for differences in brain area devoted to different senses.*

TABLE 1.1 Criteria for distinguishing sensory modalities

Modality	Physical stimulus	Receptor type	Number	Afferent path	Synapses	Cortical receiving area (Brodmann number)	Computation
Audition	Air pressure waves	Mechano-	3.5K	Vestibulocochlear nerve, cochlear division (VIII)	5	Heschl's gyrus (BA 41)	Auditory object location & recognition, orienting, social communication
Gustation (taste)	Chemical contact	Chemo-	1M	Facial, glossopharyngeal, vagus nerves (VII, IX, X)	3	Primary gustatory cortex (BA 43)	Substance edibility, nutrition
Nociception (pain)	Mechanical or chemical contact	Noci-	~100K	Spinothalamic tract Trigeminal nerve (V)	3	Primary somatosensory cortex (BA 1-3)	Harm, injury
Olfaction (smell)	Chemical contact	Chemo-	6M	Olfactory nerve (I)	2	Primary olfactory cortex (BA 28)	Stimulus approach/avoidance, substance edibility
Somatosensation (touch) Proprioception (body position) Kinesthesis (body movement)	Mechanical force	Mechano-	~100K	Lemniscal tract Trigeminal nerve (V)	3	Primary somatosensory cortex (BA 1-3)	Haptic object segregation & recognition, body position and movement
Vestibular sense (balance)	Motive force	Mechano-	~20K	Vestibulocochlear nerve, vestibular division (VIII)	3	Posterior parietal operculum (BA 40)	Head position & acceleration, visual stability, body posture & equilibrium
Vision	Electromagnetic radiation	Photo-	125M	Optic nerve (II)	4	Striate cortex (BA 17)	Visual object segregation, location, & recognition, self-motion, scene layout, orienting

FIGURE 1.2
Cortical representation of the senses. Top: Cortical receiving areas in the human brain. Bottom: Total cortical area devoted to three senses in three different animals (redrawn from Krubitzer, 1995). The broken line identifies the cortical receiving area in macaque monkey. Copyright © 1995 Elsevier. Reproduced with permission.

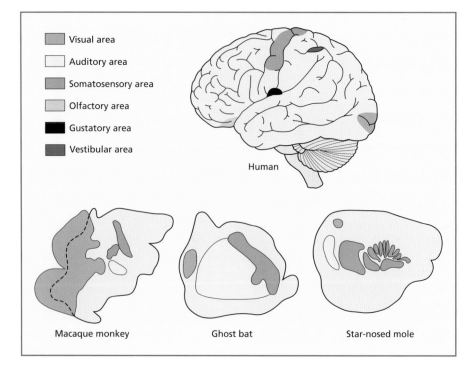

PSYCHOPHYSICS

Figure 1.3 shows the three key elements of sensation and perception. When external stimuli arrive at a sensory organ (1) they generate a neural response in sensory receptors (2) which leads to sensory and perceptual experiences (3). In this section we consider the psychophysical techniques used to study the relationship between stimuli and perceptual responses. In the following section we will turn our attention to the neuroscientific techniques that are used to study the relationship between stimuli and neural responses. Notice that there is also a direct link between neural responses and perception; neural responses are thought to underlie

FIGURE 1.3
The three key elements of perception:
(1) Sensory stimulation (light, sound, etc.);
(2) Neural responses to stimulation;
(3) Perceptual experiences which correlate with neural responses. Neuroscience studies the relation between stimuli and neural responses, and psychophysics studies the relation between stimuli and perceptual experiences. Psychophysical linking hypotheses bridge the gap between neural activity and perception.

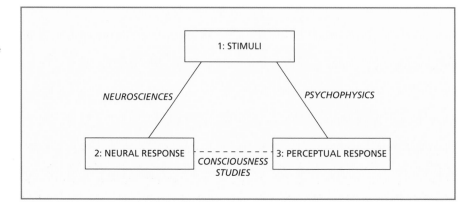

all conscious perceptual experience. Hypotheses that link these two elements are known as **psychophysical linking hypotheses**, though no one knows how and why the link exists at all (the issue of consciousness is discussed in the tutorial at the end of Chapter 14).

WEBER AND FECHNER

Psychophysical methods are so-called because they study the relation between mental events (perceptions) and physical stimulation. They were first developed by Ernst Weber and Gustav Fechner working at Leipzig University in the mid-1800s. Weber studied the ability of experimental participants to judge small differences in the heaviness of handheld weights. More specifically, he measured the smallest difference between a "standard" weight and another "comparison" weight that could be reliably detected, known as the "just noticeable difference" or JND. Weber found that the JND was a constant fraction of the standard weight. For example, if the JND for a weight of 1000g was measured at 50g, then the JND for a weight of 2000g would be 100g; a JND of 1/20. When discrimination was measured for many other sensory judgments (brightness, loudness, and so on), they were all characterized by a specific JND. This rule became known as Weber's Law, and the JND became known as Weber's Fraction. Fechner extended Weber's initial discoveries in his research into how our perception of the magnitude of a stimulus grows with stimulus intensity. Fechner reasoned that a sequence of stimuli that grows in steps that correspond to JNDs is equally spaced in terms of sensory increments though not equally spaced in terms of stimulus intensity. For example, assuming that weights must increase in steps of 1/20 in order for them to be discriminable (a JND of 1/20), the following sequence of weights is spaced at equally discriminable sensory increments: 1000g, 1050g, 1102.5g, 1157.6g, 1215.5g, 1276.3g, 1340g, and so on. The difference between the first two weights is 50g (1/20th of 1000), while the difference between the last two weights is 63.7g (1/20th of 1276.3g). So a small increment to a relatively light weight would produce the same change in perceived weightiness as a larger increment to a relatively heavy weight. This rule became known as Fechner's Law.

Fechner developed a set of experimental methods known as psychophysical methods for measuring the relation between mental and physical events. The tutorials section at the end of the chapter offers an introduction to the principles underlying these important techniques.

The discoveries made by Weber and Fechner laid the foundations of experimental psychology. They demonstrated that, using psychophysical techniques, it is possible to discover universal laws governing relationships between mental events and physical events; in other words, the link between boxes 1 (stimuli) and 3 (perceptual responses) in Figure 1.3. Given the assumption that neural responses (box 2) are also linked to perceptual responses, then psychophysical data can be used to make inferences about the neural processes underlying perceptual responses. These inferences are known as "psychophysical linking hypotheses."

SENSORY THRESHOLDS

Figure 1.4 shows data from an experiment to measure the detectability of a small light increment against a uniform background. The participant was shown a series of trials containing different increments, and at each presentation was asked to report whether they detected the increment. The horizontal axis shows the magnitude of

? *Why are special experimental techniques required to study perception?*

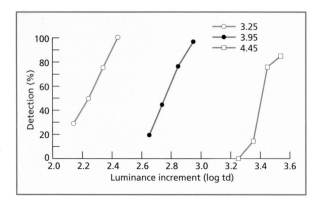

FIGURE 1.4

Psychometric function plotting the probability of a "yes" response to the presentation of a small light increment against a uniform background. The horizontal axis represents the magnitude of the light increment, and the three curves represent data obtained at three different background intensities. Adapted from Mueller (1951).

the light increment and the vertical axis shows the percentage of trials in which the participant detected the increment. The three curves represent data using three different background light levels. Each curve (also called a **psychometric function**) shows a smooth transition between no-detection and detection as stimulus level increases. This kind of detection function is called "probabilistic" rather than "all-or-none": As the size of the increment increases there is a gradual increase in the probability that the participant will detect it, rather than a sudden switch from no-detection to detection. Similarly, experiments that measure the ability of a participant to discriminate between two similar stimuli such as lights at different intensities find a smooth, probabilistic transition from perceiving no difference to perceiving a clear difference. There is no single stimulus value at which there is a step change in response from no detection or discrimination to certain detection/discrimination so there is uncertainty as to what stimulus level corresponds to the threshold for seeing it. In the face of this inherent uncertainty in the decision, the usual convention in psychophysical research is to select a given response level, such as 75% correct, as representing the threshold between no detection/discrimination and detection/discrimination. There has been a long debate as to the best explanation for the probabilistic nature of sensory thresholds, which is summarized in the tutorials section.

SENSORY MAGNITUDE

Variation in intensity affects not only the detectability of a stimulus, but also its sensory magnitude. For example, the brightness of a light, the loudness of a sound, or the heaviness of a weight increases as stimulus magnitude increases. An experimental technique called **magnitude estimation** allows us to establish the precise relationship between physical stimulus magnitude and sensory magnitude. The subject is initially presented with a standard stimulus at moderate intensity, and asked to assign an arbitrary number to it, such as 100. Other stimuli are then presented one at a time, and the subject is asked to estimate the magnitude of each relative to the standard stimulus using the same numerical scale. If, for example, a stimulus appears twice as intense as the standard (twice as bright or twice as loud), then the subject should assign the number 200 to it. The technique has been applied to a wide range of sensory stimuli. Representative data are shown on the left of Figure 1.5. The relationship between stimulus intensity and sensory magnitude is not linear.

In some sensory judgments, such as brightness, sensory magnitude increases rapidly at low stimulus intensities, but flattens off or saturates at higher intensities. In others, sensory magnitude shows the opposite pattern. If the data are plotted on logarithmic axes rather than linear axes, they fall along straight lines in the graph (right of Figure 1.5). This means that sensory magnitude data conform to a mathematical power law, in which sensory magnitude grows in proportion to stimulus intensity raised to a power

KEY TERMS

Psychometric function

A graph relating stimulus value (e.g., intensity) to the response rate of an experimental subject (e.g., proportion of "yes" responses).

Magnitude estimation

A psychophysical technique in which the subject estimates the magnitude of a given stimulus by assigning it a position along an arbitrary numerical scale (e.g., 0–100).

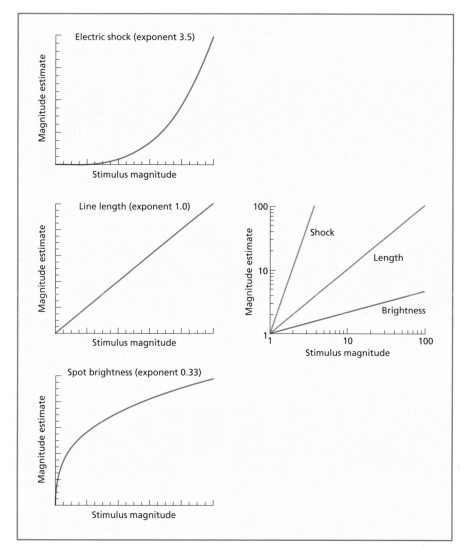

FIGURE 1.5
The relationship between stimulus intensity and sensory magnitude. The left-hand graphs are plotted using linear axes—sensory magnitude increases nonlinearly at different rates in different senses. The right-hand graph shows the same data plotted on logarithmic axes—sensory magnitude now increases linearly, showing the power-law relationship between stimulus intensity and sensory magnitude. Exponents of the plots were taken from Stevens (1961).

(the slope of each line in the logarithmic graph corresponds to the power or exponent to which intensity must be raised for that sensation). This property of sensory magnitude data is known as "**Stevens's power law**" (e.g., Stevens, 1961). The power-law relation between stimulus intensity and sensory magnitude means that equal ratios of intensity correspond to equal ratios of sensory magnitude. For example, each time light intensity increases by a factor of eight, brightness increases by a factor of two, at all levels of intensity. It seems that the sensory systems provide information about *changes* in the level of stimulation rather than about the absolute level of stimulation. Stevens's power law of sensory magnitude is closely related to Fechner's Law of JNDs.

SENSORY ADAPTATION

If there was a fixed relation between sensory magnitude and stimulus level, each stimulus level would be uniquely associated with a specific sensory magnitude. However research has shown that the relation between stimulus and sensation

KEY TERM

Stevens's power law
A nonlinear relationship between stimulus intensity and perceived magnitude, in which equal ratios of intensity produce equal ratios of magnitude.

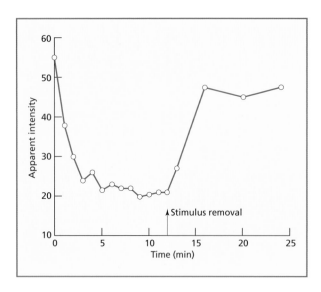

FIGURE 1.6
Adaptation to an odor. Sensory magnitude of an odor sensation was measured at regular intervals during a 12-minute exposure, showing adaptation to a constant stimulus. Once the stimulus was removed, sensory magnitude gradually recovered to former levels. From Ekman et al. (1967). Reproduced with permission from John Wiley and Sons.

is not fixed and unchanging, but varies: Any one stimulus level can give rise to a range of different sensory magnitudes; depending on the prevailing stimulus conditions. The sensory systems **adapt**. For instance, when you enter a dark cinema from a bright street, you are initially unable to see, but your visual system soon adapts to the new, dim level of illumination (and vice versa; after the film the street initially appears startlingly bright). Continuous exposure to a sustained stimulus actually has three consequences for sensation. First, sensitivity changes so that a different level of stimulus intensity is required to induce a given sensory response after adaptation than before adaptation. For example, after you have adapted to the dim cinema you require much less light to see than you did upon first entering. Second, the apparent intensity of the stimulus changes (the cinema initially appears extremely dark, but after adaptation it appears not so dark; see also the example of odor adaptation in Figure 1.6). Third, the rate at which sensory magnitude increases with stimulus level usually steepens. The response capacity of each sensory system is limited, in that it can only respond to a certain range of stimulus levels at any one time. Adaptation ensures that this restricted response is well matched to the prevailing stimulation.

PSYCHOPHYSICAL LINKING HYPOTHESES

Psychophysical data establish the relationship between stimuli and sensory experiences. But as indicated in Figure 1.3 these experiences are also linked to the neural responses generated by stimulation. Brindley (1960) recognized that any rigorous theory of sensation and perception should express this linkage in terms of explicit propositions that he called *psychophysical linking hypotheses*. More recently, Teller (1984) defined a linking proposition as "a claim that a particular mapping occurs, or a particular mapping principle applies, between perceptual and physiological states" (Teller, 1984, p. 1235).

Rigorous theories of perception usually contain at least one linking proposition of this kind. An example of such a proposition is that the loudness of a sound is coded by the rate of firing of certain cells in the auditory system. However, perceptual theories do not always spell out explicitly their linking propositions, but it is important to be aware that such propositions must form part of any theory that attempts to relate neural events to perceptual events.

COGNITIVE NEUROSCIENCE

The neurosciences can be defined as a set of scientific disciplines which are devoted to the study of the nervous system. Two branches of neuroscience are particularly relevant for sensation and perception. Cognitive neuroscience studies the parts of the nervous system that are involved in cognition, which includes sensation and perception; computational neuroscience studies the computations performed by the nervous system.

A wide range of techniques have been used in cognitive neuroscience over the last 200 years to study perception. Each technique has its particular advantages and limitations, but no one technique is preferred over the others. Different techniques complement each other, so that when considered together they allow us to construct a very detailed picture of how we perceive the world.

LESIONS

The cerebral cortex of the brain can be subdivided into many areas which specialize in certain cognitive functions, as Figure 1.2 has already shown. But in the mid-1800s, scientific opinion was that the cortex could not be subdivided in this way. Many believed that sensation, perception, and action were represented diffusely throughout the cortex. **Lesion** experiments provided some of the earliest evidence against this view, and in favor of localization of function in the brain. The procedure in such experiments is to surgically remove or destroy a specific area of an animal's brain, and then observe the consequences for behavior. If a specific behavioral function is impaired or removed following surgery, then we may infer that the relevant brain area is crucial for the maintenance of that function. However, care is needed to avoid drawing erroneous conclusions from lesion experiments. For example, one of the earliest experiments was performed by David Ferrier (1876). He examined monkeys after removal of an area on each side of the cortex known as the angular gyrus (see Figure 1.7). Ferrier concluded from his observations that the animals were completely blind following surgery. One monkey, for instance, was very fond of tea. Ferrier (1876, p. 166) noted that:

> *On placing a cup of tea close to its lips it began to drink eagerly. The cup was then removed from immediate contact, and the animal though intensely eager to drink further, as indicated by its gestures, was unable to find the cup, though its eyes were looking straight towards it.*

Later experiments, some of which are described below, indicate that Ferrier was mistaken in concluding from his observations that the monkeys were blinded by the lesion. Blindness is now known to be associated with damage to the occipital cortex, not the angular gyrus (occipital cortex is at the very back of the brain). According to Glickstein (1985), Ferrier's lesions had disrupted visually guided action, not vision itself. The monkey he described could probably see the cup, but could not perform the actions needed to drink from it. Despite such early mistakes, lesion studies have played an important part in establishing **localization of function** as a basic principle of cortical organization.

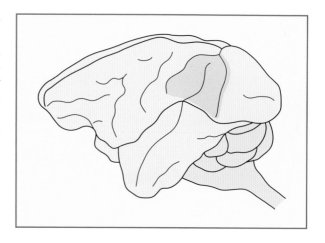

FIGURE 1.7
Site of the lesion in Ferrier's monkeys (redrawn from Glickstein, 1985). Copyright © 1985 Elsevier. Reproduced with permission.

? *How well could you infer the function of a car's components using "lesions" (disconnecting or removing components)?*

KEY TERMS

Lesion
An abnormality in structure or function in any part of the body.

Localization of function
The view that neurons underlying a specific sensory or cognitive function are located in a circumscribed brain area.

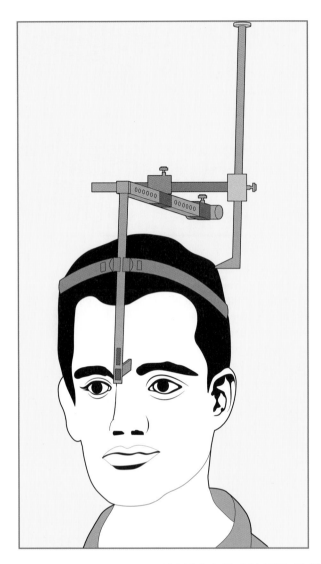

FIGURE 1.8
Inouye's instrument for tracing the path of a bullet in head wounds suffered by Japanese soldiers (drawing based on Glickstein & Witteridge, 1987).

CLINICAL CASES

Research on localization of function in humans has relied largely on clinical investigation into the consequences of accidental damage or disease to specific brain areas. The usefulness of these studies is very similar to that of lesion experiments, in that they allow inferences to be drawn about localization of function. Some of the earliest work to establish the importance of the occipital cortex for vision was undertaken by Tatsuji Inouye in the early 1900s. Inouye was a Japanese army physician, who studied soldiers wounded during combat in the Russo-Japanese war. His job was to assess their degree of blindness following bullet wounds to the head, as this determined the size of their pension (see Glickstein & Whitteridge, 1987). Inouye devised an instrument to locate precisely in three-dimensions the position of entry and exit wounds (see Figure 1.8).

Assuming a straight path for the bullet, he was then able to identify the areas of the brain that were damaged, and relate them to the impairments observed in the soldiers. Inouye was among the first to show that the visual field is mapped in a very ordered way on the surface of the human occipital cortex (see below).

Clinical studies of the consequences of brain damage are necessarily less controlled than lesion studies, since the researcher has no control over the location and extent of the damage. As a result, the inferences that can be drawn from clinical studies are limited. However, clinical studies have led to many important discoveries concerning localization of function.

SINGLE-UNIT RECORDINGS

Although a great deal was known about anatomy and about localization of function prior to the 1950s, nothing was known for certain about how individual nerve cells contributed to sensory processing. As David Hubel (1988, p. 4) remarked:

I can well remember, in the 1950s, looking at a microscopic slide of visual cortex, showing the millions of cells packed like eggs in a crate, and wondering what they all could conceivably be doing.

In partnership with Torsten Wiesel, David Hubel performed a series of ground-breaking experiments based on single-cell recordings from cells in the visual system of the cat. They were later awarded a Nobel prize for these discoveries.

Early theories of perception were inspired largely by the anatomical features of the sensory systems. The brain was known to contain huge numbers of cells, that are massively interconnected (but only over short distances) in circuits that are anatomically similar over the whole cortex. This anatomy prompted the Electrical Field Theory of perception, in which visual patterns were thought to impress corresponding patterns or fields of electrical activity on the surface of the cortex, analogous to the patterns imprinted on a photographic plate. Perceptual organization in complex displays was thought to be governed by interactions between fields of current extending across the cortical surface. Experimental tests of the theory included attempts to short-circuit the electrical fields by pinning metallic strips across the surface of the cortex in rhesus monkeys, and then performing tests of visual functioning (e.g., Lashley, Chow, & Semmes, 1951).

In the early 1950s, Stephen Kuffler was among the first to use a new **microelectrode recording** technique to monitor the activity of single sensory cells. He inserted electrodes (very fine insulated wires) through the white of the eye in an awake, anesthetized cat, and was able to record activity generated in individual retinal ganglion cells by simple visual stimuli placed in front of the animal. Kuffler's (1953) work on the cat retina, along with work by Barlow (1953) on the frog retina, and by Hubel and Wiesel (1959) on the cat visual cortex, provided the first detailed information on the way that individual sensory cells respond preferentially to certain stimuli. We now know that, despite being anatomically the same, the functional properties of individual cells vary hugely. For example, some retinal cells respond best to small, bright spots of light, while others respond best to large, dark spots. In the cortex, individual cells respond in a highly selective way to specific line orientations, or movement directions, colors, sizes, and so on (see Figure 1.9).

KEY TERM

Microelectrode recording
A technique in which electrical activity is recorded from single cells in a live animal using fine insulated wires.

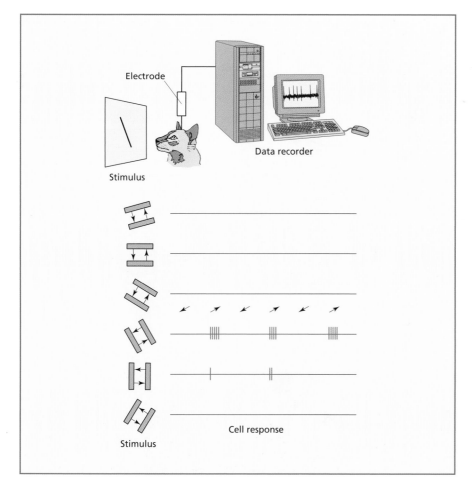

FIGURE 1.9
Single-unit recording. A stimulus is presented to the animal (in this case a visual stimulus) while a fine electrode registers activity from cells in the sensory system. The activity is recorded and analyzed by special-purpose equipment, in this case a computer equipped with appropriate hardware and software.

KEY TERMS

Feature detector
The view that individual neurons in the brain act as detectors for individual stimulus features.

Computerized tomography (CT) scan
A medical technique in which X-rays are passed through the body at different angles, and the resulting data are processed by a computer to create detailed images of body structure.

The key word is specialization rather than uniformity of function. These discoveries led to theories of pattern recognition based on neural "feature detectors." However, as we shall see in later chapters, this view of single cells as **feature detectors** is rather too simple. One must also be wary of drawing conclusions about the functioning of a huge mass of neurons on the basis of responses in single units. Indeed some argue that it is not possible to infer the functional properties of a large sensory system from knowledge of individual cell properties, however detailed (Churchland & Sejnowski, 1992). Nevertheless, single-cell recording data have had a profound influence on theories of perception.

NEUROIMAGING

Neuroimaging techniques were developed in the 1970s, primarily for use in medicine. The earliest technique to be developed was **computerized tomography** (CT). The subject is placed bodily in a long, thin, cylindrical tube (see Figure 1.10).

X-ray emitters and detectors are positioned around the circumference of the tube. A highly focused X-ray beam is emitted from one side of the cylinder so that it passes through the subject's body before being collected by detectors at the opposite side. X-rays are passed through the head from many directions around the tube. From the resulting pattern of X-ray transmission, sophisticated data analysis procedures can build up a detailed picture of the different structures inside the head, as shown in Figure 1.10. CT scans reveal areas of brain damage, and are therefore particularly useful in combination with clinical investigations into the behavioral consequences of brain damage.

FIGURE 1.10
CT scanner. The patient lies on a table that can be slid inside the scanner (left). The walls of the scanner are lined with X-ray emitters and detectors. X-rays are emitted from one side of the scanning tube so that they pass through the patient's body before being registered by detectors on the opposite side. A detailed image of the brain can be constructed from the pattern of X-ray transmission in all directions around the head.

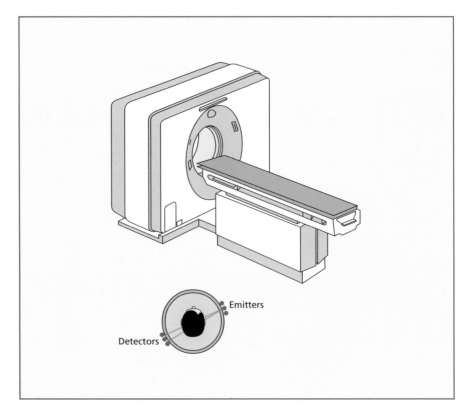

Magnetic resonance imaging (MRI) scanners detect the magnetic properties of brain molecules, revealed by passing radio waves through the head in all directions. Functional MRI (fMRI) scanning techniques use MRI scanners to detect minute magnetic changes in hemoglobin induced by variation in blood oxygen concentration (blood oxygen level-dependent or BOLD response). Since variation in blood oxygen concentration is related to neural activity (activity consumes energy) fMRI scans can inform us about brain *function*. The primary inferences from brain scanning data concern localization of function. Studies using fMRI scans often compare scans obtained while the subject is performing different tasks, in order to identify the brain areas that are associated with those tasks. An important recent development is fMRI adaptation. Repeated presentation of two similar stimuli causes a reduction in BOLD response in cortical regions containing cells responsive to both stimuli. Little or no reduction is observed if the stimuli activate different cells. So fMRI adaptation studies allow us to draw inferences about stimulus selectivity in small cortical regions (see Grill-Spector, Henson, & Martin, 2006). Neuroimaging studies are making an increasingly important contribution to sensory research, though they have also attracted a good deal of controversy about "blobology" (identification of hotspots in brain activity with little regard to their functional significance) which is being addressed using new techniques (see Poldrack, 2012).

DIRECT BRAIN STIMULATION

In recent years there has been rapid growth in other techniques to stimulate the intact human brain in a fairly localized manner, in the hope of revealing the function of the underlying neural tissue. For example, transcranial magnetic stimulation (TMS) involves directing a brief, powerful but focused magnetic pulse at the subject's head, as a way of interfering with the electrical activity of neurons in a specific brain region. Transcranial direct current stimulation (tDCS) delivers a low-level current directly to a brain region via small electrodes. This technique has known therapeutic benefits for sufferers of Parkinson's Disease, tinnitus, and damage caused by strokes, but is also being taken up as an experimental technique to interfere with brain activity.

BASIC CONCEPTS IN COGNITIVE NEUROSCIENCE

Neural impulses and transduction

Information in the nervous system is conveyed by streams of electrical signals (**neural impulses**) passed from one cell to another through the system. These impulses travel from a cell's **dendrites** and body to its **terminal buttons**, typically via an **axon**. The terminal buttons connect to the dendrites of another cell or cells at **synapses**. When the

KEY TERMS

Magnetic resonance imaging (MRI) scan
A medical technique in which short bursts of powerful radio waves are passed through the body at different angles, and signals emitted by body molecules are processed by a computer to create detailed images of body structure.

Neural impulse
A brief, discrete electrical signal (also known as an action potential) that travels rapidly along a cell's axon.

Dendrite
The branched tree-like structure projecting from a neuron's cell body, which makes contact with the terminal buttons of other cells.

Terminal button
A bud at the branched end of an axon, which makes contact with the dendrites of another neuron.

Axon
The long, thin wire-like structure that conveys neural impulses from a neuron's cell body to its terminal buttons.

Synapse
The junction between the terminal button of one neuron and the dendrite of another neuron.

impulse reaches a synapse, it causes the release of **neurotransmitter** chemicals that affect the electrical state of the receiving neuron. The neurotransmitter can be excitatory (e.g., acetylcholine, ACh), or inhibitory (e.g., gamma amino butyric acid, GABA). Excitatory neurotransmitters increase the probability that the receiving neuron will generate an impulse. Inhibitory neurotransmitters decrease the probability that the receiving neuron will fire an impulse.

Energy from the environment takes a number of forms, as Table 1.1 showed. Each sense requires specialized cells that receive one particular form of energy and convert or transduce it into neural signals. The eye, for example, contains **photoreceptors**, each of which contains photopigments (two examples are shown in Figure 1.11). The breakdown of these photopigments when struck by light results in the generation of a receptor voltage that is transmitted to neurons in the retina. The **mechanoreceptors** of the inner ear contain hair-like outgrowths (cilia). Vibrations initiated by sound pressure waves arriving at the outer ear deflect the cilia and trigger an electrical change in the receptor.

Hierarchical processing

Neural signals generated during **transduction** are transmitted to several structures in the brain. A common feature of all the senses is that ultimately at least some of the signals arrive at a receiving area in the cortex of the brain, as described earlier and pictured in Figure 1.2.

In between transduction and arrival at the cortex, signals from each sense organ pass through a series of synapses at successively higher levels of neural processing.

FIGURE 1.11
Sensory receptors. Left: Visual photoreceptors (a rod on the left, and cone on the right). Middle: Auditory inner hair cell. Right: Somatosensory Pacinian corpuscle.

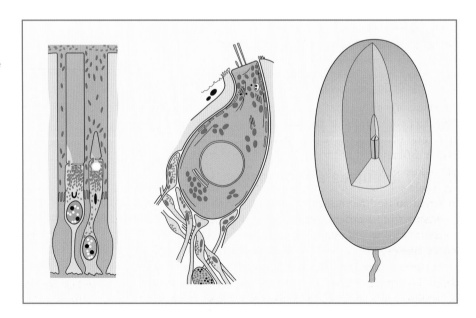

In the case of hearing, for example, there are five synapses on the route from hair cells to cortex. In the case of vision there are four levels of synapse between photoreceptors and brain. In all the senses except olfaction, one of the synapses on the route from sense organ to brain is located in the **thalamus** (olfactory signals are an exception because they pass directly from olfactory bulb to cortex). After the sensory signals arrive at a **receiving area** in the cortex, they are passed on to other cortical areas, often called **association areas**. Figure 1.12 summarizes the successive hierarchical stages characteristic of sensory processing.

Arrows in Figure 1.12 identify the direction of flow of neural signals through the system. In most cases signal flow is unidirectional up to the thalamus (at least in mammals), and bidirectional thereafter. Each stage of processing (each box in Figure 1.12) contains a large population of cells, often extensively interconnected. The input signal that arrives at each stage is modified by interactions that take place between the cells in that stage. As a result, the output signal that is passed on to the next stage differs in some way from the input signal—it has undergone a transformation during its passage through the processing stage. The successive transformations that occur as the sensory signal progresses through the hierarchy of processing refine the information it contains. For example, useful information is selectively retained and elaborated, while less useful information is lost. What information is "useful"? Theories in computational neuroscience attempt to answer this question, and are discussed later.

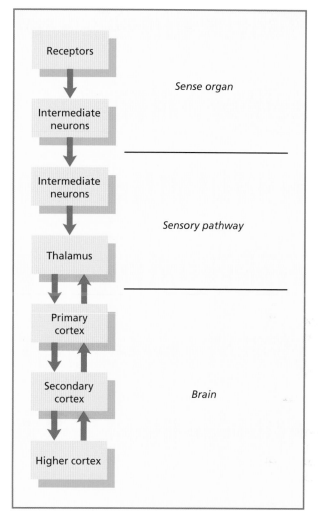

FIGURE 1.12
Hierarchical stages of sensory processing. Neural signals originate in sensory receptors and pass through a series of processing stages. Each stage consists of a large population of interconnected neurons. Arrows denote the direction of flow of the signals.

Specific nerve energy

All sense organs generate the same kind of electrical signals, as we have seen. After transduction, there is no feature of the neural signals that marks them as coming from one of the sense organs rather than any of the others. How, then, can they evoke different experiences? Differences between the senses are not reflected in the nature of the sensory signals themselves, but in their destination in the brain. As Table 1.1 and Figure 1.2 showed, signals in different sensory systems arrive at different cortical receiving areas. It is the destination that marks a particular signal as arising from a specific sense, giving the signal a characteristic sensory quality. Johannes Muller introduced this idea in 1838, and described it as the law of **specific nerve energy**.

Dramatic and direct support for the idea of specific nerve energy can be drawn from observations made during neurosurgery. The neurosurgeon removes a section of skull to expose an area of the cortex. In order to navigate the dense folds of the

? *Why are there so many processing stages in the sensory systems?*

cortical surface safely (avoiding damage to important functions), small electrical signals are often applied directly to the cortex while the patient is awake but anesthetized. This stimulation evokes sensations associated with the particular sense organ connected to that part of the cortex, such as visual or tactile sensations (see Chapter 3).

Selectivity

Neurons in the sensory systems generally respond only to a particular range of stimuli; they are highly selective. The human auditory system, for example, responds to sound pressure wave frequencies between 20 **Hz** and 16,000 Hz. Sounds outside this range are not detectable (though they may be detectable to other organisms; dogs, for example, can detect frequencies higher than 16,000 Hz). The range of effective stimuli for a particular system can be described as its sensory space. Within this sensory space, stimuli can vary along many different dimensions or parameters. A single spot of visible light can vary in, for example, its horizontal position in the visual field, its vertical position, its size, its intensity, and its wavelength characteristics. Single-unit recording techniques allow us to take an individual neuron at any one level of processing in a sensory system, and examine the particular range of stimuli within the system's sensory space to which that cell responds. Single-unit recording data reveal that sensory cells are highly selective in their response. A specific cell in the visual system, for instance, may respond only when a spot of light is presented at a specific location in the visual field, and has a particular size and color. A change in any one of these parameters causes a reduction in the cell's response (see Figure 1.13).

FIGURE 1.13
Selectivity in neural responses. The visual stimulus was a tilted bar that oscillated back and forth repeatedly (left). The upper trace on the right shows the neural impulses (short vertical lines) recorded from a cat cortical cell by Hubel and Wiesel. Time is plotted horizontally, and arrows represent the two phases in the bar's movement. The cell responded only when the bar moved up and to the right. When it moved out of the cell's receptive field (lower trace), then no response at all was recorded.

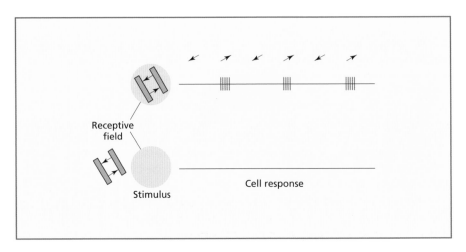

Receptive field

Stimulus

Cell response

Such selectivity is a universal property of sensory cells. Different cells have different stimulus preferences, so a stimulus change that results in a reduction in one cell's response is likely to result in an increase in another cell's response. A given cell responds to stimulation only in a limited spatial area of, for example, the visual field or body surface. This is usually called the cell's **receptive field.** Different cells have receptive fields in different locations. So as the stimulus moves about in visual space, or across the surface of the body, different cells respond to it.

Univariance and Population Coding

Although sensory neurons respond in a highly selective way to sensory stimuli, there is still an unavoidable ambiguity in their response which was first described by Naka and Rushton (1966). They measured the graded change in electrical potential produced by photoreceptors when they are struck by light, and observed that the response depends jointly on two stimulus parameters, namely the intensity of light and its wavelength. Photoreceptor response increases with intensity, but a given photoreceptor also responds more strongly to some light wavelengths than to others (as discussed in Chapter 8). The receptor has one **univariant** kind of response (electrical potential) which depends on two stimulus parameters. One cannot "read" the response to infer either intensity or wavelength unambiguously because any one response level can be produced by different combinations of the two variables. Univariance is a universal problem in sensory coding. For instance the response of many visual neurons depends on a whole constellation of stimulus parameters including position, size, contrast, orientation, and motion direction as indicated in Figure 1.13.

According to the principle of univariance, any given neuron responds to many different stimuli. The converse is also true: Any given stimulus induces activity in many different neurons. This consequence of univariance is the basis for a form of coding known as **population coding**. Neurons are activated to a greater or lesser extent by different stimuli, so the value of a given stimulus can be inferred from the relative activity of the whole population of neurons. For example, the downward visual movement of a waterfall will excite a large number of cortical cells in the visual system which respond to movement, but some cells will respond much more than others (the cells which are tuned to downward motion). People walking across your field of view from left to right will induce a different pattern of activity in the population of cells, with cells tuned to rightward motion responding the most. Population coding is thought to be ubiquitous in the sensory systems (see Pouget, Dayan, & Zemel, 2000) as you will read in later chapters.

Organization

In general, cells that respond to similar stimuli tend to be located near to each other in the brain. The most dramatic examples of this organization are so-called

KEY TERMS

Receptive field
The area of a stimulus field in which presentation of a stimulus causes a change in the firing rate of a given sensory neuron.

Univariance
A principle of neural coding in which any one level of excitation in a neuron can be produced by different combinations of stimulus values.

Population coding
A general principle of sensory processing, according to which different values of a perceptual attribute are coded by different patterns of activity in a whole population of neurons.

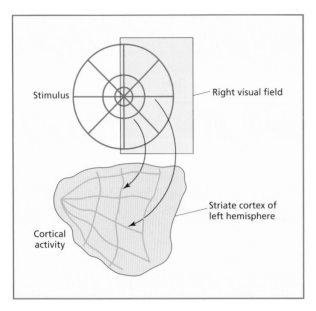

FIGURE 1.14
Topographic map in the visual system. The bull's-eye pattern in the upper part of the figure was presented to a monkey so that the area enclosed by the rectangle appeared in its right-hand visual field. The lower part of the figure is a flattened view of the animal's left cerebral hemisphere. A physiological staining technique highlights any cells that were active while the pattern was being viewed (dark areas). The pattern of activity is highly organized, and demonstrates how the animal's visual field is laid out topographically across the surface of the cortex. Based on Tootell et al. (1982).

KEY TERMS

Topographic map
A systematic projection from one neural structure to another, which preserves the spatial arrangement of neural connections (e.g., from the retina to the cortex).

Staining
A technique for identifying substances in and around cells, using chemical stains that are selectively taken up by certain kinds of tissue (e.g., cell bodies).

Cortical magnification
The exaggerated cortical representation of one part of a sensory dimension or surface compared to another.

topographic maps. Figure 1.14 shows an example from vision.

The upper bull's-eye pattern was presented to a monkey so that the area outlined by the rectangle appeared in the animal's right visual field (i.e. fixation at the center of the pattern). The lower image is a map of the left hemisphere of the monkey's cortex, showing only a portion at the rear of the hemisphere (the area where visual signals arrive—striate cortex). Tootell et al. (1982) used a physiological **staining** technique to identify which cells in this area of cortex were active while the animal viewed the bull's-eye. Regions containing active cells are darker. Neurons with receptive fields at nearby retinal positions are clearly located near to each other in the cortex, since the active regions are grouped together. The pattern of activity is so well ordered that it constitutes a map of the projection from the retina (often called a topographical cortical map). Notice that the cortical map is distorted. The small region of the image near to fixation (innermost ring of the bull's-eye) occupies a relatively large proportion of the cortical surface (left-hand third of the cortical map). This property of organization is called **cortical magnification**, and is a common feature across the senses.

Plasticity

The neural mechanisms that acquire and process sensory information are modifiable during development and during adulthood. As a human infant grows, the dimensions of his or her body change progressively. Limbs become longer and heavier, the eyes move apart. Sensory systems must be capable of adapting to these changes. Research has shown that the brain is able to tune itself into the changing sensory environment of the developing organism. Although this plasticity is only possible for a limited period during development (sometimes called a "critical period"; see Blakemore and Cooper, 1970; Maurer et al., 1999). Over much shorter time periods, each sensory system is also able to adapt itself to the specific sensory environment that the individual finds him or herself in. For example, as the sun sets the visual system's sensitivity changes progressively to match the prevailing illumination level, or, if you wear a particularly coarse-textured shirt, the initial feeling of itchiness conveyed by touch receptors in the skin soon subsides as the receptors adapt to their new environment.

Is adaptation just a by-product of depleted resources?

The graph in Figure 1.15 shows the change in response of touch receptors to a steadily applied stimulus over a period of 40 seconds. **Neural adaptability** is a universal feature of sensory systems, and is the source of the sensory adaptation effects described earlier.

Noise

The activity level of a neuron can be measured in terms of the frequency with which it generates electrical impulses. Activity level can vary between zero (no impulses at all) to approximately 800 impulses per second, though the typical rate for a very active cell is 100–200 impulses per second. In the example shown in Figure 1.15, the initial activity level of the touch receptor was about 100 impulses/s. Neural signals show a certain degree of variability, even in the absence of adaptation or short-term plasticity. The response to repeated presentation of identical stimuli differs randomly from presentation to presentation. This kind of variability is usually called "noise" because it bears no systematic relation to the incoming stimulation, or signal. There are two sources of variability (White, Rubinstein, & Kay, 2000). First, there are fluctuations in the electrical excitability of neurons, caused mainly by random opening and closing of **ion channels**. Second, there are fluctuations in synaptic transmission caused by, among other factors, the random nature of diffusion and chemical reaction across synapses.

We need to be able to detect changes in neural response since they reflect changes in the state of the outside world. However, any measure of change in neural response must take account of the inherent variability in the sensory signal. Theories of sensory coding must, as we shall see, accommodate neural noise.

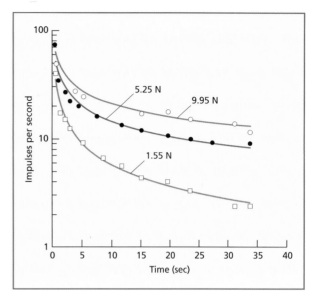

FIGURE 1.15
Time-course of the response of a pressure receptor to stimuli at three different intensities. Response rate is initially high, but declines steadily over a period of 40 seconds. Redrawn from Schmidt (1981, p. 88).

In what sense, if any, can one regard the brain as a computer?

COMPUTATIONAL NEUROSCIENCE

Three twentieth century mathematicians laid the foundations for the modern field of computational neuroscience: Alan Turing (1912–1954), Claude Shannon (1916–2001), and David Marr (1945–1980). Turing is most famous for his work as a code-breaker during the Second World War, but he also foresaw the development of modern computers. He developed the notion of universal **computation**, according to which all sufficiently powerful computing devices are essentially identical. Any one device can emulate the operation of any other device. If we accept that the brain is a form of computational device, then it follows that it can be emulated by other such devices, namely computers. This is the conceptual basis for computational neuroscience.

KEY TERMS

Adaptability
The ability of a sensory system to vary its response characteristics to match prevailing stimulation.

Ion channel
A specialized protein molecule that allows certain ions (e.g., sodium, potassium) to enter or leave a cell, so altering its electrical state.

Computation
The manipulation of quantities or symbols according to a set of rules.

Shannon was working for a US telecommunications company at about the same time as Turing was working in the UK. He developed a rigorous mathematical theory of how information is transmitted across telecommunications systems. Shannon's basic conceptual unit consists of three parts: A signal source, a transmission line or channel to carry the signal, and a receiver. Shannon identified several key properties that govern the behavior of any such system:

- Channel capacity—the number of signals it can transmit simultaneously
- Transmission rate—how quickly the signals travel along the channel
- Signal redundancy—the amount of information carried in the signal
- Noise—intrusion of information that is unrelated to the signal.

Shannon defined each of these properties in precise mathematical terms to create his "Information Theory," which has since been used to design and analyze telecommunications networks. For example, signal redundancy allows signals to be compressed with no loss of information:

> *The redundancy of ordinary English, not considering statistical structure over greater distances than about eight letters, is roughly 50%. This means that when we write English half of what we write is determined by the structure of the language and half is chosen freely.*
>
> *(Shannon, 1948, p. 392)*

Modern text messages can omit certain letters without loss of information (mny wrds cn b abbrvtd in ths wy). Cognitive scientists soon recognized that the "source–transmitter–receiver" concept can be applied to neural systems as well as to electronic systems. The neural processing stages in Figure 1.12 can be considered as a succession of source–transmitter–receiver units, and Information Theory provides the mathematical tools to analyze their behavior. For example, the concept of redundancy helps us to understand stimulus selectivity and adaptation in sensory neurons. High levels of activity incur an energy cost, so neurons tend to respond only when the activity provides the most useful (least redundant) information.

According to Information Theory, perception is above all an information processing task. David Marr accepted this view wholeheartedly. He was trained in mathematics and physiology at Cambridge in the UK before moving to the MIT Artificial Intelligence laboratory in the 1970s. Marr had initially developed mathematical models of the cerebellum, hippocampus, and cortex, before switching his attention to the visual system. Marr argued that an adequate theory of any information processing system like the visual system had to consider three levels of analysis (Marr, 1982, p. 25):

Computational theory "What is the goal of the computation, why is it appropriate, and what is the logic of the strategy for carrying it out?"

Representation and algorithm "How can this computational theory be implemented? In particular, what is the representation of the input and output, and what is the algorithm for the transformation?"

Hardware implementation "How can the representation and algorithm be realized physically?"

Cognitive neuroscience studies the hardware level of neural processing, computational neuroscience is concerned with computational theories, and psychophysics investigates the middle level of representation and algorithm. The three levels are loosely connected. A given theory can be implemented using different algorithms, which can in turn be realized in different physical systems. Indeed Turing's concept of universal computation argues that a given computation can be implemented in many different ways.

Marr's computational approach to building theories of perception has been highly influential. Some of the key concepts in computational neuroscience are unpacked in the next section.

BASIC CONCEPTS IN COMPUTATIONAL NEUROSCIENCE

Representation

Representation sits in the very center of Marr's three levels of analysis. It has long been accepted that, although the world appears to be "out there," it is in fact a pattern of neural activity evoked in our head during the act of perceiving. As Boring (1950) noted: "The immediate objects of the perception of our senses are merely particular states induced in the nerves" (p. 82).

A specific internal state of the brain, in the form of a particular pattern of neural activity, in some sense *represents* the state of the outside world. Perception must involve the formation of these **representations** in the brain. Most modern computational theories of perception are in essence theories about how the brain builds and uses representations of the world. Earlier in the chapter we discussed the idea that neural signals in sensory systems pass through a series of processing stages. According to the notion of representation, each of these stages must contain a representation of the state of the world. The transition through a series of neural processing stages can be viewed as a transition through a series of internal representations.

The idea that the state of one physical system (e.g., the brain) can in some sense represent the state of another system (e.g., the world) is very general, and can be applied to many systems. For example, the reading on a thermometer represents the current temperature; the display on a wristwatch represents the current time. As time moves on, the watch's display changes accordingly. A distinction can be drawn between two basic forms of representation, **analog** and **symbolic**. In an analog representation, magnitudes in one physical system map onto analogous magnitudes in another system. For example, height in a mercury thermometer represents temperature; the moving progress bar you see on your computer while downloading a file represents the data downloaded so far. Analog representations seem to be very common in sensory systems. One of the earliest examples was discovered by Adrian and Zotterman (1926), who measured the firing rate of sensory nerves in a frog's muscle as a function of the mechanical load on the muscle. Firing rate increased with load, so creating an analog representation of muscle load. As later chapters will show, analog **rate codes** of this kind are thought to represent many sensory dimensions such as brightness, loudness, pressure, and head acceleration. Morgan (2003) provides a detailed account of how analog spatial representations (maps) in the brain are the basis of our perception of space.

Think of another example of how the same information can be represented in both analog and symbolic form.

FIGURE 1.16
Entry for a goldfinch in a bird-spotter's handbook. The pictorial image of the bird constitutes an analog representation, while the list of attributes on the right constitutes a symbolic representation. Photo © panbazil/ Shutterstock.com.

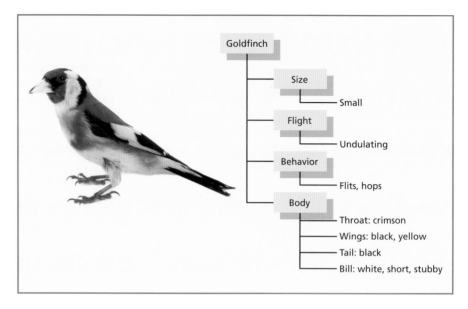

In a symbolic representation a limited vocabulary of arbitrary symbols in one system maps onto states or entities in the other system. A digital watch display represents time using the digits from 0 to 9, for example. Similar displays can be used to represent temperature, vehicle speed, altitude, and so on. As an example of the distinction between analog and symbolic representation, consider how a bird-spotter's handbook might represent a specific species of bird. The entry for that species may contain a still image of the bird, and a text list of its attributes, as illustrated in Figure 1.16. A multimedia text may also contain an audio clip of the bird's call, and a movie clip of the bird's flight. The image, audio clip, and movie clip are clearly analog representations, since they represent the bird in terms of its patterns of light or sound values. The text list of attributes is an abstract symbolic representation of the bird.

Computation

The concept of computation lies alongside the concept of representation at the heart of most present-day theories of perception (see Churchland & Sejnowski, 1992). In an abstract sense, computation can be defined as the manipulation of quantities or symbols according to a set of formal rules. It follows from this abstract definition of computation that a neural process that produces an analog quantity such as brightness, or a perceptual symbol such as an object property, can be described as a computational process. The formal rules used in computations are sometimes called **algorithms**. The idea that neural processing is a form of computation originated from the work of Alan Turing, as mentioned earlier. According to Turing, the brain can be considered as a computing device in the sense that it manipulates quantities and symbols according to sets of rules.

KEY TERM

Algorithm
A specific computational procedure used to transform one representation into another.

How exactly does the concept of computation apply to perception? We have seen that perceptual systems can be considered as *representational* systems—internal brain states represent the state of the outside world. Perceptual analysis proceeds through a series of representations, produced by a series of neural processing stages. The representation received at each processing stage is transformed into a new representation by a computational operation, and then passed onto the next stage as depicted in Figure 1.17 (a modification of Figure 1.12).

The nature of the computation that transforms one representation into the next depends on what form the two representations take, analog or symbolic. Computations performed on analog representations involve the creation and manipulation of *quantities* according to a set of rules, sometimes called signal processing. The computations involve mathematical manipulations of the values stored in the original representation. Computations performed on symbolic representations involve the creation and manipulation of *symbols* according to a set of rules. The computations involve comparisons between symbols to test for equality, and the combination of symbols to create new symbol structures. For example, the first representation may contain the symbols illustrated in Figure 1.16 (Size = Small; Flight = Undulating; etc.). The perceptual system may contain a rule that states that (IF Size = Small AND Flight = Undulating AND . . . THEN Bird = Goldfinch). An instance of the symbol for "goldfinch" would be created at the next level of representation in the processing hierarchy.

Symbolic representations and computations have traditionally been associated with human cognition, such as problem solving (Newell & Simon, 1972), and seem a natural choice for high-level perceptual representations relating to object identity. Initial perceptual representations, such as those in sense organs and cortical receiving areas, are probably best considered to be analog in form, because they involve rate codes of relatively simple stimulus properties such as intensity. Representations of perceptual objects are thought to be symbolic, but it is not yet clear where and how perceptual representations shift from analog to symbolic.

Notice the direction of the arrows in Figure 1.17. Some arrows point "upward" indicating that information flows from the bottom (receptors) to the top (cortex), so-called bottom-up processing. Other arrows point "downward," indicating that information flows back down from higher levels of analysis to lower levels, so-called top-down processing. The top-down route allows for some strategic control of processing based on, for example, context or attention.

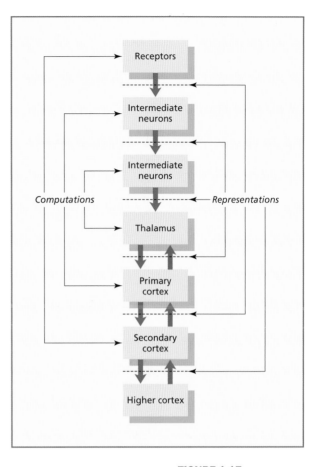

FIGURE 1.17
Representation and computation in relation to the hierarchical processing scheme depicted in Figure 1.12. Each processing stage receives a representation of the sensory stimulus as its input and creates a new representation that is passed on to the next processing stage. The modification that takes place at each processing stage can be considered as a computational operation that transforms one representation into another.

CHAPTER SUMMARY

Perception involves highly complex neural processes that consume a substantial proportion of the brain's cerebral cortex.

SENSATION, PERCEPTION, AND SENSORY MODALITY

Sensations (also known as qualia) are primitive mental states or experiences induced by sensory stimulation. Perceptions are complex, organized, and meaningful experiences of objects or events. Qualia can be divided into seven distinct sensory modalities: Audition, gustation, nociception, olfaction, somatosensation, the vestibular sense, and vision.

The modalities differ in terms of the physical stimuli that excite them, the neural structures involved in transduction and sensory analysis, and the functions they serve. In humans, a much greater area of cortex is devoted to vision than to the other senses.

The three key elements of perception are:

1. Stimuli
2. Neural responses
3. Perceptions.

Stimuli generate neural responses which in turn lead to perceptual experiences. Psychophysics studies the relation between stimuli and perceptual experience, whilst neuroscience studies the relation between stimuli and neural responses. Psychophysical linking hypotheses propose specific links between perception and neural responses, as part of theories in computation neuroscience.

PSYCHOPHYSICS

Psychophysical methods to study perception were developed by Weber and Fechner in the 1800s, who established some fundamental laws governing the relation between sensory stimuli and sensation. Basic concepts in psychophysics include:

* Sensory thresholds
* Sensory magnitude
* Sensory adaptation
* Psychophysical linking hypotheses.

COGNITIVE NEUROSCIENCE

Methods used to study sensation and perception include:

* Lesion experiments
* Clinical cases

- Single-unit recordings
- Neuroimaging
- Direct brain stimulation.

Basic concepts include:

- Neural impulses and transduction
- Hierarchical processing
- Specific nerve energy
- Selectivity
- Univariance
- Organization
- Plasticity
- Noise

COMPUTATIONAL NEUROSCIENCE

The foundations of computational neuroscience were laid by three mathematicians:

- Alan Turing introduced the concept of universal computation
- Claude Shannon developed Information Theory
- David Marr introduced the three-level distinction between computational theory, representation, and hardware implementation.

Basic concepts include:

- Analog and symbolic representation
- Computation.

TUTORIALS

PSYCHOPHYSICAL METHODS

As we saw earlier in the chapter, certain physical stimuli evoke perceptual experiences ranging from simple sensations such as "redness" or "loudness" to complex perceptions such as facial identity. How can we study the relationship between physical stimuli and perceptual experience? The simplest method is to use verbal reports, such as "it looks red" or "that is my grandmother." This phenomenological approach is severely limited in its usefulness, for several reasons. First, it obviously requires subjects who can describe their experiences in words, so excludes infants and animals. Second, even when restricted to subjects who can talk, it is contaminated by differences in the way different people use words. Third, it is open to bias introduced by each individual's assumptions, expectations, and desires.

We need precise, accurate measures of perception that can be used to establish the limits of perceptual ability, to monitor how these limits change with stimulus conditions, and to test the predictions of perceptual theories. Ideally these measurement methods should be immune to the effects of verbal ability, expectation, and attitude. Over the last 100 years or so a body of experimental techniques has been developed to provide the required measurements. Since these techniques provide quantitative, physical measures of psychological phenomena, they are called *psychophysical* methods.

Psychometric functions

Any plot relating a quantifiable response to a physical stimulus measure is known as a psychometric function. One might plot, for example, sound intensity against the probability that the subject will detect the presence of the sound. What is the typical shape of a psychometric function in a detection experiment? One might expect that below a certain stimulus level the sound is never heard, and above it, the sound is always heard—a step function. Real psychometric functions always show a gradual shift from no-detection to detection as stimulus level increases, rather than a sudden shift (as shown earlier in the chapter in Figure 1.4). Why?

Classical psychophysical theory and the psychometric function

The concept of the threshold is crucial to classical psychophysical theory. A threshold marks a transition from one perceptual experience to another, usually as a result of a simple change in the physical stimulus. For example: How intense must a sound be for us to detect it? How fast must something move for us to see the movement? How different in distance must two objects be for us to tell that one is nearer? There are two kinds of threshold, the **absolute threshold** and the **differential threshold**. The absolute threshold marks the smallest amount of stimulus energy required for an observer to just detect its presence (e.g., the minimum sound intensity or movement velocity required for detection). The differential threshold marks the minimum change in stimulus energy that can be detected by an observer. This threshold is also known as the "just noticeable difference," or JND, as discussed earlier in the chapter (e.g., the small change in sound intensity required for the observer to notice a change in loudness). Classical psychophysical methods were basically developed to measure JNDs accurately and reliably.

Classical psychophysical theory explains smooth real-world psychometric functions (as in Figure 1.4) with the following three assumptions. First, there is an ideal threshold function that relates the internal response of the sensory system ("sensory magnitude") to stimulus level. This function is a step function with two levels, "low," and "high." Second, when the internal response is "high," the observer always reports detection of the stimulus, and when the internal response is "low," the observer never reports detection of the stimulus. Third, the exact position of the threshold in relation to stimulus level is subject to some random fluctuation, due to momentary variations in neural sensitivity, arousal level, and so on. Although the threshold tends, on average, to cluster around a specific stimulus level, it occasionally falls below or above this level, so that the probability that the threshold will fall at a particular stimulus level conforms to a bell-shaped curve or **normal distribution**, as in Figure 1.18 (left).

In the figure, at a low stimulus level (top-left graph), the probability that the threshold will be lower than this level is small (arrowed area), so detection rates are low. As the stimulus level increases, the likelihood of detection improves because there is a much greater probability that the threshold will be lower than the stimulus level (lower-left graph). Consequently, if we plot probability of detection against stimulus level, a typical psychometric function is obtained (right-hand graph). At what stimulus level is threshold reached? According to classical theory, the "true" threshold coincides with the mean of the probability distribution in Figure 1.18. Since, by definition, 50% of the distribution lies below the mean, and 50% lies above it, the most logical place on the psychometric function to locate the threshold is

KEY TERM

Normal distribution
A distribution in which scores fall symmetrically and predictably on either side of the mean score.

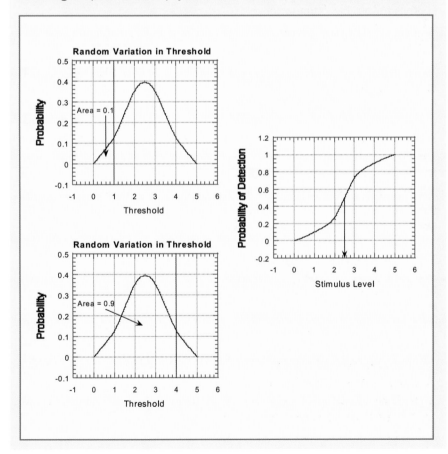

FIGURE 1.18
Explanation of the empirical psychometric function, according to classical psychophysical theory. The stimulus level at which sensory response reaches threshold is subject to some degree of random variation (left-hand graphs). A low intensity stimulus (e.g., 1.0 in the upper-left graph) is unlikely to be detected (probability 0.1), because only rarely does the threshold drop to such a low stimulus level. A high intensity stimulus (e.g., 4.0 in the lower-left graph) is very likely to be detected (probability 0.9), because most of the time the threshold is lower than this level. As a result detection rates improve gradually with stimulus level (right-hand graph).

at the 50% point. This account of thresholds applies to both absolute and differential thresholds.

Classical psychophysical methods

All classical methods aim to measure the observer's threshold. Some methods provide an estimate of the whole psychometric function. Others provide an estimate of just one point on the function, usually the 50% point. A number of classical methods were developed at the turn of the 19th century, but this tutorial will describe the only two methods that are still in use, the **method of adjustment** and the **method of constant stimuli**.

Method of adjustment

In this procedure, the observer is given control of the stimulus (e.g., a dial that controls stimulus intensity), and asked to adjust it until it is just detectable. This method is quick and easy to use, but rather unreliable. The observers have direct control of the stimulus, so are free to apply some degree of bias to their settings. Some observers may try to impress with their high sensitivity, and tend to bias dial settings toward low stimulus levels. Other observers may prefer to be cautious and careful, tending to bias their settings toward high stimulus levels.

Method of constant stimuli

The experimenter selects a range of stimulus levels at the start of the experiment. These different levels are presented to the subject repeatedly in random order, in a series of experimental trials. After each presentation, the subject is required to respond "yes" if the stimulus (or a difference between stimuli) was detected in that trial, or "no" if it was not detected. This method is more trustworthy than adjustment, since the subject has no direct knowledge of the stimulus level presented. It constructs the full psychometric function, so is reliable but more labor-intensive than the method of adjustment. Computers can be used to take care of stimulus selection, increasing the efficiency of the method.

The problem of bias in classical methods

In classical psychophysics, the subject's response to the stimulus is assumed to depend only on their sensitivity, the stimulus level at which the internal response shifts from low to high. However, responses are also likely to reflect uncontrolled bias effects. The problem is most severe using the method of adjustment, but may also intrude in the method of constant stimuli. Since a stimulus is presented in every trial, the observers are free to apply some degree of bias to their responses. They may, for example, be feeling uncooperative or lacking in confidence, and so unwilling to respond "yes" unless they are very confident of being correct. As a result, the

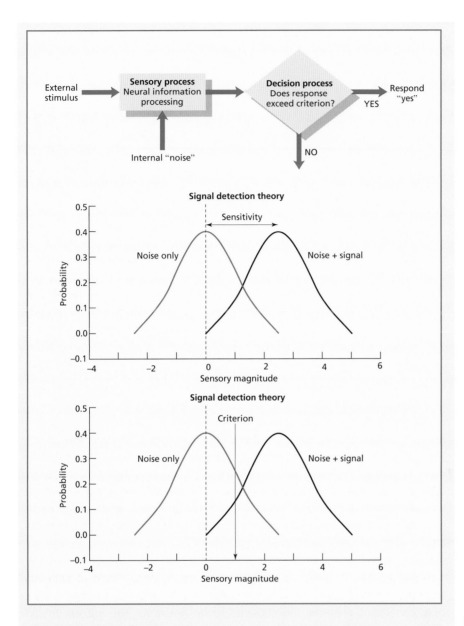

FIGURE 1.19
Signal detection theory (SDT). Top: Two hypothetical stages in detection, according to SDT. Middle: According to SDT, both stimulus-absent ("noise only") and stimulus-present ("noise + signal") trials generate a response in the sensory process of the detection system. Each response is subject to some random variation due to internal noise, shown by the two distributions. The observer's sensitivity to the stimulus is characterized by the difference between the means of the two distributions. Bottom: The decision process receives a response from the sensory process, and must decide whether the response came from the noise only distribution or from the noise + signal distribution. A specific response level is selected ("criterion"), above which the decision is that the response came from the noise + signal distribution.

measured threshold will not be a pure estimate of the subject's sensitivity to the stimulus, but will reflect some unknown combination of sensitivity and bias. Signal detection theory was developed specifically to address the problem of bias effects.

Signal detection theory (SDT)

Signal detection theory (SDT) acknowledges the importance of bias effects by assuming that stimulus detection is a two-stage process (Figure 1.19, Top). The first stage is a purely sensory process in which a specific stimulus level produces an internal sensory response that depends on the intensity of the stimulus and the sensitivity of the sensory system. This internal response is subject to random internal "noise" of the kind described earlier in the chapter. The second stage is a decision process in which the sensory response magnitude is compared to an internally set criterion. If the response magnitude exceeds this criterion, the decision process decides that a stimulus was present. If the internal response falls below the criterion, then the decision process decides that no stimulus was present. The position of the criterion is influenced by all the factors described earlier that affect bias. Highly motivated subjects may adopt a low criterion, reflecting a bias in favor of accepting rather weak stimuli. Subjects who lack confidence in their judgments may adopt a high criterion, because they are biased toward accepting only relatively intense stimuli. The experimenter is interested primarily in the sensitivity of the sensory system, rather than the subject's bias, but SDT provides methods of estimating both sensitivity and bias.

SDT methodology: Yes/no and forced-choice tasks

In classical psychophysical methods, every stimulus presentation in the experiment contains a stimulus. In SDT methods only *half* of the presentations contain stimuli, randomly selected. For example, if the subject is required to detect the presence of a visual pattern against a uniform background, then only half of the presentations contain the pattern and background, while the other half contain only the background. Presentations containing a stimulus are called *noise + signal* presentations, for reasons that will become obvious, and presentations not containing a stimulus are called noise presentations. The subject must discriminate between noise + signal presentations and noise presentations. Two kinds of task are commonly used. In a **yes/no task**, the subject is presented with a single stimulus event in each experimental trial, which may or may not contain a signal. The subject must respond "yes" if he or she decides that a stimulus was presented in that trial, and "no" otherwise. In a **forced-choice task**, the subject is usually presented with two stimulus events in each trial, side by side or one after the other. In a vision experiment, for example, two stimulus patches may be presented side by side. In a hearing experiment, two sounds may be presented sequentially. Only one event contains the stimulus to be detected. The subject must decide which of the two events contained the stimulus, and respond "left" or "right," or "one" or "two" as appropriate. Tasks of this kind are commonly called two-alternative forced choice or 2AFC tasks.

Notice that in SDT tasks the subject has no direct knowledge of which event contains the required stimulus. This reduces the possibility of bias, because when the stimulus is not detectable the subject is forced to guess as to which event contained the stimulus. However, in yes/no tasks there is a possibility of some bias in favor of "yes" responses, because of a social aversion to saying "no." Many researchers prefer to use forced-choice tasks wherever possible, because the alternative responses are fairly neutral (Green & Swets, 1966).

SDT measures of sensitivity and bias

This brief description of SDT measures is based on a yes/no task, but also applies (with appropriate modifications) to forced-choice tasks. SDT theory assumes that both noise + signal and noise events generate an internal response in the sensory process of the detection system, because this process is subject to internal noise (Figure 1.19). Noise events reflect only the contribution of internal noise to the response. Noise + signal events reflect contributions from both internal noise and external stimulation. The probability distribution of the response to each event can be plotted, as shown in Figure 1.19. Each distribution simply plots the relative probability of that event generating a specific response magnitude. The noise distribution reflects only the variable level of internal noise, which tends to cluster around a mean value (the peak of the distribution). The noise + signal distribution contains contributions from both internal noise and external stimulation. The effect of the external stimulus is to add a constant value to the noise distribution, displacing it toward higher response magnitudes. The distance over which noise + signal distribution is shifted relative to the noise distribution depends on the system's sensitivity to the stimulation. The difference between the means of the two distributions is taken as a measure of the sensitivity of the system to the stimulus, and is known as **d' (d-prime)**.

In any one trial of a yes/no task, the decision process receives a response at a particular magnitude, and must decide whether that response was drawn from the noise distribution or from the noise + signal distribution. SDT assumes that the decision process selects a specific criterion level of response, shown by the arrow in Figure 1.19. Response levels below this value are deemed to belong to the noise distribution, so are assigned a "no" response. Response levels above this value are deemed to belong to the noise + signal distribution, and are assigned a "yes" response. The level at which the criterion is set depends on biasing factors. It may be "unbiased," or midway between the two distributions, or biased in one direction or the other.

SDT provides various methods for making precise estimates of sensitivity or d' independent of criterion level or **bias** (also known as β). However, bias effects are pervasive (see Witt et al., 2015). In 2AFC tasks, a simple measure of sensitivity is given by the proportion of correct responses recorded by the subject. Readers interested in the mathematical details of SDT measures are referred to Stanislaw and Todorov (1999), who provide formulae and procedures for performing the calculations using general-purpose software such as spreadsheets.

Evaluation

SDT was first applied to psychophysical problems by Tanner and Swets in the mid-1950s and, as we have seen, it discards the classical notion of the threshold in favor of d'. Fifty years later, despite the widespread acceptance

KEY TERMS

d-prime (d')
A measure of stimulus sensitivity based on signal detection theory, it represents the increase in sensory response caused by the presence of stimulus.

Bias (β)
A measure of response bias based on signal detection theory. It represents the extent to which the subject is predisposed toward making a particular response, regardless of stimulus level.

in the scientific community of many of the ideas in SDT, much contemporary research still measures performance in terms of thresholds rather than d' (Gordon, 1997). Why should this be so? Thresholds are still a very useful, and intuitively meaningful, way of summarizing the performance of a subject, reflecting the stimulus level that is just detectable by the subject. By contrast, d' is a more abstract measure of sensitivity to a specific stimulus level, and is meaningful only if one appreciates the statistical concepts that underlie it. Despite the continuing attachment to thresholds, many researchers measure them using percentage correct responses in 2AFC tasks, having taken on board the concerns about bias effects raised by advocates of SDT.

THEORETICAL TRADITONS IN PERCEPTION RESEARCH

The previous tutorial on psychophysical methods introduced some of the techniques that have been developed for collecting perceptual data, and the rationale behind them. This second tutorial discusses the major theoretical movements that have motivated psychophysical experiments over the last 150 years. We must first define the essential properties of a theory, and discuss how the adequacy of different theories can be assessed.

At the very least, any scientific theory worthy of the name must have three properties (Popper, 1963). First, it must provide a framework for organizing and understanding the known facts in an economical manner. Second, it must attempt to provide explanations for the facts, or at least suggest causal links between them. Third, it must be capable of generating predictions that can be tested experimentally. If there are two competing theories to account for a particular set of facts, how can one select the theory that is to be preferred? Several criteria can be applied:

1. *Empirical consistency* One can compare the two theories according to their ability to explain the known facts. A theory is not much use if it cannot account for the data.
2. *Logical consistency or computability* If both theories pass the first test, one can judge their relative merits on the basis of logical consistency. Is the reasoning behind each theory tight and logically consistent? If a theory involves computational operations, can these operations be performed successfully? The inclusion of arbitrary (ad hoc) propositions, or computations that are difficult or impossible to implement, diminishes a theory's attractiveness.
3. *Occam's Razor* If both theories pass the first two tests, then one can apply the principle of Occam's Razor, which states that "Entities must not be multiplied beyond necessity." What this means is that the more parsimonious theory of the two is to be preferred. If a simple theory can explain the data as convincingly as a more complex theory then, other things being equal, the additional complexity is superfluous. Of course

this criterion begs the question: "What do you mean by simplicity?" One could interpret simplicity in computational terms, adopting a mathematical definition of computational complexity. On the other hand one could interpret simplicity in terms of the complexity of the neural structures which would be required to implement each theory.

4. **Generality** A final test of two competing theories concerns their generality. Some theories appear to exist in a vacuum, successfully accommodating the data they were devised to explain, but with no obvious connection to other phenomena or theories. Other theories attempt to place themselves in a wider context by, for example, making connections with other theories. In these circumstances, the better-connected theory is to be preferred. This criterion selects theories on the basis of higher order logical consistency. Are different theories invented ad hoc to explain phenomena in isolation, or is there some higher order rationale or structure that links different theories together? Examples of such higher order links would include energy efficiency, ecological validity.

If two competing theories cannot be separated on the basis of *any* of the four criteria, the only course of action is to return to the first criterion, empirical consistency. New predictions must be generated from each theory concerning the outcome of an experiment, formulated in such a way that (ideally) the results are bound to falsify one of the theories. In principle, the aim of any new theory is to provide the only true explanation for a particular phenomenon. However, it is worth remembering that few theories stand the test of time. Most new theories are ultimately discarded either because of empirical inconsistency, or because they prove to be unsatisfactory on the basis of one of the other criteria. Most theorists accept that the best they can hope for a particular theory is that it will provide a closer approximation to the truth than other available theories. Once a new theory appears that offers a better way of understanding the facts, then the old theory must be discarded. This does not mean that theorizing is futile and doomed to failure, for two reasons. First, it would be extremely difficult or impossible to arrive at the truth without having first absorbed the insights offered by previous theories. As Isaac Newton remarked: "If I have seen farther, it is by standing on the shoulders of giants" (letter to Hooke, 5 February 1675; see Turnbull, 1959, p. 416). Although Newton's own theories provided the foundation stones for most of the sciences, he acknowledged the debt he owed to predecessors such as Galileo and Kepler. Second, much empirical research would be aimless and trivial unless it was motivated by the need to test the predictions of new theories.

It should now be clear why it is important to understand some of the major theoretical movements in the scientific study of perception. As we shall see, each movement has made a valuable contribution to our understanding of perception. The major theoretical movements were developed in the context of vision, but the ideas can be taken to apply to all the senses. Modern theories of perception began with Structuralism 150 years ago.

Structuralist approach

Structuralism drew inspiration from the chemical decomposition of complex substances into elements. It proposed that each complex perceptual experience could be decomposed into a large collection of elementary sensations. Structuralists used introspection to break down a particular perceptual experience into its sensory components. For example, Titchener (1902) decomposed the taste of lemonade thus: "The taste of lemonade is made up of a sweet taste, an acid taste, a scent (the fragrance of lemon), a sensation of temperature, and a pricking (cutaneous) sensation" (p. 62).

Introspection proved to be an unsatisfactory basis for theories of perception for reasons that, in retrospect, appear obvious. First, introspective data are inherently qualitative rather than quantitative. Second, observers frequently disagree in their introspections. Third, many important perceptual processes cannot be studied by introspection.

Gestalt approach

Gestalt psychologists rejected the basic principles of Structuralism, and proposed instead that when a collection of elementary sensations is combined together a new perceptual entity emerges—a Gestalt. The major exponents of Gestaltism (Wertheimer, Kohler, and Koffka) were German, and the German word "gestalt" means form, figure, or configuration. According to **Gestalt psychology**, perceptual systems are not passive recipients of isolated, elementary sensations, but dynamically organize these sensations into meaningful "wholes" or Gestalts. Gestaltism emphasized the importance of structure and organization in perception. It identified a number of organizing principles or laws to describe the variety of ways that perceptual systems achieve organization. The general theme of these laws is that isolated elements that share some property in common, such as spots of the same color, or shapes that move in the same direction, or notes of similar pitch, tend to be grouped together perceptually. Elements that form a "good figure" (*pragnanz*), such as dots falling along a smooth curve or forming an enclosed regular shape, also tend to group together perceptually.

The main weakness of Gestalt psychology was that its laws tended to be descriptive rather than explanatory. Its arguments tended to be circular. For example, Gestalt psychologists would explain why certain pattern elements group together by invoking the principle of good figure or *pragnanz*. But what is the principle of *pragnanz*? It is the tendency of elements forming a good figure to group together. Despite its limitations, Gestalt psychology made a valuable contribution to perceptual theory by emphasizing the way that entirely new perceptual entities can emerge from the organization of simpler elements. Gestaltism is no longer at the forefront of perceptual theorizing, but is still influential, particularly in European psychology, and is relevant to present-day computational theories.

Constructivist approach

The German scientist Hermann von Helmholtz introduced the idea of "unconscious conclusion" in his monumental, three-volume *Treatise on Physiological Optics* published between 1856 and 1866:

> The psychic activities that lead us to infer that there in front of us at a certain place there is a certain object of a certain character, are generally not conscious activities, but unconscious ones. In their result they are equivalent to a conclusion . . . it may be permissible to speak of the psychic acts of ordinary perception as unconscious conclusions.
>
> *(1962 translation of Vol. III, p. 4)*

To expand on this idea, Helmholtz used the example of an astronomer "who computes the positions of the stars in space, their distances, etc." from his conscious knowledge of the laws of optics. He argued that "there can be no doubt" that perception involves the same kind of computation as that used by the astronomer, but at an unconscious level. Helmholtz went further, stating confidently that:

> Our ideas of things cannot be anything but symbols, natural signs for things which we learn how to use in order to regulate our movements and actions.
>
> *(1962 translation of Vol. III, p. 19)*

Helmholtz therefore advocated the view that sensory systems construct some kind of internal representation of the world, and that this representation mediates perceptual experience. Related views on the indirect and inferential nature of perception have been promoted by, among others, Gregory (1980), and Rock (1983).

It is fair to say that constructivism has had a profound impact on theories of perception. Most modern theoretical approaches rely heavily on the notions of representation and computation. Helmholtz's ideas on symbolic representation were remarkably prescient, since they appeared 100 years before representation became a cornerstone of computational neuroscience.

Ecological approach

Perception begins with physical stimulation and ends with perceptual experience. In between the two, according to the Gestalt psychologists and constructivists, are sophisticated processes that construct internal representations from the sensory information. Perceptual experience has only an indirect relationship to the sensory data. James J. Gibson took the opposite view, in rejecting entirely the need for internal representation (Gibson, 1950). He argued instead that there is sufficient information available in the visual image for unambiguous perception to be derived directly, without the need for intervening processes. He suggested that the brain as a whole "picks up" the relevant information by some kind of "resonance." Gibson used an analogy with a radio set to explain this idea. Your immediate surroundings are almost certainly filled with low-energy electromagnetic radiation broadcast by TV and radio transmitters. A radio, properly tuned, will be able to pick up some of this information and produce intelligible sounds. Gibson would argue that in this situation all the components of the radio resonate with the information available in the electromagnetic radiation. There is no need to assume that some internal representation is constructed by the radio.

Gibson's ideas were inspired by his work in aircraft pilot training during the Second World War. He noticed that conventional treatments of depth cues were of little practical value, and became convinced that the highly structured patterns of movement pilots view from the cockpit were critical for aircraft control. As a plane comes in to land, surface details in the environment, such as markings on the runway, stream across the image projected into the pilot's eyes. They radiate out from the point in the image toward which the aircraft is heading, creating an **optic flow field**. Gibson correctly deduced that this flow field contains sufficient information to specify precisely where and when the aircraft would make contact with the ground. He argued that this information is somehow picked up directly by the sensory system. Gibson identified other properties of natural images, such as texture gradients, that can be used to specify surface depth, slant, and size. Due to its emphasis on natural images, Gibson's perspective became known as the ecological approach to perception. Its denial of the relevance of mediating processes also led to the label "direct perception."

Direct perception performed a valuable service in identifying some powerful sources of information in visual images, but it drastically underestimated the difficulty of the problem posed by picking up this information. Research on **artificial intelligence** (AI) has shown that the information available in visual images is usually not sufficient by itself to recover unambiguous information about the surfaces and objects that created the image.

Computational approach

The computational approach was anticipated by Helmholtz, in his analogy between astronomical calculations and perceptual conclusions. As mentioned earlier, firm foundations for the computational approach to perception were later laid by three mathematicians (Turing, Shannon, and Marr). Turing's notion of universal computation led to the idea that the brain was an information processing device that could be emulated by other such devices, namely computers. An information processing device receives input data and performs some processing operation on the data to produce an output. An electronic calculator is a good example of an information processing device. It receives input data in the form of a sequence of numbers and symbols, and processes this data to produce an output, usually the result of a calculation. In the case of perception, the input is environmental data such as a visual image. The output is perceptual data. Intervening processes transform one into the other. Modern computational neuroscientists attempt to discover the nature of the intervening processes given the input to the system, the output it produces, and some hints about the intervening neural operations. To continue the analogy with an electronic calculator, the task is similar to trying to discover the rules of arithmetic given only the sequence of numbers and symbols providing the input, and the numbers produced by the calculator as output.

Modern computational theories of human cognition began with Newell and Simon's information processing model of problem solving (e.g., Newell & Simon, 1972). Computational neuroscientists test their theories by attempting to implement them using computer programs. In a typical test of a theory in vision, the computer is given an image and attempts to produce the required output.

The computational approach has introduced a high degree of rigor into theories of perception, but it provides no account of consciousness. There is an explanatory gap between neural computations and conscious perceptual states, as mentioned earlier in the chapter (Levine, 1983, 1999).

Phenomenology

Phenomenology lies on the opposite side of the explanatory gap from computational theories. It is the study of consciousness from the first-person perspective—how the world appears to me. There is a long tradition of phenomenology in European philosophy and psychology, but it is sometimes dismissed as a legitimate approach to the study of perception, because it is inherently subjective. Scientific approaches are usually considered to require objective methods. However, phenomenological studies can be performed using a variant of standard empirical scientific methods, including hypothesis generation and observation. There are several key differences between conventional psychophysical observations and phenomenological observations. The convention in psychophysics is to keep subjects naive as to the purpose of the experiment, and give them a well-defined task with highly constrained responses such as "yes" versus "no" (see the previous tutorial). In phenomenological experiments subjects are often fully informed about the purpose of the experiment, and their task is kept relatively open with loosely constrained responses. Response classification may occur only after the data have been examined. A key check on validity in phenomenological experiments is *intersubjectivity*, or agreement among individuals about the nature of their perceptual experience.

Many important discoveries about perception have been made using phenomenological experiments. The Gestalt school discussed earlier was founded on phenomenological observations. Prominent figures in phenomenological studies of perception include the Belgian psychologist Albert

Michotte (1881–1965; perception of causality, discussed in Chapter 12), and eminent Italian psychologists such as Vittorio Benussi (1878–1927; lightness), Cesare Musatti (1897–1989; depth from motion), Fabio Metelli (1907–1987; transparency), and Gaetano Kanizsa (1913–1993; subjective figures).

Phenomenological aspects of perception are often underplayed in psychophysical research, but modern studies would make little sense without assuming the existence of a perceptual experience in the subject that could lead to a phenomenological report. Standard psychophysical techniques typically embed phenomenological experience in an artificial task requiring simple, constrained responses. So phenomenological observation frequently underlies the subject's responses. Indeed, initial interest in a research issue is often triggered by phenomenological observations made by the experimenter.

Evaluation

In its emphasis on a specific set of issues and ideas, each theoretical movement has made its own particular contribution to our understanding of human sensation and perception. Contemporary research adopts a pluralistic approach which combines both neuroscientific and psychophysical techniques. The cognitive and computational neurosciences provide a rich set of experimental techniques and theoretical approaches, while psychophysics supplies the essential link between stimulus characteristics and perceptual experience.

Yantis (2001) has collected together many of the key papers described in this tutorial, as well as other classic papers in visual perception, and offers an excellent opportunity to study the primary sources that laid the foundations of modern perceptual theories.

The chemical senses

2

Contents

INTRODUCTION

The senses of smell and taste are called chemical senses because they extract information from the environment by means of direct chemical interactions. Molecules from external substances interact with receptor molecules in the nose and mouth, resulting in the generation of neural signals. Chemical molecules are wafted to olfactory chemoreceptors in the nose by atmospheric currents, so the stimulating substance itself can be quite remote from the perceiver. Taste, on the other hand, is a contact sense; molecules have to be in a solution that makes direct contact with the chemoreceptors. In this chapter each sense will be considered first in terms of its anatomy and physiology, and second in terms of its perceptual and functional properties. Clear relationships between anatomy and physiology, on the one hand, and perceptual and functional properties, on the other, will emerge.

SMELL

Odors are crucial for many animals. They are used to detect prey and predators, identify potential mates or competitors, and judge the palatability of food. Although smell is generally considered to be a "minor" sense for humans, we are astonishingly good at detecting odors. On January 21, 2013, residents in the southeast of England flooded the police with calls about a noxious odor of rotten cabbage, which was so bad that many feared it may be poisonous. Health officials eventually pinpointed the source of the odor to a leak at a chemical factory owned by the firm Lubrizol in Rouen, Normandy, about 160 kilometers south of the UK coastline. The leak released a chemical called ethyl mercaptan, which is normally added to domestic gas to aid the detection of gas

FIGURE 2.1
Smells can evoke powerful memories of childhood experiences. Copyright © Wavebreak Media Ltd./Corbis.

? *Why is the emotional impact of smell so great?*

leaks. The human nose is incredibly sensitive to the smell of this chemical: If three drops were added to the water in one of two Olympic-sized swimming pools, the odor would be sufficient for a human to detect which pool contained the chemical (Yeshurun & Sobel, 2010). The just noticeable difference (JND, discussed in Chapter 1) for odor is similar to that in other sensory systems, at about 5–7% (Cain, 1977).

Smell is also surprisingly effective in other ways. We can distinguish gender on the basis of breath, hand, or armpit smell (Doty et al., 1982; Schleidt, Hold, & Attili, 1981). Doctors have used the smell of a patient to help in the diagnosis of illnesses (Schiffman, 1983). Women who share accommodation have been found to synchronize their menstrual cycles as a result of chemical signals (see Wilson, 1992; Stern & McClintock, 1998).

Odors are also very effective at evoking powerful emotional responses and memories. In many people, the smell of popcorn or hotdogs evokes vivid memories of fairgrounds or movie theaters, while the smell of disinfectants and medicines brings back painful or fearful memories of spells in hospital. The size of the perfumery industry, and the volume of body perfumes and "air fresheners" manufactured, are a testament to the huge emotional impact of smell. The fragrance market in Europe was worth about £1.5bn in 2014, and about $22bn globally (*Management Today*, November 27, 2014).

ANATOMY AND PHYSIOLOGY OF SMELL

Over the last 15 years olfaction has emerged from relative obscurity as a sensory system, due to major advances in our knowledge of the genetic and molecular basis of smell. The olfactory system is remarkable for its ability to signal the presence of just a few aromatic molecules, and to discriminate between thousands of different compounds.

Receptors

Olfactory receptor neurons are found in the roof of the nasal cavity, on a patch of tissue called the **olfactory epithelium** (see Figure 2.2). In humans this tissue area covers 2–4 square centimeters, and contains about 6 million receptors (Kratskin, 1995). Each olfactory receptor cell lasts approximately 60 days, so the receptor cells are being constantly renewed. The actual receptor sites are located on cilia. These are microscopic hair-like projections that extend from the surface of each receptor cell into the moist tissue lining the inside of the nose (the olfactory mucosa). Each cell possesses about 5–40 cilia. Molecules given off by volatile substances must dissolve in the olfactory mucus in order to arrive at the receptor sites on the olfactory cilia (see Schild & Restrepo, 1998; Smith, 2000). Olfactory receptors are neurons that generate

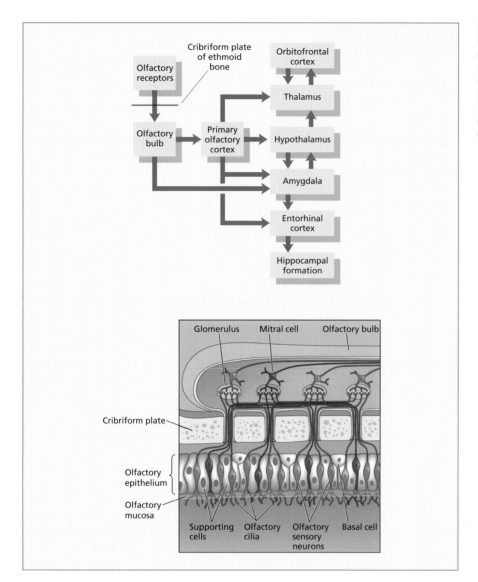

FIGURE 2.2
Sensory pathways for olfaction. Top: Flow diagram showing the organization of the pathways. Bottom: Peripheral anatomical components of the olfactory system.

an action potential when their resting potential of −65 mV depolarizes (the inside of the cell becomes positively charged) sufficiently to reach threshold. They effectively operate as molecule counters for particular kinds of chemical (Firestein, 2001).

As discussed in Chapter 1, the task of olfactory receptor neurons is to encode information about the chemical composition of odor molecules in neural signals. Small differences at the molecular level mean that different neurons are activated by different odor molecules (Ressler, Sullivan, & Buck, 1994). There are thought to be several hundred different olfactory receptor neuron types in humans. The olfactory mucosa also contains some **free nerve endings** that are

Our sense of smell is blunted when we have a cold because of the build-up of mucus in the nasal cavity that prevents odor molecules reaching the receptor cilia.

KEY TERM

Free nerve ending
A branch of a sensory nerve cell that has no specialized receptor process, but is embedded directly in tissue.

Mitral cell

A neuron in the olfactory bulb that receives signals from olfactory receptor neurons and relays them to the brain; there are 50,000 mitral cells in the human olfactory bulb.

Olfactory bulb

The mass of neural tissue protruding from the brain behind the nose, which conveys neural signals from the olfactory epithelium to the brain.

Olfactory glomerulus

A dense, spherical accumulation of dendrites and synapses, where approximately 200 olfactory receptors make contact with a single mitral cell.

Primary olfactory cortex

The cortical destination of mitral cell fibers, thought to mediate perception of smell.

Amygdala

A nucleus (dense group of neurons) lying deep in the brain, forming part of the limbic system; involved in emotional, sexual, and autonomic responses.

thought to mediate the sensations of coolness, tingling, and burning that arise from high concentrations of chemicals. Odorants are chemical compounds that have a smell or odor. Malnic et al. (1999) measured the response profiles of olfactory receptors and discovered that a single receptor responds to multiple odorants, by virtue of the fact that the odorants all contain the kind of molecule that excites the receptor. Conversely a single odorant excites multiple receptors because it contains many different kinds of molecule.

Sensory pathways

The axon of each receptor cell passes through a perforated bony plate in the skull (the cribriform plate) to project directly to a specific **mitral cell** in the **olfactory bulb**. The synapses between receptor cell axons and mitral cell dendrites bundle together to form 2000 **olfactory glomeruli** (Carlson, 2004; see Figure 2.2). Several thousand receptors converge on 5–25 mitral cells in each glomerulus (Firestein, 2001). The axons of mitral cells travel to the rest of the brain along the olfactory tract. Mitral cell axons project directly to the **primary olfactory cortex**, and also to the **amygdala**, which is associated with the generation of emotional responses.

Cortical processing

Severe blows to the head can result in a loss of the sense of smell, if the shearing force is sufficient to damage the receptor cell axons where they pass through the cribriform plate.

Smell is unique among the senses in that the neural projection from the olfactory tract is not relayed via the thalamus on the way to the cortex. This arrangement is thought to be a reflection of the relatively early appearance of olfaction during vertebrate evolution (Delcomyn, 1998). However a pathway running from the primary olfactory cortex to the orbitofrontal cortex (via the thalamus) is involved in the conscious perception of smell. Another unusual feature of olfaction is that both hemispheres of the cortex are activated by stimulation of only one nostril, whereas in other senses only one hemisphere tends to be activated by stimulation on one side of the body (usually the hemisphere on the opposite or contralateral side of the body to the stimulus). Cortical olfactory activity also seems to be modulated by breathing (see Lorig, 2002, for a review of cortical processing).

PERCEPTION AND FUNCTION OF SMELL

Detection

Some chemicals are detectable at concentrations thousands of times weaker than others. Humans are particularly sensitive to musk and to ethyl mercaptan but, for example, require concentrations up to a million times higher to detect methyl salicylate (the aromatic ingredient in the wintergreen plant).

Recognition

Memory for odor generally resembles memory for stimuli in other sensory modalities (Lawless & Engen, 1977). However, humans are quite poor at identifying odors. Cain (1982) tested the ability of men and women to recognize 80 different odors, and found that less than 50% of common household items which are used daily can be identified by smell alone. Women outperformed men in 65 of the 80 odors. Figure 2.3 plots recognition rates for the three odors that men identified best (ammonia, Brut aftershave, and sherry), and the four odors that women identified best (coconut, band-aid, fruit gum, and cat food). As well as finding recognition difficult, we often have only a minimal conscious awareness of smells (Sela & Sobel, 2010), and find it difficult to describe them (Jonsson, Olsson, & Olsson, 2005).

Theories of odor recognition

Any adequate theory to explain odor recognition must include a linking proposition to map physiological states (receptor activity) onto mental states (recognition), as discussed in Chapter 1. The simplest possible linking proposition is that each recognizable smell maps onto a specific kind of receptor. When a given receptor neuron is activated, we perceive the smell associated with it. However, we can recognize thousands of different odors with only a few hundred different kinds of olfactory receptor and mitral cell. There are clearly too few receptor cell types for each recognizable smell to be uniquely associated with a specific kind of mitral cell. In fact as described earlier most odorants contain a cocktail of different chemicals, so they will excite more than one receptor neuron type. Conversely, each receptor neuron type is able to respond to multiple odors (Sicard and Holley, 1984) As an illustration, Figure 2.4

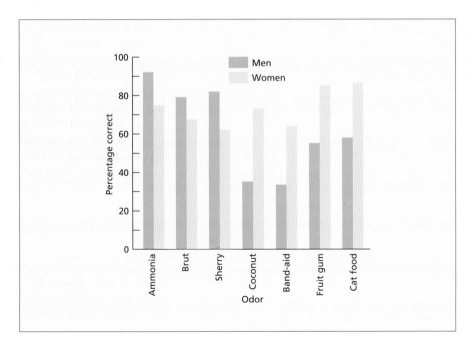

FIGURE 2.3
Odors identified most reliably by men compared with women, and vice versa, from the data set in Cain (1982).

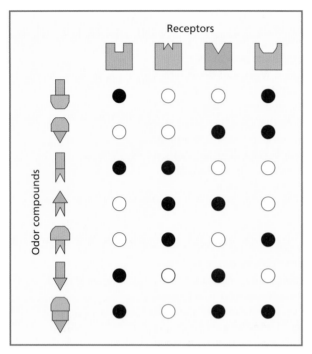

FIGURE 2.4
Combinatorial coding in olfaction. Each receptor (top row) responds to a specific odor component (denoted by a colored shape). Odor compounds are shown in the left column, depicted as a specific combination of colored shapes. Each compound activates at least two receptors (filled circles); conversely each receptor responds to several compounds. The identity of each compound is encoded by a unique combination of receptor responses (after Malnic et al., 1999).

shows seven different odor compounds (left column), each comprising a different combination of molecular features (depicted by colored shapes). Each receptor neuron type (top row) responds to a specific feature. Each row in the table shows the pattern of receptor response to each odor; a filled circle indicates that the receptor responds to the odor component. Notice that each odor compound produces a different pattern of activity across the receptor neuron types.

Malnic et al. (1999) describe this scheme as a combinatorial receptor code for odor. Even if only three receptor types contributed to each odor response, the number of odors that the system could distinguish would approach 1 billion. So the olfactory system has huge discriminatory power. This theory of odor coding is an example of *population coding*, introduced in Chapter 1: Stimulus character is carried in the responses of a whole population of cells. Linking propositions based on population coding are very common in theories of perception.

Recognition of a particular odorant amounts to recognition of a certain spatial pattern of activity across the different mitral cells in the olfactory bulb, because the anatomical positions of the glomeruli to which receptor neurons project are identical in different animals (though the different receptor cell types appear to be distributed randomly about the olfactory epithelium; Uchida et al., 2000).

Adaptation

The perceived intensity of a smell drops by 30% or more after continuous exposure. Figure 2.5 illustrates the results of an experiment by Ekman et al. (1967) in which subjects rated the intensity of a smell over a 12-minute period of continuous exposure (this graph was also used in Chapter 1 to illustrate the basic principles of adaptation). By the 12th minute, the apparent intensity of the smell had dropped to less than half its initial level. Once the smell was removed, and then presented only briefly over the next 12 minutes, its apparent intensity quickly climbed back to pre-adaptation levels. Both adaptation and recovery rates were exponential. In other words, the rate at which adaptation (or recovery) proceeded was proportional to time: As time progressed after the start of adaptation (or recovery), the rate of adaptation (or recovery) declined.

The world is never completely free of odor, so the olfactory system is never completely free of adaptation. We are continuously exposed to the odor of our own body, and often spend prolonged periods in a specific environment, such as our home. It would serve little purpose to be continually reminded of such constant odors, so adaptation ensures that they become undetectable. It is therefore not surprising that many individuals appear to be insensitive to the smell of their own body or their own house, even when those smells might appear unpleasant to others. Cigarette smokers, for example, are usually unaware of the smell of smoke on themselves or their surroundings, until they give up smoking.

Odor adaptation seems to be selective to similar smells. Moncrieff (1956) found that exposure to a specific odorant raised thresholds only for odorants with very similar smells. For example, thresholds for detecting acetone were raised nearly two hundredfold by prior exposure to acetone, but were raised by a factor of two by exposure to isopropanol. Berglund and Engen (1993) found much larger effects for self-adaptation (adapt and test on the same substance) than for cross-adaptation (adapt and test on different substances). However, Pierce et al. (1996) found that the relationship between perceptual similarity and cross-adaptation was far from simple. The complexity of adaptation effects reflects the complexity of the underlying physiological structures.

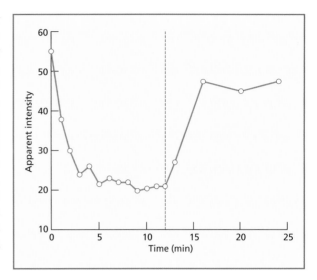

Anosmia

Odor blindness or **anosmia** can arise from a variety of sources. Partial anosmia is an inability to detect a specific odor. One person in ten in the general population is insensitive to the smell of cyanide, and one in a thousand is insensitive to butyl mercaptan. Several dozen such partial anosmias are known to exist. They are genetically transmitted, and probably reflect a deficiency in a specific type of olfactory receptor molecule (Smith, 2000).

The functional role of smell

Unlike other sensory systems, there is no agreed system for mapping physical stimulus attributes onto perception, so there is no way of predicting the smell evoked by a novel molecule (Khan et al., 2007). However people are highly consistent in the way they describe smells, so it is possible to identify the perceptual dimensions of smell. Statistical analyses of smell descriptors have revealed two dominant dimensions (Khan et al., 2007; Zarzo, 2008):

Pleasantness–unpleasantness,   also known as hedonic tone. For example, some smells are judged as pleasingly "fruity" or "flowery," while others are judged as unpleasantly "musky" or "animal."

Edible–inedible   For instance, smells associated with baked or spiced products are perceived as "edible," whereas smells associated with cleaning or cosmetic products are perceived as "inedible."

The relatively simple perceptual dimensions associated with the sense of smell, and our relatively weak ability to recognize smells despite a sophisticated sensory apparatus, indicates that this sense primarily serves as a primitive but reliable stimulus classification system. Its function is to classify smells in terms of approach–avoidance (should we get closer to the source of the smell, or avoid it?), and in terms of edibility (should we eat the substance or not?). The sense of smell allows us to classify even substances that have not been encountered before.

FIGURE 2.5
Adaptation to an odor. Sensory magnitude of an odor sensation was measured at regular intervals during a 12-minute exposure, showing adaptation to a constant stimulus. Once the stimulus was removed, sensory magnitude gradually recovered to former levels. From Ekman et al. (1967). Reproduced with permission from John Wiley and Sons.

 Think of some everyday consequences of total anosmia.

TASTE

In modern human society, taste (also known as gustation) is used mainly to define our preferences for specific foods. However, gustation is universal in the animal kingdom, and is vital for establishing whether a specific substance is edible and nutritious, or poisonous.

ANATOMY AND PHYSIOLOGY OF TASTE

Receptors

Taste receptors are chemoreceptor cells that are found on the tongue, and in the mouth and throat. They are grouped into about 10,000 **taste buds** that are located on small projections known as **papillae**. Each taste bud contains 50–150 receptor cells arranged like the segments of an orange (Smith, 2000). The receptors in each bud form synapses with the dendrites of sensory neurons whose axons bundle together to form the VIIth, IXth, and Xth cranial nerves that convey their responses to the brain.

Taste bud cells have a very short life span of less than about 10 days. This makes it difficult for investigators to establish their function. During transduction (initial reception of the chemical stimulus), molecules from a substance placed in the mouth dissolve in saliva and bind to molecules on receptor cells. The resultant change in membrane permeability causes changes in receptor potential. Different substances bind with different types of receptor neuron. The transduction mechanism appears to vary between receptor neuron types (Scott and Giza, 2000). It also varies from one species to another. Some substances have a more direct chemical effect on the receptor neuron than others (Delcomyn, 1998).

Research on taste over the last 120 years has identified five primary taste qualities: Sweet, sour, salty, bitter, and savoriness. Early recordings from the sensory neurons in the cat, rat, and rabbit matched the first four of these basic taste qualities. Fiber responses did show a preference for one type of substance over the others. Figure 2.7 (top) illustrates the four types of sensory neuron found in the cranial nerve of rats (Nowlis & Frank, 1977). Notice that although each nerve responds best to one kind of substance it also responds to some extent to other substances. This may reflect the fact that a single sensory neuron connects to more than one type of receptor.

The fifth taste receptor was identified only relatively recently, as a receptor for amino acids (Chaudhari, Landin, & Roper, 2000; Nelson et al., 2002). One particular amino acid, monosodium glutamate (MSG), mediates the taste sensation known in Japanese as **umami**, meaning "good taste" or "yummy." MSG is associated with the palatability or savory quality of food, and is present in foods such as parmesan cheese, tomatoes, mushrooms, and peas. Many snack manufacturers add MSG to

---

KEY TERMS

Taste receptor
A chemoreceptor cell found on taste buds in the mouth, tongue, and throat; there are 50–150 receptors on each bud.

Taste bud
A cluster of cells embedded in the skin of the tongue and mouth, housing taste receptors. The human tongue contains approximately 5000 taste buds.

Gustatory papilla
A small elevation on the tongue, visible to the naked eye, containing up to several hundred taste buds.

Umami
A Japanese word meaning "good taste"; recent evidence indicates that it is a fifth basic taste quality.

their products to enhance their attractiveness, and it is traditionally used as a flavor enhancer in Asian cuisine.

Some papillae contain free nerve endings that are thought to signal the spiciness of foods such as chilli peppers. Recall that free nerve endings also exist in the olfactory epithelium, and are thought to signal certain "chemical" qualities of smells such as tingle and coolness.

Sensory pathways

The VIIth, IXth, and Xth cranial nerves carrying gustatory information terminate in the nucleus of the solitary tract in the medulla (part of the brainstem). Neurons in the medulla send axons to the amygdala and to the thalamus. Projections from the thalamus terminate in the primary gustatory cortex, the anterior insula and frontal operculum (AI/FO; see Figure 2.6).

Cortical processing

Our knowledge of cortical processing in taste has benefited from all of the physiological techniques described in the previous chapter. The involvement of the AI/FO was identified clinically over 60 years ago from the loss of taste perception in individuals with bullet wounds in this region of the brain (Bornstein, 1940). Anatomical tracing in macaque monkeys has subsequently confirmed the primary role of the AI/FO in taste (Pritchard et al., 1986). The same area has been identified more recently using fMRI (e.g., Faurion et al., 1998). Single-unit recordings in the AI/FO (Scott & Plata-Salaman, 1999) indicate that the region is also involved in somatosensory and motor functions relating to taste (mouth feel; the textural and bite qualities of food).

Individual cortical cells are quite broadly tuned to taste stimuli. Scott and Plata-Salaman (1999) calculated a breadth-of-tuning coefficient from their single-unit recordings. A score of zero for a given cell would indicate total specificity in its response to one of the basic taste stimuli; a score of 1.0 would indicate equal responsiveness to all taste stimuli. Figure 2.7 (bottom) shows the distribution of scores obtained from hundreds of cortical cells. The mean score was 0.7, showing that most cells do respond to a range of stimuli, but each cell has a moderate preference for a specific taste category: 38% of the cells studied preferred sweet substances, while 34% favored salts. Much smaller proportions favored bitter or acidic substances (22% and 5% respectively). Scott and Plata-Salaman (1999) could not identify any consistent topographic arrangement in the location of cells preferring different substances within the AI/FO area. However more recent research on mice has produced evidence for topographically organized taste coding neurons, which are more tightly tuned than previously thought (Chen et al., 2011); producing a "gustotopic" map with different clusters of cells responding to different taste qualities. As we shall see in later chapters, other sensory modalities display very highly ordered cortical topography.

PERCEPTION AND FUNCTION OF TASTE

Taste adaptation

Prior exposure to one taste can affect perception of a later taste, either by diminishing that taste or by enhancing it (McBurney, 1969). For instance, adaptation to one sour

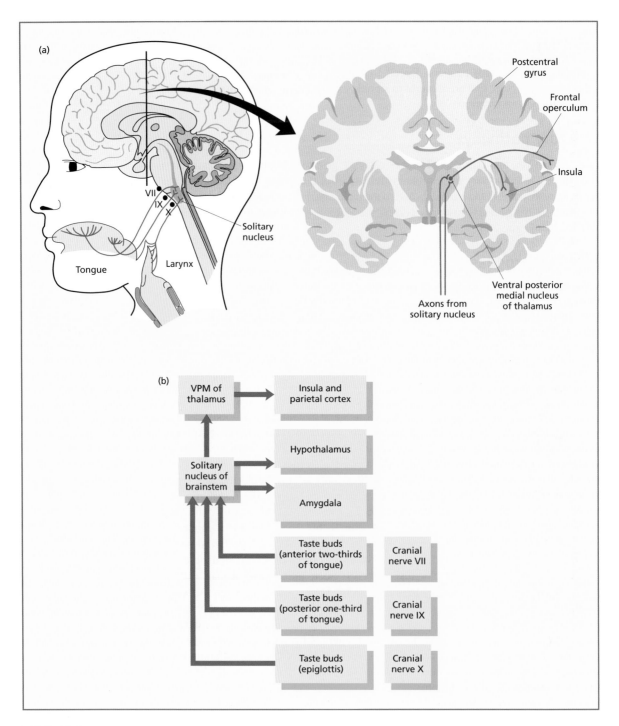

FIGURE 2.6
Sensory pathways for gustation. (a) Anatomical routes: Cranial nerves from the mouth terminate in the solitary nucleus. Central projections from here to the thalamus are shown in a sideways cross-section of the brain; fibers from the thalamus target sites in the cortex. (b) Flow diagram showing the organization of the pathways. Redrawn from Purves et al. (2001). Copyright © 2001 Sinauer Associates. Reproduced with permission.

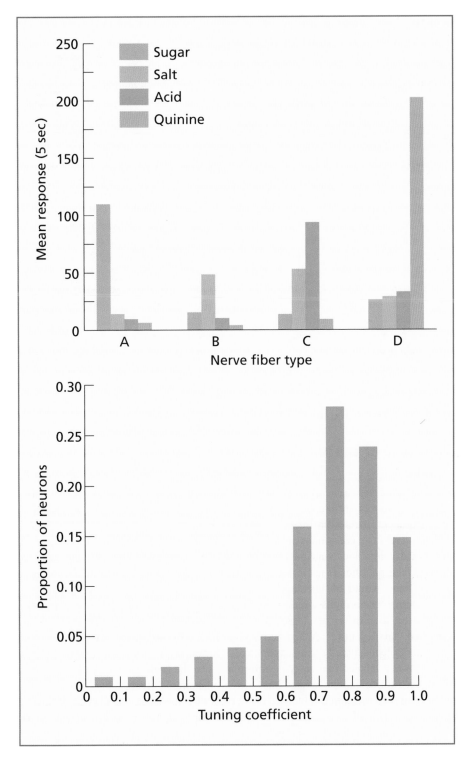

taste, such as citric acid, reduces the apparent intensity of other sour tastes such as acetic acid as well as the intensity of some bitter tastes such as quinine. On the other hand, adaptation to sour compounds will cause water to taste sweet, and adaptation to sweet compounds will cause water to taste sour (McBurney, 1969). Cross-adaptation was mentioned earlier in the discussion of smell adaptation. As we shall see in later chapters, cross-adaptation techniques are commonly used in perceptual research, because they allow us to draw some inferences about the nature of the neural mechanisms coding different sensory qualities.

Conditioned taste aversion

If a food induces illness, many animals later show an aversion to consuming that food again (Garcia & Koelling, 1966). The effect is very powerful, and requires only a single learning episode. There have been many experimental demonstrations of the effect in animals given food laced with nausea-inducing chemicals, including experiments on rats, mice, monkeys, ferrets, birds, fish, and reptiles. "Bait-shyness" in rodents can be attributed to conditioned taste aversion. Humans also show conditioned taste aversion. Many people develop an aversion to a particular food following a bout of sickness at the time they ate it. Excessive alcohol consumption can lead to a (temporary) aversion to alcohol afterwards. The aversion apparently requires no conscious awareness, and may even develop when a particular food is consumed just before a bout of sickness unconnected with consumption of the food. This is a particular problem for patients undergoing radiotherapy or chemotherapy for the treatment of cancer (Bernstein, 1978). Food aversion and loss of appetite are well known, so patients are advised not to eat within a couple of hours of treatment, and to eat nonpreferred foods (Schiffman, 1983).

Theories of taste coding

There has been a good deal of debate about how taste is coded in the human gustatory system. Some researchers have argued that taste is a "synthetic" sense, in which sensory responses are blended into an experience that cannot be broken down into its component parts (Pfaffman, 1959; Erickson, 1982). The weight of evidence suggests that taste constitutes an "analytic" sense; its sensations can be decomposed perceptually into the contributions from each of the primary sensations, with no intermediate qualities (see Bartoshuk & Beauchamp, 1994). For example, the taste of lemonade would be decomposed into contributions from sweetness, sourness, and bitterness sensations. According to this view, known as the **taste primaries** theory, the four different classes of neuron illustrated A to D in Figure 2.7 are so-called "labeled lines": When activity is present in one of the classes of neuron, that activity leads directly to an experience of the corresponding taste quality, because that class is a labeled line carrying information to the brain about a specific kind of substance (notice that the labeled lines idea is an example of a psychophysical linking hypothesis, discussed in Chapter 1). The weight of evidence favors the taste primaries theory. Cortical cells do appear to cluster into topographically organized groups on the basis of their preference for one of the stimulus categories (Chen et al., 2011).

The taste system seems to function as a nutritional gatekeeper, regulating consumption and rejection on the basis of edibility and nutritional value, as signaled by the five taste qualities:

Sweetness   Foods that contain large quantities of simple carbohydrates (sugars) which can be broken down quickly by the body and used for energy tend to be perceived as sweet. The taste of sweet is almost universally preferred and it is clearly beneficial to consume sweet-tasting substances, at least in moderation. Looy, Callaghan and Weingarten (1992) report that adults can be divided into at least two groups on the basis of their preference for sweetness. "Sweet likers" show a steadily rising preference with increasing sweetness, while another group exhibits an inverted U-shaped preference in which intermediate levels of sweetness are most preferred; the preferred level of sweetness in this latter group varies markedly from one person to another.

Saltiness   Substances that contain sodium chloride taste salty. Sodium is vital for maintaining a balanced distribution of water across cell membranes in the body, but it can be depleted by sweating or bleeding. So salt is generally perceived as palatable at moderate concentrations. Adults deprived of sodium show a heightened preference for salty foods (Beauchamp et al., 1990).

Sourness   Acidic substances taste sour, and tend to be judged as unpalatable. Acidity is associated with food which is unripe or contaminated with bacteria, so there is clearly adaptive value in avoiding it.

Bitterness   The bitter taste is associated with a diverse range of chemical compounds, including plant alkaloids that are toxic, such as strychnine, quinine, morphine, and tubocurarine (alkaloid names generally end in the –ine suffix). The unpalatable taste of bitter substances protects us from the ingestion of plant-based poisons.

Savoriness   As mentioned earlier umami is linked to the presence of amino acids, particularly monosodium glutamate (MSG), which is found naturally in a wide range of foods including seafood, tomatoes, mushrooms, peas, cheese, and walnuts. MSG serves as an indicator of protein content, and tends to increase the palatability of food. Snack manufacturers add MSG to encourage consumption, and powdered MSG is used in Asian cuisine. Powdered MSG is made from fermented sugar beet or sugar cane molasses, similar to the way in which soy sauce is made (which is also high in MSG). Some people believe that they are allergic to MSG and suffer from so-called "Chinese restaurant syndrome," but there is no scientific basis for this claim (Williams & Woessner, 2009).

FLAVOR

The sensation of eating, or *flavor*, transcends both smell and taste. It involves an interaction between several perceptual sensations including taste, smell, temperature, touch, sight, sound, and pain. These different sensations appear to interact to determine flavor, so we cannot view flavor as a simple summation of disparate sensations. However, smell and taste seem to be preeminent, in that a sensation complex that excludes them does not create a flavor. There are many examples of how the sensory components of flavor interact. For example, certain visual colors are associated with particular flavors, and when color is altered there is a change in flavor. The rated flavor intensity of foods such as yoghurt, cakes, and sucrose solutions increases with the degree of food coloration. Increases in the amount of gelling agent in a food increase its viscosity and texture thickness, but also reduce its flavor intensity, and it is difficult to relate the flavor change to the chemical effects of the gelling agent. For a review of recent perceptual research on flavor, see Delwiche (2004).

Sensory pathways in the brain for smell, taste, and vision are anatomically distinct. However, Rolls and Baylis (1994) found an area of the macaque monkey orbitofrontal cortex in which information from the three modalities converges. Cells that responded to each of the modalities were found in close proximity. Moreover, one third of the neurons had responses to a combination of two sensory modalities: Smell and taste, smell and vision, or taste and vision. These cells may form part of the neural system which is responsible for our perception of flavor.

EVALUATION

At this point it is worthwhile pausing to reflect on the general principles introduced in Chapter 1, and how they relate specifically to the chemical senses.

Qualia and modality   The smells and tastes detected by the receptors generate powerful sensory states, or qualia: The clean smell of limes, yumminess in foods containing MSG, the disgusting odor of feces. In some respects the two senses operate as distinct modalities, but they are also tightly integrated to create flavors that blend the two senses together.

Psychophysics   We are incredibly sensitive to certain smells, but thresholds vary markedly from one odorant to another. The detectability of olfactory and gustatory stimuli varies markedly over time (Figure 2.5), and helps us to adapt to specific environments. The taste primaries theory is based on a clearly articulated psychophysical linking hypothesis which proposes a direct relation between activity in sensory nerves and specific experiences.

Cognitive neuroscience   Both smell and taste are based on chemoreceptors, which show a clear preference for particular odorants (Figure 2.4) or tastes (Figure 2.7). Both senses also exhibit a clear hierarchy of processing that begins at the receptors in the nose, mouth, and throat, and ends with activity in the sensory cortex, passing through intermediate stages on the way (compare Figure 1.12 with Figures 2.2 and 2.6). Topographic maps feature in both systems.

Computational neuroscience   There are very good examples of representation in the chemical senses. In the case of smell, recall that any one receptor neuron responds to multiple odorants, and any one odorant excites multiple receptor neurons. It follows that different odorants excite different combinations of receptor neurons. We can therefore consider the pattern of activity across the population of receptor neuron types as representing the unique chemical composition of the odorant. If the odorant composition changes, the pattern of activity (representational state) in the receptors also changes. The pattern of activity actually forms a spatial representation of the odorant by virtue of the spatial arrangement of glomeruli in the olfactory bulb. Malnic et al. (1999) proposed that the pattern of activity constitutes a "combinatorial code" for odor. There are roughly 1000 different receptor neuron types. Even if we assume that just three types respond to each odor, the code would be able to discriminate nearly a billion different odors (Malnic et al., 1999). In other words, it would have nearly a billion different representational states.

In the case of taste, receptors fall into just five classes responding optimally to sugars, salts, acids (sour), plant alkaloids (bitter), and glutamic acid (umami). Activity in each receptor class appears to represent the presence of the corresponding substance; a specific state in the sensory system maps onto a specific state in the outside world (the presence of a particular kind of substance).

The psychophysical and neural characteristics of the chemical senses allow us to infer what kinds of computations they perform: Approach–avoidance, edibility, and nutritional value.

Linda Buck was jointly awarded with Richard Axel the 2004 Nobel Prize in physiology or medicine for their research on the olfactory system. Their pioneering work has given us a detailed understanding of how the nose is able to distinguish more than 10,000 smells, as well as defining the genes and proteins that control the olfactory response.

CHAPTER SUMMARY

The senses of smell and taste are known as chemical senses because their receptor neurons extract information by means of chemical interactions.

SMELL

- The sense of smell is mediated by 500–1000 different types of sensory receptor in the olfactory epithelium of the nose.
- Each mitral cell in the olfactory bulb of the brain is connected to just one type of receptor neuron. Different environmental substances create different patterns of activity across the mitral cells. The ability of humans to recognize thousands of different odors depends on the ability of the olfactory sensory system to distinguish different patterns of activity in mitral cells.
- The large number of partial anosmias found in humans is a reflection of the relatively large number of different olfactory receptors present in the sensory system.
- The function of smell is to act as an early warning system which classifies smells in terms of two dimensions: Approach–avoidance and substance edibility.

TASTE

- All tastes can be decomposed into contributions from five primary qualities—sweetness, saltiness, sourness, bitterness, and savoriness or umami.
- Gustatory receptors fall into five categories on the basis of their preference for one of five types of substance, namely sugars, salts, acids, plant alkaloids, and amino acids. These receptor neuron types map precisely onto the primary taste qualities identified perceptually.
- The taste primaries theory of taste coding proposes that the receptor neuron types are labeled lines, coding the presence of specific substances.

The properties of the sensory pathway and cortical representation of taste are consistent with the taste primaries theory.

• The function of the gustatory system is to detect different types of important substance, because there is adaptive value in regulating their intake (consuming some and avoiding others).

FLAVOR

• Food flavor during eating involves an interaction between several perceptual sensations including taste, smell, temperature, touch, sight, sound, and pain.

• Cells responsive to combinations of smell, taste, and sight may mediate flavor sensations.

TUTORIALS

SMELL AND EMOTION

The hedonic (pleasantness–unpleasantness) aspect of smell has long been regarded as its most important quality (Engen, 1982). Smells do evoke powerful emotional responses ranging from intense pleasure to extreme revulsion. In the Middle Ages it was believed that unpleasant odors actually caused diseases such as the Black Death. Doctors visiting plague victims took elaborate precautions to shield themselves from the unpleasant odor thought to cause the disease. They wore an elaborate mask shaped like a duck's head, with eye holes made of glass and a beak filled with herbs and petals (see Figure 2.8). They also carried a torch burning a potpourri of fragrant herbs.

The use of perfume to enhance attractiveness dates back to the beginning of recorded history. The ancient cultures of the Middle and Far East manufactured and traded perfumes on a large scale (Stoddart, 1990). Perfumes became synonymous with, and a substitute for, personal hygiene. Standards of personal hygiene are obviously much higher in modern society than in the Middle Ages, but washing and personal hygiene products are still sold primarily on the basis of their hedonic aromatic qualities. The continual search for clean, pleasing smells may reflect the fact that odor perception seems to be dominated by displeasure. Engen (1982) cited a Japanese study which found that only 20% of 400,000 different odors tested were judged to be pleasant. Engen and Ross (1973) reported a tendency for unfamiliar odors to be disliked by naive subjects. They used 110 different odors and found that only 11% of unfamiliar odors were liked, whereas 46% of familiar odors were liked.

FIGURE 2.8
Dress worn by doctors during the plague in 18th-century France. The leather coat was covered in honey-scented beeswax, and the beak-like mask with glass eye holes was filled with fresh herbs and dried flower petals (this may be the origin of the slang word for doctors—quacks). A potpourri of herbs was burnt in the torch. Painting by Jan van Grevenbroeck (1731–1807).

Whether a smell is pleasant or unpleasant, its emotional impact wanes with exposure. There are anecdotal reports that people who work in strong-smelling environments, such as confectionery factories, glue factories, or animal rendering plants, become adapted so that the pleasant smell of, for example, chocolate, or the unpleasant smell of animal carcasses becomes less intense. Cain and Johnson (1978) found experimental support for these anecdotal reports. Subjects were exposed to pleasant or unpleasant smells for 30 minutes. A pleasant smell (citral—lemon) was judged less pleasant after adaptation than before, and an unpleasant smell (isobutyric acid—rancid butter) was judged less unpleasant.

Why is the hedonic quality of smell so powerful? Olfaction is the only sense in which there are direct projections between the primary sensory cortex and the amygdala. In rodents 40% of neurons in the amygdala respond to olfactory stimulation (Cain and Bindra, 1972). The amygdala is well known to play a crucial role in generating emotional responses, as revealed by lesion studies and single-cell recording data (Aggleton, 1992). Zald and Pardo (1997) reported a PET neuroimaging study of the human brain regions activated by pleasant and unpleasant smells. The most significant increases in regional cerebral blood flow (rCBF) during exposure to a very unpleasant smell were bilaterally in the amygdala. Weaker activation was also found in the primary olfactory cortex. On the other hand, statistically nonsignificant increases in rCBF were found during presentation of pleasant odors. The greater power of aversive stimuli in this PET study is consistent with earlier reports that displeasure dominates odor perception, and with reports that the amygdala is particularly involved in the appraisal of danger and the emotion of fear (Scott et al., 1997). It seems that one of the primary functions of olfaction is to alert the organism to the presence of danger indicated by decomposing vegetable or animal matter.

THE VARIETY OF CHEMICAL RECEPTORS

The chemical senses are the most primitive of all senses, from an evolutionary perspective. Chemosensitivity undoubtedly emerged very early in the history of life on Earth, in primitive bacteria immersed in a watery medium awash with chemicals. Present-day bacteria are known to possess chemoreceptors that they use to guide their movement, swimming toward nutrients and away from toxins (Koshland, 1980). Gustatory receptors clearly function primarily to detect and identify food-related chemicals, whereas olfactory receptors are also used to identify other animals (mates, predators, and prey) and for localization (migration, navigation). The division of chemical senses into smell and taste has been questioned in the case of water-dwelling animals, though Atema (1977) argued that the two senses do remain distinct even in an aquatic environment. Many fish have very highly developed olfactory senses. They can detect blood and bodily fluids over considerable distances, and migrating salmon are believed to navigate to spawning grounds using olfactory signals (Smith, 2000). Birds also use odors carried by the winds for navigation, particularly over oceans (Gagliardo, 2013).

Among land-dwelling animals, olfactory receptors are remarkably similar across phyla. Glomeruli similar to those found in the human olfactory bulb are found in a wide diversity of animals, from molluscs to arthropods (Delcomyn, 1998). Gustatory receptors, on the other hand, do show marked species differences. Many animals possess two gustatory systems. As well as gustatory receptors in the mouth, they have receptors on their external body surface, such as on antennae (snails), tentacles (octopus), or legs (arthropods). The structure housing these external receptors is known as a "sensillum"—a small peg, pit, plate, socket, or hair usually open at the tip and covered in a small drop of viscous fluid in which substances diffuse before reception (Shepherd, 1988). Some female insects even have sensilli on their ovipositor (used for laying eggs in a suitable environment).

In addition to chemoreceptors that contribute to the sense of smell and taste, most animals (including humans) have a number of other chemoreceptors that monitor internal bodily chemicals, such as receptors for glucose levels, receptors for circulating toxins, and receptors for sensing the level of blood oxygenation in the carotid arteries. These receptors cannot be considered as part of a sensory system, since their responses are not processed in the same way as those of conventional sensory receptors and do not contribute to conscious experience. Many animals, especially insects, use a complex system of chemical signals to control social behavior and mating. Moths that communicate by means of sex pheromones can have as many as 75,000 chemoreceptors on each of their antennae. Only one or two molecules of pheromone are required per receptor cell over a 2-second period in order to evoke a behavioral response from the insect (Delcomyn, 1998).

The chemoreceptors found in the human gustatory and olfactory senses thus represent just a small part of a broad spectrum of chemoreceptors that serve a number of different functions in different organisms.

The body senses

3

Contents

INTRODUCTION

The body senses provide information about surfaces touching the skin (somatosensation), about the position and movement of body parts (**proprioception** and **kinesthesis**), about pain (nociception) and about the position and movement of the body itself relative to the external world (vestibular sense). As mentioned in Chapter 1, somatosensation, proprioception, kinesthesis, and nociception share significant aspects of neural processing in terms of receptor or pathways so they will be discussed together in this chapter in the section on the somatosensory system, though arguably they are different sensory modalities. The vestibular sense is distinctively different from the other body senses in terms of its neural processing, so will be discussed in a separate section.

THE SOMATOSENSORY SYSTEM

Touch mediates our most intimate contact with the external world. We use it to sense the physical properties of a surface, such as its texture, warmth, and softness. The sensitivity of this system is exquisite, particularly at the most sensitive parts of the body such as the fingers and lips. Direct contact with other people is responsible for some of our most intense and intimate sensory experiences. Individuals who lack the sense of touch due to a physical disorder are severely disabled, since they lack the sensory information that is essential to avoid tissue damage caused by direct contact with harmful surfaces.

Compared to the sense of touch, proprioception and kinesthesis seem largely invisible. We are not conscious of making use of information about the position and movement of body parts, so it is very difficult to imagine what it must be like to be deprived of proprioception. Yet proprioception is vital for normal bodily

KEY TERMS

Proprioception
The sensory modality providing information about the position of body parts, served by mechanoreceptors in the musculoskeletal system.

Kinesthesis
The sensory modality providing information about the movement of body parts, served by mechanoreceptors in the musculoskeletal system.

FIGURE 3.1
Direct physical contact mediates some of our most powerful sensory experiences. Copyright © H Team/Shutterstock.com.

functioning, and its absence is severely disabling. Some appreciation of its importance can be gained from individuals who have lost their sense of proprioception following illness. Cole and Paillard (1995) describe two such people, identified by their initials, IW and GL. IW was a 19-year-old butcher when he suffered a flu-like viral illness. He became increasingly weak and at one point fell down in the street. On admission to hospital, he had slurred speech, an absence of sensation in the mouth, no sense of touch on his body, and no awareness of body position. Although he retained an ability to move his body, he had no control over the movement. Superficially he may have appeared to be suffering from alcohol intoxication, but it soon became clear that he must have been infected by a strange virus. After recovery from the initial infection, IW spent 18 months in a rehabilitation hospital learning to control his movements, including learning to walk again, following which he was discharged and did not see a doctor for about 12 years. Later investigations established that in attacking the virus IW's immune system had destroyed the sensory nerves that supply the brain with information about touch and proprioception, though he could still sense pain and temperature. In the absence of proprioception, IW could only make controlled bodily movements with intense concentration, visual attentiveness, and imagery. Once he had learned to walk, if he sneezed, and thus broke his concentration, he would fall over. He had to monitor the position of his moving feet and legs visually while walking. Even the act of sitting in a chair required concentration to avoid falling out of it. IW avoided crowded spaces, for fear of being nudged by someone out of view. When navigating an unfamiliar environment he studied it beforehand, in the same way that a mountaineer would survey a difficult climb, to judge the degree of slope in the ground surface, to measure the size of any gaps through which he must fit, and to estimate the strength of any wind. The act of picking up an egg required intense concentration in order to avoid inadvertently gripping hard enough to crush the egg (in the absence of somatosensory feedback on grip pressure). IW made use of his acquired skills in assessing environments, and found work as an adviser for holiday care services, reporting on the suitability of possible holiday locations for disabled visitors.

The case of IW is a vivid example of the importance of intact somatosensory signals for successfully completing apparently trivial everyday activities like sitting down or picking up fragile objects.

PHYSIOLOGY OF SOMATOSENSATION

The somatosensory system includes eight different kinds of receptor and two separate pathways linking receptors to the primary receiving area in the cerebral cortex.

Somatosensory receptors

Table 3.1 lists the eight types of receptor, their location, and their primary sensory function.

TABLE 3.1 Classification of somatosensory receptors

Receptor type	Fiber	Location	Sensory function
Touch and pain:			
Nociceptors	Aδ, C	All skin, superficial	Pain, temperature, tickle
Meissner's corpuscles	RA	Glabrous skin, superficial	Light, dynamic touch
Merkel's disks	SAI	All skin, superficial	Static pressure
Pacinian corpuscles	RC	All skin, deep	Pressure, vibration
Ruffini's corpuscles	SAII	All skin, deep	Stretching of skin
Proprioception:			
Muscle spindles		Muscles	Muscle length
Golgi tendon organs		Tendons	Muscle tension
Joint receptors		Joints	Joint position

KEY TERM

Touch receptors
Mechanoreceptors below the surface of the skin, mediating perception of pressure, vibration, stretch.

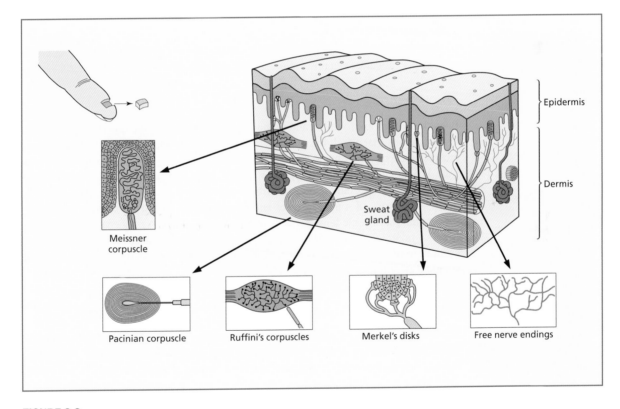

FIGURE 3.2
Cross-section through a region of hairless skin revealing five different types of touch receptor. Redrawn from Purves et al. (2001). Copyright © 2001 Sinauer Associates. Reproduced with permission.

Touch and pain receptors

Figure 3.2 illustrates the location of the five different touch and pain receptors below the surface of the skin. As indicated in Table 3.1, some lie near the surface of the skin whereas others lie deeper below the surface. Free nerve endings (**nociceptors**) do not have any structural specializations for converting stimulation into electrical responses (transduction), and it is not possible to determine their preferred stimulus on the basis of morphology. The mechanism of transduction is not well understood (Delcomyn, 1998), but they are known to mediate sensation of pain from tissue damage, as well as hot and cold. In the remaining four types of touch receptor the nerve ending is encapsulated within a specialized structure that governs the receptor's response to mechanical stimulation:

- *Pacinian corpuscles* have an onion-like capsule in which thin layers (membrane lamellae) are separated by fluid. Mechanical stimulation deforms the structure and leads to a response from the receptor. Pacinian corpuscles are able to vary their activity at a very high rate (250–350 Hz) in response to dynamic stimulation, allowing them to respond to high frequency vibration of the skin, such as that produced by the movement of a fine-textured surface across the skin.
- *Merkel's disks* and *Ruffini's corpuscles*, on the other hand, have a very sluggish temporal response, making them best suited to signal relatively stable, unchanging mechanical stimulation.
- *Meissner's corpuscles* have an intermediate temporal response (30–50 Hz), able to detect moderate dynamic stimulation.

Proprioceptors

Proprioceptors are found in and around the limbs, either in the muscles themselves, in the tendons that attach the muscles to bone, or in the joints. The proprioceptors in muscles are known as muscle spindles, and are relatively well understood, whereas little is known about the receptors in joints. Muscle spindles consist of between four and eight specialized muscle fibers surrounded by a capsule of connective tissue. The axons of sensory nerves encircle the fibers within the capsule to provide information on muscle length. Large muscles that generate fairly coarse movements possess relatively few muscle spindles, while muscles used for very fine and accurate movements, such as those in the hand and surrounding the eyes, are well supplied with muscle spindles.

Somatosensory pathways

The mechanoreceptors mediating somatosensation are modified sensory neurons. Their cell bodies are located in the **dorsal root ganglia**, which lie just outside the spinal column. Their peripheral axons end in various sensory specializations below the surface of the skin, while their central axons project toward the brain. Mechanical stimulation of a particular sensory neuron provokes a graded change in receptor electrical potential. When the receptor potential exceeds a certain minimum value an action potential is triggered, which travels along the cell's axon. The action potential is transmitted along one of two routes, known as the **spinothalamic pathway** and the **lemniscal pathway**. The flowchart in Figure 3.3 summarizes these two routes to the brain.

In the spinothalamic pathway (right-hand route in the flowchart), central axons carrying responses from nociceptors terminate in the spinal cord in areas called Rexed's laminae I and II (Purves et al., 2001). Responses are then relayed to cells in laminae IV to VI, whose axons project all the way up the spinal cord to the thalamus.

KEY TERMS

Nociceptors
Free nerve endings mediating perception of dangerously intense stimulation and temperature.

Proprioceptors
Mechanoreceptors in muscles, tendons, and joints mediating perception of body position and movement.

Dorsal root ganglia
Rounded swellings lying in the vertebrae just outside the spinal cord, each containing thousands of afferent cell bodies whose axons enter the spinal cord.

Spinothalamic pathway
The ascending sensory pathway for pain and temperature signals from free nerve endings.

Lemniscal pathway
The ascending sensory pathway for somatosensory signals from mechanoreceptors.

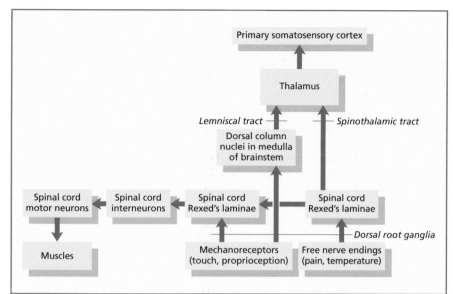

FIGURE 3.3
Sensory pathways in the somatosensory system. Responses from nociceptors (free nerve endings), mediating pain and temperature sensations, travel along the spinothalamic tract. Responses from mechanoreceptors mediating touch and proprioception travel along the lemniscal tract. Branching connections in Rexed's laminae of the spinal cord mediate reflexive withdrawal responses to harmful stimuli.

Nociceptor fibers divide into at least two types, called Aδ and C fibers (Torebjörk & Ochoa, 1990). Aδ fibers seem to mediate the initial rapid sensation of sharp pain while C fibers convey slow, duller, burning pain.

In the lemniscal pathway, some axons carrying responses from mechanoreceptors ascend the spinal cord as far as the brainstem (terminating in the dorsal column nuclei of the medulla), while others terminate in the spinal cord. Projections from the medulla terminate in the thalamus. Both the spinothalamic pathway and the lemniscal pathway contribute to cortical processing because their thalamic neurons send axons to the primary somatosensory cortex. Both pathways also contain branching projections in the spinal cord that are responsible for reflexes, such as withdrawal from painful stimuli, and the **knee-jerk reflex** (horizontal arrows in the flowchart).

The two pathways differ in their transmission speed. Axons associated with mechanoreceptors in the lemniscal pathway are myelinated (covered in a laminated wrapping) and as a result have relatively fast conduction velocities of about 20 m/s. Axons in the spinothalamic pathway are only lightly myelinated or unmyelinated, and have relatively slow conduction velocities of about 2 m/s. This difference in conduction velocity can be sensed when a drop of hot water falls on the hand. The contact of the water drop on the hand can be sensed about half a second before its temperature (Delcomyn, 1998).

It is possible to obtain direct electrophysiological recordings from the peripheral afferent nerves of human subjects, using a technique called **microneurography** (see Vallbo, Hagbarth, & Wallin, 2004). Typically, a fine recording microelectrode is inserted manually through the skin into the underlying nerve trunk of the arm or hand of a conscious subject. Recordings from the median nerve in the arm indicate that afferent

In the case of IW described earlier, all myelinated fibers were destroyed by the disease, depriving him of all sensory information from mechanoreceptors.

KEY TERM

Knee-jerk reflex (myotatic reflex)
The reflexive extension of the lower leg following a hammer tap on the knee tendon, due to activation of a simple reflex circuit in the spinal cord.

Microneurography
A technique for recording human sensory nerve activity using needle electrodes inserted through the skin into a nerve trunk.

fibers from mechanoreceptors can be divided into four types (Johansson, 1978; Johansson and Vallbo, 1979). Two types, known as rapidly adapting RA and RC fibers, respond only at the initial indentation of the skin. The other two types, known as slowly adapting SAI and SAII fibers, continue responding to constant displacement of the skin. Each type of fiber is thought to receive connections from one of the four major receptor types. Table 3.1 shows the relevant connections. Johansson and Vallbo (1979) found that RA and SAI units accounted for three quarters of the fibers they studied. Johansson (1978) found that each afferent nerve only produced a response when stimulation fell in a specific area of the hand, which defined the fiber's *receptive field*. Receptive fields were introduced in Chapter 1 to illustrate the principle of physiological selectivity. The receptive fields discovered by Johansson (1978) were roughly circular and purely excitatory; activity in the fiber increased when a stimulus was applied to the hand.

Cortical representation of somatosensation

The primary somatosensory cortex occupies a long, thin strip of cortical surface running from ear to ear across the head (the blue area in the side view of the cortex shown in the top left of Figure 3.4). The axons of thalamic neurons project to an area known as Brodmann's area 3 (subdivided into a and b), but the adjacent areas 1 and 2 also represent somatosensation. The cross-section in Figure 3.4 (middle left) is taken along the line labeled A–A' in the top left, and shows the locations of the three areas. Close inspection of the properties of neurons in area 3 reveals a very high degree of selectivity and organization.

Receptive field properties

Mountcastle (1957) found that each cell in the primary somatosensory cortex receives input from only one type of receptor. For example, one cell may be connected to Merkel disks, while another cell may receive inputs only from Meissner corpuscles. All the receptors projecting to an individual cortical neuron are located in a small area of the body, defining the cell's *receptive field*. Stimulation in some parts of the receptive field excites the cell, but stimulation in other parts inhibits the cell. Neurons in the primary somatosensory cortex often have a central excitatory region with surrounding, flanking, or offset regions of inhibition (DiCarlo, Johnson, & Hsiao, 1998). Figure 3.5 illustrates a concentrically organized receptive field (the middle neuron on the right of the schematic cortical circuit). Neural projections from sensory receptors under the skin of the forearm converge on the cortical cell by means of intermediate synapses in the brainstem and thalamus. Consequently the neuron responds only to stimulation in that region of the body (shaded area).

Projections from receptors in area A of the receptive field are excitatory, and projections from receptors in area B provide **inhibition**, by means of interneurons colored black in Figure 3.5. This kind of inhibition is a common feature in sensory pathways. The connections are organized in such a way that stimulation in the center of the receptive field excites the cell, and stimulation in the periphery of the receptive field inhibits the cell. The top recording trace in the figure shows that neural activity increases in response to stimulation at point A in the receptive field. Stimulation in area B, on the other

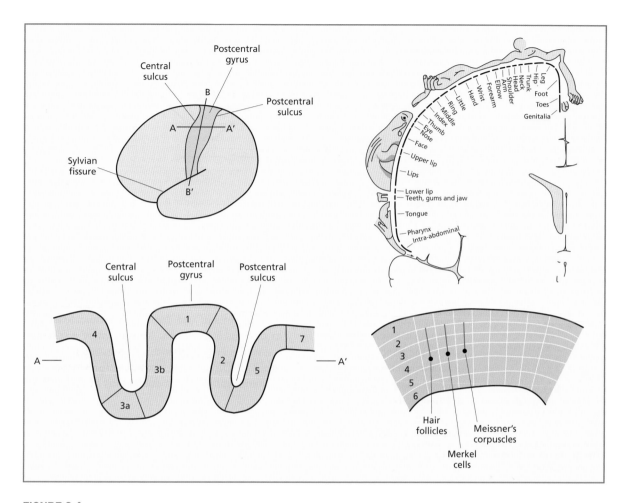

FIGURE 3.4

Cortical representation of somatosensation. Thalamic neurons project to cells in a long, thin strip extending across the cortex from ear to ear (top left; a view of the cortex from the left side). Cross-sections along the line A–A′ are shown in the lower left of the figure. In common with other areas of cortex, somatosensory cortex can be subdivided into six different layers, labeled 1–6 moving down from the surface. Thalamic axons terminate in layer 4 of area 3. Within a thin column of cortex, cells in all layers receive inputs from just one receptor type. A larger scale cross-section along line B–B′ is shown at the right of the figure. Each cell is selectively responsive to stimulation in a particular region of the body. Moving across the cortex from B to B′, there is an orderly progression in the body part covered by the cells. Top left and bottom redrawn from Smith (2000). Copyright © 2000 John Wiley & Sons Limited. Reproduced with permission. Top right from Penfield and Rasmussen (1950) © 1950 Gale, a part of Cengage Learning Inc.

hand, causes a decrease in activity (middle trace) due to the inhibition transmitted laterally in the neural circuit. Stimulation at points A and B simultaneously leads to no net change in neural response (bottom trace). Receptive fields of this kind are often called antagonistic **center–surround receptive fields**, for obvious reasons. Why is the receptive field organized in this way? Center–surround antagonism means that the cell responds best to relatively small stimuli that fill the central excitatory area of its receptive field but do not encroach on the inhibitory surround. This makes the cell's response sensitive to very small changes in the position and/or size of the stimulus.

KEY TERM

Center–surround receptive field
A receptive field containing concentrically organized regions of excitation and inhibition, as a result of lateral inhibition.

FIGURE 3.5
Cortical receptive fields. Stimulation of a small region on the forearm (left) generates a response that is recorded from the middle cortical cell on the right. This region of body surface represents the cell's receptive field. Excitation from receptors in region A of the receptive field is relayed via ascending projections in the spinal cord, brainstem, and thalamus. Inhibition from receptors in region B of the receptive field is generated by lateral connections (black in the figure). Stimulation in the central region (A) generates an increase in firing rate (top trace in the box). Stimulation in the outer region of the receptive field (B) causes a decrease in activity (middle trace). Stimulation in both A and B simultaneously does not change the activity level of the cell (bottom trace).

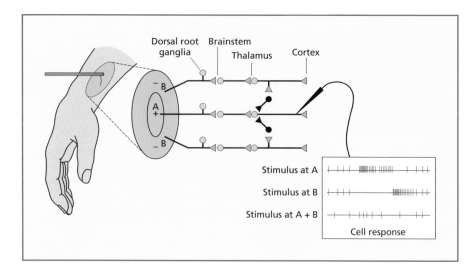

 Why is center–surround organization useful?

Hyvarinen and Poranen (1978) found cells in area 2 of monkey somatosensory cortex that responded selectively to movement direction. Movement of a stimulus across the hand in one direction produced a large response, but movement in other directions produced little or no response. Direction selectivity is preserved even when the stimulus moves in discrete jumps rather than a continuous glide (Warren, Hamalainen, & Gardner, 1986).

Cortical organization

A basic principle of sensory physiology is the high degree of order shown by the arrangement of cells at each level of processing, as discussed in Chapter 1. Somatosensation offers a supreme example of this principle. Neurons connected to receptors on the left half of the body project to somatosensory cortex in the right-hand hemisphere, and neurons connected to receptors on the right half of the body project to the left-hand hemisphere. The properties of neighboring cells in somatosensory cortex are closely related. Anatomical and electrophysiological studies over the last half century have revealed that the primary somatosensory cortex is highly organized, both vertically and horizontally.

Vertical organization Vertically, the mammalian cortex can be split into six distinct layers (see Figure 3.4, bottom), on the basis of variations in cell number, density, and morphology. The axons of thalamic neurons terminate in layer 4 of Brodmann's areas 3a and 3b. Layer 4 cells connect with cells in other layers, which in turn project to cells in areas 1 and 2 (Smith, 2000). Mountcastle (1957) found that all the cells lying within a thin column running down vertically from the surface of the cortex (**cortical column**) were connected to the same type of sensory receptor. Cells in each neighboring column were all connected to a different receptor type, as illustrated in Figure 3.4 (bottom). In addition, the cells within

KEY TERM

Cortical column
A group of cells lying within a block extending perpendicular to the surface of the cortex that share a common response property, such as receptive field location or stimulus preference.

a group of neighboring columns have receptive field locations that largely overlap on the body surface. Receptive field size varies between cortical cells, in a way that is related to the part of the body on which the receptive field lies. Receptive fields on the finger tips are very small (3–4 mm in diameter), but those on the trunk are over 100 times larger.

> The division of the whole neocortex into six layers and about 50 different areas, on the basis of histological features, was first described by the neuroanatomist Korbinian Brodmann in the early 1900s, as mentioned in Chapter 1.

Horizontal organization As one progresses horizontally (parallel to the surface of the cortex within a particular layer) along the strip of cortex devoted to somatosensation, there is a very orderly progression in the part of the body covered by the neurons' receptive fields. This horizontal organization was first described by Penfield, a neurosurgeon who performed brain surgery during the early 1950s to relieve epilepsy. The patient was anesthetized but awake during the operation, and Penfield applied small electric currents to the exposed surface of cortex by means of a small electrode. The patient reported any experiences that resulted from the stimulation. The purpose of the procedure was to identify critical areas of cortex to be avoided during surgery, but in the process Penfield made some startling discoveries. When stimulation was applied to the brain area now identified as somatosensory cortex, the patient reported tactile sensations on specific parts of the body. As Penfield systematically moved the electrode across the surface of the cortex, the bodily location of the sensation also moved systematically. Figure 3.4 is redrawn from Penfield and Rasmussen (1950), and represents a cross-sectional view of the cortex along the line B–B' in the figure. Notice that the body is mapped out across the surface of the cortex. The area of cortical surface devoted to different body parts is not in proportion to their size. For instance, relatively small areas of cortex contain cells with receptive fields on the back, or on the leg, whereas very large areas of cortex are devoted to the hands and to the lips. This effect is known as *cortical magnification*. Research on other species has discovered very different patterns of cortical magnification. In rodents, for example, the large facial whiskers are disproportionately represented in somatosensory cortex. The large spots or "barrels" apparent in the somatosensory representation of the star-nosed mole (Figure 1.2 in Chapter 1) each represent an individual whisker. The extent of cortical representation of a body part seems to reflect the importance of that body part for the survival of the animal. Recent research on "phantom limbs" has led to some surprising insights about how somatosensory sensations appear to be located on body parts, and about the capacity of the human brain to reorganize itself following injury. Phantom limbs are discussed in the tutorials section at the end of the chapter.

> Penfield's findings are a dramatic demonstration of Mueller's principle of specific nerve energy, introduced in Chapter 1.

Cortical representation of pain

Although thalamic neurons conveying information about pain do project to the somatosensory cortex, the cortical representation of pain is not well understood. Removal of the relevant region of cortex to alleviate chronic pain is not usually successful, though tactile sensation is impaired. There is a parallel transmission of pain signals from the thalamus to the reticular formation, pons, and midbrain that is probably responsible for the

> Neurons in the spinal cord conveying pain signals from the internal organs also convey information about pain near the body surface. As a result, pain from internal organs is often "referred" to a more superficial part of the body sharing the same afferent neurons. Pain in the heart muscle, for instance, is referred to the chest wall and left arm (Purves et al., 2001).

arousing effects of pain. These projections would not be affected by cortical ablation. There are also descending projections from the cortex to the spinal cord, particularly to Rexed's lamina II.

SOMATOSENSORY PERCEPTION

Detection

Bolanowski et al. (1988) measured thresholds for detecting the presence of a vibratory test stimulus applied to the hand, as a function of vibration frequency and temperature. As already mentioned, different receptor and fiber types respond over different ranges of vibration frequency. Bolanowski et al. (1988) asked whether our ability to detect vibration at a particular frequency was mediated by the fiber type most responsive to that frequency. If so, that fiber type would constitute a specialized **channel** for conveying information about a particular frequency range. Their psychophysical data indicated that detection of vibration was indeed mediated by four channels, which correspond to the four afferent fiber types (PC, RA, SAI, and SAII).

Discrimination

Our ability to discriminate fine differences in touch stimulation can be measured using a pair of calipers, placing one or both points on the skin of the subject (Figure 3.6, top). The subject's task is to report whether they can feel a single point or a pair of points. As Figure 3.6 (bottom) shows, performance varies markedly in different regions of the body. Acuity is highest on the tongue and hands, where points separated by as little as 2 or 3 mm can be discriminated. Performance is worst on the back and legs, where points have to be over 50 mm apart to be discriminated. This pattern of performance closely reflects the variation in receptive field size and cortical representation mentioned earlier in the chapter. The area of cortex devoted to the fingers contains a great many neurons having small receptive fields, typically 1–2 mm in diameter. Consequently, if the calipers are placed on the fingers and gradually moved further apart, over a range of 3 or 4 mm, the activity of an individual neuron will change markedly (refer back to Figure 3.5). In addition, the points of the calipers will very soon stimulate different neurons, since the receptive fields are so small. These changes in cortical activity mediate fine touch discrimination at the fingers. The cortical representation of the back is relatively sparse, and receptive fields are large. Consequently, a change in position of 3 or 4 mm will have very little effect on the activity of individual cells, and therefore on discrimination.

Sensation

Physiological and psychophysical data indicate that afferent fibers from mechanoreceptors can be divided into four types, each associated with a particular receptor type. Do these fibers play a role in touch sensation? To answer this question directly, Ochoa & Torebjörk (1983) and Macefield, Gandevia, & Burke (1990) extended the microneurography technique described earlier. As well as recording from afferent fibers in the arm and hand, they used the same electrode to deliver

? Think about how the activity of an individual cell varies with the position of the stimulus in its receptive field.

KEY TERM

Channel
A specific route through a processing system, usually carrying a specific kind of information.

low-voltage pulses to the fibers (known as intraneural microstimulation). The experimental subject was asked to describe any sensations evoked by the stimulation. They found that stimulation of RA and PC fibers evoked a sensation of "tapping," "flutter," "vibration," or "tingling" depending on the frequency of the stimulation. Stimulation of SAI units evoked a sensation of sustained "pressure." Curiously, stimulation of SAII units failed to evoke perceptual responses. Sensations evoked by stimulation were felt to originate in a specific area of the skin.

Intraneural microstimulation studies confirm the link between mechanoreceptor activity and perception of touch. However, it would be too simplistic to assume a direct correlation between a specific fiber type and a specific kind of touch sensation. A natural mechanical stimulus will elicit activity in several types of afferent fiber, and the resulting sensation will reflect the combined activity of the whole population of fibers. For example, the sensation of vibration can be evoked by RA activation at lower frequencies, and by PC activation at high frequencies (Ochoa and Torebjörk, 1983). Subjects report no qualitative difference between the sensations. Vibration frequency may be encoded by the relative activity levels in RA and PC fibers.

Pain

The primary sensation associated with pain is obviously its aversive quality. It is most often triggered by responses in nociceptors following tissue damage. Nociceptors are found in all parts of the body except inside the brain and bones. Their function is clearly to ensure that the damaged tissue is protected from further injury. Unlike, say, visual or auditory sensations, pain sensations do not disappear once the external stimulus has been removed, but persist to promote healing. On the other hand, debilitating pain could itself be harmful if it prevents the individual from taking appropriate action to ensure survival (soldiers in battle often deny feeling pain even after severe injury). So the link between tissue damage and pain is necessarily very complex. Melzack and Wall (1965) proposed the gate-control theory of pain. A "gate" in the spinal cord regulates incoming signals from receptors. When the gate is open, pain is felt; when it is closed, there is no pain. According to the theory, lamina II cells in the spinal cord constitute the gate. Descending nerve projections from the brain provide the signals that control the gate. Consequently, pain perception is influenced by a range of cognitive and emotional factors such as expectation, fear, and anxiety. Neuroimaging studies indicate the involvement of areas in the cingulate and prefrontal cortex (Ploghaus et al., 2003).

The importance of painful sensations for survival is illustrated by tragic instances of people who are incapable of perceiving pain due to a congenital lack

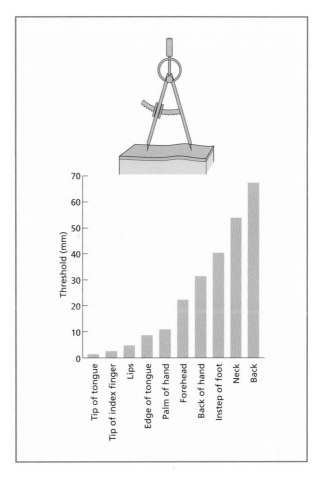

FIGURE 3.6
Two-point acuity for touch. A pair of calipers is placed on the skin surface, and the subject is required to report whether they feel a single point or a pair of points (top). The calipers are adjusted until the subject can just report the presence of a pair of points reliably (discrimination threshold). The bar graph shows the discrimination threshold on various parts of the body. Thresholds are smallest, in the region of 1–5 mm, on the mouth and fingers, and largest on the neck and back (50–70 mm).

of Aδ and C fibers (Nagasako, Oaklander, & Dworkin, 2003). They often die in childhood because they fail to notice illnesses and injuries such as burns, finger or toe mutilation, and joint damage.

Texture perception

We can perceive the texture of a surface we touch on the basis of its spatial features or its temporal features. Texture is distributed about the surface, so it has certain spatial features which include the size, shape, and density of the individual elements making up the texture (such as the distinctive texture of leather or wood). The temporal features of a texture arise from moving the skin across the surface of the texture to create vibration as the skin encounters individual elements (bumps, grooves, and so on). The character of the texture is conveyed by the frequency and the amplitude of the vibration. According to the duplex theory of tactile texture perception, coarse textures are encoded by their spatial properties, and fine textures are encoded by their temporal properties (see Hollins, Bensmaia, & Roy, 2002). To test this theory, Hollins & Risner (2000) asked subjects to distinguish between different grades of sandpaper by touch alone. Each stimulus was presented either by pressing it against the finger (a spatial cue), or by moving it along the finger pad (temporal cue). They found that fine sandpapers could be distinguished only when a temporal cue was present, but coarse textures could be discriminated equally well using spatial or temporal cues. Roy and Hollins (1998) proposed that the properties of fine textures are encoded in the relative activity of different mechanoreceptor types, as indicated in the previous paragraph.

Object recognition

Although humans normally rely on vision for object identification, touch can also be used effectively. The perception of object properties on the basis of touch is sometimes called **haptic perception**. When subjects are allowed to touch and manipulate objects without visual information, recognition rates are very high. Klatzky, Lederman, and Metzger (1985) investigated the ability of 20 blindfolded students to identify 100 common objects by touch. Objects included, for example, a ring, a golf ball, a sock, a tea bag, scissors, a fork, a key, and a screwdriver. Identification was 96% accurate, and 68% of responses occurred within 3 seconds of initial contact with the object. Subjects were clearly able to gather a great deal of useful information regarding object properties from a relatively brief manual inspection. Two objects in particular accounted for a high proportion of the errors, rice and a T-shirt.

A functional MRI study tested whether different brain regions were involved in the recognition and the localization of tactile objects (Reed, Klatzy, & Halgren, 2005). Results indicated that recognition involves **ventral** brain regions, while localization involves **dorsal** brain regions. Later chapters will show that similar distinctions between "what" and "where" processing have been proposed for audition and for vision.

KEY TERMS

Haptic perception
The perception of shape, size, and identity on the basis of touch and kinesthesis.

Ventral
Brain regions toward the front and lower part of the brain, such as the temporal lobe.

Dorsal
Brain regions toward the back and upper part of the brain, such as the parietal lobe.

THE VESTIBULAR SYSTEM

Information about the orientation and movement of the body with respect to the external environment is vital for normal bodily function. It allows us, for example, to walk and run upright without falling over, and at the same time to maintain steady fixation on an object that may itself be moving. Your ability to read information on a mobile device held in the hand while simultaneously walking across campus is made possible by the sophisticated sensory apparatus and reflex circuits of the vestibular system.

PHYSIOLOGY OF THE VESTIBULAR SYSTEM

The sensory system responsible for your ability to maintain a stable gaze while your head bobs up and down is a prime example of exquisite biological engineering. It uses receptors that are sensitive to the forces of gravity and acceleration acting on the head. These receptors are located in two organs which lie buried in deep cavities on either side of the skull known as vestibules; the **vestibular organs**.

Figure 3.7 (top right) shows the position of the vestibular organs in the head. Each organ consists of a complex set of interconnected canals and otolith organs, known as the vestibular labyrinth. Another organ, the cochlea, is connected to each vestibular organ, and shares its afferent nerve, the VIIIth cranial nerve (see Figure 3.7, top left). The cochlea is a complex spiral-shaped canal that mediates hearing (discussed in the next two chapters). In both the vestibular organs and the cochlea, sensory reception is based on minute displacements of hair-like protuberances from the receptor cells, technically known as cilia. In the vestibular canals, cilia are displaced by fluid movement caused by accelerations of the head. In the otolith organs, the cilia are displaced by inertia or by gravity. In the cochlea, fluid pressure waves cause movement of a membrane that in turn causes displacement of the cilia.

> The contiguity of the vestibular organ and the cochlea led to early ideas that both organs were devoted to hearing, with the vestibular organ mediating auditory localization. See Wade (2000).

Vestibular receptors

Figure 3.8 depicts a group of **vestibular receptor** cells on a patch of sensory epithelium. Notice that each receptor cell gives rise to a single tall, thick projection known as a **kinocilium**, and a number of smaller, narrower projections (**stereocilia**) grouped together on one side of the kinocilium. The stereocilia decrease in size with distance away from the kinocilium, and thin filaments connect the tip of each stereo- or kinocilium to the side of its taller neighbor. This arrangement is crucial to the sensory properties of vestibular receptor cells (also known as "hair cells").

Unlike mechanoreceptors, hair cells do not have axons, and do not generate action potentials. Instead, presynaptic active zones around the base of each hair cell make synaptic connections with afferent nerve cells forming part of the VIIIth cranial nerve. Stimulation of a hair cell causes the release of a

KEY TERMS

Vestibular organ
A fluid-filled organ lying in a deep cavity on the side of the skull (one on each side); it provides information about the orientation and movement of the body relative to the external environment.

Vestibular receptor
A mechanoreceptor that produces an electrical response when hair-like protrusions are deflected as a result of external forces acting on the head.

Kinocilium
The single, tall, hair-like structure projecting from each vestibular receptor.

Stereocilia
The small, hair-like structures projecting from each vestibular receptor to one side of its kinocilium; they are connected to the kinocilium by fine filaments.

FIGURE 3.7
The vestibular organs.
The two organs lie
in deep openings on
either side of the skull.
Each organ consists of
three canals (posterior,
anterior, lateral or
horizontal) and two sacs
(saccule and utricle), all
of which are filled with
fluid. Each structure also
contains a small patch
of sensory hair cells.
Head movements result
in fluid flow around the
five structures, which
displaces the hair cells
and leads to sensory
responses. The lower
part of the figure shows
the plane within which
the head must move
in order to excite each
structure. P = posterior
canal; A = anterior
canal; H = horizontal or
lateral canal; U = utricle;
S = saccule.

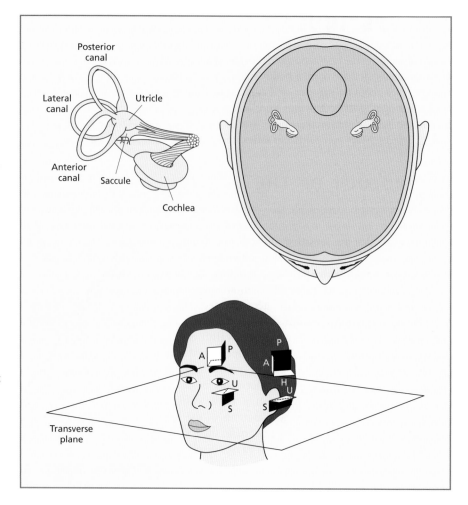

chemical neurotransmitter from its presynaptic zones. This transmitter influences the pattern of action potentials generated by the sensory neuron. Movement of the stereocilia toward the kinocilium depolarizes the hair cell and results in increases in sensory nerve activity. Movement of the stereocilia away from the kinocilium hyperpolarizes the cell, reducing sensory nerve activity. In the patch of sensory epithelium shown in Figure 3.8 the stereocilia and kinocilia are all arranged in the same order, so that deflection to the left causes excitation, and deflection to the right causes inhibition. Resting potentials in hair cells generate a high level of spontaneous neural activity in sensory nerves (about 110 spikes per second), so the firing rate of vestibular nerve fibers can accurately reflect the change in receptor potential, increasing or decreasing in accordance with the movement of the cilia. As we shall see, the significance of this biphasic response is that it allows nerve fibers to signal the direction of displacement of the cilia, which depends directly on the direction of tilt or acceleration of the head.

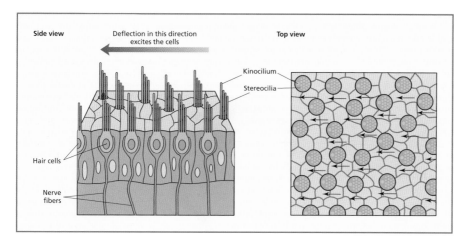

FIGURE 3.8
Vestibular hair cells
on a patch of sensory
epithelium. Each cell
consists of a single tall
hair (kinocilium) and
a number of smaller
hairs (stereocilia)
grouped on one side.
Displacement of the
hairs in the direction
of the kinocilium, as
shown, increases activity
in the sensory nerve
fiber. Displacement in
the opposite direction
decreases activity in
the sensory nerve.
Redrawn from Purves
et al. (2001). Copyright
© 2001 Sinauer
Associates. Reproduced
with permission.

The vestibular labyrinth

The labyrinth consists of two chambers (**otolith organs**), known as the utricle and the saccule, and three **semicircular canals** (see Figure 3.7). All of these membranous structures are interconnected and filled with fluid (endolymph). In each structure there is a small area of sensory *epithelium* containing hair cells described earlier. The precise arrangement of the otolith organs and canals in the head is shown in the lower part of Figure 3.7. In the saccule, the sensory epithelium is oriented vertically, and in the utricle it is oriented horizontally. The three semicircular canals are oriented at right-angles to each other, as shown in the figure. The two vestibular organs on either side of the body are mirror images of each other. The significance of this arrangement becomes apparent when one considers the physics of head movement and the vertical direction of gravitational force.

Planes and axes of head movement

Head movements can be defined in terms of three principal planes and three axes passing through the head, as illustrated in Figure 3.9.

Three principal planes   The median plane passes vertically through the head from front to back. The frontal plane passes vertically through the head from side to side. Finally, the transverse plane passes through the head horizontally.

   Three axes   The x-axis runs from front to back, the y-axis runs from side to side, and the z-axis runs vertically (see Howard, 1982).

   Three components of translation   Linear (translatory) head movements can be split into three components, corresponding to translation along each of the three axes:

- Backward and forward along the x-axis
- Sideways along the y-axis
- Up and down along the z-axis.

> ### KEY TERMS
>
> **Otolith organs**
> Two fluid-filled sacs, the utricle and saccule, in each vestibular organ.
>
> **Semicircular canals**
> Three ring-shaped canals in each vestibular organ, arranged at right-angles to each other.

FIGURE 3.9
Principal planes and axes of the human body. The body can move linearly along three possible axes; x, y, and z. The body can rotate within three possible planes: Frontal, medial, and transverse. These movements define six degrees of freedom— the body can move in six possible ways, each independent of the others. Natural movements usually contain a combination of two or more of these movement components.

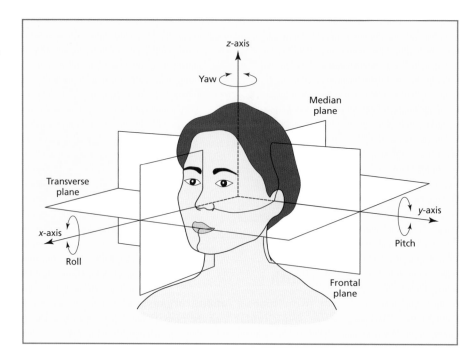

Three components of rotation Similarly, there are three possible rotational movements corresponding to rotation within each of the three planes:

- Rotation in the median plane about the *y*-axis, as in a "yes" nod, is called "pitch."
- Rotation in the transverse plane about the *z*-axis, as in a "no" shake, is known as "yaw."
- Rotation in the frontal plane about the *x*-axis, as in a sideways tilt of the head, is known as "roll."

Natural head movements Head movements therefore have six different components; in other words, they have six degrees of freedom. Each of the six components can occur independently of the others. Natural head movements frequently contain a combination of two or more of these movement components. For example, as you bend down to tie a shoelace, your head might move in a way that combines linear downward motion along the *x*- and *z*-axes, and rotational movement in the median plane as the head rotates downward. A turn of the head to one side during this movement would add a second rotational component in the transverse plane. In order to maintain proper control of body and eye position, the nervous system must split such complex head movements into their component parts. For example, the presence of a translatory component of body movement may indicate a need to adjust one's balance, while the presence of a rotational component may require compensating eye movement to maintain a stable image in the eye.

Vestibular responses to natural head movements The otolith organs and semicircular canals are shaped and located very precisely so that their responses during natural three-dimensional head and body movements effectively decompose complex movements into their translatory and rotational components. The otolith

? *Decompose another natural head movement into its movement components.*

organs provide information about linear movement components, and the semicircular canals provide information about rotational components. Precisely how they achieve this decomposition is explained in the following paragraphs.

Otolith organs

The macula   The patch of hair cells in each otolith organ is called the **macula**. It is covered by a gelatinous layer, which in turn is covered by a heavy fibrous membrane (otolithic membrane) containing calcium carbonate crystals (otoconia; see Figure 3.10). Linear acceleration of the head causes a shifting or shearing motion between the layer of hair cells and the otolithic membrane above them (similar to the movement of a loosely fitting hat placed on the head when the head is moved or tilted). The shearing motion displaces the hair cells and results in a sensory response, as shown in Figure 3.10 (right). Recall from the previous section that

KEY TERM

Macula
The patch of vestibular receptors in each otolith organ.

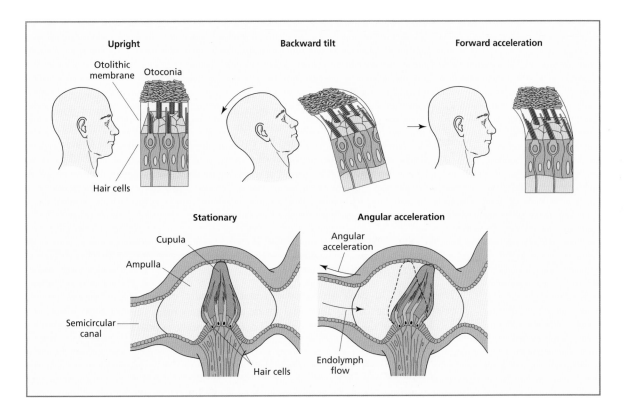

FIGURE 3.10
Sensory epithelia in the otolith organs and semicircular canals. In the utricle (top row) the hair cells are covered by a gelatinous carpet (otolithic membrane), itself covered with heavy calcium carbonate crystals (otoconia). Head tilts or accelerations lead to shearing motion between the otoconia and the hair cells, due to the inertia of the otoconia. The resulting displacement of hair cells leads to sensory responses. In the semicircular canals (bottom row), the hair cells form a bundle (crista) projecting across the canal inside a gelatinous mass (cupula). Head rotation causes a flow of fluid around the canal in the opposite direction, due to the inertia of the fluid. This current flow displaces the cupula and results in a sensory response. Redrawn from Purves et al. (2001). Copyright © 2001 Sinauer Associates. Reproduced with permission.

Invertebrates possess a structure called the statocyst, which performs the same function as the vertebrate otolith organ. In shrimps, the statocyst has an opening through which the creature takes in grains of sand that perform the same function as otoconia. In a classic study in 1893, the sand in the creature's aquarium was replaced with iron filings. The shrimp's bodily orientation could then be influenced by the presence of a strong magnet placed outside the tank (Shepherd, 1988).

individual hair cells are directional in the sense that deflections toward the kinocilium are excitatory and deflections away from the kinocilium are inhibitory. Close examination of the arrangement of hair cells in the saccule and utricle reveals that the macula in each is split down the middle. All hair cells on one side of the division are excited by deflection in one direction but inhibited by deflection in the opposite direction, whereas hair cells on the other side of the division show the opposite pattern of response. This arrangement allows the otolith organs to distinguish between opposite directions of shear on the basis of the pattern of excitation.

Responses to linear acceleration   Since the macula of the utricle is roughly horizontal, and the macula of the saccule is roughly vertical, the two organs together can signal linear acceleration along any axis, since one or the other or both will always be activated. The otolith organs respond to acceleration rather than to movement at a constant velocity, because displacement of their hair cells is due to the initial inertia of the otolithic membrane. Once a steady speed of bodily motion is reached, the otolithic membrane catches up with the macula, so the hair cells return to their resting position.

It is important to note that the information provided by the otolith organs about head tilt with respect to gravity is indistinguishable from the effect of horizontal linear acceleration. This property arises from Einstein's equivalence principle, which states that a gravitational force field is equivalent to an artificial force field resulting from linear acceleration. The effect of gravity can, of course, be described in terms of acceleration toward the ground at a specific rate. Consequently, as illustrated in Figure 3.10, the shearing motion of the otolithic membrane produced by horizontal acceleration, a, is identical to that produced by a static tilt of the head at an angle whose sine is a (Howard, 1982). This equivalence has important consequences for perception, described later in the chapter.

Semicircular canals

The crista   In each semicircular canal a bundle of hair cells (known as the **crista**) stretches across the canal inside a gelatinous mass (the cupula). Rotational acceleration of the head causes a small deflection of the cupula and the hair cells, due to the inertia of the fluid. The hair cells are deflected by about 10 millimicrons for a relatively slow head movement, as shown in Figure 3.10 (bottom).

Responses to rotational acceleration   The curved shape of the semicircular canals allows them to signal rotational acceleration of the head, because this movement will set up strong pressure against the cupula. Since there are three components of rotational movement, three canals in each labyrinth are sufficient to detect any combination of the components. The canals are roughly at right-angles because this is the optimal arrangement to signal movement about the three possible axes, which are also at right-angles of course. Unlike hair cells in the utricle and saccule, in each canal the kinocilia all point in the same direction, so all cells within a particular canal will be excited or inhibited together by movement of fluid in a

KEY TERM

Crista
The patch of vestibular receptors in each semicircular canal.

particular direction through the canal. It is important to note that each canal works in partnership with its mirror-image canal on the other side of the head, whose kinocilia point in the opposite direction. Rotation of the head about any axis will generate fluid pressure in the canals on each side of the head, but the resulting responses from canals on opposite sides will be in opposition. For example, a leftward head turn will cause an increase in firing rate in the left vestibular nerve, connected to the left horizontal canal, but a decrease in firing rate in the right vestibular nerve. Rightward rotation reverses the pattern of firing. This arrangement also applies to the other two pairs of canals (left anterior and right posterior, left posterior and right anterior), which respond well to rotation in the x- and z-axes.

> **KEY TERM**
>
> **Vestibular nuclei**
> Groups of nerve cells in the brainstem that receive axons from the vestibular receptors; they also receive inputs from the cerebellum, visual system, and somatosensory system.

The semicircular canals respond only to angular acceleration, not to a constant angular velocity of rotation. As in the case of the otolith organs, this property arises because of the initial inertia of the endolymph fluid at the start of the rotation. Once a steady rotational velocity has been reached, the fluid catches up with the canal movement, and the cupula returns to its rest position.

Central vestibular pathways

Hair cell responses are transmitted along the vestibular branch of the VIIIth cranial nerve. There are about 20,000 fibers on each side of the head (Shepherd, 1988), most of which terminate in several large groups of neurons in the brainstem called the **vestibular nuclei**. The remainder project directly to the cerebellum (see below). Projections from the vestibular nuclei can be grouped into four systems (see Figure 3.11), two ascending (thalamic and cerebellar), and two descending (spinal and ocular).

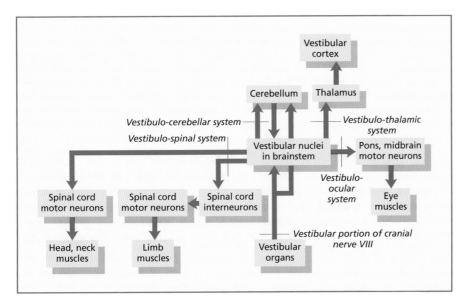

FIGURE 3.11
Sensory pathways in the vestibular system. Sensory nerve fibers from the hair cells project centrally along the vestibular portion of the VIIIth cranial nerve. Most of the fibers terminate in the vestibular nuclei of the brainstem. The vestibular nuclei act as major distribution centers, dividing responses among four major systems: Vestibulo-cerebellar, vestibulo-thalamic, vestibulo-spinal, and vestibulo-ocular. These systems control reflex movements of the eyes and body, and provide a small cortical representation for vestibular signals.

The vestibulo-cerebellar system

Cells in the vestibular nuclei project to, and receive projections from, the flocculonodular lobe of the cerebellum (see Carlson, 2004). The cerebellum is a large, complex neural structure that receives projections from, and projects to, many neurons in the cortex, brainstem, and spinal cord. One of its functions is to control movement by detecting and reducing differences between intended and actual movements. The vestibulo-cerebellar system regulates the movements that control posture and bodily equilibrium.

The vestibulo-thalamic system

This system incorporates cortical projections which mediate conscious experiences associated with vestibular activity. Neuroimaging shows that a network of cortical areas in the parietal lobe is involved in processing vestibular signals (Fasold et al., 2002). There is a strong right hemispheric dominance, consistent with this hemisphere's role in spatial attention and orientation (discussed in Chapter 14).

The vestibulo-spinal system

This system carries projections to motoneurons in the spinal cord along two tracts, medial and lateral. The medial tract carries projections mainly from the semicircular canals to motoneurons controlling muscles in the neck and trunk. These projections are thought to be involved in reflexive control of body posture and head position in space. The lateral tract carries projections mainly from the otolith organs to motoneurons controlling limb muscles. These projections are thought to be important for controlling limb movements that maintain balance. The small number of synapses between the vestibular organs and the motoneurons allows these reflexive movements to occur very rapidly. The high rate of resting discharge in vestibular afferent fibers supplies a continuous flow of excitation to the motor centers that control posture, helping to maintain the muscles in a steady state of contraction.

The vestibulo-ocular system

This system carries projections to other nuclei in the brainstem, containing motoneurons that control eye movements. This neural circuit mediates reflexive eye movements (**vestibulo-ocular reflex**) that compensate for head movement and stabilize the visual image. The importance of the vestibulo-ocular reflex can be demonstrated easily. Hold your head stationary, and oscillate this book rapidly from side to side. Notice that the print becomes an unreadable blur. Now keep the book stationary but oscillate your head from side to side at the same rate, while fixating the page. The print should remain perfectly stable and readable, because your eyes move to stabilize the image. Signals from the vestibular organs are used to drive eye movements that compensate perfectly for the head movement. The eye movements are actually driven directly by differences in firing rate between the left and right vestibular organs, without the involvement of higher brain areas.

Figure 3.12 illustrates what happens when the head is rotated about the z-axis, as in turning your head to the left. The leftward rotary acceleration displaces fluid in the left and right horizontal canals. The direction of fluid motion in the left horizontal canal causes an increase in firing rate in its afferent fibers. Fluid motion in the right horizontal canal has the opposite effect, decreasing firing rate. Note the

---

KEY TERM

Vestibulo-ocular reflex
The reflexive eye movements that compensate for head and body movement to stabilize the visual image on the retinas.

direction of fluid motion in each canal in relation to the kinocilia. These responses are collected by the left-hand and right-hand vestibular nuclei in the brainstem. Axons from the vestibular nuclei connect to the muscles surrounding each eye. There are both excitatory (+) projections and inhibitory (−) projections from each nucleus. Consequently, when the activity level in the two nuclei is equal, the eyes remain stationary. However, an imbalance between the nuclei leads to a bias in favor of signals to the muscle on one side of each eye, and a resulting eye movement. The greater level of activity in the left-hand vestibular nucleus during a leftward head turn, shown in Figure 3.12, results in compensatory eye movement to the right. Damage to the vestibulo-ocular system can cause differences in firing rates between the vestibular nuclei that results in unwanted jittering eye movements, even when the head is stationary. Damage can also result in visual disturbances such as blurred vision during head movements, due to loss of image stabilization.

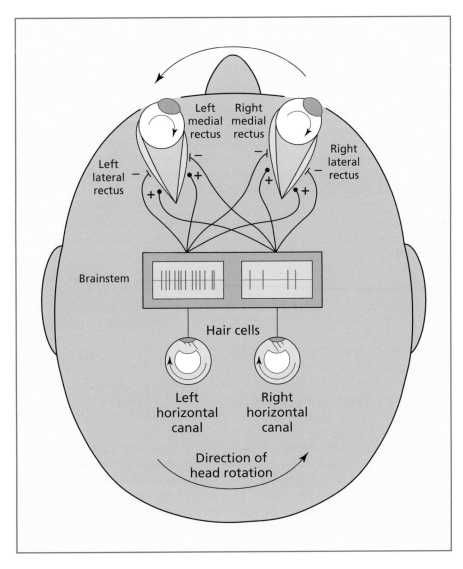

FIGURE 3.12
Schematic representation of neural circuits in the vestibulo-ocular system. During head rotation to the left, fluid movement increases activity in afferent fibers of the left horizontal canal, and decreases activity in fibers of the right horizontal canal. These responses arrive in separate groups of neurons in the vestibular nuclei of the brainstem. There are both excitatory (+) and inhibitory (−) projections from the brainstem to the external muscles of the eyes. These connections are arranged in such a way that the imbalance in activity between left and right canals is translated into an imbalance in signals arriving at lateral and medial eye muscles. This imbalance produces a rightward rotation of each eye that is sufficient to compensate for the leftward head rotation.

VESTIBULAR PERCEPTION

As we have seen above, the sensory information supplied by the vestibular system is used largely to control reflexive movements of the eyes and limbs. Its cortical representation is small relative to the representation of the other senses. However, information about the body's position and movement in the environment is available from vision as well as from the vestibular system. For example, contour orientation and texture gradients offer cues about the orientation of the ground plane relative to the body, and large-scale patterns of movement in the image ("optic flow," see Chapters 11 and 12) offer reliable information on bodily movement. Vestibular responses tend to intrude on conscious experience only when there is a discrepancy between visual information and vestibular information. The resulting sensations can, however, be very powerful, often inducing confusion, disorientation, and nausea. The situations giving rise to such discrepancies typically involve subjecting the body to movements outside the range normally experienced.

Perceptual effects attributable to vestibular responses

Vertigo

Vertigo is the sensation that you, or the environment around you, are moving or spinning when both are actually stationary. According to the sensory mismatch theory, vertigo is provoked by a mismatch between visual, vestibular, and somatosensory responses in the central nervous system (Brandt & Daroff, 1980). It is accompanied by dizziness, nausea, vomiting, postural instability, and pallor. The perceptual mismatch can arise in a variety of ways.

Height vertigo involves postural instability and nausea while standing in a high, exposed position such as on a tall building or ledge. Body sway normally causes small shifts in the retinal image, particularly involving movement of nearby objects relative to distant objects (known as motion parallax) which trigger posture corrections. These visual signals are absent in high positions; distance to the nearest stationary objects tends to be great, so there is very little retinal motion parallax due to body sway. This mismatch between visual and vestibular signals is thought to cause height vertigo.

   Motion sickness may arise when responses in one system indicates a stationary environment, while responses in another indicate motion. For example, in a moving boat or plane visual input may indicate that the immediate environment is stationary, but vestibular responses indicate body motion. In a virtual reality environment or IMAX theater, visual input may indicate body motion, but vestibular input may indicate a lack of body motion.

   Postural alcohol nystagmus In acute alcohol intoxication, small involuntary eye movements (nystagmus) and vertigo are triggered when the subject lies down. This syndrome is known as postural alcohol nystagmus (PAN), and is thought to originate in the semicircular canals. The cupula in the canals, which houses the hair cells, has the same specific gravity as the vestibular fluid (endolymph), so is not normally affected by gravitational orientation. Alcohol diffuses into the cupula, and is lighter than endolymph, making it buoyant. So when the subject lies down, the cupula moves and triggers eye movements as well as nausea due to the sensory mismatch (Brandt & Daroff, 1980; Fetter et al., 1999). As the alcohol slowly diffuses out of the cupula into the endolymph during the 12 hours after alcohol ingestion, there is a period of equilibrium followed by a further phase of PAN as the alcohol is present only in the endolymph. The second phase of PAN is associated with the hangover. It can be neutralized by a "morning after" drink, but only temporarily.

The oculogyral illusion and Coriolis effects

Everyone has experienced the dizziness that results from rotating the body about the z- (vertical) axis very rapidly. Just as the spin stops there is a strong illusory sense of bodily movement, and loss of body equilibrium, accompanied by apparent visual movement in stationary objects and reflexive movements of the eyes. Graybiel and Hupp (1946) called the illusory visual movement the "**oculogyral illusion**." These effects can be attributed to responses in the semicircular canals. During initial acceleration into the spin, "backward" deflection of the cupula due to its inertia leads to appropriate vestibular signals concerning angular acceleration. During sustained rotation the cupula returns to its resting position. During and after deceleration as the spin stops, momentum in the fluid deflects the cupula "forward" in the direction normally associated with a spin in the opposite direction. The resulting erroneous signals lead to disorientation and dizziness. The illusory impression of turning can persist for up to 30 or 40 seconds after stopping, during which time the vestibular system recovers to its resting state (Parsons, 1970).

Think about how and why a ballet dancer moves her head during a pirouette.

Coriolis effects are experienced when the head is moved *during* a spin. Head movements modify the effect that the spin has on the semicircular canals. If the head rotates about the same axis as the spin, there is a momentary increase or decrease in the total angular acceleration of the head. If the head rotates about a different axis, then the angular accelerations produced by the spin and by the head rotation interact in a complex way, under forces known as Coriolis forces. For example, if you are spinning in a leftward direction, and incline your head forward during the spin, the resultant stimulation of the canals produces a sensation that the head is being tilted sideways toward the left shoulder (see Howard, 1982, for more details). The mismatch with information supplied by the otolith organs and by vision induces dizziness and nausea.

The oculogravic illusion

Illusory tilt that is perceived during linear acceleration is known as the **oculogravic illusion**. For example, a seated individual undergoing horizontal linear acceleration will experience a strong sensation of backward tilt, and a corresponding apparent elevation of visible points positioned at eye level (e.g. Cohen, 1973). The illusion can be attributed to responses in the otolith organs. As discussed earlier, and illustrated in Figure 3.10, the macula cannot distinguish between displacements due to horizontal acceleration and displacements due to static head tilt. As a result, a displacement of the macula during rapid acceleration may be attributed, at least partially,

KEY TERMS

Oculogyral illusion
Visual disorientation and apparent movement following rapid body spins.

Coriolis effect
The apparent deflection of the head experienced when it is moved during a body spin.

Oculogravic illusion
The apparent backward head tilt and visual elevation experienced during forward body acceleration.

to head tilt. This illusion can have potentially disastrous consequences in modern transportation, as discussed in the tutorials section at the end of the chapter.

Vection

Wood (1895) described a visit to a fairground attraction called the "Haunted Swing" at the San Francisco Midwinter Fair. Visitors entered a large cubical room containing various items of furniture, and sat on a large gondola that hung in the center of the room. They experienced a swinging motion of the gondola, which eventually seemed to turn a complete revolution. In reality the swing was stationary, and the room moved (the furniture was fastened to the floor). Wood reports that "many persons were actually made sick by the illusion . . . [and could] . . . scarcely walk out of the building from dizziness and nausea." This kind of illusory motion is known as **vection** (Howard, 1982). Lishman and Lee (1973) constructed a movable room similar to that used in the Haunted Swing to study this form of vection, apparent translation or "linearvection." The subject stood on a stationary platform inside the room, the walls and ceiling of which swung back and forth slowly. Adults experienced a sensation of body sway, and tended to sway in synchrony with the room to compensate for the apparent movement of the body. Infants who had recently learned to walk fell over as soon as the room began to move. Illusions of rotary movement of the body ("circularvection") can be induced by standing inside a large textured cylinder, and setting the cylinder to rotate very slowly. One might argue that vection is not truly a consequence of vestibular responses, because the subject is stationary, and the illusion is induced by movement of the surrounding scene. However, at a neural level, the distinction between visually generated and vestibular responses disappears. Neurons in the vestibular nuclei respond to both vestibular stimulation and visual stimulation, perhaps via signals from the cerebellum (Henn, Young, & Finley, 1974). Single-cell recordings in macaque monkey ventral intraparietal cortex have also revealed neurons that respond to both visual and vestibular input (Bremmer et al., 2002). This fusion of vision and movement probably explains why visually induced sensations of body motion (involving no direct stimulation of the vestibular organs) are indistinguishable from sensations induced by actual body motion. For example, if a person tilts their head while experiencing visually induced rotation of the body, they experience the same Coriolis effect that would be induced by real rotation (Dichgans & Brandt, 1973).

? *Why is it difficult to balance on a narrow ledge high off the ground?*

CHAPTER SUMMARY

The body senses provide information about surfaces in direct contact with the skin, about the position and movement of body parts, and about the position and movement of the body relative to the outside world.

THE SOMATOSENSORY SYSTEM

- The somatosensory system contains eight different types of receptor distributed throughout the body, whose responses are conveyed to the brain along two parallel neural pathways.

- Each cortical neuron receives signals from just one of the eight receptor types, in a confined area of the body surface that defines the neuron's receptive field. Receptive fields on the hands and face are much smaller than those on the trunk and limbs.
- Cells with receptive fields at nearby body locations are themselves located near to each other in the cortex. Receptive field location changes systematically from cell to cell, so that the body is mapped out in an orderly manner across the cortex. The map is distorted so that a much larger area of cortex is devoted to some parts of the body than to others.
- Human ability to discriminate small differences in tactile stimulation varies in different regions of the body in a way that closely reflects the distortion of the cortical map.

THE VESTIBULAR SYSTEM

- The sense of balance is mediated by sensory responses from hair cells in the vestibular organs.
- Separate neural structures within each organ signal angular acceleration and linear acceleration of the head through space.
- The vestibular nuclei in the brainstem are major distribution centers for vestibular signals. Descending projections to the spinal cord control reflexive movements of the head, neck, and limbs. Projections to the extraocular muscles control eye movements that compensate for head movement. The vestibular nuclei also project to the cerebellum and to the cortex (via the thalamus).
- Mismatches between vestibular information and visual information often induce "motion sickness"—feelings of disorientation, dizziness, and nausea.

TUTORIALS

PHANTOM LIMBS

A physician treating wounded soldiers during the American Civil War noticed that his patients reported the illusion that their amputated limb was still present. He used the term "**phantom limb**" to describe the effect (Ramachandran & Blakesee, 1998). Nine out of ten amputees have such experiences. The phantom limb feels much the same as a real limb in terms of its size, movement, and tactile sensations such as itching, sweating, and pain. Indeed pain is felt in about 70% of cases over the first few weeks following amputation, and persists for years in 50% of cases (Melzack, 1990). Over time, sensations from the phantom limb may change. It may, for example, appear to telescope into the stump so that the foot is perceptually located on the thigh, or the extremity may appear to be present in the absence of an intervening limb. Prostheses such as an artificial arm or leg

KEY TERM

Phantom limb
The illusion that an amputated extremity such as a finger, leg, or penis is still present.

may appear to be real, or filled with the phantom limb. Sensations from phantom body parts are not restricted to limbs, but can include many other innervated regions of the body such as the penis, breast, and bladder.

The traditional explanation for phantom limbs is based on neural responses arising in the stump of the amputated limb. Nerve endings that once innervated the missing limb may become irritated, and generate signals that duplicate those normally arising from the limb. Once these signals arrive in somatosensory cortex, they are perceptually localized on the missing limb. We know from the work of Penfield described earlier that direct stimulation of somatosensory cortex does evoke sensations of tactile stimulation that are localized on body parts, so this explanation seems plausible. However, phantom sensations occur even in patients whose spinal cord has been cut, so that there is no route for peripheral signals to reach the brain (Melzack, 1990). We must turn to signals within the brain, rather than signals arriving from the region of the stump, for an explanation of phantom limbs.

Merzenich et al. (1984) studied somatosensory cortical maps in adult monkeys before and after surgical amputation of one or two fingers. Before amputation, each finger was represented individually in the cortex (see Figure 3.13, top). Two months following amputation of digit 3, its cortical representation had disappeared entirely. The areas devoted to the adjacent fingers had expanded to occupy the area previously devoted to the amputated finger (see Figure 3.13, bottom). Pons et al. (1991) reported more radical reorganization in the somatosensory cortex of monkeys whose sensory nerves from one arm had been severed 11 years previously. Stimulation of a monkey's deafferented hand did not excite the hand area of cortex. However, stimulation of the monkey's face did evoke a response from the "hand" area. Recall from Penfield's map (Figure 3.4) and from Figure 3.13 that the face area of cortex is adjacent to the hand area. The "face" area of cortex had expanded to incorporate an area previously devoted to the hand.

These remarkable results demonstrate that even during adulthood the cortex is able to reorganize itself in response to altered sensory input. Recall that human tactile acuity in a particular body region is closely related to the area of cortex devoted to that region (see Figures 3.4 and 3.6). If cortical reorganization also occurs in humans following amputation, one might expect improved acuity in the region surrounding the amputated limb. Haber (1955) reported just such an improvement in acuity.

It is tempting to relate the experimental findings of Merzenich et al. (1984) and Pons et al. (1991) to the phantom limb syndrome. On the basis of these studies we can assume that following amputation of a hand, for example, cortical cells formerly responsive to hand stimulation become responsive to stimulation in another part of the body (e.g., the face). We must also assume that, despite this rewiring, activity in these "hand" cells can still evoke a sensation that is localized on the missing hand. As a result, the amputee may experience sensations from a phantom hand when the face is stimulated. Ramachandran and Blakesee (1998) report observations

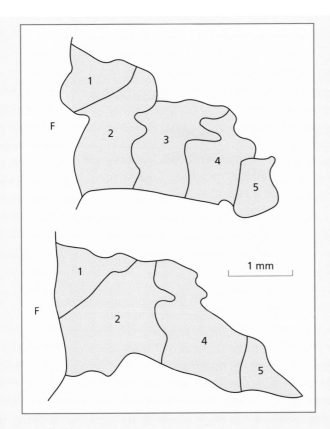

FIGURE 3.13
Maps of the somatosensory area of monkey cortex, showing the region devoted to the fingers of one hand before (top) and after (bottom) amputation of finger 3. Before amputation, each finger was represented individually in the cortex. After amputation, the representation of finger 3 disappeared, and the region devoted to adjacent fingers expanded to occupy its space. Redrawn from Merzenich et al. (1984). Reproduced with permission from John Wiley & Sons, Inc.

that are consistent with this explanation. However, cortical remapping is unlikely to be a full explanation of the phantom limb syndrome. Haber (1955) did not find perceptual localization errors with stimulation of the area surrounding an amputation. In addition, pain is a prominent feature of the syndrome and, as we saw earlier in the chapter, the central representation of pain is complex.

MODERN TRANSPORTATION AND THE VESTIBULAR SYSTEM

The vestibular system evolved to deal with the restricted range of conditions that apply to natural bodily movements. The fastest human being can run no faster than about 50 km/h (31 mph), and gravitational acceleration is 9.8 m/s^{-2} (32.2 ft/s^{-2}, or 1 G). Modern transportation can subject the body to velocities and accelerations far beyond these values. Surface transportation can reach speeds in excess of 500 km/h (310 mph), whereas the escape velocity for spacecraft is 40,000 km/h (25,000 mph). To reach this speed during take-off, spacecraft accelerate with a force of up to about 9 G. This means that the astronaut is pressed back into the seat by a force equal to nine times his or her body weight. Modern fairground attractions

Sustained acceleration in excess of about 5 G actually causes loss of vision and consciousness, if applied in a standing position; astronauts lie in a reclined position during take-off to avoid blacking out.

generate accelerations of several G. Velocities and accelerations outside the natural range can create abnormal vestibular responses that result in dizziness, disorientation, nausea, unstable vision, and disturbed motor control. These disturbances can obviously have disastrous consequences when experienced by a person in control of a vehicle.

Effects of constant velocity

As we saw earlier in the chapter, bodily movement at a fixed velocity does not generate a vestibular response. Consequently humans can subject themselves to extreme velocities with no perceptual disturbances, as long as there is no acceleration or deceleration. "Speed" sensations are really due to speed change. Passengers in cars, airliners, and spacecraft feel no vestibular sensation of speed even at extreme velocities. One can argue that it would make no sense to possess a vestibular system that was sensitive to constant velocity. As Einstein's theory of relativity made clear, in an abstract sense any measure of movement at a constant velocity is arbitrary since it depends on the frame of reference. If humans possessed a vestibular system that did signal constant velocity, would it report our speed relative to the surface of the Earth, or the speed of the Earth traveling in space? The latter is constant, so neural responses to it would be completely redundant. Indeed any response to constant speed is redundant.

Humans can, of course, gain some sense of movement at constant velocity from the visual system. However, this information specifies relative velocity; speed in relation to the visible surroundings. Our perception of constant velocity movement is therefore vulnerable to variation in visual input. Underestimation of road vehicle speed in foggy conditions is due to the lack of both visual and vestibular information regarding velocity. A heightened sense of road speed is experienced in open or low-slung vehicles, such as motorcycles and racing cars, where visual movement cues are particularly powerful.

Effects of variation in velocity

Perceptual disturbances due to abnormal vestibular responses all arise from *changes* in vehicle velocity (either speed or direction). Aircraft pilots are at particular risk of perceptual disorientation, leading to inaccurate perception of the attitude or motion of the aircraft relative to the Earth's surface. According to one estimate, disorientation accounted for nearly 40% of fatal accidents in civil aviation in the period 1964–1972 (*United States Naval Flight Surgeon's Manual*, 1991). The oculogyral and oculogravic illusions described earlier in the chapter are common experiences for aircraft pilots.

The oculogyral illusion can occur following aircraft maneuvers that involve complete revolutions in any of the three principal axes (turns, rolls, and spins). The pilot may experience an illusion of turning in the opposite direction just after the turn is completed. During and after such maneuvers, the vestibulo-ocular reflex is likely to trigger eye movements, in an attempt to stabilize vision during the spin. Since the aircraft's cockpit instrumentation obviously remains in a fixed position relative to the pilot's head, such eye movements succeed only in producing visual instability that obscures the instruments. Any head rotations executed during the spin heighten disorientation, due to Coriolis effects discussed earlier.

The oculogravic illusion can lead to the pilot mistakenly perceiving the aircraft to be level when it is in fact banking, or tilted when it is actually level. In the situation illustrated in Figure 3.14(a), the aircraft is executing a bank and turn. The pilot is subject to both gravitational and centrifugal forces, which combine to create a resultant force that is slightly tilted from gravitational vertical. The pilot may interpret this resultant force as gravitational vertical, and therefore perceive the plane to be flying straight and level. A second example is illustrated in Figure 3.14(b). During a catapult launch from an aircraft carrier, the aircraft is subjected to a peak forward linear acceleration that presses the pilot back in his or her seat with a force

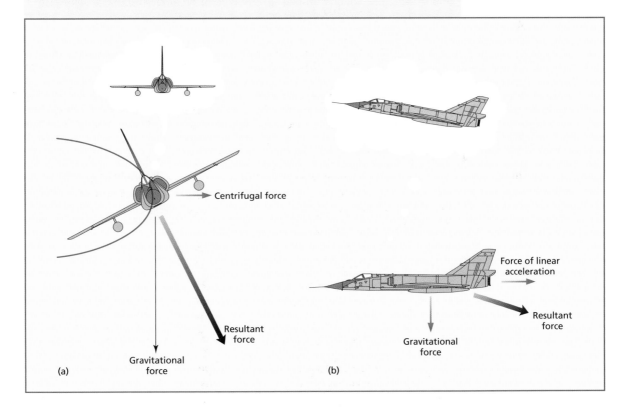

FIGURE 3.14

The oculogravic illusion in aviation. (a): During a bank and turn, the vestibular apparatus is subjected to both vertical gravitational force and horizontal centrifugal force. These forces combine to produce a resultant force that is slightly tilted from vertical. The pilot may interpret this resultant force as corresponding to gravitational vertical, and consequently perceive the plane to be flying straight and level. (b): During a catapult launch from an aircraft carrier, the vestibular apparatus is subjected to vertical gravitational force and to horizontal linear acceleration. The direction of the resultant force is tilted, and can lead the pilot to perceive the aircraft to be tilted backward.

equal to 4.5 G. When combined with the downward gravitational force of 1 G, the resultant force acting on the otolith organs indicates a backward tilt of the aircraft (though perceived tilt is much less than would be predicted by the direction of the resultant force). Inexperienced pilots may attempt to compensate for this apparent tilt by pitching the plane down toward the sea. The extreme disorientation experienced by pilots can impair and confuse their motor control to such an extent that they report an invisible "giant hand" interfering with their command of the control column.

Flying instruction draws attention to the dangers of misinterpreting vestibular signals. Pilots are taught to avoid flying "by the seat of the pants," and to rely on instrumentation for information about the attitude and motion of the aircraft.

Space motion sickness

Motion sickness is an acute problem for astronauts. In the first few hours of weightlessness 70% of astronauts suffer from nausea, vomiting, fatigue, and drowsiness which can last up to 96 hours (Lackner & DiZio, 2006). In short space flights motion sickness may have a significant impact on the mission. The origins of motion sickness in space are not fully understood. In general terms it is thought to be caused by the sensory conflicts described earlier, but lack of gravity poses unique challenges for the nervous system. Weightlessness changes the pattern of activity in the vestibular organs in two ways: First, the resting load on the utricular and saccular membranes is removed; second, the shear forces associated with changes in head orientation are removed. Furthermore, the patterns of muscular activity required to change body position change drastically in the absence of gravity. In this context it is not surprising that so many astronauts suffer space motion sickness. As yet there is no reliable way of screening astronauts for their susceptibility to space motion sickness (Lackner & DiZio, 2006).

The physics and biology of audition

4

Contents

INTRODUCTION

Humans are generally considered to be highly visual animals. However, visual information is restricted to the immediate field of view (an angle of approximately 200° centered on the line of sight in humans; see Chapter 7), and obviously relies on the presence of an adequate light source. Sound can be sensed in all directions around the body, and can even be sensed (within limits) through opaque occluding objects. Social and cultural communication in humans relies heavily on sound stimuli, in the forms of language and music (see Figure 4.1).

Individuals lacking the sense of hearing are severely limited in their ability to communicate with others, and are also at greater risk of injury from hazards outside the field of view. Indeed recent research indicates that the increased use of headphones while walking in urban environments is a significant risk factor in pedestrian injuries, particularly among young people (Lichtenstein et al., 2012).This chapter provides an introduction to the physical properties of sound, and to the biology of the sensory apparatus that humans use to sense sound. The following chapter concentrates on perceptual aspects of audition, building on the knowledge acquired here.

FIGURE 4.1
Auditory communication is an essential element of social interaction.
Copyright © Leland Bobbe/Corbis.

KEY TERM

Sine wave
A wave whose height varies smoothly so that it conforms to a mathematical sine function of time or distance (adjective: sinusoidal).

SOUND AS A PHYSICAL STIMULUS

Sound consists of pressure waves carried by vibrating air molecules. It is usually produced by a vibrating surface. For example, when a gong vibrates after being struck, it pushes to and fro on the surrounding air molecules. The resulting pressure changes are passed on by collisions between air molecules, and the sound wave travels away from the gong at a speed of approximately 335 meters per second. Parts of the wave where air pressure is increased are called compressions, and parts where pressure is decreased are called rarefactions, as shown in Figure 4.2.

SIMPLE SOUNDS

The air pressure wave produced by the gong is called a longitudinal wave, because the particles that cause it vibrate back and forth in the same direction as the wave. The repetitive variation in air pressure in the simplest sound wave, such as the pure tone produced by a tuning fork, can be described mathematically as a **sine wave.** This means that the repetitive alternation between compression and rarefaction as a function of distance from the sound source has the same shape as the variation in $sin(\theta)$ as a function of angle θ, shown in Figure 4.3. Since sound pressure waves

FIGURE 4.2
The vibrating surface of a gong creates waves of fluctuating air pressure that emanate from the gong. The pressure wave consists of alternating phases of increased pressure (compression) and decreased pressure (rarefaction).

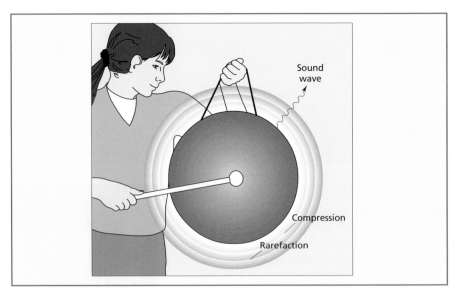

FIGURE 4.3
A simple sound wave (left) can be described mathematically as a sine wave (right). Two critical parameters of the sound wave are its period (1/frequency) and its amplitude.

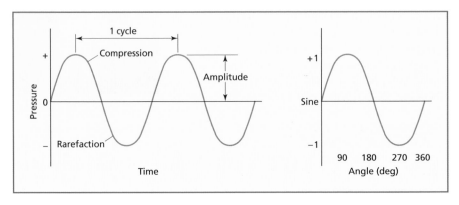

travel through air at a constant speed of 335 m/s, the horizontal axis of the waveform plot in Figure 4.3 can be scaled in terms of time, so representing the rate at which the alternations between compression and rarefaction are generated by the vibrating surface. The sinusoidal variation in sound pressure level has three important features: frequency, amplitude, and phase.

Frequency

A single alternation between compression and rarefaction is called one cycle of the wave. The wave's **frequency** corresponds to the number of alternations between compression and rarefaction that are generated in a one-second period; in other words, the number of cycles per second. The unit of frequency is *hertz*, named after the 19th century German physicist Heinrich Hertz. A sound pressure wave having a frequency of 1 Hz contains one compression/rarefaction cycle per second, a wave at a frequency of 2 Hz contains two cycles per second (as in Figure 4.3), and so on. The rate of vibration of the sound source determines the frequency of the resulting sound pressure wave. Variation in frequency relates perceptually to variation in perceived pitch. Low frequencies tend to be perceived as deep bass pitches, and high frequencies tend to be perceived as high treble pitches. However, the relation between frequency and pitch is complex, as we shall discover in the next chapter.

? What is the mathematical relationship between frequency and wavelength (period)?

Amplitude

The **amplitude** of a wave corresponds to the amount of change in pressure created by it (see Figure 4.3). Amplitude is usually expressed on the **decibel (dB)** scale, named after Alexander Graham Bell, the Scottish-American inventor of the telephone. The box gives the formula for calculating dB as applied to sound pressure levels, known as **dB SPL**, which will be used in the remainder of this chapter. The dB SPL scale has two important properties.

The dB SPL scale is relative

The dB **sound pressure level (SPL)** scale measures sound pressure relative to a fixed reference pressure, chosen because it is close to the minimum sound pressure detectable by humans (at 1000 Hz). So the dB SPL scale specifies that the amplitude of a particular sound is a certain number of times higher or lower than the standard pressure.

The dB SPL scale is logarithmic

Equal ratios of pressure level correspond to equal increments in dB level. For example, each tenfold change in pressure equates to a decibel change of 20 dB. Similarly, each doubling (or halving) of pressure adds (or subtracts) 6 dB to the sound's decibel level.

The precise formula for dB SPL is:

$$N_{dB} = 20 * \log_{10}(P_e/P_r)$$

Where N_{dB} is decibel level, P_e is the SPL to be expressed in dB, and P_r is the reference pressure. P_e and P_r are commonly expressed in the standard physical unit of pressure, dynes per square centimeter. P_r is fixed at 0.0002 dynes/cm^2 (minimum sound pressure detectable by humans at 1000 Hz). The dB sensation level (SL) scale expresses dB above an individual's threshold at a given frequency.

KEY TERMS

Frequency
The number of cycles (periods) of a wave per unit of time or distance.

Amplitude
The maximum height of a wave, measured from its mean value to its maximum value.

Decibel (dB)
A measure of the difference between two quantities, based on the logarithm of their ratio (so equal ratios between the quantities correspond to equal dB differences).

Sound pressure level (SPL)
A decibel measure of sound pressure relative to a fixed reference pressure.

A logarithmic scale is used because it allows a very wide range of pressure levels (from 1 to 10 million) to be expressed in a compact range of dB values (from 0 to approximately 140).

Perceptually, SPL corresponds roughly with the loudness of a sound, although, as in the case of frequency and pitch, the relation between SPL and loudness is a complex one, to be discussed in the next chapter. The SPL produced by normal conversation is approximately 60 dB. The SPL of loud thunder or heavily amplified rock music is approximately 120 dB. Note that, because of the logarithmic nature of the dB scale, the pressure amplitude of the rock music is 1000 times greater than the amplitude of normal conversation. SPLs in the region of 140 dB can cause pain and hearing loss.

Phase

Phase defines a particular point on a waveform, and is measured in degrees (or equivalent radian values). One complete cycle of a repeating waveform occupies 360° of phase (or 2π radians), as shown in Figure 4.3. Conventionally a phase value of 0° corresponds to the point on a sound wave where pressure is at resting level. Maximum pressure occurs at one quarter of a cycle (90° or π/2), and minimum pressure occurs at three quarters of a cycle (270°). Phase is an important factor in the interaction of two waves; if two superimposed waves have similar phase values they tend to augment each other, whereas if the two waves differ by 180° they tend to cancel each other out. Phase also describes the relative timing of two sound waves, in terms of one leading or lagging behind the other; waves with smaller phase values are normally considered to lead those with larger values.

Rows (b) to (d) in Figure 4.4 show three sound waves that differ in their timing from the wave in row (a). The angle at the end of each row specifies the phase of that sound wave relative to the wave in row (a). Each wave is phase-shifted relative to wave (a) by a specific angle. For example, wave (d) is phase-shifted relative to wave (a) by an angle of +270°. Note that, since sine waves are repetitive or periodic, we can also say that wave (d) is phase-shifted relative to wave (a) by −90°(270°–360°).

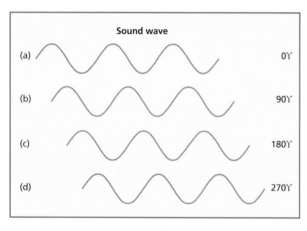

FIGURE 4.4
Phase differences between sine waves. Each wave (a) to (d) differs from wave (a) by the phase angle shown on the right. Angles are based on the sine wave plot shown in Figure 4.3, so each point on wave (b) is shifted relative to the corresponding point on wave (a) by an angle of 90°, or one quarter of a complete cycle of the wave.

COMPLEX SOUNDS

Natural sound sources hardly ever produce sounds that conform to the simple sinusoidal waveforms shown in Figures 4.3 and 4.4. Plots of sound pressure as a function of time reveal much more complex variation, as illustrated in Figure 4.5. However, any complex sound can be treated as a large collection of simple sine waves added together. The particular frequencies, amplitudes, and phases of the sine waves determine the overall form of the **complex wave**, and hence complex sound, they create. Figure 4.6 breaks the clarinet sound from Figure 4.5 into its component sine waves. The waveform in the top graph contains the series of sine waves shown in the middle graph. Notice how the components vary in frequency, amplitude, and phase.

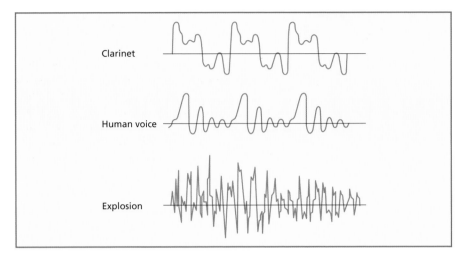

FIGURE 4.5
Complex sound waves produced by a musical instrument, the human voice, and an explosion.

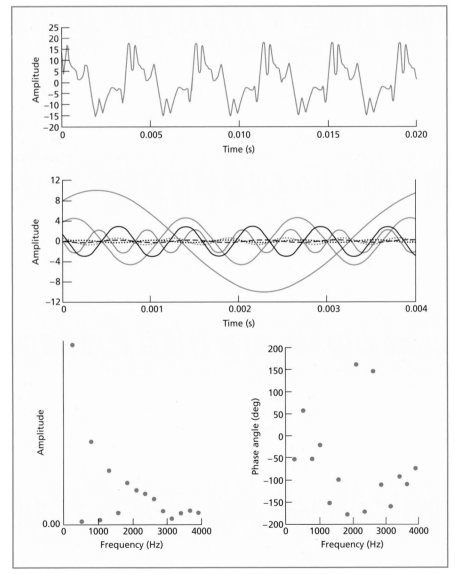

FIGURE 4.6
Top: A clarinet note. Middle: The series of sine wave components that add together to make the note. Bottom: Plots of the amplitude and phase of each component in the clarinet note. The component with the lowest frequency is called the fundamental, and gives the note its characteristic pitch. Higher frequency harmonics convey the timbre of the note.

Fundamental frequency
The lowest sinusoidal frequency in a complex wave.

Harmonic frequency
A sinusoidal component of a complex wave, having a frequency that is an integer multiple of the fundamental frequency.

Fourier analysis
The mathematical procedure by which a complex signal is decomposed into its magnitude spectrum and phase spectrum.

Fourier spectrum
A representation of the magnitude of individual frequency components present in a signal such as a sound wave; it is also known as the *magnitude spectrum*.

Phase spectrum
A representation of the phases of individual frequency components present in a signal.

The graph at the bottom left summarizes the different sine wave frequencies contained in a single clarinet note. The position of each dot on the horizontal axis identifies the frequency of that component, and the height of each dot specifies the component's amplitude. The graph at the bottom right plots the phase of each component, so the height of each dot specifies phase angle. The lowest frequency in the series is called the sound's **fundamental frequency**. The higher frequency components in any musical note are equally spaced along the frequency axis, at integral multiples of the fundamental frequency. These components are known as **harmonics**, and are conventionally numbered in order of distance from the fundamental, which is assigned harmonic number 1. The fifth harmonic, for example, has a frequency that is five times higher than the fundamental frequency. Musicians sometimes call harmonics above the fundamental "overtones." The fundamental frequency of the note relates to its perceived pitch. A note with a higher fundamental frequency would appear to have a higher pitch. The pattern of amplitudes in the harmonics relates to the timbre of the note played by the instrument. Different instruments playing a note at the same pitch (i.e., at the same fundamental frequency) sound different because they differ in terms of the relative levels of their harmonics.

Many natural sounds are not periodic, and do not contain a harmonic series of frequency components. Instead they contain a continuous "spectrum" of components in which all frequencies are represented. The particular amplitudes and phases of these components determine the overall form of the complex wave representing the sound.

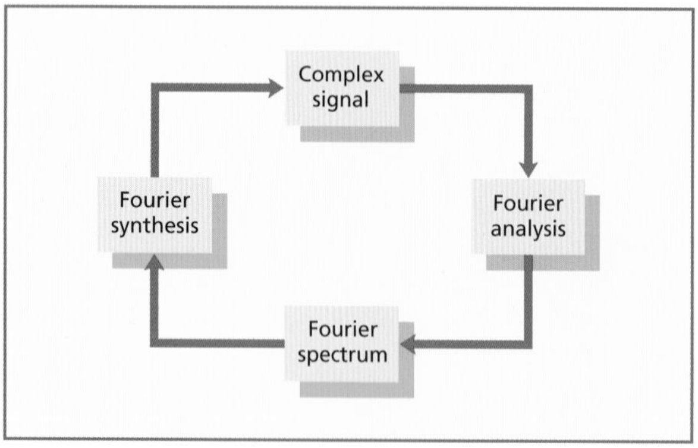

Fourier theory

A well-established mathematical procedure allows any complex sound, whether periodic or nonperiodic, to be broken down into its sine wave components. The mathematic theory underlying this procedure is called Fourier theory, after the 18th century French mathematician who first developed it, Joseph Fourier. An acquaintance with Fourier theory is crucial for a full understanding of the physical properties of sound, and of the biological system that processes sound. Indeed, Fourier theory has very wide scientific applications in many fields, including human vision.

FIGURE 4.7
Fourier analysis decomposes a complex signal into its frequency components, which can be displayed visually in a Fourier spectrum. The original signal can be recovered by the reverse operation, called Fourier synthesis.

Fourier spectrum

As illustrated in Figure 4.7, any complex signal can be broken down into sine wave components by a procedure called **Fourier analysis**. Figure 4.6 illustrates part of the results of Fourier analysis, namely the *magnitude spectrum* (**Fourier spectrum**) that contains information about the amplitude (or its square, called power) in the original signal at each frequency. Fourier analysis also generates a **phase spectrum** that contains information about the phases of the sine wave components making up the signal. Textbooks rarely present phase spectra, because component amplitudes are usually considered the most important features of complex signals. The magnitude spectrum and the phase spectrum together provide a complete representation of the original signal. It follows, then, that the original signal can be reconstituted perfectly by recombining the components, using a procedure called Fourier synthesis.

Many software packages include functions for performing Fourier analysis on waveforms. However it is important to understand some of the fundamental principles behind this important technique in order to interpret the results of the analysis correctly. The tutorials section at the end of the chapter contains a detailed introduction to Fourier analysis.

Spectrogram

Strictly speaking the mathematical techniques used to compute Fourier spectra assume that the sound signal extends over an infinite period of time. Real signals obviously do not remain unchanged. A single note produced by a musical instrument, for example, starts at a specific point in time, and different harmonics start at different times. The complex variation in harmonic amplitude at the start of a note is known as its "attack." Different instruments sound distinctive partly because they differ in their attack. Human speech sounds also contain many frequency components that vary in their amplitude over time. A simple magnitude spectrum clearly cannot depict variations in the acoustic signal that occur over time. So it is necessary to analyze changes in the frequency content of the signal over a succession of small time intervals. The time-varying spectrum is displayed graphically in a **spectrogram**. Time is plotted horizontally, and frequency is plotted vertically. Magnitude is represented by the darkness (or color) of the plot. Figure 4.8 shows spectrograms of a musical note (top), and a speech sound (bottom). It is easy to see how the frequency content of each signal changes over time by inspecting the dark contours in each plot.

The spectrogram is essentially a series of Fourier spectra from brief samples of the acoustic signals, taken over successive time windows. The restriction of each spectrum to such a short period of time limits its ability to distinguish between certain frequency components. In general, the frequency resolution of the spectrogram depends on the sampling window. For example, a sampling window of 10 milliseconds would allow a frequency resolution of 100 Hz (two frequency components would have to differ by at least this amount to be resolvable as separate peaks in the spectrogram; see Moore, 1997). Spectrograms therefore must trade off their ability to resolve variations over time with their ability to resolve variations

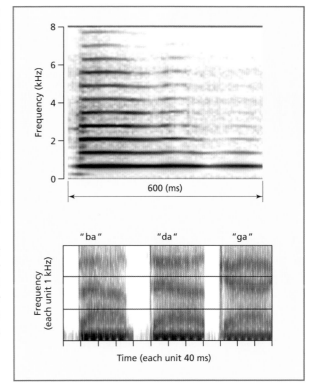

FIGURE 4.8
Spectrograms of two complex sounds: A note on a musical instrument (clarinet, top), and brief segments of human speech (bottom). Time is plotted horizontally and frequency is plotted vertically. Dark regions in the plot represent high amplitude components. Each spectrogram shows how the frequency components of the signal change progressively over time.

KEY TERM

Frequency filter
Any process that modifies the frequency content of signals passing through it.

over frequency. "Wideband" spectrograms opt for very good time resolution (typically around 3.3 ms) but this is at the expense of a relatively coarse frequency resolution (typically around a band of 300 Hz).

Filters

As indicated in Figure 4.7, after Fourier analysis has been applied to a signal to yield its spectrum, the signal can be reconstituted exactly by the reverse procedure of Fourier synthesis. However, Fourier theory can be used to investigate how a particular transmitting device or medium modifies or "**filters**" acoustic signals. The modification involves changes to the amplitude of certain components in the signal's spectrum. If a component's amplitude is reduced to zero, then the component is removed from the filtered signal. When Fourier synthesis is then applied to the modified spectrum, the resulting complex signal differs from the original because of the attenuation that has been applied to the removed component. To give an example, suppose we wish to know what happens to a sound when it passes over a medium such as the human head (sounds arriving at the right ear from sources to the left of the head must pass around the head first). We can generate a complex sound and record its variation in pressure level at the source and at the ear (top row of Figure 4.9). What precisely has happened to the sound? Fourier analysis of the signal before and after passing around the head (bottom row of Figure 4.9) reveals that the obstruction caused by the head removes the higher frequency components from the

? Think of another example of an obstruction that acts as an acoustic filter.

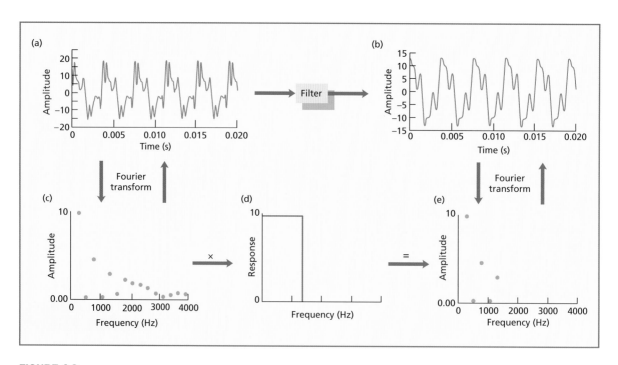

FIGURE 4.9
Filtering using Fourier methods. When a complex sound signal (a) is transmitted through a linear acoustic filter such as the head, the output that results (b) is a modified version of the input. The effect of the filter on the frequency components of the signal can be computed by taking the Fourier spectrum of the input (c), and multiplying this spectrum by the transfer function of the filter (d). The resulting output spectrum (e) corresponds to the Fourier spectrum of the output signal (b).

signal. In Fourier terms, the head is said to act as a *filter* that allows low frequencies to pass by but attenuates or removes high frequencies; a low-pass filter.

Transfer functions

The head is basically a physical obstruction that blocks or attenuates some sound frequencies more than others. The middle plot in the bottom row of Figure 4.9 shows the **transfer function** of the head, in terms of the relative amplitude of the signal that passes by the head as a function of frequency. Values close to 1 indicate very little attenuation. Values close to zero indicate that very little of the sound is transmitted around the head. If the transfer function of the head is known, then its effect on *any* complex signal can be calculated by (a) taking the spectrum of the signal; (b) multiplying the spectrum by the transfer function; and (c) applying Fourier synthesis to the output spectrum. The filtered signal transmitted around the head is revealed. This illustrates the power of Fourier analysis as a tool for studying the effect of filters on any arbitrary signal.

It is obviously crucial that the transfer function of the filter is known. How can it be derived? As mentioned earlier, the transfer function plots the amount of attenuation that is applied by the filter at each sine wave frequency present in a signal. The simplest way to derive the transfer function is to present the filter with a simple sinusoidal signal at a known frequency and amplitude, and measure the amplitude of the sine wave that is transmitted through the filter. The ratio of input amplitude to output amplitude defines the filter characteristic at that frequency. This procedure is repeated at a wide range of sine wave frequencies, to construct a complete representation of the filter's properties.

Filtering techniques provide powerful methods for describing the properties of acoustic filters and predicting their effects on an unlimited range of sound signals. They can be applied both to simple transmitting media and to more complex physical devices such as microphones and amplifiers. They can also be applied to the human auditory system. Each stage of auditory processing can be investigated to determine the way in which it filters the incoming acoustic signal.

Linearity

The use of Fourier theory to analyze the properties of an acoustic filter depends critically on the assumption that the filter is **linear.** Such a filter must obey three rules:

1. The output of the filter never contains any frequency component that was not present in the input signal. In the simplest case, if a sine wave input is applied, then the output must consist only of a sine wave at the same frequency (though its amplitude and phase may differ from the input).
2. If the amplitude of the input to the filter is changed by a certain factor, then the output should change by the same factor. For example, if the amplitude of a sine wave input is doubled, then the amplitude of the sine wave output should also double.
3. If a number of sine wave inputs are applied to the filter simultaneously, then the resulting output should match the output that would be produced if the inputs had been applied separately, and their individual outputs summed.

The application of Fourier theory to linear systems that obey these rules is often called *linear systems theory.* A filter that violates at least one of these rules is called

? *Why does truncating a waveform add new frequencies?*

a **nonlinear filter**. A nonlinear system adds distortions, in the form of additional frequency components that were not present in the input. Consequently, the filter's response to complex signals cannot be predicted straightforwardly from its response to simple sine wave inputs.

Figure 4.10 shows examples of linear and nonlinear filter outputs in response to a pure sine wave. The leftmost graphs show the temporal waveform (upper), and the frequency spectrum (lower) of the signal. A pure sine wave contains only one frequency component. The output of a linear filter (middle graphs) is also a sine wave, though it may be delayed in time (phase-shifted), as the graph shows. One form of nonlinearity is a failure to respond to low-intensity parts of the signal. The rightmost graphs show the output of a filter having such a nonlinearity. The upper graph shows that parts of the input waveform below a certain intensity are truncated because the filter does not respond to them. The frequency spectrum of the truncated waveform is shown in the lower graph. It contains many other frequencies in addition to the original sine wave frequency, violating one of the rules of linearity.

Later in this chapter, and in the next chapter, it will become clear that some parts of the human auditory system can be considered approximately linear, while others are highly nonlinear. Linear systems theory provides us with powerful mathematical tools to identify the nonlinear parts of the auditory system, and to define the precise nature of the nonlinearities.

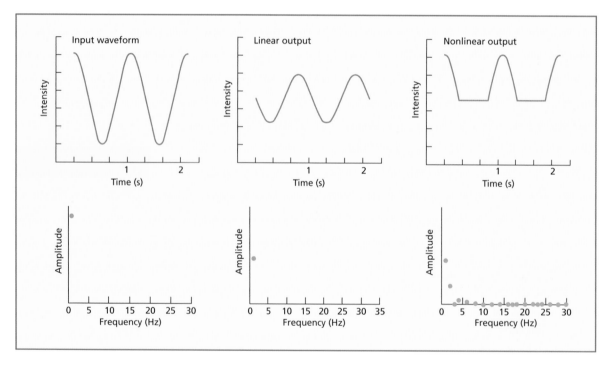

FIGURE 4.10
Examples of linear and nonlinear responses to simple stimuli. The left-hand pair of graphs show a single sine wave in terms of its waveform (upper) and its frequency spectrum containing a single component (lower). The middle pair of graphs show the output of a linear filter in response to the sine wave. The output is itself a sine wave. A nonlinear filter may produce a nonsinusoidal output that contains a range of frequency components. The right-hand pair of graphs show the output of a nonlinear filter, which does not respond to intensities below the mean intensity of the sine wave. The output waveform (upper) shows no modulation at lower intensities; the output spectrum (lower) shows the addition of many high frequency components that were not in the signal.

THE PHYSIOLOGY OF THE AUDITORY SYSTEM

Everyone knows that we hear sounds using our ears, two slightly flexible flaps on either side of the head surrounding openings into the skull. The outer ear is the only visible part of the peripheral auditory system, a complex and sophisticated biological system that detects and encodes sound pressure waves. The peripheral auditory system includes the outer ear, the middle ear, and the inner ear. Neural responses generated by the inner ear are transmitted to the central auditory system, which includes populations of neurons in the brainstem and cerebral cortex.

It is fair to say that we know a great deal about how the peripheral auditory system detects and encodes sound, but less is known about how the central auditory system mediates perception of sound. This brief introduction will cover the whole auditory system, but will necessarily devote more space to those parts of it that are best understood.

The components of the peripheral auditory system are shown in Figure 4.11. The **outer ear** gathers sound energy and focuses it down the **ear canal.** A thin

KEY TERMS

Outer ear
The outermost components of the auditory system: the pinna, meatus, and ear canal.

Ear canal
The S-shaped tube leading from the meatus to the tympanic membrane; it is approximately 0.6 cm wide and 2.5 cm long.

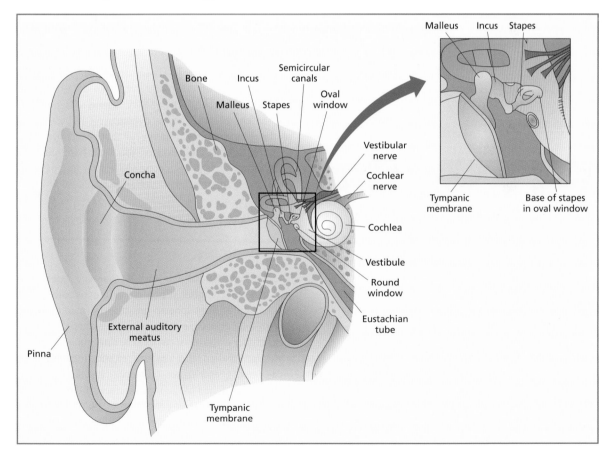

FIGURE 4.11
Component parts of the human ear. The outer ear consists of the pinna, concha, and meatus. The middle ear includes the tympanic membrane and three ossicles. The inner ear includes the cochlea, a coiled structure filled with fluid. The vestibulo-cochlear nerve carries sensory responses toward the brain. Redrawn from Purves et al. (2001). Copyright © 2001 Sinauer Associates. Reproduced with permission.

flexible membrane (the **tympanic membrane**, commonly known as the ear drum) is stretched across the canal 2.5 cm inside the skull. Air pressure waves cause the membrane to vibrate. Three tiny interconnected bones (ossicles) in the middle ear transmit these vibrations to the cochlea, a spiral-shaped bony structure filled with fluid. Mechanical energy applied by the ossicles sets up ripples of movement in the cochlear fluid. Sensory hair cells in the cochlea generate electrical signals when they are displaced by the fluid movement. These responses are transmitted to the brainstem and then to the cerebral cortex, to create our conscious experience of sound.

THE OUTER EAR

The flexible flap surrounding the outer ear is known as the **pinna** (also known as the auricle). Its funnel-shaped inner part is known as the concha. The pinna is made up mostly of cartilage, and is attached to the skull by ligaments and muscles. In humans the pinna is virtually immobile, whereas other mammals such as horses and cats are able to move the pinna to orient it in the direction of a sound source. The shape and size of the human pinna, concha, and ear canal have two consequences for hearing. First, they act as an amplifier, boosting sound pressure for frequencies between 1500 and 7000 Hz, or 1.5 and 7 kHz (Yost, 2000). Second, the complex folds of the pinna act as an acoustic filter that attenuates high frequency sound components. The extent of attenuation depends on the elevation of the sound source relative to the head, providing a cue as to the elevation of the sound source. The tympanic membrane is a cone-shaped semitransparent membrane covering an area of approximately 55 mm^2.

The muscles attached to the ossicles contract reflexively when the ear is exposed to intense sounds. The middle ear reflex is controlled by neurons in the brainstem, and may help to protect the ear from damage. However, the reflex acts too slowly to offer protection against sudden impulsive sounds such as gunshots. Another function of the reflex may be to dampen down the audibility of self-generated sounds to ensure that we are not deafened by the sound of our own voice.

KEY TERMS

Meatus
The opening into the ear canal.

Tympanic membrane
The flexible cone-shaped membrane extending across the inner end of the ear canal; it transmits sound energy to the middle ear.

Pinna
The external ear visible on each side of the head; its funnel-shaped inner part (concha) funnels sound into the meatus.

Middle ear
The air-filled cavity containing the bones and associated supporting structures that transfer sound energy from the outer ear to the inner ear.

Oval window
The point of entry for sound energy into the inner ear; it is a small membrane-covered opening in the cochlea.

THE MIDDLE EAR

The ossicles

The three bones of the **middle ear** are housed in an air-filled chamber. Pressure in the middle ear is maintained at atmospheric pressure by means of the 3.5 cm long eustachian tube, which connects the middle ear chamber to the nasal cavity. The three interconnected bones are called the malleus (Latin for hammer), incus (anvil), and stapes (stirrup). The handle of the malleus is attached to the inner surface of the tympanic membrane. Its head is connected to the next ossicle, the incus. The smallest bone, the stapes (actually the smallest bone in the body), is connected to the incus at one end and to the cochlea at the other end. The point of attachment between the footplate of the stapes and the cochlea is a membrane-covered opening in the cochlea known as the **oval window**. The three ossicles are held in position by ligaments and muscles.

Impedance matching

The tympanic membrane is thus connected mechanically to the oval window of the cochlea by the three ossicles. At first sight, this arrangement seems overly complicated. Why not have the tympanic membrane bear directly on the oval window? The reason is that the outer and middle ear cavities are filled with air, while the inner ear is filled with fluid. Air offers much less resistance to movement than does fluid. Consequently, if sound energy were to impinge directly on the oval window the fluid would offer resistance and virtually all of the energy would be reflected back out of the ear. The bones of the middle ear act to maximize the transmission of sound from the outer ear to the inner ear. Technically, air and fluid differ in their acoustic **impedance**, or resistance to movement of the air or fluid. The function of the middle ear is to match up the low acoustic impedance of the tympanic membrane with the high acoustic impedance of the oval window, known as **impedance matching**.

The middle ear achieves impedance matching in two ways. First, the diameter of the tympanic membrane (55 mm^2) is much larger than the area of the stapes in contact with the oval window (3.2 mm^2; Yost, 2000). Consequently, the force per unit area at the footplate of the stapes is much higher than that at the tympanic membrane. Second, the ossicles act as levers that increase the mechanical force at the tympanic membrane by a factor of 1.3. Buckling movement in the tympanic membrane also acts to increase pressure. Yost (2000) calculated that the combined effect of these actions is to increase pressure by a factor of 44, or 33 dB SPL, counteracting the high impedance of the fluid behind the oval window. The middle ear is usually considered to be an approximately linear transmitter of sound energy, at least at normal listening levels.

THE INNER EAR

Each **inner ear** consists of a series of bony, fluid-filled cavities in the temporal bone incorporating the sense organs of both hearing and balance. As Hudspeth (1989) commented, the inner ear is a remarkably sophisticated inertial guidance system, acoustic amplifier, and frequency analyzer occupying no more space than a child's marble. The semicircular canals and otolith organs form the vestibular organ used to sense body position and movement (covered in the previous chapter). The **cochlea** is the sense organ for hearing, converting sound energy into neural impulses. Many critical features of hearing can be related directly to the mechanical properties of the cochlea.

Structure of the cochlea

The cochlea (Latin for snail) is a small, coiled tube about 10 mm in diameter. If the tube were straightened out it would be about 34 mm long in humans. The coiled shape of the cochlea minimizes the space it occupies in the head, maximizes the

KEY TERMS

Scala vestibuli

The tube running along the cochlea that contains the oval window at its base.

Scala tympani

The tube running along the cochlea that contains the round window at its base.

Scala media

The tube that runs between the scala vestibuli and scala tympani.

Cochlear partition

The flexible structure that separates the scala tympani and scala media, and houses the scala media.

Basilar membrane

The flexible structure on the cochlear partition that houses mechanoreceptors; it forms part of the organ of Corti.

Traveling wave

The ripple of displacement that travels along the basilar membrane when sound vibrations are applied to the oval window.

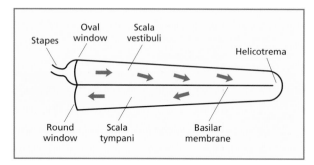

FIGURE 4.12

Simplified cross-section through an uncoiled cochlea. Arrows indicate the direction of fluid displacement when the stapes pushes on the oval window. The basilar membrane lies between the two scala. It is narrow and stiff near the base, and wide and flexible near the apex.

supply of blood and nerves, and boosts its response to low frequency sounds (Manoussaki et al., 2008). The cochlear tube or "duct" is divided along its length into three chambers: the **scala vestibuli** and **scala tympani** are separated by the smaller third chamber, the **scala media**, in the **cochlear partition** (see Figure 4.15).

The basal (outermost) end of the scala vestibuli contains the flexible oval window. The basal end of the scala tympani contains another flexible window called the round window. A small opening between the scala vestibuli and scala tympani known as the helicotrema allows the two chambers to share the same fluid, perilymph, which has the same composition as cerebrospinal fluid. The cochlear partition houses the **basilar membrane**, the structure that contains the cochlea's sensory hair cells. Before discussing the properties of these hair cells in detail, it is important to consider the mechanical response of the cochlea to vibrations applied to the oval window.

Mechanical properties of the cochlea

Traveling waves on the basilar membrane

Sound vibrations picked up by the tympanic membrane cause the stapes to push back and forth on the oval window at the same frequency as the sound wave. When the stapes pushes on the oval window, it displaces the fluid in the scala vestibuli. Since this fluid is incompressible, the pressure is transmitted to the scala media, which in turn displaces the cochlear partition as the pressure is transferred to the scala tympani, deforming the basilar membrane. The increase in pressure in the scala tympani causes the round window to bulge outward (see the arrows in Figure 4.12). When the stapes pulls back from the oval window, pressure is transferred through the cochlear chambers in the opposite direction, again causing a displacement of the basilar membrane.

The mechanical properties of the basilar membrane vary considerably from base to apex. The displacement of the basilar membrane takes the form of a wave that travels along the membrane from the basal end (where the wave originates) to the apical end. Figure 4.13 shows an example of a **traveling wave** at four successive instants in time. The envelope of the wave is drawn through all the points of maximum displacement along the membrane as the wave travels along it.

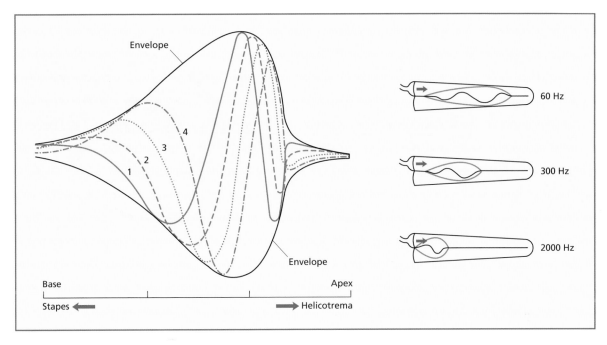

FIGURE 4.13
Vibration of the stapes disturbs cochlear fluid and creates traveling waves of displacement along the basilar membrane. Left: A traveling wave on the basilar membrane at four instants in time. Right: Instantaneous waves and envelopes of traveling waves at three different frequencies. Redrawn from Yost (2000). Copyright © 2000 Elsevier. Reproduced with permission.

Frequency-to-place conversion

Displacement is greatest at a particular place along the membrane. At the basal end, the membrane is relatively narrow and stiff, while at the apical end it is much wider and more flexible. As a result, the position of maximum displacement of the membrane depends on the frequency of vibration. Georg von Bekesy was the first to discover that the point of maximum displacement is near the apex for low frequencies, and near the base for high frequencies, as illustrated in Figure 4.13. This frequency-dependent displacement pattern is the key to the cochlea's ability to encode sound frequency.

When a pure sinusoidal input is applied to the cochlea, each point on the basilar membrane vibrates in an approximately sinusoidal manner, at the same frequency as the input sine wave. As we have seen in Figure 4.13, the magnitude of displacement is greater at some places on the membrane than at others. In a normal healthy ear each point on the basilar membrane is relatively sharply tuned to frequency, in that large displacements occur only for a relatively narrow band of sound frequencies. The left-hand plot in Figure 4.14 shows the sensitivity to sound at a specific place on the basilar membrane, as a function of sound frequency. Over a very narrow range of frequencies near 18 kHz, this particular place on the membrane requires very little sound in order to produce a displacement. At other frequencies, much greater sound levels are required to produce the same displacement. Such sharp frequency tuning is unlikely to reflect just the passive mechanical properties of the basilar

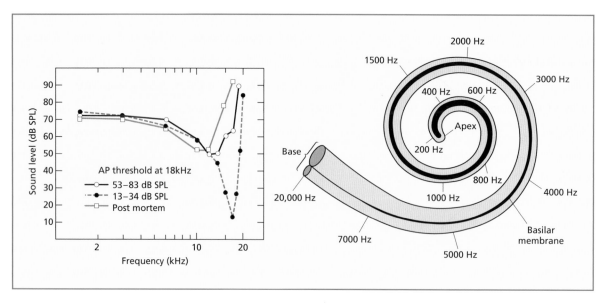

FIGURE 4.14

Left: Frequency tuning curves at a specific point on the basilar membrane in a live animal (circles), and post mortem (squares). Adapted from Moore (1997). Right: Map of the frequencies that produce maximum displacement at points along the basilar membrane (after Culler et al., 1943). High frequencies displace the base of the membrane, and low frequencies displace the apex. Note the approximately logarithmic variation in frequency with distance along the membrane. For example, the distance between the 1000 Hz and 2000 Hz points is equal to the distance between the 2000 Hz and 4000 Hz points.

membrane. As we shall see, an active physiological process involving outer hair (cilia) cells contributes to the sharpness of tuning (bandwidth of auditory filters). The right half of Figure 4.14 is a drawing of the cochlea showing the place of maximum displacement over the full spectrum of audible frequencies. The basilar membrane achieves a "**frequency-to-place**" conversion (Moore, 1997). The frequency of vibration is encoded in terms of the place of maximum displacement.

Linearity of basilar membrane displacement

One criterion for linearity is that the amplitude of basilar membrane displacement should double when the amplitude of the input wave doubles. The membrane obeys the rule only at very low and very high input amplitudes (Robles, Ruggiero, & Rich, 1986). At intermediate amplitudes the active physiological process mentioned above amplifies the response of the basilar membrane.

A second criterion for linearity is that when two pure sinusoidal tones are presented together the membrane should vibrate in a way that reflects the sum of the two individual responses. In other words it should show two peaks in displacement, at the locations appropriate for the two component frequencies. The basilar membrane obeys this rule only when the two tones are widely separated in frequency. When the tones are relatively close in frequency, their vibration patterns interact to produce nonsinusoidal displacements at certain locations. When the frequency difference is sufficiently small, the basilar membrane fails to resolve the components. It produces a single broad peak in displacement rather than two individual peaks.

KEY TERM

Frequency-to-place conversion

An encoding scheme in which the place of maximum displacement on the basilar membrane codes the frequency of sound vibration.

The organ of Corti

The basilar membrane forms part of a complex structure known as the **organ of Corti**, which separates the scala vestibuli from the scala tympani (see Figure 4.15). Sensory hair cells lie on top of the basilar membrane. Some of their stereocilia are embedded in the underside of a flexible overhanging structure called the **tectorial membrane**. The hair cells form four neat rows running along the length of the basilar membrane. One row lies on the inner

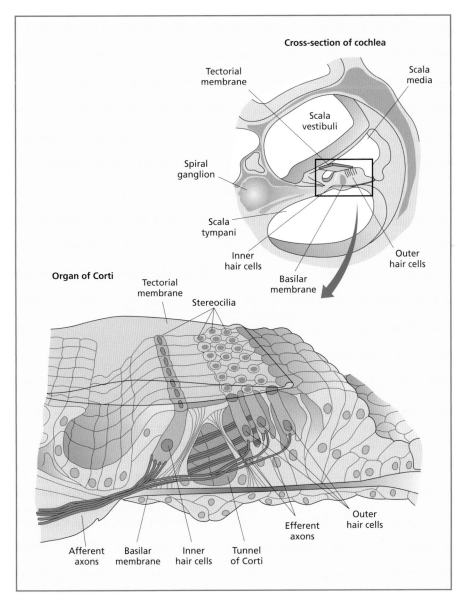

FIGURE 4.15
The organ of Corti, showing the detailed structure of the basilar membrane. Rows of inner and outer hair cells run along the length of the basilar membrane. Their stereocilia project into the space between the basilar membrane and the tectorial membrane. Outer hair cell stereocilia are actually embedded into the tectorial membrane. Redrawn from Purves (2001). Copyright © 2001 Sinauer Associates. Reproduced with permission.

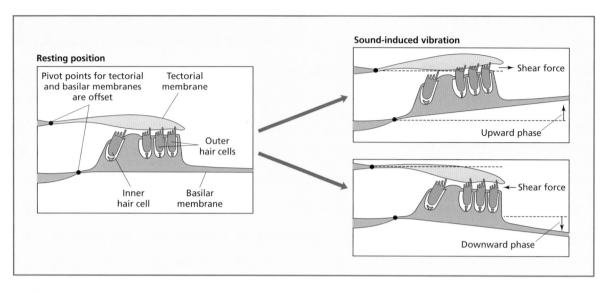

FIGURE 4.16
Basilar membrane displacement produces shearing motion between the tectorial and basilar membranes, due to their different pivot points. Hair cells protruding into the gap between the two membranes are displaced by the shearing motion. Redrawn from Purves et al. (2001). Copyright © 2001 Sinauer Associates. Reproduced with permission.

side of the cochlear spiral (**inner hair cells**), and contains approximately 3500 hair cells. The other three rows lie closer to the outside of the spiral (**outer hair cells**) and contain about 12,000 hair cells (Moore, 1997). When fluid vibrations cause a displacement of the basilar membrane, it pivots about a point that is offset from the pivot point of the tectorial membrane. The up-and-down displacement of the two membranes is consequently transformed into a shearing motion between them, as shown in Figure 4.16. The inner hair cells are displaced by the fluid. The tips of the outer hair cells are embedded in the tectorial membrane, so are displaced by the relative motion of the basilar membrane and tectorial membrane.

Inner hair cells

Cochlear hair cells are similar to the hair cells found in the vestibular organs, described in detail in the previous chapter, except that adult cochlear cells do not possess a single tall kinocilium (it disappears early in development). As in the vestibular system, cochlear hair cells produce graded receptor potentials in response to displacement of their stereocilia. Displacement toward the tallest stereocilia depolarizes the cell (increasing voltage), and displacement in the opposite direction hyperpolarizes the cell (decreasing voltage). It is remarkable that stereocilia displacements as small as 0.3 nanometers alter receptor potential, sufficient to reach the threshold of hearing. This distance corresponds to the diameter of atoms, and is equivalent to a displacement at the top of the Eiffel Tower by only a thumb's width (Hudspeth, 1989). Moreover, transduction can occur over a time period as small as 10 microseconds. Fluctuations in receptor potential can therefore reflect basilar membrane displacement quite faithfully. Palmer and Russell (1986) recorded receptor potentials in the guinea pig in response to pure tones. They found that

KEY TERMS

Inner hair cells
The mechanoreceptors on the basilar membrane that provide afferent signals to the auditory system when the membrane is displaced.

Outer hair cells
Motile hair cells spanning the gap between the basilar membrane and tectorial membrane; they control the mechanical coupling between the two membranes.

receptor potential could follow the waveform of the tone only for frequencies up to 3000 Hz (note that one period of a 3 kHz tone lasts 300 microseconds).

The base of each inner hair cell makes synaptic contact with afferent fibers of the auditory nerve. Approximately 90–95% of the estimated 50,000 afferent auditory nerve fibers make contact with inner hair cells. Each fiber attaches to a single inner hair cell. Since there are only 3500 inner hair cells, each hair cell has approximately 10 fibers attached to it. Most of the sensory information about sound is conveyed by inner hair cells.

Outer hair cells

Since so few afferent fibers (5–10%) are connected to outer hair cells, the responses of these cells must convey very little useful sensory information about sound. On the other hand, there are far more outer hair cells than inner hair cells. What is the function of outer hair cells? Outer hair cells are able to change their size, expanding and contracting along their length, whereas inner hair cells cannot. Outer hair cell motility seems to arise from two sources (Yost, 2000). First, they contain some crucial proteins supporting muscle-like contractions in response to stereocilia displacement. Second, they receive efferent stimulation from the cochlea nerve. It is known that there are about 1800 efferent fibers in the auditory nerve, which convey signals from the central auditory system out to the cochlea. Many of these fibers make contact with outer hair cells.

> It is a remarkable fact that the ear itself can generate sounds, which can be detected by very sensitive microphones placed in the auditory meatus. These sounds are known as **oto-acoustic emissions** or *cochlear echoes*, since they are usually detected some 5–60 ms after the ear is stimulated with a click. Although the exact source of oto-acoustic emissions has not been identified, they are thought to originate in the nonlinear amplification supplied by outer hair cells.

Since outer hair cells bridge the gap between the basilar membrane and the tectorial membrane, outer hair cell motility alters the mechanical coupling between two membranes. It is thought that the alteration in mechanical coupling effectively amplifies the response of the basilar membrane, so increasing the response of inner hair cells. The filled symbols in Figure 4.14 show the SPL required to produce a fixed basilar membrane displacement in the presence of outer hair cell motility (live animal). The open symbols show SPL required in the absence of outer hair cell motility (postmortem). Outer hair cell motility clearly increases the mechanical sensitivity of the basilar membrane, and narrows its frequency response.

Sound frequency coding in the auditory nerve

The intracellular resting potential of hair cells is −70 mV. Movement of the basilar membrane toward the tectorial membrane depolarizes the inner hair cells, increasing their receptor potential. Movement of the basilar membrane away from the tectorial membrane hyperpolarizes the hair cells. Neurotransmitter is released only when the hair cells are depolarized. As a result, auditory nerve fibers fire only when the basilar membrane moves toward the tectorial membrane. Since the basilar membrane vibrates in synchrony with an input sound wave, auditory nerve fibers fire during each positive phase of the wave, at least for low frequency waves, as shown in the top half of Figure 4.17. This property of nerve fiber activity is known as **phase locking**. Neurons cannot produce action potentials at rates greater than 1000 spikes/s, since they have an absolute refractory period of 1 ms. Consequently auditory nerve fibers cannot fire at every cycle of the wave for sound frequencies higher than 1 kHz. Although a particular nerve fiber does not fire at every cycle for sounds above 1 kHz, when it does fire the impulses occur at roughly the same phase of the wave each time. As a result, the interval between successive impulses is an integral multiple of the period of the waveform, as illustrated in the lower half of Figure 4.17. The response of the fiber is still phase-locked to the auditory signal. Even this form of phase locking collapses above frequencies of 4–5 kHz, because the inner hair cells cannot change their voltage fast enough (Palmer & Russell, 1986).

? *Think of a linking proposition (described in Chapter 1) to relate auditory nerve fiber responses to perceived pitch.*

A fundamental function of the ear is to encode the frequency of sound waves that enter the ear. The mechanical and neural properties of the cochlea are suitable for using two different methods of encoding sound frequency of sound wave stimuli, known as place coding and rate coding.

FIGURE 4.17
Phase locking of auditory nerve fiber activity in response to sounds at low frequency (top) and at high frequency (bottom). Since hair cells release neurotransmitter only when displaced in one direction, auditory nerve fibers fire only to one phase of the sound wave (the phase creating the necessary displacement). At low frequencies, a response can occur at every cycle of the sound wave (top). At high frequencies each fiber's response cannot occur at every cycle, but responses are still phase-locked. The combined response of a number of fibers can recover the frequency of the stimulating waveform (bottom).

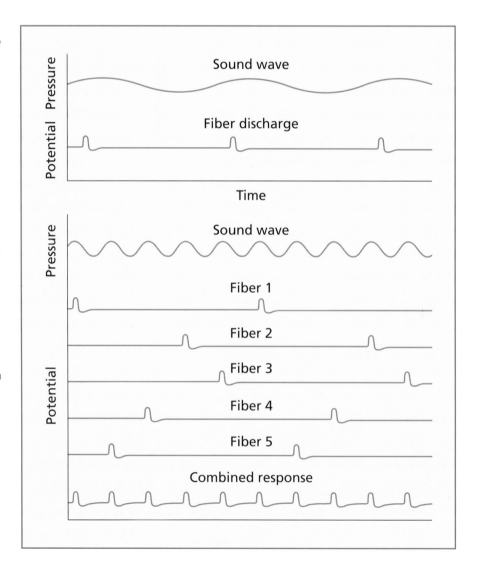

Place code

Earlier in the chapter we saw that the basilar membrane performs a frequency-to-place conversion. As shown in Figure 4.14, each sound wave frequency is associated with a particular place of maximum displacement on the membrane. Since hair cells are distributed along the length of the membrane, the distribution of hair cell activity along the membrane provides an orderly *place code* for sound frequency. The place of maximum hair cell activity represents the frequency of the input sound wave. Each auditory nerve fiber connects to only a small number of hair cells in a particular region of the membrane. So the place code is preserved in the response pattern of auditory nerve fibers. The sound frequency that produces the greatest response from a particular nerve fiber is known as its *characteristic frequency*. The orderly spatial arrangement of characteristic frequency along a neural structure such as the basilar membrane is known as *tonotopic organization*. We have already seen (Figure 4.13) that quite a large portion of the basilar membrane is displaced in response to a single input frequency, particularly at low frequencies. Consequently, any one auditory nerve fiber will respond to a broad range of sound frequencies, though it responds best to its characteristic frequency. Figure 4.18 plots frequency tuning curves derived from recordings in single auditory nerves of the cat (Palmer, 1995).

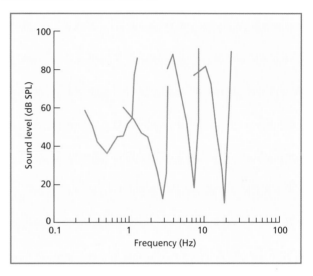

Rate code

Phase locking provides a second possible mechanism for encoding sound frequency. Since auditory nerve fiber impulses are phase-locked to the sound wave, the response rate of a particular fiber should reflect the frequency of the stimulus. It should be noted that it is not necessary for an individual fiber to fire at every single cycle of the wave, only that when it does fire the impulse is locked to a particular part of the cycle. If the activity pattern from a whole ensemble of nerve fibers is combined, then the combined response should reconstruct the frequency of the stimulating waveform. Wever (1949) called this method of rate coding the volley principle, illustrated in Figure 4.17.

Perceptual evidence on the roles of place coding and rate coding in pitch perception is discussed in the next chapter.

Intensity coding in the auditory nerve

In the absence of stimulation, each auditory nerve fiber discharges at a steady spontaneous rate. Different fibers vary widely in their spontaneous firing rate. Most fibers have high resting firing rates (18–250 spikes/s), but a small number have very low spontaneous firing rates (below 0.5 spikes/s). In each fiber, SPL must exceed a certain threshold value in order to register a change in firing rate. At the other end of the intensity scale, above a certain SPL the fiber's activity level saturates, so that further increases in SPL result in no change in activity. The range of sound levels between threshold and saturation defines the fiber's **dynamic range.** Auditory nerve

FIGURE 4.18
Frequency tuning curves of auditory nerve fibers in the cat. Each curve represents a single auditory nerve fiber, and plots the sound pressure level required to produce an above-threshold response from the fiber at different stimulating frequencies (adapted from Palmer, 1995, figure 1).

KEY TERM

Dynamic range
In auditory nerve fibers, it is the difference between the minimum SPL to which a fiber responds, and the SPL at the fiber's maximum firing rate.

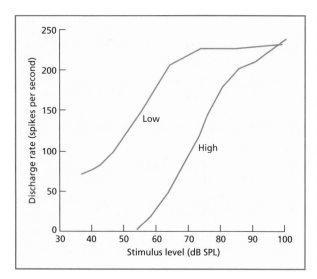

fibers have a dynamic range of between 20 and 60 dB. Human hearing has a dynamic range of at least 100 dB. How is this possible? Auditory nerve fibers with a high spontaneous firing rate have low thresholds, so they are sensitive to very quiet sounds, but their dynamic range extends only up to approximately 60 dB SPL (upper curve in Figure 4.19). Fibers with a low spontaneous firing rate have relatively high thresholds (up to 50 dB SPL), but their dynamic range extends up to about 100 dB SPL (lower curve in Figure 4.19). It appears that information about sound intensities at different levels may be carried by different groups of fibers (Plack & Carlyon, 1995). Recall from earlier in the chapter that each inner hair cell connects to a number of different afferent fibers, which could vary in their sensitivity.

FIGURE 4.19

Activity as a function of sound pressure level, for a low-threshold and a high-threshold auditory nerve fiber (adapted from Palmer, 1995, figure 9).

Is the ear a Fourier analyzer?

At the beginning of the chapter we discovered that, according to Fourier theory, each and every sound can be decomposed into a unique set of one or more sine wave frequency components. Neural activity in the auditory nerve seems to encode input sounds in terms of their Fourier spectra. Frequency is encoded by the frequency-to-place conversion that occurs on the basilar membrane. Phase and intensity appear to be encoded directly in the patterns of activity in auditory nerve fibers. Although on this basis it is tempting to describe the ear as a Fourier analyzer, such a view would be an oversimplification. The ear violates all three rules that must be satisfied by linear filters.

- According to the first rule described earlier, the ear should not introduce any frequency component that was not present in the input signal. One example of how the ear violates this rule is the phenomenon of combination tones. When the basilar membrane is stimulated with two tones at different frequencies, it creates a distortion product at a third frequency, which is sometimes clearly audible (Plomp, 1965; Kim, Molnar, & Matthews, 1980).
- The second rule of linearity requires that the amplitude of the ear's output should vary in direct proportion to variations in input amplitude. But the basilar membrane's displacement is nonlinear due to the cochlear amplifier described earlier in the chapter (the limited dynamic range of auditory nerve fibers, illustrated in Figure 4.19, also violates this rule).
- The third rule states that the ear's response to a combination of components should be equal to the sum of its responses to those components when applied separately. A number of researchers have studied auditory nerve responses to pairs of tones. They find that the response of a single fiber to one tone can be suppressed by the presence of a second tone (Sachs & Kiang, 1968). **Two-tone suppression** depends on the relative frequencies of the two tones. For example, when one tone is at or near the characteristic frequency of a particular fiber, suppression occurs when the second tone has a frequency that lies just outside the range of frequencies to which the fiber responds (in other words, just outside the tuning curve depicted in Figure 4.18).

KEY TERM

Two-tone suppression
Suppression of an auditory nerve fiber's response to a tone during presentation of a second tone.

Such gross departures from linearity clearly rule out the view that the ear performs a strict Fourier analysis on the incoming sound signal. However, the signal that the ear transmits to the brain can be viewed as an *approximation* to a Fourier analysis of the sound, so the Fourier approach is still very useful. The frequency-to-place conversion of the basilar membrane does attempt to decompose sound signals into frequency components, and some representation of phase and intensity is carried in the patterns of firing in auditory nerve fibers. The nonlinearities that rule out a faithful Fourier analysis can be viewed as adaptations that maximize the dynamic range of the system, or improve its ability to detect very faint sound signals. Given that the ear did not evolve with mathematical purity in mind, the extent of the similarity between the mathematical process of Fourier analysis and the physiological processing of sound is remarkable.

THE ASCENDING AUDITORY PATHWAY

Cell bodies associated with the auditory nerve are located in the spiral ganglion of the cochlea. Each spiral ganglion cell makes contact with one or more hair cells, and a central process to form an auditory nerve fiber. Figure 4.20 provides a simplified schematic view of the complete ascending pathway. Auditory nerve fibers terminate in the brainstem, where they form synapses with large groups of neurons in the **cochlear nuclei**. Fibers from the right ear arrive at the right cochlear nucleus, and fibers from the left ear arrive at the left cochlear nucleus. Most of the fibers leaving each nucleus cross over to the opposite (contralateral) side of the brain. The remaining fibers stay on the same side (ipsilateral). One group of fibers from each cochlear nucleus ascends directly to the contralateral inferior colliculus in the midbrain. Another group of fibers

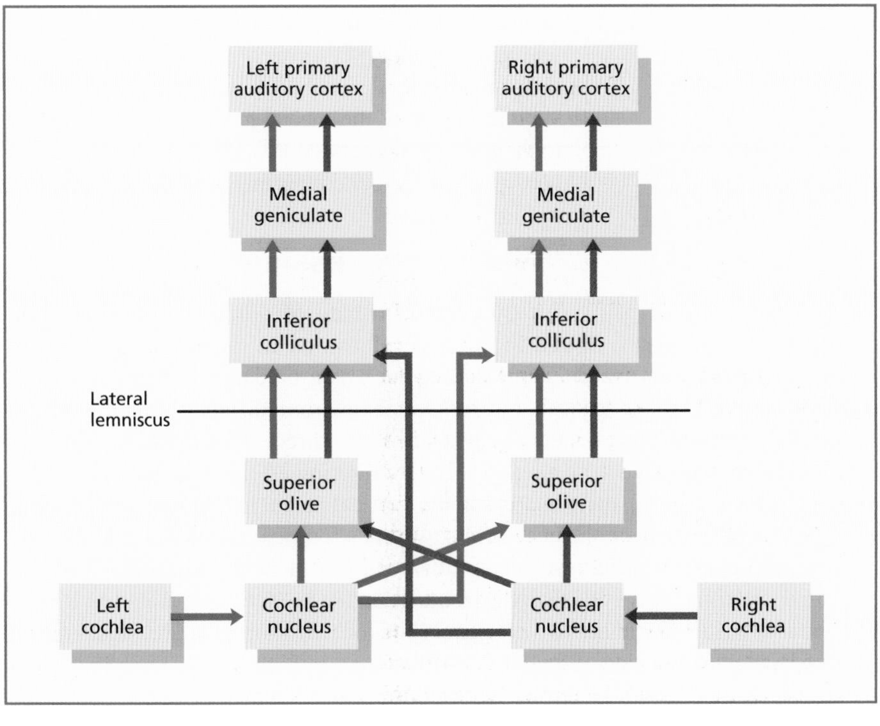

> **KEY TERM**
>
> **Cochlear nucleus**
> The mass of nerve cells in the brainstem where auditory nerve fibers terminate.

FIGURE 4.20
Schematic diagram of the ascending auditory pathway. Binaural responses appear first in the superior olive, which contains special neural circuits that compute "where" a sound originates in auditory space. The monaural projection from each cochlear nucleus to the inferior colliculi may carry information about "what" the sound is. Adapted from Moore (1997) and Yost (2000).

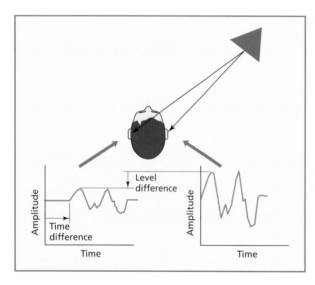

FIGURE 4.21
Cues for auditory localization in the transverse plane (azimuth). The signal arriving at the ear on the far side of the head has a lower amplitude and is slightly delayed relative to the signal arriving at the nearer ear. Redrawn from Yost (2000). Copyright © 2000 Elsevier. Reproduced with permission.

projects only as far as the **superior olive** in the pons. Most fibers in this group project to the contralateral superior olive, while the rest project ipsilaterally. Neurons in the superior olives therefore receive inputs from both ears. Projections from each superior olive carry auditory responses centrally to the lateral lemniscus, then onward to the inferior colliculus, and **medial geniculate nucleus**. Auditory signals finally arrive bilaterally in the primary auditory cortex.

The ascending auditory pathway involves a complex combination of serial and parallel processing stages. In the interests of simplicity, we will concentrate on how two important aspects of the sound stimulus are processed in the auditory pathway: *what* the sound is, and *where* it originates.

"What" processing

The "what" attributes of a sound include its frequency composition and its temporal features such as phase properties, onset, and duration. Some neurons in the cochlear nuclei have a complex response to sound frequency and a much wider dynamic range than auditory nerve fibers. Higher up in the auditory pathway, both the inferior colliculus and the medial geniculate nucleus contain cells that appear to convey "what" information, responding only to sounds coming from one ear (monaural) that vary in frequency, or sounds of a specific duration. Some cells respond to more than one sense modality, by virtue of incoming signals from the somatosensory, vestibular, and visual systems. The ventral regions of the medial geniculate nuclei project to the primary auditory cortex. Other regions project to cortical areas surrounding primary auditory cortex.

"Where" processing

An important attribute of a sound is the direction from which it originates. Sound localization allows us to orient ourselves to the potential danger of an unseen sound source such as a predator. It also helps us to segment complex sound stimuli into components from different sound sources. Unlike the retina of the eye, the cochlea offers no direct representation of sound location. However, as we have already seen, the filtering effect of the pinna provides a cue for the location of sound sources in the vertical plane. In addition, the physical arrangement of the ears on the head offers two cues for localization in the transverse or horizontal plane (hearing researchers often call this plane the **azimuth**). The two ears are approximately 14 cm apart horizontally on the head, and separated by a mass of bone and tissue. There are two consequences for reception of sound signals from sources located to one side of the head, as illustrated in Figure 4.21. First, the sound signal has to travel slightly further to reach the contralateral ear than to reach the ipsilateral ear. As a result, the signal arriving at the contralateral ear is delayed or phase-shifted relative to the signal arriving at the ipsilateral ear. Second, the signal arriving at the contralateral ear must pass around the head, and may suffer some degree of attenuation as a result.

Specialized neural circuits in the auditory pathway detect the very small differences in phase and intensity that can be used for sound localization. Cells in the superior olive receive bilateral projections from the anteroventral region of each cochlear nucleus. Circuits in the medial superior olive compute the minute time differences between the auditory signals arriving at the two ears (**interaural time differences**, or ITD). Circuits in the lateral superior olive compute the difference in intensity between the signals arriving at the two ears (**interaural level differences**, or ILD).

Interaural time differences

Sounds originating directly opposite one ear arrive at that ear approximately 700 microseconds before they arrive at the opposite ear. This ITD becomes progressively smaller as the location of the sound source moves closer to the median plane (directly in front of or behind the head). Humans can detect ITDs as small as 10 microseconds. Such remarkable performance is mediated by neural circuits of the kind illustrated in Figure 4.22, first proposed by L. A. Jeffress in 1948 (Yin & Chan, 1990). Figure 4.22

KEY TERMS

Interaural time difference (ITD)
A difference in the time of arrival of an auditory stimulus at one ear relative to the other.

Interaural level difference (ILD)
A difference in the intensity of an auditory stimulus arriving at the one ear relative to the other.

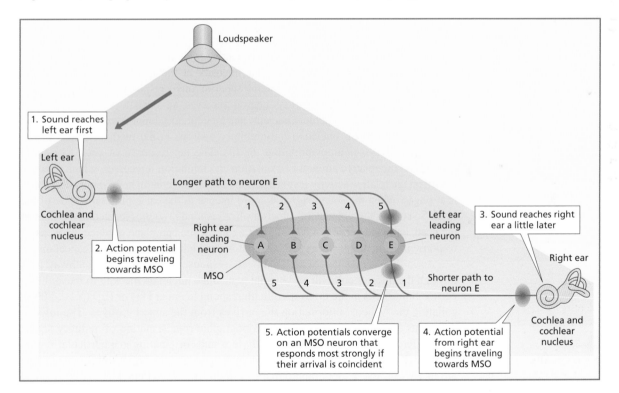

FIGURE 4.22
Schematic diagram of a neural circuit in the medial superior olive that computes interaural time differences. Each neuron (A–E) receives one excitatory input from the left cochlea and a second from the right cochlea. Axon length varies systematically, so that the axon to neuron A from the right cochlea is longer than the axon from the left cochlea. The reverse applies to neuron E. As a result, neuron A responds best to sound located near to the right ear—although the sound reaches the right ear before the left, its signal is delayed due to the greater axon length. Right and left ear signals arrive at neuron A together. Neuron E responds best to sound located near the left ear. Responses in the array of neurons A–E create a map of sound location. Redrawn from Purves et al. (2001). Copyright © 2001 Sinauer Associates. Reproduced with permission.

shows a row of cells (labeled A to E) in the right medial superior olive. Each cell receives one input from the ipsilateral cochlear nucleus (lower lines) and another from the contralateral cochlear nucleus (upper lines). Both inputs are excitatory (excitation–excitation, or EE), and each EE cell only fires when it receives coincident signals from the two cochlear nuclei. The axons projecting to the superior olive vary systematically in length, compensating for differences in the arrival time of signals at each ear. For example, a long axon projects to neuron E from the left (contralateral) cochlear nucleus, and a short axon projects to it from the right (ipsilateral) cochlear nucleus. As a result, a sound located nearer to the left ear than to the right ear will arrive at the left ear first, but its signal will take longer to travel up to the superior olive. Neuron E will fire strongly when the two signals arrive together. Activity in neuron E therefore encodes an ITD consistent with a sound source located near the left ear. Cells A to D are sensitive to other ITDs. Cell A, for example, will respond strongly to sound sources located nearer to the right ear because the axon carrying signals from that ear is longer than the axon carrying signals from the left ear.

Responses based on ITDs require that the signal arriving from the ear is phase-locked to the auditory stimulus. As we saw earlier in the chapter, phase locking is only possible for sound frequencies below approximately 3 kHz.

Interaural level differences

Sound frequencies above approximately 2 kHz are attenuated by the human head, which acts as a low-pass filter. Consequently, high frequency signals originating on one side of the head have a higher intensity at the ipsilateral ear than at the contralateral ear. Neurons in the lateral superior olive respond according to these ILDs. Each lateral superior olive neuron receives an excitatory input from the ipsilateral anteroventral cochlear nucleus, and an inhibitory input from the contralateral anteroventral cochlear nucleus (via inhibitory neurons in the medial nucleus of the trapezoid body; excitation–inhibition, or EI). The net response of each EI neuron depends on the relative amount of excitation and inhibition it receives, which depends in turn on the relative activity levels in the ipsilateral and contralateral inputs. Response is strongest when the sound signal is more intense in the ear on the same side of the head. So cells in the right lateral superior olive respond to sounds located to the right of the head, and vice versa. Sounds originating in the median plane produce the weakest response in EI neurons, because the excitatory and inhibitory influences cancel out.

As in the case of the "what" pathway, responses in the "where" pathway pass through the inferior colliculi and medial geniculate nuclei on the way to the auditory cortex. Some cells in the inferior colliculi respond to either ITD or ILD (Yost, 2000), collating the "where" information that arrives from the superior olives. The inferior colliculus of the barn owl contains a topographic representation of auditory space, with different cells responding optimally to sounds originating in a particular region of space (Knudsen & Konishi, 1978). Many believe that the brains of other mammals are likely to possess topographic maps of auditory space (Purves et al., 2001). The superior colliculi lie adjacent to the inferior colliculi, and contain cells that respond to visual stimuli. Neural connections between the superior and inferior colliculi are important for coordinating responses to visual and auditory stimuli.

? *Think of linking propositions (described in Chapter 1) to relate responses in the superior olive to perceived direction.*

AUDITORY CORTEX

The **primary auditory cortex** is located on Heschl's gyrus in primates, which lies on the superior temporal lobe, hidden from view in the lateral sulcus. Two areas of auditory association cortex surround the primary auditory cortex. The area immediately surrounding the primary auditory cortex is known as the "belt" region. This region is itself partially encircled by the "parabelt" region (see Kaas & Hackett, 2000). The top of Figure 4.23 shows a side view of the macaque cerebral cortex. Only the parabelt region is visible on the superior temporal gyrus. The bottom of Figure 4.23 also shows the areas hidden from view in the lateral sulcus.

The primary auditory cortex is mapped **tonotopically**. Cells with similar frequency preferences lie close to each other on the cortical surface. There is an orderly progression of preferred frequency across the cortex. The cortical surface can be divided into a series of bands containing cells with the same characteristic frequency (isofrequency bands), as shown in Figure 4.23. Cells within a column extending down from the surface of the cortex have similar characteristic frequencies. Figure 4.23 shows that there are actually three abutting "maps" of frequency space in primary auditory cortex, allowing the area to be subdivided into three "core" areas (Kaas & Hackett, 2000). Cells in these core areas respond well to pure tones (Whitfield & Evans, 1965), and have narrow frequency tuning.

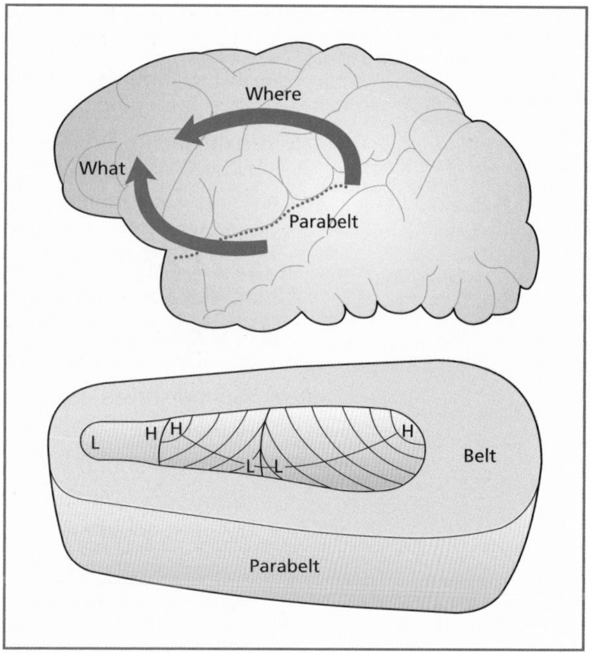

The belt regions surrounding primary auditory cortex (the **auditory association cortex**) are densely interconnected to it. Cells in these regions typically respond better to narrowband noise and frequency-modulated sweeps than to pure tones. Detailed examination of cells in the belt regions, and their connections with other areas of cortex, suggests that the distinction between "what" and "where" pathways is preserved in the cortex (Poremba et al., 2003). Rauschecker and Tian (2000) propose that the "what" pathway involves projections from the anterior part of the parabelt region to orbitofrontal cortex. The "where" pathway involves projections from the posterior part of the parabelt region to posterior parietal cortex and dorsolateral prefrontal cortex (see Figure 4.23). A neuropsychological study by Clarke et al. (2002) supports the "what" versus "where" distinction in human auditory cortex. Patients with lesions in parietal, frontal, and superior temporal cortex had a selective deficit in "where" processing, while patients with lesions in fusiform and temporal cortex were deficient in "what" processing. As we shall see in later chapters, the visual system also appears to contain separate streams of neural information processing for "what" and "where" attributes.

FIGURE 4.23
Macaque auditory cortex. Top: A side view of the cerebral cortex reveals only one visible area of auditory cortex, the parabelt region. Other areas of auditory cortex lie hidden in the lateral sulcus. Arrows indicate separate processing streams for the "what" and "where" attributes of sound stimuli. Bottom: Arrangement of three areas of auditory cortex in the lateral sulcus.

THE DESCENDING AUDITORY PATHWAY

Descending fiber tracts run all the way from the auditory cortex to the cochlea, following a very similar route to the ascending fibers. En route, descending fibers form synapses in reverse order to those found in the ascending fiber tracts (cortex–medial geniculate nuclei–inferior colliculi–superior olives–cochlear nuclei–cochleas). The descending pathway contains both excitatory and inhibitory

KEY TERMS

Tonotopic organization
An organized arrangement of neurons, so that cells with similar frequency preferences lie close together in a neural structure.

Auditory association cortex
Two concentric bands of cortex encircling primary auditory cortex, containing cells responsive to auditory stimuli.

connections, and probably acts as a control system to select and shape the sensory input (Yost, 2000). Since the pathway extends all the way down to the ears, it probably contributes to the amplifying action of the inner hair cells and the acoustic reflex of the middle ear. It may also be involved in our ability to attend selectively to certain auditory stimuli.

CHAPTER SUMMARY

PHYSICS OF SOUND

- Sound waves consist of fluctuations in air pressure created by vibrating surfaces.
- A simple sound wave can be described as a sine wave having a specific frequency, amplitude, and phase.
- According to Fourier theory, a complex sound wave can be regarded as a collection of many simple sine waves added together. Fourier spectra and spectrograms offer graphical representations of the sine wave frequency components of complex sounds.
- Any transmitting device or medium can be viewed as a filter that preserves some Fourier components in a sound, and attenuates or removes other components.
- The transfer function of the filter defines its ability to transmit sound components at different frequencies.
- Fourier theory can be used to characterize a filter's properties only if the filter can be assumed to be linear. The output of nonlinear filters contains frequency components that were not present in the input.
- The auditory system can be viewed as a complex processing system that contains both linear and nonlinear components.

PHYSIOLOGY

The auditory system can be divided into a peripheral part and a central part.

Peripheral auditory system

- The peripheral auditory system includes the outer ear, middle ear, and inner ear.
- The outer ear gathers sound energy and focuses it down the ear canal onto the tympanic membrane.
- Vibrations of the tympanic membrane are transmitted by the middle-ear ossicles to the inner ear. A major function of the middle ear is impedance matching.
- The organ of the inner ear, the cochlea, is spiral-shaped and filled with fluid.

- The cochlea is divided along its length into three chambers. The basilar membrane forms part of one of the partitions. Its mechanical response achieves a frequency-to-place conversion of sound signals.
- Inner hair cells distributed along the basilar membrane are tuned to different characteristic frequencies, by virtue of their location on the membrane, and their responses are phase-locked to the incoming sound waveform, for frequencies up to 1 kHz.
- Outer hair cells in the cochlea act to amplify and fine-tune the responses of the inner hair cells.
- Sound frequency is coded in the auditory nerve by the tonotopic organization of the basilar membrane, and by phase locking of auditory nerve fiber impulses to the incoming sound wave.
- Sound intensity is coded in the auditory nerve by two populations of fibers, one responding at SPLs up to 60 dB, and the other responding to SPLs up to 100 dB.

Central auditory system

- The central auditory system consists of several populations of cells in the brainstem and cerebral cortex.
- Auditory nerve responses from the hair cells arrive at the cochlear nuclei in the brainstem.
- A complex series of serial and parallel processing stages in the brainstem then conveys these signals to their destination in the auditory cortex.
- The "what" attributes of sound (frequency composition and temporal structure) are encoded by tonotopically organized neurons in the cochlear nuclei, and at higher levels of processing.
- The "where" attributes of sound (location of the sound source in auditory space) are encoded by binaural cells in the superior olive and higher levels of processing. Some binaural cells are sensitive to time differences, and others are sensitive to level differences.
- The auditory cortex preserves the distinction between "what" and "where" stimulus attributes in two streams of neural analysis.

TUTORIALS

FOURIER ANALYSIS

The mathematical foundations of Fourier analysis were established nearly 200 years ago by the French mathematician Jean Baptiste Joseph Fourier (1768–1830) from his work on the conduction of heat through solid bodies (see Bracewell, 1989). Fourier analysis is now widely used as a mathematical tool to solve a range of problems in science and engineering. It aids in understanding such physical phenomena as heat transfer, vibration, electrical current flow, sound conductance, and optical imaging. Fourier analysis is also a crucial tool in the fields of hearing and vision research. It provides a rigorous method for specifying the physical properties of stimuli and, with certain assumptions, how the stimuli are processed by sensory systems. This tutorial will introduce the basic concepts underlying Fourier analysis. A more rigorous mathematical introduction, including derivation of equations, can be found in Bracewell's (1978) standard text.

Fourier analysis, in essence, decomposes or divides up a waveform or function into sinusoidal waves of different frequency, known as frequency components or Fourier components. It identifies the different frequencies, amplitudes, and phases of the components. These components can, in turn, be summed to recreate the original waveform or function. In the context of hearing, the waveform represents sounds, such as a note produced by a musical instrument, or the call of a bird. Individual frequency components correspond to pure tones. Sound waveforms vary as a function of time, so the frequency components used in the examples below will be defined in terms of cycles per second or Hertz (Hz).

KEY TERMS

Even function
A function that is symmetrical with respect to the y-axis, so the value of y at a given value of x is the same as its value at $-x$: $f(-x) = f(x)$ for all x. The function $y = \cos(x)$ is even.

Odd function
A function that is asymmetrical with respect to the y-axis, so the value of y at a given value of x is opposite to its value at $-x$: $f(-x) = -f(x)$ for all x. The function $y = \sin(x)$ is odd.

Inner product
A number whose value represents the degree of correspondence between two functions.

Even and odd functions

A function is **even** if it is symmetrical about the vertical axis. In other words, when it is folded about zero on the horizontal axis, the positive and negative portions of the function match exactly. Figure 4.24 (top left) shows the even function $y = \cos(2\pi ft)$. The frequency term f defines how rapidly the function modulates over time (t). Notice that the negative part of the waveform is a mirror image of the positive part. A function is **odd** if it is not symmetrical about the vertical axis; its positive and negative portions are not mirror images. Figure 4.24 (top right) shows the odd function $y = \sin(2\pi ft)$. The two functions in Figure 4.24 (top) are both sinusoidal. Notice that the cosine wave is identical to the sine wave except that it is shifted in phase by one quarter of a cycle of the wave.

Inner products

The sine and cosine functions shown in Figure 4.24 (top) lie at the core of Fourier analysis. When a sound signal is subjected to Fourier analysis, the strength of a signal component at a given frequency is measured by calculating its **inner products** with sine waves and cosine waves at that frequency. The inner product of two functions is calculated by multiplying the two functions together point by point, and then summing the result of each multiplication. The inner product tells us how much one function has in common with the other. If the inner product is large, then the two functions are very similar, whereas if the inner product is zero then the two functions are unrelated. Decomposition of the signal waveform into frequency components therefore involves calculating inner products of the

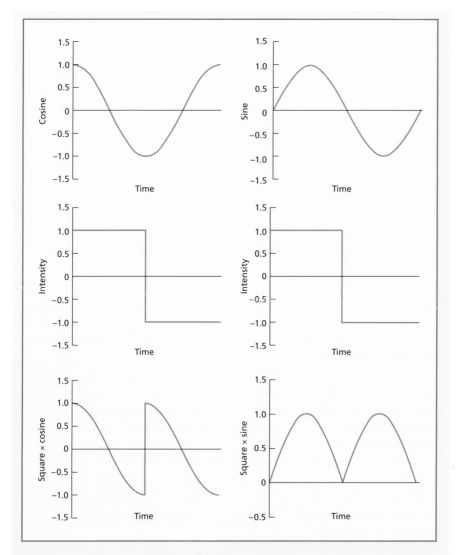

FIGURE 4.24
Top: Cosine function (left) and sine function (right). The cosine function has even phase, because it is symmetrical about zero on the x-axis. The sine function has odd phase, because it is asymmetrical about zero on the x-axis. Middle: A square wave arranged to have odd phase (at zero on the x-axis the wave is at the start of its high-intensity phase). Bottom: Point-by-point multiplication of the square wave with the cosine function (left) shows both positive and negative values that sum to zero. Point-by-point multiplication of the square wave with the sine function (right) has only positive values and a positive sum.

waveform with sine waves and cosine waves at all possible frequencies. The reason why inner products are calculated using both sine waves and cosine waves becomes clear when one considers how the result varies according to whether the original waveform itself is odd, or even, or intermediate between odd and even.

Odd waveforms

If the waveform is odd, then the inner product of a sine wave (also odd) and the waveform is likely to be large, especially if the period of the waveform matches the period of the sine wave. Peaks in the waveform align with peaks in the sine wave. On the other hand, the inner product of an odd waveform and a cosine wave (even) of the same frequency will be zero. Peaks in the waveform align with zero in the cosine wave.

For example, the middle row of Figure 4.24 shows one cycle of a square-wave stimulus. Over the first half-cycle stimulus intensity is high, and over the second half-cycle it is low. Notice that the square wave is arranged in odd phase (zero on the horizontal axis corresponds to the start of the high-intensity part of the wave). The bottom row shows the result of multiplying the square wave point by point with the cosine and sine waves in the top row. The lower left graph is the product of the odd square wave and the even cosine wave. The sum of these products (inner product) equals zero, because for each positive value there is a matching negative value elsewhere in the product. The lower right graph shows the product of the odd square wave and the odd sine wave. Now all the products are positive, and the inner product sums to 1.273 (corresponding to $4/\pi$ in this simple waveform).

Even waveforms

Similarly, if the waveform is even its inner product with a sine wave will be zero, whereas its inner product with a cosine wave will be large. Many waveforms are intermediate between odd and even, so their inner products with sine waves and cosine waves will both be nonzero.

If the square wave in Figure 4.24 was shifted to have even phase (so that zero on the time axis aligned with the middle of a peak or a trough rather than with the beginning of a peak), then the inner product with the cosine wave would become 1.273, and the inner product with the cosine wave would become zero.

Sines and cosines are thus used to ensure that frequency components are identified whether they be in odd phase, or in even phase, or in any intermediate phase. The relative magnitudes of the even and odd inner products specify the phase of the frequency component.

Complex numbers

It follows from the preceding discussion that two values are required to represent the strength of a sinusoidal component at a given frequency, one representing its even part and the other representing its odd part. Mathematicians represent these even and odd pairs of values as a **complex number**, which contains a so-called *real* part and an *imaginary* part. The real (*R*) part of the number corresponds to the even, cosine part of the component. The imaginary (*I*) part of the number corresponds to the odd, sine part.

Magnitude, energy, and phase

The real and imaginary parts can be combined to calculate the overall **magnitude** (sometimes called *amplitude*) of the component regardless of

---

KEY TERMS

Complex number
A number having two parts, called real and imaginary, from which other numbers can be computed; in Fourier analysis the parts represent the cosine and sine contributions to each component.

Magnitude
The strength of the contribution of a given frequency component in a waveform; it is calculated from the complex number for each component.

its particular phase. Magnitude is calculated by taking the square root of the sum of the two parts squared,

$$\sqrt{(R^2 + I^2)}.$$

The *energy* of the component at a given frequency is conventionally defined as the sum of the two parts squared, $(R^2 + I^2)$. Fourier analysis also provides a means to calculate the precise phase of a component at a given frequency from its even and odd parts. **Phase** is given by arctan (I/R).

Periodic waveforms

A periodic waveform, as we saw earlier, repeats itself at regular time intervals. The time interval separating successive repetitions defines the period of the waveform. The sound of a clarinet and of the human voice, depicted in Figure 4.5, are both periodic. Fourier theory states that all periodic waveforms can be decomposed into a set of discrete frequency components known as a **Fourier series**. The lowest frequency in the waveform is called the fundamental, and all other components in the waveform are at integer multiples of the fundamental frequency. The exact frequency, amplitude, and phase of the components depend on the particular form of the periodic waveform.

Table 4.1 shows how the frequency content of a complex wave can be calculated using inner products. It shows the inner product of the square wave in Figure 4.24 with sines and cosines at nine frequencies above the fundamental frequency (f). The first row at f contains the inner products described previously. The square wave contains odd-numbered harmonic frequencies at $3f$, $5f$, $7f$, $9f$, and so on. All the components have odd phase, so all the cosine inner products are zero. Magnitude relative to the fundamental declines with frequency in the sequence 1/3, 1/5, 1/7, 1/9, and so on. The magnitude and phase values in Table 4.1 can be plotted in graphs, as shown in Figure 4.25. The plot of magnitudes is known as a

TABLE 4.1 Frequency components in a square wave

Component	Sine (*I*)	Cosine (*R*)	Magnitude	Phase (°)
f	1.273	0	1.273	90
2*f*	0	0	0	0
3*f*	0.424	0	0.424	90
4*f*	0	0	0	0
5*f*	0.255	0	0.255	90
6*f*	0	0	0	0
7*f*	0.182	0	0.182	90
8*f*	0	0	0	0
9*f*	0.14	0	0.14	90

FIGURE 4.25
Magnitude and phase spectra showing the first five components of a square wave. Values correspond to those given in Table 4.1. In common with all periodic waves, the square wave contains a discrete sequence of frequency components.

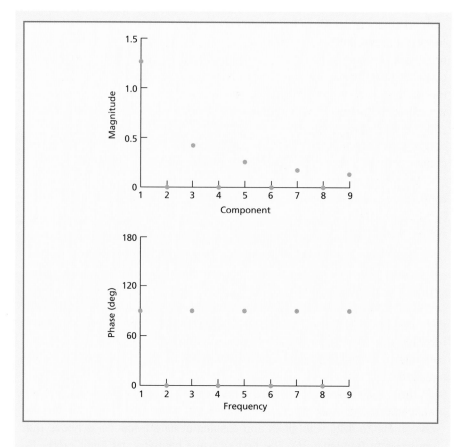

magnitude spectrum, and the plot of phase is known as a phase spectrum. Compare Figure 4.25 to Figure 4.6, which shows the magnitude and phase spectra of a more complex periodic waveform. The complex waveform has components at many different frequencies and phases.

The standard formula for the Fourier series of a function $x(t)$ is:

$$x(t) = a_0 / 2 + \sum_{n=1}^{\infty}(a_n \cos 2\pi nf_0 t + b_n \sin 2\pi nf_0 t) \tag{4.1}$$

where a_0 is the mean value of the function, a_n and b_n are the cosine and sine amplitudes of the nth frequency component, f_0 is the lowest (fundamental) frequency. The periodic waveform is composed of a series of sine and cosine components at integer multiples of the fundamental (the $nf_0 t$ term), at appropriate amplitudes (the a_n and b_n terms). The exact frequency, amplitude, and phase of the components depend on the particular form of the periodic waveform.

Nonperiodic waveforms

Fourier analysis can also be applied to signals that do not have a repetitive periodic structure, called nonperiodic signals. A simple example of a nonperiodic waveform is a single pulse, as illustrated in Figure 4.26. As an auditory stimulus, this waveform would correspond to the sound of a click. Recall that the magnitude spectrum of any periodic waveform contains discrete components at intervals that are an integer multiple of the fundamental frequency. The magnitude spectrum of any nonperiodic waveform contains a continuous array of frequency components, rather than a discrete series of components. Figure 4.26 shows the magnitude spectrum of the pulse. Although it contains energy at all frequencies, energy tends to decline progressively as frequency increases.

Whereas periodic signals are analyzed using a Fourier series, nonperiodic signals are analyzed using a **Fourier integral**. The Fourier transform of a function of time, $x(t)$, is a function of frequency $F(f)$. The formula for the Fourier transform $F(f)$ of $x(t)$ is:

$$F(f) = \int_{-\infty}^{\infty} x(t)\exp(-j2\pi ft)\,dt \qquad (4.2)$$

This formula appears markedly different from the formula for the Fourier series (4.1), in two ways. First, the summation term in formula (4.1) is replaced with an integral term in formula (4.2), because the Fourier integral contains an infinite array of frequency components. Second, the cosine and sine terms in formula (4.1) are replaced by a complex exponential in formula (4.2). According to **Euler's relation**, the sine and cosine parts of a complex number can be replaced by a complex exponential:

$$\cos\theta + j\sin\theta = \exp(j\theta) \qquad (4.3)$$

KEY TERMS

Fourier integral
A continuous spectrum of frequency components making up a nonperiodic (nonrepeating) waveform.

Euler's relation
A mathematical rule that allows a sine and cosine pair to be represented as an exponential.

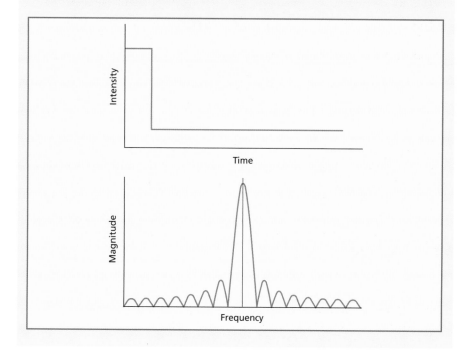

FIGURE 4.26
Top: A brief pulse, which would be heard as a click. Bottom: The amplitude spectrum of the pulse. Since the pulse is nonperiodic, its amplitude spectrum contains energy at all frequencies, in contrast to periodic waves such as the square wave in Figure 4.25.

The standard form of the Fourier integral (4.2) makes use of Euler's relation. A fundamental property of the Fourier transform is that the original function x(t) can be recovered by an inverse Fourier transform, written mathematically as:

$$x(t) = \int_{-\infty}^{\infty} F(f) \exp(j2\pi ft) df \qquad (4.4)$$

The presence of integrals extending to infinity in formulas for nonperiodic waveforms (4.2 and 4.4) has two important consequences:

1. Both F(f) and x(t) are defined over times and frequencies from minus infinity to plus infinity. Negative time in x(t) is a familiar concept, since it represents time in the past rather than time in the future. The concept of negative frequency in F(f), on the other hand, may seem rather odd but is a mathematical consequence of the Fourier integral. Negative frequencies are displayed in the magnitude spectrum of the pulse (Figure 4.26). Fortunately negative frequencies make little difference to the interpretation of spectrum plots. Notice from Figure 4.26 that the magnitude of each negative frequency component exactly matches the magnitude of its positive counterpart. This property is generally true for real physical auditory or visual signals.

2. The second consequence of the integrals is that the signal waveform is assumed to be infinitely long. No real sensory stimulus can be assumed to extend to infinity. Instead, we must assume that the signal extends for long enough to be considered effectively infinite.

Fourier analysis in sensory systems

Both periodic and nonperiodic signals are frequently encountered by all sensory systems. Isolated clicks, flashes of light, taps on the skin, and jerks of the head are all nonperiodic. Voices, visual textures, rough surfaces drawn across the skin, and head bobs during running are all periodic. All sensory stimuli, whether periodic or nonperiodic, can be subjected to Fourier analysis to identify the frequencies they contain. The neural response of each sensory system can also be subjected to Fourier analysis to discover which stimulus frequencies are attenuated, or whether the response contains frequencies not actually present in the stimulus:

- In the case of touch, neural responses depend on the vibration frequency of a mechanical stimulus. Some somatosensory neurons can respond to rapidly changing stimulation (high vibration frequencies), others can respond only to slowly changing stimulation (low vibration frequencies).
- In audition, cells in the cochlea respond according to the frequency and phase of incoming sound signals, described earlier in the chapter.

- In vision, neural receptive fields respond selectively to certain frequencies of luminance modulation over time and over space (discussed in more detail in Chapter 9)

Sensory neurons can therefore be viewed as frequency-tuned filters that respond to some stimulus frequencies but not others.

Fourier techniques help us to understand how a complex sensory stimulus is represented in the response of a population of sensory neurons (see Figure 4.9). However successful this approach is, it does not mean that the sensory system is actually performing Fourier analysis on the stimulus. As we saw earlier, Fourier analysis assumes strict linearity, but sensory systems exhibit many forms of nonlinearity. Nevertheless, Fourier analysis helps us to identify the linear and nonlinear parts of a sensory system, and to define the precise nature of the nonlinearities.

Calculating Fourier transforms

Although formulas have been included here in order to introduce the basic principles behind the technique, researchers do not need to know them in order to apply Fourier analysis to a data set. Standard numerical techniques have been developed that allow Fourier transforms to be computed quickly and easily from any array of numbers. A procedure known as the "**fast Fourier transform**," or FFT, is implemented in many scientific software packages, including spreadsheets. The Fourier transform in Figure 4.26 was produced using Excel's "fourier" function. For those wishing to add Fourier analysis to their own computer programs, code listings and libraries are widely available. As in the case of statistical analysis, modern software takes care of the computations, so researchers can concentrate on understanding what the results of the computations mean.

> **?** *Think of other examples of sensory signals that can be subjected to Fourier analysis.*

> **KEY TERM**
>
> **Fast Fourier transform (FFT)**
> A numerical computational technique for performing Fourier analysis on an array of signal values.

Perception of sound

5

Contents

INTRODUCTION

The stimulus for hearing is a pair of complex sound pressure waves entering the two ears. In a natural sound field, these pressure waves are made up from a mixture of sounds generated by a variety of sources. Imagine that you are sitting in a bar talking with some friends. In addition to the sounds produced by

FIGURE 5.1
In a noisy environment, the acoustic waveform may contain sounds emanating from many sources. Copyright © Ted Streshinsky/Corbis.

your friends, perhaps talking simultaneously, each acoustic waveform may well include sounds from other conversations, from music playing on a sound system, and from passing traffic. The computational task facing the auditory system is to extract from these complex waveforms the discrete auditory objects that created them, such as individual voices, musical melodies, and car horns. Only by solving this problem will you be able to understand what each of your friends is saying, as well as enjoy the music playing in the background.

The previous chapter described how the acoustic waveform is picked up by the peripheral auditory system and encoded as a stream of neural impulses traveling up the approximately 50,000 fibers that make up the auditory nerve. The impulses carry information about the frequency content of the waveform (frequencies, amplitudes, and phases), which is a jumbled mixture of components contributed by the different sound sources. From this encoded stream of components the brain builds a representation of basic perceptual attributes for each sound source, such as loudness and pitch, and of more complex objects, such as speech sounds and musical melody. This chapter will present some of the theories that have been developed to bridge the gap between auditory nerve activity and perception. These theories make extensive use of concepts introduced in Chapter 1, including representation, computation, and linking propositions.

The chapter begins with a discussion of basic perceptual attributes (loudness, pitch, and location), before considering more complex representations (speech, auditory objects). The chapter ends with a discussion of hearing dysfunction.

LOUDNESS PERCEPTION

Loudness is the perceptual attribute of a sound that corresponds most closely to its physical intensity. Experimental studies of loudness perception have generally used two techniques to compare the loudness of different sounds: Loudness matching and loudness scaling.

LOUDNESS MATCHING

In this technique, the subject is required to adjust the intensity of a sound (called the comparison stimulus) until it sounds as loud as a standard stimulus with a fixed intensity. The frequency dependence of loudness can be investigated by manipulating the frequency difference between the comparison stimulus and the standard stimulus. For example, a standard tone may be fixed at 1 kHz and 40 dB SPL, and the subject is asked to adjust the intensity of a 2 kHz comparison tone until it appears equally loud (the dB SPL measure of

KEY TERM

Loudness
The perceptual attribute of a sound that relates to its intensity (SPL).

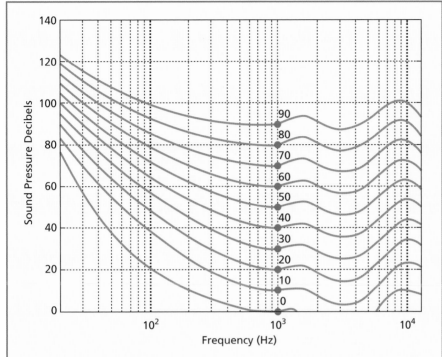

FIGURE 5.2
Equal-loudness contours for a range of comparison frequencies (shown on the abscissa), in relation to a standard frequency of 1 kHz. Different curves represent data at different standard SPLs. For this reason, reading up from 1 kHz (10^3Hz) on the abscissa (same frequency as the standard) each curve is at a height that matches its SPL (see Suzuki & Takeshima, 2004).

intensity was introduced in the previous chapter). If this procedure is repeated for a range of comparison frequencies, then the resulting plot of comparison SPL as a function of frequency is known as an **equal-loudness contour**. The curve labeled "40" in Figure 5.2 shows the equal-loudness contour for a 1 kHz standard tone at 40 dB SPL. The whole procedure can be repeated at different standard intensity levels, to generate a family of equal-loudness contours, representing matched loudness at different sound levels. The other curves in Figure 5.2 show examples of these contours. Note that the lowest curve in the plot actually represents the absolute threshold for detecting the presence of a tone at different frequencies. The highest curve shows that loudness matches are still possible at standard intensities in excess of 100 dB, indicating that the human auditory system has a very wide dynamic range.

It can be seen that equal-loudness contours tend to follow the absolute threshold curve at lower standard intensities, but flatten out at high intensities. At lower standard intensities low frequency sounds must be set to a high intensity to appear equal in loudness to higher frequency sounds. The "bass boost" control in audio reproduction equipment is an attempt to compensate for the lack of loudness in the low frequency region at low intensities. At high intensities the bass signal tends to appear relatively loud, due to the flattening of the equal-loudness curve.

KEY TERM

Equal-loudness contour
A curve plotting the SPLs of sounds at different frequencies that produce a loudness match with a reference sound at a fixed frequency and SPL.

The loudness level of a tone is sometimes expressed in phons, defined as the level (in dB SPL) of a 1 kHz tone to which the tone sounds equally loud. Each equal-loudness contour in Figure 5.2 defines a specific phon level. For example, a 50 Hz tone must be set to an SPL of approximately 60 dB in order to attain a phon level of 40.

LOUDNESS SCALING

Stevens devised the sone unit to define the loudness of a sound; 1 sone was arbitrarily defined as the loudness of a 1 kHz tone at 40 dB SPL. A sound judged to be twice as loud as this has a sone value of 2.

Equal-loudness contours provide a means of comparing the loudness of different sounds, but they cannot tell us how rapidly the loudness of a sound increases with its intensity; in other words, how loudness *scales* with intensity. The simplest method of estimating a loudness scale is to ask the subject to assign numbers to sounds at different intensities. For example, if the loudness of a standard tone is assigned the arbitrary number 100, and a second tone appears twice as loud, the subject should rate the loudness of the second tone with the number 200. This technique is known as magnitude estimation, and was discussed in Chapter 1. In common with other sensory magnitudes (see Figure 1.5), loudness does not increase linearly with intensity. Instead, loudness obeys a mathematical power law in which sensory magnitude grows in proportion to stimulus intensity raised to a power. According to Stevens (1961), the exponent for loudness is 0.3. This means that each time sound intensity increases by 10 dB, loudness increases by a factor of two, at least for sound levels above 40 dB SPL (Plack & Carlyon, 1995).

MODELS OF LOUDNESS PERCEPTION

Auditory nerve fiber responses are known to be frequency selective, due to the frequency-to-place conversion performed by the cochlea which was discussed in the previous chapter. The simplest account of intensity coding in the peripheral auditory system is that intensity in a particular frequency region is coded by the firing rate of fibers tuned to that frequency region. As the firing rate of auditory nerve fibers increases, so does encoded intensity. How is encoded intensity linked to perceived loudness? The most successful model of loudness perception, the **excitation pattern model**, proposes that the overall loudness of a given sound is proportional to the total neural activity evoked by it in the auditory nerve. This model can account for experimental data on the loudness of both simple and complex sounds (Moore, 1997). Loudness meters incorporate a computation similar to that proposed by the excitation pattern model.

A potential problem for the excitation pattern model of loudness is that auditory nerve fibers have a relatively narrow dynamic range (about 60 dB; see Figure 4.19) compared to the dynamic range of loudness perception (about 120 dB; see Figure 5.2). However, as discussed in Chapter 4 and illustrated in Figure 4.19, different auditory nerve fibers cover different ranges of intensity. Fibers with low spontaneous firing rates saturate at intensities higher than approximately 60 dB SPL, and fibers with high spontaneous firing rates do not saturate until SPL exceeds 100 dB. Although individual auditory nerve fibers have a restricted dynamic range, the range covered by the whole population of fibers together is sufficient to account for the range of loudness perception.

A number of computational studies have investigated whether responses in auditory nerve fibers can account for human ability to discriminate different intensity levels. They have found that responses in as few as 10 auditory nerve fibers predict performance that is superior to human listeners over a wide dynamic range (e.g., Viemeister, 1983). This raises the question of why human performance is not better than one would expect on the basis of auditory nerve responses. Plack and Carlyon (1995) suggest that central limitations in the brain prevent it from making optimal use of the incoming neural information. One possible limitation is memory. Loudness comparisons require the listener to

KEY TERM

Excitation pattern model
A theory of loudness perception in which the loudness of a sound is proportional to the summed neural activity it evokes in the auditory nerve.

retain a memory trace of one sound in order to compare its loudness with that of a second sound. Decay of the trace may inject "memory noise" into the system, degrading the psychophysical judgment (see Chapter 1 for a discussion of noise in psychophysics).

PITCH PERCEPTION

Pitch is the perceptual attribute of a sound that corresponds most closely to its frequency. In the case of pure tones, pitch is related to the frequency of the tone. In the case of complex tones, pitch is related to the frequency of the fundamental (lowest frequency, as discussed in Chapter 4). Pitch perception allows us to order sounds on a musical scale extending from low bass notes to high treble notes. Since pitch is closely related to frequency, we shall begin by discussing frequency selectivity and discrimination by the auditory system as revealed by perceptual studies.

FREQUENCY SELECTIVITY

Following on from earlier work by Ohm in the 19th century, Helmholtz (1877) believed that:

> *the human ear is capable, under certain conditions, of separating the musical tone produced by a single musical instrument, into a series of simple tones, namely, the prime partial tone, and the various upper partial tones, each of which produces its own separate sensation.*
>
> *(Helmholtz, 1877, translation by Ellis, 1954, p. 25)*

The assertion, now often called Ohm's law, that the auditory system constructs a separate representation for each frequency component of a complex sound has driven much psychophysical research since the time of Helmholtz.

Psychophysical studies of frequency selectivity

There must, of course, be some limit to the auditory system's ability to select out the frequency components of a complex sound wave. The main psychophysical technique used to investigate the limits of frequency selectivity is **masking**. Everyday experience provides many examples of how one sound can be obscured by another. For example, ambient noise from the immediate environment can make it very difficult to hear the voice of a friend talking on your mobile phone. Systematic studies of masking typically measure a listener's ability to detect a simple sinusoidal signal in the presence of a noise mask. Noise in this context has a very particular meaning. It refers to a stimulus containing a wide range of frequency components with random phases but equal amplitudes. Subjectively, this kind of noise produces an unstructured hissing sound, similar to a de-tuned radio.

KEY TERMS

Pitch
The perceptual attribute of a sound that relates to its frequency.

Masking
An experimental effect in which a participant's ability to detect a sound signal is impaired in the presence of noise.

FIGURE 5.3
Critical-band masking. The signal was a 2 kHz pure tone. The mask contained noise centered at 2 kHz. The abscissa plots the bandwidth of the noise, and the ordinate plots the threshold for detecting the signal in the presence of the noise. For very narrowband noise (50–400 Hz), detectability worsens as noise bandwidth increases. Once the noise bandwidth reaches 400 Hz further increases have no effect on signal detectability (adapted from Schooneveldt & Moore, 1989).

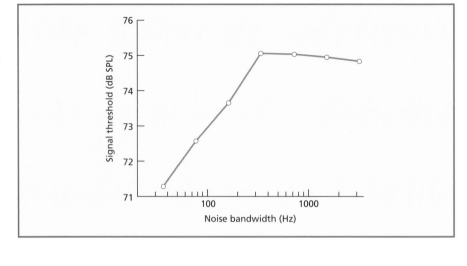

? Think about why frequency discrimination should be related to critical-band masking.

In the 1940s Fletcher used **band-pass noise** as a mask, centered on the frequency of the sinusoidal signal that the subject was required to detect. Band-pass noise contains only frequencies that fall within a certain band above and below its center frequency. For example, band-pass noise with a center frequency of 2000 Hz and a bandwidth of 400 Hz contains energy at all frequencies between 1800 and 2200 Hz, but no energy below 1800 Hz and above 2200 Hz.

Fletcher found, as illustrated by data from Schooneveldt and Moore (1989) in Figure 5.3, that a listener's ability to detect the signal became progressively worse as the noise bandwidth increased up to a certain bandwidth, after which detectability remained constant. Wider bandwidths had no effect on threshold. Fletcher inferred that the listener detects the signal using a band-pass filter somewhere in the auditory system that admits certain frequencies but removes others. He assumed that the most effective filter for detecting the signal is one centered on the same frequency as the signal. Only noise frequencies within the pass band of the filter interfere with the listener's ability to hear the signal. The noise bandwidth at which detectability flattens off can then be taken as an estimate of the bandwidth of the auditory filter. Fletcher called this bandwidth the *critical bandwidth*.

More recent masking experiments have used pure tone masks, and systematically varied the difference between mask frequency and signal frequency. The signal is fixed at a relatively low sound level (e.g., 10 dB SPL). Mask SPL is varied to find the level at which the signal can just be detected. Data from these experiments can be plotted as psychophysical tuning curves. Examples are shown in Figure 5.4, for several different signal frequencies. Notice that masking is most effective when the mask frequency is very close to the signal frequency. As mask frequency moves away from signal frequency, progressively higher mask SPLs are required to maintain the signal at threshold. Data of this kind have led to the view that hearing is served by a bank of overlapping band-pass filters stretching from low frequencies to high frequencies. The psychophysical tuning curves can be viewed as estimates of the filter shapes.

KEY TERM

Band-pass noise
A sound stimulus containing equal energy within a certain band of frequencies above and below its center frequency.

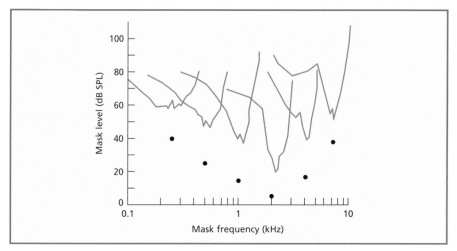

FIGURE 5.4
Psychophysical tuning curves. The signal was a pure tone at one of six frequencies, fixed at a relatively low intensity (shown by the filled circles in the plot). The mask was also a pure tone, at one of the frequencies shown on the abscissa. Each curve represents the intensity of the mask required to just mask each signal, as a function of mask frequency. Low mask intensities are needed when the mask has a similar frequency to the signal, but progressively more intense masks are needed as mask frequency departs further from signal frequency (adapted from Vogten, 1974).

Physiological basis of frequency selectivity and masking

Ever since the time of Helmholtz, the mechanical properties of the cochlea have been invoked to explain frequency selectivity. The point of maximum displacement on the basilar membrane varies with stimulus frequency (see Figure 4.14). So the frequency tuning of auditory nerve fibers is governed by their place of innervation on the basilar membrane. It is therefore reasonable to propose a link between frequency-tuned responses in the peripheral auditory system, as revealed by physiological studies, and the auditory filters revealed by psychophysical studies. The frequency tuning curves of cat auditory nerve fibers shown in Figure 4.18 are remarkably similar to the psychophysical tuning curves shown in Figure 5.4. Evans, Pratt, and Cooper (1989) compared the bandwidths of guinea-pig auditory nerve fibers with filter bandwidths measured behaviorally using noise masking. There is very good agreement between the neural data and the behavioral data, as shown in Figure 5.5.

The simplest explanation of **critical-band masking** in psychophysical tasks makes three assumptions:

- The presence of the signal increases the level of activity in auditory filters tuned to its frequency.
- When this response increment exceeds some minimum value, the signal is detected by the listener.
- The mask also produces excitation in auditory filters, but this activity is obviously unrelated to the presence or absence of a signal.

If the mask and the signal activate *different* filters, then the presence of the mask should have no effect on the excitation produced by the signal, and therefore on its detectability. If the mask excites the

KEY TERM

Critical-band masking
An experimental effect in which masking of a sinusoidal signal occurs only when the centre frequency of the noise falls within a certain band of frequencies surrounding the signal.

FIGURE 5.5
Estimated auditory
filter bandwidth as a
function of characteristic
frequency, in the guinea
pig (adapted from Evans,
Pratt, & Cooper, 1989).
Filled circles represent
estimates based on
recordings directly from
auditory nerve fibers.
Open symbols represent
estimates based on
behavioral responses in
a masking experiment.

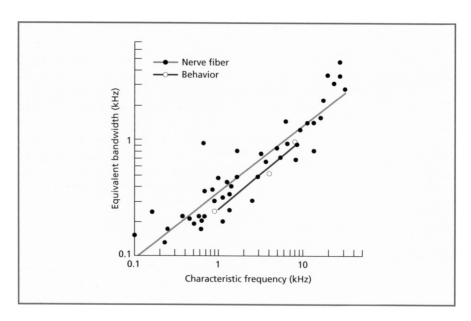

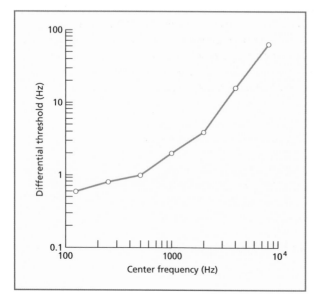

same filter as the signal, the resultant activity will
swamp the activity produced by the signal, impairing
detectability. A more intense signal is required to
reach the minimum increment in filter response
required for detection.

FREQUENCY DISCRIMINATION

Studies of frequency discrimination measure a
listener's ability to detect small changes in frequency.
A common technique involves the successive
presentation of two tones with slightly different
frequencies. The listener is required to report whether
the first tone or the second tone had a higher pitch.
The differential threshold is taken as the change
in frequency required for the listener to achieve a
fixed percentage of correct responses (e.g., 75%; see
Chapter 1 for more details on differential thresholds).

FIGURE 5.6
Human differential
threshold for frequency
as a function of
reference frequency,
summarized from a
number of early studies
(adapted from Moore,
1997, figure 5.1).

Figure 5.6 shows differential threshold as a function of frequency, obtained in
several studies.

It is clear that frequency discrimination is remarkably good at low frequencies.
A change in frequency of less than 1 Hz can be detected reliably at frequencies
below 1000 Hz. Discrimination deteriorates as frequency increases, but does not
exceed 100 Hz even at frequencies over 10 kHz. This corresponds to a 1% change
in frequency at threshold.

What information do listeners use when making frequency discriminations?
Experiments on frequency discrimination explicitly instruct the subject to attend to
the pitch of the two tones. An adequate theory of pitch perception must therefore be
able to explain why the differential threshold for frequency is so small.

THEORIES OF PITCH PERCEPTION

A given sound stimulus produces a characteristic pattern of activity across neurons in the peripheral auditory system tuned to different frequencies. In simple terms, this activity pattern can be viewed as a smoothed sample of the sound's magnitude spectrum. The activity pattern is smoothed because each neuron responds to a range of frequencies centered on its characteristic frequency. It can be assumed, as the preceding section indicated, that frequency-tuned neurons bear a direct relation to the bank of auditory filters identified by psychophysical experiments. How is this activity pattern linked to our perception of the sound's pitch?

Pure tones

The relation between neural activity and perceived pitch is relatively straightforward in the case of pure tones. The peripheral auditory system provides two ways to encode the frequency of pure tones:

* The frequency-to-place conversion of the basilar membrane (see Figure 4.14).
* The response rate auditory nerve fibers (see Figure 4.17).

The place and timing theories of pitch perception in pure tones are linked directly to these two frequency-coding strategies.

Place coding theory

Helmholtz (1877) believed that the basilar membrane vibrated in sympathy with the frequency of an incoming sound wave. He understood the implications of the membrane's variation in width, and noted that:

> *the parts of the membrane [vibrating] in unison with higher tones must be looked for near the round window, and those with the deeper, near the vertex of the cochlea.*
> *(Helmholtz, 1877, translation by Ellis, 1954, p. 146)*

From this fact he proposed the first theory of pitch perception, now called the **place theory**:

> *Hence every simple tone of determinate pitch will be felt only by certain nerve fibres, and simple tones of different pitch will excite different fibres . . . The sensation of pitch would consequently be a sensation in different nerve fibres.*
> *(Helmholtz, 1877, translation by Ellis, 1954, pp. 147–148)*

Rate coding theory

As explained in Chapter 4, auditory nerve responses are phase-locked to the frequency of an incoming sound wave, at least for frequencies below 4–5 kHz. The response rate of neural impulses therefore carries information about sound frequency. The rate coding theory of pitch perception assumes that the listener discriminates the pitch of pure tones by means of differences in the response rate or time intervals between neural firings.

KEY TERM

Place theory
A theory of pitch perception, according to which pitch is determined by the place of maximum excitation on the basilar membrane; also known as frequency-to-place conversion.

Evidence

Several lines of evidence indicate that both theories are correct: Pitch in low frequency pure tones is conveyed by a rate code, namely phase locking, and pitch in high frequency tones is conveyed by the place of maximum activation on the basilar membrane.

- Phase locking breaks down at frequencies above 4 kHz, so pitch perception based on timing information is possible only for low frequency sounds.
- Moore (1973) measured frequency discrimination for very briefly presented tones. Such stimuli produce very broad patterns of displacement on the basilar membrane (brief pulses contain very many frequency components; see the tutorials section of Chapter 4). If frequency discrimination relies on the place of maximum displacement, performance should be relatively poor because the membrane displacement is so broad. However Moore (1973) found that below 5 kHz discrimination was much better than that predicted on the basis of place coding.
- In Sek and Moore's (1995) data on frequency discrimination (Figure 5.6), there is a marked deterioration in performance above 4 kHz. They interpret their results in terms of rate coding below 4 kHz, and place coding above 4 kHz.

Why do brief pulses of sound contain so many frequency components?

Complex tones

As explained in the previous chapter, complex tones contain a series of harmonic frequency components spaced at intervals equal to the frequency or repetition rate of the fundamental. The pitch heard in a complex sound mainly corresponds to the frequency of the fundamental, but several findings show that pitch perception in complex sounds is far from simple. The auditory system appears to combine information from across a complex sound's spectrum in order to estimate its pitch. Complex sounds with different spectra can have the same pitch, and conversely complex sounds with similar spectra can have different pitches (Plack, Barker, & Hall, 2014).

Listeners can even hear the pitch corresponding to a complex sound's fundamental frequency when that component is *not* present (though higher harmonics are present). This phenomenon is known as the "**missing fundamental**." For example, a complex tone containing frequencies at 1000, 1200, and 1400 Hz appears to have a pitch corresponding to the fundamental at 200 Hz. You can still perceive the relatively low pitch of a male friend's voice over the telephone, despite the fact that the fundamental frequency of his voice may be at about 150 Hz and the small speaker in your phone's handset cannot generate frequencies below 300 Hz.

Helmholtz attempted to explain the missing fundamental effect in terms of the place theory by arguing that the ear has a nonlinearity which reintroduces energy at a frequency corresponding to the fundamental (nonlinearities were discussed in the previous chapter). This explanation cannot be correct, because the missing fundamental is still heard even when masking noise is introduced in the region of a sound's spectrum corresponding to the fundamental frequency. If the fundamental is reintroduced by a nonlinearity, then it should be masked by the noise.

The ability of the cochlea to resolve the harmonics of a complex sound is limited to the first ten components, which have the lowest frequencies. Higher harmonics are too close together in frequency for the basilar membrane to resolve; each stimulates multiple hair cells. However, the unresolved harmonics generate a combined response that repeats or "**beats**" at the fundamental frequency of the sound (when sine waves at different frequencies and phases combine together, they can cancel each other out or augment each other, depending on their frequencies and phases; see the tutorials section of Chapter 4). The beat frequency for a set of harmonically related sine waves carries information about their fundamental frequency. The temporal pattern of firing in the auditory nerve is known to follow the beat frequency. Consequently the pitch of a complex sound can be encoded in responses synchronized to its beat frequency. The beat frequency is present in a complex sound even when the fundamental component is absent because the beat is produced by higher harmonics, so rate theory can explain the missing fundamental. Schouten called the pitch sensation produced by beats in higher harmonics "**residue pitch**."

However resolved harmonics can also play a role in complex pitch perception. Plomp (1967) created complex harmonic stimuli in which the lower (resolved) harmonics specified one pitch, and the higher unresolved harmonics specified a different pitch. Listeners heard the pitch defined by the resolved harmonics, so it seems that they tend to dominate pitch perception. Pitch can be heard when only resolved or only unresolved harmonics are present, so both kinds of harmonic can play a role in pitch perception (Moore & Glasberg, 1986).

The timing of responses in auditory nerve fibers seems to be the most important source of information about pitch in complex sounds, in other words a rate code rather than a code based on frequency-to-place conversion. Moore, Glasberg, and Shailer (1984) found that the JND for harmonics in complex sounds was much smaller than that predicted on the basis of frequency-to-place conversion. Furthermore, a model of pitch perception based entirely on rate codes has proved itself to be quite successful (Meddis & O'Mard, 1997).

Is there a "pitch center" in the brain?

Although cortical neurons are selectively tuned to sound frequency, it is not clear how this tuning is based on the temporal code supplied by the auditory nerve. Primate cortex is mapped tonotopically (Kaas & Hackett, 2000), and this ordered arrangement may play a role in estimating pitch from frequency-selective responses, but it is not clear how. Neuroimaging studies have searched for a "pitch center" in human auditory cortex. Current evidence points to a region of secondary auditory cortex lying beside primary auditory cortex (Penagos, Melcher, & Oxenham, 2004), but the question of a pitch center in human auditory cortex is still unresolved (Plack, Barker, & Hall, 2014).

AUDITORY LOCALIZATION

Auditory localization refers to a listener's ability to judge the direction and distance of a sound source. This information can be used to orient attention toward the source of the sound, such as a predator or prey animal. It can also be used as an aid in the segregation of individual sound sources from the complex wave arriving at the ears.

> **KEY TERMS**
>
> **Beat**
> Regular changes in the amplitude of a wave when two or more sine waves at different frequencies are added together.
>
> **Residue pitch**
> The pitch heard in a complex wave due to beats rather than to resolvable harmonic components.

Think about why some animals have larger ears than others.

The direction of a sound source can be specified relative to two principal planes passing through the head. The direction of a sound source in the horizontal (left–right) plane is specified by an *azimuth* angle relative to straight ahead. Direction in the vertical (up–down) plane is specified by an angle of *elevation* relative to horizontal. For example, a sound source having an azimuth angle of 0° and an elevation of 90° would be located directly above the head. A sound source at 90° azimuth and 0° elevation would be directly opposite the left ear.

Perceptual research typically investigates sound localization in one plane at a time, manipulating horizontal location while keeping vertical location constant, or vice versa. As we shall see, results indicate that horizontal localization relies on binaural cues (comparisons between the signals arriving at the two ears). Vertical localization relies on monaural cues (information available in the signal arriving at just one ear).

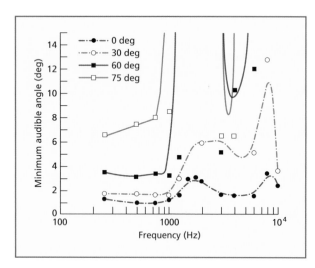

FIGURE 5.7
Minimum audible angle as a function of signal frequency. A pure tone was presented at one of four azimuth angles, and the ordinate plots the minimum change in angle that listeners could detect reliably (adapted from Yost, 2000).

LOCALIZATION IN THE HORIZONTAL PLANE

Minimum audible angle

Many psychophysical studies have measured the smallest change in azimuth angle that can be detected reliably by listeners, relative to a particular reference angle. The threshold angular change is known as the **minimum audible angle** (MAA). Figure 5.7 shows the MAA for sine wave stimuli as a function of stimulus frequency, for four different reference angles. The 0° data (filled circles) represent the smallest change in direction from straight ahead that listeners could reliably detect. Below approximately 1000 Hz a shift as small as 1° can be detected. There is a pronounced elevation of thresholds for frequencies in between 1500 and 1800 Hz. This region of poor performance is also present for all the other reference angles plotted in the figure.

The duplex theory

Over 120 years ago, John William Strutt (Lord Rayleigh) identified two potential cues for the localization of sound sources in the horizontal plane, which were mentioned in the previous chapter, interaural level differences (ILD) and interaural time differences (ITD):

- ILDs arise because the ear further from the sound source lies in the acoustic shadow cast by the listener's head. As a result the intensity of the signal arriving at the further ear is lower than the intensity of the signal arriving at the nearer ear.
- ITDs occur because the two ears are approximately 14 cm apart, so sounds from a source nearer to one ear will arrive at that ear slightly before they arrive at the other ear.

Rayleigh's **duplex theory** proposed that the two cues are complementary: ITDs are effective at low sine wave frequencies, and ILDs are effective at high frequencies. The neural coding of ILD and ITD was considered in detail in Chapter 4 (see Figure 4.21). Specialized neural circuits in the superior olive encode the ILDs and ITDs created by lateralized sound sources. Responses in these neural circuits are the presumed neural substrate of Rayleigh's duplex theory. Central processes in the auditory cortex must compute a single estimate of azimuth angle on the basis of information concerning ILD and ITD.

We can infer that the deterioration in performance shown in Figure 5.7 occurs at the transition between localization based on ITDs (below 2 kHz), and localization based on ILDs (above 2 kHz). In this frequency region neither cue operates effectively. The MAA of 1° obtained at low frequencies corresponds to an ITD of only 10 microseconds.

For complex natural sounds such as speech, ITDs in lower frequencies appear to dominate the computation of azimuth angle. Wightman and Kistler (1992) generated stimuli in which ITDs indicated one azimuth angle, but ILDs indicated another azimuth angle. When the stimuli contained low frequencies, ITDs determined apparent direction. When low frequencies were removed, ILDs were more important for apparent direction.

Cones of confusion

Despite the obvious utility of binaural cues for sound localization, they are not sufficient to define direction uniquely. A given set of cue values is usually consistent with a range of possible sound directions, in addition to the true direction. For example, a sound source located directly in front of a listener provides the same binaural cue values as a sound source located directly behind the listener. The curved line in Figure 5.8 (left) is drawn through all locations in the horizontal plane (seen from above) that yield the same ITD between the ears. This curve can be rotated to sweep out a **cone of confusion**, shown in Figure 5.8 (right). All sounds located on the cone's surface yield the same ITD, so their locations are confusable.

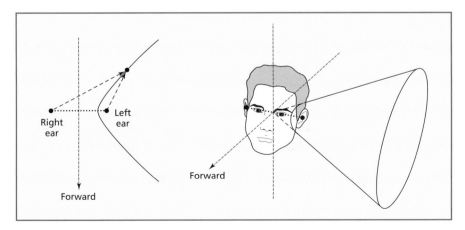

FIGURE 5.8
The cone of confusion. Left: The curved line is drawn through all horizontal locations (seen from above the head) that yield the same ITD between the two ears. Right: The curve on the left has been rotated to sweep out a conical surface. Sound sources located anywhere on the surface yield the same ITD. These locations are therefore confusable.

How is this ambiguity resolved? The key lies in the observation that each position of the listener's head relative to the sound source has its own cone of confusion. If the listener moves his or her head, then only a very small number of possible directions would be consistent with the different cones of confusion. Listeners can also use cues for localization in the vertical plane.

LOCALIZATION IN THE VERTICAL PLANE

The ability of listeners to judge elevation is much better than would be expected on the basis of binaural cues and head movements (Moore, 1997). The auditory system must therefore exploit other cues to establish elevation. The main cue for vertical localization is thought to be the interaction of the sound with the external ear. This cue is necessarily monaural, and is based on the way that sound waves are reflected off the external ear into the ear canal. The complex folded structure of the pinna acts as an acoustic filter, selectively modifying both the amplitude and phase properties of frequency components in the incoming sound wave. The small, asymmetrical shape of the human pinna has two crucial effects on its filtering properties. First, the effect of the pinna is restricted to frequencies above 6 kHz, because only these frequencies have sufficiently short wavelength (below 6 cm) to be affected by the pinna. Second, the filtering effect of the pinna depends on the direction of the sound source. Given a complex broadband stimulus, the pinna tends to introduce peaks and valleys in the high frequency region of the sound's spectrum. As the elevation of the sound source increases, these peaks and valleys tend to move toward higher frequencies.

> Sounds heard via headphones tend to appear localized inside the listener's head, because they bypass the pinna. The pinna appears to alter sounds in a way that leads them to be perceived as external to the listener. Sounds recorded using microphones placed in the ear canal of a dummy head with realistic outer ears still appear externalized even when played through headphones.

Gardner and Gardner (1973) compared localization performance with and without pinna effects. They removed any contribution of the pinna by filling the cavities in the outer ear with molded rubber plugs. Localization was worse when the effect of the pinna was removed, especially for bands of noise with high center frequencies.

THE PRECEDENCE EFFECT

In a cluttered natural environment, the sound emanating from a given source may reach our ears via several paths. As well as the direct path from the source to the ear, there may be many other paths that involve reflections off nearby surfaces such as rocks or walls (echoes). With several echoes from different directions, there is a great deal of scope for confusion about the true direction of the sound source. However, listeners do not normally experience such confusion. Sounds can be localized accurately even in highly reverberant conditions. This accuracy is achieved because the earliest arriving sound wave is given precedence over later echoes. If two brief sounds are presented to an observer, 5–50 ms apart in time, they appear fused as a single sound. The apparent direction of the fused sound is determined by the direction of the first sound. This is known as the **precedence effect**.

Precedence can be demonstrated easily at home using stereo reproduction equipment to listen to a monophonic signal, such as a mono radio station. When the listener is facing the two speakers and positioned midway between them, the sound appears to come from directly ahead. When the listener moves closer to one speaker than the other, the sound appears to come entirely from the nearer speaker. However, the further, unheard speaker still makes a contribution to the loudness and apparent spatial extent of the sound. This can be verified by listening to the effect of unplugging the further speaker.

? Demonstrate the precedence effect using your own stereo system.

DISTANCE JUDGMENTS

Perceptual research has demonstrated that four cues are used by the auditory system to estimate the distance of a sound source (see Zahorik, 2002). Other things being equal, more distant sounds are quieter than nearer sounds. In fact, sound intensity decreases by a factor of four each time distance doubles (the inverse square law). So sound intensity provides a simple cue to distance, and it is well known that louder sounds appear closer than quieter sounds. In environments containing sound-reflecting surfaces, the proportion of acoustic energy reaching the listener directly rather than via reverberation decreases as source distance increases. This direct-to-reverberant energy ratio offers a second cue to distance. Third, distance also alters the spectrum of sounds. Air molecules absorb energy at higher sound frequencies more than at lower sound frequencies. As a result sounds from more distant sources appear muffled. Thunder, for example, is heard as an extremely loud crack from nearby, but as a quiet rumble from a far distance. Finally, at distances closer than 1 meter ILD increases substantially as distance declines, while ITD is not affected (Brungart & Rabinowitz, 1999).

Zahorik (2002) studied intensity and direct-to-reverberant energy, and found that the relative weight attached to the two cues depended on the nature of the sound signal and the angular position of the source. He also reported that distance judgments consistently underestimated the true distance.

SPEECH PERCEPTION

THE PRODUCTION OF SPEECH SOUNDS

Both speech and musical sounds are produced by a vibrating sound source that is filtered by a resonating chamber. In the case of speech, the vibration is produced by air that is forced through the vocal cords by the diaphragm. This vibration creates a harmonic sound whose fundamental frequency depends on the rate of vibration. When the harmonic sound reaches the vocal tract, its spectrum undergoes radical modification because the vocal tract acts as a resonator. Certain frequencies are amplified, because the vocal tract tends to vibrate or resonate more at those frequencies than at other frequencies. These resonant frequencies are called **formant frequencies**, and show up as distinct peaks of energy in the sound's frequency

> **KEY TERM**
>
> **Formant frequency**
> The distinctive frequency at which the vocal tract (the tube of air between the larynx and lips) vibrates to create a certain vowel sound.

FIGURE 5.9

Simplified spectrograms of three speech sounds, /ba/, /da/, and /ga/. Each sound contains concentrations of energy at particular frequencies (formants), due to resonance in the vocal tract. The frequency of each formant changes progressively over the first 50 ms or so of the sound (formant transition). Different speech sounds are distinguishable in terms of their formant frequencies and transitions.

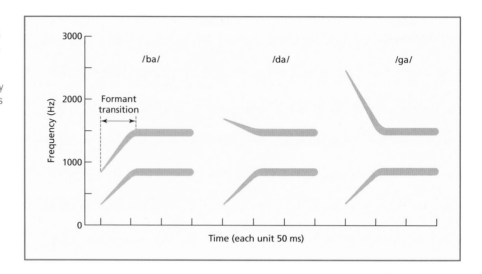

The smallest unit of sound that allows different words to be distinguished is defined as the phoneme. The word "dog," for example, contains three phonemes. Changes to the first, second, and third phoneme respectively produce the words "log," "dig," and "dot." English is said to contain 40 different phonemes, specified as in /d/, /o/, /g/ for the word "dog."

spectrum. Formant frequencies are numbered in ascending order starting with the formant at the lowest frequency. Formants often display a smooth change in their frequency during the first 50 ms or so of the speech sound. These frequency glides are known as formant transitions. Figure 5.9 shows a simplified spectrogram for three different speech sounds, heard as /ba/, /da/, and /ga/. The sounds differ in terms of their formant transitions.

SPEECH MODE

It has long been argued that speech perception involves a special mode of auditory processing, known as the **speech mode**. Advocates of the existence of a speech mode make two claims about speech processing. First, they argue that the perceptual processing of speech sounds is qualitatively different from the processing of nonspeech sounds. Second, they argue that specialized neural structures are dedicated to speech processing.

Qualitative differences between speech and nonspeech processing

Processes that differ *qualitatively* use completely different kinds of computation. It should not be possible to convert one process into the other by changing some details of the computation, such as increasing the bandwidth of a filter, or adding an extra step in the computation (see the distinction between analog computation and symbolic computation in Chapter 1). Some have argued that the speech processing is qualitatively different from the processing of nonspeech sounds

KEY TERM

Speech mode

A mode of auditory processing that is specialized for processing speech sounds.

because only speech processing supports **categorical perception**.

Categorical perception

When the frequency content of nonspeech sounds is altered in some way, listeners report relatively gradual and continuous changes in their perceptual attributes. For example, the pitch of a sound varies smoothly with changes in its fundamental frequency. A small change in frequency produces a slight change in pitch, while a large change in frequency produces a very marked change in pitch. Different speech sounds vary in terms of their formant frequencies or formant transitions, as we have seen in Figure 5.9. It is possible to create synthetic speech stimuli that contain formants lying in between those defining different speech sounds. Liberman et al. (1957), for example, created a set of 14 stimuli in which the formant transition of the second formant varied continuously between the three values illustrated in Figure 5.9. The spectrograms at the bottom of Figure 5.10 show the stimulus set.

What do listeners perceive when presented with these intermediate stimuli? Do they report a gradual change in their perception of the phoneme (defined in the box earlier), similar to the change in pitch of nonspeech sounds? The answer is no—there is no gradual shift from perception of one phoneme to perception of another. Instead, there is a sudden switch when the formant frequency reaches

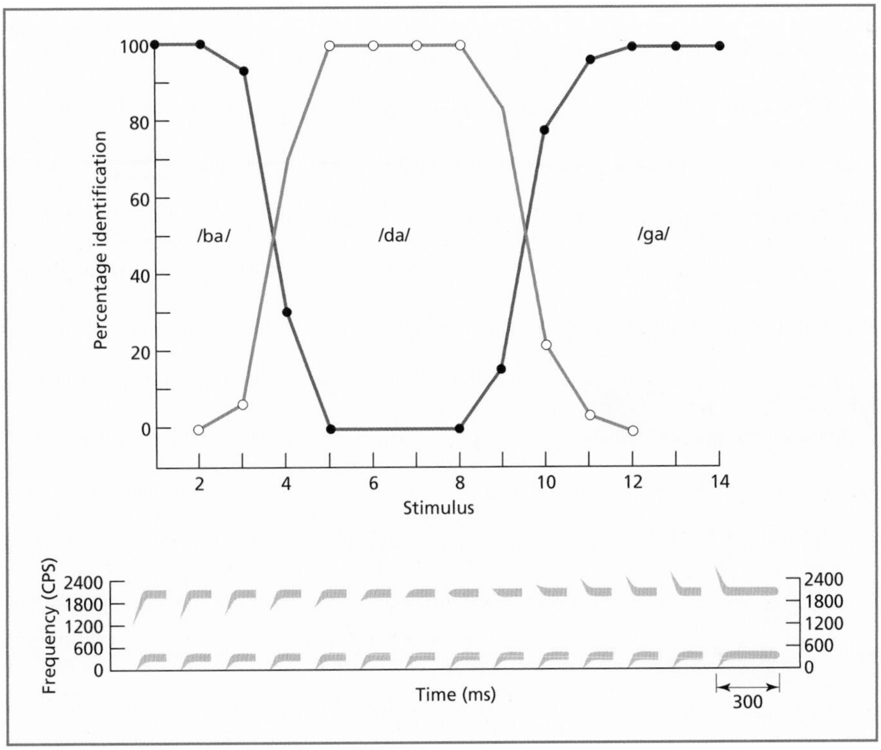

> **KEY TERM**
>
> **Categorical perception**
> Each stimulus is perceived as a member of a discrete category, in an all-or-nothing fashion, rather than occupying a position along a continuous dimension.

FIGURE 5.10
Phoneme boundaries. Liberman et al. (1957) created a set of 14 synthetic speech sounds in which the formant transition of the second formant varied continuously between the values specifying the three sounds shown in Figure 5.9. Spectrograms of the 14 sounds are shown along the bottom of the figure. Listeners were asked to identify each synthetic sound as a /ba/, /da/, or /ga/. Identification data show very sharp transitions between perceived phonemes. (From Liberman et al., 1957, adapted with permission from APA.)

a particular value. The three curves in Figure 5.10 show the percentage of time each stimulus was identified as /ba/, /da/, and /ga/ in Liberman et al.'s (1957) experiment. The transition from one phoneme to the next was very sudden, as seen in the steepness of the curves. The sharpness of the perceptual boundary between phonemes has been taken as evidence that listeners group speech sounds into discrete perceptual categories (e.g., Liberman et al., 1957). The switch from one category to another occurs when the formant frequency reaches a **phoneme boundary**. On this basis it has been argued that there is a special speech mode of auditory processing. The argument is weakened by evidence for categorical processing of nonspeech sounds. For example, Locke and Kellar (1973) studied the identification and discrimination of chords by musicians and nonmusicians. Stimuli were musical chords containing three pure tones. The frequency of the middle tone was manipulated to create a continuum of sounds in between A minor (440/523/659 Hz) and A major (440/554/659 Hz). Musicians in particular tended to categorize the sounds as either A minor or A major despite the relatively small changes in frequency involved.

Evaluation

Other perceptual effects have also been taken as support for a special speech mode of processing (Moore, 1997). However, as in the case of categorical perception, these effects are not unique to speech, but are also found using nonspeech signals. Thus, although a range of different studies does indicate that there is something special about speech, evidence is not strong enough to conclude that there is a mode of auditory processing that is unique to speech. Speech may be special because it is encountered so frequently that listeners become expert at processing speech signals. This expertise leads to differences between speech and nonspeech perception. In a similar way, pitch perception in expert musicians may differ from pitch perception in nonmusicians.

Physiological specialization in the processing of speech sounds

Evidence that specialized neural structures are dedicated to processing speech sounds has come from two sources: Neuropsychological studies of brain damage, and brain imaging.

Neuropsychology

Neuropsychological research has identified an area in the left hemisphere of the human brain, where damage is associated with disturbed speech perception. In the late 1800s the German neurologist Carl Wernicke found that damage in a small area of the left cortical hemisphere resulted in an inability to comprehend speech. The area he discovered became known as **Wernicke's area**, and the disorder is commonly called Wernicke's aphasia.

Figure 5.11 shows that Wernicke's area lies on the posterior portion of the temporal lobe, posterior

---

KEY TERMS

Phoneme boundary
A formant frequency defining the boundary at which perception switches from one phoneme to another.

Wernicke's area
An area in the left hemisphere of the human cortex where damage results in disordered speech perception (Wernicke's aphasia).

to primary and secondary auditory cortex. Patients suffering from Wernicke's aphasia are unable to understand speech, but do not show evidence of marked sensory impairments of hearing. Note that Wernicke's aphasia does not provide unambiguous evidence for a special speech mode of auditory processing. The disorder may reflect a disturbance in the neural system that links the auditory representation of speech sounds with their meanings.

Neuroimaging

Research in this area has attempted to isolate regions of the cortex where activity is uniquely associated with auditory processing of speech sounds. Scott et al. (2000), for example, used PET to study the brain areas activated solely by intelligible speech, regardless of acoustic complexity. They used a variety of speech and speech-like sounds that were carefully designed to be equivalent in terms of acoustic complexity, but variable in terms of their intelligibility as speech. In addition, Scott et al. used a passive listening task in which subjects were not required to make semantic decisions regarding the content of the speech stimuli. In keeping with earlier neuropsychological research, Scott et al. (2000) found preferential activation of the left hemisphere by speech stimuli. Intelligible speech activated an area in the left anterior superior temporal sulcus. Unintelligible speech activated nearby areas in the left hemisphere, but nonspeech sounds activated the superior temporal gyrus in the right hemisphere. Scott et al.'s results are consistent with single-cell recording studies in primates that reveal a "what" auditory processing stream that advances anteriorly from primary auditory cortex, extracting more complex features from auditory stimuli (see Chapter 4).

Hickok and Poeppel (2007) have proposed that speech processing divides into two cortical streams; namely the familiar dorsal and ventral routes. The dorsal stream translates acoustic speech signals into articulatory representations which are essential for speech production, and is strongly left-hemisphere dominant. The ventral stream is bilaterally organized, and maps acoustic speech input onto conceptual and semantic representations.

SPOKEN WORD RECOGNITION

Word recognition is a fundamental aspect of speech perception. Recognition requires the listener to map a continuously varying stream of acoustic energy onto a discrete set of meaningful symbols, known words. When you are sitting in a bar talking with friends you effortlessly break up the acoustic energy from their voice into words. On the other hand, if you overhear someone talking in a language you have not learnt it is impossible to discern any kind of discrete structure at all. The task is far from trivial. It is complicated by the fact that the sound of each word is partly dependent on the sounds of preceding and succeeding words, due to the interaction of motor commands (coarticulation). Further difficulties are introduced by variations in the way the same word is spoken due to prosody (speech rhythm, stress, and intonation), and to the sex, age, size, and accent of the speaker.

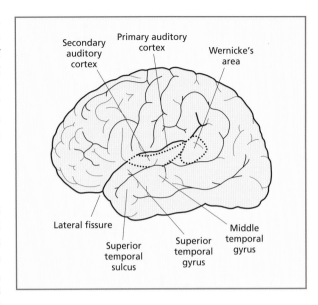

FIGURE 5.11

Human cortical areas involved in speech processing. Primary auditory cortex lies on Heschl's gyrus, hidden on the upper surface of the temporal lobe inside the lateral fissure. Secondary auditory cortex encircles this primary area, covering part of the superior temporal gyrus. Wernicke's aphasia (inability to understand speech) is associated with damage to the posterior portion of the left temporal lobe, posterior to auditory cortex. Brain-imaging studies of cortical activation in response to speech stimuli (e.g., Scott et al., 2000) find activity in auditory cortex and in an area anterior to secondary auditory cortex on the superior temporal gyrus.

The mental lexicon is the brain's internal dictionary. It is a central concept in explanations of spoken word recognition. It contains a representation of each word we have learnt in terms of its physical characteristics (sound) and its symbolic properties (meaning). Current theories of word recognition assume that the process of recognition begins with a prelexical analysis to break up the acoustic signal into primitive speech units (phonemes). Candidate words in the mental lexicon are then activated in a graded manner according to the number of matching and mismatching features emerging from the analysis. Eventually sufficient evidence accrues to rule out all except the correct word. Many experiments support the notion of multiple activation early in analysis. For example, in recognition memory experiments subjects make false positive responses to words that had not been presented previously but begin in the same way as words that had been presented earlier (Wallace, Stewart, & Malone, 1995).

Theories of word recognition differ in their treatment of bottom-up and top-down information (this distinction was introduced in Chapter 1). Some theories argue that recognition involves only bottom-up information flow; phonemes and words are extracted entirely on the basis of information contained in the auditory stimulus (Norris, McQueen, & Cutler, 2000). Others argue that a top-down route also exists, in which the results of higher levels of analysis are fed back down to lower levels to influence early processing (Marslen-Wilson & Tyler, 1980; McClelland & Elman, 1986). The issue is still controversial, and centers on the interpretation of context effects such as the phoneme restoration effect. Warren (1970) presented listeners with sentences in which a small sound segment had been removed and replaced with noise. Listeners reported hearing a word consistent with the context. For example, in the sentence "It was found that the *eel was on the axle," where * indicates noise, listeners reported hearing "wheel." On the other hand, in the sentence "It was found that the *eel was on the table," listeners reported hearing "meal." One explanation for context effects is top-down feedback from the lexical level to increase activation of contextually consistent words. An alternative explanation is that recognition involves high-level "decision" units that receive only bottom-up information from both prelexical and lexical levels (Norris, McQueen, & Cutler, 2000). There have been arguments supporting both sides of the debate (see McQueen, 2005; McClelland, Mirman, & Holt, 2006; Myers & Blumstein, 2007).

A recent survey of neuroimaging studies favors a hierarchical processing system involving the ventral regions of the cortex (DeWitt & Rauschecker, 2012). Initial analysis of the spectral content of speech sounds takes place in the primary auditory cortex. Spectral features are used to form a representation of speech formants and phonemes in the midsuperior temporal gyrus, and then word representations are constructed in the anterior part of the superior temporal gyrus, based on the temporal sequence of phonemes. This kind of hierarchical processing scheme has much in common with theories of visual object recognition, discussed in later chapters.

AUDITORY SCENE ANALYSIS

This chapter began with an example of a natural acoustic environment, likely to be encountered while sitting in a bar talking with some friends. The sound waves reaching each ear may include contributions from friends' voices, from music playing on a sound system, and from passing traffic (see Figure 5.1). The auditory system must partition the incoming complex signal into each of these components in order to build separate perceptual representations of the objects or events generating the sounds. Only then will the listener be able to follow the conversation, enjoy the music, and so on. Bregman (1990) called the perceptual process that achieves this decomposition *auditory scene analysis*. Parts of the complex acoustic signal that are grouped together form an **auditory stream**, in Bregman's (1990) terminology, which is identified with a discrete object or event in the world that created the sound (your friend, the jukebox, a car outside the bar). The auditory system groups sound components into streams on the basis of three physical characteristics.

KEY TERM

Auditory streaming
Grouping of parts of a complex acoustic signal into discrete auditory objects.

SPATIAL LOCATION

In a crowded bar you are able to separate out the voice of the person with whom you are talking from the cacophony of other voices in the room on the basis of your ability to assign different locations to sound sources (Hawley, Litovsky, & Culling, 2004). As discussed earlier, sound source localization is based on two complementary cues, ITD and ILD. However, ITDs are surprisingly ineffective for auditory grouping. Darwin (1997) suggested that ITDs rely on prior grouping, rather than act as a cue to grouping. ITDs are encoded by frequency-selective neurons in the brainstem (see Chapter 4). Natural sounds usually contain many frequency components. If several sounds are present simultaneously, the auditory signal will contain many frequency components having a range of ITDs. The auditory system can only deduce location from the ITDs of a set of components after those components have been grouped together as belonging to the same source. ITD cannot therefore act as a grouping cue itself.

SPECTRAL CONTENT

The conversation in the bar also provides a very good example of grouping on the basis of pitch. Men tend to speak at a lower pitch (fundamental frequency) than women, and individuals differ in the precise pitch of their voice. So if two friends are talking simultaneously, the difference in the pitch of their voices is a major cue enabling the listener to correctly separate the utterances into two streams.

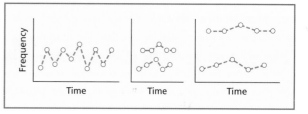

The fundamental frequency of each complex sound is so important for simultaneous grouping because it determines the frequencies of all the sound's harmonics. As we saw in Chapter 4, the harmonics of a complex sound are equally spaced in frequency at exact multiples of the fundamental frequency. So if two complex sounds have different fundamentals, their harmonics form different harmonic series, which can be segregated into different auditory streams.

Some simple examples of streaming based on spectral content are shown in Figure 5.12. The stimulus consists of six tones presented in a repeating sequence, with three tones at higher pitch interleaved with three tones at lower pitch. In the case of the left-hand sequence, listeners perceive a single auditory stream in which the "melody" contains alternating high- and low-pitched notes. When the same sequence of tones is presented more rapidly (middle stimulus) the tones tend to separate into two streams, one containing the higher-pitch notes and the other containing the lower-pitch notes. A similar effect occurs when the presentation rate stays constant, but the frequency difference between the two sets of notes increases (right-hand stimulus).

The stimuli in Figure 5.12 illustrate two spectral grouping cues, based on temporal proximity (middle), and frequency similarity (right). Other cues include harmonic similarity and amplitude (Darwin, 1997; Carlyon, 2004). In the case of complex

FIGURE 5.12
Auditory grouping. The stimulus contains a repeating sequence of six notes, with three low-pitch notes alternating with three high-pitch notes. In the left-hand stimulus, the notes form a single perceptual stream or melody whose pitch rises and falls alternately (dashed line). If the time interval between notes is shortened (middle), or if the frequency difference between the high notes and the low notes is increased (right), the stimulus tends to segregate into two streams, one containing the high notes and the other containing the low notes.

? *Think about the auditory streams you perceive in emergency sirens. Are they stable?*

harmonic sounds, unlike the pure tones in Figure 5.12, streaming is influenced by the overall spectral properties or timbre of harmonic sequences. A recent fMRI study showed activation in the intraparietal sulcus during auditory streaming (Cusack, 2005). Grouping on the basis of spectral cues seems to reflect the probability that the two components could be emitted by a single source (Bregman, 1990).

TIME OR ONSET

Sounds from independent natural sources generally start and stop at different times. In doing so, all the spectral components of each sound necessarily start and stop at the same time. Shared onset and offset is a powerful grouping cue for partitioning a complex sound wave into components from different sources, even when the components are otherwise very similar (Darwin & Ciocca, 1992). As mentioned in the previous chapter, the attack and decay of a sound influences its perceived timbre. For example, guitar notes and cymbal sounds have a sudden attack and very gradual decay, whereas a trombone note has a much more gradual attack.

HEARING DYSFUNCTION

Human hearing is mediated by a complex system of mechanical and neural structures. Consequently there are many sources of dysfunction that result in hearing loss. Dysfunctions are broadly classified into two categories, *conductive* and *sensorineural*. **Conductive hearing loss** is associated with problems in the mechanical structures of the outer and middle ear. **Sensorineural** dysfunction arises from damage to neural structures in the cochlea, auditory nerve, or central auditory system. Tinnitus, or ringing in the ears, cannot be readily classified as a conductive disorder or a sensorineural disorder, since its origin has not yet been identified. Figure 5.13 summarizes the main forms of dysfunction.

KEY TERMS

Conductive hearing loss
Deafness caused by impaired conduction of sound energy by the outer and middle ear.

Sensorineural hearing loss
Deafness caused by damage to the inner ear, especially cochlear hair cells.

FIGURE 5.13
Classification of hearing dysfunction.

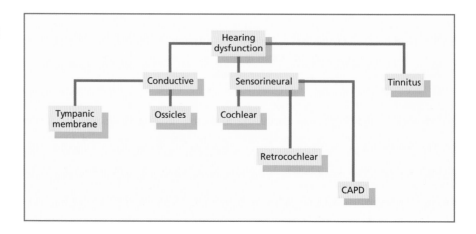

CONDUCTIVE HEARING LOSS

Apart from blockages in the outer ear due to wax or a foreign body, conductive hearing loss is usually associated with damage to the tympanic membrane or impeded transmission via the ossicles.

Damage to the tympanic membrane

Holes or perforations in the eardrum can be caused by violent stimulation or by infection. This damage reduces the efficiency with which the eardrum transmits sound pressure waves to the middle ear. Scar tissue formation during healing may increase the stiffness of the membrane, again reducing its efficiency.

The ossicles

Infection or otosclerosis can impede the ability of the ossicles to transmit energy, by restricting their ability to move. Infection is common in childhood, and may result in the development of scar tissue around the bones. Otosclerosis may fuse the ossicles against the bony structure of the middle ear.

The middle ear cavity is normally filled with air, which allows free movement of the ossicles. Fluid build-up in the middle ear can impede the movement of the ossicles, and is the most common cause of hearing loss. It arises from blockages that prevent fluid produced by the lining of the middle ear from draining into the nasal cavity through the Eustachian tube.

Consequences and treatment of conductive hearing loss

All conductive dysfunctions impede the conduction of sound energy to the cochlea. As a result, auditory thresholds are raised by as much as 40–50 dB in the most severe cases. Subjectively, very quiet sounds will be inaudible, while louder sounds will seem muffled. A crucial feature of conductive hearing loss that aids diagnosis is the relatively uniform elevation of threshold at all sound frequencies.

Fortunately, most forms of conductive hearing loss can be treated either by drugs to attack the infection, or by some form of mechanical intervention. Damaged tympanic membranes heal or can be repaired using grafting techniques. Damaged ossicles can be replaced with prosthetic ossicles. Fluid in the middle ear can be drained by inserting a grommet (tiny plastic tube) through the eardrum (though resulting damage to the eardrum is a risk).

All these interventions can return hearing sensitivity to normal or near-normal levels. In cases that cannot be treated by drugs or surgery, a simple hearing aid can be effective because it amplifies the signal to compensate for the loss in conduction efficiency.

SENSORINEURAL HEARING LOSS

Neural damage can be located in the cochlea, in the auditory nerve, or in central structures. Damage located in the auditory nerve is usually called *retrocochlear dysfunction*. Damage to central structures is sometimes termed *central auditory processing disorder* (CAPD).

[?] *Why is it a good idea to wear earplugs at heavily amplified music concerts?*

Grommet surgery has become so common that healthcare providers now consider the financial implications of the procedure carefully before approving surgery.

Cochlear damage

The delicate sensory structures of the cochlea are vulnerable to damage resulting from:

1. Exposure to intense sounds
2. Exposure to ototoxic drugs (e.g., antibiotics, solvents)
3. Infection
4. Metabolic disturbance
5. Allergy
6. Genetic disorders
7. Age (presbyacusis).

Very high noise levels, for example, can cause the elastic limit of the organ of Corti to be exceeded. This may result in structural damage to the stereocilia, tectorial membrane, and basilar membrane. Damage consequently has a major impact on the sensory function of the hair cells, particularly outer hair cells.

Cochlear damage usually has three perceptual consequences:

- Raised thresholds
- Broader frequency tuning
- Loudness recruitment.

As in the case of conductive disorders, cochlear damage leads to elevated thresholds for detecting sounds. Unlike conductive losses, however, the problem cannot be solved satisfactorily by simply amplifying the incoming signal. Sufferers report that sounds appear unclear and distorted, and find understanding speech particularly difficult. These problems can be attributed to the effect of cochlear damage on frequency tuning in the auditory nerve. Loss of outer hair cell function leads to a broadening in the frequency tuning of individual nerve fibers (see Figure 4.14). Broader tuning means that the listener cannot separate simultaneous frequency components in complex signals. The ability to segregate a speech signal from background noise and from other speech signals is severely impaired.

Loudness recruitment refers to an abnormally rapid growth of loudness as the intensity of a sound is increased. Sufferers find very quiet sounds difficult to hear, but may be able to hear louder sounds as well as normal listeners. Hence raising your voice so that it can be heard by an elderly relative often leads to the complaint "no need to shout!" Loudness recruitment is closely associated with cochlear damage and, as in the case of broadened frequency tuning, is probably related to outer hair cell damage. The cochlear amplifier described earlier enhances sensitivity to faint sounds, but has little effect on sensitivity to louder sounds. Outer hair cell motility is thought to be responsible for this effect. Without the amplification of faint sounds, loudness grows very rapidly as sound intensity increases.

As mentioned earlier, one cause of cochlear hearing loss is aging. **Presbyacusis**, as it is known, probably starts when a person is in their 20s, but may

Mammalian hair cells do not regenerate once they have been damaged, so cochlear hearing loss is permanent. On the other hand, some species such as birds and fish do have the ability to regenerate hair cells following damage. The origin of these species differences is not clear.

? *Think about how outer hair cell loss affects the functioning of the basilar membrane.*

KEY TERM

Loudness recruitment
Abnormally rapid growth in loudness with SPL, resulting from damage to outer hair cells in the cochlea.

not become noticeable until they have reached 50. Hearing loss begins at extremely high frequencies, and progresses down the frequency scale with advancing age. The effect is thought to reflect a progressive loss in hair cell efficiency. In other words, the hair cells deteriorate and become less effective. Hair cells at the base of the cochlea bend in response to all sound frequencies, whereas cells at the apex only bend at low frequencies. Cells at the base are therefore likely to wear out sooner than those at the apex. Since, according to the place theory of frequency coding, cells at the base code high frequencies, presbyacusis progresses from high to low frequencies.

Retrocochlear dysfunction

Retrocochlear dysfunction arises from disorders that affect the auditory nerve. The vestibular nerve runs alongside the auditory nerve. Tumors growing on the vestibular nerve can damage the auditory nerve, resulting in unilateral hearing loss and tinnitus (ringing in the ears). Treatment involves surgical intervention to remove the tumor, which results in complete and permanent hearing loss in the affected ear.

Central auditory processing disorder

A group of clinical patients present themselves with hearing problems in noisy environments, yet standard tests reveal no sensory deficits. This condition is gradually becoming known as *central auditory processing disorder*, or CAPD (e.g., Paul-Brown, 1996). The precise cause or causes of the disorder have not yet been identified. Treatment is confined to measures that improve the perceptibility of the signal against noisy backgrounds.

Tinnitus

Tinnitus is the perception of a ringing sound that appears to originate inside the head, and to occur in the absence of any obvious external source. Transitory episodes of tinnitus are quite common, but in a small number of individuals the experience is so persistent that it becomes debilitating. Although the phenomenon probably originates in the peripheral auditory system, its exact causes have proved very difficult to identify (apart from tinnitus associated with retrocochlear dysfunction). One form of tinnitus is due to otosclerosis causing changes in impedance across frequency. Current therapeutic approaches emphasize a three-way interaction between the auditory system, the limbic system (involved in emotional responses), and the sympathetic nervous system (involved in arousal). Therapy may involve measures to intervene in each system. Auditory interventions may include the use of in-ear sound generators to promote habituation to the sound. Relaxation techniques, counseling, and cognitive behavior therapy attempt to minimize the arousal and anxiety produced by the phenomenon.

Cochlear implants

Cochlear implants have been used to treat sensorineural deafness since the 1980s, and have been fitted to hundreds of thousands of patients worldwide. They convert sound energy into electrical signals which are delivered directly to the spiral ganglion neurons. A microphone picks up sounds from the environment, and the resulting electrical signals are processed to prioritize audible speech before being sent to an array of 20 or so electrodes, which transmits the signals to the auditory nerve. Implants perform complex information processing on the auditory input, compressing its huge dynamic range and reducing its bandwidth. Cochlear implants are normally offered to patients with profound bilateral sensorineural hearing loss exceeding 70 dB. Users benefit from greater awareness of sounds, improved speech intelligibility, and assistance with lip-reading. However implants incorporate a very small number of electrodes, and cannot hope to adequately replace the sophisticated transduction and encoding processes that are normally performed by the thousands of hair cells in the cochlea. Wide differences in performance are found, due to variations in signal quality and encoding algorithms. Mismatch with a user's preexisting memories of sounds may also affect performance.

CHAPTER SUMMARY

LOUDNESS

- Perception of loudness is studied experimentally using matching and scaling tasks.
- Sound intensity appears to be coded by the rate of firing in frequency-tuned auditory nerve fibers. The excitation pattern model of loudness perception proposes that the overall loudness of a given sound is proportional to the total neural activity evoked by it in the auditory nerve.
- Human loudness discrimination is worse than one would expect on the basis of auditory nerve responses, indicating that central factors limit the ability of the brain to make use of intensity information.

PITCH

- Pitch is related to a sound's frequency.
- Psychophysical tuning curves are remarkably similar to the frequency tuning curves of individual auditory nerve fibers.
- Pitch is coded in two ways:
  - Frequency-to-place conversion of resolved lower frequency sound components.
  - Temporal patterns of firing in the auditory nerve evoked by unresolved higher harmonics.

LOCALIZATION

- Rayleigh's influential duplex theory proposes that localization in the horizontal plane makes use of two different binaural cues over different frequency ranges:
  - Interaural time differences are used at low frequencies.
  - Interaural level differences are used at high frequencies.

- Localization in the vertical plane depends on the filtering effect of the pinna.
- Localization is accurate even in highly reverberant environments, because the earlier arriving direct sound wave takes precedence over later echoes.

SPEECH PERCEPTION

- Speech sounds are complex harmonic sounds that vary continuously over time.
- Evidence for a special speech mode of auditory processing is inconclusive: Effects previously considered to be unique to speech (e.g., categorical perception) are also obtained using nonspeech sounds.
- Neuroimaging studies indicate that speech is processed by two parallel streams in the cortex, a dorsal stream and a ventral stream.
- Spoken word recognition involves a prelexical stage in which the sound energy is broken up into primitive speech units, and a lexical stage in which the speech units are mapped onto known words.

AUDITORY SCENE ANALYSIS

- Auditory scene analysis involves dividing up the components of a complex sound wave into auditory objects, on the basis of grouping cues.
- Grouping of sounds is based on:
  - Spatial location
  - Spectral content
  - Time or onset.

HEARING DYSFUNCTION

- Disorders of hearing can be grouped into two categories: Conductive and sensorineural.
- Conductive hearing loss is associated with disorders in the mechanical structures of the outer and middle ear.
- Conductive disorders impede the transmission of sound energy to the cochlea, and can be treated with an amplifying hearing aid.
- Sensorineural dysfunction arises from damage to neural structures in the cochlea, auditory nerve, or central auditory system.
- Sensorineural disorders can cause abnormal growth in loudness with stimulus intensity and broadened frequency tuning, usually due to damage in the outer hair cells of the cochlea. Simple amplifying hearing aids are therefore of limited utility. Cochlear implants have proved to be a useful aid for sufferers of profound sensorineural hearing loss.

TUTORIALS

MUSIC PERCEPTION

Music is a universal feature of all human cultures, both past and present. Crude musical instruments have been found in the remnants of the earliest civilizations. Music is so important in present-day culture that it supports a huge worldwide industry. In the UK alone, annual turnover in the music industry amounts to several hundred million pounds.

Curiously, there is no universally agreed definition of what constitutes music. Carterette and Kendall (1999, p. 726) provide a general definition of music as "temporally organized sound and silence that is areferentially communicative in a context." A crucial distinction between music and speech is that speech is referential because speech sounds act as references to words. Setting aside issues of definition, certain acoustic stimuli are recognized as musical by most members of a given culture, even when those stimuli have never been heard before:

> You are browsing, let us imagine, in a music shop, and come across a box of faded pianola rolls. One of them bears an illegible title, and you unroll the first foot or two, to see if you can recognize the work from the pattern of holes in the paper. Eventually you decide that the only way of finding out is to buy the roll, take it home, and play it on the pianola. Within seconds your ears have told you what your eyes were quite unable to make out—you are the proud possessor of a piano arrangement of "Colonel Bogey."
>
> (Longuet-Higgins, 1979, p. 307)

How do we recognize a sound as a piece of music? Recognition is based on a set of universal perceptual features of musical sounds.

Features of musical sounds

Musical tone

Tone is the primary quality of musical sound in western music. It has three important characteristics: Musical pitch, loudness, and timbre (Rasch & Plomp, 1999).

*   *Musical pitch* is related to the fundamental frequency of a complex harmonic sound, and is heard for fundamental frequencies between 20 Hz and 5000 Hz.
*   *Loudness* is less important than pitch. Western musical notation allows for only five levels of loudness (from soft or pianissimo to loud or forte).

- *Timbre* gives a musical tone its distinctive character, and allows two tones to be distinguished even if they have the same pitch and loudness. Timbre is related to the harmonic composition of the tone, as well as to its temporal properties such as rise time and vibrato.

Theories of how pitch, loudness, and timbre are analyzed by the auditory system were discussed in detail earlier in the chapter.

Consonance

When two tones are played simultaneously, they may sound pleasant and harmonious, or *consonant*. Alternatively the combination may sound unpleasant and rough, or *dissonant*. Pure tones separated by more than one critical bandwidth (described earlier in the chapter) sound consonant. Tones having smaller differences in frequency sound dissonant (Rasch & Plomp, 1999). Complex tones blend harmoniously to produce chords when their fundamental frequencies are in simple ratios, such as 2:1, so that several of their harmonics coincide in frequency. Otherwise the harmonics tend to beat.

Melody

When the pitch of a musical sound varies progressively over time, it creates a pitch "contour" that is heard as a melodic, flowing form. This contour retains its character even when the sequence of tones defining it is transposed to a different pitch range. Rosner and Meyer (1982) found that untrained subjects classify musical melodies into a small number of standard schemes, such as a "gap-fill" scheme involving a melodic leap (usually upward) followed by a gradual progression back to the starting note. Melodic contours are probably constructed by listeners using the processes of auditory scene analysis described earlier in the chapter.

? What role does auditory streaming play in melody perception?

Rhythm

Melody involves musical structure over time periods extending over many seconds. Rhythm relates to relatively short-term temporal structures. Lerdahl and Jackendoff (1983) argued that rhythm has two components:

- *Segmentation* or the grouping of repeating elements over different time scales.
- *Metre* or the regular alternation of strong and weak elements.

The strong beat heard in popular music is a good example of meter. Metrical music has a prominent motor component—listeners respond to the beat by tapping their feet or by moving their body in synchrony. The association between music and dance is ancient.

Functional significance of music

Our ability to hear the distinctive features of music can be explained using the same perceptual processes discussed earlier in the chapter in the context of nonmusical sound processing, such as pitch and loudness analyzing mechanisms, and auditory grouping processes. However, these explanations do not address the fundamental question as to why music has become such a powerful feature of human culture. It is plausible to suppose that music is a biological adaptation, since its features are universal across cultures and recorded history, and it can be appreciated with no formal training. There are two alternative accounts of the origin of this biological adaptation.

Music and language

One account draws on the close parallels between language and music. Both are forms of communication found in all human cultures, and involve discrete acoustic elements structured hierarchically into sequences according to a set of rules. The assumption is that our ability to perceive music is a byproduct of the evolution of language, and has no evolutionary function of its own. This view is exemplified in Pinker's (1997) provocative remark that music is no more than "auditory cheesecake." The perceptual characteristics of music also play a role in language processing. Pitch and timbre, for example, are useful for identifying the properties of individual voices. Melody and rhythm in music relate to intonation and prosody in speech. Saffran et al. (1999) presented evidence that a learning mechanism known to be involved in word segmentation can also be used to segment tone sequences, reinforcing the link between music and language.

Music and evolution

The alternative view is that music evolved because it is adaptive. There are several variants of this argument (see Miller, 2000; Cross, 2001). One advocates the Darwinian view that music is important for sexual selection, because it functions as a courtship display to attract sexual partners. Another variant emphasizes the role of music in promoting social cohesion and cooperation. Rhythmic songs help a group of people to work together in a coordinated way, perhaps improving teamwork in hunting or reducing intergroup conflict. A third variant of the evolutionary argument proposes that music plays a central role in socialization. Musical communication is prominent in early mother–infant interactions and, according to this view, promotes emotional bonding and social awareness (see Schulkin & Raglan, 2014).

Research on the syntactic structure of music and on the brain areas involved in music favor the linguistic view of music (Patel, 2003). An area of cortex known as Broca's area (BA 44) has long been known to be associated with language processing. Damage in this area leads to an inability to produce language, either spoken or written (Broca's aphasia). Recent neuroimaging studies have shown that Broca's area is also important for several aspects of music processing (Abdul-Kareem et al., 2011). On the other hand, some neuropsychological case studies have shown that some individuals can have impaired music perception but no impairment in language processing, or vice versa (Peretz & Coltheart, 2003), indicating that at least part of music processing is distinct from language processing.

The physics of vision—light and the eye

6

Contents

INTRODUCTION

Before we can begin to understand visual perception, we must consider the basic properties of the physical stimulus, light. Answers to fundamental questions about vision, such as why we have a light sense and how our sense organs gather information from light, depend on understanding the nature of the physical stimulus.

The physical nature of light has puzzled philosophers and scientists throughout history, and is still not completely understood. The Ancient Greeks believed that vision was due to a "fire" that is emitted by the eyes to strike objects and so reveal their shape. Plato distinguished three kinds or "fire": Daylight from the sun, fire of the same kind emitted by the eye, and fire streaming off objects to interact with the fire emitted from the eyes (see Gregory, 1981). We now know, of course, that the eye does not emit light

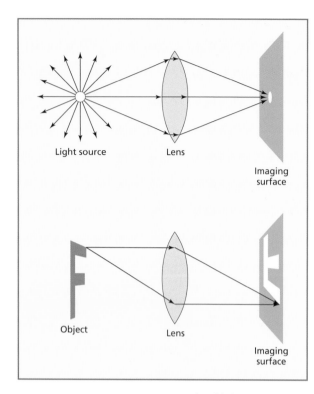

FIGURE 6.1
Image formation by lenses.
Top: Light emanates
from a point source in
all directions. When
some portion of the rays
passes through a lens,
refraction causes the
rays to converge back to
a point. An image of the
point is created on an
appropriately positioned
imaging surface. Bottom:
An extended object can be
considered as a spatially
distributed collection of
points. The lens produces
a spatially distributed
image of the object on the
imaging surface.

but only receives and reflects it, and that light behaves as both a wave and a particle. Issues concerning the nature of light itself have taxed some of the greatest minds in the history of science, including Isaac Newton, Christian Huygens, Max Planck, and Albert Einstein. The following few pages outline the scientific quest to understand the nature of light. If you prefer not to delve into it, skip forward to "Light is a wave *and* a particle."

WHAT IS LIGHT?

Light is a form of radiant energy that is capable of stimulating receptors in the eye and evoking a visual sensation. The behavior of light can be described in three apparently incompatible ways: As rays, as particles, and as waves. One of the major successes of modern theoretical physics has been to resolve the apparent inconsistencies between these descriptions.

LIGHT AS RAYS

Everyday experience tells us that light normally travels in straight lines or rays from a light source at such a high speed that it can be considered instantaneous. Light rays are emitted from a point on a source in all directions (see Figure 6.1). Opaque occluding objects in the path of the rays create well-defined shadows. Light rays are deflected (**refracted**), as they pass from one transmitting medium, such as air, into another, such as glass or water. This behavior is crucial to our understanding of how images can be formed by lenses and mirrors.

Lenses

A suitably shaped lens will refract incident rays emanating from a point so that they converge back to a point after they emerge from the lens. An image of the point on the source is created if an imaging surface is placed at the correct distance from the lens. If the source is a spatially distributed object comprising many points, then the lens will form a spatially distributed image of the object on the imaging surface.

The image will be inverted relative to the object, but it will preserve the topology of the object (the geometrical relations between individual points), as shown in Figure 6.1. The field of geometrical optics provides very precise descriptions of the ray behavior of light. If you would like to know more about geometrical optics, the tutorials section of this chapter provides a more detailed introduction.

LIGHT AS PARTICLES: ISAAC NEWTON

The question of what light rays contain was addressed by Isaac Newton (1642–1727). He believed that light rays were composed of a stream of particles or "corpuscles" that traveled in straight lines. He argued that reflections occurred when these particles bounced off an opaque surface. Refractions occurred as the particles entered a transparent medium at an oblique angle and were deflected in their path. Newton explained the spectrum of colors observed when sunlight is refracted through a prism by supposing that rays of different colors are "differently refrangible" (capable of being refracted).

LIGHT AS WAVES

Christiaan Huygens

Christiaan Huygens (1629–1695), who was a contemporary of Newton in the 1600s, proposed that light propagates from a source in waves similar to water waves. This wave theory was seen as a direct competitor to Newton's particle theory.

Thomas Young

The authority of Newton was such that Huygens' wave theory received little attention for a long period, until a critical experiment was published by Thomas Young in 1801. He passed light through two adjacent slits in an opaque screen, and observed the distinctive striped pattern that appeared on a second screen behind the first (see Figure 6.2, left).

The pattern contained alternating dark and light bands. It seemed, strangely, that when light is added to light it can result in darkness. Young had observed the

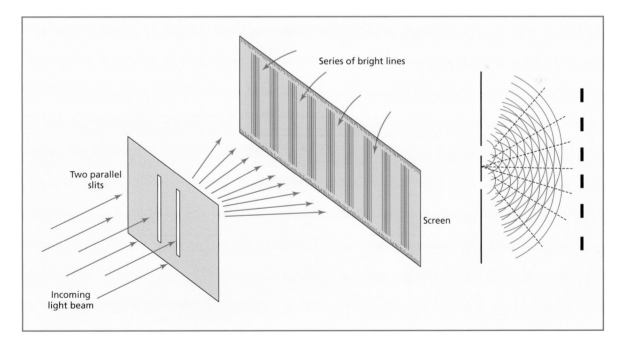

FIGURE 6.2

Young's double-slit experiment. Left: When light is passed through two adjacent slits in a screen, the image formed behind the screen consists of alternating light and dark lines. Right: The lines are created by interference between the two wavefronts emanating from the slits. Where the peaks in the two wavefronts coincide (dotted lines on the right), bright bars are created on the screen. Young's experiment provided strong evidence for the wave properties of light. Copyright © 1982 John Wiley & Sons Limited. Reproduced with permission.

phenomenon now known as **interference**, which can be explained by supposing that light travels in waves. When two wavefronts cross, they can either augment each other to heighten the wave or cancel each other to dampen it out (see Figure 6.2, right), in the same way that water waves can interact to create a bigger wave or to cancel each other out. Notice from Figure 6.2 that as the original wavefront passes through each slit, it spreads laterally to create two new wavefronts. This effect is known as **diffraction**. The concentric circles emanating from each slit in Figure 6.2 (right) represent adjacent peaks in the advancing wavefronts. The radiating lines are drawn along directions in which peaks in the two wavefronts add together (constructive interference). Bright lines appear at locations where these lines strike the screen. In between the lines the waves tend to cancel each other out (destructive interference) because peaks in one wave meet troughs in the other wave.

James Clerk Maxwell

What kind of waves make up light? This question was answered by James Clerk Maxwell's (1831–1879) famous electromagnetic field equations, according to which light waves can be described as transversely oscillating electrical and magnetic fields that propagate at finite speed. Maxwell described light as "an electromagnetic disturbance in the form of waves."

The full **electromagnetic spectrum** of wavelengths extends from wavelengths as small as 10^{-13} m (γ-rays) to wavelengths spanning several kilometers (radio waves), as shown in Figure 6.3. Wavelengths that can stimulate the receptors in the eye to produce a visual sensation occupy only a very narrow band of wavelengths in this spectrum (between 400 and 700 nm). As we shall see later, the wavelength of light is closely associated with visual sensations of color.

THE DUALITY OF LIGHT

By the end of the 19th century, Newton's corpuscular theory had been eclipsed by the electromagnetic wave theory developed by Maxwell. However, a series of major empirical and theoretical developments in the first decade of the 20th century redefined views on the nature of light, and led to the development of quantum mechanics.

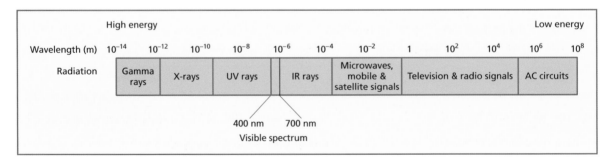

FIGURE 6.3
The electromagnetic spectrum. The wavelength of electromagnetic radiation spans a huge range. The energy associated with the radiation co-varies with wavelength, so very short wavelength gamma rays have extremely high energy. The portion of the spectrum capable of producing a visual sensation occupies a narrow band of wavelengths, from 400 to 700 nm.

Max Planck

At the turn of the century the German physicist Max Planck (1858–1947) was attempting to derive equations which describe the radiation emitted by a black body at different temperatures. He found that his equations worked only if he assumed that the radiation was emitted as a stream of discrete packets or **quanta** of energy. According to Planck's equation, the energy of a quantum is proportional to its frequency, so short wavelength particles such as X-rays are high in energy (this is why they are so damaging when they strike the body).

Philipp Lenard

At about the same time another German physicist, Philipp Lenard (1862–1947), was making empirical observations that were entirely consistent with Planck's quantum theory and inconsistent with wave theory. He reported a phenomenon known as the *photoelectric effect*. He found that electrons can be released from a metal surface when it is struck by light. Observations of the kinetic energy measured in the released electrons did not agree with predictions of the wave theory of light. According to the theory, the energy of a light is proportional to its intensity. This would predict that the kinetic energy of electrons released in the photoelectric effect should be proportional to light intensity. Observations indicated that as light intensity increased more electrons were emitted, but the kinetic energy of each electron remained constant. Changing the frequency of the light, on the other hand, did produce a change in kinetic energy.

Albert Einstein

Albert Einstein (1879–1955) used Planck's notion of quanta to explain the photoelectric effect in a major theoretical paper published in 1905. This paper laid the foundations of the theory of quantum mechanics, according to which light (and indeed all matter) can be considered to be both a stream of particles and a wave.

Light is a wave *and* a particle

How can light be both a particle and a wave? The behavior of light is certainly consistent with both descriptions, since it propagates through space as a wave, which causes interference, yet behaves like discrete particles during emission and absorption. It must be recognized that quanta of light are fundamentally different from the particles that we can see and touch in everyday experience, such as pebbles or grains of sand. Light quanta are submicroscopic units of energy that have no mass and do not even have a well-defined location. Light is a ray, a wave, and a stream of particles.

This story about the fundamental nature of light is relevant here because all three aspects of its behavior are important for understanding visual perception, in different ways:

1. Ray properties are especially useful when attempting to understand how images are formed by optical devices such as eyes, as described in the discussion of geometrical optics in the tutorials section.
2. Wave properties are important when considering the behavior of light at a much finer scale, such as when dealing with passage through small apertures (e.g., the pupil) or along very narrow waveguides (e.g., photoreceptors). Wave or physical optics allows us to understand the blurring effects seen with very small pupils, as described in the tutorial.

Planck's equation is one of the most famous in physics:

$$E = hf$$

Where E is the energy transferred by a quantum, f is the frequency of the quantum, and h is Planck's constant (6.63×10^{-34} Joules).

Einstein published two other theoretical papers in 1905, while working as a clerk in the Swiss Patent Office in Bern. One paper concerned the random motion of small particles, and the other concerned the special theory of relativity. Einstein received a Nobel Prize for his work on the photoelectric effect in 1921. Lenard and Planck also received Nobel Prizes for their work, in 1905 and 1918 respectively.

KEY TERM

Quantum
The smallest discrete unit of energy in which radiation may be emitted or absorbed.

> Light quanta are also known as photons. This term was introduced by Lewis (1926).

3. The quantal nature of light intrudes on visual perception when light intensity is so low that quantum absorptions can be counted individually. Visual sensitivity and resolution in very dim light is limited by "photon noise," discussed later in the chapter.

Both wave and particle models of light can be related to the color sensations produced by light. According to wave theory, color depends on frequency (the frequency of violet light is about twice that of red light). According to particle theory, color depends on energy (violet quanta transfer twice as much energy as red quanta). The two models are related via Planck's equation (see the box). Discussions of color vision generally prefer to use the wave model.

SOME IMPORTANT PROPERTIES OF LIGHT

ABSORPTION, REFLECTION, TRANSMISSION

When light strikes the interface between two substances (e.g., between air and glass), it may be transmitted, absorbed, or reflected, as shown in Figure 6.4. All three fates play a crucial role in vision.

FIGURE 6.4
How light interacts with surfaces. Top: When light strikes an interface between two media, such as air and glass, it may be transmitted, absorbed, or reflected. All three possible events are important for vision. Bottom: Reflections can be either specular (such as those seen in mirrors) or diffuse (such as those seen on rough surfaces like wood and fabric).

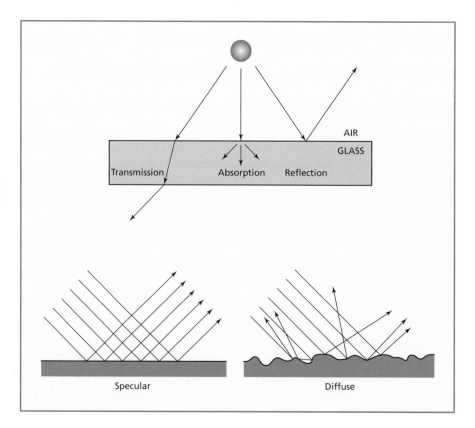

Absorption

During absorption, light quanta are taken up by the substance and converted into thermal energy. Substances that absorb a high proportion of incident radiation, such as dark clothing and black-painted metal, heat up rapidly when exposed to sunlight.

Light must be absorbed by photoreceptors in the eye and converted into electrical signals, otherwise the process of vision cannot begin.

Reflection

During reflection, light rays are scattered backward at the interface between the two surfaces. According to the first law of reflection, rays are reflected so that the angle of incidence equals the angle of reflection. Rays can be reflected in two ways (lower part of Figure 6.4):

* *Specular reflection* occurs when the surface is smooth (irregularities are small relative to the wavelength of light). Light rays are reflected regularly in a predictable direction.
* *Diffuse reflection* occurs when the surface contains larger irregularities. Each ray obeys the law of reflection, but rays are reflected in random directions.

Reflected light is crucial for vision, since it conveys information about the properties of surfaces present in the environment. Specular reflections create mirror-like images and highlights which give us information about smooth, shiny surfaces; diffuse reflections tell us that the surface is rough or textured.

Transmission

During transmission through a medium, quanta of certain wavelengths may be scattered by the molecules they hit. In low-density media such as air, light is scattered laterally. Air molecules scatter light in the blue region of the spectrum, resulting in the bluish appearance of the sky. In dense, uniform media such as glass there is very little lateral scattering, due to destructive interference. Scattering occurs mostly in the forward direction. The interference between the original wave and waves produced by forward scattering results in a retardation of the wavefront as it passes through the medium.

Refraction

An important consequence of the retardation of light during transmission through a medium is *refraction*, a change in the direction of the path of light rays as they enter a transmitting medium obliquely. The degree of change in direction depends on the extent to which the wavefront is retarded, and this in turn depends on the **refractive index** of the transmitting medium. Materials with higher indices retard light more, and consequently produce greater angles of refraction. Air has a refractive index close to 1.0, meaning that light is retarded very little during its transmission. Glass has a refractive index of approximately 1.5, so when light strikes an interface between air and glass it will change direction.

Heat is, of course, radiant energy that is re-emitted from the hot surface in the infrared region of the spectrum. In a greenhouse, or a car, short wavelength sunlight heats up the interior, but the glass of the greenhouse or vehicle is opaque to the infrared heat radiation, trapping the energy inside. A similar effect occurs when sunlight enters the Earth's atmosphere and heats the surface of the Earth—hence the "greenhouse effect."

? *Think about why your vision is blurred under water.*

KEY TERM

Refractive index
The ratio of the velocity of propagation of an electromagnetic wave in a vacuum to its velocity in a given transmitting medium.

FIGURE 6.5
Refraction. When rays of light from a wavefront strike a transmitting medium such as glass obliquely, their direction of travel is deflected (refracted) due to the retardation in the wavefront. When parallel rays strike two glass prisms, they begin converging when they emerge from the prisms. This illustrates the basic principle behind image formation by lenses.

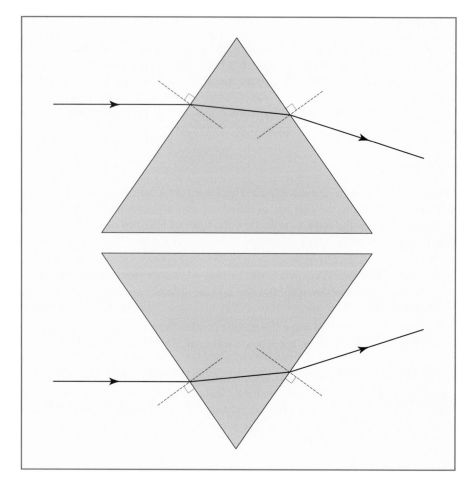

Refraction is a crucial property of light for vision, because it is the principle underlying the formation of images by lenses. Figure 6.5 shows two glass prisms receiving parallel light rays. Due to refraction, as the light rays enter and leave the glass, the rays converge when they exit the prisms. This effect illustrates the basic principle underlying the ability of lenses to form images, as seen in Figure 6.1 earlier. The surface of the lens is curved so that parallel light rays entering the lens from a distant point will converge on a point behind the lens. The distance of this point of focus from the lens defines the lens's **focal length**. Further details can be found in the tutorials section later in the chapter.

INTENSITY

The intensity of a light source ultimately depends on the number of quanta it emits per unit of time. A range of physical units, known as **radiometric** units, has been developed to measure intensity. However, the effectiveness of light quanta as a stimulus for vision depends on their wavelength, since the human visual system is more sensitive to some wavelengths than to others. So, in the context of vision, light intensity is usually specified in **photometric** units that take account of human sensitivity. The most commonly used unit is "candelas per square meter" (abbreviated to cd/m², or equivalently cd/m⁻²), which measures the intensity of the light emanating from a surface relative to that of a standard light. Further details on different measures of light intensity can be found in the tutorials section.

Table 6.1 gives typical **luminance** values (in cd/m²) for a piece of white paper under four illumination levels (based on data in Makous, 1998, and Land & Nilsson, 2002). Corresponding numbers of photons emitted per second are shown in the fifth column, calculated according to formulae given in the tutorials section. Photons are shown as log values, so "15" in the table corresponds to 10^{15} photons. Light intensities experienced by organisms living on the surface of the Earth seem very high indeed when measured in terms of quanta emitted. Even viewed in moonlight, white paper emits 10^{15} quanta per second (10^6 is a million) over a fixed area known as a steradian (defined in the tutorials section). In sunlight the paper emits nearly a million times more quanta.

One might assume that quanta are so plentiful in most conditions that quantum catch by the eye has little bearing on visual perception. However, it is important and instructive to consider natural light intensities in terms of the number of quanta available for vision. As we shall see below, the human eye responds to light by means of many photoreceptor cells distributed around its inner surface. Light reaches the receptors after passing through the various optical components of the eye (cornea, pupil, lens, intraocular fluids). Column 6 of Table 6.1 estimates the number of quanta hitting each receptor per second at the different light levels (based on Land & Nilsson's, 2002, estimate that quantal numbers are reduced by a factor of 10^{15} when one takes into account the optics and dimensions of photoreceptors). In bright conditions, each photoreceptor receives 100,000 quanta per second. In the dimmest borderline conditions that can support human vision, each receptor receives only 0.0001 quanta per second. In other words, many minutes may elapse between successive strikes on any one receptor. The quantal nature of light thus becomes an important issue at low light levels (individual photoreceptors are capable of responding to individual quantum strikes).

We can see from Table 6.1 that the visual diet experienced by an organism on Earth spans a very wide range (increasing by a factor of 100,000,000 from the lowest

KEY TERM

Luminance
A photometric measure of the energy emitted or reflected by an extended light source, in candelas per square meter of surface (cd/m⁻²).

? *Why do so few photons reach each photoreceptor, relative to the number entering the eye?*

TABLE 6.1 Luminance properties of paper at four light levels

1 Source	2 Luminance (cd/m²)	3 Pupil diameter (mm)	4 Retinal luminance (log td)	5 Log photons/ m²/sr/s	6 Photons per receptor per second	7 Visual range
Absolute threshold	0.000001	7.1	−4.3	11	0.0001	
	0.0001	6.6	−2.4	12	0.001	Scotopic (rods only)
Paper in starlight	0.0003	6.4	−1.9	13	0.01	
	0.01	5.5	−0.5	14	0.1	Mesopic
Paper in moonlight	0.2	4.5	0.6	15	1	(rods and
	1	4.0	1.2	16	10	cones)
Paper in room light	100	2.4	2.8	18	1,000	
	10,000	2.0	4.6	19	10,000	
Paper in sunlight	40,000	2.0	5.2	20	100,000	Photopic (cones
	1,000,000	2.0	6.6	21	1,000,000	only)
Damage possible	100,000,000	2.0	8.6	23	100,000,000	

levels detectable to levels high enough to cause damage). At any one instant a single photoreceptor can respond to light over a tiny fraction of this range of intensities (roughly two rows of the table; this range is known as "dynamic range"). Yet humans can see adequately both by starlight and in the midday sun. How, then, does the visual system cope successfully with such a huge range of light levels? Fortunately, we are not exposed to the full range all at once. At any one moment the intensity in a scene, from the darkest shadow to the brightest surface, varies only by a factor of less than 1 in 100 (see below), a tiny fraction of the full range available on Earth. As one moves from well-shaded, interior, or night-time conditions into bright outdoor conditions, the relatively narrow range of light levels experienced slides up the intensity scale. The visual system possesses mechanisms that adjust the dynamic range of photoreceptors so that it too slides up and down the intensity range, and thus receptor responses remain well matched to prevailing illumination conditions. This process of adjustment is known as light and dark adaptation, and is discussed in detail in Chapter 8.

The proportion of incident light reflected by a surface is known as **reflectance**. Highly reflecting surfaces appear whitish, and have values approaching unity. Snow, for example, has a reflectance of 0.93, whereas newspaper has a reflectance of 0.38 (Makous, 1998). Surfaces with reflectance values approaching zero appear very dark.

CONTRAST AND REFLECTANCE

Unless the observer looks directly at a light source (not recommended in the case of the sun, as it is likely to result in permanent eye damage), the pattern of light and dark entering the eye is due to reflections from surfaces in the scene. Some surfaces reflect a very high proportion of the light that strikes them. For example, white paper reflects approximately 75% of the incident light. Other surfaces absorb a high proportion of the incident light. Black paper and paint, for instance, reflect only 5% of the incident light. Black velvet reflects about 2%.

Consequently, even in a scene containing the extreme combination of both black velvet and white paper, intensity will vary only by a factor of 1 in 38 (the paper will reflect 38 times more light than the velvet). A useful and very widely used measure of relative luminance in patterned scenes is Michelson Contrast, sometimes abbreviated to "**contrast**" (C), it is defined as:

$$C = (L_{max} - L_{min})/(L_{max} + L_{min})$$

? *Think about why luminance is less informative about objects than contrast.*

where L_{max} is the higher luminance value and L_{min} is the lower luminance value. Contrast can vary between 0 and 1.

It is very important to realize that contrast is independent of the absolute level of illumination and (in the absence of variations in illumination such as shadows) is determined by surface reflectance. For example, let's assume that you have a sample of black velvet and a piece of white paper and are viewing them in moonlight: L_{max} corresponds to the luminance of the paper, 0.2 cd/m^{-2}; L_{min} corresponds to the luminance of the velvet, 0.0053 cd/m^{-2}. The contrast between the paper and the velvet is 0.948, according to the equation above. When viewed in sunlight, the luminances of the paper and velvet are 40,000 cd/m^{-2} and 1066.7 cd/m^{-2} respectively. Contrast is again 0.948.

KEY TERMS

Reflectance
The proportion of incident light reflected from a surface.

Contrast
A measure of the difference between the highest luminance and the lowest luminance emitted or reflected from a surface.

Absolute luminance tells us about the power of the illuminating light source, but is uninformative about the properties of surfaces, whereas contrast provides information about surface reflectance. So the initial stages of neural processing in the visual system are specialized to encode contrast but discard information about absolute luminance.

WAVELENGTH

Humans are able to detect wavelengths in the spectral region between 400 nm and 700 nm. Wavelength is correlated with sensory impressions of color. Moving down the wavelength scale from 700 to 400 nm, color varies through the following sequence: red–orange–yellow–green–blue–indigo–violet. The acronym ROYGBIV is sometimes used as a mnemonic. The wavelength composition of light actually reflected from a surface depends jointly on the spectral power distribution of the illuminating light and the spectral reflectance of the surface, and our impression of color depends on wavelength in a complex way. Chapter 8 discusses color vision in detail.

Spectral power distribution of light sources

Commonly experienced light sources emit radiation across a broad spectrum of wavelengths. Figure 6.6 plots relative energy as a function of wavelength (spectral power distribution) for sunlight and for an incandescent lamp. The vertical lines mark the limits of the visible spectrum. Notice from Figure 6.6 that incandescent lamps such as those once widely used in domestic lighting have much more energy in the yellow–red end of the spectrum than daylight.

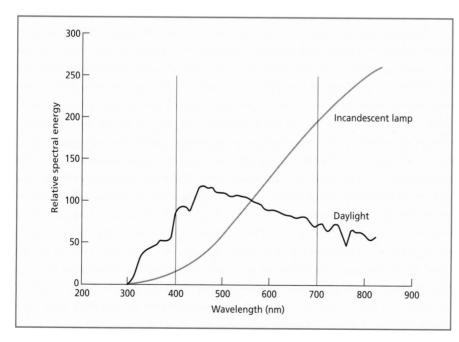

FIGURE 6.6
Emission spectra of two common light sources, the sun and an incandescent lamp (domestic lightbulb). Vertical lines represent the borders of the visible spectrum. Daylight has a peak in energy at wavelengths in the short wavelength region (450 nm) that appears bluish to humans, whereas lamps emit more and more energy at higher wavelengths that appear yellowy–red (graphs based on CIE standard illuminants A and D$_{65}$).

FIGURE 6.7
Spectral reflectance functions of several familiar surfaces. Notice that some surfaces such as snow reflect a much higher proportion of incident radiation than other surfaces. In addition, the preponderance of different wavelengths in the reflected energy varies between surfaces. Grass, for example, has a peak in the green part of the spectrum (550 nm) (adapted from Wyszecki & Stiles, 1982).

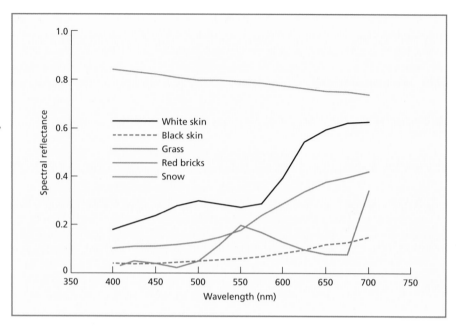

Spectral reflectance functions

Surface reflectance (the proportion of incident light reflected) generally varies as a function of wavelength to define the surface's spectral reflectance function. Figure 6.7 plots **spectral reflectance functions** for a range of surfaces. Snow reflects a high proportion of light at all wavelengths, whereas grass absorbs light quite efficiently at most wavelengths. Notice the distinct peak in the reflectance of grass at wavelengths in the green region of the spectrum. Natural surfaces tend to have smooth, slowly changing reflectance functions, and generally reflect more light at longer wavelengths than at shorter wavelengths.

Spectral power distribution of reflective surfaces

As stated earlier, the spectral power distribution of light reflected from a surface depends jointly on the spectral power distribution of the illuminating light source (often called "illuminant"; e.g., Figure 6.6), and the surface's reflectance function (e.g., Figure 6.7). The two functions are multiplied, wavelength by wavelength, to arrive at the power distribution of the reflected light. Changes in the power distribution of the illuminant can therefore result in marked changes in the power distribution of light reflected from a surface. Surfaces viewed under artificial light, for instance, reflect much more energy in the yellow region of the spectrum than when viewed under daylight, due to the marked differences in incident energy shown in Figure 6.6. However, our perception of surface color tends to remain constant in the face of such changes. This phenomenon is known as *color constancy*, and is discussed in detail in Chapter 8.

THE EYE

The eye is the peripheral organ of vision. Its function is to catch photons and direct them onto photoreceptors in order to begin the process of vision. Animals have evolved a huge variety of organs that respond to light, only some of which can be

KEY TERM

Spectral reflectance function
The proportion of light reflected from a surface as a function of the wavelength of the incident light.

classed as eyes. Some invertebrates such as worms have isolated receptors distributed on the surface of their skin. The minimum qualification for such an organ to be called an eye is that it must form some kind of image on a sheet of photoreceptors. Images are vital for effective vision because they preserve the spatial arrangement of the points in space from which the light rays emanated. With suitable neural processing, a great deal of information about the structure of the world can be extracted from images, as we shall discover in the rest of the book.

STRUCTURE OF THE HUMAN EYE

Humans, in common with other mammals, birds, and reptiles, have single-chambered eyes. Figure 6.8 shows the main structures of the human eye. It is a roughly spherical, light-tight chamber about 24 mm in diameter, about three quarters of the inside surface of which is lined with a sheet of photoreceptors known as the retina. An opening in the chamber, covered by a transparent membrane, admits light.

The transparent membrane, known as the cornea, is about 12 mm in diameter and 0.55 mm thick at its center. Having passed through the **cornea** and into the anterior chamber behind, incoming light then enters an aperture known as the **pupil**. The pupil is formed by a muscular diaphragm known as the iris (idiosyncratic pigmentation in the iris determines eye color, and is increasingly used as a form of identification). After passing through the lens, situated behind the pupil, light travels through the posterior chamber before striking the photoreceptor sheet, known as the retina. The structure of the retina is very complex, and will be described in detail in the next chapter.

The two chambers of the eye on either side of the lens are filled with two substances, vitreous humor and aqueous humor. Vitreous humor is a viscous gel that fills the large posterior chamber of the eye, maintaining its shape and holding the retina against the inner wall. The watery aqueous humor is pumped into the eye continuously, entering the eye near the

KEY TERMS

Cornea
The transparent membrane through which light enters a single-chambered eye.

Pupil
The circular aperture formed by a muscular diaphragm in the eye, through which light passes after entering the cornea.

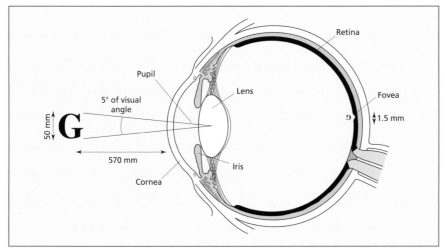

FIGURE 6.8
Major components of the human eye. Dimensions are also shown for the image produced by a 50 mm tall letter viewed at a distance of 570 mm (similar to a large newspaper headline viewed at arm's length). The angle subtended by the letter at the nodal point of the eye is 5°. The retinal image of the letter is 1.5 mm tall, and spans approximately 500 photoreceptors.

Abnormally high pressure in the eye is known as glaucoma, often caused by blocked outflow of aqueous humor. If untreated, glaucoma causes permanent loss of vision, because the increased pressure impedes blood flow into the eye.

attachment of the lens to the eye (called ciliary processes) and leaving near the margins of the iris (canal of Schlemm). It flows in both the small anterior chamber (behind the cornea) and the main posterior chamber. Rate of flow is such that the entire volume of the fluid is replenished approximately every 45 minutes. The functions of the aqueous humor are to nourish the lens and to keep the eye inflated. If the outward flow of aqueous humor is impeded in some way, fluid pressure in the eye can build up to cause a disorder known as glaucoma, in which pressure on nerve fibers in the eye causes damage which compromises sight.

VISUAL ANGLE

How should we measure the size of an object? Linear size in millimeters or inches is obviously the most appropriate measure for most everyday situations, such as when deciding whether a given item of furniture will fit into an available space in your home. However, when studying the images of objects as stimuli for vision, the relevant measure gives the size of the image projected onto the retina. The most frequently used measure is **visual angle**, which corresponds to the angle formed or subtended by the object at the center (nodal point) of the lens. Visual angle depends jointly on the size of the object and its viewing distance; a small object such as a coin held just a few centimeters from the eye projects a relatively large image on the retina, whereas a very large object such as the moon viewed from a great distance projects a relatively small image. If visual angle is relatively small (10° or less) it can be calculated easily from trigonometry using the formula:

$$\tan \theta = s/d$$

where θ is visual angle, s is object size, and d is viewing distance. One degree is divided into 60 minutes (abbreviated to 60′, and one minute is divided into 60 seconds (abbreviated to 60″). So 0.25° can also be expressed as an arc of 15′, and 0.01° can be expressed as 36″ of arc.

A one pound or one euro coin (diameter 2.25 centimeters) viewed from 60 centimeters (about arm's length) subtends a visual angle of arctan (2.25/60) = 2.15 degrees at the eye. The moon (diameter 3476 kilometers) is a vastly larger object, but is normally viewed from a very large distance; it is 378,000 kilometers from the Earth, and so subtends a visual angle of only 0.53 deg at the eye. A pound or euro coin would have to be positioned 225 centimeters from the eye in order to subtend 0.53 deg. At this distance it would just be large enough to occlude your view of the moon, so creating your own lunar eclipse.

The significance of the nodal point of the lens lies in the fact that light rays pass through it without being refracted (because they strike the surface of the lens at right-angles so are not deflected in their path). So the angle subtended by the image on the retina is equal to the angle subtended by the object at the nodal point.

It is sometimes useful to convert the angular size of an image on the retina into linear units, typically millimeters. For a given visual angle the further away the retina is from the lens (in other words, the larger the eye), the larger will be the retinal image in linear units. In the case of human eyes, one degree of visual angle is equal to approximately 0.288 mm on the retina. The issue of eye size is discussed in more detail later in the chapter. Retinal image size will be specified in either angular or linear units or both in the remainder of this chapter, as appropriate.

? *Which would be preferable, a television 50 cm wide viewed from 3 m away, or a cinema screen 6 m wide viewed from 40 m?*

KEY TERM

Visual angle
The angle an object subtends at the center of a lens; it is used to measure the size of an object as a stimulus for vision.

To give an example, Figure 6.8 depicts a letter G and the image it projects onto the retina. Values given correspond to a 50 mm tall headline in a newspaper viewed at approximately arm's length (570 mm). The letter subtends a visual angle of 5°, and projects an image 1.5 mm tall on the retina. The width of a thumb held at arm's length corresponds to an image occupying approximately 2° of visual angle on the retina.

OPTICAL PROPERTIES OF THE EYE

Cornea and lens

Optical power

Refraction occurs at an interface between media having different refractive indices. In the case of the eye, refraction occurs at four surfaces, namely:

* Anterior (front) corneal surface
* Posterior (back) corneal surface
* Front surface of the lens
* Rear surface of the lens.

The combined effect of these surfaces is to create an optical system with a focal length of 16.8 mm. This means that in a normal, relaxed eye the image of a distant object will fall into focus 16.8 mm behind the center of the lens system, a distance that corresponds precisely to the location of the retina. A lens's optical power refers to its ability to converge or diverge light rays. As discussed in detail in the tutorials section, optical power is conventionally expressed in **diopters** (D), which correspond to (1/focal length in meters). A lens with high optical power has a short focal length, expressed as a large value of D. Converging lens systems, like that in the eye, have positive power because they converge light rays; diverging lens systems have negative power. The power of the eye's optical system is therefore ($1/16.8 \times 10^{-3}$), or 59.52 D. Spectacle prescriptions add or subtract a small amount of power to correct for errors of accommodation, discussed in the next section.

The degree of refraction at an interface between two media depends on the difference in refractive index of the media, as described in the tutorial. The refractive indices of air, cornea, ocular fluid, and the lens are 1.009, 1.376, 1.336, and 1.413 respectively. We can therefore see that the greatest degree of refraction in the eye's optical system occurs at the interface between air and the cornea, because of the large difference in refractive index. In fact, approximately 48 D of the eye's optical power is contributed by refraction at the anterior surface of the cornea.

Accommodation

Although the optical power of the eye is sufficient to focus parallel rays from far objects on the retina, diverging rays from near objects come into focus behind the retina. There are two ways to bring the image back into focus on the retina. The first is to move the lens further away from the retina. Certain fish (and cameras) adopt this strategy. The alternative is to increase the optical power of

KEY TERM

Diopter
A measure of the refractive power of a lens; it corresponds to (1/f) where f is its focal length in meters.

KEY TERMS

Accommodation
The process by which the shape of the eye's lens is changed to alter its focal length.

Presbyopia
The age-related change in accommodative range, resulting from loss of flexibility in the lens.

Myopia
A condition in which the refractive power of the eye's lens is too great, causing the image of distant objects to be de-focused.

Hyperopia
A condition in which the refractive power of the eye's lens is too weak, causing the image of near objects to be defocused.

How can presbyopia be treated?

What kinds of lenses must spectacles contain?

the lens. This latter strategy is adopted by reptiles, birds, and mammals, including humans. The lens is deformable, and ciliary muscles located around the margins of the lens where it attaches to the eye can adjust its shape to accommodate objects at different distances. The process of focusing is actually known as **accommodation**. So-called zonular fibers attach the lens to the ciliary muscles. When the muscles are relaxed, intraocular pressure stretches the zonular fibers, which in turn pull the lens into a thin shape. In this shape the lens has a focal length of 59.52 D, appropriate for far objects. When the muscles are tense, they relieve the pressure on the zonular fibers, which allows the lens to relax into a thicker shape with a shorter focal length. In young healthy eyes accommodation can increase the optical power of the eye by up to approximately 8 D, allowing objects as close as 250 mm to be brought into focus. This distance is known as the *near point*. Lens flexibility declines with age, so that the near point moves progressively further away. Beyond the age of 50 there is typically little scope for accommodation left, a condition known as **presbyopia** (see Glasser & Campbell, 1998).

Accommodative errors Two kinds of error are commonly found. The optical power of the eye can be either too great or too weak, given the size of the eye, resulting in image blur at the retina.

- **Myopia**, or short-sight, occurs when the optical power is too great. Rays from distant objects come into focus in front of the retina, and accommodation is no help because it increases optical power and brings the point of focus even further forward. Near objects do fall into focus without accommodative effort, which is required only for very near distances.
- **Hyperopia**, or long-sight, occurs when the optical power is too weak. Rays from distant objects come into focus behind the retina. In this case accommodation does help, but it comes into play at distances that should not normally require it.

Both kinds of accommodative error can be corrected in two ways. The traditional solution is to wear corrective lenses, either as spectacles or as contact lenses, which add or subtract optical power to remove the error. A more recent solution, known as *photorefractive keratectomy*, is to shave a very small amount of material from the surface of the cornea using a laser. This has the effect of altering the radius of curvature of the cornea in such a way as to alter the optical power of the cornea and correct the accommodative error.

Pupil

The diameter of the pupil varies between approximately 7 mm and 2 mm as light level drops from the highest to the lowest levels perceptible, as shown in column 3 of Table 6.1. The resultant change in area equates to a sixteenfold variation in retinal illumination. Since this is an insignificant fraction of the range of illumination levels experienced on Earth, as shown in Table 6.1, we can safely assume that the function of the pupil is not solely to control retinal illumination. Its function may be more subtle, in regulating the balance that must be struck between maximizing the eye's sensitivity and retaining its resolution (ability to resolve detail), as explained later in the chapter.

Pupil size is influenced by emotional responses. Initial studies suggested that large pupils are associated with positive or pleasurable emotions, whereas small pupils are associated with negative emotions (Hess and Polt, 1960). However more recent research paints a more complex picture. Pupils dilate (grow larger) in response to arousing images, regardless of whether they are perceived as pleasant or unpleasant (Bradley et al., 2008).

> Other old studies (e.g., Hess, 1975) also claim that large pupils make female faces appear more attractive, perhaps because they indicate an interest in the viewer.

Photoreceptors

The retina of each eye contains over 100 million photoreceptor cells, responsible for converting light energy into neural activity (transduction). Each photoreceptor is a long, thin tube consisting of an outer segment that contains light-sensitive pigment and an inner segment that in effect forms the cell body. A detailed discussion of how photoreceptors achieve transduction will be postponed until the next chapter. The discussion here will concentrate on the optical properties of photoreceptors.

Rods and cones

Human photoreceptors fall into two classes, called **rods** and **cones** on the basis of the shape of their outer segments. Rods and cones differ in several important respects:

> Curiously, there is a cone-rich rim at the extreme edge of the retina, where the far lateral periphery of the visual field is imaged; it may form part of a rapid early warning mechanism (Williams, 1991).

- They contain different light-sensitive pigments (discussed in the next chapter). Rod pigment is very sensitive at low light levels. Cones are 30–100 times less sensitive, so function only at high light levels.
- There are far more rods in each eye (approximately 120,000,000) than cones (approximately 6,000,000).
- They differ in width, length, and retinal distribution. An important landmark on the retina is the *fovea*, a small pit at the optical center of the retina, 1.5 mm (5.2°) wide. The central area or *foveola* (0.5 mm or 1.7° wide) is entirely devoid of rods and contains only cones (more details below).

As column 7 of Table 6.1 indicates, rods operate at light levels ranging from the lowest detectable to bright moonlight. Cones operate at all levels down to starlight. So at the lowest light levels (known as "scotopic"), vision is served only by rods; at the highest "photopic" light levels vision is served only by cones; and at intermediate levels corresponding to dusk and bright starlight, both photoreceptor classes operate (mesopic vision).

KEY TERMS

Rod
A type of photoreceptor that is specialized to respond at low light levels.

Cone
A type of photoreceptor that is specialized to respond at high light levels.

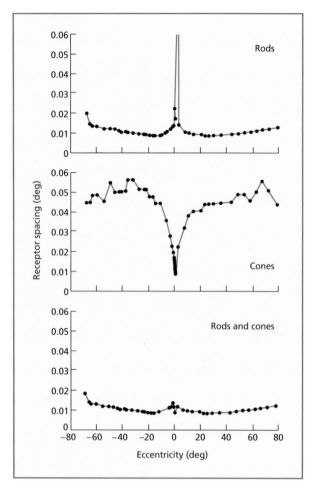

FIGURE 6.9
Distance between adjacent photoreceptors in the human retina as a function of retinal position for rods, cones, and all receptors combined. Cones are concentrated in the fovea, where no rods are found. Taking both receptor types together, spacing remains fairly stable across the retina (data taken from Osterberg, 1935, which were expressed as photoreceptors per square mm; the data plotted were calculated as the square root of his values, to give an approximate value for spacing).

? *How well would a miniature person, say 20 cm tall, be able to see?*

Photoreceptor width

The light-sensitive portion of each cone has a diameter of approximately 1–4 micrometers (μm) in the fovea, and 4–10 μm outside the fovea. Rods have a diameter of 1 μm near the fovea (Wandell, 1995). The width of each photoreceptor obviously imposes a limit on the spacing between adjacent photoreceptors. Spacing, in turn, determines the ability of the retina to resolve detail. As we shall see shortly, reducing the spacing between receptors (packing them more densely across the retina) increases their ability to resolve fine spatial detail. So why are the photoreceptors not narrower still? The answer to this question lies in the wave properties of light. If the width of a photoreceptor becomes so narrow that it approaches the wavelength of visible light (0.4–0.7 μm) the receptor becomes unable to retain light by total internal reflection. Instead, some of the light spills out through the sides of the photoreceptor, and excites adjacent receptors. This "cross-talk" between receptors reduces the effective resolution of the retinal mosaic, because each photoreceptor's response depends not just on the light striking it, but also on the light striking its neighbors. There is consequently nothing to be gained in terms of resolution from having photoreceptors narrower than 1 μm, and indeed none have been found in the eyes of any animal.

Photoreceptor length

The light-sensitive portion of each human cone is up to 80 μm long in the fovea and 40 μm long outside the fovea; rods are 60 μm long (Wandell, 1995). The proportion of incident light absorbed by a photoreceptor depends on its length. Inside the fovea, cones absorb up to 50% of incident light. Outside the fovea, cones absorb 33% of incident light. Rods absorb 42% of incident light (see Warrant & Nilsson, 1998).

Photoreceptor spacing

Figure 6.9 plots photoreceptor spacing for cones, for rods, and for both combined, as a function of retinal location. Cone spacing is smallest in the fovea—0.003 mm (0.01°, or 0.6′ arc). Moving outside the fovea, cone spacing increases fourfold to approximately 0.013 mm (0.045°, or 2.7′ arc), while rod spacing is 0.003 mm (0.01°, or 0.6′ arc). Taking both classes of photoreceptor together, Figure 6.9 indicates that the distance separating adjacent receptors is surprisingly stable across the entire retinal surface, at a value (3 μm) approaching the minimum available given the wavelengths of visible light.

Resolution and sensitivity

The *resolution* of the eye is its ability to pick out fine spatial details in the retinal image. *Sensitivity* refers to the eye's ability to detect light at very low illumination levels. Both aspects of performance are important for vision; adequate sensitivity is important for us to see anything at all, whereas high resolution is crucial for our ability to see spatial detail. These two goals place quite different, indeed conflicting, demands on the optical components of the eye.

KEY TERM

Grating
A pattern of alternating light and dark bars, widely used in vision research.

Resolution

Figure 6.10 illustrates how photoreceptor spacing limits the resolution of the receptor array. It shows a black-and-white test image (upper left) along with corresponding patterns superimposed on three imaginary retinal mosaics with different receptor spacing. Each circle represents an individual photoreceptor.

The test image includes a **grating** consisting of alternating black and white bars, and a "C" like broken circle. Gratings are used very frequently to assess spatial resolution, for reasons that will become clear in Chapter 9. Notice that the finest mosaic (top right) can represent both the grating pattern and the broken circle faithfully. The coarsest mosaic (bottom right) cannot resolve individual grating bars, and provides only a very crude rendition of the broken circle. Mathematical procedures allow us to calculate the finest grating bars that can be resolved by a given photoreceptor spacing. In simple

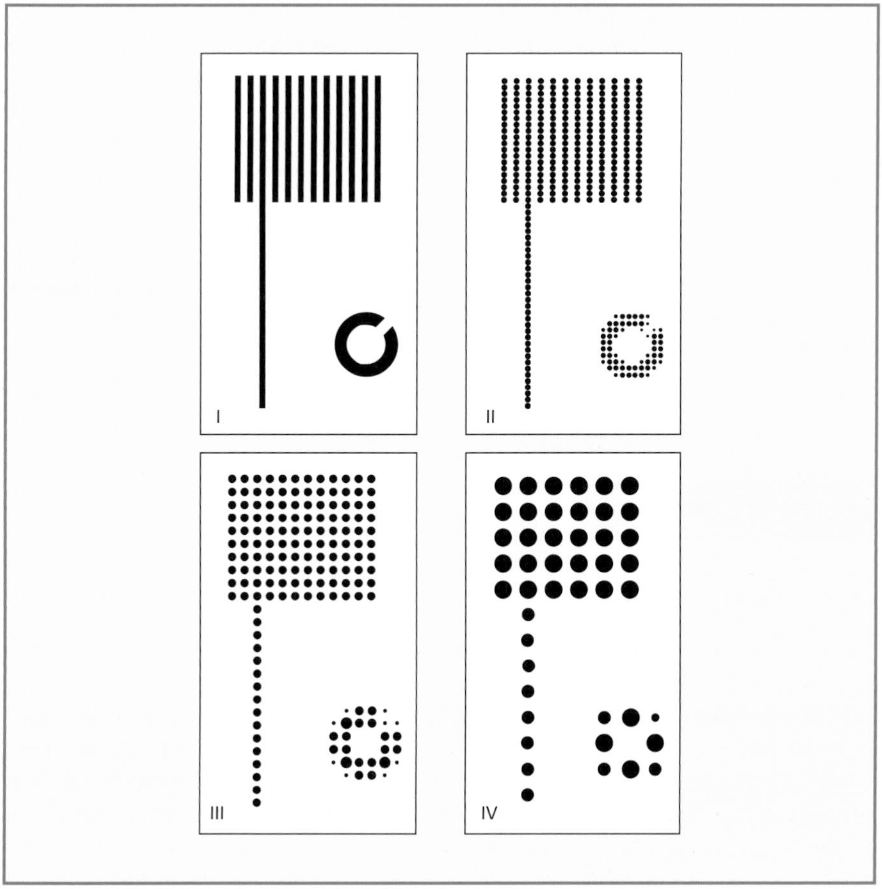

FIGURE 6.10
Effect of receptor spacing on the resolution of the receptor array. The stimulus pattern (top left) consists of a vertical grating and a broken circle. This pattern was superimposed on retinal mosaics at three different spacings: small (top right), medium (bottom left), and large (bottom right). Each circle represents a receptor positioned over an element of the pattern. Small receptor spacing permit a faithful rendition of the pattern on the array of receptors—all grating bars and the break in the circle are available. At the largest receptor spacing individual grating bars cannot be resolved, and the break in the circle is highly degraded (redrawn from Pirenne, 1948). Used with permission of Taylor & Francis, Inc.

terms, the bars of a grating can be resolved faithfully if each adjacent light and dark bar falls on a separate receptor. Each pair of light and dark bars constitutes one cycle of the grating pattern. So there must be at least two receptors per grating cycle in order to accurately represent the grating (the so-called Nyquist limit). With fewer receptors it is not possible to represent all the bars of the grating faithfully, indeed it is likely that the grating will appear to have a different bar spacing (frequency). This phenomenon is known as "spatial aliasing" (an alias of the grating frequency is available to the receptor array, not the correct frequency itself). Within the upper bound set by the Nyquist limit, the acuity of the human visual system is actually remarkably high; so high in fact that it is sometimes called "hyperacuity." Chapter 9 discusses the neural processing which allows the system to perform so well.

Photoreceptor spacing is limited by photoreceptor width which, in turn, is limited by the wavelengths of the visible spectrum. Once the minimum photoreceptor width is achieved, the only other way to increase the resolving power of the retina is to increase the size of the image. Larger images allow greater detail to be resolved because they are sampled by more photoreceptors. Larger images require larger eyes, since image size or **magnification** is a function of focal length (as mentioned earlier; see the tutorials section at the end of the chapter). In the case of the human eye (focal length 16.8 mm), an object 50 mm tall viewed from a distance of 570 mm (such as the headline in a newspaper held at arm's length; see Figure 6.8) would cast an image 1.5 mm tall on the retina. This image would span 500 photoreceptors. An eye half the size of the human eye would produce an image half as tall, spanning half as many photoreceptors (assuming constant photoreceptor spacing).

Interreceptor spacing Receptor spacing (s) and eye size or focal length (f) jointly determine the **interreceptor angle** ($\Delta\Phi = s/f$). This angle is the defining feature of the eye's resolving power. For example, eyes with an interreceptor angle $\Delta\Phi$ of 0.01° can accurately resolve successive dark bars in a grating no closer than 0.02° before aliasing sets in, corresponding to a grating spatial frequency of 50 cycles per degree of visual angle (abbreviated to cpd). Assuming that photoreceptor spacing is close to its optical limit, resolution is governed by eye size. Other things being equal, animals with small eyes have less acute vision than animals with large eyes. Cats, for example, have poorer spatial resolution than humans.

Sensitivity

Sensitivity is limited by **photon noise**, as Figure 6.11 illustrates. It shows an array of 400 photoreceptors (small circles), receiving an image of a central dark disk (large circle) on a light background. Each white small circle represents a photon strike on a receptor. At high illumination levels (IV, bottom right), photon strikes define the image accurately. As light level falls toward the absolute threshold for vision (I, upper left), the image becomes less distinct due to the uncertainty associated with individual photon strikes (photon noise).

Retinal illumination at low light levels naturally depends on pupil diameter; wider pupils catch more photons. Some species have eyes capable of very large pupil diameters, which have an advantage in terms of sensitivity since they admit more light. Image degradation due to lens imperfections at wide apertures

---

KEY TERMS

Magnification
The size of the image produced by a lens; it depends on the focal length of the lens.

Interreceptor angle
The visual angle between two neighboring photoreceptors; it determines the resolving power of the eye.

Photon noise
The inherent natural variation in the rate at which photons strike a receiving surface such as the retina.

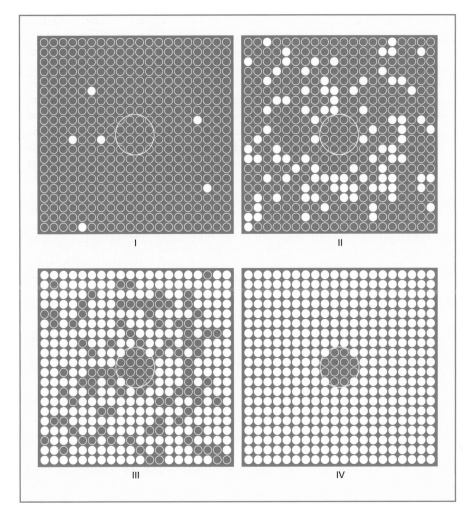

FIGURE 6.11
Effect of photon noise on acuity. The small circles represent locations of individual photoreceptors, with white circles representing active receptors. The large circle in the center of each panel shows the position of a large dark disk presented as an image against a white background for a short time. The four panels represent photoreceptor responses at four different light levels. Under extremely dim illumination (top left), when few photons are emitted, the probability that any one receptor will be struck by a photon is very low. Just six active receptors are shown. As illumination level and photon numbers rise, the probability of activity in each receptor also rises. At the highest level (bottom right), so many photons are emitted that all receptors are activated by the light region of the image. The ability of the photoreceptor mosaic to resolve the pattern at low light levels therefore depends on the number of photons emitted, not on the fineness of the mosaic or blur in the image (redrawn from Pirenne, 1948). Used with permission of Taylor & Francis, Inc.

is not an issue, since resolution is limited by photon noise as Figure 6.11 illustrates. At higher illumination levels there are so many photons available that photon noise is no longer relevant. In these conditions smaller pupil diameters are called for in order to minimize the deleterious effects of lens imperfections. A pupil diameter of 2–3 mm is considered to be optimal for retinal image quality. Pupil diameters smaller than 2 mm suffer increased blur due to the effects of diffraction. At diameters greater than 3 mm the effects of **chromatic** and **spherical aberration** become more pronounced (a detailed discussion of diffraction and aberrations can be found in the tutorials section).

Optimal eye size

The foregoing discussion would suggest that both resolution and sensitivity are best served by larger eyes, which have the smallest possible interreceptor angles and large maximum pupil diameters. This observation begs the question—why are human eyes

---

KEY TERMS

Chromatic aberration
The property of an optical system that causes light rays at different wavelengths to be focused in different planes, so degrading the image.

Spherical aberration
The failure of light rays striking all parts of a lens to converge in the same focal plane, so degrading the image.

not larger than 24 mm in diameter? Eyes are expensive organs, because they occupy a significant amount of space in the head (especially in small animals), and they consume a large amount of energy. It has been estimated, for example, that 10% of the oxygen consumption of a walking fly is devoted to phototransduction (Laughlin, de Ruyter van Stevenınck, & Anderson, 1998). It therefore makes sense for eyes to be no larger than strictly necessary given the visual requirements of their host. Once the eyes have achieved the level of resolution required by their host in order to catch prey, avoid predators, and so on, pressures on energy consumption and cranial space limit further increases in eye size. Nocturnal and deep-sea dwelling animals have the largest eyes, in the interests of maximizing sensitivity at low levels of ambient illumination. Deep-sea squid possess the largest eyes of all, with a diameter of 40 cm (Land & Nilsson, 2002).

Rods versus cones

The relatively constant spacing of rods and cones combined (Figure 6.9) might lead one to expect that our ability to resolve detail is also constant across the retina. However, as mentioned earlier, rods and cones operate at different light levels, with rods operating at low light levels and cones operating at high light levels (see column 7 of Table 6.1). The differing distributions of rods and cones aim to strike a balance between maximizing resolution and retaining sensitivity. In high illumination, resolution is very high (near the 50 cpd optical limit of the eye) but only in central vision, since this is where cone spacing is smallest. Outside the fovea, resolution drops to a value dictated by rod spacing—only 11 cpd. On the other hand, the fact that we have any sensitivity at all at low illumination levels is due to rods outside the fovea.

EYE MOVEMENTS

The eye muscles

Humans have six extraocular muscles that allow the eyes to rotate quickly and accurately about any combination of the three possible axes. Figure 6.12 illustrates the attachment points of the muscles. They work as three antagonistic pairs. The

FIGURE 6.12

The extraocular muscles. Six muscles working in three pairs allow each eye to rotate in its socket about the three possible axes (based on Walls, 1963).

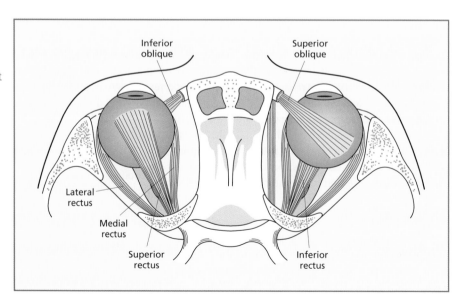

medial and lateral recti control side-to-side rotation about the vertical axis (known as adduction and abduction); the superior and inferior recti control up-and-down rotation around the horizontal axis running from side to side across the head (known as elevation and depression); and the superior and inferior obliques control rotation about the visual axis itself (the horizontal axis running from front to back through the head; the two directions of rotation are known as intorsion and extorsion).

Types of eye movement

Large-scale eye movements have been classified into six types, distinguished in terms of whether they are voluntary (under conscious control) or involuntary (under reflex control), and whether they are conjugate or disjunctive.

In conjugate movements, the two eyes move by the same amount and in the same direction (e.g., both eyes turn to the left). In disjunctive movements, the two eyes move by the same amount but in opposite directions (e.g., the eyes both turn inward toward the nose, so that one becomes cross-eyed).

Table 6.2 categorizes the six different types of large-scale movement with reference to the two classifications (voluntary/involuntary, conjugate/disjunctive):

- **Saccades** are rapid, voluntary conjugate shifts in eye position between steady fixations, which typically last only 45 ms or less. Saccade means "jerk" in French.
- Voluntary conjugate pursuit movements are engaged when the eyes lock on to a moving target and track it as it moves across the visual field. It is impossible to initiate smooth pursuit movements without having a target to track.
- Vergence eye movements are voluntary disjunctive movements and can be divided into convergent movements in which the visual axes of the two eyes move further away from parallel (becoming more cross-eyed), and divergent movements in which the visual axes of the eyes move toward parallel (becoming less cross-eyed).
- Vestibulo-ocular movements are involuntary conjugate movements triggered by signals generated in the vestibular system in response to head acceleration or deceleration. These reflexive movements were considered in detail in Chapter 3.
- Optokinetic nystagmus is triggered by image motion. It consists of an alternating series of saccadic and smooth pursuit movements. Optokinetic nystagmus is easily experienced when looking sideways out of a moving train or car. Your eyes involuntarily latch onto a stationary point in the scene outside, track it back smoothly for a short distance, and then flick or saccade forward to latch onto another stationary point.

TABLE 6.2 Classification of eye movements

	Conjugate movement	Disjunctive movement
Voluntary	Saccade	Convergence
	Pursuit	Divergence
Involuntary	Vestibulo-ocular	
	Optokinetic	

KEY TERM

Saccade
The rapid, jerky eye movement used to shift gaze direction.

In addition to the large-scale movements, the eyes also engage in small, rapid, involuntary movements known as microsaccades.

Why do the eyes move?

Microsaccades seem to be essential for refreshing visual responses, perhaps preventing adaptation to unchanging stimulation. When the retinal image is perfectly stabilized by using special procedures such as optical stabilization, visual sensations disappear entirely (Heckenmueller, 1965). Turning to large-scale movements, there are three general reasons why it is useful to have mobile eyes: For shifting gaze, for keeping gaze still, and for seeing depth.

Shifting gaze

As we saw in the previous section, the ability of the retina to resolve fine spatial detail varies with retinal location and with illumination level. Cones operate only in bright conditions, so resolution is much higher near the visual axis in the fovea than elsewhere on the retina. Eye movements allow us to shift our gaze so that the most acute portion of the retina is brought to bear on a particular region of interest in the visual field. Humans tend to adopt a "fixate–saccade" strategy. Short periods of fixation, typically lasting 300 ms, alternate with saccades to ensure that the eyes are always directed at the center of current interest. It seems that relatively little specific detail about the content of the visual scene is stored in the visual system from one saccade to the next, though more general information may be retained. This explains why saccades occur so frequently—if detailed information is required, the eye simply executes a saccade to acquire it.

Keeping gaze still

It may seem paradoxical that eye movements can keep gaze still, but it is true. Things in the real world tend to move about, whether they are animate creatures or inanimate objects affected by gravity or other forces. If one wishes to keep gazing at a moving thing then the eyes must move to keep pace with it. This gaze centering has to be very accurate if it is to preserve our ability to see details on the moving object. Any movement of the image across the retina degrades the quality of the information provided by photoreceptors, because photoreceptor responses are relatively slow. Figure 6.13 shows the time course of responses in photoreceptors to a brief flash of light. It can take a tenth of a second or more for receptor response to reach its peak, and each response lasts at least 100 ms even for very brief flashes. Imagine that you are fixating steadily on a stationary point as a person walks across your field of view at a distance of 10 meters. If we assume a walking speed of 5 kph, or 140 cm s^{-1}, the image of the person will move across your retina at a speed of 8° s^{-1}, passing over photoreceptors at a rate of one every 1.25 ms. At this speed the image of the person will not dwell on each photoreceptor long enough for that receptor to reach its maximum response before the image moves on—there will be a reduction in effective contrast. Since each

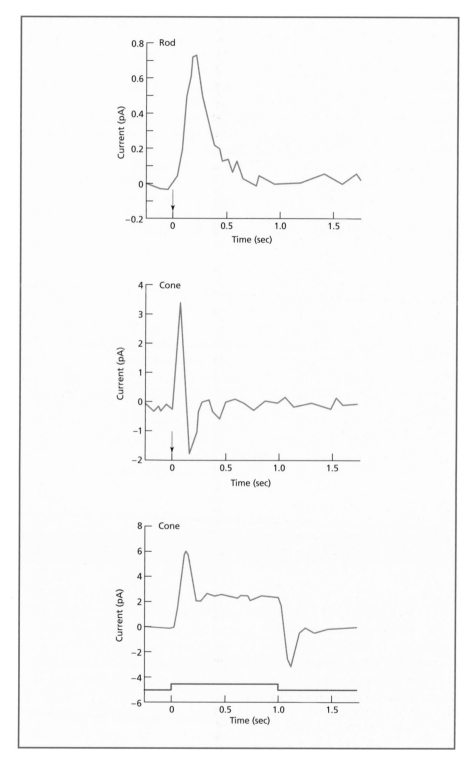

FIGURE 6.13
Time course of
photoreceptor responses
to a brief, dim flash of
light (top two traces),
and a 1-second pulse
of light (bottom trace)
(replotted from recordings
in macaque monkey
photoreceptors reported
by Schnapf & Baylor,
1987).

Saccadic eye movements themselves generate motion of the image across the retina. Chapter 12 on motion perception contains a discussion of why we are not aware of this motion.

photoreceptor's response lasts tens of milliseconds, at any one instant in time a whole array of receptors will be responding. Receptors that were passed over many milliseconds ago will still be responding when new responses are just building in other receptors. Consequently, the "neural" image of the moving figure will be spread over many receptors, an effect known as **motion blur**. Eye movements compensate for object motion and stabilize the position of the image on the retina. Voluntary pursuit movements and optokinetic nystagmus keep the center of interest—a moving object—stationary on the retina (at the cost of blurring and contrast reduction in the background). Vestibulo-ocular movements stabilize the retinal image of the stationary world during head movements.

Land (1999) also argues that eye movements during self-motion such as walking serve to simplify the complex pattern of retinal movement that accompanies self-motion (optic flow, discussed in Chapter 12), which helps us to judge our direction of heading as well as the distances of objects in the scene.

Seeing depth

We have already seen that in order to maximize acuity each eye must be positioned so that the center of interest in the image is projected onto the fovea. The eyes are necessarily located a short distance apart in the head. This means that if both eyes are to engage in foveal fixation on the same point in the world, their visual axes must be made to converge using vergence eye movements. The degree of convergence depends on viewing distance. Points very close to the observer require large convergence angles, while very distant points require extremely small convergence angles.

Even when converged to fixate on the same object, the two eyes receive slightly different views of the world, due to their different positions in the head. These slight differences provide a very powerful visual depth cue, discussed in detail in Chapter 11, which also contains more information about convergence.

CHAPTER SUMMARY

LIGHT

Light is a form of energy that can be described as a ray, a wave, and a stream of particles:

- The particle or quantal nature of light is important for understanding how light is emitted and absorbed, especially at low intensities. Absorption by receptors is essential for vision.
- Ray properties are useful for understanding large-scale properties of light, including how it is refracted during transmission through the optical components of the eye to create a retinal image.
- Wave properties are useful for understanding much finer scale effects such as diffraction, as well as color sensations.

KEY TERM

Motion blur
Smearing in an image caused by movement of an object relative to the imaging surface.

Three important measures of light as a stimulus for vision are:

* Intensity (number of quanta emitted per second)
* Contrast (ratio of the lightest to the darkest parts of an image)
* Wavelength (emission spectra of light sources, and reflectance functions of object surfaces).

THE EYE

* Humans have single-chambered eyes. The cornea and lens refract incoming rays to form an image on the light-sensitive inner surface of the eye (the retina). Over two thirds of the optical power of the eye is provided by the cornea.
* Variation in lens shape allows the eye to adjust its optical power to maintain a focused image of objects at different distances.
* Photoreceptor cells called rods and cones catch incoming photons and generate electrical currents that are transmitted through the network of neurons in the retina to the optic nerve.
* The optical properties of the photoreceptors (width, length, and distribution) place fundamental limits on the information transmitted up the optic nerve.
* The structure of the eye represents a compromise between properties that maximize spatial resolution and those that maximize sensitivity to light.
* Eye movements are mediated by six extraocular muscles. Eye movements serve to shift our gaze to objects of interest, to stabilize our gaze when objects move, and to achieve binocular fixation on objects at different distances.

TUTORIALS

The sun bombards the surface of Earth with high levels of electromagnetic radiation. The lawful way that this radiation interacts with matter offers great potential for providing detailed information about the world around us. So the visual system evolved neural structures to capture radiation in a narrow band of the electromagnetic spectrum—light. In order to properly understand the process of vision we need to appreciate some of the basic physical characteristics of light, and the structures which capture it. Armed with this knowledge we can answer such questions as:

* What determines the sharpness of the retinal image, and why?
* Why does eye size matter for vision?
* What is the best way to measure light as a stimulus for vision?

OPTICS

Lenses

The surface of an illuminated or self-luminous object can be regarded as a large collection of point sources. Rays emanate from each point radially in all directions. Figure 6.1 shows one such point, placed in the vicinity of a lens. Hecht (2002) defines a lens as "a refracting device that reconfigures a transmitted energy distribution" (p. 150). Some portion of the rays emanating from the point passes through the lens. In the case of a convex or converging lens, the bundle of rays from a far object converges on a point some distance behind the lens, known as the focal point (F_1 at the top of Figure 6.14). A *real image* of the point would be formed if an imaging surface were placed at the focal point, to form a focal plane. In the case of a concave or diverging lens, the bundle of rays diverges on leaving the lens, as if emanating from a point in front of the lens (F_2 in Figure 6.14). No image would appear on a screen placed at focal point F_2, since it is just a projection from the path of the diverging rays, so the image at F_2 is known as a *virtual image*. The distance of the focal point from the center of the lens is known as the *focal length, f,* of the lens. The power of a lens is often expressed in terms of the reciprocal of focal length ($1/f$). If f is expressed in meters, then power is measured in *diopters* (D).

FIGURE 6.14
Converging and diverging lenses. Top: A converging lens forms a real image of an object at its focal point (F_1). An imaging surface placed at this point would show an image of the object. Bottom: In a diverging lens, rays emanate as if from an object positioned at focal point F_2. The image at F_2 is known as a virtual image, since no image would appear on a surface placed at F_2 (the rays do not actually reach F_2).

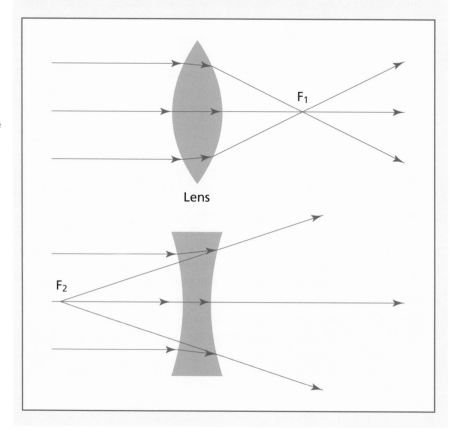

Refraction

Refraction is the principle underlying the formation of images by lenses. As mentioned earlier in the chapter, the effective speed with which a light wavefront passes through a medium may be retarded, due to interference between the original wave and waves produced by forward scattering. An important consequence of the retardation of light during transmission through a medium is *refraction*, a change in the direction of the path of light rays as they enter a transmitting medium obliquely (see Figure 6.15). Refraction occurs because the retardation of the wavefront skews its direction of travel as it enters the medium, similar to the way a moving vehicle's direction would be skewed if one front wheel left the road and entered gravel at the roadside. Imagine that rays *a* and *f* in Figure 6.15 were the wheel tracks of a vehicle as it left the road (air), and entered gravel (glass). Wheels in track *a* would reach the gravel and begin slowing down before the wheels in track *f*. As a result, the direction of the vehicle's travel would be skewed toward the slow side of the vehicle.

Media that transmit light have an *index of refraction*, which defines the extent to which a light wavefront is retarded during transmission. The index of refraction, *n*, is defined as follows:

$$n = c\,/\,v$$

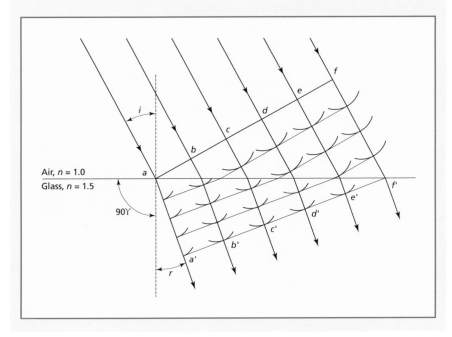

FIGURE 6.15
Refraction. A wavefront containing the bundle of rays *a–f* is shown striking a glass surface. The wavefront is retarded as it enters the glass. Since waves in one part of the wavefront (*a*) are retarded before waves at other parts (e.g. *f*) have reached the glass, the direction of the wavefront is skewed once it enters the glass. The angle of each refracted ray (*r*) differs from the angle of each incident ray (*i*) by an amount that depends on the refractive indices of air and glass.

where c is the speed of light in a vacuum, v is its speed in the medium. Air has a refractive index n of 1.00029. For water n equals 1.333, for glass n equals approximately 1.5, and for the cornea (outermost surface of the eye) n equals 1.376. The degree to which light rays are deflected or refracted as they pass from one medium into another depends on the refractive index of each medium. The angle of refraction is defined in Snell's Law:

$$\sin i \, / \sin r = n_2 \, / \, n_1$$

where $\sin i$ is the angle of the incident light ray as it strikes the interface between medium 1 and medium 2, $\sin r$ is the angle of the refracted light ray traveling through medium 2, and n_2, n_1 are the indices of refraction of the two media (see Figure 6.15). The angle through which light rays are refracted on entering a given medium is higher for media with larger refractive indices.

Airy disk

According to ray or geometric optics, the real image of the point source in Figure 6.1 should itself be a point. However, images formed by actual lenses never conform to this ideal. Even in the best lenses, the image of a point is always slightly blurred. To understand why this is so, we must consider image formation in terms of wave or physical optics rather than geometrical optics. Light from a point strikes the lens as a wavefront, shown as W_1 in Figure 6.16 (rays are lines at right-angles to the wavefront).

The part of the wavefront passing through the center of the lens is delayed more than the part passing through the edge of the lens,

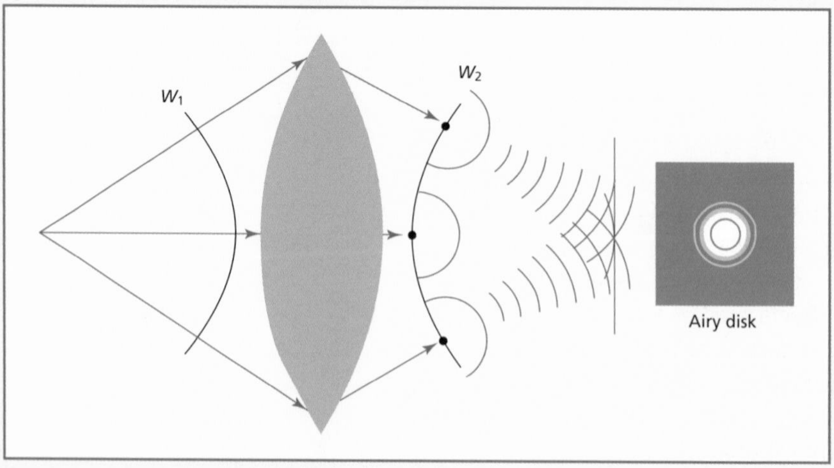

FIGURE 6.16

Formation of the Airy disk. The wavefront (W_1) emanating from a point is curved in an arc centered on the point. After this wavefront has passed through a lens, it is curved in an arc centered on the focal point of the lens (W_2). Each point on a wavefront can be considered as the source of new wavefronts. Three points are shown on W_2. As these wavefronts interact when they reach the focal point, constructive and destructive interference produces a central bright disk (the Airy disk) surrounded by dimmer rings.

W_1 W_2

Airy disk

because the lens is thinner at its edges. Consequently, the wavefront that emerges from the lens is curved in an arc centered on the focal point (W_2 in Figure 6.16). As the various parts of the wavefront meet at the focal point, they interfere to create an interference pattern of the same kind as that observed by Thomas Young. The pattern has a central bright spot, known as the **Airy disk**, surrounded by an alternating series of faint dark and bright rings. Figure 6.16 illustrates how interference produces the Airy disk. Each point on the wavefront emanating from the lens (W_2 in the figure) can be considered as the source of a new wavefront. Three such wavefronts are shown in the figure. Just as in the case of Young's double slit experiment (see Figure 6.2), when these different wavefronts cross they interact to either cancel out or augment each other. All of the wavefronts combine constructively at the focal point to create a bright spot, but alternating destructive and constructive interference creates a series of rings surrounding this spot.

Optical systems, including eyes, usually have a circular aperture placed between the light source and the lens in order to control light intensity and depth of field. The radius of the Airy disk depends on the diameter of the aperture, according to the following equation:

$$r \approx 1 \times 22 \cdot f\lambda / D$$

where r is the radius of the disk (radius to the first dark ring), f is focal length, D is aperture diameter, and λ is the wavelength of the light (all measures in mm). The width of the Airy disk is inversely proportional to aperture diameter—wider apertures create smaller disks. You may be able to understand why this is so from inspection of Figure 6.16. An aperture placed in front of the lens limits the size of the wavefront emanating from the lens. A narrow aperture, for example, would remove the more peripheral (top and bottom) wavefronts and so broaden the interference pattern at the focal point.

The solid line in Figure 6.17 plots the intensity of the retinal image created by a very thin line, at two different pupil diameters, as measured by Campbell and Gubisch (1966). The dotted line is the **linespread** expected on the basis of diffraction effects alone. At the narrower pupil diameter, the actual linespread is very close to that predicted by diffraction—the image is said to be *diffraction-limited*. At the wider pupil diameter, diffraction effects predict a narrower spread, according to the equation above. Actual linespread at wider pupil diameters is much worse than that predicted by diffraction—optical imperfections play a much greater role in determining image quality. Small pupil diameters are therefore optimal for preserving image quality.

KEY TERMS

Airy disk
The image of a point light source created by an optical system; it contains a bright central spot surrounded by several faint rings.

Linespread function
The image (or a mathematical function describing the image) of a very thin line created by an optical system.

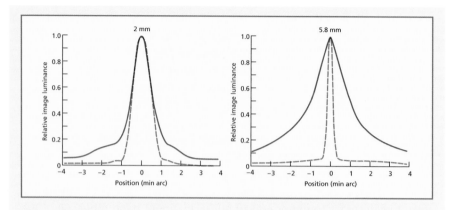

FIGURE 6.17
Linespread functions. These functions plot the luminance profile across the retinal image formed by a thin bright line. The functions on the left relate to a pupil diameter of 2.0 mm, and the functions on the right relate to a pupil diameter of 5.8 mm. The solid functions show the actual luminance profile of the line. The broken functions show the profiles predicted on the basis of diffraction effects illustrated in Figure 6.16. The difference between the solid and broken functions can be attributed to aberrations of the kind shown in Figure 6.18, which become more severe as pupil diameter increases (adapted from Campbell & Gubisch, 1966).

Aberrations

The two most significant optical imperfections that affect image quality are spherical aberration and chromatic aberration.

Spherical aberration

A lens with a spherical surface will not bring all rays to focus at the same point. Peripheral rays are refracted more than central rays (see top of Figure 6.18), so the image of a point will be a blurred circle. One solution to this problem is to use an appropriately nonspherical surface. The surface of the human cornea has a hyperbolic shape for this reason. A second solution, also adopted in human and other eyes, is to vary the refractive index of the lens material, adjusting the angle of refraction across the lens to compensate for the focusing error. This solution requires that the lens has a gradient of refractive index from high in the center to low at the periphery. Even after such measures are taken to avoid spherical aberration, slight deviations from a perfect hyperbolic shape, or refractive index, will introduce some degree of blurring in the image.

Chromatic aberration

Chromatic aberration arises from the manner in which the wavefront emanating from a light source is retarded during its passage through a refracting medium. The degree to which the wavefront is retarded varies with frequency, because the retardation is due to interference between the original wave and forward scattered waves. Shorter wavelengths are retarded more than longer wavelengths. Since refraction (a change in the direction of the path of light rays as they enter a transmitting medium obliquely; refer back to earlier in the chapter) depends on retardation, the angle through which a light ray is refracted depends on its frequency. Shorter (violet) wavelengths are deflected more than longer (red) wavelengths. If

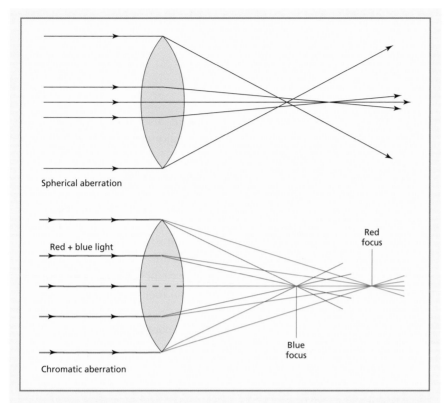

Spherical aberration

Red + blue light

Red focus

Blue focus

Chromatic aberration

FIGURE 6.18
Lens aberrations. Top: Spherical aberration. Light rays passing through the lens near its center come into focus at a further distance than rays that pass through the lens near its edges. Consequently, an imaging surface placed at either distance will reveal a blurred image. Bottom: Chromatic aberration. Light rays at longer (red) wavelengths come into focus at a further distance from the lens than rays at short (blue) wavelengths. Hence an imaging surface placed at a particular distance will show color fringes from out-of-focus wavelengths.

the refracting device is a prism, then white light (composed of many wavelengths) will be dispersed into a rainbow spectrum of colors, as observed by Newton. If the refracting device is a lens, then each different wavelength will have a different focal point (see bottom of Figure 6.18). The image of light from a white point will be a blurred circle of colored fringes. Cameras attempt to compensate for this effect by combining two lenses of different material and different shape, so that their aberrations cancel out. Eyes attempt to deal with the problem by reducing sensitivity to wavelengths at the short end of the visible spectrum.

One might expect that people whose eyes have the smallest optical aberrations, and therefore the best image quality, should have the best visual acuity. Intriguingly it seems that this is not the case, leading to suggestions that the human eye has self-correcting mechanisms which can compensate for the aberrations present in individual eyes (Artal, 2014).

Lens equations

Lens equations allow us to calculate the size and location of the image produced by a lens. For a thin lens, the distance (d_i) of the image from the focal plane depends on the distance of the object (d_o), as defined in the Newtonian lens equation (which first appeared in Isaac Newton's *Opticks* in 1704):

$$d_i = f^2 / d_0$$

For an object very far away from the lens (d_o essentially infinite), d_i is effectively zero, so the image falls in the focal plane of the lens. As the object approaches the lens, d_i grows progressively because the point of focus falls beyond the focal plane of the lens. An imaging surface fixed in position at the focal plane would render a blurred image of the object. In order to maintain a focused image, one of two things must happen. The imaging surface could be moved back away from the lens until it coincides with the point of focus. This is the solution used in many cameras. Alternatively, the power (focal length) of the lens could be adjusted to maintain focus on a fixed imaged plane. As objects move closer to the lens, its power must be increased to maintain focus. This is the solution adopted in human eyes.

The size of the image, H_i, is an important consideration for eyes. The following equations specify image height:

$$H_i / H_0 = f / d_0, \text{ or}$$
$$H_i = H_0 \times (f / d_0)$$

Thus, for a given size of object (i.e., H_o fixed), at a given distance away (i.e., d_o fixed), the size of the image scales directly with focal length f. Lenses with small focal lengths project smaller images than those with long focal lengths. The human eye has a focal length of approximately 16.77 mm (59.6 D, see Land & Nilsson, 2002). So a person 1.8 m (6 ft) tall standing 15 m away would project an image in your eye that was 2 mm tall. The ability of an eye to resolve fine detail is partly governed by the size of the image projected by the lens, so animals with smaller eyes are inherently limited in their ability to resolve detail.

MEASURING LIGHT INTENSITY

Light intensity can be measured according to two different systems, the *radiometric* system and the *photometric* system.

The radiometric system

The radiometric system for measuring light intensity uses physical energy units that can be traced back to photons. Measures fall into four categories, as shown in the left-hand column of Table 6.3.

TABLE 6.3 Photometric and radiometric measures of light intensity

Measure	Radiometric term	Radiometric unit	Photometric term	Photometric unit
Total energy emitted	Radiant energy or flux	Watts (W)	Luminous flux	Lumen (lm)
Energy from a point source	Radiant intensity	Watts per steradian ($W \cdot sr^{-1}$)	Luminous intensity	Lumens per steradian ($lm \cdot sr^{-1}$), known as candelas (cd)
Energy from an extended source	Radiance	Watts per square meter per steradian ($W \cdot m^{-2} \cdot sr^{-1}$)	Luminance	Lumens per square meter per steradian ($lm \cdot m^{-2} \cdot sr^{-1}$), or candelas per square meter ($cd \cdot m^{-2}$)
Energy received at a surface	Irradiance	Watts per square meter ($W \cdot m^{-2}$)	Illuminance	Lumens per square meter ($lm \cdot m^{-2}$), known as lux

Total radiant energy

The total energy emitted by a source, also called *radiant energy* or *radiant flux*, is measured in watts. One watt corresponds approximately to 10^{18} photons at a wavelength of 555 nm.

Radiant energy from a point source

Energy emitted by a point source emanates in all directions, so it is usually more convenient to specify the range of directions over which the measured amount of energy is emitted. The convention is to consider a point source as positioned at the center of a sphere, and to divide the sphere into conical sectors. These sectors are measured in units of solid angle known as *steradians*. A complete sphere contains 4π steradians. Energy emitted by a point source, also called *radiant intensity*, is therefore specified in watts per steradian.

Radiant energy from an extended source

Most light-emitting sources, such as TV and computer screens, are extended over space. The appropriate measure of intensity for such sources must therefore specify the unit of surface area over which it applies. Energy emitted by an extended source, also called *radiance*, is therefore specified in watts per square meter per steradian.

Radiant energy received at a surface

Energy falling on a receiving surface can simply be specified in terms of watts received per square meter of surface area, also called *irradiance*. The amount of energy received depends on both the energy emitted by the source and the distance between the receiving surface and the source. Irradiance E_e can be calculated from radiant intensity I_e using the following relation:

$$E_e = I_e / r^2$$

where r is the distance between the source and the receiving surface. Energy falling on the surface declines according to the square of the distance, known as the *inverse square law*. Each doubling in distance results in a fourfold decline in irradiance. This occurs because as distance increases, energy emanating over a particular range of directions falls on a progressively greater area of the receiving surface (the same effect occurs with sound intensity, for the same reasons). Strictly speaking, the inverse square law holds only for point sources. Practically speaking, it operates with an error of less than 1% if the diameter of the source is less than 1/10th of the distance to the receiving surface (Pokorny & Smith, 1986).

The photometric system

Light was defined at the beginning of the chapter as energy that is capable of evoking a visual sensation. Since this definition includes a reference to perception, purely physical radiometric measures of light are not sufficient. The majority of frequencies in the spectrum of radiant energy are invisible to humans, and even the visible frequencies vary in their effectiveness. Radiometric measures do not therefore accurately represent light intensity as a stimulus for vision. The photometric system of light measurement was developed by the Commission Internationale de l'Eclairage (CIE) to take account of human sensitivity to different wavelengths.

Spectral luminous efficiency functions: V(λ) and V'(λ)

The spectral *luminous efficiency function* specifies the relative sensitivity of the eye to different wavelengths. There are a number of ways to estimate the spectral luminous efficiency function, but in 1924 CIE adopted a standard function V (λ) based on the average of estimates obtained in a number of different laboratories. Most of the estimates were obtained using a technique known as heterochromatic flicker photometry, in which a fixed reference light alternates rapidly with a comparison light to create flicker. The observer adjusts the intensity of the comparison light to minimize or eliminate the sensation of flicker. In this way lights of many different

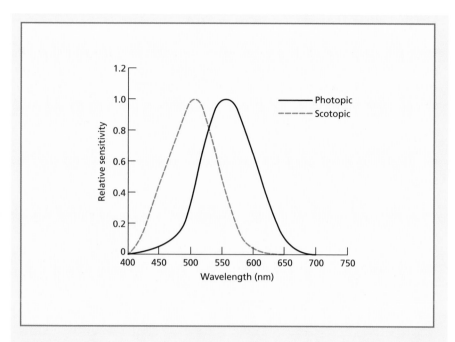

FIGURE 6.19
Photopic and scotopic
luminous efficiency
functions, as defined
by CIE. These show
the relative sensitivity
to light of different
wavelengths at high
(photopic) illumination
levels (solid line), and low
(scotopic) illumination
levels (broken line).
The peak sensitivity of
human vision shifts to
shorter wavelengths
under scotopic viewing
conditions.

wavelengths can be defined in terms of their sensory "efficiency" relative to a light of standard intensity. Figure 6.19 shows the luminous efficiency function for the standard observer defined by CIE in 1924. This function was obtained at high light levels, known as **photopic vision**. But relative sensitivity has been found to change at low light levels (and you may have some ideas about why this should be so after reading the next chapter). So in 1951 CIE introduced a second standard function $V'(\lambda)$ appropriate for lower light levels, known as **scotopic vision**, also shown in Figure 6.19.

Units in the photometric system of measurement are based on corresponding units in the radiometric system, adjusted for the relative efficiencies defined in $V(\lambda)$ and $V'(\lambda)$, as shown in Table 6.3.

Total luminous energy

Total energy emitted, or *luminous flux*, is specified in *lumens*. One lumen is defined as the luminous flux of 1/683 W of monochromatic radiation at a wavelength of 555 nm (Makous, 1998), or approximately 4×10^{15} photons. The total luminous flux emitted by a source is calculated by multiplying the radiant flux at each wavelength by its luminous efficacy defined on the luminous efficiency function, and summing the products.

Luminous energy from a point source

Energy emitted by a point source, or *luminous intensity*, is specified in lumens per steradian, also known as candelas (cd).

Luminous energy from an extended source

Energy emitted by an extended source, or *luminance*, is specified in candelas per square meter (lumens per square meter per steradian), abbreviated to cd/m^{-2}. Luminance values of white paper at different illumination levels are shown in column 2 of Table 6.1.

Luminous energy received at a surface

Energy received at a surface, or *illuminance*, is specified in lux (lumens per square meter).

Photometric units are used very frequently in the research literature on visual perception, the most commonly used unit being candelas per square meter (cd/m^{-2}), since this measures surface luminance of visual stimuli. Luminance is usually measured by pointing a telescopic spot photometer at the surface to be measured. The photometer is similar in size and shape to a small camcorder. The center of its viewfinder contains a small gray spot. A digital display on the photometer reports the luminance of the area covered by the spot, in cd/m^{-2}.

Retinal illumination

Even photometric luminance units may not provide a sufficiently precise measure of stimulus intensity in certain situations. Light enters the eye via the pupil, and variation in the diameter of the pupil can result in significant variation in the amount of light that falls on the retina of the eye (see earlier in the chapter for a discussion of the pupil). **Troland** units (td) specify retinal illuminance, taking pupil size into account. One troland is defined as the retinal illumination that would result from viewing a surface at 1 cd/m^{-2} through a pupil with an area of 1 mm^2 (Makous, 1998). If the calculation is done using the photopic luminosity function, the result gives photopic troland values; if done using the scotopic luminosity function the result gives scotopic trolands. Column 4 of Table 6.1 shows luminance in log trolands, taking into account the pupil diameters shown in column 3.

Troland value does not take into account the part of the pupil through which light enters the eye. Light entering near the edge of the pupil is less effective than light entering near the center of the pupil, due to the optical properties of the retinal photoreceptors (light rays that strike the photoreceptors obliquely are less effective than rays that strike them straight on). This effect is known as the **Stiles–Crawford effect**.

Visual physiology

Contents

INTRODUCTION

When light strikes the network of cells that line the inside surface of the eye, it initiates a chain of neural events in the visual system that leads, 100 milliseconds or so later, to a conscious visual experience. The visual system comprises all the neurons responsible for seeing, which can be divided into three major components: The retina, the visual pathway, and the visual cortex, as illustrated in Figure 7.1.

- The retina contains the neural circuitry connecting photoreceptors to the ganglion cells, whose fibers form the optic nerve.
- The visual pathway includes the optic nerve, the cell nuclei to which its fibers project, and the onward projection to the cortex.
- The visual cortex includes all cortical areas that contain cells responsive to visual stimuli.

This chapter will review the major features of each component, following the route of neural signals as they travel through the system from the photoreceptors to cortical cells.

FIGURE 7.1
The visual system includes the retinas, the visual pathway connecting the retinas to the brain, and the visual cortex. The two eyes' fields of view overlap (top). The human visual system is arranged so that binocular information from the right half of the visual field arrives in the left hemisphere, and binocular information from the left half of the visual field arrives in the right hemisphere. Note that onward connections from the superior colliculi are not shown.

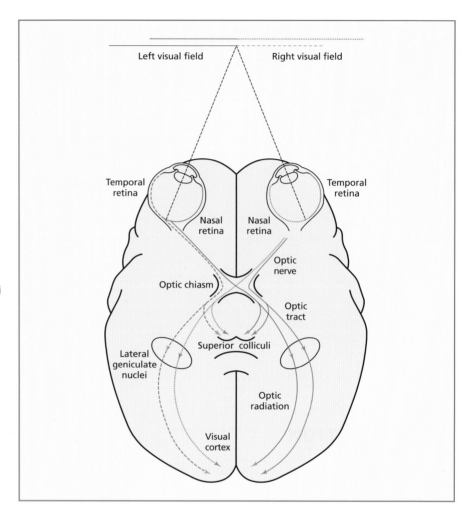

THE RETINA

Figure 7.2 contains a cross-section sketch of the human eye. It is covered by a tough, flexible tissue called the sclera, except at the anterior part where the transparent cornea admits light to the interior. The inside surface of the sclera is lined with the choroid, which provides nutrients to the next layer, the retina. As befits its name (thought to be derived for the Latin word *rete*, meaning net), the retina is a layered network containing five different types of neuron, which are distributed across the inner surface of the eye in a fairly regular lattice. The nuclei of these cells are clustered into three layers:

- Photoreceptor cells in the outer nuclear layer (nearest the choroid) are responsible for transducing light energy into neural signals.
- Ganglion cells in the ganglion cell layer supply the nerve fibers that carry neural signals out of the eye and along the visual pathway towards the brain.

- The inner nuclear layer contains bipolar cells, amacrine cells, and horizontal cells. Its complex neural circuitry connects photoreceptors to ganglion cells.

Separating these layers are plexiform layers that contain the fibers and synapses which connect the cell layers together. There are far more photoreceptors (over 100 million) than there are ganglion cells (approximately 1 million) in each eye. The massive convergence of signals from the outer nuclear layer to the ganglion cell layer is achieved by the cells in the inner nuclear layer. This convergence is executed with such precision and selectivity that by the time signals travel up the fibers of ganglion cells towards the brain, they contain a highly encoded representation of the retinal image, the first stage of image analysis in the visual system. Our journey through the visual system begins with photoreceptors in the outer nuclear layer.

OUTER NUCLEAR LAYER

Photoreceptor components

As you learnt in the previous chapter, receptors in the outer nuclear layer fall into two classes, rods and cones. The outer segment of each receptor contains a stack of disks packed with light-sensitive pigment molecules. The inner segment contains the cell nucleus and synaptic terminals (see Figure 7.3).

The synaptic terminals contain pockets or synaptic clefts that receive processes from bipolar cells and horizontal cells in the adjacent retinal layer. Each rod contains a single synaptic cleft that admits two horizontal cell processes and between two and five bipolar processes. Cones, on the other hand, have several synaptic clefts, each admitting two horizontal cell processes and two or more bipolar processes.

Notice from Figure 7.2 that the photoreceptors actually face away from the incoming light. The tip of each outer segment adjoins a layer of the retina known as the retinal pigment epithelium (RPE), which serves several vital functions (Strauss, 2005). One of its tasks is to regenerate light-sensitive pigment in the photoreceptor discs after the pigment has been isomerized (its molecules change configuration) by quantal absorption (a process known as the "visual cycle"), and so maintain visual sensitivity. To maintain proper retinal function, photoreceptors also undergo a daily renewal process in which 10% of their volume is shed at the tip and digested by the RPE; material is recycled and returned to the receptors so new disks can be regenerated at the base of the outer segment.

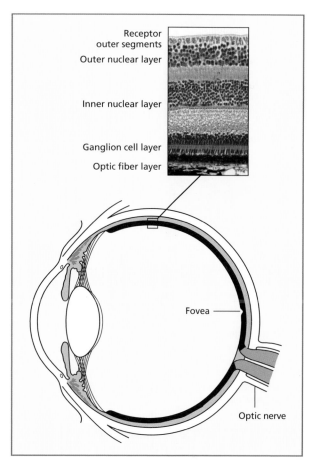

FIGURE 7.2
A cross-section through the human eye, with a photomicrograph of the area of retina indicated showing the retina's layered structure. Light entering the eye from the left must pass through all the cell layers before it reaches the rod and cone photoreceptors. Based on a figure in Lee (2011). Micrograph © Steve Gschmeissner/Science Photo Library.

Disk turnover is such that all the disks in each photoreceptor are replaced approximately every 12 days (Purves et al., 2001).

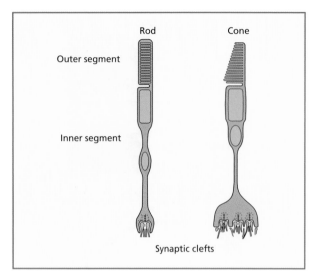

FIGURE 7.3
Components of rod and cone photoreceptors. The outer segment is a stack of disks containing light-sensitive pigment molecules. The inner segment includes the cell nucleus, and synaptic terminals housed in pockets called clefts.

Photon absorption

The probability that a light quantum (photon) will be absorbed by a photoreceptor depends on its direction of travel and on its frequency.

Photon direction

Photons arrive at the photoreceptors from a range of directions, depending on where they pass through the pupil. Photons traveling through the center of the pupil arrive in a direction that is nearly parallel to the long axis of each receptor, while photons traveling near the edge of the pupil arrive at a slight angle to the receptor's long axis. Photons arriving from nonparallel directions are less likely to be absorbed by the receptor, an effect known as the Stiles–Crawford effect (discussed in Chapter 6). This effect occurs because photons are guided onto the receptor's outer segment as they pass through the inner segment. This guidance is most effective when photons travel the full length of the photoreceptor. The Stiles–Crawford effect is more marked for cones than for rods, so rods absorb 60% more photons from a dilate pupil than do cones.

Photon frequency

The probability that a photon at a given frequency will be absorbed by a photopigment molecule depends on the spectral sensitivity of the molecule. As shown in Figure 8.8, there are three distinct classes of cone photopigment, which have different spectral sensitivities from each other and from rod photopigment. If a photon happens to have a frequency near the peak sensitivity of the receptor it strikes, it is more likely to be absorbed.

Photoreceptor responses

Once a photon has been absorbed, there is no guarantee that it will lead to a visual response. Only two thirds of the photons absorbed by a photoreceptor actually result in a response. Energy from the remaining photons is dissipated as heat (Rodieck, 1998). Any responses that do occur are mediated by a process known as *photoisomerization* in the receptor's visual pigment molecules.

Photoisomerization

Each pigment molecule consists of a protein portion (known as opsin), and a light-catching portion (known as a chromophore). Visual responses are initiated when an absorbed photon causes a change in the shape of the chromophore molecule (photoisomerization). No chemical bonds are broken, but a cascade of biochemical events occurs within the outer segment of the photoreceptor, which results in a change in receptor membrane potential. All mammalian pigment molecules use 11-*cis* retinal as their chromophore, and are known as rhodopsins. Rods and cones contain different variants of rhodopsin, giving them different wavelength sensitivities.

Graded potentials

The distance over which signals are transmitted through the layers of retina from photoreceptors to ganglion cells is so small (less than 0.2 mm) that it does not require the generation of action potentials. Instead, photoreceptors generate graded changes in membrane potential and correspondingly graded changes in the rate of neurotransmitter release within their synaptic cleft. In total darkness photoreceptors have a membrane potential of –40 mV. Increases in retinal illumination cause the potential to become more negative (hyperpolarization), until it reaches saturation at –65 mV. So the rate of neurotransmitter release is actually higher in the dark than it is in the light.

At very low light levels, rods can produce a reliable change in potential after a single photon strike, but they reach saturation with the absorption of only approximately 100 photons per second. Cones require approximately 30–100 photons to produce a reliable change in potential, but can respond without saturating at very high rates of absorption (50,000 photons per second).

Rods and cones also differ in the way their response changes over time. The two traces of Figure 7.4 show the change in membrane current in a rod and a cone in response to a very brief flash of light (marked on the trace below each response; the black bar represents 500 ms; redrawn from Schnapf & Baylor, 1987). The rod does not reach its peak response until roughly 200 ms after the flash. The cone responds about four times faster. A number of other differences between rods and cones were discussed in Chapter 6, including their retinal distribution and spectral sensitivity, all of which have important consequences for sensation and perception which will be discussed later in this chapter and in the next.

Univariance

Each photon that photoisomerizes a pigment molecule has the same biochemical effect on the molecule as any other photon that photoisomerizes it, regardless of photon frequency. The photoreceptor has no way of distinguishing between photoreceptors at different frequencies. All it can do is report the rate at which it is catching photons. This principle of photoreceptor behavior is known as the "principle of **univariance**." Of course the probability that a photon will be absorbed by a given receptor depends jointly on its frequency and the spectral sensitivity of the photoreceptor's pigment. Photons of a particular frequency will tend to be captured more by some receptor types than by others. So later stages of visual processing must integrate information

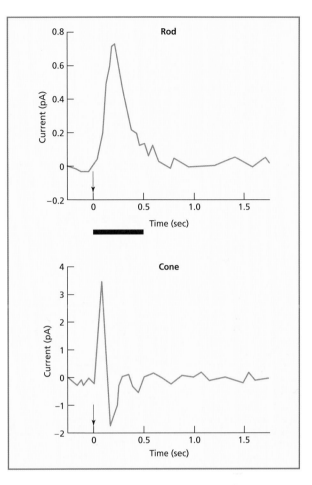

FIGURE 7.4
The time course of responses in rod (top) and cone (bottom) photoreceptors. A brief flash of light was presented at the point marked by the arrow on the horizontal axis. The bar between the two plots represents 500 ms. Adapted from Schnapf and Baylor (1987).

KEY TERM

Univariance
When a photon is absorbed, its effect on a photoreceptor is the same regardless of the photon's wavelength.

Think about how later processes could infer wavelength from receptor activity, using ideas developed in Chapters 2 and 3.

across the different photoreceptor types in order to infer the frequency characteristics of the incident photons, and this is discussed in the next chapter.

INNER NUCLEAR LAYER

Cones connect to a complex network of cells in the retina, whereas rods' connectivity involves relatively simple retinal circuitry. So although there are far fewer cones than rods in the retina, there are 8–10 cone-driven neurons for every rod-driven neuron. Figure 7.5 is a highly schematic representation of the pattern of connectivity in the inner nuclear layer. It shows how bipolar, horizontal, and amacrine cells collect the signals from receptors and funnel them towards the ganglion cells.

Bipolar cells

Bipolar cells transmit responses "vertically" through the retinal network from photoreceptors down towards ganglion cells. Like the photoreceptors to which they are connected, bipolar cells transmit graded potentials.

ON versus OFF bipolars

Bipolar cells can be subdivided into two types, ON and OFF.

FIGURE 7.5
Retinal circuitry connecting photoreceptors (top: rods, R; and cones, C) to ganglion cells (bottom: GC). Circuitry differs between the different receptor types. Cone bipolars (CB) connect cones to ganglion cells; ON variants (ON CB) increase transmitter release when cone photon catch increases, while OFF variants (OFF CB) decrease transmitter release when photon catch increases. Rod bipolars (RB) are all ON, and connect rods to ganglion cells via AII amacrine cells and cone bipolars. The laterally spreading dendrites of horizontal cells (H, HI) terminate in the synaptic clefts of photoreceptors alongside bipolar cell processes. Amacrine cells (A, AII) connect to each other, to bipolar cells, and to ganglion cells. Large dots indicate excitatory connections, small dots indicate inhibitory connections.

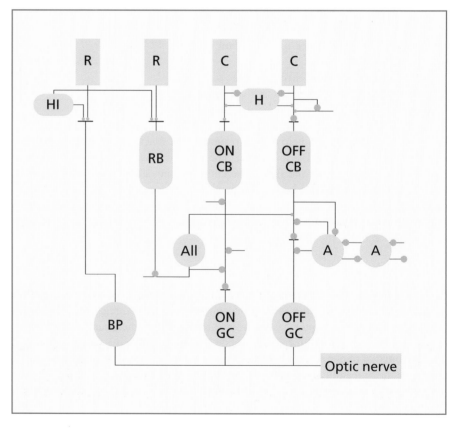

TABLE 7.1 Changes in the graded potential of photoreceptors and bipolars in response to increases or decreases in photon catch

	Increase in photon catch	Decrease in photon catch
Photoreceptors	Hyperpolarize (more negative)	Depolarize (more positive)
	Decrease in neurotransmitter	Increase in neurotransmitter
ON bipolars	Depolarize (more positive)	Hyperpolarize (more negative)
	Increase in neurotransmitter	Decrease in neurotransmitter
OFF bipolars	Hyperpolarize (more negative)	Depolarize (more positive)
	Decrease in neurotransmitter	Increase in neurotransmitter

KEY TERMS

Cone bipolar
A class of retinal cell that conveys activity from cone photoreceptors to ganglion cells.

Rod bipolar
A class of retinal cell that conveys activity from rod photoreceptors to amacrine cells.

- ON bipolars are activated by an increase in the photon catch of receptors, so they respond to light onset. In other words, they depolarize (increase the rate of transmitter release).
- OFF bipolars are activated by a decrease in the photon catch of receptors, so they respond to light offset. In other words, they hyperpolarize (decrease the rate of neurotransmitter release).

Table 7.1 summarizes the change in the graded potential of photoreceptors and bipolars in response to increases or decreases in photon catch.

Notice that the response of OFF bipolars has the same sign as the response of photoreceptors, whereas the response of ON bipolars is inverted relative to the photoreceptors. This distinction between ON and OFF responses is of major importance for visual processing because it relates to our perception of increases and decreases in light level, and is preserved at later levels of analysis.

Rod versus cone bipolars

Some bipolar cells connect only to cones. Others connect only to rods. Each cone bipolar makes contact with between 1 and 10 cone photoreceptors, whereas rod bipolars contact 30–50 rods.

- **Cone bipolars** can be divided into ON and OFF variants, and connect with ganglion cells, as shown in Figure 7.5 (labeled ON CB and OFF CB).
- **Rod bipolars** (RB in Figure 7.5), on the other hand, have only ON responses, and mainly connect to a class of amacrine cells known as AII, rather than to ganglion cells. These amacrine cells in turn make connections with cone bipolar cells. Some connect to ON cone bipolars; others connect to OFF cone bipolars.

So ON signals from rods "piggyback" onto both the ON and OFF bipolar circuitry that connects cones to ganglion cells (Rodieck, 1998). It seems that the relatively simple circuitry for rod signals is superimposed on preexisting cone circuitry (there is also evidence for some direct connections between rod and cone receptors at their inner segments; Sharpe & Stockman, 1999).

? *Why is retinal circuitry dominated by cones?*

Horizontal cells

Horizontal cells each have an axon that extends laterally across the retinal network up to a distance of 1 mm or more. Dendrites reach out from both the cell body and the axon, terminating in the synaptic clefts of photoreceptors. These clefts also receive processes from bipolar cells, and horizontal cells serve to modulate the signals that are passed from photoreceptors to bipolar cells. Stimulation of horizontal cells by photoreceptors is fed back to reduce the influence of the photoreceptors on bipolar cells. This effect is known as lateral inhibition; it spreads across the retina along horizontal cell axons. Consequently, activation of any one photoreceptor tends to reduce the activation of the surrounding photoreceptors.

Amacrine cells

Amacrine cells make synaptic contacts with bipolar cells, with other amacrine cells, and with ganglion cells. Amacrine cells outnumber both horizontal cells and **ganglion cells**, and account for the majority of synapses onto ganglion cells. They can be classified into many different types that appear to serve different roles, mostly still ill-defined (Masland, 2001, 2012). One of the most well-known types is the "starburst" amacrine cell, which is responsible for direction-selective responses in mouse and rabbit retinal ganglion cells (Briggman, Helmstaedter, & Denk, 2011). Another type, the AII amacrines, conveys rod signals to cone bipolars, as we have seen. Yet other types of amacrine cell may serve to modulate the signal carried by bipolar cells and ganglion cells, over both short and long periods of time.

GANGLION CELL LAYER

As its name suggests, this layer contains the cell bodies of retina ganglion cells (RGCs), though it also contains some amacrine cell bodies.

Cell types

The retina contains about 20 different classes of RGC (Dacey, 2004). Three classes, known as **midget**, **parasol**, and **small bistratified** make up at least three quarters of all RGCs (Wässle, 2004). The myriad other types each make up a tiny percentage of the population. Despite their low numbers they are likely to play significant roles in visual processing, but relatively little is known about them. Recent research has identified a class of RGC that expresses melatonin and senses light directly, and seems to be involved in functions that require information about illumination level, such as diurnal body rhythm and pupil size (Berson, Dunn, & Takao, 2002; Dacey et al., 2005). Some of these cells connect directly to the suprachiasmatic nuclei in the brain, others project to the lateral geniculate nuclei (see below) and have complex receptive field properties (Dacey et al., 2005). A different class of RGC responds selectively to movement direction, mediated by starburst ganglion cells (at least in rabbits and mice; see Vaney, Sivyer, & Taylor, 2012).

Bistratified, midget, and parasol cells

These three types of RGC are the most numerous and best understood. Their distinctive response properties are crucial for higher-level processing of spatial, time-based (temporal), and chromatic information. All three cell types generate action potentials at a rate that is influenced by activity levels in the amacrine and bipolar cells that connect with them. The precise response properties of each ganglion cell type arise from the specific connections they make with amacrine and bipolar cells, which in turn make contacts with photoreceptors.

Response properties of bistratified, midget, and parasol cells

Table 7.2 summarizes the major response properties of midget, parasol, and bistratified ganglion cells.

Luminance response

As explained in the previous chapter and illustrated in Table 6.1, only rods respond at the lowest light levels (scotopic); cones respond at the highest levels (photopic); and both receptor classes respond at intermediate levels (mesopic). All three ganglion cell types receive signals from cones, so all are active during twilight and daylight (mesopic and photopic light levels). In darkness (scotopic light levels), only the parasol cells remain active, due to rod input via rod bipolars and AII amacrine cells (Lee et al., 1997). Vision at night is mediated by only a small fraction of the optic nerve fibers projecting to the brain, since parasol cells account for just 8–10% of all ganglion cells. Midget ganglion cells account for 70–80% of all ganglion cells, so it seems that the primate retina is designed primarily for daytime vision.

We have already seen that there are far fewer cones than rods in the primate retina (7 versus 120 million), both connecting to approximately 1 million optic nerve fibers. Given the relative incidence of different ganglion cell classes, and their luminance response, we can infer the following. During daylight, an average of seven cone photoreceptors must converge onto each active ganglion cell. At night, an average of 600 rod photoreceptors must converge onto each active parasol ganglion cell. It is therefore inevitable that the eye's resolving power is much lower at night than during daylight. However, such simple ratios do not allow for the fact that different ganglion cells may receive information from different numbers of receptors.

Spatial response

Every ganglion cell has a receptive field, which defines the area of retina within which light must fall in order to influence the response of the cell (receptive fields were introduced in the context of somatosensation in Chapter 3). This area corresponds to the array of photoreceptors whose responses can find a route to the ganglion

TABLE 7.2 Major response properties of midget, parasol, and bistratified ganglion cells

	Midget ganglion	Parasol ganglion	Bistratified ganglion
Incidence	70–80%	8–10%	Below 10%
Luminance response	Photopic only	Photopic and scotopic	Photopic only
Spatial response	Opponent	Opponent	Nonopponent
Spectral response	L versus M (central)	L + M	S versus (L + M)
	L + M (peripheral)		
Temporal response	Sustained	Transient	
Projection	Parvo LGN	Magno LGN	Konio LGN

cell through the intervening retinal cell network. Many ganglion cell receptive fields exhibit a crucial property known as **spatial opponency**, in which the cell's activity is excited when light falls in one part of its receptive field, and inhibited when light falls in another part. The excitatory and inhibitory regions of the receptive field are arranged in a center–surround configuration, as shown in Figure 7.6 (left).

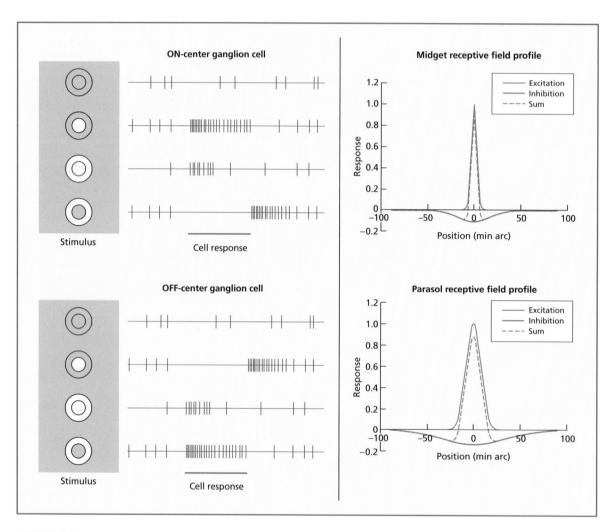

FIGURE 7.6
Spatial responses in ganglion cells. Left: Stimuli are shown superimposed on concentrically organized receptive fields. The trace adjacent to each stimulus shows neural activity as a function of time. The thick horizontal bars mark the duration of each stimulus. Cells with an excitatory center and inhibitory surround (top four traces) respond best to the onset of small light spots and offset of small dark spots. Cells with an inhibitory center and excitatory surround (bottom four traces) show the opposite pattern of response; they respond best to the onset of small dark spots and the offset of small light spots. Right: Cross-sections of midget and parasol ganglion cell receptive fields. Midget ganglion cells have smaller receptive fields than parasol ganglion cells. In both cell types the center and surround influences conform to a spatial Gaussian (bell-shaped or normal) distribution. The center is more dominant than the surround.

Center–surround organization in ganglion cells is largely a consequence of the bipolar and horizontal cell influences described earlier. The center response reflects the influence of bipolar cells, and the opposing surround response is due to lateral inhibitory signals from horizontal cells. We saw earlier that there is a distinction between ON bipolars and OFF bipolars. This distinction is inherited by ganglion cells.

Which other sensory system is known to possess center–surround receptive fields?

- ON-center ganglion receptive fields have an excitatory center and inhibitory surround (as in Figure 7.6, top left). Small light spots that fill the center of the receptive field produce the best response.
- OFF-center receptive fields have the opposite arrangement; an inhibitory center and excitatory surround (bottom left). Small dark spots produce the best response.

Midget RGCs have smaller receptive fields than parasol RGCs; near the fovea the center of each midget cell's receptive field receives input from a single cone, whereas parasol cell receptive field centers are 6–8 cones in diameter (Lee, Martin, & Grünert, 2010). The small size of midget cell receptive fields maximizes acuity in central vision (see below under "Information processing"). Receptive field size increases towards the retinal periphery.

The two right-hand profiles in Figure 7.6 show cross-sections of typical ON-center midget and parasol receptive fields (taken across the middle of the receptive field map on the top left). The red lines show the excitatory input to each receptive field, and the gray lines show the inhibitory input. Notice that the strength of each input follows a bell-shaped or normal distribution across the receptive field. Individual ganglion cells vary in the height and width of the two components, but the surround is always much wider than the center (usually by a factor of four or more), and the center input is always more dominant than the surround input.

Center–surround ganglion cell responses were first observed in a mammal (the cat) by Stephen Kuffler in 1953, at Johns Hopkins Hospital, USA.

Spectral response

Cone photoreceptors can be divided into three classes on the basis of their spectral sensitivity (see Chapter 6 and Chapter 8):

- S-cones are most sensitive to short wavelength light in the blue spectral region
- M-cones are most sensitive to medium wavelengths in the green spectral region
- L-cones are most sensitive to long wavelengths in the red spectral region.

The manner in which a given ganglion cell responds to the wavelength properties of incident light depends on how the different cone classes contribute to the different regions of its receptive field. If the excitatory and inhibitory inputs to the cell are each drawn from all three cone classes, then the cell will not show any selectivity in its response to different wavelengths; it responds to variations in illumination across the receptive field. If there is an imbalance between the cone classes in their contributions to excitation or inhibition, then the ganglion cell will exhibit some degree of **spectral opponency**: The cell will be excited by light from one portion of the spectrum, and inhibited by light from another portion of the spectrum. Spectral opponency in RGCs can be broadly classified into two types:

- "Blue–yellow" opponent, with S-cone input opposed by the sum of M- and L-cone input
- "Red–green" opponent, with L- and M-cone inputs of opposite sign.

KEY TERM

Spectral opponency Wavelengths from one portion of the spectrum excite a response, and wavelengths from another portion inhibit a response.

Relation between spectral opponency and spatial opponency

Figure 7.7 summarizes the various receptive field types found in bistratified, midget, and parasol ganglion RGCs.

Blue–yellow opponency is a property of bistratified ganglion cells (Figure 7.7, bottom). Most of the cells discovered so far are excited by blue and inhibited by yellow (so-called blue–ON cells; see Dacey, 2000), and do not show spatial opponency.

Red–green opponency is mediated by midget ganglion cells in the center of the retina. Parasol cells, and midget cells in the peripheral retina, do not show spectral opponency, but do show spatial opponency.

Notice that S-cones have their own class of ganglion cell. The segregation of S-cone responses in bistratified RGCs probably has an evolutionary origin. The S-cone pathway is present in all nonprimate mammals, and may represent a very

FIGURE 7.7
Summary of the spatial, spectral, and temporal response properties of the three major ganglion cell types. Percentages represent the relative preponderance of different cell types. L, M, and S refer to the cone classes providing inputs to each region of the receptive fields (L = long; M = medium; S = short); either excitatory (+) or inhibitory (−). Temporal responses show the effect of presenting a small spot of light at the center of the receptive field for 450 ms (horizontal traces; adapted from de Monasterio, Gouras, & Tolhurst, 1976).

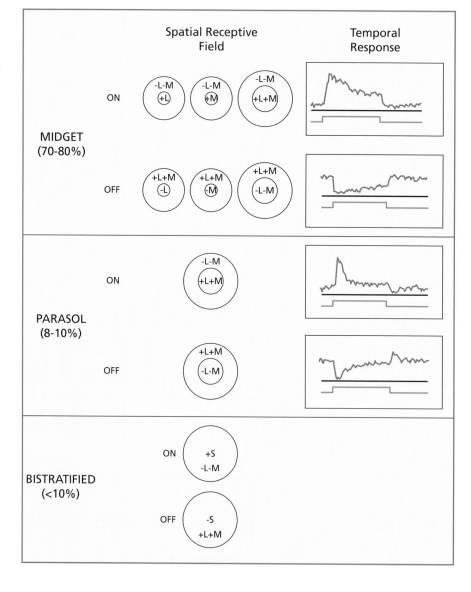

early mammalian color coding circuit. The L and M pathway is mostly restricted to Old World monkeys and is associated with the more recent evolution of separate L- and M-cone types (Dacey, 2000).

Why is the red–green opponent system restricted to central vision? An answer may lie in the distribution of cone types on the retina, and how they connect to ganglion cells. Roorda et al. (2001) created photographic images of the living human retina that revealed the spatial arrangement of S-, M-, and L-cones. Photoreceptors are arranged in an approximately hexagonal lattice pattern. S-cones appear to be distributed nonrandomly, but are relatively rare. On the other hand, the distribution of M- and L-cones is fairly random, allowing clumps of cones of the same pigment type.

A central unresolved issue is the extent to which L- and M-cone inputs to RGCs are selective in order to create well-defined spectrally opponent responses. A moderate degree of selectivity in the connections between cones and RGCs may be sufficient to create spectral opponency, at least in the small receptive field sizes found in central retina (Lee, Martin, & Grünert, 2010). Here, midget cell receptive fields are created from a dominant input from a single M- or L-cone at the center of the receptive field, and weak nonselective inputs from M- and L-cones in the surround (horizontal and amacrine connections are not selective for cone type). This could be sufficient to create strong red–green opponency (Lennie, Haake, & Williams, 1991). Figure 7.8 shows two midget receptive fields superimposed on the retinal mosaic from which they are drawn. The center of both receptive fields is dominated by input from a single L-cone. In the receptive field on the right, the surround is largely drawn from M-cones, so the cell will show strong spectral opponency. The receptive field on the left shows surround inputs from L-cones, and will therefore show weak spectral opponency. Further into the retinal periphery, ganglion cells connect with many tens of cones, most likely drawn randomly from M- and L-cones on the basis of their retinal distribution. Both center and surround will include contributions from both L- and M-cones, so the receptive fields will lack wavelength selectivity. Although the scheme in Figure 7.8 is attractive in its simplicity and has some support (Buzas et al., 2006), the origin of spectral opponency in the retina is still not fully understood (Reid & Shapley, 2002; Dacey & Packer, 2003; Sun et al., 2006; Lee, Martin, & Grünert, 2010).

L-cones outnumber M-cones by a ratio of 1.6:1, but this ratio varies by at least a factor of four between individuals. Nevertheless, color perception seems relatively stable across individuals (Lennie, 2000).

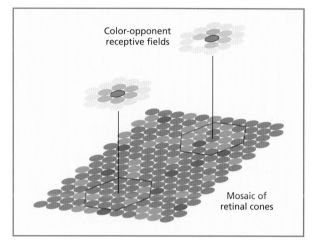

Color-opponent receptive fields

Mosaic of retinal cones

FIGURE 7.8
Origin of spectral opponency in small midget ganglion cell receptive fields. Dominant center input from a single photoreceptor and weak surround inputs from a random mixture of photoreceptor types are sufficient to confer spectral opponency (after Lennie, 2000). Key: blue = S-cones; green = M-cones; red = L-cones. Copyright © 2000 Elsevier. Reproduced with permission.

Temporal response

The temporal response of a cell relates to the time course of its activity following the appearance or disappearance of a stimulus. Midget and parasol cells have distinctively different temporal responses. Midget ganglion cells have a so-called tonic or **sustained temporal response**, which means that their level of activity remains at a relatively high

KEY TERM

Sustained temporal response
A change in response is sustained at a relatively high level for the whole duration of stimulation.

? *What is the functional significance of a cell's temporal response?*

level during the presence of a visual stimulus. Parasol ganglion cells have a phasic or **transient temporal response**, which means that they show a brief change in activity at stimulus onset and offset, but relatively little activity during constant stimulation. Figure 7.7 includes examples of midget and parasol temporal responses to a small spot of light presented in the center of the receptive field for 450 ms (from de Monasterio, Gouras, & Tolhurst, 1976). ON-center cells respond with an increase in firing level, and OFF-center cells respond with a decrease in firing level. Amacrine cell influences may play a role in generating the distinctive temporal responses of ganglion cells.

Information processing by ganglion cells

Ganglion cell responses carry a very selective representation of the retinal image. Certain aspects of the image are preserved, while others are removed. In this sense ganglion cells act as information processing filters (discussed in Chapter 1).

Spatial filtering

A ganglion cell's activity level reflects the combined responses of all the photoreceptors within its receptive field. Since small receptive fields sum over a smaller retinal area than large receptive fields, they can resolve finer spatial details. This is illustrated in Figure 7.9.

The left-hand column shows the ON-center midget and parasol receptive fields also plotted in Figure 7.6, this time as net response (the difference between excitation and inhibition at each point in the receptive field). The top row shows two retinal light distributions: A pair of thin bars (left), and a step change of intensity (right). The profiles below each retinal stimulus show the response of each receptive field type to the stimulus.

Consider first the response of the midget receptive field to the double-bar stimulus. The graph plots the response generated by receptive fields centered on each retinal position shown on the horizontal axis. Receptive fields positioned at the middle of each bar generate a high response, because the bright bar just fills the ON center. Receptive fields positioned in the dark surround generate a lower level of response, since there is less light falling on them. The larger parasol receptive field's response to the double-bar stimulus is markedly different. The receptive field is so large that its response combines the two bars into one. In other words, the large receptive field filters out fine-scale detail in the image (the gap between the bars), and retains coarse-scale detail (the general shape of the pair of bars). The right-hand column in Figure 7.9 shows responses to a step edge. The parasol response is spread over a greater retinal area than the midget response. Because of this, large receptive fields are sometimes said to create **neural blur**.

Center–surround receptive fields are sometimes called edge finders, because they are described as responsive to edges but not to regions of even illumination. This description is only correct when there is perfect balance between the excitatory and inhibitory influences on the receptive field. Ganglion cell receptive fields are invariably weighted in favor of the center, producing edge responses of the kind shown in Figure 7.9; a peak on one side of the edge and a trough on the other side. The tutorials section of this chapter explains how receptive field profiles are defined mathematically, and how they are used to compute the activity levels shown in Figure 7.9.

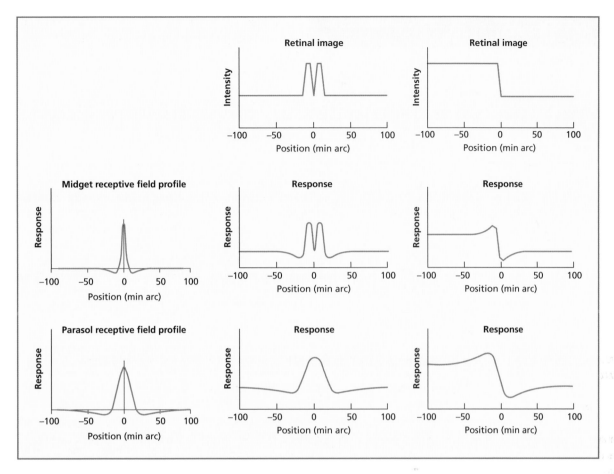

FIGURE 7.9
Examples of ganglion cell responses. The two plots in the leftmost column show cross-sections of midget and parasol spatial receptive fields (the same cells as plotted in Figure 7.6). The two plots in the top row show two stimulus profiles, a double-bar stimulus (left) and a step edge (right). Reading down from each stimulus, and across from each receptive field, the plot at each intersection shows the response of the receptive field to the respective stimulus.

Chromatic filtering

The opponent nature of chromatically selective ganglion cell responses creates antagonistic pairs of colors that cannot coexist. The antagonistic pairs isolate three dimensions or "cardinal directions" of color coding in separate information process-ing channels, two **chromatic channels** and one **achromatic channel**:

Relate channel structure to the theoretical principles introduced in Chapter 1.

- Red versus green (midget ganglion cells)
- Blue versus yellow (bistratified ganglion cells)
- Dark versus light (parasol cells and midget cells).

The implication is that perception of color along the red–green direction is mediated by activity in the red–green channel. Similarly perception along the blue–yellow direction depends on activity in the blue–yellow channel, and perception of intensity is mediated by the achromatic channel. Chromatic opponency forms the basis of one theory of color perception, known as *opponent-process* theory, which was actually developed long before ganglion cells were discovered. The next chapter discusses this account of color sensations.

Temporal filtering

The characteristically different temporal responses of parasol and midget cells (see Figure 7.7) have led to the view that there are two separate channels conveying temporal information to the brain. The two channels have become known as the parvo (P) and magno (M) systems, on the basis of the lateral geniculate neurons to which midget and parasol ganglion cells connect, respectively. The P system has sluggish, sustained temporal responses inherited from midget cells, and is thought to convey information primarily about static form. The M system has fast, transient temporal responses inherited from parasol cells, and is thought to convey information primarily about motion. The M versus P distinction is discussed in more detail later in the chapter.

ON and OFF systems

It is important for the visual system to respond both to light increases and to light decreases. As we saw earlier, ON and OFF cells both respond to increases and decreases, but in opposite directions. For example, ON cells increase their firing rate and OFF cells decrease their firing rate in response to light increases in their receptive field. Since both cell classes respond to both directions of luminance change, why are separate ON and OFF systems required? In the absence of stimulation, ganglion cells are almost silent and produce few action potentials. Consequently, a given cell has much more scope to convey information by raising its activity level than by lowering it: Both light increases and light decreases have to be signaled by increases in activity. Light increases are signaled by ON cells, and decreases are signaled by OFF cells (Schiller, Sandell, & Maunsell, 1986).

THE VISUAL PATHWAY

The fibers of retinal ganglion cells form the optic nerve. In all vertebrates these fibers terminate at six locations within the brain. Each termination site consists of a large agglomeration of neuronal cell bodies called a nucleus. The relative numbers of fibers arriving at each site vary across species. In primates the major projection is to the lateral geniculate nuclei, which receives approximately 90% of ganglion cell fibers. The remaining 10% is shared among the other subcortical nuclei, though most goes to the superior colliculi (Perry, Oehler, & Cowey, 1984). The importance of these minor projections should not be underestimated. There are so many optic nerve fibers that even 10% of them exceeds the combined central projections in the hearing, taste, and smell pathways.

DESTINATIONS OF OPTIC NERVE FIBERS

Lateral geniculate nuclei

Two nuclei in the thalamus, known as **lateral geniculate nuclei** (LGN; also called the dorsal LGN or LGN_d) receive the major projection from the retina in primates (see Figure 7.1). LGN cell fibers project in turn to the cortical receiving area for vision, known as striate cortex or V1. Signals traveling along the path through the LGN to the cortex (the geniculostriate pathway) are thought to be responsible for conscious visual awareness. This pathway is discussed in much more detail in a later section.

Superior colliculi

Two nuclei in the midbrain known as the superior colliculi also receive major projections from the retina. It is the most important projection site in many nonprimate species such as birds, reptiles, and fish. The superior colliculi are thought to be involved in integrating visual and auditory signals, and in directing visual attention (discussed in later chapters).

Suprachiasmatic nuclei

The suprachiasmatic nuclei form part of the hypothalamus, and project to the pineal gland. They are thought be the brain's "biological clock," regulating the daily rhythms of sleep and wakefulness. Visual input to the suprachiasmatic nuclei should allow the body clock to remain synchronized to the cyclical variation in light levels at the Earth's surface. Berson, Dunn, & Takao (2002) found a class of ganglion cell that seems to respond directly to light (without the involvement of photoreceptors) and connects directly to the suprachiasmatic nuclei.

Pretectum

The pretectum lies in the path of optic nerve fibers traveling towards the superior colliculi (in nonmammalian vertebrates the superior colliculus is known as the tectum). Neurons in the pretectum project to neurons in the Edinger–Westphal nucleus that play a role in controlling the constrictor muscle in the iris. Hence the pretectum is thought to be important for regulating pupil diameter.

Pregeniculate

The pregeniculate in primates lies adjacent to the LGN_d, and probably corresponds to the ventral lateral geniculate nucleus (LGN_v) of other vertebrates. The function of the pregeniculate/LGN_v remains mysterious. It does not project to the cortex, but to the suprachiasmatic nuclei, so may be involved in regulating the biological clock.

Accessory optic system

Some optic nerve fibers branch away from the main tract to terminate in midbrain nuclei that form the accessory optic system. The precise function of the accessory optic system is not known, though it seems to play a role in stabilizing the retinal image during head movements (Rodieck, 1998).

THE GENICULOSTRIATE PATHWAY

Representation of the visual field

Binocular convergence

Figure 7.1 shows that in primates, as in many other predators, the two eyes face forward so their fields of view overlap substantially. Consequently, a given object will project images onto the retina of both the right eye and the left eye. For example, the words to the right of the word you are presently reading will project an image onto the outer (temporal) half of your left eye's retina, and onto the inner (nasal) half of your right eye's retina. Important information about depth and distance can be inferred from comparisons between the images projected onto the two eyes (see Chapter 11). The left eye's view of a given image feature must be compared to the right eye's view of the same feature in order to extract this information. The comparison is achieved by neurons in the visual system that receive signals from both eyes, so-called **binocular neurons**. These neurons are located in the visual cortex, as we shall see below. The arrangement of neural connections in the visual pathway is designed to achieve convergence of signals from the two eyes onto binocular cortical neurons.

Notice from Figure 7.1 that the left visual field (solid lines) is represented binocularly in the right cortical hemisphere. The right visual field (dashed lines) is represented binocularly in the left cortical hemisphere. This crossover between eye and brain is achieved by partial decussation.

Partial decussation

When the optic nerve fibers from each eye meet at the optic chiasm (from the Greek letter *chi*, or X) half the fibers from each eye cross over to the other (contralateral) hemisphere of the brain, and half remain in the same hemisphere (ipsilateral), so achieving **partial decussation** or partial crossing-over. The eye of origin and retinal location of each ganglion cell's receptive field determine whether its fiber crosses over or not, as shown in Figure 7.1.

Left visual field Fibers originating in the left visual field of each eye (solid lines in Figure 7.1) converge on the right hemisphere:

- Fibers in the left visual field of the left eye (nasal retina) cross over.
- Fibers in the left visual field of the right eye (temporal retina) do not cross over.

Right visual field Fibers originating in the right visual field of each eye converge on the left hemisphere:

- Fibers in the right visual field of the left eye (temporal retina) do not cross over.
- Fibers in the right visual field of the right eye (nasal retina) cross over.

Consequently, the left LGN, and the cortex to which it projects, receive information from both eyes, but only from the right half of the visual field. The right LGN, and the cortex to which it projects, receive information from the left half of the visual field in both eyes.

Structure of the LGN

LGN layers

Figure 7.10 (top) is a cross-section through the LGN revealing its six major layers, numbered from 1 to 6. Layers 1 and 2 contain large cell bodies, so these layers are called magnocellular or **magno layers**. Layers 3 to 6 contain small cell bodies, so these layers are called parvocellular or **parvo layers**. Each major layer contains two sublayers. The upper,

> **KEY TERMS**
>
> **Magno layers**
> Layers in the LGN with large cell bodies; they receive projections from parasol ganglion cells.
>
> **Parvo layers**
> Layers in the LGN with small cell bodies; they receive projections from midget ganglion cells.

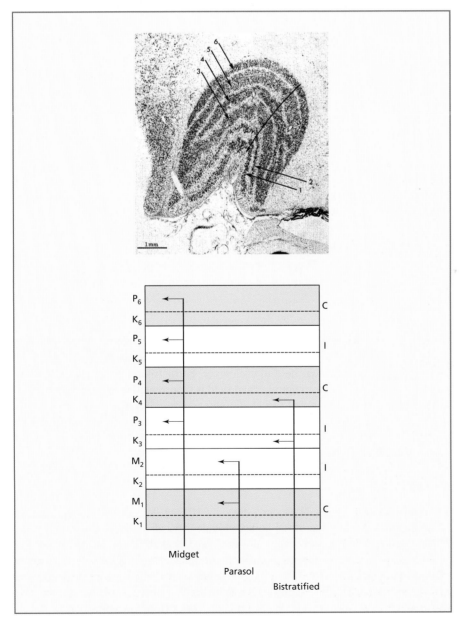

FIGURE 7.10
The lateral geniculate nucleus (LGN). Top: A cross-section through the LGN reveals six major layers. The bottom two layers are magnocellular layers, because they contain large cell bodies; the top four layers are parvocellular layers, because they contain small cell bodies. Bottom: Each layer contains a principal sublayer (labeled M_1 to M_2 and P_3 to P_6), and a koniocellular sublayer (labeled K_1 to K_6). Eye of origin varies from layer to layer: Layers 1, 4, 6 receive input from the contralateral eye (C, shaded); the rest receive input from the ipsilateral eye (I). (Cross-section from Hubel & Wiesel, 1977, by permission of the Royal Society.)

The names attached to different layers are based on Latin or Greek words. Magnus means large and parvus means small in Latin; konis means dust in Greek. Fitzpatrick, Itoh, and Diamond (1983) found that average cell body size in LGN magno layers was 154 µm². Parvo cell bodies measured 119 µm², and cells in the intercalated or konio layers were 76 µm².

principal sublayer contains most of the cell bodies, and the lower koniocellular or **konio sublayer** contains fewer, smaller cell bodies. Each sublayer can be identified by a letter—P for principal parvo, M for principal magno, and K for konio—and a number between 1 and 6. So there is a total of 12 LGN layers—M_1 to M_2, P_3 to P_6, and K_1 to K_6 (bottom of Figure 7.10).

There are four important features of the LGN's layered structure: Eye of origin, ganglion cell type, topography, nonretinal input.

Eye of origin

Each LGN cell within each major layer receives information originating from only one eye. With one exception, the eye of origin alternates in successive layers, as shown in the Figure 7.10. Cells in layers 1, 4, and 6 receive optic nerve fibers from the contralateral eye. Cells in layers 2, 3, and 5 receive optic nerve fibers from the ipsilateral eye.

Ganglion cell type

There is a highly organized projection from different ganglion cell types to LGN layers. Although there is still some uncertainty about connections to the LGN, the following points appear to be well established:

* Midget ganglion cell fibers terminate in the four principal parvo layers, P_3–P_6.
* Parasol ganglion cell fibers terminate in the two principal magno layers, M_1–M_2.
* Small bistratified ganglion cell fibers terminate in two koniocellular layers, K_3 and K_4.

Topography

The receptive fields of cells within each layer of the LGN are arranged topographically, creating a map of the visual field in each layer. Furthermore, the maps in different layers are in register. So the central visual field is represented near the center of each layer. Consequently, if a small visual stimulus is presented at a particular location in the visual field, it will activate cells lying along a line passing through the layers of the LGN perpendicular to its surface (approximately parallel with the column of numbers in Figure 7.10, top, as shown by the arrow).

Nonretinal input

The retinal input to the LGN accounts for only 10% of the synapses on its neurons. Descending fibers from the visual cortex provide 30% of the input (Sillito & Jones, 2002). Cortical input is topographically organized, and different groups of cortical neurons provide input to the magno, parvo, and koniocellular layers of LGN. Other inputs to the LGN also arrive from midbrain sites such as the superior colliculus and reticular formation. The descending input is thought to be important for altering incoming responses on the basis of processing needs in the cortex (top-down processing).

Signal processing in the LGN

No new response properties emerge at the level of the LGN. Cells have center–surround receptive fields similar to those of the incoming optic nerve fibers. The preponderance of nonretinal inputs indicates that the function of the LGN is to modulate the flow of information from retina to cortex. Three particular functions have been proposed (Sillito & Jones, 2002):

- To sharpen spatial responses by modifying the center–surround organization of the receptive fields, perhaps increasing surround inhibition.
- To begin the process of integrating information across larger retinal areas by promoting synchronous activation of ascending LGN signals.
- To enhance the salience of sudden changes in stimulation by modulating the firing patterns of LGN neurons.

THE VISUAL CORTEX

Much of the posterior half of the cerebral cortex is devoted to vision. Anatomical, electrophysiological, and neuroimaging studies have revealed at least 10 distinct areas, each with its own retinotopic map of the visual field. Area V1, also known as **striate cortex**, is the receiving area for the majority of LGN fibers. All the other areas (often called **"extrastriate" cortex**) largely depend on V1, either directly or indirectly, for their visual input, though recent studies have found a direct projection from koniocellular LGN cells to extrastriate area MT (Sincich et al., 2004; Jayakumar et al., 2013). The next section discusses striate cortex in detail. Extrastriate cortex is discussed later in the chapter.

STRIATE CORTEX

Anatomical connections

Layers

Striate cortex is approximately 1.5 mm thick, and is divided into six layers numbered from 1 (nearest the surface) to 6 (deepest). Layer 4 is actually subdivided into separate sublayers labeled 4A, 4B, 4Cα, and 4Cβ (see Figure 7.11).

LGN inputs

Fibers from the LGN terminate in different layers (Fitzpatrick, Itoh, and Diamond, 1983; Chatterjee & Callaway, 2003):

- Magno fibers terminate primarily in layer 4Cα.
- Parvo fibers terminate primarily in layer 4Cβ.
- Konio fibers terminate in superficial layers 2, 3, and 4A.

Internal connections

There are rich interconnections between cells in different cortical layers, particularly from layer 4 cells to cells in layers 2 and 3, and from these superficial layers down to layers 5 and 6.

Striate cortex is so called because of its characteristically striped appearance in anatomical sections, such as the example at the top right of Figure 7.11.

KEY TERMS

Striate cortex
The primary receiving area for visual signals from the LGN; it is also known as V1 or area 17.

Extrastriate cortex
Areas of secondary visual cortex that receive signals from striate cortex.

FIGURE 7.11
Primary visual cortex, or V1, contains six anatomically distinct layers. Layer 4 is divided into four sublayers (4A, 4B, 4Cα, 4Cβ). Parvo, magno, and konio divisions in the LGN project selectively to different layers. The predominant input is to layer 4C (magno to 4Cα and parvo to 4Cβ). Konio cells project to superficial layers. There are forward projections from V1 to extrastriate cortex, as well as descending projections to the LGN and the midbrain. (Cross-section from Hubel & Wiesel, 1977, by permission of the Royal Society.)

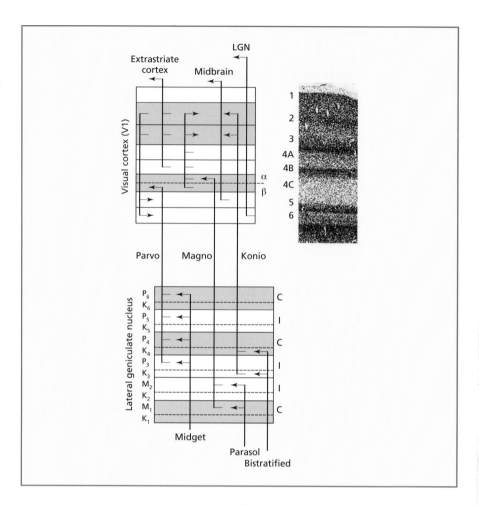

Connections to extrastriate cortex

Fibers project from the striate cortex to several destinations:

- Cells in layers 2, 3, and 4B project to extrastriate cortex.
- Cells in layer 5 project to midbrain structures such as the superior colliculus and pons.
- Cells in layer 6 project to the LGN. Projections are highly selective, with cells in different parts of layer 6 projecting to different layers in the LGN.

Striate cortex also receives reciprocal connections from extrastriate cortex. The extensive connections between cortical cells allow them to generate new forms of stimulus selectivity, particularly selectivity for spatial orientation, motion direction, binocularity, and wavelength.

? *What is the functional significance of cortical cell selectivity?*

Cell properties

Striate cortical cells have much larger receptive fields than LGN cells (Sceniak, Hawken, & Shapley, 2001; see Table 7.6 in the tutorials section). Indeed the difference in receptive field size is so great that it cannot be explained solely by the spread of connections within striate cortex. Sceniak, Hawken, and Shapley (2001) suggest that feedback connections from extrastriate cortex play a role in shaping striate receptive fields. The relatively large receptive fields of cortical cells have a high degree of stimulus specificity.

Orientation tuning

The majority of cortical cells show selectivity for stimulus orientation. For a given cell, lines or bars at a specific orientation produce the greatest response. A change in orientation away from the cell's preferred orientation, even by a few degrees, produces a marked drop in response, as shown in Figure 7.12.

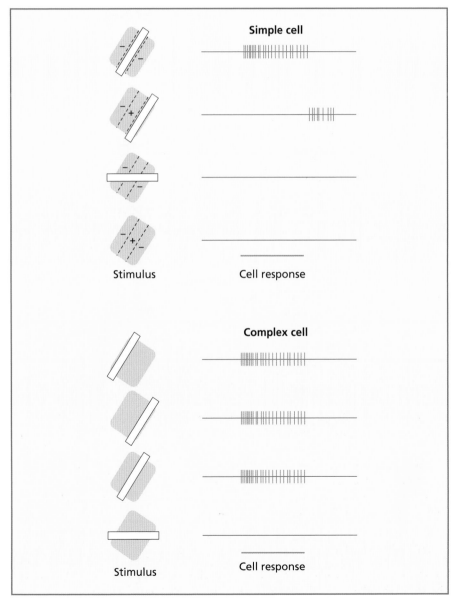

FIGURE 7.12
Orientation tuning in cortical cells. The leftmost column shows bar stimuli at different orientations and positions, superimposed on a simple cell receptive field (top) and a complex cell receptive field (bottom). The trace adjacent to each stimulus shows neural activity as a function of time. The thick horizontal bars mark the duration of each stimulus. Simple cell receptive fields have elongated excitatory and inhibitory zones, and produce the strongest response to a line or edge at the optimal orientation and position. Different cells prefer different orientations. Complex cells also respond best at certain orientations, but their receptive fields cannot be mapped into excitatory and inhibitory regions. Their response does not depend critically on stimulus position.

KEY TERMS

Simple cell

An orientation selective cell in visual cortex with an elongated retinal receptive field containing excitatory and inhibitory zones.

Complex cell

A cell in visual cortex with a relatively large receptive field that does not contain identifiable excitatory or inhibitory zones, but nonetheless is orientation selective.

Direction-selective cell

A visual cell that responds more strongly to retinal movement in one direction than to movement in the opposite direction.

Hubel and Wiesel (1962) also described a third, rare, class of cells called *hypercomplex*, whose response seemed to depend critically on stimulus length as well as orientation (also called end-stopped cells). More recent research indicates that some degree of length tuning is present in many cortical cells (Sceniak, Hawken, & Shapley, 2001), and that some of these cells may actually be tuned to stimulus curvature rather than length. The "hypercomplex" label is no longer widely used.

Orientation-tuned cells can be classified as either **simple** or **complex**, using Hubel and Wiesel's (1962) original criteria. Simple cells have receptive fields that can be mapped into excitatory and inhibitory zones just like retinal ganglion and LGN cells. Orientation tuning arises because the zones are elongated rather than circularly symmetrical (see Figure 7.12, top), so that the optimal stimulus is also elongated. The stimulus must be aligned appropriately with the cell's excitatory and inhibitory zones in order to produce a strong response. Complex cells respond to the same kinds of stimuli as simple cells but their receptive fields are much larger, and they do not contain identifiable excitatory and inhibitory zones. Each cell's response does not depend critically on the precise position of the stimulus in the receptive field (see Figure 7.12, bottom). Complex cells are the most common type of cortical cell, accounting for over two thirds of striate cells. Simple cells are relatively uncommon, at about one in ten striate cells (Hubel & Wiesel, 1968). Our understanding of the origins of orientation tuning is still incomplete (Pugh et al., 2000).

Direction selectivity

Some striate cortical cells respond selectively to motion direction. Figure 7.13 shows the response of a typical **direction-selective cell.** The cell responds vigorously when the stimulus moves up towards the right (preferred direction), but does not respond when the stimulus moves in the opposite direction

FIGURE 7.13
Direction selectivity in cortical cells. The stimulus (leftmost column) was a bar that oscillated back and forth repetitively, shown by the arrows. The trace adjacent to each stimulus denotes neural response. The cell responded only during phases when the bar moved up and to the right.

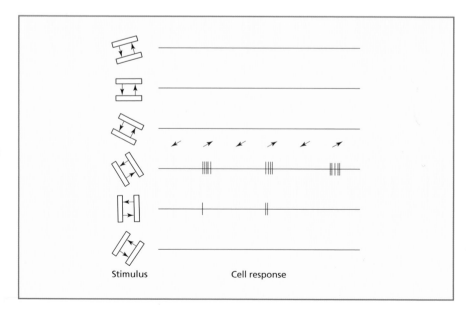

Stimulus   Cell response

(nonpreferred or null direction). Direction selectivity is discussed in greater detail in Chapter 12.

Binocularity

Each cortical hemisphere receives signals originating from both eyes, by virtue of partial decussation in the visual pathway described earlier. A given cortical cell can be assessed in terms of its ability to respond to stimulation presented to each eye. Some cells respond equally well to stimulation of either eye. Others respond much more vigorously to stimulation of one eye than to stimulation of the other, a property known as **ocular dominance**. Hubel and Wiesel devised a classification scheme in which a cell's ocular dominance was rated on a seven-point scale. A cell in group 1 is influenced only by the contralateral eye, and a cell in group 7 is influenced only by the ipsilateral eye. Cells in group 4 are driven equally by both eyes. Figure 7.14 plots the relative proportions of striate cells belonging to each group, in monkey cortex. Simple cells tend to belong in groups 1 or 7, while complex cells are spread more evenly across ocular dominance groups (Hubel & Wiesel, 1968).

As mentioned earlier, binocularity is important for depth coding. Three-dimensional scenes project slightly different images to the two eyes, creating a depth cue known as **binocular disparity**. Some binocular cortical cells do have receptive fields in slightly different locations in the two eyes, making them disparity-tuned. Disparity tuning and depth coding are discussed in much more detail in Chapter 11.

Wavelength

Our understanding of wavelength responses in striate cortex is still incomplete. It is clear, however, that a significant proportion of cortical cells show selective responses to wavelength. Johnson, Hawken, and Shapley (2001) found that 41% of striate cells gave chromatically opponent responses. Some cortical cells show single opponency, with opposing responses to different cone inputs as in the LGN. Other cells exhibit **double opponency**, in which the cell has opponent responses to different cone inputs, but the sign of the response is reversed in different regions of the receptive field (Shapley & Hawken, 2011). For example, a given cell's receptive field may have one zone in which it is excited by L-cone inputs and inhibited by M-cone inputs, and an adjacent zone in which it is inhibited by L-cones but excited by M-cones. The role of chromatically opponent cells in color vision is discussed in Chapter 8.

Surround suppression

The receptive fields originally mapped by Hubel and Wiesel (1962) are sometimes called "classical receptive fields" or CRFs. Many cortical neurons have an additional region surrounding the CRF

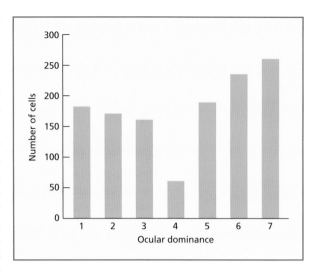

FIGURE 7.14
The distribution of ocular dominance in striate cortical cells. Cells in group 1 are driven only by the contralateral eye; cells in group 7 are driven only by the ipsilateral eye; cells in group 4 are driven equally by the two eyes. The great majority of cells show a clear preference for one eye or the other (data from Hubel & Wiesel, 1968).

where preferred stimuli actually suppress their response (see, for example, DeAngelis, Freeman, & Ohzawa, 1994). Surround suppression is thought to play a role in regulating neural responsiveness in order to maximize stimulus sensitivity and discrimination ("normalization"; see Carandini & Heeger, 2012), and in the analysis of higher order visual features such as texture-defined borders, which will be discussed in Chapters 9 and 12 (Tanaka & Ohzawa, 2009; Hallum & Movshon, 2014).

Origin of cortical cell receptive field properties

Hubel and Wiesel favored a hierarchical scheme to explain the construction of cortical receptive fields. A simple cell with an orientation-tuned receptive field could receive inputs from several LGN cells whose concentric receptive fields are aligned on the retina to form a row at a specific orientation. Cells with large, complex receptive fields could be constructed using inputs from a group of simple cells with overlapping, small retinal receptive fields that have the same orientation tuning. Although attractive, there is no direct evidence in favor of the hierarchical scheme, and some contradictory evidence. As mentioned at the start of this section, Sceniak, Hawken, and Shapley (2001) found that cortical receptive fields are too large to be explained by simple convergence of LGN receptive fields. In addition, several lines of evidence indicate that complex receptive fields are created in parallel with simple receptive fields, rather than in series (see Wilson et al., 1990). It is likely that striate receptive fields emerge from a combination of complex circuitry within striate cortex, and reciprocal connections with extrastriate cortex.

Functional architecture

The previous section detailed some of the stimulus specificities that emerge in individual striate cortical cells. In this section we consider how these neurons are distributed within the cortical tissue, an aspect of the cortex known as its functional architecture. Are cells that share certain stimulus specificities grouped together, and, if so, how? It is important to bear in mind that a given cell is selectively responsive to a combination of stimulus attributes, such that the optimal stimulus must have an appropriate retinal location, orientation, binocularity, and (frequently) motion direction. If grouping principles do apply to the layout of cells in the cortex, we must also consider how the ordered arrangements of different preferences intersect.

> [?] Compare the architecture of striate cortex with the architecture of somatosensory cortex outlined in Chapter 3.

Topography

Topographic maps are a common feature in sensory cortex, as demonstrated in previous chapters. So it should come as no surprise to learn that cells are distributed across the visual cortex so that their receptive field locations form an ordered topographic map of the visual field. Figure 7.15 (right) shows the right half of the visual field. Central, foveal locations are at the center of the bull's-eye pattern at 0°. The black circle shows the location of the optic disc, where optic nerve fibers leave the eye. Figure 7.15 (left) shows the surface of the contralateral (left) striate cortex in humans, marked with the visual field location of receptive fields at each point on the cortical surface. Although the visual field is mapped in a very orderly way, the map is hugely distorted. About half of the cortical surface is devoted to the central 10° of the visual field, which occupies only 1% of the visual field.

Layers

As mentioned earlier, the gray matter of the cortex can be divided into six layers of neurons lying parallel to its surface, numbered from 1 at the surface down to 6. Hubel and Wiesel (1962, 1968) found that different cell types tended to be more numerous in some layers than in others. Cells in layer 4 tended to have either circularly symmetrical receptive fields, or elongated "simple" receptive fields. Cells in the more superficial (1–3) and deeper (5–6) layers tended to have "complex" receptive fields. Wavelength selective cells are found in all layers, but are concentrated especially in layers 2 and 3 (Johnson, Hawken, & Shapley, 2001). This organization makes sense in the context of the anatomical connections between layers described earlier, with LGN fibers terminating mostly in layer 4.

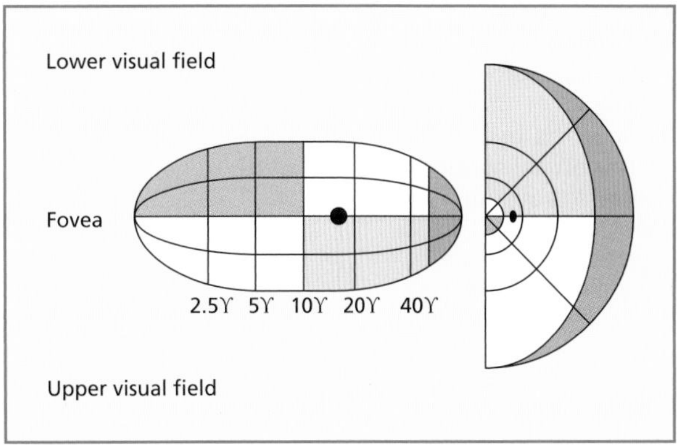

Columns

Hubel and Wiesel (1962, 1968) discovered that the cortex can also be partitioned into columns running perpendicularly to its surface, demarcated by alternations in **ocular dominance** and **orientation**. Recordings from electrodes which advanced through the cortex along a line perpendicular to its surface revealed that successive cells had similar ocular dominance and orientation preferences. Electrode penetrations along a more oblique angle found sequences of cells that alternated repetitively in ocular dominance between left-eye and right-eye dominant. At the same time, preferred orientation changed progressively from cell to cell. Ocular dominance columns are much wider than orientation columns. A distance of 1 mm on the cortical surface is sufficient to cover a complete ipsilateral–contralateral cycle of ocular dominance, and a total shift in preferred orientation of 180°.

Figure 7.16 (top) is a schematic depiction of striate cortical architecture, showing the columnar arrangement of orientation and ocular dominance columns. Orientation columns generally cross the borders between ocular dominance columns perpendicularly to them, and converge in pinwheel-like patterns at the centers of ocular dominance columns (not shown in Figure 7.16). Viewed from above the surface of the cortex, the tops of ocular dominance columns form a striped pattern across the cortex, as shown in Figure 7.16 (bottom).

Blobs

Layers 2 and 3 of striate cortex contain clusters of cells, called cytochrome oxidase **blobs**, that were identified over 30 years ago (Wong-Riley & Carroll, 1984) using a histological stain that detects high levels of metabolic activity. These blobs have been the subject of intense scrutiny, and some controversy, since their discovery. They are cylindrical pillars roughly 0.5 mm apart, and

FIGURE 7.15
Relative area of the striate cortex devoted to different regions of the visual field. The right half of the visual field is shown on the right, subdivided into zones centered on the fovea. The surface of the contralateral striate cortex is shown on the left, marked and shaded to match the visual field diagram. A very small central portion of the visual field occupies a large proportion of cortical surface.

KEY TERMS

Ocular dominance column
A slab of cortical tissue running perpendicular to the cortical surface, in which all binocular cells share the same degree of ocular dominance.

Orientation column
A slab of cortical tissue running perpendicular to the cortical surface, in which all orientation-selective cells share the same preferred orientation.

Blob
A cluster of cells in the superficial layers of striate cortex identified by a staining technique, many of which are color selective.

FIGURE 7.16
Top: Schematic depiction of a striate cortical hypercolumn, covering a 1 mm × 1 mm region of the cortical surface. Cells are grouped according to their ocular dominance, with the dominant eye alternating roughly every millimeter. Preferred orientation changes progressively but more rapidly than ocular dominance, so that a complete set of orientation preferences occupies approximately 1 mm of cortical distance. Cytochrome oxidase blobs are found in superficial layers, centered on the ocular dominance columns. Bottom: View of the cortical surface from above, showing how the tops of ocular dominance columns form a swirling, striped pattern not unlike a fingerprint.

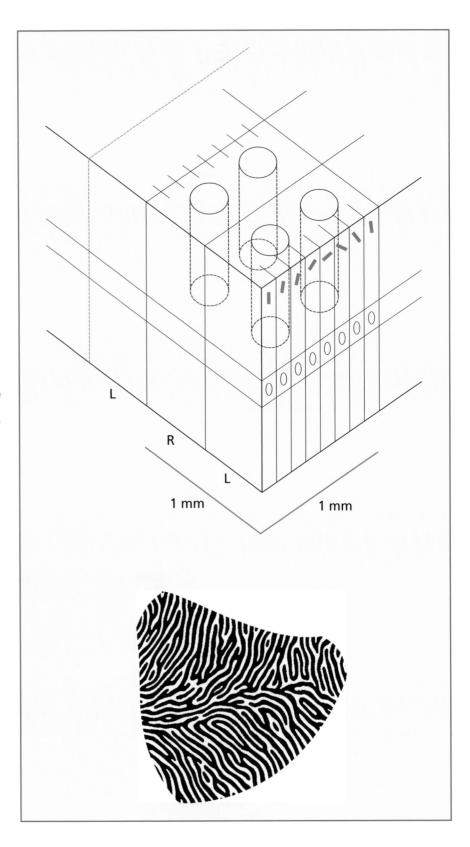

arranged in parallel rows centered on ocular dominance columns (Livingstone & Hubel, 1982; see Figure 7.16). Cells in the blobs receive afferents from koniocellular LGN fibers, as well as from other cells within striate cortex. The receptive fields of cells within the blob regions are often poorly tuned for orientation, and many are color selective (Landisman & Ts'o, 2002). However there is no consensus in the literature regarding the degree to which color-selective cells cluster in the blobs (Shapley & Hawken, 2011).

Hypercolumns

Cells in all layers below a particular location on the cortical surface have receptive fields in approximately the same location in the visual field. Advancing across the surface, receptive field location changes progressively to create the topographic map described earlier. However, the local scatter in receptive field position is such that one must traverse a distance of approximately 2 mm on the cortical surface to move from one region of the visual field to the next. This distance is sufficient to include one complete cycle of ocular dominance, and a full range of preferred orientations. Hubel and Wiesel (1974) therefore argued that a 1 mm^2 region of cortex can be viewed as a functional unit called a **hypercolumn** that contains all the neural machinery required to analyze a particular region of the visual field. In central vision, each hypercolumn would cover an area of the visual field spanning about 0.25° or less. In peripheral vision (20° eccentricity), each hypercolumn would cover an area over 30 times this size.

KEY TERM

Hypercolumn
A block of cortex containing one complete cycle of ocular dominance and a full range of orientation preferences.

EXTRASTRIATE CORTEX

Beyond striate cortex, a large number of visually responsive cortical areas have been identified on the basis of several criteria, including topographic organization, anatomical connections, and cell response properties. Figure 7.17 illustrates the 30 cortical areas identified in the macaque monkey.

Some of these areas have close homologues in human cortex, identified using neuroimaging techniques (Tootell et al., 1998a). The functional significance of these diverse areas is still unclear. Some researchers have attempted to organize the visual areas hierarchically on the basis of anatomical connections, to reveal the order in which visual processing advances from one area to the next (Felleman & van Essen, 1991). However, with approximately 300 projections between different areas, the number of possible hierarchical schemes is extremely large, making it difficult to draw firm conclusions about hierarchical processing, at least beyond the first five or six areas (Hilgetag, O'Neill, & Young, 1996). Indications about the role of areas closest to V1 can be gleaned from their detailed properties, some of which are summarized in Figure 7.18 (based on Lennie, 1998; and Schmolesky et al., 1998).

> There is still some debate about the best way to characterize areas V3, V3A, and VP. Some authors view V3 and VP as a single area, since they both share borders with V2, and cover the lower and upper visual field respectively (VP is shown in Figure 7.17). Others prefer to include V3A in the grouping. For simplicity, all three areas will be treated as a single complex labeled V3/V3A in this discussion.

FIGURE 7.17
Cortical areas of the macaque monkey that contain cells responsive to visual stimuli (shaded areas redrawn from Felleman & van Essen, 1991). The small insets show an intact brain, viewed from each side. The large map represents a flattened view of one hemisphere. Reproduced by permission of Oxford University Press.

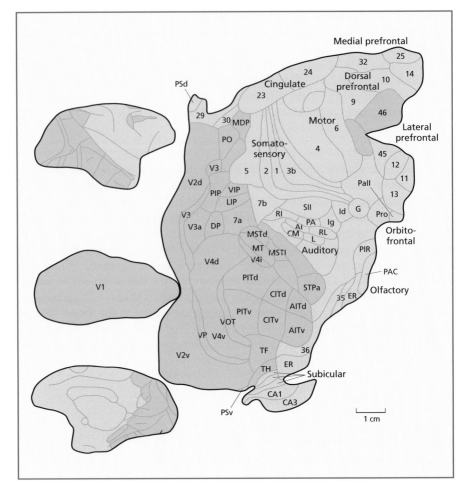

Size

Each cortical area in Figure 7.18 is drawn in proportion to its relative area. On this basis alone it can be seen that areas V1, V2, and V4 are responsible for the bulk of early visual processing.

Connectivity

The values adjacent to the arrows connecting areas in Figure 7.18 show estimates of the percentage of fibers in each projection pathway (calculated in the manner described by Lennie, 1998). V1 projects primarily to V2. V2 in turn has roughly equal projections to V3/V3A and to V4. V3/V3A projects predominantly to V4. The largest projection from V4 is to IT. Area MT receives very small projections from V1, V2, and V3. It projects to MST as well as to several other areas (not shown), including the frontal eye fields (FEF).

Response latency

Response latency of a cell refers to the time interval between the presentation of stimulus on the retina and the initiation of a response in the cell. The vertical position

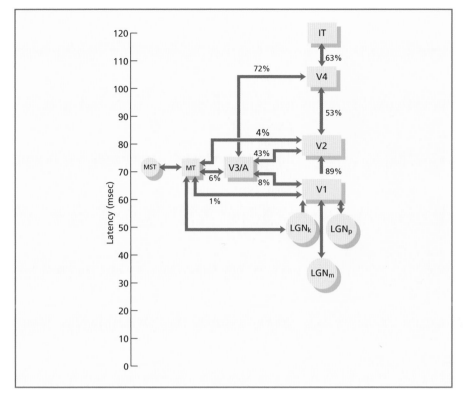

FIGURE 7.18
Some distinctive features of the largest visual cortical areas. The relative size of the boxes reflects the relative area of different regions. The arrows labeled with percentages show the proportion of ascending fibers in each projection pathway. Connections are reciprocal or bidirectional (not shown). The vertical position of each box represents the response latency of cells in each area, as measured in single-unit recording studies. V3/A includes areas labeled as V3, V3A, and VP in Figure 7.17; IT includes areas labeled as PITd, PITv, CITd, CITv in Figure 7.17.

of each area in Figure 7.18 represents the response latency of its cells (indicated by the scale on the left), as reported by Schmolesky et al. (1998) from single unit recordings (see also Lamme & Roelfsema, 2000). Area V1 responds earliest, as befits its role as the primary receiving area for LGN fibers. However, a succession of dorsal areas (V3/V3A, MT, and MST) have response latencies only a few milliseconds longer than that of V1, and at least one area (MT) receives a direct projection from the LGN (Sincich, Park, Wohlgemuth, & Horton, 2004). More ventral areas (V2, V4, and IT) have slower latencies.

Response properties

Figure 7.19 shows the percentage of cells in each area displaying selectivity for orientation, motion direction, color, and binocular disparity. All these selectivities are found in all areas. Areas V1, V2, and V3 are broadly similar in terms of the preponderance of different stimulus preferences. Area V4 has a higher proportion of color selective cells than any other area, and MT has the highest proportions of motion and disparity selective cells.

Notice that the values in Figure 7.19 exceed 100%. This means that cortical cells have multiple stimulus preferences. A given cell may show selective responses to both orientation and movement direction, or binocular disparity. So although cells show a high degree of specificity, they cannot be viewed as "feature detectors" that respond only in the presence of a single stimulus attribute.

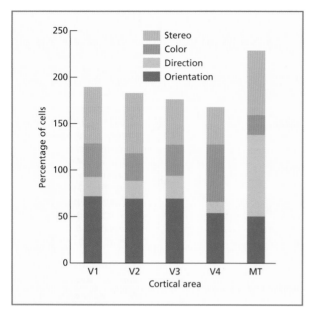

FIGURE 7.19
Percentage of cells in each of the first five cortical areas selective for orientation, motion direction, color, and binocular disparity. Total percentage in each area exceeds 100% because cells respond selectively to more than one stimulus attribute. The full range of stimulus specificities is found in all areas, though relative proportions vary from area to area.

Although cells in different areas have broadly similar stimulus specificities, closer inspection reveals some marked differences. For instance, receptive field sizes are substantially larger in extrastriate cortex, as shown in Table 7.3 (figures from Lennie, 1998).

Extrastriate cells also show more sophisticated response properties than striate cells. Motion selective cells in MT, for instance, respond to more complex motion properties than striate cells (discussed in more detail in Chapter 12). Cells in MST appear to prefer large-field motion such as expansion or rotation (Tanaka & Saito, 1989). Cells in IT prefer highly specific spatial patterns, such as geometrical shapes or even faces (Tanaka, 1993; Perrett, Rolls, & Caan, 1982).

Selective sensory attention is known to modulate the strength of a cortical neuron's response to its preferred stimulus (discussed in Chapter 14). Extrastriate neurons show much larger attention effects than striate neurons (Maunsell, 2004). The source of this modulation is still unclear.

Architecture

Detailed study of extrastriate cortex has revealed highly ordered architectural features. Cytochrome oxidase staining of V2 reveals **stripes**, in contrast to the blobs of V1 (Tootell et al., 1983). The nature of the projection from V1 cells to V2 cells is still not clear (Xiao & Felleman, 2004). MT cells appear to be grouped according to speed preference (Liu & Newsome, 2003) and disparity tuning (De Angelis & Newsome, 1999), whereas V2 cells show some grouping according to color preference (Xiao, Wang, & Felleman, 2003).

KEY TERM

Stripes
Groups of cells in area V2 of visual cortex identified by a staining technique.

TABLE 7.3 Relative receptive field size in different cortical areas

Relative RF size	Cortical area
1	V1
2–3	V2
4–5	V3/VP
5–6	V4
7–10	MT

Lesion studies

Lesions have been used in many studies as a way to infer the functional role of different cortical areas. Several studies have used reversible lesions, in which area V1 is temporarily deactivated by cooling before neural responses in adjacent areas are recorded. Results of these experiments are consistent with the pattern of connections shown in Figure 7.18. Deactivation of V1 causes a complete loss of responsiveness in V2 and V4 neurons, and partial loss in V3 (Girard, Salin, & Bullier, 1991). There is relatively little change in MT responses during V1 deactivation (Girard, Salin, & Bullier, 1992).

Behavioral studies shed light on the perceptual consequences of cortical lesions (e.g., Newsome et al., 1985; Merigan, Nealey, & Maunsell, 1993; Merigan, 1996):

- V1 lesions result in a complete loss of visual function in the affected area.
- V2 lesions produce impaired form and texture discrimination.
- V4 lesions also produce impaired form and texture discrimination.
- MT lesions cause pronounced deficits in motion perception.

"Two streams" theories of cortical function

The predominant view of visual cortical function is that beyond V2 it divides into two parallel **streams of processing** which perform different roles, each containing several successive stages of analysis in different cortical areas. The two streams are known as the **ventral** stream, which follows a lower route into the temporal lobe (including areas V4 and IT), and the **dorsal** stream, which follows a higher route into the parietal lobe (including areas V3, MT, and MST). The division into two parallel streams was first proposed by Ungerleider and Mishkin (1982) but over the intervening years there has been continuing debate as to the best way to characterize the difference between the two streams.

"What" versus "where"

Ungerleider and Mishkin, (1982) based their proposal on the results of lesion experiments in monkeys. They found that lesions in the temporal cortex caused severe deficits in shape and object discrimination but did not affect performance in visuospatial tests such as visually guided reaching. Parietal lesions, on the other hand, had no effect on visual discrimination but did cause deficits in visuospatial tasks. Ungerleider and Mishkin (1982) proposed a "what" versus "where" distinction: The ventral "what" stream specializes in processing information about object features and identity, and the dorsal "where" stream specializes in visuospatial analysis, including movement and visually guided reaching. Recall from Chapter 5 that a similar division into "where" and "what" streams has been proposed in auditory cortex.

Magno versus parvo

Following Ungerleider and Mishkin's (1982) original proposal, some authors have argued that the specialization can be better described in terms of the attributes which are processed in the two streams: Motion in the dorsal stream, form and color in the ventral stream. This distinction is a direct continuation of the distinctive response properties of magno and parvo cells, that can be traced right down to the parasol and midget cells of the retina (Livingstone & Hubel, 1988; Van Essen & Gallant, 1994). Magno cells are associated with motion processing, while parvo cells are associated with form processing. However it has become clear in recent years that the two streams process the same visual attributes, combining both magno and parvo inputs, but for different purposes (Malpeli, Schiller, & Colby, 1981; Nealey & Maunsell, 1994; Nassi & Callaway, 2006). For example, motion and depth information can be used both for "dorsal" tasks such as navigation, and for "ventral" tasks such as shape analysis.

"Perception" versus "action"

More recently the debate has focused particularly on the functions of the dorsal stream. Goodale and Milner (1992) described it as an action-focused "how" stream which specializes in the unconscious control of action. The ventral stream, on the other hand, serves conscious perception. Goodale and Milner (1992) based

KEY TERMS

Processing stream
A series of neural processing stages in a sensory system specializing in the extraction of certain stimulus attributes.

Ventral stream
A processing stream including cortical areas V4 and IT, which is claimed to specialize in the analysis of spatial form.

Dorsal stream
A processing stream including cortical areas V3, MT, and MST, which is claimed to specialize in the analysis of movement, depth, and action.

their proposals on human clinical cases. Patients with damage that includes the occipitotemporal region (ventral) cannot describe or recognize objects, but patients with damage in posterior parietal cortex (dorsal) have difficulty in reaching for objects, adjusting for object size, shape, and orientation.

Kravitz et al. (2011) have argued that the dorsal stream is involved in several functions including visually guided action, spatial navigation, and spatial memory. An fMRI study by Zachariou, Klatzky, & Behrmann (2014) concluded that both streams contribute to shape perception, but location processing ("where") is a particular function of the dorsal stream.

Evaluation

Thirty years after the dorsal versus ventral distinction was first proposed, debate continues as to its functional significance. The following observations are consistent with the view that the dorsal stream has a specific function that requires fast processing, but information is shared extensively between the two streams:

1. There is a large disparity in size between areas in the two streams. The total cortical area devoted to the ventral stream areas in Figure 7.18 (V4, IT) is 2.5 times larger than the area devoted to the dorsal stream areas (V3/A, MT, MST). This indicates that the dorsal stream has a more specialized and/or simpler function than the ventral stream.
2. There is a marked difference in latency between the two streams. The three dorsal areas have almost identical, fast latencies. Responses in ventral areas are up to twice as slow. This indicates that the two streams do not act in parallel, at least in the sense of response timing. Whatever the dorsal stream does, it has to be done fast (Chen et al., 2007).
3. There are extensive reciprocal connections between areas forming the two streams, indicating a high degree of cross-talk between them.
4. There is no clear dichotomy between the streams in terms of cell response properties. The full range of stimulus specificities is found in both streams, though in different proportions. Along with the previous observation, this indicates that the two streams are not strictly segregated modules dedicated to processing separate stimulus attributes. They may specialize in different tasks (action guidance, shape analysis, and so on), rather than in attribute processing.

CHAPTER SUMMARY

The visual system can be divided into three major components: The retina, the visual pathway, and the visual cortex.

THE RETINA

The retina is a layered network of cells lining the inner surface of each eye:

*   The outer nuclear layer contains over 120 million photoreceptor cells that generate graded changes in neurotransmitter release in response to changes in illumination.

- The inner nuclear layer contains a complex network of bipolar, horizontal, and amacrine cells through which the photoreceptor responses converge onto ganglion cells.
- The ganglion cell layer contains 1 million cell bodies of ganglion cells, whose axons form the optic nerve.
- Midget, parasol, and small bistratified ganglion cells supply over 75% of optic nerve fibers, and their activity carries information about spatial and temporal variations in the luminance and spectral properties of the light striking the retina.
- Other ganglion cell types are also likely to play important functions, but relatively little is known about them.

THE VISUAL PATHWAY

The visual pathway carries responses from the retina to the visual cortex:

- In mammals the major termination site for optic nerve fibers is the lateral geniculate nucleus (LGN) in the thalamus.
- Due to partial decussation, fibers carrying responses from the left visual field of each eye terminate in the right LGN, and responses from the right visual field arrive in the left LGN.
- Each LGN contains two magnocellular layers and four parvocellular layers, each separated by a koniocellular layer.
- Parvo, magno, and konio layers receive selective projections from midget, parasol, and bistratified ganglion cells respectively.
- LGN cells project to the primary receiving area in visual cortex, V1, and to extrastriate MT.
- The preponderance of nonretinal input to the LGN indicates that its main function is to modulate incoming responses on the way to the cortex.

THE VISUAL CORTEX

- The visual cortex comprises the major receiving area V1, also known as striate cortex, and numerous extrastriate areas.
- Cortical cells respond selectively to stimulus orientation, movement direction, color, and binocular disparity.
- Extrastriate cortical cells have larger receptive fields and more complex responses than striate cells.
- In all cortical areas, cells are distributed in a highly ordered pattern.
- The precise function of many extrastriate areas is not clear, but a broad division between two parallel streams is a central element in current theories. One stream includes a series of ventral areas, and the other passes through more dorsal areas.
- The ventral stream is thought to specialize in the analysis of spatial pattern and form; the dorsal stream seems to be important for visually guided action and navigation, though its function is still debated.

TUTORIALS

WHY DO WE NEED TO KNOW ABOUT VISUAL PHYSIOLOGY?

This chapter has presented a very detailed introduction to the physiology of the visual system. Since this book is really concerned with visual perception rather than visual physiology, many students might wonder why such a detailed knowledge of physiology is important for understanding vision.

One way to answer this question is to look back at theories of vision that predated single-cell studies. The gross anatomy of the connections between eye and brain has been known since the turn of the 20th century. However, knowledge of neural circuit layout alone is not enough to infer function. Before recordings of activity in individual cells became available in the 1950s, theories of perception were inspired by anatomy. The brain was known to contain huge numbers of cells, massively interconnected (but only over short distances) in circuits that are similar over the whole cortex. Studies of localized brain damage (e.g., following gunshot wounds) also showed that the visual cortex was mapped topographically. These facts inspired the *Electrical Field Theory* of perception. Visual patterns were thought to set up corresponding fields of electrical activity across the surface of the cortex. Perceptual organization in complex displays was said to be governed by interactions between these current fields. Experimental tests of the theory included attempts to short-circuit the electrical fields by pinning metallic strips across the surface of the cortex in rhesus monkeys, and then performing tests of visual functioning (e.g., Lashley, Chow, & Semmes, 1951).

Of course we now know that, despite anatomical uniformity, functional properties vary markedly from cell to cell and from area to area in the cortex. The key word is specialization rather than uniformity of function. The known functional properties of cells, and the architecture of the cortex, place fundamental constraints on the nature of perceptual theories.

However it is important to be aware of potential pitfalls when applying physiological findings to perception. A highly influential book on visual processing by David Marr, published posthumously in 1982, took issue with the efforts of many researchers which sought to understand perception on the basis of the known properties of cells in the visual cortex. He argued that:

> *trying to understand perception by studying only neurons is like trying to understand bird flight by studying only feathers: It just cannot be done. In order to understand bird flight, we have to understand aerodynamics; only then do the structure of feathers and the different shapes of bird's wings make sense.*
>
> (Marr, 1982, p. 27)

Marr argued that theories of perception must consider, in abstract computational terms, what information is required for a given perceptual task, why that information is useful, and how it is used. However, computational considerations alone are not sufficient, at least for understanding human perception. An elegant computational theory that would be impossible to implement in neural hardware would have little to say about how humans perceive the world. The underlying neural structures place fundamental constraints on the computations that the visual system could or should perform, so it is crucial to give due consideration to the physiology when building theories.

Neural hardware can itself suggest computational theories. To return to Marr's analogy with bird flight, it has been observed that the feathers at the tips of eagle wings curl up consistently, which suggests that this feature serves a useful function. Aerodynamic studies of this design have found that curled wing tips maximize lift while minimizing wingspan (and therefore aiding maneuverability). Designers of the Airbus A380 incorporated this natural feature in the design of their aircraft to minimize its wingspan, so that it can land at smaller airports. Likewise studies of nature's solutions to processing problems can lead to breakthroughs in our understanding of the underlying computations. It is no coincidence that Marr's favored computational device for detecting luminance edges in images (his "Laplacian-of-Gaussian" operator) bears a striking resemblance to the center–surround receptive fields of RGCs. The next tutorial shows how to build a simple computational model of RGC response using Marr's device.

Marr's (1982) crucial insight was that a full understanding of perception requires us to consider both computational issues and the known physiology. One or the other by itself is not sufficient. Many times in later chapters you will come across an explanation for a well-known perceptual phenomenon in visual perception which attempts to combine knowledge of physiological entities such as photoreceptors, receptive fields, stimulus-specific neurons, or cortical processing with computational concepts such as population coding and Bayesian inferences.

MODELING CELL RESPONSES

Mathematical techniques are available that allow us to compute precisely how an array of cells in the visual system responds to a specific visual stimulus. Computational modeling was advocated by Marr (1982), as discussed in the previous tutorial, and has become a crucial tool in vision research. It can reveal exactly which aspects of the stimulus are preserved in cell responses, and which are discarded. As such it provides a rigorous method for comparing the predictions of theoretical models against actual data (obtained either from cells, or from behaving organisms). Textbooks on perception rarely offer any detail on how computational modeling is performed, and this tutorial is intended to fill the gap by offering a general introduction to the field, at least in the context of relatively low-level cells in the visual system. It makes minimal assumptions about prior mathematical knowledge. Read on if you are comfortable dealing with some mathematical concepts (even those you barely understand), and are interested in finding out how computational models can be used to understand what cells may be doing.

Cells in the visual system can be viewed as simple **information processing devices**, described in terms of an input, an output, and a process that transforms one into the other. In order to compute the output (response) of a given cell to a given visual stimulus, we need to specify:

- *Input*—A description of the stimulus.
- *Process*—A description of the cell's receptive field, and a mathematical process for applying the receptive field to the stimulus.
- *Output*—A description of the output corresponding to the cell's response to the stimulus.

Visual stimuli

Stimuli are represented by arrays of numbers, corresponding to the intensity of the image at regular intervals or sample points across the retina. A one-dimensional cross-section through a visual image can be represented using a one-dimensional array of numbers. For example, Table 7.4 shows the intensity of the image in the region of the double bar plotted in Figure 7.9. Intensity is constant at 100 (arbitrary) units, except at the locations of the bars (5 to 10, and −5 to −10′ arc) where intensity rises to 200 units.

Receptive fields

A one-dimensional cross-section through a receptive field can also be represented by an array of numbers which specify the cell's responsiveness at each location. Table 7.5 shows the responsiveness profile of the midget receptive field plotted in Figure 7.9.

TABLE 7.4 Intensity profiles in a double-bar luminance profile

Position (min)	−40	−35	−30	−25	−20	−15	−10	−5	0	5	10	15	20	25	30	35	40
Intensity	100	100	100	100	100	100	200	200	100	200	200	100	100	100	100	100	100

TABLE 7.5 Responsiveness profile of a midget receptive field

Position (min)	−20	−15	−10	−5	0	5	10	15	20
Response $R(x)$	−0.052	−0.073	−0.091	0.098	0.888	0.098	−0.091	−0.073	−0.052

As shown in Figure 7.6, many receptive fields can be decomposed into opposing excitatory and inhibitory regions. In the case of RGCs, these regions are formed from two bell-shaped, or Gaussian, distributions (also known as "normal distributions"; Rodieck, 1965). The peaks of the two distributions, one positive (excitation) and one negative (inhibition), are aligned but the center distribution is narrower than the surround distribution. The responsiveness of the cell can therefore be calculated as the sum of the positive and negative distributions (or equivalently as the difference between two positive Gaussian functions; often called a **difference-of-Gaussians**, or *DoG* function). A convenient mathematical formula for a one-dimensional DoG function is:

$$R(x) = \exp(-x^2/\sigma_c^2) - (k\sigma_c/\sigma_s) \exp(-x^2/\sigma_s^2)$$

where x represents retinal position. Only three parameters, σ_c, σ_s, and k, are needed to specify the receptive field profile. σ_c and σ_s are **space constants** that determine the width of the center and surround components respectively (Wilson, 1978). They specify the space constant (standard deviation) of each distribution. The scaling factor k sets the balance between the center and surround components, based on the total area under each component. If k equals 1.0, then the center and surround are perfectly balanced (areas equal). This means that there is no net response from the cell when the whole receptive field is evenly illuminated. If k is less than 1.0, then the response is biased in favor of the center, so the cell does respond to even illumination.

Many different estimates of the three parameters are available in the single-cell recording literature. Table 7.6 shows some typical values, based

TABLE 7.6 Representative estimates of concentric receptive field parameters

Paper	Cell type	σ_c (min arc)	σ_s (min arc)	k
Enroth-Cugell and Robson (1966)	Cat X ganglion (p. 536)	23.2	156.4	0.90
Linsenmeier et al. (1982)	Cat X ganglion (fig. 14)	21.6	86.4	0.94
	Cat Y ganglion (fig. 14)	52.8	79.2	0.75
Derrington and Lennie (1984)	Macaque parvo LGN (table 1)	1.72	10.14	0.65
Croner and Kaplan (1995)	Macaque midget Ganglion (table 1, fig.10)	3.0	25.2	0.55
	Macaque parasol Ganglion (table 1, fig. 10)	10.2	48	0.55
Sceniak et al. (2001)	Macaque V1 (figs. 2, 3, 5A)	60	132	0.63
Xu et al. (2002)	Owl monkey K (p. 707)	18.6	54.6	0.83
	Owl monkey M (p. 707)	10.8	46.2	0.74
	Owl monkey P (p. 707)	7.2	33.6	0.74

on the means or medians of samples of cells studied in each of the research papers. Estimates vary due to differences between species, cell classes, visual stimuli, retinal location, and even the anesthetic employed.

The profiles plotted in Figures 7.6 and 7.9 were calculated using typical values from published papers. For the midget cell, σ_c = 3.97 min arc, σ_s = 22.98 min arc, and k = 0.647. For the parasol cell, σ_c = 10.5 min arc, σ_s = 47.1 min arc, and k = 0.645.

As mentioned earlier in the chapter, computational models frequently use receptive fields that are perfectly balanced (k = 1.0), so that they respond only in the region of luminance edges. However, balanced cells are encountered only rarely in single-cell studies, as is clear from the values for k in Table 7.6. The example responses used here are more representative of realistic cells.

Receptive field responses

Table 7.5 quantifies the responsiveness of the cell at each position in its receptive field relative to the center of the receptive field (0 min arc). The response of the cell to a stimulus that covers its receptive field can be calculated by summing the responses at each point in the receptive field. The response at each point is found by multiplying the responsiveness at that point by the intensity of the stimulus at the same point.

The second row of Table 7.7 shows the intensity profile of a step-edge stimulus, with higher intensity to the left of position zero. The third row is the responsiveness of a receptive field centered at zero. Values represent responsiveness at each location in the receptive field (taken from Table 7.5). The fourth row is the product of stimulus intensity and responsiveness at each position. The fifth row contains the net response of the receptive field centered at position zero (obtained by summing all the responses in the fourth row). It is possible to compute the response of cells with receptive fields centered at each other location using the same procedure. The bottom row shows net response of receptive fields at different locations on either side of the edge. The leftmost and rightmost responses show the response

TABLE 7.7 Computed response of concentric receptive fields to a step edge (convolution)

Position (min)	−40	−35	−30	−25	−20	−15	−10	−5	0	5	10	15	20	25	30	35	40
Intensity	200	200	200	200	200	200	200	200	100	100	100	100	100	100	100	100	100
Responsiveness at 0					−0.052	−0.073	−0.091	0.098	0.888	0.098	−0.091	−0.073	−0.052				
Response					−10.4	−14.6	−18.2	19.6	88.8	9.8	−9.1	−7.3	−5.2				
Sum									53.4								
Response sum at each				130.4	135.6	142.9	152	142.2	53.4	43.6	52.7	60	65.2	65.2			

of receptive fields positioned wholly on the light side and wholly on the dark side of the edge, respectively. Two points are worthy of note:

- First, the receptive field does respond to even illumination, since the leftmost response is higher than the rightmost response (due to the receptive field's imbalance in favor of the receptive field center).
- Second, the influence of the edge extends some distance on either side, reaching out at least to $+/-20$ min arc from the edge. The receptive field introduces "neural blur," as described earlier in the chapter.

The mathematical procedure illustrated in Table 7.7 is known as **convolution.** It is the standard technique for modeling receptive field responses, and is easy to apply using standard spreadsheet formulas such as SUMPRODUCT(). Some of the plots in Figure 7.9 are graphical representations of the arrays in Table 7.7.

MODELING WITH MORE DIMENSIONS

The stimulus and receptive field profiles used so far have been cross-sections which show intensity or responsiveness along one dimension of space. Natural images and receptive fields actually vary in three dimensions: Two spatial dimensions (x and y), and one temporal dimension (t). The computational method described in the previous section extends readily to two or three dimensions. Consider a two-dimensional image, which contains variation of intensity in both x and y. Table 7.8 shows luminance values that define a simple 2-D image of a light bar tilted 45 degrees anticlockwise from vertical.

The responsiveness of a receptive field can also be described in two dimensions. Indeed center–surround receptive fields are 2-D by definition. The upper 3×3 cells of Table 7.9 show a simple version of a small cortical receptive field in which the excitatory and inhibitory zones confer

TABLE 7.8 A simple 2-D image containing a tilted light bar

					x-position					
	200	100	100	100	100	100	100	100	100	100
	100	200	100	100	100	100	100	100	100	100
	100	100	200	100	100	100	100	100	100	100
	100	100	100	200	100	100	100	100	100	100
y-position	100	100	100	100	200	100	100	100	100	100
	100	100	100	100	100	200	100	100	100	100
	100	100	100	100	100	100	200	100	100	100
	100	100	100	100	100	100	100	200	100	100
	100	100	100	100	100	100	100	100	200	100
	100	100	100	100	100	100	100	100	100	200

TABLE 7.9 Response profiles of simple orientation-selective receptive fields		
2	−1	−1
−1	2	−1
−1	−1	2
−1	−1	2
−1	2	−1
2	−1	−1

a preference for the same orientation as the line in Table 7.8; notice that the positive region of the receptive field defines a line. Summed excitation exactly balances inhibition (the summed responsiveness of the cell is zero).

We can compute the response of this receptive field to the stimulus in Table 7.8 using convolution, as before:

- The center of the receptive field is superimposed on a specific cell of the stimulus array.
- Response at each point is computed by multiplying stimulus intensity in each cell by responsiveness in the corresponding cell of the receptive field.
- Overall response is computed by summing responses at each point.
- This procedure is repeated at each location in the stimulus array.

Table 7.10 shows the convolution output (the location of the line is shown by white cells). The balanced receptive field produces zero response in locations where it is covered uniformly, but a very high response at the location of the line. For comparison, Table 7.11 shows the response of the lower receptive field in Table 7.9, whose optimal orientation is perpendicular

TABLE 7.10 Result of convolving the upper receptive field in Table 7.9 with the image in Table 7.8

600	−200	−100	0	0	0	0	0
−200	600	−200	−100	0	0	0	0
−100	−200	600	−200	−100	0	0	0
0	−100	−200	600	−200	−100	0	0
0	0	−100	−200	600	−200	−100	0
0	0	0	−100	−200	600	−200	−100
0	0	0	0	−100	−200	600	−200
0	0	0	0	0	−100	−200	600

TABLE 7.11 Result of convolving the lower receptive field in Table 7.9 with the image in Table 7.8

0	−200	200	0	0	0	0	0
−200	0	−200	200	0	0	0	0
200	−200	0	−200	200	0	0	0
0	200	−200	0	−200	200	0	0
0	0	200	−200	0	−200	200	0
0	0	0	200	−200	0	−200	200
0	0	0	0	200	−200	0	−200
0	0	0	0	0	200	−200	0

to the line. In this case there is no response at the location of the line, and weak, inconsistent responses nearby.

These examples illustrate how to perform computational modeling in two spatial dimensions. But natural images vary over time as well, when objects in the scene move. The temporal response of a receptive field can be specified by an array representing responsiveness as a function of time after stimulus onset. Figure 7.7, for example, plots the temporal response of midget and parasol RGCs. It is therefore possible to model cell responses to stimuli that vary over time, as well as over space, by performing convolutions in two or three dimensions. Researchers in motion perception often find it sufficient to compute responses to motion over just two-dimensions, the time dimension plus one spatial dimension (x–t space). Chapter 12 describes x–t space in much more detail.

Color vision

8

Contents

INTRODUCTION

The power of color as a perceptual experience is vividly illustrated by a painter who lost his ability to see in color following a closed head injury he suffered in a minor traffic accident. Sacks and Wasserman (1987, p. 26) describe his experiences as follows:

> *He saw people's flesh, his wife's flesh, his own flesh, as an abhorrent gray; "flesh-colored" now appeared "rat-colored" to him . . . The "wrongness" of everything was disturbing, even disgusting . . . He turned increasingly to black and white foods—to black olives and white rice, black coffee and yoghurt.*

These at least appeared relatively normal, whereas most foods, normally colored, now appeared horribly abnormal.

He confused many things, such as gray and yellow socks, red and green peppers, mustard and mayonnaise. He could no longer see clouds, since they were indistinguishable from the apparently pale-gray sky.

As this person's experiences indicate, color is especially important for distinguishing between objects that are otherwise hard to tell apart. A simple scientific definition of color vision is "the ability to distinguish between lights of different spectral composition, regardless of intensity." This definition captures an important aspect of color vision, and helps us to understand color deficiencies which are discussed later in the chapter. However color vision involves much more than wavelength discrimination. Natural surfaces vary intrinsically in terms of their propensity to absorb electromagnetic energy at some wavelengths and reflect it at other wavelengths, as discussed in Chapter 6 (spectral reflectance; see the functions in Figure 6.7). For example, the chlorophyll in leaves causes them to reflect light predominantly at wavelengths around 555 nm, while the flavonoids in fruit and berries cause them to reflect most strongly around 600 nm. Estimates of surface spectral reflectance would therefore be very useful for the task of picking out ripe fruit from a leafy bush. Color vision involves neural computations which endow us with the ability to estimate the spectral reflectance properties of surfaces.

Before proceeding it is important to recall Isaac Newton's observation that light waves or particles are not colored. Colors are entirely a construction of neural processes in the brain and there is no simple, fixed relation between light wavelength and color. The term "color perception" is tautological, because color *is* a perception. The chapter begins with a consideration of the basic perceptual dimensions of color, and then moves on to discuss the mechanisms that the visual system uses to estimate the spectral composition of light striking the retina.

? *Review the physics and physiology of color in Chapters 6 and 7.*

COLOR SPACE

A **color space** is a two- or three-dimensional geometric construct in which each point represents a particular color, and different colors are distributed along the axes of the space according to some organizing principle. It has long been acknowledged that color can be described in terms of just three independent perceptual attributes: Hue, saturation, and brightness:

- *Hue* corresponds to the color itself, such as "red," or "blue."
- *Saturation* corresponds to the purity of the color, often described in terms of how much neutral color (white) is present. Pink, for example, is a desaturated red.
- *Brightness* corresponds most closely to the perceived intensity of the light.

Traditionally these three attributes are depicted in a three-dimensional space, as shown in Figure 8.1.

KEY TERM

Perceptual color space
A graphical representation of the hue, saturation, and brightness dimensions of color.

The vertical axis represents brightness, with light colors at the top and dark colors at the bottom. Radial distance from the center represents saturation; with neutral white light lying at the center of the circle and more saturated colors lying further out from the center. Angle around the circumference represents hue, ordered in terms of similarity. Most colors around the circumference of the circle can be described as intermediate between other colors. Orange, for example, is intermediate between red and yellow—a reddish yellow; aquamarine is intermediate between green and blue—a greenish blue. But four particular colors are said to be "unique hues": Red, green, blue, and yellow. Any color can be described in terms of its redness or greenness, and its blueness or yellowness.

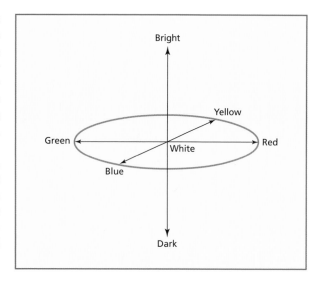

FIGURE 8.1
Perceptual color space. Brightness varies vertically, hue varies around the circumference of the circle, and saturation varies radially (from neutral at the center of the circle).

OPPONENT COLORS

The existence of unique hues in color descriptions led Ewald Hering, a German physiologist (1834–1918), to propose an opponent theory of color, as follows:

> *Therefore, since redness and greenness, or yellowness and blueness are never simultaneously evident in any other color, but rather appear to be mutually exclusive, I have called them opponent colors. To begin with, this term is used to characterize the way they occur without implying any sort of explanation.*
>
> *(Hering, 1905–1911/1964, p. 50)*

Hering also proposed an opponency between light and dark sensations. The notion of opponency along the red–green and blue–yellow axes of color space has been very influential in the development of color theories, as later sections in the chapter will show. The color space in Figure 8.1 is a useful way of summarizing the ways that humans describe specific pure colors. However, it is of limited use in understanding what happens when colors are mixed. What color is seen in the mixture, and what, if anything, does that imply for theories of color?

COLOR MIXTURE

There are two fundamentally different ways of mixing colors. One is known as subtractive mixing, and the other is known as additive mixing. Additive mixing is much more useful than subtractive mixing as a tool for developing theories of color appearance, as you will discover. Subtractive mixing is the chemical basis for the colors seen in almost all painting and printing.

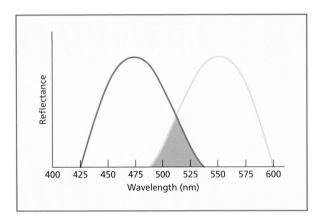

FIGURE 8.2
Hypothetical illustration of subtractive color mixture. The two curves represent the reflectance spectra of two pigments, one "blue" and the other "yellow." A mixture of the two appears green because only these wavelengths are reflected by both pigments (shaded area).

SUBTRACTIVE MIXTURES

Subtractive color mixing involves the removal of wavelength components from a stimulus patch by absorption or by scattering. Colors created using pigments or dyes are based on **subtractive color mixture**. A simple hypothetical example is shown in Figure 8.2.

The two curves show the reflectance spectra of two ink pigments. One pigment appears blue when illuminated in isolation by broad-spectrum (white) light, because it absorbs all wavelengths except those in the blue region, which are reflected. The other pigment appears yellow because it absorbs all wavelengths except those in the yellow region. When the two pigments are mixed together the result appears green in broad-spectrum light, because the only wavelengths which are reflected by both pigments are in this part of the spectrum (shaded region). If more pigments were put into the mix, the resulting color would become a murky gray as a wider range of wavelength components were absorbed. Ink-based color reproduction systems, such as those in inkjet printers, use three differently colored inks, called subtractive primaries, chosen because their mixture gives the broadest gamut of available colors. Figure 8.3 illustrates three typical subtractive primaries (cyan, magenta, and yellow), and the colors that result from their combination.

Subtractive color mixing is of great practical value for painted or printed reproduction of color, but is of limited use as a tool for developing color theories. Unlike **additive mixture**, the color seen in one subtractive mixture cannot be predicted straightforwardly from the color seen in other mixtures. The process is a purely physical one determined by the (sometimes complex) reflectance properties of the pigments.

ADDITIVE MIXTURES

Additive mixing involves the addition of wavelength components to a stimulus by the superimposition of multiple light sources. To give an example, a stimulus patch emitting light at a wavelength of 700 nm appears red (in a neutral context; see "color constancy" below). A patch emitting light at 560 nm appears green. What color is seen when the two patches are superimposed to create a stimulus that emits both 560 nm and 700 nm wavelengths? Yellow is seen. If a third wavelength is available in the blue region of the spectrum, then seven different colors are seen in the various combinations of the three wavelengths, as illustrated in Figure 8.4.

Color mixture is investigated in the laboratory using the apparatus illustrated in Figure 8.5. The observer views a circular stimulus patch that is split vertically into two halves. One half receives monochromatic light of a given wavelength and intensity, known as the test light. The other half of the stimulus patch receives light containing a mixture of

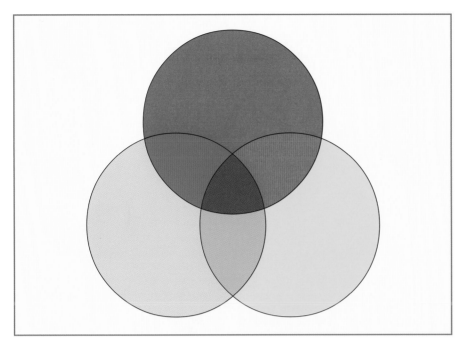

FIGURE 8.3
Typical colors used in reproduction systems based on subtractive mixing. Areas of overlap indicate the color seen in mixtures of the primary colors.

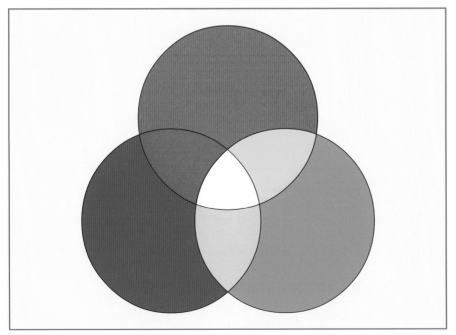

FIGURE 8.4
Additive mixtures of three primary lights. The areas of overlap show the color seen in mixtures of the primary colors.

wavelengths, known as primaries. The observer adjusts the intensity of the test light and the relative intensities of the primaries until the entire stimulus patch appears uniform (a so-called Rayleigh match).

Once a color match is achieved, the two apparently matched halves of the stimulus patch contain **metameric colors**, or metamers, defined as a pair of stimuli that have matching colors but physically different spectra. In the example of

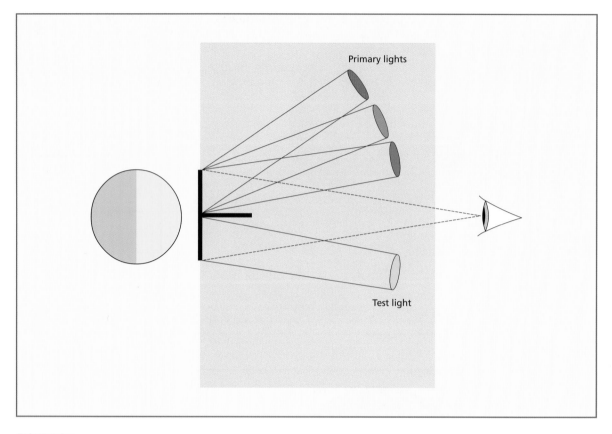

FIGURE 8.5
Apparatus used to study additive color mixing. The observer views a bipartite field. One side of the field is illuminated by a monochromatic (single-wavelength) test light. The other side is illuminated by a mixture of three primary wavelengths. The subject can achieve a subjective match between the two halves of the field by adjusting the relative intensities of the primary lights.

Metamers were studied by Maxwell (1855) using disks painted with various color and rotated very rapidly to create additive color mixture.

Figure 8.5, the yellow appearance of a mixture of 560 and 700 nm may appear identical to a monochromatic light from the yellow region of the spectrum, provided that the relative intensities of the 560 and 700 nm components are appropriate. Metameric color mixtures can tell us a great deal about the color computations performed by the visual system, and obey two simple laws.

Laws of additive metameric mixture

Linearity

In a linear system, the response to a stimulus containing several components corresponds to the sum of the responses produced when the components are presented separately. For example, assume that the relative intensities of a combination of primary lights are set so as to make a perceptual match with a patch of test light (A), using the apparatus in Figure 8.5. A second match is then made with a different test light (B). Finally, a third match is made against a test patch created by adding together the light from patches A and B. What primary intensities are required to match this third test patch? Matching intensities can be found simply by adding together the primary intensities that were required to match the original tests A and B when they were presented separately. A further consequence of linearity is that when a new wavelength component is added equally to both members of a metameric pair of colors, then their metameric identity is preserved (though their apparent color may change).

Trichromacy

Observers with normal color vision can make a match with any given test color using a combination of no more than three appropriately chosen primary colors. Metameric matching is therefore said to be trichromatic (three-colored). The choice of primaries is restricted by the condition that one primary cannot be metameric to a mixture of the other two. In practice, primaries are chosen on the basis of empirical convenience, and are usually as widely spectrally separated as possible.

> The choice of red, green, and blue primaries in color displays was largely pragmatic because it allowed the largest gamut of colors to be reproduced. No specific attempt was made to match the spectral properties of the primaries with the spectral sensitivities of photoreceptors.

Uses of additive mixture

These two laws of additive color mixing play an essential role in modern image reproduction systems such as flat-panel displays (used in televisions, computers, cameras, and phones), and projectors. Such systems are based on additive mixing of three primaries. In the case of liquid-crystal displays (LCDs), for example, a white light source (back light) sits directly behind the LCD panel itself. Each picture element ("pixel") in the display is composed of a triplet of adjacent cells which controls the light wavelengths that are transmitted through the panel at the pixel location. The three cells are each covered by a filter which admits light in either the red, green, or blue spectral regions. The triad of cells is too small to be resolved by the visual system, so the color seen in the light transmitted by the triad at each pixel is equivalent to an additively mixed color based on the three primaries. A wide gamut of colors can be seen on these displays simply by varying the relative intensities of the red, green, and blue components.

> ? *Why might the color of a garment appear different in a photograph or on TV?*

COLOR MATCHING: THE CIE CHROMATICITY DIAGRAM

The highly lawful nature of additive color matching makes it possible to create a color space based on color matching data, rather than the descriptive dimensions used in Figure 8.1. A universally agreed, metric color space was produced by the Commission Internationale de l'Eclairage (CIE) in 1931 using matching data from large groups of observers. Unlike the color space shown in Figure 8.1, the **CIE chromaticity diagram** is two-dimensional. There is no need to include the brightness axis because mixture linearity means that color matches are independent of intensity. The CIE chromaticity diagram plots proportions of light rather than absolute intensities. It is reproduced in Figure 8.6.

Pure spectral colors are plotted along the perimeter of the space, labeled with their wavelength. Mixtures of wavelengths lie inside the perimeter. Saturation decreases toward the center until, at the location marked W, mixtures appear

KEY TERM

CIE chromaticity diagram
A standard graphical representation of the hue and saturation attributes of color, based on color matching data obtained from large groups of observers.

FIGURE 8.6

The CIE chromaticity diagram. Pure spectral colors are arranged around the perimeter of the shape. Additive mixtures of wavelengths lie inside the shape. The color seen in a mixture of two wavelengths lies along a straight line joining the two wavelengths. Mixtures falling on the location labeled W appear white. The small triangle in the space represents the gamut of colors available in a typical LCD display.

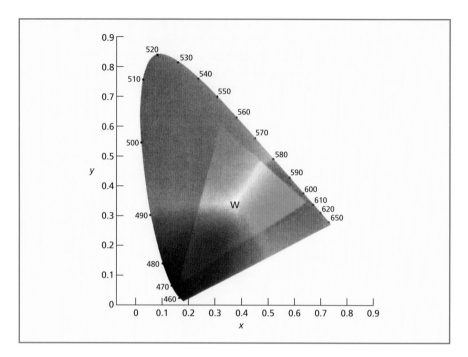

neutral or white. The diagram is designed so that the color created by an additive mixture of any two primary wavelengths lies along a straight line across the space joining the two wavelengths. The location of the mixture along the line is determined by the relative intensities of the two primaries. If a mixture line passes through the neutral point at the center of the space, the wavelengths at each end are said to be **complementary**, since the color of one can be balanced out completely by the other to produce white.

The shape of the chromaticity diagram

Notice that the CIE space is not circular like the color space in Figure 8.1. Its characteristic shape is designed so that it depicts color mixtures along straight lines. The straight section in the lower part of the perimeter arises because the most saturated purples can only be created by a mixture of the shortest and longest visible wavelengths (440 nm and 700 nm respectively). The line represents differing proportions of the two wavelengths.

Chromaticity coordinates

The color space in Figure 8.6 is located within two axes, labeled x and y. Any color can be identified by its location on the x- and y-axes, known as its **chromaticity coordinates**. This provides a universally agreed system for specifying color, which is essential for reproducibility both in scientific research and in industrial applications. Modern instruments can be used to identify the chromaticity coordinates of a given color patch, allowing researchers to reproduce each other's stimuli. Table 8.1 shows the chromaticity coordinates of some light sources.

The vertices of the pale triangular inset in Figure 8.6 are located at the chromaticity coordinates of the three LCD display components given in Table 8.1.

The gamut of colors available with these three primaries is defined by the area lying inside the triangle. Colors outside the triangle cannot be seen in a computer display. They generally correspond to colors having the most extreme levels of saturation.

ORIGIN OF ADDITIVE COLOR MIXTURE

Additive color mixture can be explained by retinal processes. As Chapter 7 explained, the human eye contains three classes of cone photoreceptor, with differing spectral sensitivities (S-, M-, and L-cones; see Figure 8.8). The response of each cone class obeys the principle of univariance; the response of the photopigment is the same regardless of light wavelength. However, the cone classes differ in terms of the probability that they will respond to a quantum of a given wavelength. For instance, an S-cone is much more likely to respond to short-wavelength light than is an M- or L-cone. The wavelength of the incident light can be inferred by comparing the responses of different cone classes: Any given color corresponds to a particular ratio of excitation across the three cone classes. Blue colors, for example, activate S-cones more than M- and L-cones. Metameric color mixtures can be explained very simply in these terms: Metamers have the same color appearance because they create the same ratio of responses across the triad of cone classes.

Figure 8.7 illustrates this very important idea. The first three groups of bars in Figure 8.7 show hypothetical activation levels of three cone classes to three

TABLE 8.1 Chromaticity coordinates of some standard light sources

Source	x	y
Fluorescent lamp	0.35	0.37
Sun	0.32	0.33
Red LCD display	0.64	0.34
Green LCD display	0.28	0.61
Blue LCD display	0.14	0.06

Although mixture of pigments is subtractive, there is one way to create a form of additive color mixture using pigments. The pointillist technique in art involves constructing a painting by placing very small dots of color next to each other. When viewed from a distance at which the individual dots cannot be resolved, the dots merge together additively to create new colors.

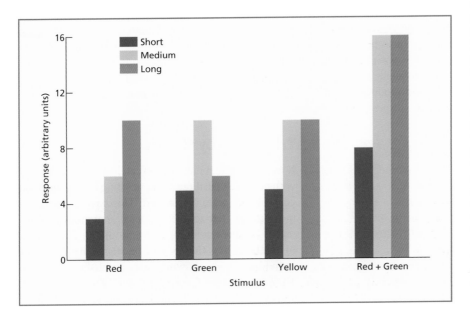

FIGURE 8.7

A simple explanation of additive color mixture. The leftmost group of three bars shows the triad of cone responses to a "red" wavelength light. The middle-left group shows the triad of cone responses to a "green" wavelength. The middle-right group shows the triad of cone responses to a "yellow" wavelength. The rightmost group shows the triad of responses to an additive combination of the "red" and "green" wavelengths. Notice that the relative response of the three cone classes to the mixture is identical to that produced by the pure "yellow" wavelength. Hence the mixture appears yellow.

FIGURE 8.8

Top: Helmholtz's estimate of three kinds of "fiber" responsible for color sensations, produced in the later 1800s. Bottom: Estimates of cone photoreceptor spectral absorbances based on direct measurements taken in the late 1900s (adapted from Stockman & Sharpe, 2000).

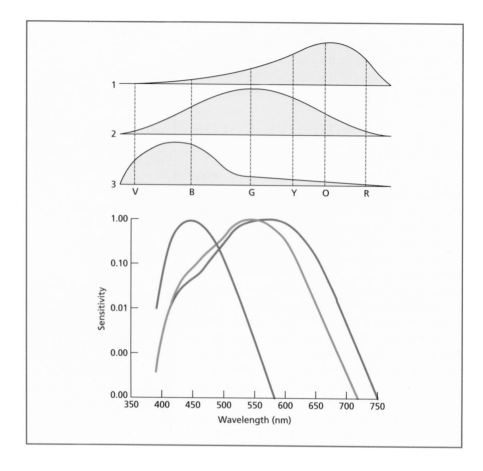

different wavelengths. The leftmost bars show relative responses to a light in the red portion of the spectrum. The light appears red because it produces the greatest activation in L-cones. Similarly, the green wavelength activates M-cones most and the yellow wavelength produces the greatest activation in both the M- and L-cones. The rightmost bars show the pattern of cone response to a combination of the red and green wavelengths. The pattern of activation corresponds to the sum of the two individual activations (see "Linearity" above). It is identical to the pattern of activation produced by spectral yellow. Consequently, this combination will appear identical to spectral yellow.

Maxwell and Young were renowned British physicists who made major contributions in several fields (see Chapter 6 on the physics of light). Helmholtz was a hugely influential German physiologist. Palmer, by contrast, was an obscure figure, better known in Continental Europe than in his native Great Britain. He was a glass merchant specializing in colored glass, who spent much of his time in Europe, and also published in French (Mollon, 1993).

Trichromacy theory

It was known that metameric matches can be achieved with no more than three primaries long before the three cone classes were discovered. This basic property of metamerism led to the proposal that human color vision is "three-colored" or trichromatic. The origins of **trichromacy theory** can be traced back to four individuals, whose work was published between 1777 and 1911: George Palmer, Thomas Young, James Clerk Maxwell, and Hermann von Helmholtz.

The earliest account of trichromacy was published in 1777 by Palmer. He believed that light was actually composed of only three differently colored rays (red, yellow, and blue), and proposed that:

> *the surface of the retina is compounded of particles of three kinds, analogous to the three different rays of light; and each of these particles is moved by its own ray.*
> *(quoted in Sherman, 1981, p. 17)*

In 1802, Thomas Young (who may have encountered Palmer's work while a student in Gottingen, according to Mollon, 1993) proposed that the three primary colors were red, green, and violet. To test his theory, Young performed additive color mixing experiments using rapidly spinning disks with sectors painted in different colors (with spinning disks the retinal responses to the different sectors overlap in time, effectively creating an additive mixture). Maxwell also conducted many quantitative experiments on additive color mixture using spinning disks. Writing in 1856, Maxwell supported Young's trichromacy theory as follows:

> *We are capable of feeling three kinds of color-sensations. Light of different kinds excites these sensations in different proportions, and it is by the different combinations of these three primary sensations that all the varieties of visible color are produced.*
> *(quoted in Helmholtz, 1911/1962, p. 143)*

Helmholtz (1911/1962) proposed that the three primary sensations were conveyed to the brain by three kinds of nervous fiber, and estimated the spectral response of the fibers using the graph reproduced in Figure 8.8 (top).

He called the three fibers red-sensitive, green-sensitive, and violet-sensitive, on the basis of their peak response. The curves in Figure 8.8 (top) are remarkably similar to modern estimates of the spectral absorbance curves of the three cone classes (Figure 8.8, bottom). Direct measurements of cone sensitivities were first made in the 1960s using a technique known as microspectrophotometry (Brown & Wald, 1964; Marks, Dobelle, & MacNichol, 1964): A piece of excised retina is mounted on a microscope slide and a thin beam of light is directed at the outer segment of an individual photoreceptor. Some of the light is absorbed by photopigment, and the rest passes through to be picked up by a light sensor. Careful measurement of the amount of light absorbed by different receptors yields estimates of the spectral sensitivity of cone photopigments.

The durability of trichromatic theory is a tribute to the insights and empirical ingenuity of Palmer, Young, Maxwell, and Helmholtz. The theory is often called the *Young–Helmholtz Theory*, but this name does not give due recognition to the contributions of Palmer and Maxwell.

DUAL-PROCESS THEORY

Notice that there is an apparent discrepancy between trichromacy and the perceptual color space depicted in Figure 8.1. Color space has two chromatic axes and so two pairs of colors, red–green and blue–yellow, which inspired Hering's opponency theory. Yet trichromacy implicates only three colors: Red, green, and blue. The inconsistency between trichromatic and opponent theories was a perplexing problem for many years, but was resolved in the second half of the 20th century by

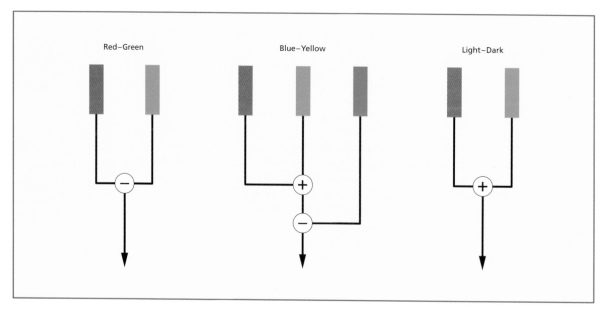

FIGURE 8.9
Schematic diagram of the early stages of neural color processing. Three cone classes supply three "channels."
The achromatic (light–dark) channel receives nonspectrally opponent input from L- and M-cone classes. The two
chromatic channels receive spectrally opponent inputs to create the L–M or "red–green" channel and S–(L + M) or
"blue–yellow" channel.

Hurvich and Jameson (1957). They developed a dual-process theory that contained
trichromatic photoreception in the first stage, and opponent-process neural coding
in the second stage. Like its predecessors, Hurvich and Jameson's model was
developed without the benefit of modern electrophysiological data. Instead, Hurvich
and Jameson estimated the spectral response of theoretical opponent mechanisms
using a perceptual cancellation technique. For the red–green pair, for example,
Hurvich and Jameson measured the amount of light from the green region of the
spectrum that was required to cancel the reported "redness" of a patch containing
light from the red region of the spectrum. Similar measurements were made using
many other pairs of wavelengths, until Hurvich and Jameson were able to estimate
the spectral sensitivities of the color-opponent channels.

The later discovery of three classes of cone photoreceptor, and color opponent
responses in ganglion and LGN cells, is consistent with Hurvich and Jameson's
dual-process theory. As shown in Figure 8.9, the trichromatic stage involves three
photoreceptors with peak sensitivities at long, medium, and short wavelengths. The
opponent stage involves three opponent pairs; L–M, S–(L + M), and L + M. The
three pairs are sometimes called "channels," two **chromatic** and one **achromatic**:

- The L–M chromatic channel (red–green) receives opposing input from L- and
  M-cones.
- The L–(S + M) chromatic channel (blue–yellow) receives opposing input from
  S-cones, and the sum of L- and M-cones.
- The L + M achromatic channel (light–dark) receives input from the sum of
  L- and M-cones. The light–dark response of this channel is spatially segregated to
  produce spatial opponency.

Compare the schematic diagram of Figure 8.9 with the ganglion cell receptive fields shown in Figure 7.7. The fibers of midget ganglion cells carry the L–M opponent signal to the LGN; bistratified ganglion cell fibers carry the S–(L + M) opponent signal (Dacey, 2000). The tuning of these two opponent signals defines two axes or "cardinal directions" along which neural color signals vary (Derrington, Krauskopf, & Lennie, 1984), which were in agreement with earlier psychophysical data on the detection of changes in color (Krauskopf, Williams, & Heeley, 1982).

However, the cardinal directions are at the center of a long-standing mystery in color science. They do not map readily onto the "unique hue" sensations, and no neuroimaging or neurophysiological studies have found evidence for cells tuned to the unique hues (Wachtler, Sejnowski, & Albright, 2003; Wuerger, Atkinson, & Cropper, 2005). A good deal of evidence points towards higher-order cortical color mechanisms which recombine the LGN signals to create neural tuning that is intermediate between the cardinal axes, such as "orange" or "blue–green," and narrowly tuned cells have been found, but many questions remain about the nature of cortical color coding (Krauskopf et al., 1986; Wachtler, Sejnowski, & Albright, 2003; Eskew, 2009).

You may be wondering why color vision relies on just three classes of photoreceptor to encode all the colors we can perceive. This question has prompted a great deal of debate in vision science, and can be answered in a number of different ways. The tutorials section at the end of the chapter summarizes the debate.

Dual-process theory is concerned with how the visual system encodes the wavelength composition of light. However, color vision is really concerned with estimating the reflective properties of surfaces, not just the spectral composition of light striking the retina, and this is a very complex task for reasons that were outlined briefly in Chapter 6. To reiterate here, the spectral composition of the light striking the retina from an object depends jointly on the spectral reflectance of the object's surface (its tendency to reflect some wavelengths more than others) and the spectral composition of the illuminating light (relative energy at different wavelengths). In extreme conditions it can be virtually impossible to disentangle these two factors. For example, yellow sodium street lights emit a very narrow range of wavelengths in the yellow region of the visible spectrum. During daylight, cars parked along a street may show wide variations in color (reds, greens, blues, and so on) because their pigmented metal surfaces reflect only a specific portion of the broad-spectrum sunlight. But under sodium street lighting all the colors tend to appear as lighter and darker shades of yellow, because only yellow wavelengths are available in the light source, and are therefore reflected from the cars' surfaces.

? Color processing involves ratios of cell responses. What other perceptual dimensions appear to involve ratio coding?

To overcome these problems the visual system performs computations that take into account the spatial and temporal distribution of wavelengths in the scene under view. Research on color interactions has helped to reveal the nature of these computations.

COLOR INTERACTIONS

COLOR CONTRAST AND ADAPTATION

Metameric color matches between pairs of stimuli can be explained lawfully by triplets of cone responses only when the stimulus surfaces are viewed against a chromatically neutral gray background, and without prior exposure to any particular colors. When a colored surface is viewed against a colored background (spatial context), or after exposure to a particular color (temporal context) the color of the context interacts with the color of the surface to alter the latter's appearance. Several forms of **color interaction** have been described.

Simultaneous color contrast

When a colored surface is placed against a colored background, the background may change the surface's hue, saturation, and brightness. A green disk placed against a more saturated green background appears less green than when it is placed against a red background (Figure 8.10, upper left). Similarly, a blue disk placed against a more saturated blue background appears less blue than when it is placed against a yellow background (Figure 8.10, upper right). Particularly vivid effects can be created using patterned surrounds, as shown in the lower half of Figure 8.10. In general, color contrast shifts the hue of a surface away from the hue of its background and in the direction of the complementary hue.

FIGURE 8.10
Color contrast. Top: The saturation of a color patch is influenced by the surrounding color. Bottom: Particularly strong contrast effects can be created by patterned figures. The ring in the center of this annulus is uniform, but takes on a different color in the top left and bottom right quadrants compared to the other two quadrants, because of the patterned surround (based on displays in Monnier & Shevell, 2003).

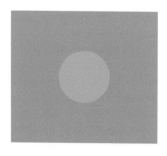
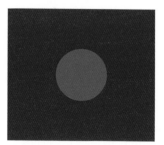

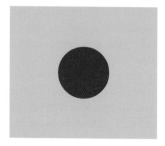
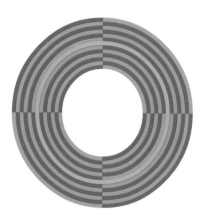

FIGURE 8.11
Color after-images. After fixating on the center of the upper display for approximately 60 seconds, transfer your gaze to the lower display. You should experience a color after-image.

Color adaptation

When one color is viewed for a short time, and then replaced by a differently colored test surface, the color of the test surface is influenced by the adapting color. Similar test colors appear less saturated than before adaptation. Neutral test colors take on the complementary hue to the adapting color. An example of the latter effect is shown in Figure 8.11.

ORIGIN OF COLOR INTERACTIONS

Contrast and adaptation effects demonstrate the importance of context for color vision. The hue of a surface is determined not just by the triad of L-, M- and S-cone responses currently being generated in the area of retina stimulated by the surface, but by a comparison of those responses with others at different retinal locations and at recent points in time. For example, a surface may appear more red if the triad of responses to it shows a greater preponderance of L-cone activity than the triad of responses to its spatial or temporal context. Figure 8.12 shows in more detail how comparisons of response triads can explain contrast and adaptation. The vertical bars containing red, green, and blue sections depict the relative L-, M- and S-cone response to the stimulus respectively, arrowed below each bar. The upper half of Figure 8.12 illustrates the explanation for simultaneous color contrast, and the lower half illustrates the explanation for color adaptation.

FIGURE 8.12
Explanations of color contrast (top) and adaptation (bottom) based on triads of cone responses. Each vertical bar is divided into three sections representing the relative responses of the three cone classes to a given stimulus. The dotted lines between vertical bars highlight the way in which the preponderance of cone responses varies between stimuli, accounting for contrast and adaptation effects. See the text for detailed explanations.

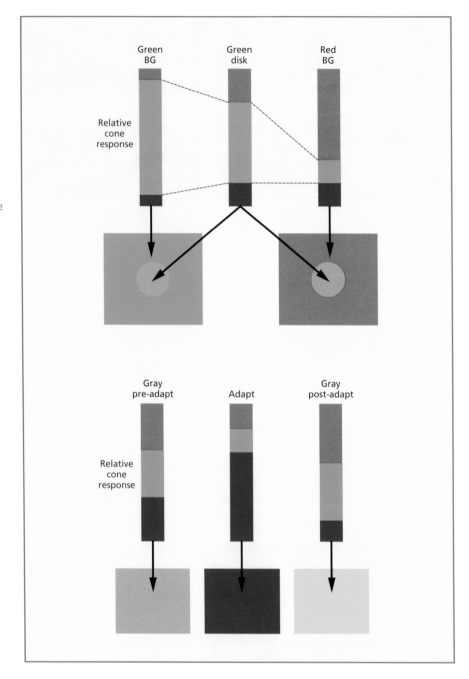

Explaining color contrast

Consider the contrast effect in Figure 8.12 (reproduced from Figure 8.10, upper left). The central bar in Figure 8.12 (upper) depicts the relative responses of L-, M-, and S-cone classes to the green disk. The right-hand bar in Figure 12.12 (upper) depicts the relative cone responses to the red background. The disk appears a saturated green because of the relatively large M-cone response to the disk compared with the background. The left-hand bar in Figure 8.12 (upper) depicts the relative cone responses to a saturated green background. Now the disk appears desaturated, because of the lower preponderance of M-cone signal in the response to it compared with the response to the background.

Explaining color adaptation

To explain adaptation, we must assume that the adapting color reduces the responsiveness of the cone classes sensitive to it. The triad of responses to subsequently viewed colors will be biased in favor of the other two cone classes. The lower-left bar in Figure 8.12 shows the unadapted response to a gray surface. Roughly equal responses from the three cone classes mean that the surface appears a neutral color. The middle bar in Figure 8.12 (lower) shows the relative cone responses while adapting to a blue field. S-cones are most active, and will show the greatest reduction in responsiveness. When the gray surface is viewed after adaptation, the S-cone response is weak compared with the response of the L- and M-cone classes. Hence the gray field takes on a yellowish hue.

COLOR CONSTANCY

What is the functional significance of color contrast and adaptation? As indicated earlier, these effects are thought to reveal some of the computations performed by the visual system to estimate the spectral reflectance of surfaces. Setting aside the extreme example of sodium lighting described earlier, significant changes in the illuminating spectrum are not uncommon in everyday life. For instance, the spectrum of daylight varies markedly during the day from daybreak, through midday, to sunset. Some interior lights have a greater preponderance of longer wavelengths than daylight, as shown in Figure 6.6. Despite such large changes in illumination, an object's color (namely, our perception of its spectral reflectance) remains relatively stable. This effect is known as **color constancy**.

How does the brain achieve color constancy? The starting point for building stable representations of surface color is the ratio of L-, M- and S-cone responses (cone excitation ratio). Foster and Nascimento (1994) found that the cone excitation ratio generated by different surfaces remains stable under different illuminants. For example, if surface *a* excites L-cones twice as much as surface *b* under a given illuminant, it will also excite L-cones twice as much under other illuminants. An important element of building stable visual representations of surface color involves a comparison between the cone excitation ratio in the retinal region stimulated by a given surface and the excitation ratio of its spatial and temporal context. Let's say that surface *a* above belongs to a strawberry and surface *b* belongs to the surrounding leaves. The strawberry will look red because it reflects relatively more energy at long wavelengths than do the leaves, in a wide range of lighting conditions. Local contrast and adaptation basically nullify the biasing effect of the spectral composition of the illuminating light, which affects the entire visual image and remains relatively stable over time. Contrast and adaptation thus play an important role in color constancy. A study of color constancy by Kraft and Brainard (1999) produced evidence that local color contrast makes the largest contribution to color constancy though other cues are also used, including (Hurlbert, 1999):

- Global contrast, based on cone responses averaged over the whole scene.
- Luminance maxima or highlights, which are often used by specular reflections from glossy surfaces. As mirror reflections of the light source, highlights reflect its full spectrum.

- Mutual reflections from one object to another in the scene, creating secondary light sources.
- The range of colors in the scene, which is indicative of the range of wavelengths in the illuminant.

Kraft and Brainard (1999) showed observers a realistic scene containing various small objects and papers. Their task was to adjust the chromaticity of a test surface in the scene until it appeared neutral gray. Kraft and Brainard varied the illuminant and the cues available. Baseline observations revealed that color constancy was by no means perfect (i.e., 100% resistant to illuminant changes), but attained a level of 83%. Kraft and Brainard found that when local contrast cues were removed, constancy fell to 53%. When global contrast and luminance maxima were removed as well, constancy was further reduced but still above zero, at 11%. As yet there is no universally agreed, comprehensive computational theory of color constancy.

CORTICAL PHYSIOLOGY

Color processing up to the level of the cortex is relatively straightforward, and consistent with dual-process theory. As outlined earlier, separate neural channels encode the cardinal directions of color space. R–G opponent midget ganglion cells project to the parvocellular layer of the LGN. Cells in this layer then project to primary cortical layer 4Cα. B–Y opponent bistratified ganglion cells terminate in the koniocellular layer of the LGN, which in turn projects to primary cortical layers 2, 3, and 4A.

The situation with regard to cortical processing of color is less clear. Many cortical neurons show tuning to directions other than the cardinal axes, and the unique hues have no special status in terms of neural responses (Wuerger, Atkinson, & Cropper, 2005). Color opponency is, however, a core feature of cortical processing in all the early visual areas, no doubt derived from opponency in the LGN. Cortical cells exhibit two different kinds of opponency, called single- and double-opponency. Single-opponent cortical cells are similar to their counterparts in the LGN in that they exhibit opposing responses to different cone inputs. These cells respond best to large areas of uniform color and to the interior of large color patches. Double-opponent cortical cells also show opponency between cone inputs, but the sign of the opponency is reversed in different regions of the cell's receptive field. So in one part of the receptive field the cell's inputs might be $-L + M$, while in another part of the receptive field the inputs might by $+L–M$. Double-opponent cells respond best to color patterns, textures, and boundaries, which would make them ideally suited for signaling surface and object color. The cell above, for instance, would respond best to a color pattern in which long-wavelength light fell on the ($+L–M$) part of the receptive field, and medium-wavelength light fell on the ($-L + M$) So double-opponent cells are a plausible physiological substrate for the local color contrast cue to color constancy (Shapley & Hawken, 2011). Consistent with this view, Wachtler, Sejnowski, and Albright (2003) reported that the response of color opponent cells in macaque V1 was affected by stimuli that produce color contrast. The similarity between neural and perceptual contrast effects supports the view that V1 "plays an important role in the neural processing that leads from the sensory signals to our percept" (Wachtler, Sejnowski, & Albright, 2003, p. 689).

The prevailing view of modular processing in the cortex has shifted over the past 30 years or so, and is still subject to change. In the 1970s and 1980s the dominant theory held that color, form, and motion were processed in segregated neural compartments in the cortex (Livingstone & Hubel, 1988). More recent approaches favor the view that processing of these attributes is likely to be closely linked (Shapley & Hawken, 2011). Cortical area V4 was once viewed as specializing in the visual analysis of color, as one of the segregated cortical processing streams (Zeki, 1978). Cases of achromatopsia such as the one which was described at the start of the chapter were once thought to arise from damage to V4. Evidence has since accumulated to show that area V4 also plays an important role in form analysis (Orban, 2008) and may function to integrate color and form information. For example, lesions in area V4 of macaque monkeys do not cause severe deficits in color discrimination, and analyses of human clinical cases have called into question the purity of their color deficits. Achromatopsia is frequently accompanied by deficits in form perception, such as prosopagnosia (inability to recognize faces; see Bouvier & Engel, 2006).

COLOR DEFICIENCY

A frequently asked question about color vision is "How do I know that the color I see is the same as the color you see?" There is no way to answer this question definitively, of course, since colors are mental states. Most people use color names in the same way, and make the same judgments of the similarities and dissimilarities between colors. A fabric that I might describe as "crimson," for example, would be given the same description by most other observers. However, about one in 12 people have very different color experiences from the rest of us. They may confuse crimsons with blues, and scarlets with greens. Such individuals are commonly called "color-blind," though this label is a misnomer since most of them do see colors, but in a different way from typical observers. The more accurate clinical term is *color deficient*, because there is a reduced capacity to discriminate between colors. The existence of **color deficiency** has been known for centuries, but only in the last century was its cause traced to the properties of cone photopigments.

As discussed earlier, normal color vision is trichromatic in the sense that typical observers require three primaries to achieve a subjective match with any color. Color deficient observers behave differently in color matching experiments. They can be divided into three groups on the basis of their performance:

- *Anomalous trichromats* require three primaries to achieve metameric matches, but in proportions that are different from those required by typical observers.
- *Dichromats* require only two primaries to achieve metameric matches.
- *Monochromats* require only one primary.

Color deficiency is linked to abnormal properties in the cone photopigments.

ANOMALOUS TRICHROMACY

The eye of the anomalous trichromat possesses three cone classes, but the spectral sensitivity of the cones is shifted relative to typical trichromats. The two major forms of **anomalous trichromacy** are protanomaly and deuteranomaly:

- In *protanomaly* the peak response of the L-cones is shifted to shorter wavelengths, so that it is closer than normal to the peak of the M-cones. As a result, protanomalous observers are more sensitive to green wavelengths than typical observers.

KEY TERMS

Color deficiency
A reduced capacity to discriminate between colors, caused by an abnormality in cone photopigments.

Anomalous trichromacy
A form of color deficiency in which the individual possesses three different cone classes, but their spectral sensitivity is shifted relative to normal trichromats.

- In *deuteranomaly* the peak response of the M-cones is shifted to longer wavelengths, so that it is closer than normal to the peak of the L-cones. As a result, deuteranomalous observers are more sensitive to red wavelengths than typical observers.

Both protanomalous and deuteranomalous observers have poorer than normal color discrimination, due to the greater overlap in the spectral sensitivities of the M- and L-cone classes.

DICHROMACY

The eye of an individual with **dichromacy** contains a normal number of cones, but lacks cones of one class. Any one of the three cone classes may be missing:

- In *protanopia*, L-cones are missing.
- In *deuteranopia*, M-cones are missing.
- In *tritanopia*, S-cones are missing.

Protanopes and deuteranopes cannot distinguish between reds and greens, since one or the other arm of the red–green chromatic axis is missing. They have no ability to distinguish between wavelengths greater than 520 nm (Ruddock, 1991). Tritanopes cannot distinguish between blues and yellows, since one arm of the blue–yellow chromatic axis is missing. They have no ability to distinguish wavelengths between 450 nm and 480 nm.

All dichromats have a neutral point on the spectrum; a wavelength that appears neutral gray to them. Normal trichromats, of course, have no neutral point because each wavelength is associated with a color experience. For protanopes, the neutral point is at 492 nm, while for deuteranopes it is at 498 nm. Tritanopes have a neutral point at 575 nm (Ruddock, 1991).

MONOCHROMACY

Individuals with **monochromacy** have no ability to distinguish different colors, and can match any given color with a single primary wavelength of the appropriate intensity. Monochromats presumably experience the world as shades of gray, rather like the view on a black and white television. The poor visual acuity of most monochromats is consistent with the view that their vision is mediated entirely by rods. A few monochromats appear to have near-normal acuity, and at least some receptors that resemble cones, though in relatively small numbers (Ruddock, 1991).

INCIDENCE OF COLOR DEFICIENCIES

A great deal is also known about the genes coding photopigments; see Nathans (1989).

Color deficiency is genetically transmitted. The relevant genes behave recessively (a copy must be inherited from both parents for color deficiency to occur) and are located on the X chromosome; the normal allele is dominant. Males have only one X chromosome, inherited from their mother, so males are color deficient if their mother's X chromosome carries the trait. Females have two X chromosomes (one from each parent), so are color deficient only if both carry the trait. It is not, therefore, surprising that male color deficients outnumber female color deficients by a factor of 22:1.

The prevalence of color deficiency varies markedly between racial groups, with Caucasians showing a higher incidence than other racial types. For example,

Caucasian males have the highest prevalence of red–green deficiency, at nearly 8%, while Native Americans have the lowest prevalence, at 2.5% (Jaeger, 1972). Table 8.2 shows the incidence of the different forms of color deficiency in the Caucasian population, taken from Piantanida (1991).

Anomalous trichromacy is much more common than dichromacy or monochromacy, accounting for three quarters of all reported color deficiencies.

DIAGNOSIS OF COLOR DEFICIENCY

A range of clinical tests has been developed to assess color vision. One of the most common tests involves so-called **pseudo-isochromatic plates**, on which are printed dots of varying hue, brightness, and saturation. The dots are arranged so that dots of similar color form a recognizable shape, such as a letter against a background of dissimilar dots. An example is shown in Figure 8.13. The observer's task is to identify the number. The number seen depends on the form of color vision possessed by the observer. The most well-known test is named after its inventor, Ishihara.

TABLE 8.2 Incidence of colour deficiency in the Caucasian population

Deficiency	Prevalence (%)
Protanomaly	1.73
Deuteranomaly	4.78
Protanopia	0.81
Deuteranopia	0.48
Tritanopia	0.45
Rod monochromacy	0.30
Monochromacy (cones)	0.0001
Total	8.55

KEY TERM

Pseudo-isochromatic plate
A pattern of colored dots, used in the diagnosis of color deficiency; the shape seen in the dots varies according to the observer's color vision.

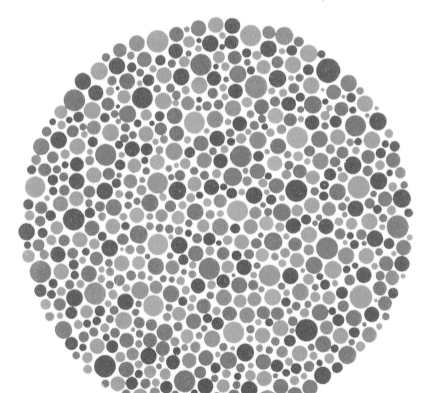

FIGURE 8.13
Example plate from the Ishihara test for color deficiency. The dots are grouped together on the basis of hue to create a recognizable shape such as a letter or number. Individual differences in color vision can lead to the appearance of different shapes in the plate. Normal observers should see the number 6, but observers with a deficiency involving medium and long (R–G) photoreceptors may see the number 3.

CHAPTER SUMMARY

COLOR SPACE

* Color descriptions are based on three dimensions: Hue, saturation, and brightness.
* Hering proposed that the hue dimension contains two opponent pairs of colors, red–green and blue–yellow.

COLOR MIXTURE

* Subtractive mixtures of pigments involve the removal of wavelength components from a stimulus.
* The colors seen in subtractive mixtures cannot be predicted straight-forwardly from their constituent pigments.
* Additive mixtures of light sources involve the addition of wavelength components to a stimulus.
* The colors seen in additive mixtures can be predicted on the basis of two rules: Linearity, and trichromacy.
* The CIE chromaticity diagram represents additive color mixtures in a standardized, metric color space.
* A metameric match to any color can be achieved with an additive mixture of no more than three primaries. This fact led to the trichromatic theory of color vision.
* Metameric matching can be explained by the ratio of responses across the three cone classes. Two colors with matching cone ratios appear identical.

DUAL-PROCESS THEORY

* The apparent discrepancy between Hering's opponent colors theory and the trichromatic theory can be reconciled by a two-stage theory in which trichromacy forms the first stage and opponent-processing forms the second stage. Dual-process theory can explain how the visual system estimates the spectral composition of lights.

COLOR INTERACTIONS

* When a surface is surrounded by another color, its hue may be altered (contrast).
* When one color is viewed for a short time and then replaced by a test color, the latter may be influenced by the first color (adaptation).
* Color contrast indicates that the color of a surface is not determined solely by the triad of cone signals it generates. Instead, a surface's color is determined by comparing its triad of cone responses with the triad of responses generated by the surrounding color.

COLOR CONSTANCY

- Color contrast and adaptation are thought to play an important role in color constancy, in which the color of an object remains stable even in the face of changes in the spectral composition of the illuminating light.
- Several other cues are also involved in the computations that achieve color constancy, including global contrast, luminance maxima, and mutual reflections.

PHYSIOLOGY

- Dual-process theory offers a good account of color processing up to the level of the cortex.
- Cortical processing involves single-opponent cells which respond to large areas of uniform color, and double-opponent cells which respond to color patterns and borders. Color opponent cells are thought to play a role in color constancy.
- Evidence for a specialized color center in the human cortex is not convincing; color processing is closely linked to the processing of other attributes.

COLOR DEFICIENCY

- Observers with deficient color vision fall into three categories:
  - Anomalous trichromats, who require three primaries for metameric matches, but in abnormal proportions.
  - Dichromats, who require only two primaries to achieve metameric matches.
  - Monochromats, who require only one primary and therefore cannot discriminate color at all.
- Color deficiency is inherited genetically via a recessive gene on the X chromosome, so its incidence is much higher in males than in females.

TUTORIALS

WHY THREE CONE CLASSES?

An ability to detect variations in the spectral composition of light reflected from objects (*chrominance*) is extremely useful for distinguishing between objects in natural scenes. As an example, Figure 8.14 shows a photograph of natural foliage. The original image is shown at the top. The version in the lower left contains only the original image's luminance signal, while the version in the lower right shows only the chrominance signal. It is clear that leaves, flowers and berries can be discriminated much better on the basis

FIGURE 8.14
Luminance and chrominance signals in a natural scene. The original image is shown at the top. The lower-left image shows only its luminance signal. The lower-right image shows only its chrominance signal. The original image is basically the sum of the luminance and chrominance components.

of chrominance than on the basis of luminance. One complication with luminance variation is that it confuses variation in surface reflectance with variation in illumination (shading and shadows), while chrominance is unaffected by illumination level. In general terms, then, color vision has obvious benefits. The minimum requirement for chrominance discrimination is the presence of two photoreceptor classes with different spectral sensitivities. A change in wavelength composition will then produce a change in relative photoreceptor response even when there is no change in illumination. In principle, chrominance discrimination should improve as the number of receptor classes increases. Two specific questions are frequently asked about human color vision:

- Why do we possess only three different classes of cone?
- Why are their spectral sensitivities distributed in the manner shown in Figure 8.8, namely two largely overlapping and one set apart?

Spatial resolving power

One way to answer these questions is to consider the consequences of possessing many photoreceptor classes having relatively narrow spectral sensitivities. The problem with this arrangement is that each cone class would have to share the retina with all the others. The average spacing between adjacent receptors of the same class would necessarily be relatively large. This could have a disastrous effect on the spatial resolving power of the retina, as discussed in Chapter 6 (see Figure 6.11). Each doubling of receptor spacing would halve the maximum spatial resolution of the receptor array. Moreover, the effective resolving power of the retina would vary with the spectral composition of the stimulus. Stimuli that excited only one photoreceptor class would be resolved very poorly, whereas stimuli that excited several classes would be resolved much better.

Fine spatial discriminations are best served by having very few photoreceptor classes (ideally just one), while fine chromatic discriminations are best served by having more photoreceptor classes. At high luminance levels the visual system strikes a balance between these competing requirements by having three classes with relatively broad spectral sensitivities. In fact, the central retina possesses just two photoreceptor classes (L- and M-cones) whose spectral sensitivities overlap extensively, and S-cones are entirely absent. As discussed in Chapter 6, at low luminance levels the visual system sacrifices chromatic discrimination in favor of maximizing spatial resolution, having just one photoreceptor class (rods).

Visual ecology

We can also gain clues about trichromacy by considering its evolutionary origins. The dominant view is that color vision evolved for finding food. Indeed, the spectral sensitivity of the L- and M-cone classes seems to be finely tuned to detect small differences between the leaves and fruit eaten by our ancestors. Leaves and fruit tend to have high reflectance in the red–green part of the spectrum (Osorio & Vorobyev, 1996). It was even suggested by Grant Allen in the 1800s that trichromacy in primates and the reflectance functions of certain fruits are well matched because they co-evolved as a seed dispersal system. Both parties benefited from this relationship, since the animal acquired food while dispersing the plant's seeds. According to this idea, the colors we see in fruits such as apples and oranges actually arose because of the color sensations themselves. Regan et al. (2001) found evidence consistent with the co-evolution hypothesis from their investigation of primate trichromacy and fruit coloration. For example, many plants from different branches of the evolutionary tree produce similar fruits. However, trichromatic vision is also found in primate species that eat only leaves, so it likely that our cone classes evolved for discriminating young leaves as well as fruit.

More recently Changizi, Zhang, and Shimojo (2006) offered a different account of the evolution of the L- and M-cone classes, based on the social importance of judging the emotional state of fellow humans. Blushing and blanching in the face are significant indicators of emotion and their detection requires a finely tuned ability to judge redness, as would be possible with closely spaced M- and L-cones. In support of this idea, Changizi, Zhang, and Shimojo (2006) noted that primate species with bare faces tend to be trichromatic, while those with furry faces tend to be dichromatic.

In a slightly different take on the issue of ecology, a number of research studies have measured the spectral reflectance curves of natural materials such as grass and wood, and have analyzed the number of color axes that would be needed in a coding system in order to represent their spectral properties economically and accurately for the purposes of discrimination and recognition. Results have shown that only three axes are required, and they bear a close similarity to the axes of human color vision (Lennie & D'Zmura, 1988; Lee, Wachtler, & Sejnowski, 2002).

Evolutionary genetics

Another reason for the similarity in spectral sensitivities of the M- and L-cone classes is their evolutionary genetics. They are thought to have evolved from a common ancestor relatively recently (35 million years ago), long after the emergence of the S-cone class. S-cone photopigment is coded by an autosomal (not sex-linked) gene. The genes coding L- and M-cone photopigments are adjacent to each other on the X chromosome, and are 98% identical in terms of their DNA.

As this brief discussion shows, there is still a great deal of debate concerning the evolutionary origin of the L- and M-cones, and about the evolutionary benefits of trichromatic vision. See also Gegenfurtner and Kiper (2003), and Surridge, Osorio, and Mundy (2003).

Spatial vision

9

Contents

INTRODUCTION

Many basic phenomena in spatial vision can be linked directly to the characteristics of the neural structures surveyed in Chapter 7. We know, for example, that vision at high light levels is mediated by cones, while vision at low light levels is mediated by rods. Fundamental aspects of vision at different light levels can be related to the properties of the cone and rod photoreceptor systems. This chapter begins by discussing some of these fundamental perceptual phenomena, which provide a platform in the perceptual domain on which we can build later discussions of more complex phenomena in spatial vision.

FUNDAMENTAL FUNCTIONS

PHOTOPIC AND SCOTOPIC VISION

As shown in Table 6.1, visual function can be divided into three zones, known as **scotopic**, **mesopic**, and **photopic**. In scotopic vision light levels are so low that only rod photoreceptors can function; in natural conditions this range would cover the

TABLE 9.1 Differences between scotopic and photopic vision

	Scotopic vision	Photopic vision
Photoreceptors	Rods (120,000,000)	Cones (6,000,000)
Light levels	Below 0.01 cd/m^2	Above 10 cd/m^2
Dark adaptation	Slow (35 min)	Fast (10 min)
Color vision	Monochromatic	Trichromatic
Peak spectral sensitivity	507 nm	555 nm
Peak spatial and temporal sensitivity	1 cpd low-pass below 3Hz	3 cpd 8 Hz

meager illumination provided by starlight during the hours of darkness. Photopic vision involves higher light levels beyond the saturation point for rods, in which only cone photoreceptors can function, as experienced during daylight hours. At the border between scotopic and photopic vision there is a "mesopic" zone in which the two photoreceptor systems overlap; at these twilight levels rods have not quite saturated, but there is just enough light to generate responses in cones. Table 9.1 lists some of the most important functional differences between rod-mediated scotopic vision and cone-mediated photopic vision.

Dark adaptation

The shift from photopic to scotopic vision as ambient illumination declines at sunset takes over half an hour to complete. So when moving abruptly from daylight into a darkened room such as a movie theater, we initially experience blindness. Very little of the visual scene in the theater is perceptible at first because light levels are too low for cones, but more detail gradually becomes visible as cones adapt to the lower illumination and rods begin to function. The process of adjusting to dark conditions is known as dark adaptation.

The two photoreceptor systems adapt at different rates. Cones adapt more rapidly than rods, so if one measures the time course of dark adaptation using a method that allows contributions from both rods and cones, the dark adaptation curve has a characteristic scalloped shape. The solid line in Figure 9.1 shows such a dark adaptation curve, obtained by measuring the detectability of a small spot of light placed 7° into the periphery (which contains both rods and cones; see Figure 6.9).

When rod and cone contributions are isolated, the two limbs of the dark adaptation curve are revealed. The dotted line shows results when the experiment is repeated in the rod-free fovea, and the dashed line shows results in the periphery at 10° eccentricity, where cones are scarce. When the process of dark adaptation is incomplete (after 5 to 10 minutes of adaptation, or around dusk), neither system of photoreceptors is operating at its peak efficiency. Subjectively, the visual world takes on a murky, indistinct character during mesopic light levels.

? Think of other differences between rod and cone systems that might affect driving performance.

The Purkinje shift

Figure 6.19 in Chapter 6 showed the differing spectral sensitivities of the rod and cone photoreceptors. Rods are most sensitive to light wavelengths in the region of 507 nm, whereas cones are maximally sensitive in the region of 555 nm. This

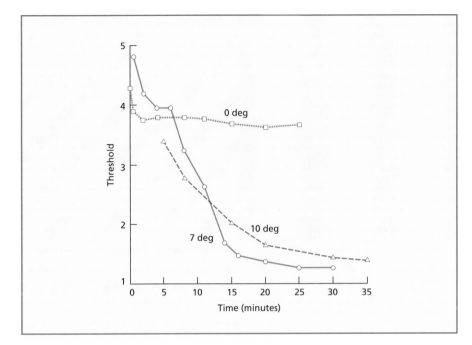

FIGURE 9.1
Dark adaptation curves adapted from Pirenne (1962). The solid line shows results using a 3° diameter spot viewed at an eccentricity of 7° (both rods and cones); the dotted line shows results using a 2° spot at an eccentricity of 0° (cones only); and the dashed line shows results using a 2° spot at an eccentricity of 10° (rods only). Threshold is expressed in picolamberts (1 lambert = 3183 cd/m²). The vertical position of the 7° data has been shifted to facilitate comparison with the other data.

difference in maximum sensitivity has consequences for the appearance of colored surfaces at different illumination levels. In photopic conditions, a surface emitting wavelengths near 555 nm will appear brighter than one emitting wavelengths near 507 nm, because cones are more sensitive to wavelengths of 555 nm. In scotopic conditions, wavelengths near 507 nm will appear brighter, since their perception is mediated by rods. This shift in brightness is called the Purkinje shift, after the Bohemian physiologist J. E. Purkinje who first observed it in 1825.

Figure 6.19 also reveals why vehicle instrument panels are often illuminated by red light at night. Long wavelengths are visible to the high-acuity cone system, provided that intensity is high enough. They fall beyond the rod system's sensitivity range, so do not affect the driver's state of dark adaptation, and his or her ability to see in the darkness outside.

SPATIAL CONTRAST SENSITIVITY

Spatial vision is based on the detection of spatial features in the image. We would not be able to perform everyday tasks, such as recognizing an object from its outline shape, or judging a person's facial expression, without some representation in the visual system of spatial image features. Spatial features are defined by spatial variations of image intensity. A simple measure of the salience of a spatial feature is the contrast between its brightest and darkest parts (contrast was defined more precisely in Chapter 6). Our present understanding of how the visual system builds representations of spatial features is based on studies of the minimum amount of contrast in a simple spatial pattern required for an observer to detect its presence. The standard laboratory stimulus for measuring contrast detection thresholds is the **luminance grating**.

KEY TERM

Luminance grating
A laboratory stimulus used to study spatial vision; it is a striped pattern containing alternating light and dark bars, commonly with a sine wave luminance profile.

FIGURE 9.2
Stimulus dimensions of luminance gratings. The two left-hand gratings differ in luminance contrast, with the lower contrast at the bottom. They also differ in spatial phase, as revealed by the misalignment of their bars. The two left-hand gratings have a low spatial frequency, while the two right-hand gratings have medium (top) and high (bottom) spatial frequencies. The two right-hand gratings differ in orientation.

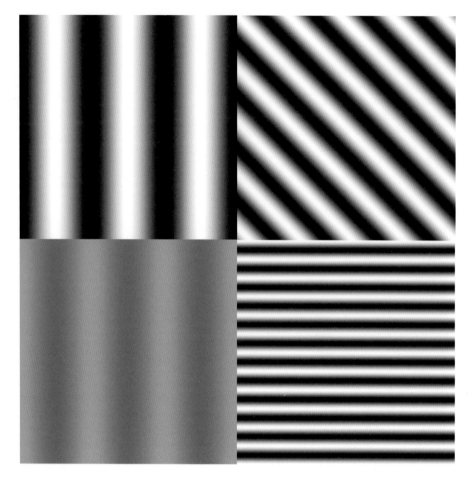

Luminance gratings

Luminance gratings contain alternating bright and dark bars. Four defining properties of a grating are its contrast, spatial frequency, orientation, and phase (illustrated in Figure 9.2).

Contrast

Contrast relates to the magnitude of the intensity difference between the lightest part of the luminance distribution (peak) and the darkest part (trough). The lower left grating in Figure 9.2 has low contrast, and the upper left grating has high contrast. Contrast can vary between 0 and 1.0. A contrast of zero corresponds to a uniform field (no difference between peak and trough in the luminance distribution), and very high contrast patterns approach a contrast of 1.0 (contrast can only reach 1.0 if the darkest part of the luminance distribution has a luminance of zero). The formula for calculating contrast can be found in Chapter 6.

Spatial frequency

The **spatial frequency** of a grating relates to the fineness of its bars, since it specifies how many bars the grating contains per unit of distance. The two left-hand gratings in Figure 9.2 have a low spatial frequency, and the right-hand gratings have a high spatial frequency. We saw in Chapter 6 that distances in retinal images are expressed in degrees of visual angle. Spatial frequency is therefore defined as the number of grating cycles per degree of visual angle, where one cycle of the grating is the distance from a given point on the waveform to the nearest corresponding point (e.g., between adjacent peaks). The fingers of an outstretched hand held at arm's length create a grating pattern with a spatial frequency of 0.25 cycles per degree (cpd); each finger is approximately 2° wide, so adjacent fingers (one cycle of your hand grating) are roughly 4° apart. If you hold a ruler between your hands at arm's length, the millimeter markings on it create a grating with a spatial frequency of approximately 10 cpd (one centimeter subtends 1 degree at a distance of 57 centimeters).

> Psychophysical experiments often use sinusoidal gratings in which luminance varies smoothly from bright to dark and back again, with a profile that conforms to a mathematical sine function. You may recall that sine waves were also discussed in Chapter 4 in the context of sound waves (see Figure 4.6). To learn more about sinusoidal gratings, and why they are used so frequently in experiments, refer to the tutorials section at the end of the chapter.

Orientation

Orientation relates to the slant of the grating's bars. Two gratings in Figure 9.2 are vertical, one is horizontal, and the fourth has an orientation of –45° with respect to vertical.

Phase

As discussed in Chapter 4, phase defines a particular point on a waveform. The two vertical gratings on the left of Figure 9.2 differ in phase, because the waveform defining one grating is shifted on position relative to the other. Phase is usually specified in phase angle. One complete cycle of a grating corresponds to 360°. So a phase difference of, say, 180° corresponds to a difference in position of one half a cycle. The gratings on the left of Figure 9.2 differ by 180° of phase; bright bars in the top grating line up with dark bars in the bottom grating.

> **?** *What is the auditory equivalent of a sine wave grating?*

Contrast thresholds for gratings

Grating sensitivity at a given spatial frequency is established by measuring the minimum amount of contrast required for an experimental observer to reliably discriminate the grating from a uniform field. In a classic psychophysical experiment, Campbell and Robson (1968) generated a grating pattern on a display screen much like a television. At each of a range of spatial frequencies, the observer adjusted the contrast of the grating until the pattern was barely detectable. The mean of either five or ten such settings defined the observer's contrast threshold for that spatial frequency.

Figure 9.3 (left) plots contrast threshold as a function of spatial frequency at two levels of illumination. In photopic conditions (500 cd/m²; open symbols) the observer required the least contrast to detect gratings of 3 cpd, but could not detect gratings higher than about 40 cpd whatever their contrast. In borderline scotopic conditions (0.05 cd/m²; closed symbols) more contrast was needed to detect gratings at any frequency. Thresholds were lowest at 1 cpd, and the

> Since the advent of computer-controlled psychophysical techniques, the preferred method of measuring thresholds is the Method of Constant Stimuli. See the tutorials section of Chapter 1.

FIGURE 9.3

Grating sensitivity, as measured in psychophysical threshold experiments. The left-hand graph shows the luminance contrast required to detect a grating, as a function of its spatial frequency and mean luminance. The subject requires least contrast to detect gratings at medium spatial frequencies. The right-hand graph re-plots the data in terms of contrast sensitivity (1/contrast) as a function of spatial frequency. Data are taken from Campbell and Robson (1968). The gray line plots the optical transfer function of the eye at a pupil diameter of 2.5 mm as used in Campbell and Robson's experiment, calculated using formulae in Watson (2013). The line shows the ratio between contrast in a grating stimulus and contrast in its image, as a function of stimulus spatial frequency. Ratios close to 1.0 indicate that the stimulus is transmitted with relatively little attenuation. Ratios close to zero indicate that the stimulus is severely attenuated during its passage through the system. The optics of the eye act as a low-pass filter. Low spatial frequencies are transmitted well, but attenuation increases progressively as spatial frequency increases.

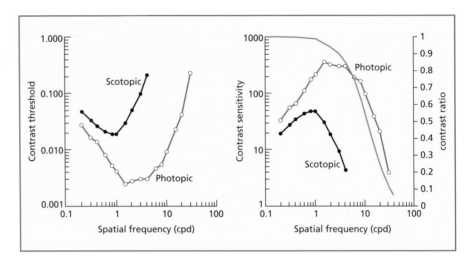

high frequency cut-off (beyond which gratings were no longer visible at any contrast) fell to about 8 cpd. These curves have been replicated in numerous studies.

Contrast sensitivity

Contrast threshold values are often converted into contrast sensitivity values by calculating the reciprocal of **contrast threshold** (1/contrast threshold). For example, a threshold contrast of 0.05 becomes a **contrast sensitivity** of 20, and a threshold of 0.2 becomes 5. The right-hand graph of Figure 9.3 plots the data in the left-hand graph in terms of contrast sensitivity. These plots are called **contrast sensitivity functions**, or CSFs. The main reason that data is plotted in terms of CSFs is that higher sensitivity (better performance) corresponds to higher values in the graph.

Origins of the spatial contrast sensitivity function

What determines the shape of the CSF? Sensitivity is governed by two factors: optical limitations and neural responses.

Optical limitations

In Chapter 6 you learnt that all optical systems suffer from diffraction and aberrations, which introduce image blur. The image of a very thin bright line is spread over a certain distance in the image to form a line spread function, as shown in Figure 6.18. If a second line is placed sufficiently close to the first, then their blurred images merge into each other; the two lines are not resolved. Similarly, gratings of sufficiently high spatial frequency disappear entirely from the image because their bars are too close together. The ability of an optical system to resolve a high contrast grating of a given spatial frequency is assessed by comparing the original contrast of the grating with the contrast present in its image. The ratio between the contrast of the grating's image and its original contrast specifies how well the optical system transmits the grating. **Contrast ratios** close to 1.0 indicate near-perfect transmission; ratios near zero indicate that the grating is very poorly resolved by the optical system. The gray line in Figure 9.3 (right) plots contrast ratio as a function of spatial frequency for the human eye at the 2.5mm pupil diameter employed by Campbell and Robson (1968), as specified by Watson (2013). This plot is called an **optical transfer function**. Low frequency gratings are transmitted with no loss of contrast, but beyond about 2 cpd progressively more contrast is lost from the image as spatial frequency increases. The optical transfer function clearly sets an upper limit on the highest spatial frequencies that human observers can detect, and is responsible for the sharp drop in the CSF at high frequencies which is evident in Figure 9.3 (see also Campbell & Green, 1965).

Neural responses

The shapes of the CSFs in Figure 9.3 are very different from the optical transfer function. There is a marked decline in low frequency sensitivity even though low frequencies are preserved best in the optical image, which must be due to the neural machinery used by the observer to detect the presence of the gratings.

The response of a neuron in the visual system depends on how well its retinal receptive field matches the spatial pattern in the image (see Figures 7.6 and 7.12). Many neurons in the initial stages of visual analysis (at least up to simple cells in the striate cortex) have receptive fields made up of excitatory and inhibitory subregions. A grating of a given spatial frequency will selectively activate cells whose receptive field subregions match the width of its bars. As Figure 9.4 illustrates, a low spatial frequency grating (left) will activate large receptive fields well (a bright bar fills the excitatory center, with relatively little light falling in the inhibitory flanks), but produces little response in small receptive fields (a bright bar fills the whole receptive field). On the other hand, a high spatial frequency grating (right) will be ineffective for large receptive fields (no difference in average illumination between the center and flanks), but will drive small receptive fields very well. The shape of the CSF is presumed to reflect the responsiveness of the underlying receptive fields. From the CSFs in Figure 9.3 we can infer that:

1. There are fewer, less responsive very large receptive fields, resulting in the inverted-U shape of the CSF.
2. Receptive field sizes are larger in scotopic conditions, since peak sensitivity occurs at a lower spatial frequency in scotopic conditions than in photopic conditions. This may reflect the greater role played by parasol ganglion cells at low light levels (see Table 7.2 and Figure 7.6).

KEY TERMS

Spatial contrast threshold
The minimum contrast between the lightest and darkest parts of a pattern required for it to be reliably detected by an observer; lower values indicate better performance.

Spatial contrast sensitivity
The reciprocal of spatial contrast threshold (1/threshold); higher values indicate better performance.

Contrast sensitivity function (CSF)
A graph of spatial contrast sensitivity to luminance gratings, plotting sensitivity as a function of grating spatial frequency.

Contrast ratio
The ratio between the amount of contrast in an optical image, and the contrast in the original stimulus; values near unity indicate near-perfect transference.

Optical transfer function (OTF)
A graph of an optical system's ability to transfer luminance gratings, plotting contrast ratio as a function of grating spatial frequency.

? Why does pupil diameter affect the OTF?

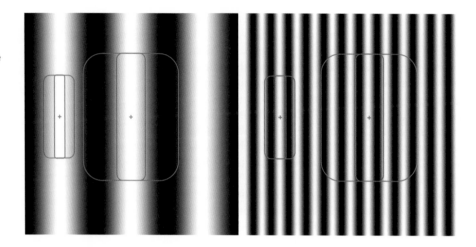

FIGURE 9.4
Spatial frequency selectivity in cortical cell receptive fields. The left-hand panel shows a low spatial frequency grating, and the right-hand panel shows a high spatial frequency grating. Two receptive fields are shown in each panel, one small and one large. Each receptive field will only generate an excitatory response if more light falls on its center than on its surround. The small receptive field is well matched to the width of the bars in the high frequency grating, but is swamped by the bars of the low frequency grating. The large receptive field, on the other hand, is best suited to the low frequency grating.

TEMPORAL CONTRAST SENSITIVITY

Natural visual images are never entirely stationary on the retina. Our eyes move incessantly, and real-world objects have a tendency to move either under their own steam or due to the effect of gravity. It is therefore important to establish how well the visual system responds to images that vary over time—its **temporal contrast sensitivity**. The simplest way to measure temporal sensitivity is to present an observer with a flickering light, and find the smallest amount of flicker that the observer can detect. In other words, we find the smallest luminance contrast between the bright phase and the dark phase of the flicker that is required for the observer to just detect that the light is flickering rather than steady. Sensitivity has been found to depend on the rate of flicker, usually called the **temporal frequency** of the light.

Figure 9.5 illustrates different flicker rates. The intensity of a light is shown over the course of two seconds. In the bottom line the light is bright for 1000 milliseconds, and dark for 1000 milliseconds. In the middle line the light is bright (or dark) for periods of 500 milliseconds, and in the top line the light is bright (or dark) for periods of 250 milliseconds. Flicker rate is expressed as cycles per second, or hertz, where one cycle is a single alternation from bright to dark. The lights in the three lines have flicker rates of 2, 1, and 0.5 Hz reading from top to bottom.

FIGURE 9.5
An illustration of flicker rate in a small spot. The spot alternates in intensity between light and dark. The rate of alternation defines its flicker temporal frequency. When each light and dark phase lasts 1000 milliseconds (bottom), one cycle of alternation lasts 2 seconds, so temporal frequency is 0.5 Hz. When each light and dark phase lasts 500 milliseconds (middle) one cycle lasts 1 second so temporal frequency is 1 Hz. When each light and dark phase lasts 250 milliseconds (top) one cycle lasts 500 milliseconds, so temporal frequency is 2 Hz.

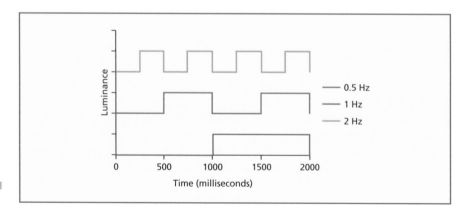

Temporal contrast sensitivity function

The results of an experiment to measure flicker sensitivity at a range of flicker rates can be plotted as a **temporal contrast sensitivity function**; an example is shown in Figure 9.6 (from de Lange, 1958). The figure shows sensitivity at two different illumination levels: Photopic (159 cd/m²; open symbols), and borderline scotopic (0.06 cd/m²; closed symbols). Sensitivity declines rapidly at high temporal frequencies, and frequencies above 50 Hz are not visible at any contrast. In photopic vision peak sensitivity occurs at approximately 8 Hz, and sensitivity drops away gently at lower frequencies.

Origins of the temporal contrast sensitivity function

The shape of the temporal contrast sensitivity function is determined entirely by neural responses in the visual system. Rods and cones have different temporal responses, as shown in Figure 7.4. Both receptor types contribute to retinal ganglion cells, and the complex neural circuitry associated with these cells has a major bearing on their temporal response (Masland, 2001). For example, differences in the timing of excitatory and inhibitory inputs to a cell will influence how its response fluctuates over time. So even at the ganglion cell level, temporal responses represent a complex interaction between multiple inputs. Temporal responses at the next level in the neural hierarchy, the LGN, will show additional influences as a result of descending inputs from the cortex. Further modifications to temporal responses occur in the cortex, due to intracortical circuitry.

Psychophysically measured temporal sensitivity therefore represents the combined effect of multiple neural processing stages. A clearer understanding of the origin of the contrast sensitivity function emerges when one considers temporal sensitivity and spatial sensitivity together—*spatiotemporal sensitivity*.

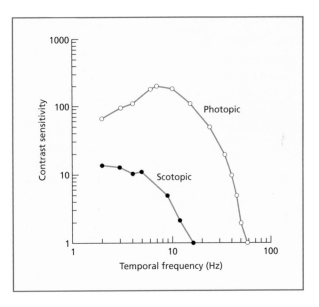

FIGURE 9.6
Temporal contrast sensitivity as a function of flicker rate, at two illumination levels. Sensitivity is highest (in other words, thresholds are lowest) at a flicker rate of approximately 8 Hz in photopic conditions. Adapted from de Lange (1958).

SPATIOTEMPORAL SENSITIVITY

The previous two sections showed how we can investigate spatial sensitivity and temporal sensitivity using very similar techniques. Both involve the measurement of contrast thresholds for a periodic stimulus. In the case of spatial sensitivity, the stimulus is periodic over space (a grating). In the case of temporal sensitivity, the stimulus is periodic over time (a flickering light). Contrast sensitivity in the two domains looks very similar. Figures 9.3 and 9.6 show that in both cases sensitivity is optimal at intermediate frequencies, declines rapidly at higher frequencies,

KEY TERMS

Temporal contrast sensitivity
The reciprocal of the amount of contrast between the brightest and darkest phases of a flickering stimulus required for a subject to detect the flicker.

Temporal frequency
The alternation rate of a flickering stimulus, measured in hertz, or the number of flicker cycles (bright–dark alternations) per second.

Temporal contrast sensitivity function
A graph of temporal contrast sensitivity, plotting sensitivity as a function of flicker temporal frequency.

and declines more gradually at lower frequencies. The link between the spatial and temporal domains is closer still. In both, the subject's task is simply to detect the presence of a stimulus. One can therefore measure sensitivity to stimuli that contain both spatial *and* temporal periodicity (**spatiotemporal contrast sensitivity**).

Stimuli

Spatiotemporal sensitivity is measured with a flickering grating. The spatial alternation between black and white bars of the grating define its spatial periodicity. Over time, each light bar gradually becomes dark at the same time as each dark bar becomes light, so the grating reverses in contrast. The bars then reverse in contrast again to return to their original intensity, as shown at the top of Figure 9.7. The

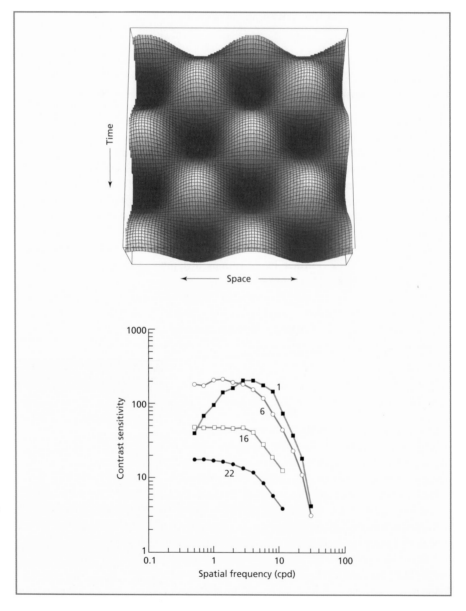

FIGURE 9.7
Spatiotemporal contrast sensitivity. Top: Space–time plot of a spatial grating that repetitively reverses in contrast over time. The grating's spatial frequency is defined by the rate of contrast alternation across space (horizontal slices through the panel). The grating's flicker temporal frequency is defined by the rate of contrast alternation across time (vertical slices through the panel). Bottom: Contrast sensitivity for flickering gratings as a function of their spatial frequency (horizontal axis) and temporal frequency (different curves), adapted from Robson (1966). Spatial sensitivity is band-pass at low temporal frequencies (filled squares), but low-pass at high temporal frequencies (filled circles).

rate at which each bar completes one cycle of contrast reversal defines the temporal frequency of the grating. Notice that a horizontal slice through the **space–time plot** in Figure 9.7 represents a spatial pattern at an instant in time, and shows the spatial periodicity of the grating. A vertical slice through the *space–time* plot represents a temporal pattern at a given location, and shows the temporal periodicity of the grating.

Sensitivity

Experiments to measure spatiotemporal sensitivity have found that the spatial and temporal properties of the grating interact: Spatial contrast sensitivity depends on the grating's temporal frequency, and vice versa. Figure 9.7 plots contrast sensitivity as a function of spatial frequency for gratings at four different temporal frequencies, taken from Robson (1966). The low temporal frequency curve (filled squares) is similar to that shown in Figure 9.3, with a pronounced peak at medium spatial frequencies (known as band-pass). However at the highest temporal frequency (filled circles), spatial sensitivity becomes low-pass.

Origins of variation in spatiotemporal sensitivity

Neural factors influence the shape of the spatial and temporal CSFs. The interaction between spatial and temporal frequency evident in Figure 9.7 can also be attributed to the properties of visual neurons. There are two alternative accounts of how the properties of center–surround receptive fields can explain the **spatiotemporal CSF**. One account is based on changes in the receptive field organization of a single cell population, and the other is based on differing responses of two distinct populations of center–surround cells.

Receptive field organization

Center–surround receptive fields can be broken down into the separate contributions from their center and surround. Figure 7.6 showed that each component conforms to a normal or Gaussian spatial distribution. Excitation and inhibition tail off gradually from their maximum values at the center of the receptive field. The net response of the receptive field is given by the difference between the excitatory and inhibitory distributions. Figure 9.8 (left) shows another example of center, surround, and net responses. The center and surround components have different widths, so they respond to different ranges of spatial frequency. Both have a low-pass frequency response, but the center responds to higher frequencies than the surround. The red and green lines in Figure 9.8 (overleaf) show the spatial frequency response of each component. The difference between them (thick black line) has a band-pass response (peak sensitivity at intermediate frequencies).

This explanation of the spatiotemporal CSF assumes that the balance between excitatory and inhibitory components varies with temporal frequency (Kelly, 1985). At low temporal frequencies, the two components have similar weight, so the receptive field has a band-pass characteristic (filled squares in Figure 9.7). If inhibition is less effective at high temporal frequencies, the influence of the surround becomes weaker so the low-pass spatial response of the center becomes dominant.

Evidence in support of this theory comes from single-unit recording data. Derrington and Lennie (1984) measured the contrast sensitivity of individual primate

FIGURE 9.8
Decomposition of center–surround receptive fields into center and surround components (left) that have different spatial frequency responses (right). The center is narrower, and therefore responds to higher spatial frequencies. The overall shape of the receptive field, and its spatial frequency response (thick lines), is given by the difference between the center and surround responses (left). The spatiotemporal contrast sensitivity function shown in Figure 9.7 can be explained by an alteration in the relative weights of center and surround components at different temporal frequencies, either in a single population of cells or in separate populations of cells. Equal weighting between the center and surround produces narrow frequency selectivity, whereas unequal weights produce broad, lower-pass selectivity. (Based on Bruce, Green, & Georgeson, 2003.) Copyright © 2003 Psychology Press.

Compare the response properties of the psychophysical transient and sustained channels with the magno and parvo systems (Chapter 7).

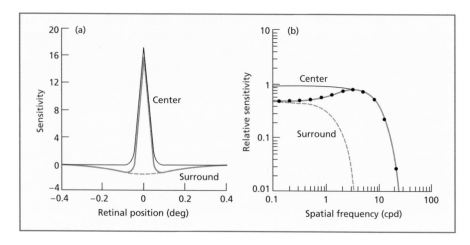

parvo and magno LGN cells. They found the minimum contrast of a flickering grating required to produce a criterion level of response in each cell, as a function of spatial and temporal frequency. Both parvo and magno cells showed a band-pass spatial frequency response at low temporal frequencies, and a low-pass temporal response at high temporal frequencies. The optimum spatial frequency was approximately 8 cpd for parvo cells, much like the human psychophysical data shown in Figure 9.7, and 1 cpd for magno cells.

Parallel pathways

According to this explanation, the spatiotemporal CSF actually reflects the contributions of two different populations of cells. Psychophysical experiments conducted after Robson's (1966) study led to the idea that information is processed in two separate and parallel pathways or *channels* in the human visual system (Tolhurst, 1973). One channel conveys information about pattern and shape, and is the most sensitive channel at high spatial frequencies and low temporal frequencies (filled squares in Figure 9.7; also known as the **sustained channel** due to the nature of its temporal response). The other channel conveys information about movement, and is the most sensitive channel at low spatial frequencies and high temporal frequencies (filled circles in Figure 9.7; also known as the **transient channel**). The characteristics of the proposed sustained and transient channels map neatly on to the differing response properties of cells in the midget/parvo and parasol/magno divisions of the visual pathway respectively (refer back to Figure 7.7). This idea is attractive because it provides a linking hypothesis between a large body of human psychophysical data and the neurophysiological parvo versus magno division that, according to some views, runs right through to extrastriate visual cortex.

Merigan and Eskin (1986) attempted to establish the neural substrate of contrast sensitivity in an experiment that combined psychophysical observations with physiological intervention. They trained macaque monkeys to perform a task measuring their contrast sensitivity. The monkeys were presented with a grating on one of two screens and pressed a button to select the screen containing the grating. One group of monkeys was given a neurotoxin that causes selective degeneration of ganglion cells projecting to the parvo layers of the LGN. When the treated monkeys were compared with untreated monkeys, they showed reduced contrast sensitivity only for gratings that were both high in spatial frequency and low in temporal frequency. Sensitivity at combinations of low spatial and high temporal frequency was barely affected by the neurotoxin. Contrast sensitivity losses in patients suffering certain clinical conditions mirror the selective losses observed by Merigan and Eskin (Plant, 1991).

These results favor the parallel pathways interpretation of the contrast sensitivity function. They indicate that basic perceptual functions can be dissected into contributions from cells in the parvo and magno divisions of the visual pathway. However, there are two important limitations:

- It would be an oversimplification to assume that the visual system just switches between the two cell divisions as stimulus parameters change. Contrast sensitivity is likely to reflect contributions from both divisions, though their relative importance may vary with stimulus conditions. Bright, centrally viewed but spatially extended visual stimuli, for example, are likely to activate both cell divisions in different regions (parvo cells at the fovea, and magno cells in the periphery).
- Contrast sensitivity experiments, by definition, tell us only about the detectability of visual stimuli. Experiments that require *discrimination* of stimulus attributes such as orientation, size, motion direction, and velocity, are likely to reflect more complex cortical processes in which parvo and magno responses are combined in some way.

REPRESENTATION AT MULTIPLE SPATIAL SCALES

SPATIAL SCALE

Visual images contain detail at many different spatial scales. Coarse-scale detail carries information about the general shape and structure of objects in the image, while fine-scale detail carries information about sharp edges and surface textural properties.

For example, the left-hand image of Figure 9.9 shows a photograph of a human face. The middle image represents only the coarse-scale information in the

FIGURE 9.9
Left: A photograph of a face. Middle: A low-pass filtered version of the face, retaining only coarse-scale or low spatial frequency information. Right: A high-pass filtered version of the face, retaining only fine-scale or high spatial frequency information.

The preponderance of low frequencies in the spectrum of the face in Figure 9.9 is typical of natural images. In general, amplitude falls in proportion with the reciprocal of spatial frequency (1/f). There has been much debate in the literature on the significance of this fact (Field, 1987).

? *Think of other examples of natural scenes in which information at different spatial scales can be used in different ways.*

photograph (created by applying spatial blur to the photograph). The only information preserved at this scale conveys the general shape of the head and hair, and the locations of relatively large features such as the eyes and mouth. The right-hand image represents only the fine-scale information, which conveys the precise shape of the eyes and mouth but discards large-scale luminance variation such as the darkness of the hair (it was created by taking the point by point difference between the original image on the left and the blurred image in the middle). Coarse-scale information may be useful for identifying the shape as a human face, and locating the approximate positions of the eyes, nose, and mouth. Fine-scale information, on the other hand, may be useful for estimating the age of a person from the skin texture of their face. Natural images generally contain different kinds of information at different spatial scales. In images of landscapes, for instance, coarse-scale detail might allow identification of trees and rock formations, while fine-scale detail conveys textural properties such as leaf shape and rock surface markings. In a traffic scene, coarse-scale detail may indicate the location of vehicles and road signs, while fine-scale detail reveals the make of the vehicle, and the lettering on road signs.

SPATIAL SCALE AND SPATIAL FREQUENCY

Fourier theory

Fourier theory was introduced in Chapter 4 in the context of hearing. Any complex sound waveform can be decomposed into a collection of simpler periodic components (repetitive fluctuations in air pressure over time) known as pure tones, as illustrated in Figure 4.6. Fourier decomposition of sounds helps us to understand the filtering effects of barriers such as the human head, which removes high frequency sound components while preserving lower frequencies (see Figure 4.9). Exactly the same general principle applies to complex visual images, which can also be decomposed into simpler periodic components. In the case of vision the components are repetitive fluctuations in image luminance over space and over time, which can be defined in terms of their sine wave spatial and temporal frequencies as described earlier in this chapter. Any natural image can be decomposed into a large collection of sine wave components at various frequencies, contrasts, orientations, and phases that is unique to that image.

? *What is the visual equivalent of an auditory click? Think about their frequency content.*

There is an intimate relation between spatial scale in natural images and Fourier component spatial frequency. Coarse-scale image content is carried by low frequency Fourier components, and fine-scale content is carried by high frequency components. Neurons in the visual system can be described in terms of their spatial (and temporal) frequency tuning, so Fourier analysis in vision helps us to understand the information content of images, and the likely neural response to them by the visual system. Fourier theory is widely used in vision science as a tool for analyzing images and modeling responses to them. The tutorials section at the end of the chapter offers a primer in this essential research technique.

Spatial filtering

As the flowchart in Figure 4.7 shows, when Fourier analysis is applied to a complex signal the resultant Fourier spectrum identifies the frequency components present in the signal. In spatial vision the complex signal is a two-dimensional image, and

 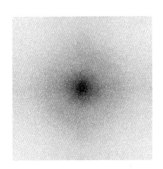

FIGURE 9.10
Fourier spectra of
the images shown in
Figure 9.9. Each point
represents a spatial
frequency component.
Spatial frequency
increases with radial
distance from the
center of the plot.
Orientation is given by
the angle of the line
joining each component
to the center of the
plot. The amplitude
of each component
is represented by its
intensity (darker points
have higher intensity).
The spectrum of the
original image (left)
contains a full range of
frequency components,
while in the filtered
spectra (middle and
right) components within
a certain range have
been removed.

the frequency components in the Fourier spectrum are sine wave gratings. Fourier synthesis reconstitutes the image. As Figure 4.9 goes on to demonstrate, it is possible to remove certain components from the Fourier spectrum before synthesizing the image. This operation amounts to removing or filtering some spatial frequencies from the image.

Returning to the example of the face on the left of Figure 9.9, the left-hand plot in Figure 9.10 shows its Fourier spectrum. Each point in the plot represents a particular spatial frequency component. Distance from the center of the plot corresponds to spatial frequency, with lower frequencies nearer the center. The angle of the line joining each component to the center of the plot corresponds to the orientation of the component. The intensity of each point represents the amplitude of the corresponding component (darker points indicate higher amplitudes). The original photograph contains a wide range of component frequencies and orientations, though lower frequency components have the greatest amplitude.

When the photograph is blurred to preserve only the coarse-scale information (Figure 9.9 middle) the effect is to filter out all the higher frequencies, as can be seen in the middle of Figure 9.10. The filter which produces this effect is called a low-pass filter. The version of the photograph that contains only fine-scale detail has been high-pass filtered to attenuate all the low frequencies and preserve all the high frequencies.

Multiple spatial filters in the visual system

The visual system distributes the diverse information present at different spatial scales in the responses of different populations of neurons. In frequency terms, different populations of neurons encode information over different ranges of spatial frequency in the Fourier spectrum; in other words, the neurons act as narrowly tuned spatial frequency filters. The CSF of a given neuron in the visual system can be viewed as an estimate of its spatial frequency response, since it represents how well the neuron responds to gratings at various frequencies.

Figure 9.11 (top) shows the CSFs of parvo and magno LGN cells recorded by Derrington and Lennie (1984). These functions are so broad that they basically divide up the frequency spectrum into just two components—too coarse a representation for detailed spatial frequency analysis. Figure 9.11 (bottom) shows the CSFs of cells in the striate cortex, recorded by De Valois, Albrecht, and Thorell (1982). Cortical CSFs are much narrower than those in the

The contrast in tuning width between LGN and cortical cells bears out the observation in Chapter 7 that cortical cell receptive fields are not simply created by aggregating LGN receptive fields. Intracortical processing is required, and this is likely to involve operations that combine magno and parvo signals in various ways.

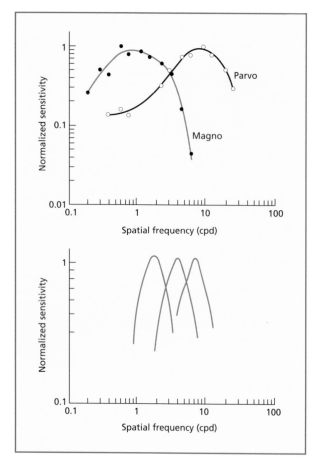

FIGURE 9.11
Contrast sensitivity functions of cells in the visual system. Top: Parvo (open symbols) and magno (filled symbols) LGN cells, adapted from Derrington and Lennie (1984; curves are based on best-fitting difference-of-Gaussian functions). Bottom: Striate cortical cells (adapted from De Valois, Albrecht, & Thorell, 1982). Cortical cells have much narrower spatial frequency tuning than LGN cells.

LGN, and do a much better job of dividing up the frequency spectrum into bands of spatial frequency.

In the next section we consider psychophysical evidence that the human visual system also contains such narrowly tuned spatial frequency filters. Later sections consider how the visual system makes use of these filters in the early stages of visual processing. There are two major caveats to bear in mind. First, in the interests of simplicity, the foregoing discussion has disregarded temporal sensitivity. However, it was emphasized earlier that spatial sensitivity cannot be regarded as independent of temporal sensitivity. A more comprehensive treatment of spatial vision would consider *spatiotemporal* frequency analysis. This would require consideration of three-dimensional Fourier spectra (two spatial dimensions, plus a third dimension to represent temporal frequency). A discussion of such spectra is beyond the scope of this chapter, though simple spatiotemporal receptive fields will be introduced in the context of motion perception (Chapter 12). Second, the idea that the visual system performs a frequency analysis on the image using frequency-tuned filters should not be taken to mean that the visual system actually uses Fourier analysis to represent and recognize objects. Fourier transforms involve some strict assumptions:

- They are global, combining information across the whole image, whereas visual receptive fields are local.
- They represent each frequency component in the image independently of all other components, while the receptive fields of visual neurons admit a range of components (Figure 9.11), and neurons interact with each other.
- They assume that the response of the system is linear. Linearity was discussed in Chapter 4, and the same restrictions apply in the case of vision as in the case of hearing. Some aspects of visual responses can be considered linear, but many others are grossly nonlinear.

Fourier analysis is best viewed as a powerful and extremely useful mathematical tool for analyzing the information content of visual images and characterizing certain response properties of visual neurons, it should not be confused with a theory of visual function.

PSYCHOPHYSICAL EVIDENCE FOR MULTIPLE SPATIAL FILTERS

Psychophysical evidence for the existence of multiple spatial filters in the human visual system is based on two techniques: Adaptation and masking.

Adaptation

Adaptation is one of the most widely used techniques in visual psychophysics. The basic paradigm involves three stages:

- Pre-adaptation psychophysical measurement
- Adaptation to an inducing stimulus
- Post-adaptation psychophysical measurement.

A comparison between pre-adaptation and post-adaptation measurements reveals the effect of the adapting stimulus on performance. Measurements involve either threshold or suprathreshold stimuli.

Threshold measurements

If an observer views a high-contrast grating for several minutes, their ability to see a low-contrast test grating is reduced for a while afterwards. A comparison of contrast thresholds before and after the period of adaptation reveals **threshold elevation**: more contrast is required for detection after adaptation than before adaptation. Blakemore and Campbell (1969) measured threshold elevation as a function of the difference in spatial frequency between the adapting and test gratings. They found that threshold elevation was generally maximal when adapting and test spatial frequencies matched, and declined progressively as the difference between the two frequencies increased. Figure 9.12 (a) shows some of their data. The solid curve shows contrast sensitivity before adaptation. The dashed curve shows sensitivity after adapting to a spatial frequency of 7.1 cpd (arrowed on the abscissa). Sensitivity is depressed only for similar spatial frequencies.

We can assume that adaptation depresses the sensitivity of neural filters in the visual system which are responsive to the adapting spatial frequency. So the specificity of the adaptation effect reflects the specificity of the underlying filters. When adapting and test frequencies are very similar, the *same* filters respond to both, so threshold elevation occurs. On the other hand, when adapting and test frequencies are very dissimilar, they stimulate *different* filters and no threshold elevation is measured. The spatial frequency specificity of contrast adaptation is therefore evidence for the existence of multiple spatial filters.

Contrast adaptation is orientation tuned. When adapting and test gratings are sufficiently different in orientation then no threshold elevation is found, even if the gratings have the same spatial frequency (Movshon & Blakemore, 1973). Contrast adaptation is also binocular, in the sense that it can be obtained when the adapting grating is presented to only one eye, and the test grating is presented to the other eye (Blakemore & Campbell, 1969). These findings indicate that the spatial filters involved in contrast adaptation correspond to binocular, orientation-tuned cells in striate cortex.

Suprathreshold measurements

Adaptation can also affect the appearance of high-contrast stimuli, also known as suprathreshold stimuli. Figure 9.2 showed several examples of *suprathreshold* sine wave grating stimuli. The reader should have no difficulty in detecting these

FIGURE 9.12
Adaptation to gratings.
(a) The solid line shows
contrast sensitivity as
a function of spatial
frequency, prior to
adaptation. Note the
similarity with the
graph in Figure 9.3.
The broken line shows
contrast sensitivity after
a period of adaptation to
a high-contrast grating
at the spatial frequency
shown by the arrow
on the horizontal axis.
Adaptation reduces
sensitivity to gratings
whose frequency is
similar to the adapting
spatial frequency.
Adapted from Blakemore
and Campbell (1969).
(b) An explanation of
the size after-effect,
based on population
coding in an array of
spatial frequency tuned
filters. The population
response to a medium
spatial frequency test
grating is shown by the
purple lines. Population
responses to adapting
gratings are shown
in solid blue (upper
graph, high-frequency
adapter; lower graph,
low-frequency adapter),
with depth of adaptation
plotted as broken blue
lines. Test responses
after adaptation
(broken gray lines) are
skewed away from the
spatial frequency of
the adapting stimulus,
causing shifts in
apparent spatial
frequency.

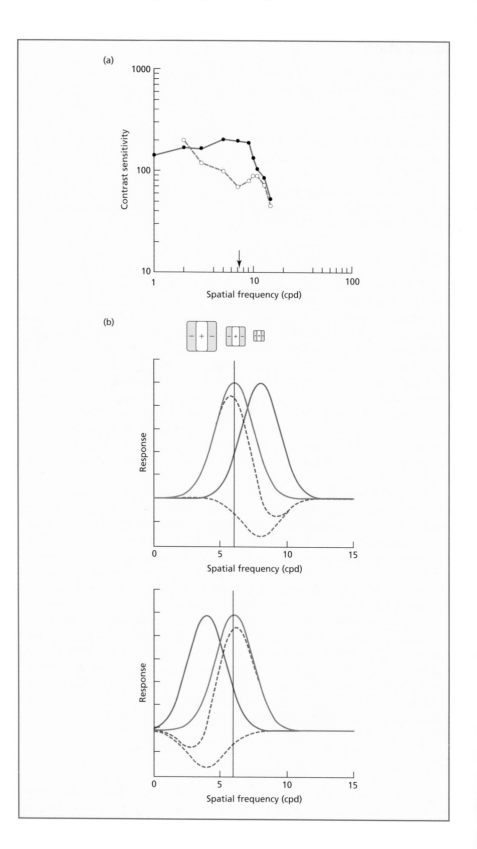

gratings, and judging their frequency and orientation accurately. However, the apparent frequency or orientation of a grating can be influenced by prior exposure to an adapting grating:

- **Size after-effect** Blakemore and Sutton (1969) reported that a given test spatial frequency grating appears to have a lower frequency following adaptation to a high frequency grating, and appears to have a higher frequency following adaptation to a low frequency grating.
- **Tilt after-effect** An analogous effect is found in judgments of orientation (Gibson & Radner, 1937). Adaptation to lines tilted slightly clockwise from vertical makes vertical lines appear tilted slightly anticlockwise; adaptation to anticlockwise lines makes vertical lines appear tilted clockwise from vertical.

These after-effects can be explained using spatial filters selectively tuned to spatial frequency and orientation, as illustrated in Figure 9.12(b) for the size after-effect. Both graphs show the response of any array of tuned neural filters to various spatial frequency gratings. The receptive field sketches along the spatial frequency axis at the top indicate that neurons with large receptive fields signal low spatial frequencies and neurons with small receptive fields signal high spatial frequencies, as illustrated earlier in Figure 9.5. According to the principle of population coding discussed in previous chapters, our perception of spatial frequency is based on the relative response of the population of tuned filters. The solid purple lines show relative filter response to a medium-frequency test grating. Filters tuned to medium frequencies respond best, so dominate our perception of this spatial frequency. The solid blue line in the upper graph shows relative filter response to a higher spatial frequency. If the observer is exposed to this stimulus for a period of time, the activated filters show reduced responsiveness, or adaptation (as introduced in Chapter 1). The broken blue line in the upper graph shows the extent of adaptation in different filters; filters that respond most to the adapting stimulus show the greatest adaptation. If the medium frequency test grating is presented after adaptation, the population response is distorted by the adaptation. The broken grey line in the upper graph shows the population response to the medium frequency after the adapting to the high frequency grating (it is actually created by subtracting the broken blue line from the solid purple line). Notice the skew in response away from the adapting stimulus. In the lower graph the adapting stimulus (blue line) has a lower frequency than the test stimulus, and the adapted population response (broken grey line) is skewed towards higher spatial frequencies. Notice that the population response to a fixed test grating can be shifted either towards higher or towards lower frequencies, depending on the nature of the adapting stimulus, offering an explanation for the size after-effect. The same explanation can be used for the tilt after-effect. Indeed, adaptation effects in motion perception can also be explained by a tug-of-war between filters tuned to different directions (see Figure 12.5 for an illustration of the tug-of-war explanation).

Masking

Contrast threshold at a given spatial frequency is elevated when a high-contrast masking grating is superimposed on the test pattern. The magnitude of elevation depends on the difference in frequency between the test grating and the masking

KEY TERMS

Size after-effect
A change in the apparent spatial frequency of a test grating following exposure to an adapting grating.

Tilt after-effect
A change in the apparent tilt of a test stimulus following exposure to an adapting stimulus.

? *Relate this explanation for after-effects to the population coding ideas discussed in the first three chapters.*

Masking techniques were also discussed extensively in Chapter 5, because they can be used to infer the selectivity of filters in the auditory system tuned to narrow ranges of sound frequency. As in the case of vision, the similarity between physiological and perceptual estimates of filter bandwidth is remarkable (see Figure 5.5).

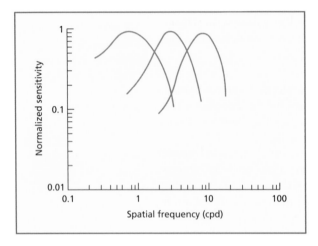

grating. Masks at the same frequency as the test stimulus produce the greatest threshold elevation. The masking effect declines steadily as the difference in frequency increases, in much the same way that adaptation declines as the difference between adapting and test gratings increases.

We can assume that **masking** is effective because it corrupts the response of filters tuned to the test spatial frequency (it injects activity that is not correlated with the presence of a signal). When the mask and test frequencies are sufficiently close in frequency to stimulate the same filter, threshold elevation occurs. When the two frequencies are so different that the mask stimulates a different filter from the test, no threshold elevation occurs. So the specificity of masking provides an estimate of the spatial frequency selectivity of the underlying filters. Figure 9.13 shows estimates of the frequency selectivity of spatial filters, based on masking data (Wilson, McFarlane, & Phillips, 1983). The similarity with the frequency tuning of cortical cells (Figure 9.11) is striking.

FIGURE 9.13
Spatial frequency tuning curves of spatial filters in the visual system, estimated psychophysically using contrast masking. The similarity with cortical cell tuning (Figure 9.11) is remarkable. Adapted from Wilson, McFarlane, and Phillips (1983).

USES OF SPATIAL FILTERS

So far we have seen that natural images contain information at many different spatial scales or frequency ranges. Psychophysical studies show that the human visual system possesses filters that respond selectively to narrow bands of spatial frequency. In neural terms these mechanisms correspond to populations of spatial frequency-selective neurons in the visual cortex, as found in single-unit studies. In this section we consider in more detail how the visual system might make use of the information provided in spatial frequency-tuned neural filters.

FEATURE LOCALIZATION

Images formed in the eye contain patterns of light and dark that vary continuously across the retina. Even the sharpest contours on visible surfaces are rendered in the retinal image as continuously varying luminance distributions (see, for example, the linespread functions in Figure 6.17). Yet in most situations we perceive the visual world to be divided into discretely different surfaces and objects, defined by collections of features. A major computational goal of low-level spatial vision is thought to be the construction of a neural representation of features in the image. Features can be defined as "physical aspects of the image that are discretely represented and which have a measurable position" (Morgan, 2011, p. 738). Psychophysical and computational research on how the visual system detects features and assigns a location to (or "localizes") them has focused almost entirely on three particular types of luminance feature: Edges, bars, and blobs. Edges are often considered to be the most fundamental type of feature, because bars and blobs can be described

KEY TERM

Masking
A rise in the contrast threshold for a test stimulus in the presence of a second, masking stimulus.

as collections of edges in different spatial configurations. Spatial frequency-tuned filters have played a key role in theories of edge localization.

The importance of edges

Intensity edges in an image correspond to the points at which luminance changes most steeply across space. Figure 9.14 shows a grayscale image. The graph below the image plots luminance as it varies along the horizontal line drawn across the middle of the image. The edges (steepest luminance changes or gradients in the profile) mark the boundaries of surfaces and objects in the scene. Information on edge location can be used to distinguish objects from their background, and establish their shape and position, so edge localization is a crucial early step in the process of scene analysis.

Observers are highly efficient at locating edges. A standard laboratory test of edge localization is **Vernier acuity**, illustrated in Figure 9.15. The observer's task is to report whether the top line is displaced to the left or to the right of the bottom line. In optimal conditions observers can reliably report displacements as small as

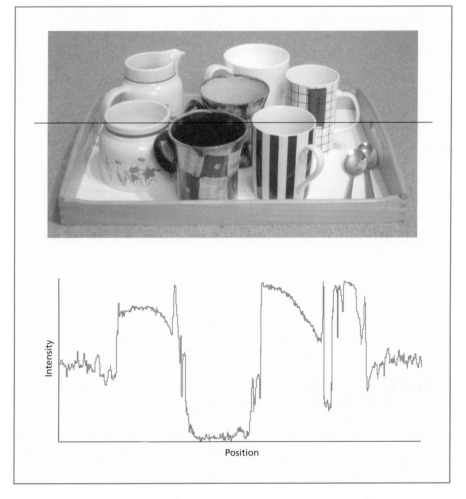

FIGURE 9.14
Intensity edges in images are defined by steep changes in luminance across space. The graph below the image plots luminance along the horizontal line drawn across the image. Edges occur at the boundaries of surfaces and objects, as well as at surface markings.

FIGURE 9.15
A standard psychophysical test of edge localization performance involves Vernier alignment. In each trial a pair of lines is presented, one above the other. The observer must report whether the upper line is displaced to the left of the lower line (as on the left) or to the right (as on the right). Vernier acuity is defined by the displacement that reaches a criterion level of response, usually 75% correct reports of displacement direction.

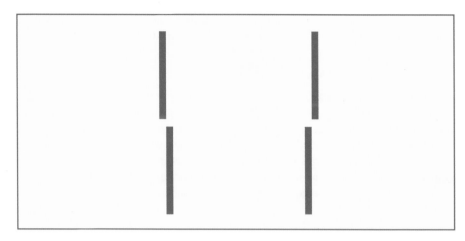

5″ arc (Westheimer & McKee, 1977). In linear units, this distance corresponds to an offset of less than 1/70th of a millimeter at arm's length, or of 5 mm viewed from a distance of 200 meters. A 5″ arc is also less than one sixth of the distance between adjacent photoreceptors on the retina. Performance at such high levels of precision has been called **hyperacuity** (Westheimer, 1975).

Explaining hyperacuity

How can observers perform acuity tasks with a precision that seems to defy the resolution of the retinal mosaic? Figure 9.16 (top) shows the retinal luminance profile of a thin line at two positions, 0′ and 0.2′ arc (12″ arc). Due to the optical effects discussed in Chapter 6 (see Figure 6.17), the line's profile is spread over a distance spanning more than 4′ arc. Foveal cones are spaced at intervals of approximately 0.6′ arc (36″ arc), and the vertical dashed lines in the top graph represent the centers of adjacent cones in the retinal mosaic. The middle bar graph shows the response of each photoreceptor in the presence of the line at its two positions (given by summing the light that falls in each 0.6′ arc interval). Notice that the shift in line position causes a slight change in the response of each photoreceptor. Some receptors increase their response, while others decrease their response. The bottom bar graph shows the ratio of photoreceptor responses at the two line positions. Some receptors increase their response by over 25% and others decrease their response by a similar amount, even though the change in line position is much smaller than the distance between adjacent photoreceptors. This shift in the pattern of photoreceptor response can be detected by a mechanism that compares the responses of nearby photoreceptors (Lee et al., 1993). Receptive fields containing adjacent excitatory and inhibitory zones compute the change in retinal illumination at neighboring locations; in other words they compute the "spatial-derivative" of retinal luminance, as discussed earlier in this chapter and in Chapter 7. So the response of spatial-derivative receptive fields carries information that should be sufficient to achieve hyperacuity, provided that an appropriate computational process reads out the response and encodes it in terms of edge location (see Barlow, 1979; Morgan & Watt, 1982 for more detailed discussions).

[?] *Why are center–surround receptive fields important in explaining hyperacuity?*

KEY TERM

Hyperacuity
Acuity performance in which the observer can detect changes in spatial location that are smaller than the distance between adjacent retinal photoreceptors.

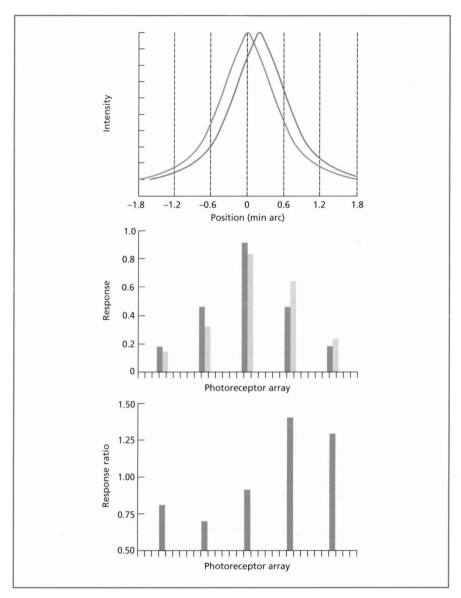

FIGURE 9.16
How to explain our ability to detect Vernier displacements much smaller than the distance between adjacent photoreceptors. Top: Retinal light distributions across two lines displaced by a distance of 12″ arc (typical of Vernier acuity thresholds). The vertical dashed lines mark the centers of adjacent photoreceptors. Light from each line is spread over more than 4′ arc and six photoreceptors, but the shift in the peak of the distribution is a fraction of the spacing between photoreceptors. Middle: Response at each photoreceptor, assuming that response is given by summing the light over each 0.6′ arc interval in the top graph. Blue bars correspond to the left-hand line, and purple bars correspond to the right-hand line. Bottom: The change in response at each photoreceptor caused by the shift in line position. Some receptors increase their response by about 25%, while others decrease their response by the same amount. Thus, even though the line displacement is relatively small, there is a significant change in response across a number of photoreceptors.

Theories of edge localization

A number of computational theories have proposed encoding schemes which infer edge location from the pattern of responses in spatial-derivative receptive fields (reviewed in Morgan, 2011). Most theories involve the series of processing stages illustrated in Figure 9.17.

Spatial filtering

All theories begin by applying a bank of spatial derivative filters to the image. Filters at many different spatial scales (receptive field sizes) are required, for two reasons. First, edges can occur at many scales, ranging from relatively steep, sharply defined luminance steps at object boundaries to the shallow, blurry shoulders of shadows.

FIGURE 9.17
Processing stages involved in current theories of edge localization in the visual system. A bank of spatial frequency-tuned filters extracts image detail at different spatial scales. Filter outputs are used to detect the presence of features in the image, such as edges, lines, and bars. Finally, the features extracted at each spatial scale are reconciled to create a single, integrated feature map. Specific theories differ in the detailed operations performed at each stage, and one model argues that filter outputs are combined before feature extraction, rather than after.

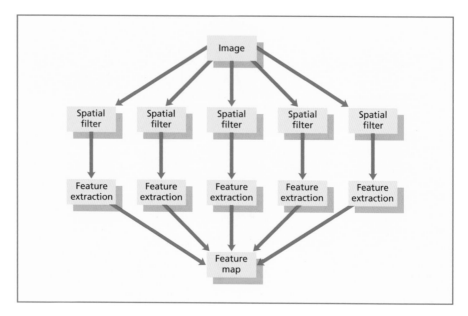

? *At what stage does the representation in each model become symbolic?*

KEY TERMS

Peak
A point where the value of a function such as a receptive field response reaches its maximum.

Primal sketch
A relatively primitive representation of local spatial structure in an image, produced by the initial stages of visual processing.

Filter size must be matched to edge width in order to detect the edge. Second, as Marr (1982) pointed out, filter responses at any given scale can be unreliable, picking up phantom edges which do not exist in the image, so filter outputs at different scales have to be compared or combined in some way to minimize errors.

Early theories such as Marr and Hildreth's (1980) model assumed that these filters corresponded to neurons in the visual pathway (retina or LGN). More recent analyses acknowledge that retinal and LGN cells are too broadly tuned, and that the most likely candidates are cortical cells (Morgan & Watt, 1997). All the models use balanced center–surround receptive fields, which produce no net response to uniform illumination, and have narrow frequency tuning (see Figures 9.8 and 9.22).

Feature extraction

Models of edge localization also contain a feature extraction stage, in which the filter outputs are interpreted to encode a limited set of features describing the spatial structure of the image, such as edges, lines, and bars. The rules governing this interpretation are based on the distinctive "signatures" in the responses that distinguish between different spatial features. An edge, for example, causes the filter response to have a **peak** on one side of the edge and a trough on the other (see Figure 7.9, right-hand column). Marr and Hildreth's (1980) and Georgeson et al.'s (2007) models use the midpoint between the peak and trough to encode edge location, whereas Watt and Morgan's (1985) model uses peaks.

Feature map

The output of the feature extraction stage is a map containing the locations of all extracted features. Grouping processes (discussed in Chapter 10) are assumed to use the feature map to extract large-scale spatial structures and shapes. Marr and Hildreth (1980) called the output of their model the **primal sketch**, and this term is now often used to refer to any low-level map of local spatial structure (Bruce, Green, & Georgeson, 2003).

Filter combination

A distinctive aspect of different models concerns when and how filter outputs are combined. Some theories propose that feature extraction occurs *before* filters at different spatial scales are combined, as depicted in Figure 9.17. Others favor the reverse order: Feature extraction *after* filter combination. The precise way that filter outputs are combined also varies between models; for example some models keep ON- and OFF-center responses separate, while others combine them.

Which model is best?

Comparisons between the different localization models are difficult because the models differ in quite complex ways, have been applied to different kinds of images, and have been tested against different psychophysical measures. A definitive empirical test of all the models would have to implement all of them, apply them to the same range of images, and compare their predictions against a single set of psychophysical measures. Such a test would be a major undertaking, and it has not so far been conducted. A deeper problem is that many of the differences between models are rather subtle, making it extremely difficult to devise a single critical test (or at least a test that can withstand attempts to iron out wrinkles by tweaking details of specific models, a favored pastime of modelers).

Block quantization effects

The effect As an example of the difficulty in distinguishing between the models, let's consider the well-known "Abraham Lincoln" demonstration, which once seemed to offer the prospect of telling us about how the outputs of spatial frequency-selective filters are combined in early spatial vision. In the original demonstration, a photograph of Abraham Lincoln was subjected to block quantization as follows. The image was divided up into an array of equal-sized tiles or blocks. The intensity of each tile was set to the average intensity of the region of the photograph covered by the tile.

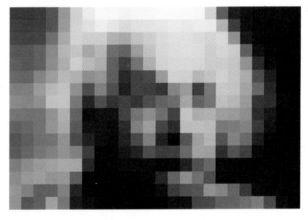

Block quantization preserves the low spatial frequency content of the image, at a scale that corresponds to the size of the blocks. But the edges of the blocks introduce spurious high spatial frequencies that are not related to the content of the image. As you can see from Figure 9.18, block quantization makes it very difficult to identify the person in the photograph. However, low-pass filtering the image (by removing your spectacles, if you wear spectacle corrections, or defocusing your eyes) allows the person's identity to become more apparent (a famous theoretical physicist).

FIGURE 9.18
A photograph that has been block-quantized by dividing the image into blocks, and setting the intensity of each block to the average intensity of the region covered by the block. It is very difficult to identify the subject of the photograph, unless the image is blurred (Harmon & Julesz, 1973).

Explanations Both early and late feature extraction models have offered explanations for block quantization effects:

* Watt and Morgan's (1985) model proposed that the outputs of filters in different frequency bands are combined *early* in the process of edge localization. So prior to edge extraction the spurious high frequency information introduced by the blocks

is summed with the low frequency information correlated with the photograph, consequently interfering with recognition. Blurring improves recognition because it optically removes the spurious high frequencies that influence edge extraction.

• Advocates of *late* filter combination such as Morrone, Burr, and Ross (1994) argued that features are first extracted at each scale, and a final feature map is derived by combining the scale-specific maps. The high frequency features defining the blocks "drag" the features at coarser scales with them, so distorting the representation in the final feature map and causing interference.

The Abraham Lincoln demonstration is not a very good testbed for theories of edge localization. It does tell us that information in different frequency bands is combined, as all models assume, but it cannot tell us much more.

TEXTURE ANALYSIS

In everyday terms, texture refers to the physical properties of an object's surface, such as whether it is rough or smooth, glossy or matt, patterned or uniform. If two visible surfaces differ in physical texture, the images of those surfaces will differ in spatial structure or **visual texture** (provided that the texture can be resolved by the imaging system). The visual system can use visual texture to segment a surface, shape, or object from its background. Spatial frequency-selective filters can play a role in texture analysis because their output depends on spatial structure in the image. If two regions of the image differ in spatial structure, and we apply an array of spatial frequency- and orientation-selective filters to them, we can assume that at least some of those filters will respond more to one region than to the other. This variation in filter response forms the basis for computational models of texture segregation (reviewed in Landy & Graham, 2004). The general scheme is known as **filter–rectify–filter (FRF)**, after the three successive processing stages involved.

As an example of a FRF process, consider how it would operate on an image containing a large shape defined by broad stripes (low spatial frequency) against a background of narrow stripes (high spatial frequency), as in an image of a tiger or zebra standing in front of long grass. In the first stage the image is filtered by applying relatively large receptive fields responsive to low spatial frequencies. The resulting response pattern (neural image), contains strong responses in the region containing the zebra, and weak responses in the region containing the grass (as demonstrated in Figure 9.4). But all the responses fluctuate across the image because of the way that individual receptive fields align with the stripes; responses are strongest in regions where the excitatory center of the receptive field aligns with bright stripes (and weakest where it aligns with dark stripes). The second and third steps (rectify and filter) remove this fluctuation. In the second step, the filter responses are rectified to reduce the response variation by converting negative responses into positive ones, or by ignoring one sign of response entirely (refer back to the discussion of ON and OFF receptive fields in Chapter 7). In the third step, a very low spatial frequency filter is applied to the neural image to smooth out the fluctuations and isolate the relatively large shape defined by the stripes.

Psychophysical evidence on texture edge localization

The FRF scheme can be used to localize edges defined by many different kinds of texture variation, as opposed to the luminance edges localized in the scheme in

Figure 9.17. The low frequency third-stage filters wipe out any representation of the individual texture elements themselves, but retain a representation of texture boundaries. Nothdurft (1993) provided psychophysical evidence that texture segmentation depends specifically on the differences between texture elements at the borders between texture regions, as would be expected on the basis of an edge localization scheme. Evidence for low frequency second-stage filtering was provided by Gray and Regan (1997) and Mather and Smith (2002):

- Gray and Regan (1997) compared Vernier acuity for luminance- and texture-defined edges. Acuity for texture edges was an order of magnitude worse than acuity for luminance edges (6′ arc or more for the former, compared to 300' arc or less for the latter), as expected on the basis of low frequency second-stage filtering. Morgan (1986) had previously reported Vernier thresholds in the region of 40″ arc for stereoscopically defined texture edges.
- Mather and Smith (2002) measured observers' ability to discriminate different degrees of blur in luminance edges and in texture edges. Blur discrimination thresholds were much larger for texture edges than for luminance edges, consistent with the idea that lower frequency filters are used for texture edges than for luminance edges.

? Why should acuity be worse using lower frequency filters?

Recent studies of neural responses in the visual cortex have identified a possible neural substrate for FRF-style texture analysis (Tanaka & Ohzawa, 2009; Hallum & Movshon, 2014). As mentioned in Chapter 7, many cortical neurons show surround suppression; a stimulus presented outside the classically defined receptive field (CRF) can suppress responses to preferred stimuli which fall inside the receptive field. The suppressive surround is sometimes called the extra-classical receptive field (ERF). The response of the CRF may constitute the initial filtering stage of the FRF mechanism. The CRF and ERF are often arranged asymmetrically and are elongated parallel to each other (Tanaka & Ohzawa, 2009), so their combined response may constitute the second FRF stage of relatively low spatial frequency filtering (the opposing CRF and ERF contributions effectively produce a response which is tuned to contrast modulations over a larger region).

SCENE GIST

The "gist" of a scene refers to its basic level semantic categorization as, for example, a kitchen, or a street, or a mountain. We are very adept at gist recognition, as you probably experience every time you rapidly flip through television channels searching for something to watch. A very brief glimpse of each image is sufficient for you to grasp the essential nature of the scene being broadcast. Psychophysical studies have found that observers can recognize scene gist in a fraction of a second (Potter, 1976; Rousselet, Joubert, & Fabre-Thorpe, 2005). Oliva and collaborators studied the image properties that support rapid gist processing, and particularly investigated the role played by information at different spatial scales. Their results indicated that relatively coarse scale (low spatial frequency) information from the entire image is sufficient to allow categorization, though it is not adequate for identifying individual objects (see Oliva, 2005).

Gist computation is thus likely to be based on holistic processing of the scene's global spatial frequency content, as would be available in the responses of an array of spatial frequency-tuned filters of the kind described earlier in the chapter. Torralba and Oliva (2003) had previously analyzed the spatial frequency spectra of 14 different image categories, such as portraits, indoor scenes, street scenes, natural objects, and so on, and found that each category has a characteristic spectral "signature." Portraits, for instance, contain a preponderance of low frequency energy that is evenly distributed across all orientations (as evident in Figure 9.10), while indoor scenes contain much more energy at horizontal and vertical orientations than at all other orientations. Thus the relative activity of a population of frequency- and orientation-tuned cortical cells should contain enough information to make rapid gist judgments. Scene gist computations based on spatial frequency analysis are likely to play an important role in future theories of recognition and attention (discussed in later chapters).

STEREO AND MOTION

Spatial frequency-selective receptive fields lie at the heart of stereoscopic depth and motion computations:

- Stereoscopic vision relies on the visual system correctly matching features extracted from the image in one eye with the corresponding features extracted in the other eye. This matching problem is very difficult to solve. Some computational theories make use of spatial frequency selectivity to simplify the problem by restricting the search for matches to certain bands of spatial frequency.
- Motion analyzing processes must deal with images that move across the retinal mosaic at high speed. For example, the image of a human walking across your field of view at a distance of 10 meters will traverse 800 photoreceptors per second (assuming the eyes are stationary). Precise localization is not a priority for motion processes so relatively large, low spatial frequency receptive fields can be used. They have the advantage that they are able to integrate over a greater portion of the motion trajectory and therefore produce a more reliable estimate of velocity and direction.

These processes will be discussed at length in later chapters.

CHAPTER SUMMARY

FUNDAMENTAL FUNCTIONS

- The shift from cone vision to rod vision (dark adaptation) takes approximately 30 minutes. Dark adaptation is accompanied by a shift in the relative brightness of surfaces that reflect different wavelengths, due to the differing spectral sensitivities of rods and cones (the Purkinje shift).
- The spatial contrast sensitivity function shows that human observers are most sensitive to gratings of medium spatial frequency (3 cpd). Sensitivity to spatial frequency declines rapidly at higher frequencies, and gradually at lower frequencies.
- The temporal contrast sensitivity function shows maximum sensitivity to medium flicker rates (8 Hz). Sensitivity to temporal frequency declines rapidly at higher frequencies and more gradually at lower frequencies.

- Spatiotemporal contrast sensitivity depends jointly on spatial frequency and temporal frequency: Sensitivity to spatial frequency is band-pass at low temporal frequencies, and low-pass at high temporal frequencies. The shape of the spatiotemporal contrast sensitivity function can be explained by the properties of parvo and magno cells in the visual pathway.

REPRESENTATION AT MULTIPLE SPATIAL SCALES

- Natural images contain information at many different spatial scales, or spatial frequencies.
- Fourier theory provides a method of decomposing complex images into their spatial frequency components.
- Cells in the visual system can be viewed as spatial frequency filters tuned to respond to only a subset of spatial frequencies.
- Psychophysical evidence for multiple spatial filters in the human visual system comes from contrast adaptation and from masking experiments.

USES OF SPATIAL FILTERS

- Spatial frequency-tuned filters in the human visual system are used in several computations: For feature localization, for texture analysis, scene gist analysis, and in the early stages of stereo and motion processing.
- Theories of luminance edge localization combine the outputs of multiple spatial filters to infer the presence of features such as edges and lines. Some theories extract features before combining information at different spatial scales, others extract features after combining the outputs of filters at different spatial scales.
- Theories of texture analysis include additional intermediate processing stages in which a nonlinear transform is applied to the filter outputs before second-stage low spatial frequency filtering and feature extraction.
- Experimental evidence indicates that rapid processing of scene gist is based on the pattern of responses in spatial frequency- and orientation-tuned cortical filters.

TUTORIALS

FOURIER ANALYSIS APPLIED TO VISION

Fourier analysis was introduced in Chapter 4 as a tool for studying complex auditory waveforms and their representation in the auditory system. Fourier analysis is widely used in the study of vision as well. This tutorial introduces the basic principles of Fourier analysis in the visual domain. It assumes that the reader has already studied the tutorial on Fourier analysis in Chapter 4.

One-dimensional (1-D) spatial images

Auditory stimuli can be described in terms of variation along a single dimension, namely time. So Fourier analysis of an auditory waveform produces a frequency spectrum that contains variation in amplitude along a single temporal dimension which represents temporal frequency (cycles per second, measured in hertz). The direct spatial equivalent in vision is a one-dimensional image that contains variation in light intensity along a single spatial dimension, which has the appearance of a stripy texture. Fourier analysis decomposes any complex one-dimensional spatial pattern into sinusoidal component waves of different spatial frequency, amplitude, and phase. Visually, each spatial frequency component is a sine wave grating. Figure 9.19 shows a simple example.

The thick black line shows the luminance profile of a one-dimensional pattern containing a sharp edge separating a light bar on the left from a dark bar on the right (a small fragment of a repeating "square wave" pattern). The other lines show some of the sine wave component gratings which compose the pattern. The grating with the lowest frequency and highest amplitude (F1) is called the fundamental frequency (you may recognize this terminology from the chapters on hearing). The other components are whole-number (integer) multiples of this frequency, at progressively lower amplitude (F3 at 3x frequency and 1/3 amplitude, F5 at 5x frequency and 1/5 amplitude, and so on). The thick line shows the sum of the five components plotted. As you can see it is an approximation to a square wave pattern; the addition of further components in the sequence would progressively sharpen up the edge. Notice the edge is created by the phase alignment of all of the components at the location of the edge. All of the waves have a positive-going

FIGURE 9.19
Summation of 1-D spatial frequency components to create complex spatial waveforms. As a series of components are added progressively to the waveform, the resultant image approximates a square wave more closely. The components correspond to those shown in Table 4.1 and in Figure 4.25.

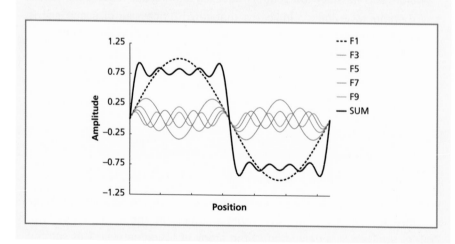

gradient at that point. If one of the components shifted in phase there would be a visible effect on the summed profile.

If you compare Figure 9.19 with Figure 4.6, which shows the harmonic content of a clarinet note, you will see how Fourier analysis applies equally well to auditory and visual stimuli. The auditory equivalent of the Fourier series in Figure 9.19 was shown in Table 4.1 and Figure 4.25. Any periodic one-dimensional spatial pattern can be decomposed into a Fourier series of sine wave gratings (as in the case of audition, a strict application of Fourier theory requires that the waveform is infinitely long, though this restriction is often disregarded).

Two-dimensional (2-D) spatial images

Natural images vary in two spatial dimensions, vertically (*y*-axis) and horizontally (*x*-axis). Fourier analysis can also be applied to these images, and results in two-dimensional spectra. Each component in the frequency spectrum of a 2-D pattern has both a vertical spatial frequency and a horizontal spatial frequency. Consider the case of the spatial frequency grating shown in Figure 9.20 (top). Vertical and horizontal cross-sections

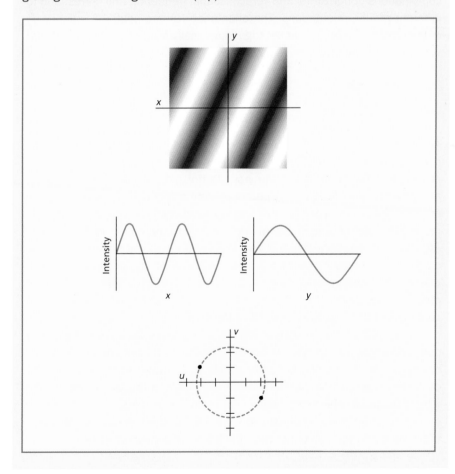

FIGURE 9.20
Top: A tilted sine wave grating. Middle: The vertical and horizontal spatial frequencies of the grating, given by its modulation along the vertical and horizontal lines through the middle of the grating. Bottom: Representation of the grating in a 2-D frequency spectrum. The *y*-axis represents modulation along the vertical axis, and the *x*-axis represents modulation along the horizontal axis. Each point identifies the vertical and horizontal frequency of the grating. As discussed in Chapter 4, frequency spectra contain both positive and negative frequencies at symmetrically opposite locations.

across this grating (Figure 9.20, middle) reveal the horizontally and vertically oriented spatial frequencies of the grating respectively. The representation of this component in a 2-D frequency spectrum is shown in Figure 9.20 (bottom). The y-axis represents luminance variation of this component along the vertical axis (horizontally oriented frequency, conventionally labeled v), and the x-axis represents its luminance variation along the horizontal axis (vertically oriented frequency, conventionally labeled u). As with the spectra shown in Chapter 4, the frequency spectrum contains both positive and negative frequencies. The component in Figure 9.20 is represented by a pair of points at the appropriate uv locations in frequency space. Notice that if the grating was rotated to a different orientation, its vertical and horizontal spatial frequencies would change, even though the width of its bars remained constant. If the grating was rotated to a vertical orientation, its spatial frequency along the vertical axis would become zero (no variation along the y-axis), and its spatial frequency along the horizontal axis would correspond to the frequency given by the width of its bars. As the orientation of the grating changes, its location in uv space moves around a virtual circle in the frequency spectrum. Different points around the circle involve different combinations of horizontal and vertical spatial frequency, and correspond to different grating orientations. The orientation (θ) and spatial frequency (f) of the grating can be calculated trigonometrically from its horizontal (u) and vertical (v) spatial frequencies as follows:

$$\theta = \arctan (u/v)$$

$$f = \ddot{O} (u^2 + v^2)$$

According to Fourier theory, any complex 2-D spatial pattern can be decomposed into a specific set of frequency components. Each component is identified by its vertical frequency, its horizontal frequency, its phase, and its amplitude. Frequency spectra provide a very useful visual summary of the information content of images. Most natural images contain a preponderance of amplitude at low spatial frequencies. In fact power (defined as the square of amplitude) falls linearly with log frequency roughly as $1/f$. But energy can vary markedly in terms of the preponderance of energy at different orientations. Different kinds of visual scene have characteristic 2-D Fourier spectra, as outlined earlier in the chapter, which could be used to establish the gist of the scene.

Figure 9.21 shows several simple 2-D images and their frequency spectra, organized in two columns. One column has been randomly reordered. As a test of your understanding of Fourier spectra, try to pair up each image in one column with its spectrum in the other column. An interesting point, which may help you to solve the problem, is that an image and its spectrum form a Fourier transform pair—one is the Fourier transform of the other. So you can either treat the left-hand column as images and the

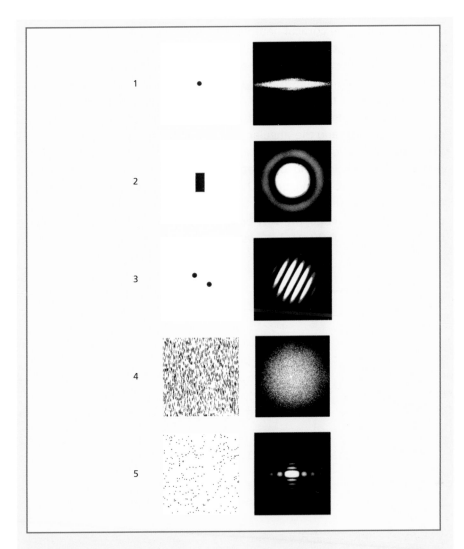

FIGURE 9.21
A collection of 2-D images and their Fourier transforms. One column represents the images, and the other represents their transform (the two labels are interchangeable, since one column is the Fourier transform of the other). The order in one column has been randomly reordered relative to the other column. The correct order is given at the end of the tutorial. Images are based on those in Harburn, Taylor, and Welberry (1975).

right-hand column as frequency spectra, or vice versa. The solution can be found at the end of the tutorial.

Spatial frequency filtering

As Figures 9.9 and 9.10 demonstrated earlier in the chapter, spatial frequency filtering amounts to the removal of certain spatial frequencies from an image by setting the amplitude of components at those frequencies to zero. An inverse Fourier transform applied to the modified spectrum reveals the effect on the spatial image. When high frequencies are removed (Figures 9.9 and 9.10, middle), the image appears blurred and lacking detail. When low frequencies are removed (Figures 9.9 and 9.10, right), the image contains only fine-scale lines.

Individual visual cortical neurons can be viewed as spatial frequency filters tuned to respond only to certain grating frequencies and orientations. The response selectivity of these neurons can be visualized in the spatial frequency domain, as shown in Figure 9.22 (bottom). Each ellipse in the plot represents the responsiveness of an individual neuron. The distance of each ellipse from the center of the plot represents each neuron's preferred spatial frequency, and the angular position of each ellipse represents its preferred orientation. The area enclosed by each ellipse represents the range of frequencies and orientations to which the neuron responds. Each cortical neuron in Figure 9.22 samples a relatively small region of frequency space, though some cells are more selective than others. LGN cells, on the other hand, are very broadly tuned for spatial frequency and orientation. Figure 9.22 (top) shows the selectivity of two such cells.

FIGURE 9.22
Polar plots of LGN (top) and cortical (bottom) cell receptive fields estimated from single-cell recordings, arranged to resemble a 2-D spatial Fourier spectrum. Each ellipse encloses the spatial frequencies and orientations to which a single cell responds. Cortical cells are much more selectively tuned than LGN cells (adapted from De Valois, Albrecht, & Thorell, 1982).

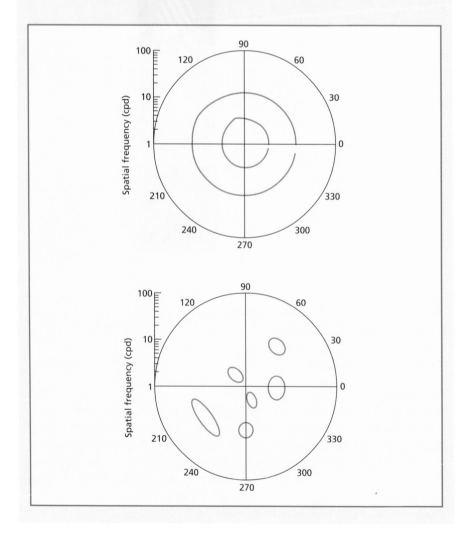

Spatiotemporal images

Visual images vary over time as well as over space. We can therefore add a third, temporal, dimension to our representation of visual images, to create a *xyt* representation. The Fourier transform of a *xyt* image is also three-dimensional. Two dimensions correspond to horizontal and vertical spatial frequency, as described in the previous section. The third dimension corresponds to temporal frequency. The tutorial on spatiotemporal approaches to motion processing in Chapter 12 contains examples of *xyt* images. Three-dimensional *xyt* images and their Fourier transforms are difficult to interpret, so many researchers restrict themselves to two of the three dimensions of the *xyt* space, according to the task in hand. The 2-D *xy* representation discussed in the previous section is useful for studying spatial vision, and can be viewed as a cross-section through *xyt* space in the *xy* (spatial) plane. We can also slice *xyt* space in the *xt* (or *yt*) plane, illustrated in Figure 12.14. A *xt* image contains the temporal dimension (*t*) and one spatial dimension (*x*), and is particularly useful for studying motion processing.

If we return to Figure 9.20 (top), the vertical axis can be relabeled to represent the temporal dimension. In this new depiction, the plot represents a grating that shifts progressively along the *x* (spatial) axis as one advances along the *y* (temporal) axis. In other words, the grating *moves* along the horizontal axis. Consider the vertical slice through the grating, shown in the middle of Figure 9.20. This now represents how the intensity at a specific *x* location in the image varies over time (*y*). Notice that the intensity of the point modulates repetitively at a particular temporal frequency as successive grating bars drift past (recall Figure 9.7). So in the frequency spectrum of the *xt* image the *v* axis becomes temporal frequency. The pair of points representing the grating component in the frequency spectrum (Figure 9.20, bottom) now identify its spatial frequency (*u*) and its temporal frequency (*v*), which jointly specify the grating's velocity.

Visual movement therefore creates oriented contours in *xt* space (spatiotemporal orientation). If the grating in Figure 9.20 was redrawn to move at a higher velocity, its orientation in *xt* space would be further away from vertical (stationary), and its temporal frequency would be higher. Changes in the velocity of a grating at a fixed spatial frequency shift the position of its Fourier component vertically along the temporal frequency axis. Note that this is a subtle but important difference between changes of grating orientation in *xy* plots and changes of velocity in *xt* plots. Changes to a grating's orientation correspond to rotations in the *xy* spatial domain, and produce rotations of its frequency component's position in the Fourier domain. Changes to a grating's position in the *xt* domain (motion) correspond to shearing of the grating along the *x*-axis, and produce shearing of its frequency component in the Fourier domain along the *v*-axis (both of which preserve its *x* spatial frequency; only temporal frequency changes).

Fourier analysis in theories of vision

Two-dimensional Fourier representations of visual images, whether as *xy* or as *xt* space, are widely used in vision research. As in the case of audition, Fourier techniques have allowed researchers to develop theories in which responses at certain processing stages faithfully represent the Fourier energy in the stimulus, while responses at other stages contain significant nonlinear components. This approach has proved valuable in the development of theories of texture segmentation (see the discussion of texture analysis earlier in this chapter, and in Chapter 10) and of motion processing. Theories of motion processing, for instance, distinguish between Fourier and nonFourier motion detectors. Fourier-based motion detectors are also known as first-order detectors. Their response is thought to be governed by energy in the spatiotemporal Fourier spectrum. The response of nonFourier detectors, also known as second-order detectors, contains significant nonlinear components so the relation between Fourier energy in the stimulus and detector response is much more complex (see Chapter 12).

Solutions for Figure 9.21

Images are paired (L–R) as follows:

1–2
2–5
3–3
4–1
5–4

Shape and object perception

10

Contents

INTRODUCTION: THE THREE-STAGE MODEL

The processes described in Chapter 9 compute piecemeal representations of visual structure, containing information about the local features present at different places in the image. This representation is sometimes called the *primal sketch*, because it provides a simple description of local image features (see Morgan, 2011). However, most visual tasks, such as recognition and visually guided action, require sophisticated representations of discrete, meaningful objects rather than an unstructured patchwork of locally encoded detail. Theories of visual processing therefore propose at least two further levels of analysis after the primal sketch, as shown in Figure 10.1, to create a three-stage model of shape and object processing. In the second stage the visual system builds a representation of the larger-scale shapes and surfaces visible in the scene. In the third stage, the visual system constructs representations of the objects present in the scene.

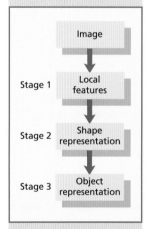

FIGURE 10.1
Three stages of visual processing. The first stage, discussed in Chapter 9, builds a piecemeal representation of local image properties. The second stage builds a representation of larger-scale shapes and surfaces. The third stage matches shapes and surfaces with stored object representations to achieve recognition.

There is some evidence that people with scotomas can, when pressed, reveal access to some primitive perceptual representation, probably in subcortical structures (blindsight; see Weiskrantz, 1986; and the visual pathways described in Chapter 7).

NEUROPSYCHOLOGICAL EVIDENCE

Neuropsychological case studies provide general support for the three-stage model of visual analysis shown in Figure 10.1:

1. People with damage to the earliest visual cortical areas, particularly striate cortex, are blind in the area of the visual field lying in the damaged area. These areas of cortical blindness are called scotomas.
2. People with brain damage to extrastriate visual cortical areas seem to have intact lower level visual functions, including complete visual fields, and near-normal color, depth, and movement detection and acuity (stage 1 in Figure 10.1), but suffer from disordered object perception or **agnosia** (stages 2 or 3 in Figure 10.1).

Lissauer (translated in Yantis, 2001) drew a distinction between two forms of agnosia, *apperceptive* and *associative*, which seem to map onto the two higher stages of the three-stage model:

- Apperceptive agnosia involves deficient shape representation (stage 2). A person studied by Benson and Greenberg (1969), for example, could not name, copy, or match even simple shapes. In a shape-matching task he incorrectly matched a triangle with a circle.
- People suffering from associative agnosia are able to copy and match shapes normally but cannot identify objects from their images (stage 3). Recognition based on touch or sound is unimpaired.

"Gestalt" is a German word whose closest English equivalents are "pattern," "shape," or "configuration." The Gestalt movement began with the work of Wertheimer in Germany in the early 20th century (see Wertheimer, translated in Yantis, 2001; and Rock & Palmer, 1990).

There is a continuing debate among neuropsychologists about how many other forms of agnosia can be distinguished, and precisely what functional impairments they involve (reviewed in Farah, 1999). Some argue in favor of a finer grained distinction between agnosias, which would indicate that the three-stage model of Figure 10.1 is too coarse. Furthermore, there is no universal agreement among researchers as to what visual processes are involved in shape analysis and object representation, as we shall see in this chapter. Nevertheless, it is convenient for the present purposes to partition visual processing into the three broad stages illustrated in Figure 10.1. Stage 1 was considered in the previous chapter. The various proposals for stages 2 and 3 are surveyed in the following sections. A crucial distinction between stages 2 and 3 is that operations performed in stage 2 do not involve any knowledge about the objects present in the scene, whereas stage 3 involves stored representations of objects.

KEY TERM

Agnosia
A clinical condition characterized by disordered visual perception of shapes and/or objects.

SHAPE REPRESENTATION

GESTALT LAWS

The process that computes a representation of larger shapes must necessarily integrate local information provided over relatively long distances in the image. In the first part of the 20th century the Gestalt psychologists formulated a set of rules or "laws" of perceptual organization, which demonstrate how the visual system seems to have in-built preferences for grouping parts of the image together on the basis of certain visual properties. These properties include:

- Proximity
- Similarity of color
- Similarity of size
- Common fate
- Good continuation.

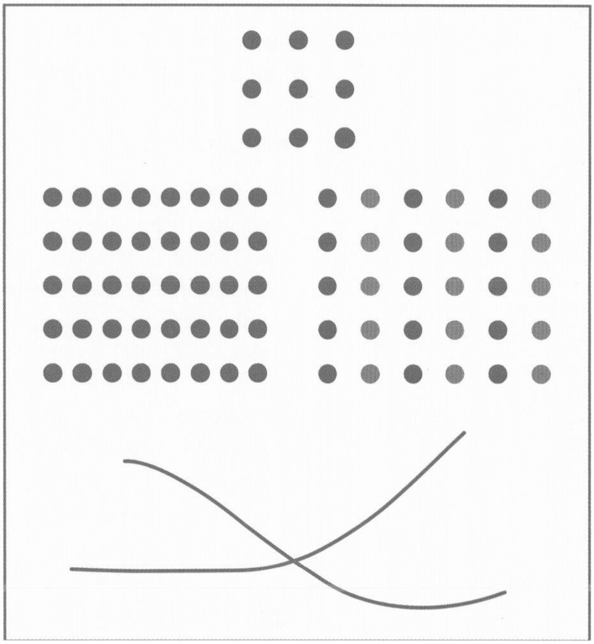

Figure 10.2 illustrates some of these principles in operation (common fate, not illustrated, involves grouping on the basis of common movement properties). The Gestalt psychologists attempted to relate their grouping laws to events in the brain that are isomorphic to the corresponding perceptual experience. Isomorphism assumes that the brain event has the same shape as the perceptual event, so that a perceived circle, for instance, creates a circular trace in the brain. Gestalt theories were obviously handicapped by lack of knowledge concerning the physiology of the visual system (see the tutorials section of Chapter 7). Later discoveries concerning the physiological substrate of perception offered no support for the Gestaltists' ideas about isomorphism, leaving behind a set of descriptive principles with no theory of perceptual processing.

Nevertheless, Gestalt laws do capture some consistent aspects of perceptual organization. It is therefore worth asking why and how the laws work. In answer to "why," it is plausible to argue that Gestalt laws are built into the visual system because they reflect the properties of real-world scenes and objects.

FIGURE 10.2
Examples of Gestalt grouping laws in action.

Proximity

Most surfaces are made of cohesive, opaque material. So in general two nearby points in the image are more likely to originate from the same object than two points that are far apart. The law is not cast-iron, of course. Translucent or transparent bodies such as mist or snow violate this law and are known to stretch theories of shape analysis to their limit.

Similarity

Object surfaces tend to be made of relatively few materials, so their visual texture is relatively uniform. It therefore makes sense to group local image regions together if they contain similar visual texture (e.g., size and color). Animals and military vehicle designers try to avoid detection by breaking up their surface into discordant textures (camouflage).

Common fate

As in the case of proximity, this law is motivated by the fact that objects are made of cohesive, opaque material. If an object moves, its parts tend to move together. Consequently, if different image regions contain movement that has a common direction and velocity, they are likely to have originated from the same object. The transparent objects mentioned in the case of proximity also raise issues for models of motion analysis (discussed in Chapter 12).

Good continuation

Object shape tends to vary smoothly, with relatively few very sharp corners or edges, especially if the object has been molded by natural forces of erosion. A very good natural example would be a beach pebble. When attempting to delineate the contours of objects, it therefore makes sense to bias grouping in favor of contours that vary smoothly rather than sharply (Geisler et al., 2001).

Marr's (1982) computational theory of vision recognized the value of Gestalt laws as assumptions about the world. Marr built Gestalt-like grouping constraints into his computational theory. Having answered the "why" of Gestalt grouping, we are left with the question of how perceptual grouping is achieved. There are probably several answers to this question.

SHAPE SEGMENTATION PROCESSES

Texture-based segmentation

The outputs of spatial frequency-tuned filters can be used to unify image regions on the basis of visual texture, as discussed in Chapter 9, using a filter–rectify–filter (FRF) processing sequence. Grouping on the basis of proximity and similarity can be explained by FRF processing.

Proximity

When texture elements are closer together in one region than in another, the spatial frequency content (and average luminance) of the two regions is likely to differ. Spatial frequency-tuned filters are sensitive to these differences, so FRF processing would achieve segmentation.

Similarity

Grouping on the basis of similarity in size, shape, or color can also be driven by variations in the output of spatial frequency-tuned filters, since filter response will vary as a function of these attributes.

Motion- and depth-based segmentation

The Gestalt law of *common fate* can be explained by specialized motion and depth processes. In both cases, cooperative interactions between motion- or depth-sensitive neurons lead to segmentation on the basis of common motion or stereoscopic disparity. Detailed discussions of motion and stereo processing can be found in later chapters, but it should be borne in mind that they provide important routes to shape segmentation.

> The Gestalt psychologists did not actually describe a grouping law based on common disparity, perhaps because the nature of this cue was not fully understood at the time.

Symbolic segmentation

Texture, motion, and depth processes operate in the domain of neural images. The outputs of spatial frequency-, motion-, or disparity-selective filters form a neural image of the corresponding image attribute. Specialized processes such as

FRF sequences can be applied to the neural image to achieve segmentation. An alternative, influential approach to segmentation is based on symbolic computations (the distinction between image-based and symbolic computations was introduced in Chapter 1 during the discussion of representation).

Marr's (1982) original conception of the primal sketch was as a symbolic representation. It consisted of a list of the local features or **primitives** in the image (edges, bars, and so on), each annotated with its properties (position, orientation, contrast, length, width).

Collections of primitives can be grouped on the basis of similarities in their symbolic properties. Marr (1982) proposed that grouping is based on:

- Average local intensity
- Average size
- Local density
- Local orientation
- Local distances between neighboring pairs of similar items
- Local orientation of the line joining neighboring pairs of similar items.

Marr (1982) described the grouping process as follows (p. 91):

> *One initially selects roughly similar items from [the primal sketch] and groups or clusters them together, forming lines, curves, larger blobs, groups, and small patches to the extent allowed by the inherent structure of the image.*

The result of grouping, according to Marr, is a new set of symbolic primitives representing the larger spatial structure of more localized primitives.

CONTOUR INTEGRATION

The segmentation processes discussed so far divide up the image into regions on the basis of shared texture, motion, or depth properties. The contours between regions are important because they describe the boundaries of objects or their parts. Silhouettes, for example, present only the bounding contours of an object, yet they are often sufficient to support identification. Figure 10.3 shows some objects represented as silhouettes.

Contour representation at the earliest levels of visual analysis (stage 1 in Figure 10.1) is limited to local information about the position, contrast, and orientation of edges and lines. In order to represent extended contours, the visual system must integrate this local information over relatively long distances in the image. The Gestalt law of good continuation is an example of a rule which seems to govern contour integration. It is based on the assumption that natural objects generally have smoothly varying contours: Animal bodies tend to have rounded bulges defined by muscle or fat; natural surfaces formed by erosion also tend to be rounded and smooth.

FIGURE 10.3
The silhouettes of objects are often sufficient for recognition, demonstrating the importance of bounding contours in object representation.

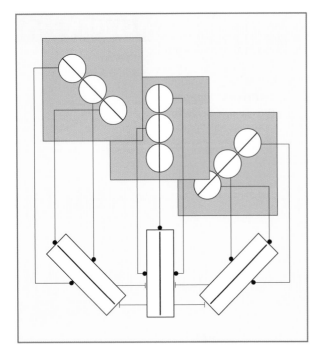

FIGURE 10.4
Hypothetical collector units with long receptive fields (large rectangles) integrate contour signals from smaller receptive fields (circles) to construct responses to extended contours (after Morgan & Hotopf, 1989).

The basic task of contour integration processes is to bind together local edge responses to create a representation of extended contours. Observers are quite good at binding together disconnected line or bar segments that follow a smooth path across the image against dense backgrounds of randomly oriented segments (Field, Hayes & Hess, 1993). Different theories of contour integration achieve this binding in different ways. Some theories (Morgan and Hotopf, 1989; Moulden, 1994) basically sum the local responses (illustrated in Figure 10.4). Other theories propose that neurons responding to local edges propagate their signals laterally to other neurons at the same processing level to produce mutual facilitation when all neurons are active simultaneously. The result is enhanced responses in the presence of a long, smooth contour. In support of this proposal, Polat and Sagi (1994) found that contrast thresholds to detect a patch of grating were lower when another grating was present at an adjacent location, provided that the bars of the two gratings were lined up to create a longer contour (see also Pettet, McKee, & Grzywacz, 1998). Recent psychophysical research on the timing of this kind of facilitation is consistent with lateral cooperative interactions (Cass & Alais, 2006). For more discussion of feature binding theories, see Chapter 14's discussion of Triesman's Feature Integration Theory.

"Bottom-up" interactions are unlikely to be the whole story of contour integration, and a number of researchers have proposed mechanisms which incorporate feedback from higher cortical areas which modulates the activity of striate cells in such a way as to enhance responses to long contours (Angelucci et al., 2002; Stettler et al., 2002).

SURFACE PARSING

Nakayama, He, and Shimojo (1995) argue that shape segmentation alone is insufficient to serve as a precursor for object representation. The problem is that natural scenes are cluttered with numerous surfaces, many of which occlude each other and interrupt their smooth contours. Consequently, segmented regions and shapes are likely to have arbitrary configurations that depend partly on the spatial arrangement of surfaces as well as on their intrinsic shapes. Nakayama, He, and Shimojo (1995) therefore argue that surface parsing is an essential step in midlevel visual processing (stage 2 in Figure 10.1). Shapes that are disconnected in the image, yet belong to the same surface on an object, are grouped together by the visual system. Nakayama, He, and Shimojo (1995) call this grouping operation **parsing**. It can be achieved with no knowledge of the objects to which the surfaces belong.

KEY TERMS

Parsing
A process that divides input signals into discrete, meaningful units.

Generic viewpoint
A viewpoint providing a perspective on an object that is typical of many other viewpoints.

Accidental viewpoint
A viewpoint providing a highly unusual, perhaps unique, perspective on an object.

Depth cues are crucial for parsing image regions into surfaces and assigning the ownership of an occluding edge to one surface or another, since they provide information about the depth ordering of different regions. One particularly important cue is known as stereoscopic disparity: The two eyes are separated in the head by about 6 centimeters, and consequently have slightly different views of the world. These small image differences indicate the depth order of surfaces in the scene and the next chapter contains a detailed discussion of this cue, called stereoscopic disparity. It is a particularly powerful parsing cue, as illustrated in Figure 10.5 (based on Nakayama, Shimojo, & Silverman, 1989). The figure shows an image of a face interleaved among horizontal strips of texture. When stereoscopic disparity indicates that the face is located behind the strips of texture, the face strips are parsed into a common surface and the face is readily perceived. When disparity indicates that the face strips are nearer than the texture the face strips are no longer parsed into a single surface, disrupting our perception of the face. Thus disparity indicates surface occlusion: It identifies which of the two surfaces that are divided by a contour actually "owns" the contour. Contour ownership can in turn provide information for surface parsing. Qui and von der Heydt (2005) studied single-unit responses in cortical area V2 and found cells that seemed to signal contour ownership: Some cells tuned to, say, vertical contours also preferred the contour to be owned by the surface to its left, while others preferred the contour to be owned by the surface to its right. These cells could therefore play a role in surface parsing.

Though it can be a powerful cue, stereoscopic disparity is not essential for surface parsing. The line drawing in Figure 10.5 shows a collection of arbitrary closed forms. We do not perceive three arbitrary shapes, but two surfaces arranged in depth, with one partially occluding the other. There are no disparity cues in this case; parsing is based on the intersections between contours. "T"-junctions are strong occlusion cues. The surface to which the top of the "T" belongs is parsed as in front of the surface to which the upright of the "T" belongs.

In some situations, several alternative surface interpretations of an image may be available. In these circumstances, Nakayama, He, and Shimojo (1995) propose that the visual system selects the most likely interpretation, which assumes that the surfaces are being viewed from a "generic" vantage point as opposed to an "accidental" vantage point. A **generic viewpoint** is one of a large set of possible vantage points that all give roughly the same view. An **accidental viewpoint** is one that is uniquely associated with a very specific view of the scene. In Figure 10.5, for example, the generic constraint would parse the image into two shapes. It is also possible, though extremely unlikely, that the scene does actually consist of three separate shapes whose contours happen to line up with each other precisely at a specific vantage point.

The issue of ambiguity, and the consequent need to draw perceptual inferences based on the most plausible interpretation of the sensory data (for example,

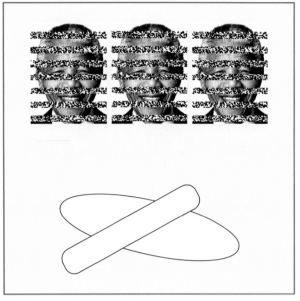

FIGURE 10.5

Demonstrations of surface parsing. Top: The image of a face is interleaved with strips of texture. When the strips belonging to the face have far disparity, allowing them to be parsed into a single surface, the face is readily perceived (stereo viewing of this demonstration requires crossed free fusion, described in the next chapter). Bottom: Monocular cues from T-junctions of contours are sufficient for surface parsing.

? *Think of some examples of generic and accidental views of everyday objects, such as a bucket or pen.*

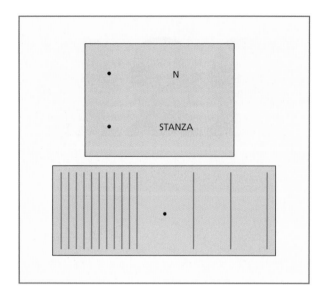

FIGURE 10.6

Upper panel: While fixating the dot at the top, the letter N to the right can be seen clearly. While fixating the dot below, the letter N cannot be seen clearly, because of crowding by the other letters in the word. Lower panel: While fixating on the central spot, it is possible to attend to each of the bars on the right individually, and count them. Although the bars on the left can be resolved, it is not possible to attend to each individually, or to count them.

generic viewpoints are much more likely than accidental ones), has wide applicability across all of the modalities. The tutorials section of the chapter explains the dominant theoretical approach to handling perceptual inference, based on a mathematical formula know as Bayes' theorem.

CROWDING

Each word in this line is legible at the point where you fixate, but words a short distance to the left or right of fixation are not legible. The effect is not due simply to limitations in visual acuity; an effect known as "crowding" also contributes to illegibility. When a single letter is placed by itself away from the center of gaze, it may be legible, as in the top panel of Figure 10.6 (fixate on the upper dot at the left). When the same letter forms part of a word, it is no longer possible to distinguish it clearly (fixate on the lower dot at the left of the top panel). The letters appear to crowd each other out in peripheral vision, perhaps because their features get jumbled up rather than allocated to the correct shapes (Pelli, Palomares, & Majaj, 2004). Another interpretation of crowding is that it reflects a limit on how finely we can focus our spatial attention (He, Cavanagh, & Intriligator, 1997). An example consistent with this idea is shown in the bottom panel of Figure 10.6. When the central spot is fixated, it is possible to resolve the individual bars in the gratings both to the left and to the right. However, the bars on the left are so closely spaced that we cannot count through them without moving fixation from the central spot. The bars on the right are more widely spaced, so each bar can be counted individually. Chapter 14 discusses spatial attention and crowding effects.

OBJECT REPRESENTATION

Imagine that you have made some teas and coffees for a group of friends, and have carried the mugs, milk, sugar, and so on, to the table (Figure 10.7). In order for each of your friends to pick up the correct drink, they need to:

1. Identify the mugs in the presence of other items such as milk jugs, sugar bowls, spoons, and biscuits.
2. Distinguish between their personal mug and other mugs.
3. Reach out and pick up their mug.

This everyday example illustrates some of the visual tasks that require the visual system to compute object representations, namely:

*   Identification of an object as belonging to a particular class (e.g., a mug versus milk jug).

KEY TERMS

View-independent representation
An object representation that reflects only the intrinsic structure of the object; also known as an object-centered representation.

View-dependent representation
An object representation that reflects the structure of the object as seen from a specific viewpoint; also known as a viewer-centered representation.

- Discrimination of different objects within a class (e.g., my mug versus your mug).
- Interaction with objects (pour the milk without spillage).

Although most people complete these tasks without apparent difficulty or effort, the underlying complexity of the tasks is revealed when computer scientists attempt to build machines that can perform them. Computer vision systems are still incapable of human-like, general-purpose recognition, which involves coping with a very large set of possible objects (many thousands), a significant number of which could be present in any given scene. If you look around the scene before your eyes, wherever you happen to be, and begin counting every single object to which you would assign a different name, you will probably reach a number in the hundreds before too long. The popular game of "I spy" relies on the fact that there are often many objects in sight with names that begin with the same letter.

A major computational difficulty facing any recognition system arises from the fact that images of objects reflect both intrinsic factors and extrinsic factors (Riesenhuber & Poggio, 2000):

- Intrinsic factors define the character of an individual object, in terms of its shape and surface properties.
- Extrinsic factors cause significant changes in the image of the object that are not related to its intrinsic properties. They include the viewpoint of the observer relative to the object; the nature of the light source such as its direction; the presence of occluding surfaces; and the nature of the background. Figure 10.8 illustrates the effect of extrinsic factors on the image of a mug.

Low-level features and surfaces extracted during earlier stages of visual processing reflect both intrinsic and extrinsic factors. Theories of object processing vary in the way they accommodate extrinsic factors. **View-independent** theories attempt to remove all extrinsic influences and build representations of objects that reflect only their intrinsic properties. **View-dependent** theories incorporate viewpoint effects into their object representations. Both kinds of theory include propositions for how an internal representation of an object in view is created, and then compared against stored representations of previously viewed objects.

FIGURE 10.7
A collection of objects, illustrating the various tasks that require object representations: Recognition (a mug versus a jug); discrimination (my mug versus your mug); interaction (pour the milk from a jug into a mug).

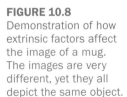 *Relate the different theories of object representation and recognition back to the different kinds of representational systems described in Chapter 1.*

FIGURE 10.8
Demonstration of how extrinsic factors affect the image of a mug. The images are very different, yet they all depict the same object.

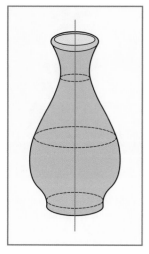

FIGURE 10.9
Marr and Nishihara's generalized cones, used to represent the shape of a vase. (From Bruce, Green, & Georgeson, 2003, figure 9.15, p. 277.) Copyright © 2003 Psychology Press.

FIGURE 10.10
Marr and Nishihara's structural description of the human figure as a hierarchical arrangement of cylindrical shapes. From Marr and Nishihara (1978), by permission of the Royal Society.

VIEW-INDEPENDENT THEORIES

View-independent theories propose that the visual system represents objects in terms of a **structural description** of their component parts, and the relations between those parts, independent of extrinsic factors. They are symbolic, containing a list of parts descriptors with associated properties. Marr and Nishihara (1978) offered an influential analysis of models based on structural descriptions, and some specific proposals for human vision.

Marr and Nishihara's (1978) generalized cones

In Marr and Nishihara's (1978) theory, the basic descriptor for all object parts is a three-dimensional generalized cone, as illustrated in Figure 10.9.

A generalized cone corresponds to the volume created by moving a cross-section of constant shape but variable width along an axis. The shape in Figure 10.9 was created using a circular cross-section. Generalized cones can form a variety of shapes including pyramids, spheres, and cylinders. Marr and Nishihara's description of a human figure, for example, is similar to a stick figure as shown in Figure 10.10. Generalized cones forming cylinders capture the relative lengths and positions of the limbs.

Marr and Nishihara's 3-D object models are hierarchical in that component parts can themselves be decomposed into parts. Figure 10.10 shows models of the body, the arm, and the hand. Recognition is achieved by matching a model description derived from the image with stored 3-D model descriptions.

A crucial step in Marr and Nishihara's theory involves establishing the axis along which to sweep the cross-section of the generalized cone describing the object. Marr and Nishihara restricted their analysis to objects whose primary axis can be derived from its axis of symmetry or elongation. Marr (1977) had previously shown that the outline or silhouette of an object is sufficient to derive its primary axis (hence Marr's statement quoted earlier on the importance of contour integration). However, perceptual evidence that the visual system uses axis-based descriptions is not convincing (Quinlan & Humphreys, 1993).

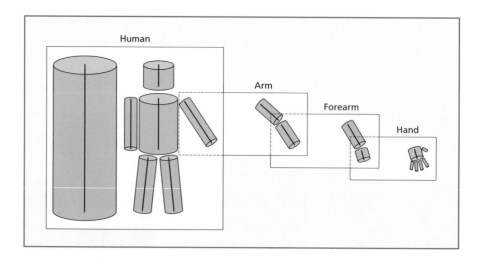

Biederman's (1987) geons

Marr and Nishihara's approach has been highly influential, even though their specific proposals have been disputed. Biederman's (1987) model of recognition is also based on structural descriptions, and owes a large debt to Marr and Nishihara's analysis. In contrast to Marr and Nishihara's generalized cones, Biederman's parts descriptors are a limited set of basic geometric shapes, or *geons*. Examples of proposed geons include wedges, cylinders, and bricks, as shown on the left of Figure 10.11. Example objects containing these geons are shown on the right of Figure 10.11. Geons are derived from a 2-D image representation, rather than the 3-D representation proposed by Marr and Nishihara.

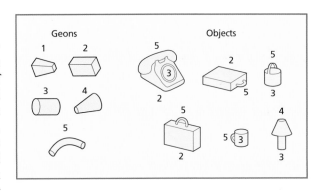

FIGURE 10.11

A selection of Biederman's geons, and their combination to form objects. From Biederman (1987). Copyright © American Psychological Association. Reproduced with permission.

Biederman proposed that geons are detected on the basis of certain "nonaccidental" properties of contours in the image, such as linearity, parallelism, curvilinearity, and symmetry. His assumption was that these image properties are more likely to reflect certain regularities in the world than to arise accidentally. For example, curved contours in the image usually reflect curved edges on objects, and parallel contours reflect parallel edges on objects. Specific nonaccidental properties are used to detect the presence of specific geons. Parallel contours, for example, are used to detect the presence of brick-shaped geons. The structural description of a given object defines the spatial arrangement of the geons which make it up.

Biederman and his coworkers reported a series of psychophysical experiments, which they interpreted as providing support for the role of geons in object representation. Biederman and Cooper (1991), for example, studied repetition priming. When subjects are presented with pictures to name, repetition of the same picture in different trials results in faster, more accurate responses. Biederman and Cooper (1991) found that priming is reduced when depicted objects do not share geon components. A limitation of these experiments is that they were not designed to critically test predictions from competing models. It is therefore not clear how well other models can account for the results.

Models based on structural descriptions have several weaknesses:

- Since all objects are described using the same limited set of components, it may be difficult to make fine discriminations between objects in the same class.
- It is often possible to decompose an object in a number of different ways, depending on the choice of component parts to extract. An "A," for example, can be decomposed into either three lines or five lines (Edelman, 1997). Indeed some objects, such as a shoe or a loaf, may have no structural decomposition at all.
- It has proven to be extremely difficult to find the lines and junctions from which to infer the presence of components in a natural (photographic) image. Implementations of Biederman's geon model have therefore restricted themselves to labeled line drawings.

VIEW-DEPENDENT THEORIES

This kind of theory does not attempt to construct a view-invariant, abstract model of objects. Instead, known objects are stored in terms of a small number of discrete

> Biederman's use of nonaccidental properties is an example of Bayesian approaches to vision, discussed in the tutorials section of this chapter.

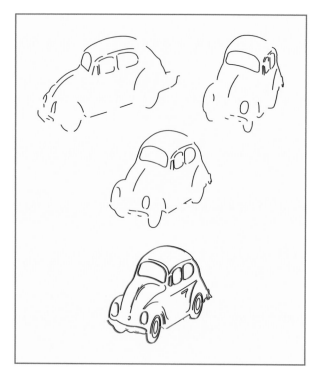

FIGURE 10.12
Recognition by alignment of candidate views with a novel view of an object. Top: Two prototypical views of a car. Middle: An intermediate view created by combining the two prototypical views. Bottom: A match between the intermediate view (blue) and a novel view (black). Modified from Ullman (1998).

prototypical forms or views. Recognition is achieved by comparing a novel view of an object against stored prototypical views.

Alignment

Ullman's (1998) model uses features such as surface markings and junctions between surfaces, which are particularly informative about the disposition of the object's surfaces. The relative positions of these features are recorded in each stored prototype. Views which are intermediate between the stored prototypical views can be computed by interpolating between the positions of corresponding features in different prototypes. During recognition of an object from a novel viewpoint, the system attempts to create an intermediate view that matches the novel view. Figure 10.12 (top), for example, shows two prototypical views of the same car. Figure 10.12 (middle) shows a view that is intermediate between the two stored views, created by combining the positions of certain features in the two views. Figure 10.12 (bottom) shows a novel view of the car superimposed on the intermediate view (blue). The interpolated view is a good match with the novel view.

Shape space

Edelman and Duvdevani-Bar's (1997) model is also based on comparisons between novel views and interpolated prototypical views, but uses a more complex form of prototype representation based on "**shape space**," and different mathematical procedures to achieve matching. You are familiar with the concept of three-dimensional color space (hue, saturation, brightness) from Chapter 8, in which similar colors lie close together and dissimilar colors are far apart. The similarity between any pair of colors can be measured by the metric distance between their positions in the space. Shape space has many more dimensions, because shapes can vary in more ways than colors, but the basic principle is the same. Each prototypical shape occupies a specific location in multidimensional shape space, and the metric distance between shapes reflects their similarity. A viewed shape is assigned a location in shape space, and can be categorized according to the prototypical shapes which lie closest to it. In the example of Figure 10.13, the shapes of different animals are positioned according to their similarity.

There is convincing support for the general idea that human object recognition involves view-dependent representations of some kind. Palmer, Rosch, and Chase (1981) found that many objects have "canonical" views, from which subjects prefer to imagine, view, or photograph them. Object naming is faster using canonical views. Bulthoff and Edelman (1992) required subjects to learn complex unfamiliar shapes. Later recognition was poorer when the shapes were presented from novel viewpoints, even though the learning phase was sufficient to form a 3-D view-independent representation.

The main weaknesses of view-dependent theories are that:

- The precise geometrical structure of objects is usually not made explicit in the representation. This makes the representation unsuitable for tasks requiring such information.
- Present implementations include only a limited set of object prototypes. It is not clear how well view-dependent theories can be scaled up to accommodate a large set of object prototypes.

NEURAL BASIS OF OBJECT REPRESENTATION

The debate in the cognitive science literature between advocates of view-independent and view-dependent theories has been a lively one (see Biederman & Gerhardstein, 1993; Tarr & Bulthoff, 1995). For example, advocates of structural descriptions have criticized experiments such as Bulthoff and Edelman's (1992) on the grounds that they used objects with no distinguishing geons. On the other hand, advocates of structural description theories tend to restrict themselves to objects that have a clear decomposition into component parts.

Testing for viewpoint dependence in recognition is not a decisive way to discriminate between theories, since all current models predict some perceptual effect of viewpoint. According to Marr and Nishihara's view-independent theory, viewpoints that obscure an object's major axis can be expected to impair the process of creating a structural description. Biederman's geon theory predicts worse performance using viewpoints that introduce accidental properties leading to inappropriate geon decomposition.

Some researchers have attempted to resolve the controversy by proposing that the visual system uses multiple object representation systems for different tasks and/or different classes of object (Logothetis & Sheinburg, 1996; Foster & Gilson, 2002). Others have sought clarification from the neurophysiology of object processing. It is widely believed that object processing is mediated by the ventral pathway in the visual cortex, which runs through areas V1, V2, V4, and IT (see Chapter 7). Agnosia (described at the beginning of the chapter) is associated with ventral stream damage (Farah, 1999), and TMS delivered in occipitotemporal cortex disrupts object processing tasks such as face discrimination (Pitcher at al., 2009).

The response properties of cells in cortical area IT are consistent with view-based theories of object processing. Logothetis, Pauls, and Poggio (1995) reported that most of the IT cells they found responded maximally to one particular view of complex patterns of objects such as faces or body parts, with some tolerance to changes in scale or position of the object. Very few cells responded in a view-independent manner. Logothetis, Pauls, and Poggio (1995) concluded that a population of cells each tuned to a different aspect of an object could, as an ensemble, encode at least some kinds of three-dimensional objects. Riesenhuber and Poggio (2002) and DiCarlo, Zoccolan, and Rust (2012) argue for a two-stage population-coding scheme in which: (i) Different views are stored as different patterns

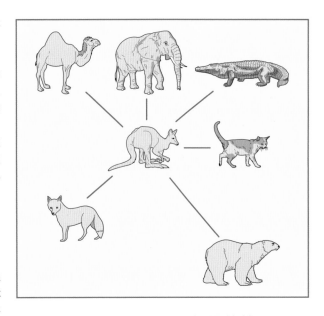

FIGURE 10.13
Recognition by interpolation between a novel object view and stored prototypical views. Each prototypical animal shape occupies a specific location in a multidimensional representation space (collapsed onto just two dimensions in the figure). The distance between prototypical shapes reflects their similarity. The similarity of a viewed shape (kangaroo) to stored prototypes is measured by their distance apart in the shape space. The kangaroo is more similar to a cat than to a polar bear. Redrawn from Edelman (1995). Reproduced with kind permission from Springer Science and Business Media.

of activity in a cell ensemblage; and (ii) view invariance is then achieved by cells which take a weighted sum of outputs in the first stage. The neurophysiological evidence thus points towards a serial processing scheme involving *both* view-dependent and view-independent representations.

It is unclear whether object processing in the visual cortex involves a single truly general-purpose system which can handle any kind of object equally well (a computationally difficult task), or is structured as a collection of subsystems which each specialize in specific object classes (computationally more tractable). Several such possible subsystems have already been identified in fMRI studies, including areas that appear to be specialized for faces, places, body parts, and specific object classes (see Spiridon & Kanwisher, 2002). The disruption to object processing caused by TMS described above and reported by Pitcher et al. (2009) was task selective. For example, TMS over the "occipital face area" disrupted discrimination of faces but not objects or bodies, while TMS over the "extrastriate body area" disrupted discrimination of bodies but not faces or objects. So it seems that there may be specialized processing subsystems at least for some biological important object categories.

SCENE PERCEPTION

The theories of recognition discussed in the preceding section take no account of the visual context in which objects appear. Objects are almost never encountered in complete isolation but appear in the context of a larger scene, and many studies have found that objects in a consistent or familiar background scene are processed more quickly and recognized more accurately than those seen against an inconsistent background (e.g., Biederman, Mezzanotte, & Rabinowitz, 1982; Davenport & Potter, 2004). Information about the background presumably allows the visual system to estimate the probability of an object's presence, position, and scale. For example, tables and chairs often occur together in scenes, so the presence of one raises the probability that the other is also present. A lamp post is much more likely to be present in a street scene than is a giraffe. Context effects can be mediated either by associations between objects that occur together in scenes (tables and chairs) or by holistic scene properties which do not require representations of individual objects (vertical and horizontal contours in streets). The latter can be conveyed by patterns of activity in a large population of spatial frequency- and orientation-tuned neurons, as discussed in the previous chapter under scene gist. Several processing schemes have been proposed to explain how context can affect recognition (see Bar, 2004). One possibility is that rapid categorization of scene gist sensitizes or primes the representations of all possible objects associated with it, improving recognition performance. Another possibility, which is not mutually exclusive with the first, is that analysis of the object and its context occurs in parallel, with each facilitating the other.

What information about a scene is extracted by the visual system, and is therefore available to facilitate recognition? Subjective impressions are unreliable: You may believe that your visual impression of a scene is complete, accurate, and persistent, rather like a mental photographic snapshot. But research has found that this belief is far from the truth. Scene perception is actually highly selective, transitory, and abstract. A number of experiments indicate that the visual system retains relatively little detailed information from one glance to the next. Observers are unable to detect even gross changes in image content when they occur during saccades or simulated saccades, especially if the change occurs away from the focus of interest. This effect is called "inattentional blindness," and has been demonstrated using a variety of experimental paradigms (see Simons & Levin, 1997, and Chapter 14). It indicates that observers never form a complete and detailed representation of the scene before them. Only partial representations are constructed, and scene details are not retained from one glance to the next.

Although detailed pictorial information about the scene seems to be lost quite quickly, more abstract properties are retained. Observers can extract and remember the gist of a scene and its overall layout very well (see Tatler, Gilchrist, & Rusted, 2003), even when recognition is poor. For example, after a series of pictures is presented very rapidly (four per second) subjects are relatively poor at subsequent recognition, but much better at a more abstract decision ("Look for an animal," "Look for a picture that is not of house furnishings and decorations"; see Intraub, 1981). We seem to retain a conceptual understanding of the scenes we have viewed, rather than detailed pictorial information.

CHAPTER SUMMARY

Higher levels of processing in spatial vision can be divided into two broad stages:

- Shape representation
- Object representation.

SHAPE REPRESENTATION

- Gestalt laws describe the tendency for image elements to be grouped together on the basis of such properties as proximity, similarity, common fate, and good continuation. Gestalt laws reflect the properties of real-world objects, such as cohesiveness and opacity.
- Shape segmentation can be achieved using texture analysis, common motion and depth properties, and symbolic grouping.
- Shape representation may also involve a parsing operation to link together disparate shapes that belong to the same, partially occluded object surface. Motion, depth, and T-junctions of contours are powerful parsing cues.

OBJECT REPRESENTATION

- Object representations serve several purposes: Recognition of an object as belonging to a general class; discrimination of particular objects within a class; interaction with objects.
- Object processing is computationally difficult because images of objects reflect both intrinsic factors and extrinsic factors. Theories of object processing differ in how they deal with extrinsic factors.
- View-independent theories propose that the visual system removes all extrinsic influences to create a structural description of objects in terms of their component parts and the relations between parts.

- View-dependent theories store objects in terms of a few discrete prototypical views. Recognition involves comparing a novel 2-D view against stored views of known objects, to find the closest match.
- Neurophysiological evidence favors view-based theories; object processing is mediated by the ventral pathway, and cells in area IT appear to have view-based stimulus preferences. However view independence may arise in higher order cell populations.

SCENE PERCEPTION

- Background context is known to facilitate object recognition, either by activating representations of objects that are likely to occur together in a scene or by rapid categorization of scene gist.
- Research on "inattentional blindness" has found that very little is retained about a scene from one glance to the next, apart from gist and layout.

TUTORIALS

BAYESIAN MODELS OF VISUAL PERCEPTION

Visual images are generally ambiguous in the sense that the same sensory data can be interpreted in many different ways. An extremely simple example is shown in Figure 10.14 to illustrate this point. It depicts a dark rectangular

FIGURE 10.14
An image containing an arbitrary geometrical shape, and four 3-D objects that could all have given rise to it.

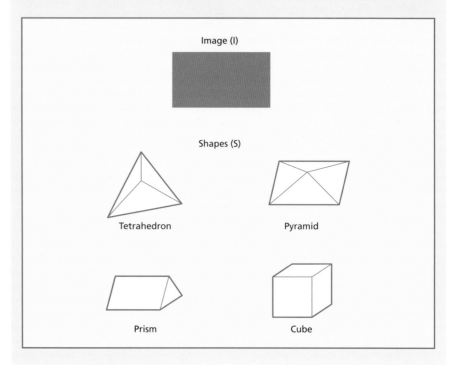

shape projected onto an imaging surface (the retina). What real-world object could have created this image? Formally the number of possible 3-D objects is so large as to be effectively infinite. To appreciate why there are so many alternatives, consider just one possible 3-D object, a brick. If the long axis of the brick was parallel to the optical axis of the imaging system (pointing directly at the image) then a brick of any length would produce the image shown; an infinity of bricks. To simplify the argument, the toy world in Figure 10.14 contains just four possible objects (denoted S).

How does the visual system select one of these alternative objects as its interpretation of the image? Bayes' theorem provides a rigorous mathematical framework for modeling ambiguity resolution in sensory processing, and so offers a logical answer to the question. It was first described in 1763 by an 18th century clergyman called Thomas Bayes. The theorem provides a mathematical framework for inductive logic, which is a type of reasoning that involves drawing a general conclusion from a specific set of facts. For example: "Most of the professors I have met are clever, therefore this professor must be clever." Bayes devised a simple mathematical formula for estimating the probability that an inference is true, which combines two probability values, a *"prior"* and a *"likelihood."* As its name implies, the *prior* is a probability estimate based on prior experience of the world (Are most professors clever?). The *likelihood* measures how well the current facts match the inference (Does this professor appear to be clever?). The probability that the inference is true (its *"posterior probability"*) is calculated by multiplying the *prior* and *likelihood* together. (It should be borne in mind that Bayes' theorem is a way of arriving at a best-guess, it is not foolproof).

For the sake of argument, let's assume that, in the imaginary world depicted in Figure 10.14, prism shapes are more commonly encountered than other shapes (high prior probability). The column labeled P(S) in Table 10.1 summarizes the prior probabilities of different shapes, S. If we also assume that the shape, whatever it might be, is viewed side-on to one of its sides, then the likelihood associated with each shape is based on the proportion of its sides having a silhouette that matches the image I. The cube has the highest likelihood because all of its sides match the silhouette. Table 10.1 shows all the likelihoods in column P(I|S). The posterior probability of each interpretation is shown in column P(S|I). The best interpretation (technically

TABLE 10.1 Illustrative Bayesian probabilities for the shapes in Figure 10.14

Object	P(S)	P(I|S)	P(S|I)
Tetrahedron	0.1	0	0
Pyramid	0.3	0.2	0.06
Prism	0.4	0.6	0.24
Cube	0.2	1	0.2

known as the "*maximum posterior probability*") is the prism. Using the labels in Table 10.1, Bayes' theorem can be summarized as:

$$P(S|I) \approx P(S) \times P(I|S)$$

The $\approx$ symbol means "approximately equal" and is in the equation because a constant has been omitted in the interests of clarity.

Bayes' theorem offers a simple mathematical procedure for combining information from previous experience with currently available information. If experience in the toy world of Figure 10.14 had indicated that cubes are a little more common (say, a prior probability of 0.3), then its posterior probability would rise to 0.3 [$P(S) = 0.3$; $P(I|S) = 1$; $P(S|I) = 0.3$], enough to win the competition. On the other hand if the image had been a triangular shape (and the priors were unchanged), then the likelihoods of all the shapes would change dramatically and as a result the pyramid would win [$P(S) = 0.3$; $P(I|S) = 0.8$; $P(S|I) = 0.24$].

Bayesian inference is widely used in modern theories to explain how the brain makes perceptual inferences. The flow diagram in Figure 10.15 summarizes the flow of information in these models. Incoming sensory data is combined with prior knowledge to compute a probability associated with each inference. In some models the posterior probability is fed back down to the early sensory processing stage to test how well it fits the data and, potentially, to influence the course of low-level analysis. This downward route may be particularly important if the sensory data is not very reliable

FIGURE 10.15
Functional diagram for a Bayesian inference system in sensory processing. Decisions about features and objects are made by combining knowledge about the world (priors) with sensory evidence (likelihoods) using Bayes' rule.

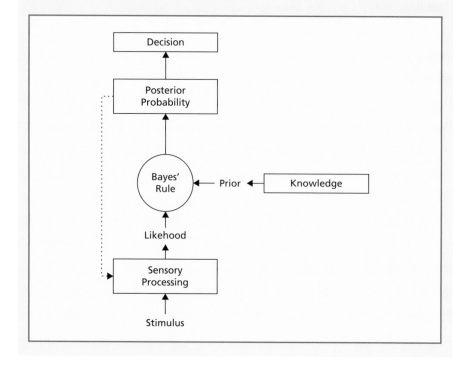

(noisy or incomplete), so there is some give-and-take in terms of the relative importance of prior knowledge and incoming data.

When thinking about applying Bayes' theorem to neural processing, it may not be obvious how neural codes can store probability values. Population codes are ubiquitous in sensory system, and they can be viewed as representing the relative probabilities of different stimulus values given the current input; the most likely values lie near the peak of the response distribution. A neural implementation of Bayesian inference could therefore involve combining the responses of a population of cells that holds likelihood values with responses from another population that holds priors. This kind of system has had some success in explaining motion illusions and object perception (Weiss et al., 2002; Kersten & Yuille, 2003).

Bayesian inference can also be used to combine information from different sources, such as different depth cues or different sensory modalities. Each cue provides its own estimate of the stimulus, and has a likelihood value attached to it (Jacobs, 2002). The contribution of each cue to the combined estimate is weighted by its likelihood so that the most reliable cues have a greater influence on the estimate (Hillis et al., 2004; Drewing & Ernst, 2006).

Because Bayesian coding schemes make statistically optimal use of the information available, they have come to be used as a benchmark or ideal observer against which to compare the performance of real observers.

Depth perception

11

Contents

INTRODUCTION

The world is three-dimensional (3-D), but the images cast onto our retinas vary in only two spatial dimensions, vertical (y) location, and lateral (x) location. The third dimension of depth, or z location, is missing. Yet this dimension is crucial for many visual tasks such as reaching out to pick up objects, walking over uneven terrain, or assessing how far away a dangerous predator may be (Figure 11.1). The visual system has to build three-dimensional representations of the world from the two-dimensional (2-D) images it receives. Four important computational goals of depth processing are to:

FIGURE 11.1
Many everyday activities require perceptual judgments of three-dimensional depth and distance. Copyright © My Good Images/ Shutterstock.com.

- Establish the depth order of the visible surfaces—which is nearest, which furthest and so on.
- Estimate the depth intervals between surfaces—how much further away one surface is than another.
- Estimate the absolute distance of surfaces and objects from the viewer.
- Derive estimates of three-dimensional surface geometry and object shape.

To complete these tasks the visual system must use cues available in the two-dimensional retinal image, and in the state of the muscles both inside and outside the eye. There are multiple cues available, which vary in their utility for completing the different tasks. Table 11.1 lists 11 cues to depth, and their relevance to the four computational goals listed above. The most basic task is to determine depth order,

TABLE 11.1 Utility of depth cues in depth computations				
	Depth order	**Depth interval**	**Absolute depth**	**Shape**
Interposition	☑	☒	☒	☒
Height	☑	☑	☒	☒
Atmosphere	☑	☑	☒	☒
Size	☑	☑	☑	☒
Texture gradient	☑	☑	☒	☑
Blur	☑	☑	☑	☒
Accommodation	☑	☑	☑	☒
Motion	☑	☑	☒	☑
Shadows	☑	☑	☒	☑
Vergence	☑	☑	☑	☑
Stereo	☑	☑	☑	☑

and all cues can contribute to it. Most cues can also supply some information about depth intervals, but relatively few are useful for estimating absolute depth and surface shape. However the devil is in the detail—the utility of each cue is limited in certain respects, such as in terms of the ranges of distances over which the cue operates. The following sections discuss each cue in turn.

THE MULTIPLICITY OF DEPTH CUES

The first nine cues in Table 11.1 are available in the image projected onto a single retina, or in the position of a single eye, the so-called **monocular cues**. The last two cues require information to be combined across the two eyes, the so-called **binocular cues**.

MONOCULAR CUES

Interposition

Interposition is a monocular depth cue that is also discussed in Chapter 10 in the context of surface representation. As Figure 10.5 shows, the partial occlusion of a far surface by a near surface creates characteristic "T"-shaped intersections of contours. These intersections provide a simple cue to the depth order of the surfaces to which the "upright" and "top" contours of the T belong: The surface to which the top of the T belongs is usually closer than the surface to which the upright belongs. The cue cannot provide information about the size of depth interval between the surfaces.

Height in the visual field

Imagine that you are standing on a level surface outdoors (usually called the ground plane in the perceptual literature) and looking toward the distant horizon. The position in the visual field of surface markings or of objects resting on the ground depends on their distance. We can express visual field position in degrees, where 0° corresponds to the horizon, and 90° corresponds to a position at your feet (perpendicular to your line of sight). As the distance of elements on the surface increases, their position in the visual field rises progressively from near 90° to near zero. Figure 11.2 plots **height in the visual field (HVF)** as a function of horizontal distance. HVF varies with the tangent of visual field position (shown in the inset). HVF therefore offers an indication both of depth ordering (ground plane elements located higher up in the image are further away than those at lower positions) and of depth interval (the vertical distance between elements in the image scales with their relative distance on the ground plane).

The upper plot represents HVF from the point of view of a human of average height (160 cm). The lower plot represents HVF from the point of view of a crawling infant, or a domestic cat (20 cm). Cue variation is much more rapid when the eyes are closer to the ground. Equivalent distances also project to more central locations in the image. A point 400 cm away on the ground plane is only 3° below the line of sight from the point of view of a cat, but over 20° away from the line of sight from the viewpoint of an adult human.

The cue plotted in Figure 11.2 can be used either as a visual cue to relative depth (the difference in the vertical position of two elements in the visual field) or as a nonvisual cue (the change in angle of elevation of the eyes as one shifts fixation between the two elements, signaled by the extraocular muscles which control eye position).

There has been relatively little psychophysical research on the use of HVF as a depth cue (Epstein, 1966; Wallach & O'Leary, 1982; Ooi, Wu, & He, 2001). In one paper, Ooi, Wu, and He (2001) measured apparent distance using two tasks. One task required a blindfolded subject to walk to a previously seen spot on the ground. The other task required the subject to throw a beanbag to a visible target on the ground. Ooi, Wu, and He (2001) manipulated the HVF cue by having subjects wear prisms that displaced the image vertically. They found evidence that HVF does indeed influence depth perception.

The utility of height in the visual field as a depth cue has a major limitation. The relation between height and distance shown in Figure 11.2 applies only to objects or markings on horizontal ground plane surfaces. When objects move off the ground plane and into the air, height in the image is obviously an unreliable indicator of distance. When surfaces depart from horizontal, height is determined by surface slant as well as distance. While reading a page in a book held up in front of you, for example, text on different lines varies markedly in vertical position but relatively little in viewing distance. On the other hand, the rate at which text varies in *size* at different vertical positions in the image (an example

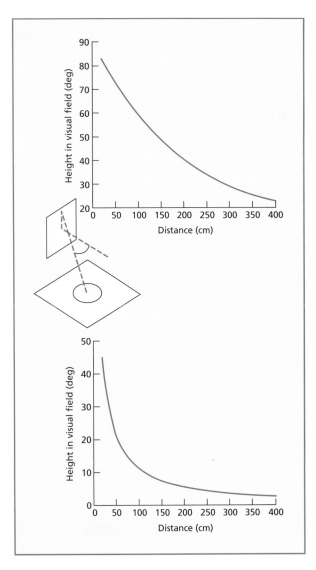

FIGURE 11.2
Height in the visual field (HVF) of an object on the ground surface as a function of its distance from the viewer, assuming a horizontal ground plane and fixation on the horizon. The upper plot shows HVF from the point of view of a human of average height (160 cm), while the lower plot shows HVF from the point of view of a crawling infant or domestic cat (20 cm). The inset shows the angle plotted in the graphs.

KEY TERMS

Ordinal depth cue
A depth cue in which cue value varies in discrete ordinal steps, such as "nearer" versus "further."

Texture gradient
A monocular cue to the orientation and depth of a textured surface; it is based on graded variation in the size, shape, and density of texture elements.

Leonardo da Vinci was a pioneer in the use of atmospheric perspective in paintings. He developed a technique known as s*fumato* ("smoky" or "hazy" in Italian), which involved the application of thin translucent glazes to reduce contrast and so create a sense of distance.

of a texture gradient) can be used to infer surface slant, described in a later section.

Atmospheric perspective

Light from distant objects has to travel through more atmosphere than light from nearby objects. Atmospheric particles, including dust, air, and water molecules, scatter light. Consequently, distant objects appear reduced in contrast, as shown in Figure 11.3 (there is also a slight shift toward bluish hues). The degree of attenuation in contrast depends on the atmosphere's attenuation coefficient. Figure 11.3 (bottom) plots contrast as a function of distance for different attenuation coefficients. A difference in contrast can serve as a cue to **ordinal depth**; the magnitude of the difference scales with the size of the depth interval.

O'Shea, Blackburn, and Ono (1994) reported that higher contrast shapes are judged as nearer than lower contrast shapes. Given the relatively slow change in contrast with distance, atmospheric perspective can serve as a depth cue only for very large distances.

FIGURE 11.3
Contrast attenuation due to light scattering by atmospheric particles (dust, air, and water molecules). The photograph at the top demonstrates the reduction in contrast in the image of more distant hills compared with nearer hills. The graph at the bottom plots contrast as a function of distance for two different atmospheric conditions: Clear (solid line), and light fog (dashed line; adapted from Fry, Bridgman, & Ellerbrock, 1949). Notice that the distance scale covers several kilometers.

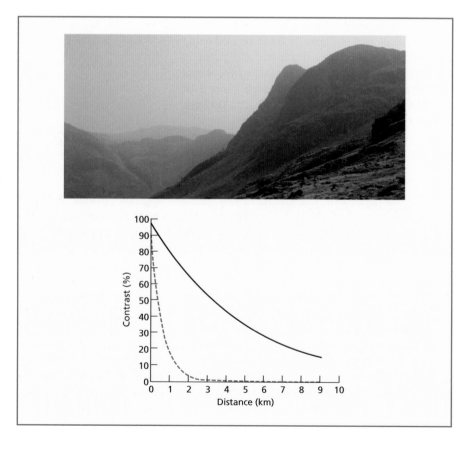

Retinal image size

This cue is based on the geometric fact that an object of fixed actual size will project a progressively smaller image onto the retina as it is viewed from more distant viewpoints (see Chapter 6 to review geometrical optics). The retinal area covered by the object decreases at a faster rate than its size, as illustrated in Figure 11.4.

The graph shows the angular diameter and area of a soccer ball as a function of its distance from the eye (starting from a distance of 20 cm, a typical value for the near point of accommodation). Notice that the variation in size and area is highly nonlinear. Retinal size is halved each time distance doubles. Once the ball reaches a distance of approximately 260 cm, 90% of its range of variation in size has occurred. The range of variation in area asymptotes more quickly; 90% of its range of variation is reached at a distance of 80cm.

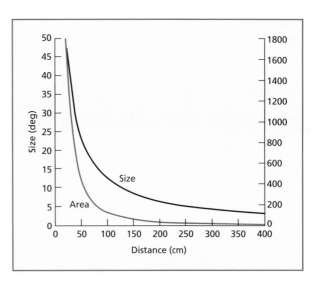

Retinal image size varies in a lawful and systematic way with distance, and therefore offers information about depth order and depth interval. If we are viewing two objects of equal actual size, and the image of one is half the size of the other, we can infer that it is twice as far away. If one knows the actual size of an object and the optical properties of the eye, it would in principle be possible to estimate its absolute distance from the size of its retinal image (see the section on lens equations in the tutorials of Chapter 6). So the utility of the cue depends on prior knowledge about object size. Nevertheless, in many viewing conditions size does appear to be used as a depth cue; many commonly viewed classes of object, such as trees, humans, and cars, are similar in size. Figure 11.5 is based on the experiment of Ittelson (1951).

FIGURE 11.4
Graph showing the variation in projected image size and area of a soccer ball as a function of distance from the viewer. Variation in size and area is highly nonlinear. Most of the range of variation is confined to distances of less than 80cm.

Texture gradient

The image of a textured surface that is slanted away from an observer, such as the ground plane, contains highly structured variations in the shape and density of elements located on the surface. Gibson (1950) noted that **texture gradients** provide visual cues about surface orientation and depth. Figure 11.6 (top) shows an example of a textured surface slanted away from the viewpoint. Three separable components of texture gradient are evident as one moves across the image in the direction of surface slant (vertically in Figure 11.6).

FIGURE 11.5
Demonstration of relative size as a distance cue. The three playing cards appear to be at different distances because their images differ in size. This effect relies on the assumption that the three cards have the same actual size.

Perspective gradient

Element *width* or separation at right-angles to the slant varies systematically. Convergence or linear perspective is a special case of this gradient, the most familiar example of which is the convergence of rail tracks as they disappear into the distance.

FIGURE 11.6

Top: The image of a textured surface slanted away from the viewer. There is a graded variation in texture properties as one moves across the image in the direction of increasing distance: Element width or separation decreases (perspective gradient); element height decreases (compression gradient); and texture density (elements per unit area in the image) increases. (From Bruce, Green, & Georgeson, 2003.) Middle and bottom: Graphs plotting the three components of texture gradient for a ground plane surface from the point of view of a human of average height (middle), and a crawling infant or domestic cat (bottom). Perspective (element width) and compression (element height) are measured in degrees of visual angle (the drawings on the right indicate the angles plotted); density is measured as the number of elements per unit area in the image.

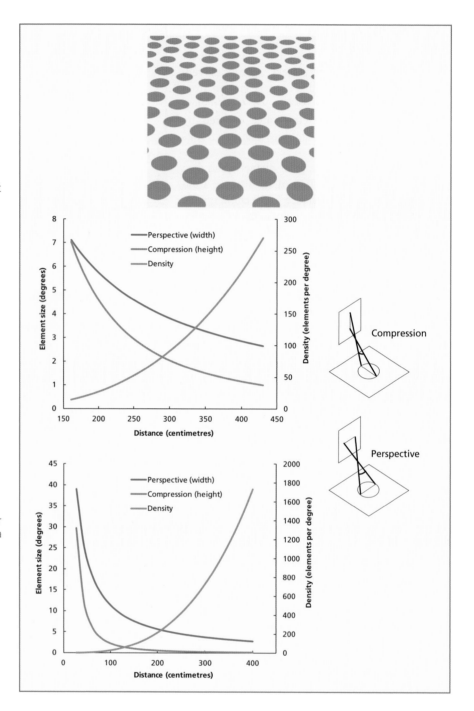

Compression gradient

Element *height* in the direction of slant varies progressively, due to the foreshortening effect of surface slant.

Density gradient

The number of elements per unit of area in the image varies progressively. At the bottom of the image in Figure 11.6 (nearest part of the surface), there are relatively few texture elements per unit of image area, while at the top of the image (furthest part of the surface) there are many texture elements in an equal-sized image area.

The graphs in Figure 11.6 plot these three components of texture gradient for a ground plane surface as a function of distance from the viewer's eyes. The upper graph plots texture variation from the point of view of an adult human, and the lower graph plots texture variation from the point of view of a domestic cat or crawling infant. Both graphs plot the projected height (compression), width (perspective), and density of equally sized and spaced elements on the ground plane. All three texture cues change much more over shorter distances than over longer distances (the curves flatten out). Note also that cue variation is more gradual for taller observers, because the degree of slant in the surface along a given line of sight is lower. The angular size of the elements is also much larger for the cat or infant, because they are much closer to the ground surface.

The projection in the visual image of texture elements distributed on any planar surface, such as the wall of a building, obeys the same functions as those shown in Figure 11.6. The steepness of the functions depends on surface slant. Knill (1998) measured the ability of observers to discriminate small changes in the slant depicted in a planar textured surface, for slants ranging from zero (a vertical surface parallel to the plane of the image) to 70° (nearly horizontal). He found that performance was very poor for slants near vertical, but improved markedly as depicted slant increased. Knill (1998) concluded that texture gradients were useful only for slants in excess of 50°. When viewing a horizontal ground plane from the height of an adult, this would correspond to the slant visible when fixating on a point on the ground at least 2 meters away. From the point of view of a cat, this slant would occur while fixating at a distance of only 25 cm. Of the three gradients described above, Knill (1998) found that compression seemed most important for slant judgments.

The lawful relation between distance and cue value evident in Figure 11.6 demonstrates that texture gradients offer cues about depth order and interval. For example, image areas having lower texture density should be nearer in the scene than areas having a higher density, with the difference in density indicating the size of the depth interval. Variations in texture can also provide information about surface geometry and object shape. For example, the dimples on a golf ball and the stitched panels on a soccer ball give a very clear impression of spherical shape.

The utility of texture gradients clearly relies on the presence of regular texture on surfaces. Strictly speaking, elements should have uniform size, shape, and spacing on the surface for the cue to operate most reliably. However, Knill (1998) and others have shown that the visual system is able to make use of texture gradient cues even when texture elements vary somewhat in size, shape, or spacing.

Image blur

In a real retinal image of a slanted surface, such as that depicted in Figure 11.6, some parts of the scene will inevitably be more spatially blurred than others. Eyes, like cameras, have a limited **depth of field**. Assume that the eye (or camera) is focused on a point at a given distance. Within a certain range of distances, points lying nearer or further away than the point of focus will appear sharply defined in the image. This range of distances defines the optical system's depth of field. Points lying beyond these limits will appear blurred in the image, by an amount that depends lawfully on distance. The graph in Figure 11.7 (b) shows how the

KEY TERM

Depth of field
The range of distances either side of the point of focus within which there is no perceptible blur in the visual image.

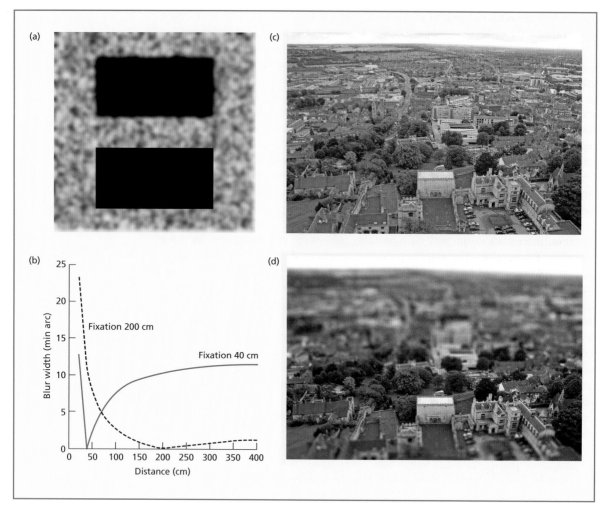

FIGURE 11.7

Image blur as a depth cue. (a) Two black rectangles against a blurred texture background. The rectangle with sharply defined borders appears closer than the rectangle with blurred borders. (b) The degree of blur in the image of a point in a 3-D scene as a function of the distance of the point from the viewer. The solid line shows image blur when the observer fixates on a point at a distance of 40 cm; the broken line depicts blur assuming fixation at 200 cm. Blur is absent for scene points at fixation distance, but increases for nearer or more distant points. Values were calculated using equations in Mather and Smith (2000). (c) A photograph of a natural scene. (d) The same image as in (c) manipulated digitally to simulate tilt-shift photography. Note that the image appears to depict a model or miniature.

magnitude of blur varies with distance from the point of fixation. Two fixation distances are plotted, 40 cm and 200 cm. Blur is absent at fixation distance, and increases more sharply for nearer distances than for further distances. Depth of field is defined by the smallest increase in blur on either side of fixation that is perceptible to the observer (Campbell, 1957).

Variations in image blur therefore offer cues to depth order, depth interval, and absolute distance (Pentland, 1987). Several computational algorithms have been proposed for estimating depth from image blur. Perceptual evidence indicates that image blur does influence depth perception (Marshall et al., 1996; Mather, 1996). Figure 11.7 (a) shows a synthetic image in which blur provides a cue to the differing depths of the black rectangles.

The utility of blur as a depth cue is limited by several factors. First, as you read in Chapter 6, some degree of blur is always present in retinal images, even at the point of focus, complicating the interpretation of blur. Second, depth of field depends on the diameter of the entrance pupil. A point at a given distance from fixation will appear more blurred when viewed through a relatively wide pupil than when viewed through a narrow pupil. Pupil size also has to be taken into account when interpreting metric blur information. Third, many eyes have accommodative errors which introduce blur and also need to be taken into account when interpreting retinal blur. Fourth, human observers are relatively insensitive to small changes in blur extent (Mather & Smith, 2002).

Some of these limitations can be addressed by a calibration process which adjusts the interpretation of blur according to the prevailing level that is present in a given eye, and there is evidence from adaptation studies for the operation of such a process (Webster, Georgeson, & Webster, 2002). Blur can be quite effective in manipulating apparent depth. In tilt-shift photography a blur gradient is added to a natural scene to manipulate its apparent depth. Figures 11.7 (c) and (d) show a natural scene before and after the addition of blur which increases steadily from the center towards the top and bottom of the image. Notice that the blurred image seems to be a model or miniature (an effect known as "tilt-shift miniaturization"; Held et al., 2010; Vishwanath & Blaser, 2010). The blur simulates a very narrow depth of field; as the graph in Figure 11.7 (b) shows, the steepest blur gradient (and narrowest depth of field) occurs for very short viewing distances, as when viewing a model. Although image blur does seem to play a role in depth perception, it probably provides only relatively coarse depth information.

Accommodation

If an observer shifts fixation between points which lie at different distances, the lens of the eye must change shape (accommodate) in order to maintain a focused image of the fixated point. Accommodation is controlled by the ciliary muscles of the eye. The lens is at its thinnest when the muscles are relaxed, optimal for distance vision (shown at the top left of Figure 11.8). Fixation on a relatively near point requires that the muscles contract to release the tension on the lens's suspensory ligaments, allowing the lens to assume a thicker shape (top right of Figure 11.8). Information on the state of the ciliary muscles therefore offers a nonvisual cue to absolute fixation distance. When fixation shifts between objects at different distances, changes in accommodation give information about depth order and interval; within limits set by the accommodative range of the eye, the greater the depth interval the larger the change in accommodation.

Figure 11.8 also shows a plot of accommodation (change in optical power of the lens) as a function of fixation distance. In an eye free of refractive error, no accommodation is required for objects at very far distances. The nearest distance to which young adults can accommodate is approximately 15 cm. Accommodative range (the range of distances over which accommodation changes significantly with distance) extends only from about 15 to 300 cm. Fisher and Ciuffreda (1988) and Mon-Williams and Tresilian (2000) report that within this range accommodation probably provides only relatively coarse depth information.

The range of accommodation shrinks with age. By the time most people reach their fifties, there is virtually no accommodative range left, due to loss of flexibility in the lens (hence the need for reading glasses).

FIGURE 11.8
Top: The eye's lens changes shape to maintain a sharply focused retinal image of scene points at different distances. When fixating distant points (left), the ciliary muscles are relaxed and the lens is quite thin, producing relatively little convergence of incoming light rays; for near points (right), the ciliary muscles are tensed to allow the lens to take on a thicker shape, producing greater convergence of incoming rays. Bottom: Graph showing accommodation in diopters (D) as a function of object distance from the eye (adapted from Charman, 1991; recall from the tutorial section of Chapter 6 that the converging power of a lens is measured in diopters).

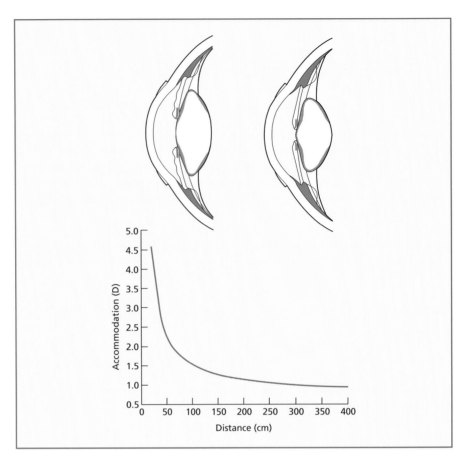

Motion parallax

The cues discussed so far are available in static scenes. If the observer moves through the scene, the movement of image elements across the retina provides powerful depth cues. Movement through the world creates motion gradients in the retinal image, which bear a close relation to the texture gradients described earlier. The graphs in Figure 11.6 show the projected height and width of equally sized elements located on the ground plane. Projected height and width decrease for elements located at progressively further distances. We can also view the graphs as representing the retinal velocity of elements that move through equal distances on the ground plane (i.e., at constant velocity), rather than arrays of constant-sized static elements. So motion provides the same depth ordering and interval cues as texture gradients and size cues. For example, if two human figures walk across your field of view, one twice as far away from you as the other, the further walker will be half as tall in the retinal image, and will translate across your field of view at half the retinal velocity of the nearer walker.

Optic flow

In the case of height variation (compression), the graphs show the projected velocity of points on the ground at different distances, moving toward or away from the

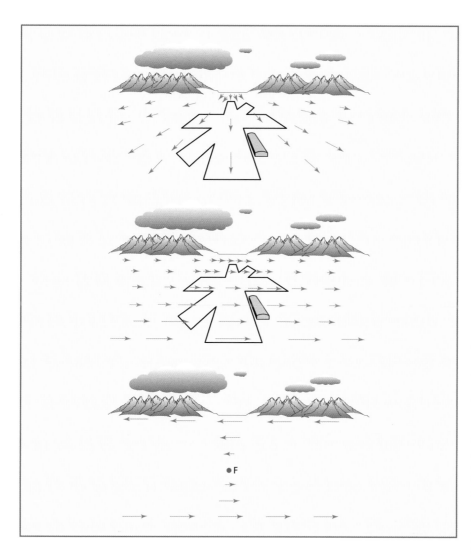

FIGURE 11.9
Motion parallax provides powerful depth cues, illustrated by these images depicting an outdoor scene from the viewpoint of a moving observer (based on illustrations in Gibson, 1950). Top: When the observer translates across the ground plane towards the horizon, while fixating on the horizon, scene points translate across the image in a highly structured expanding pattern, often called optic flow. Retinal velocity increases as scene points approach the observer. Middle: When the observer translates to the left, while maintaining fixation on the horizon, the pattern of retinal flow again provides information about distance. The retinal velocity of a given point depends on its distance from the viewer. Bottom: When the observer fixates on a point in the middle distance (F) while translating leftwards, point F becomes stationary on the retina, while other points move leftward or rightward. Image points that were moving rightward more rapidly than the point in the middle distance continue to move rightwards; points that were moving more slowly now move leftwards.

observer at a constant speed. The lengths of the arrows in Figure 11.9 (top) show velocity in different parts of the image. This pattern of movement is often called *optic flow* (which is discussed in more detail in the next chapter).

Motion parallax

In the case of width variation (perspective) plotted in Figure 11.6, the graphs show the projected velocity of points at different distances moving *across* the observer's field of view at a constant speed. The lengths of the arrows in Figure 11.9 (middle) show velocity at different distances. This pattern of movement is often called **motion parallax**.

The examples in Figures 11.6 and 11.9 assume that the observer's gaze remains fixed on the horizon.

KEY TERM

Motion parallax
Movement in one part of an image relative to another, as can be produced by objects moving at different distances from the observer.

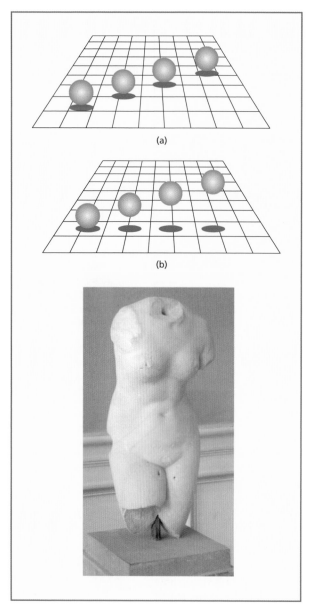

(a)

(b)

FIGURE 11.10

Top: Texture and shape cues provide a 3-D context for the spheres, but each sphere's apparent position in the scene is influenced by its cast shadow. If the shadow is close to the spheres, then the spheres are perceived as near the ground plane. Bottom: Attached shadows provide information about 3-D form.

If the observer fixates on one of the moving points, then that point becomes a stationary reference in the image, and the projected movement of all other points in the field will be expressed relative to that point. For example, in the case of motion parallax, if the observer tracks a point in the middle distance, the movement pattern shown in Figure 11.9 (bottom) will result. Points nearer than the fixated point are moving more rapidly, so will continue to move in the same direction as previously. Points further away than the fixated point are moving more slowly, so will move in the opposite direction. Psychophysical experiments have shown that optic flow and motion parallax are sufficient to support high-precision depth perception even when no other depth cues are available (Rogers & Graham, 1979; M. G. Harris, 1994). The success of Imax theaters is testament to the power of dynamic depth cues. Motion processing is discussed in more detail in the next chapter, which also discusses a phenomenon known as the kinetic depth effect, in which the three-dimensional structure of an object can be inferred solely on the basis of its movement properties, just as it can from texture variation.

Shadows

Directional illumination creates two kinds of shadow. Cast shadows are shadows from one object that fall on the surface of another object. Attached shadows are those cast by the object onto its own surface. Both kinds of shadow provide depth information. Kersten et al. (1996) demonstrated how the position and movement of cast shadows influence the perception of depth ordering and intervals. Figure 11.10 (top) reproduces the effect studied by Kersten et al. (1996). The texture gradient on the surface provides a 3-D context for the spheres, but the perceived position of the spheres in relation to the tiled surface depends on their cast shadows.

Figure 11.10 (bottom) shows how attached shadows provide powerful cues to 3-D object shape. Koenderink, van Doorn, and Kappers (1996) found that shading cues are important for judging 3-D shape (though their stimuli also contained texture cues). Many sculptures are carved from materials that provide no cues to depth other than attached shadows, yet convey a strong impression of three-dimensional form.

When interpreting shadow effects, the visual system tends to assume that light is directed from above, and that objects are convex rather than concave. Correct interpretation of shading also requires assumptions that the illumination is uniform, and that object surfaces are uniform, diffuse reflectors. In situations where these assumptions do not hold, interpretations based on shadows alone are liable to be inaccurate.

 Analyze a painting of an outdoor scene in terms of the cues used by the artist to convey an impression of depth.

BINOCULAR CUES

Two depth cues are available only when information from both eyes is combined. One cue is nonvisual (vergence), and the other cue is purely visual (binocular disparity).

Vergence

When both eyes fixate on the same point in space, their visual axes must converge in order to project an image of the point onto the fovea in each eye. The **vergence angle** formed by the intersection of the two visual axes depends on distance, as shown at the top of Figure 11.11.

The graph at the bottom of Figure 11.11 plots vergence angle as a function of distance. Vergence angle is controlled by the extraocular muscles (see Chapter 6). Information on the state of the extraocular muscles therefore offers a cue as to the absolute distance of the fixated point, and shifts in vergence angle indicate depth ordering and interval. As with other depth cues, vergence angle varies nonlinearly with distance. By a distance of 200 cm, 90% of the full range of vergence angles has been used up.

There has been a longstanding debate in the literature regarding the importance of vergence angle as a depth cue. It appears weak beyond 2 meters (not surprising, given the physical cue variation plotted in Figure 11.11), and seems to lead to depth underestimation at these distances. Viguier, Clement, and Trotter (2001) investigated vergence cues at relatively near distances (below 80 cm). They found that distance perception mediated by vergence was accurate below 40 cm, but showed consistent underestimation at greater distances. One difficulty facing those studying vergence cues is that vergence and accommodation are yoked together in the visual system. When accommodation changes, so does vergence, even when one eye is occluded (an effect called *accommodative vergence*). It can therefore be difficult to separate out the contributions of the two cues to distance perception.

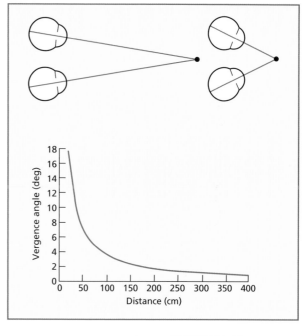

FIGURE 11.11
Top: The eyes must converge to fixate on a near object. (From Bruce, Green, & Georgeson, 2003, figure 7.2, p. 171.) Bottom: Graph showing converge angle as a function of object distance. Notice that most of the range of variation in vergence angle is confined to distances that are within 2 meters from the observer. Copyright © 2003 Psychology Press.

Binocular disparity

In humans, the two eyes are typically 6.3 cm apart. Consequently, they receive slightly different views of the world. These slight differences provide one of the most powerful cues to depth, binocular disparity, which is responsible for stereo vision (stereopsis). Figures 11.12 and 11.13 illustrate the detailed basis of the cue. They show two eyes viewing a pair of

KEY TERM

Vergence angle
The angle at which the visual axes of the two eyes intersect while the observer fixates on a point binocularly; it offers a cue to fixation distance.

FIGURE 11.12
Top: Plan view of a simple scene in which a binocular observer views a small vertical rectangle positioned in front of a larger rectangle. The observer is fixating on the center of the nearer rectangle. Middle: The scene as viewed from the left eye and the right eye. Bottom: The left- and right-eye views are superimposed to show the small differences resulting from the slightly different viewpoints of the two eyes. While the observer fixates on the nearer rectangle, there are differences in both the horizontal and the vertical positions of the edges of the far rectangle.

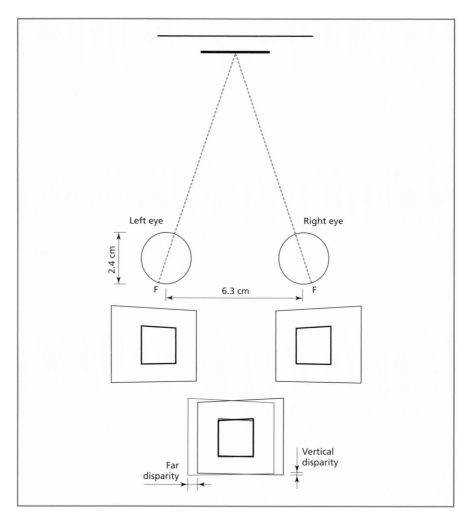

rectangles, one slightly closer than the other. The view from each eye is shown below. The two views are superimposed at the bottom, with the left eye's view in blue, and the right eye's view in black. The slight difference in viewing position produces small differences between the two eyes' images.

While fixating on the center of the small *near* rectangle (Figure 11.12), its vertical edges fall on corresponding positions in the two eyes (the blue and black edges are superimposed). Notice that the vertical edges of the far rectangle fall on noncorresponding locations in the two eyes. The right eye's view of these edges is displaced to the right relative to the left eye's view. The difference in horizontal image position between the two eyes is called **horizontal binocular disparity.**

Horizontal binocular disparity

When fixation shifts to the large *far* rectangle (Figure 11.13), its vertical edges now fall on corresponding positions in the two eyes, but the vertical edges of the nearer nonfixated rectangle fall on noncorresponding positions. Now the right eye's view is displaced to the left relative to the left eye's view, in the opposite direction to the

KEY TERM

Horizontal binocular disparity

A binocular depth cue based on the difference in the horizontal retinal position of an image point in one eye relative to the other; often abbreviated to disparity.

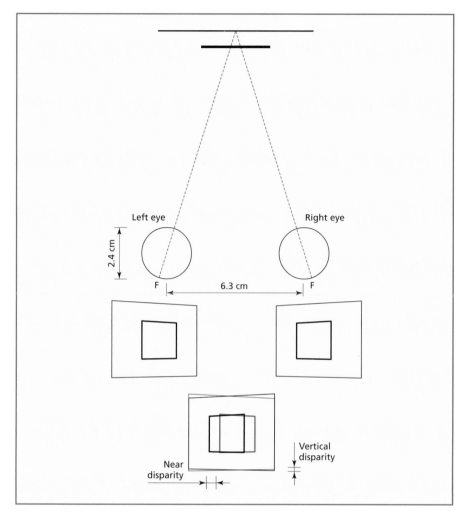

FIGURE 11.13
The same scene as depicted in Figure 11.12, with the observer fixating on the far rectangle. Notice that the pattern of disparities between the two eyes' views is different: The edges of the near rectangle now show horizontal disparities.

displacement shown in Figure 11.12. In general, the sign of horizontal binocular disparity depends on the sign of the difference in depth between fixated and nonfixated points in the image:

- **Far (uncrossed) disparity**: The nonfixated point is further away, and the right eye's view of the point is shifted to the right relative to the left eye's view.
- **Near (crossed) disparity**: The nonfixated point is nearer, and the right eye's view of the point is shifted to the left relative to the left eye's view.

The magnitude of the disparity or, in other words, the magnitude of the shift in position of a nonfixated point in one eye's image compared to the other eye's image, depends on the difference in distance between the fixated and nonfixated points. Disparity is usually expressed in terms of angular displacement, with negative values denoting near disparities and positive values denoting far disparities. More details on the geometry of disparity, and how to simulate disparity using stereo viewing techniques, is provided in the tutorials section at the end of the chapter. It is important to understand the

KEY TERMS

Far disparity
The horizontal binocular disparity created by an item that is further away than fixation distance; it is also known as uncrossed disparity.

Near disparity
The horizontal binocular disparity created by an item that is nearer than fixation distance; it is also known as crossed disparity.

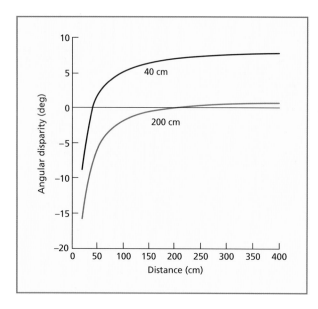

FIGURE 11.14

Horizontal binocular disparity as a function of distance, for two fixation distances. Notice that disparity is zero at fixation distance, is negative for distances nearer than fixation, and is positive for distances further than fixation. Binocular disparity provides information about distance relative to fixation.

general nature of binocular disparity, as demonstrated in Figures 11.12 and 11.13, in order to appreciate its importance as a depth cue.

Recent research in stereo vision draws a distinction between *absolute disparity* and *relative disparity*. Absolute disparity is depicted in Figures 11.12 and 11.13, and corresponds to the shift in the imaged position of a nonfixated point in one eye relative to the other eye. Relative disparity refers to a situation in which there are two nonfixated points; the relative disparity of the two points corresponds to the difference in their absolute disparities. Both kinds of disparity can provide information about the depth ordering and intervals between pairs of points at different depths. Relative disparity may be particularly useful for computing 3-D surface geometry and shape.

Figure 11.14 shows absolute horizontal binocular disparity as a function of the distance of the nonfixated point, for two fixation distances (40 cm and 200 cm). Two important properties of absolute horizontal disparity are apparent in Figure 11.14. First, absolute disparity specifies depth relative to fixation, not absolute depth. For example, a near disparity of −1.0° corresponds to a distance of 36 cm when fixating at 40 cm, but a distance of 130 cm when fixating at 200 cm. Second, disparity changes much more rapidly at near distances than at far distances, regardless of fixation distance, and 90% of the total variation in disparity has been consumed at a distance of approximately 300 cm (assuming fixation at 40 cm).

Vertical disparity

The rectangles in the lower half of Figures 11.12 and 11.13 appear trapezoidal because each eye views them from a slightly oblique angle (the slightly nearer side of each rectangle appears longer in the image than the opposite side). Consequently, when the two eyes' views are superimposed there are slight differences in the vertical location of features between the eyes, such as the corners of the rectangles. These differences are called vertical disparities. The opposite keystone effects in the two eyes are due to the fact that the eyes are converged; as viewing distance increases and convergence angle diminishes, the keystone effect becomes negligible. So the magnitude of vertical disparity carries information about absolute depth (convergence angle and vertical disparity declines as distance increases), and does appear to influence depth estimates (Rogers & Bradshaw, 1993). The question of whether and how the human visual system exploits vertical disparities has attracted some controversy, and is discussed in the tutorials section at the end of the chapter.

Random-dot stereograms

Far more research on depth perception has been devoted to binocular disparity than to any other depth cue partly because, as evident in Table 11.1, it is the only cue that can potentially provide information for all the major computational tasks in depth perception. A second factor that has had a major influence on research is the introduction of a powerful experimental stimulus for studying stereo vision,

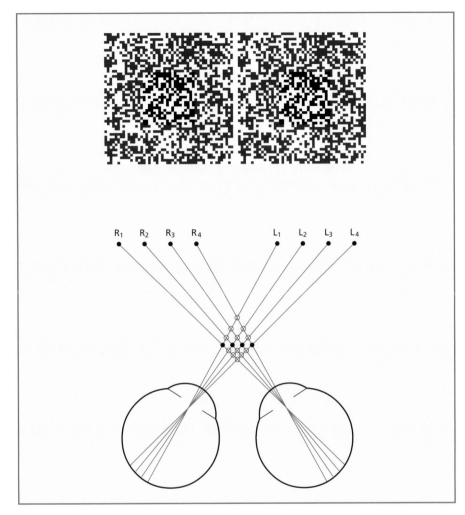

FIGURE 11.15
Top: Construction of a random-dot stereogram. One image is delivered to each eye (see Figure 11.20 for delivery methods). The two images contain identical arrays of dots, except that a subset of dots in one image is shifted in position relative to their position in the other image (black dots; color for illustration only). The shift introduces a disparity cue when the images are viewed binocularly. Bottom: The correspondence problem. When a row of four identical dots is viewed binocularly, the visual system must match each dot's image in the left eye (L_1–L_4) with its corresponding partner in the right eye (R_1–R_4). Perceived depth is correct only if the correct matches are made (filled circles). Each false match (open circles) lies at an incorrect depth. (From Bruce, Green, & Georgeson, 2003, figure 7.7, p. 178.) Copyright © 2003 Psychology Press.

the **random-dot stereogram (RDS)** first developed by Bela Julesz in the early 1960s (though see Bergua & Skrandies, 2000). An RDS (shown in Figure 11.15) typically contains two dense arrays of random dots. A stereo viewing technique is employed to deliver one array of dots to the left eye, and the other to the right eye.

If the two arrays are identical, the observer perceives a single fused image of a vertical planar surface. It is possible to create a horizontal disparity cue by selecting a subset of dots and shifting their horizontal position in one eye's view relative to the other eye's view. The direction of the shift (left versus right) determines whether the displacement creates a far disparity or a near disparity. In the example of Figure 11.15, a central rectangular region of dots is shifted to the right in the left eye's view (the region vacated by some of the dots is filled with new dots). When subjects view the RDS, they perceive the rectangle of dots to be nearer than the remaining dots. It is important to appreciate that any arbitrary shape can be depicted in this way, though textbook examples generally involve simple rectangular shapes.

The crucial aspect of a RDS is that it presents disparity in isolation from all other depth cues, and therefore demonstrates that disparity alone can be sufficient to mediate depth perception.

KEY TERM

Random-dot stereogram (RDS)
A stereogram containing pseudo-randomly arranged dots; some dots are in disparate locations in one eye's view relative to the other eye's view.

The correspondence problem in RDS

When researchers began to consider in detail how a visual processing system (whether natural or artificial) can extract depth from RDS stimuli, they encountered a severe problem, known as the **correspondence problem**. Figure 11.15 illustrates a very mild form of the problem. It shows a row of four dots presented to two eyes. The left-eye images of the dots are labeled L_1 to L_4, and the right-eye images are labeled R_1 to R_4. The left image of the leftmost dot (L_1) could, in principle, be matched with any one of the four dots visible in the right eye. Only the correct match (shown by the leftmost filled circle) will be encoded at the correct depth. Each of the other possible matches will be encoded at incorrect depths defined by the retinal positions of the two images. These incorrect or false matches are shown by open circles. Across all four left- and right-eye dots, there are four correct pairings, and 12 incorrect pairings. How does the visual system select the correct matches and reject the incorrect matches? This is the correspondence problem. It has been the subject of much psychophysical and computational research.

The problem is much more severe in the case of full RDS arrays, since they contain many thousands of dots in each eye's image. From a purely computational viewpoint, the information available in the image is not sufficient to arrive at a unique solution that rejects all false matches and retains only correct matches. However, it is possible to arrive at a correct solution if certain assumptions are made that rule out many potential matches on the grounds that they are impossible (or at least extremely unlikely to occur) in images of real three-dimensional scenes. A number of constraining assumptions have been identified in both psychophysical and computational research, including similarity, continuity, and epipolar geometry.

Similarity Binocular matches are only admissible if they involve elements in each eye that have similar spatial properties such as contrast and orientation (Marr & Poggio, 1976; Mayhew & Frisby, 1981).

Continuity If there are several candidate matches, the visual system selects the match offering the smoothest and/or least change in disparity across the image (Marr & Poggio, 1976; Pollard, Mayhew, & Frisby, 1985).

Epipolar geometry A plane passing through a point at a given depth and the optical centers of the two eyes defines a plane (**epipolar plane**) which projects to a straight line in each eye's image. These lines are called **epipolar lines**. For a given image point in one eye, all the points in the other eye which could possibly match it must lie along the same epipolar line (more details on epipolar geometry can be found in the tutorials section). On this basis the search for correspondence can be restricted to epipolar lines, greatly simplifying the problem. The epipolar constraint has received a great deal of attention in computational research (e.g., Zhang et al., 1995), but its relevance for stereopsis is unclear (Stevenson & Schor, 1997; Schreiber et al., 2001).

Some constraints, such as similarity and continuity, can be implemented readily in terms of the properties of or interactions between cortical cells tuned to binocular disparity (described below). No firm conclusions have been reached regarding which assumptions are the most important for human vision. Human stereopsis is not captured adequately by current computational models (e.g., Gillam & Borsting, 1988; Weinshall, 1989; Bruce, Green, & Georgeson, 2003), and surprising new discoveries are still being made (May, Zhaoping, & Hibbard, 2012).

KEY TERMS

Correspondence problem
The problem of matching up two images point by point; the two images may depict the same scene at different viewing positions or times.

Epipolar plane
The plane that passes through a given point in front of the viewer, and through the nodal points of the two eyes.

Epipolar line
The projection of the epipolar plane onto the retinal image.

Psychophysics of stereopsis in RDS stimuli

A great deal of psychophysical research has been conducted on the ability of observers to discriminate depth in RDS stimuli. The smallest disparity that can be discriminated reliably (the lower disparity limit) is typically less than 6″ of arc (Howard & Rogers, 1995; Badcock & Shor, 1985). When fixating at arm's length (57 cm), this corresponds to a change in distance of less than 1/60th of a centimeter. At the other extreme, the largest disparity that can be discriminated reliably in RDS stimuli, known as the upper disparity limit, is in the region of 20′ arc (Glennerster, 1998). With fixation at arm's length, this upper limit corresponds to a change in distance of 3 cm. Disparity limits are influenced by a range of stimulus parameters (e.g., Wilcox & Hess, 1995; Burt & Julesz, 1980). The typical values obtained psychophysically for the lower and upper disparity limits imply that stereopsis is particularly useful for making very fine discriminations of depth at distances quite close to fixation distance.

Diplopia

At very large (or small) disparities vision tends to become **diplopic**; we see double images. To demonstrate this effect, fixate on the end of a finger held about 30 cm in front of the eyes. If you direct your attention to objects further away, while maintaining fixation on the finger, you will see two images of each object. Similarly, if you place another finger much closer to your eyes it will also appear diplopic while fixating on the more distant finger.

Physiology of stereopsis

As mentioned in Chapter 7, many cells in the visual cortex are selectively sensitive to disparity, because they are binocularly driven and their receptive fields lie in disparate positions in the two eyes. Poggio and Talbot (1981) found that these cells can even respond appropriately to RDS stimuli. Disparity tuning is found in all areas of visual cortex (see Figure 7.19 in Chapter 7). No single area seems to be dedicated to stereo vision. Recent electrophysiological studies have examined the response of individual cortical cells to absolute disparity and relative disparity. Cells in V1 respond only to absolute disparity, but cells in other visual areas (V2, V3, V4, MT) seem to respond to both absolute and relative disparity; no cells have been found that respond purely to relative disparity (Parker, 2007; Anzai & DeAngelis, 2010), though the issue is complicated by the fact that there are many different ways to generate stimuli containing relative disparities.

Although the ubiquity of disparity-tuned cells indicates that both the dorsal and ventral processing streams process stereo information, some believe that different stereo computations are performed in the two streams, with the dorsal stream performing simple computations such as absolute distance to support orienting and navigation, and the ventral stream performing fine computations such as 3-D shape and curvature which support object perception (Parker, 2007).

Stereoblindness

In order to make use of binocular disparity in depth estimation, the observer obviously must possess two eyes that can execute vergence eye movements, and disparity selective neurons in their visual cortex. Surprisingly, around 5% of the general population does not satisfy these requirements, and is consequently stereoblind. The most common etiology of stereoblindness is as follows. In the first few years of life, an imbalance in the extraocular muscles results in poorly coordinated eye movements. The infant has a squint (technically known as a *strabismus*), and is unable to maintain binocular fixation. Consequently, the images projected onto the retinas of the two eyes contain very little of the correlation that is required to drive binocular cortical neurons. These neurons shift their sensitivity to become monocularly driven.

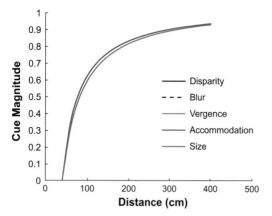

If strabismus is not corrected in the first 5 years of life, during which cortical responses are malleable, then no binocular cortical neurons will be left in the cortex, and stereopsis will not be possible. In adulthood, individuals with this history are often unaware of their lack of stereo vision until they encounter RDS stimuli, but have relied on the many alternative cues to depth and distance.

CUE COMBINATION

CORRELATIONS BETWEEN CUES

Looking back over the depth cues surveyed in the previous section, two general trends emerge. First, each cue has its own advantages and disadvantages. Second, cue magnitude often varies in a highly lawful way, with a surprising degree of correspondence between the cues. Both static and dynamic cues derived from elements lying on the ground plane (perspective and compression cues, with corresponding motion cues of flow and parallax) vary at a rate that depends on eye height (see Figure 11.6). If one compares the metric information available in the other cues it becomes clear that different cues are very highly correlated. Figure 11.16 re-plots cue values for absolute disparity, blur, vergence, accommodation, and size from previous figures as a function of distance, in a manner that

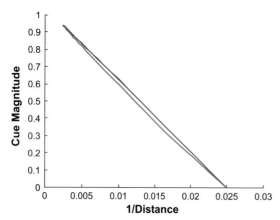

allows direct comparisons between cues. It plots cue magnitude relative to its value at fixation (40 cm in Figure 11.16), as a proportion of its maximum value (estimated at a distance of 1000 cm). In this plot all cues are zero at fixation distance, and rise towards their maximum at far distances. Remarkably, the cues collapse onto a single function. Cue magnitude initially rises sharply, and then levels off. As the lower graph shows, cue magnitude varies linearly with the reciprocal of distance (1/distance). An interesting implication of the nonlinear function in Figure 11.16 is that depth judgments should be most precise at distances within about 3 or 4 meters, because cue value varies most at close range.

FIGURE 11.16
Top: Cue variation for disparity, blur, vergence, accommodation, and size as a function of distance, re-plotted from previous figures (assuming fixation at 40 cm). Cue magnitude relative to its value at fixation is expressed as a proportion of its maximum value (1.0). Different cues are very highly correlated. Bottom: In all cases, cue magnitude varies linearly with the reciprocal of distance.

COMBINING CUES

Neurophysiological evidence indicates that neurons in higher order cortical regions integrate information from different cues (Tsutsui, Taira, & Sakata, 2005). However, despite the similarities evident in Figure 11.16, the information provided by different depth cues is often incomplete, imprecise, or even contradictory, and the cues available vary with context. For example:

* Interposition is unambiguous about ordering but cannot specify depth interval;
* Size cues rely on knowledge about real size;
* Texture gradients are available only in scenes containing evenly textured surfaces;
* Image blur varies with ambient illumination (pupil diameter);
* Accommodation varies with the age (and refractive state) of the observer;
* Motion parallax cues are available only when objects or the observer move;
* Horizontal disparity cannot specify absolute distance.

No single cue is adequate by itself, and different combinations of cues are relevant for different tasks, as shown in Table 11.1. So the visual system adopts a flexible strategy in which cues are combined with variable relative weights, depending on the context and task (see Bulthoff & Mallot, 1988). Heavily weighted cues have a greater influence on the combined depth estimate. A great deal of recent research on depth perception has studied the ways that different cues are combined. Psychophysical studies indicate that the weight assigned to a given cue varies with stimulus conditions, and across observers (Buckley & Frisby, 1993; Johnston, Cumming, & Landy, 1994; Girshick & Banks, 2009). For example, Johnston, Cumming, & Landy, (1994) studied stereo and motion cues, and found that stereo cues were more heavily weighted at near distances, but motion cues were more heavily weighted at far distances. Cue combination is a complex, context-dependent, and idiosyncratic process.

Think of other factors that might influence the weight attached to particular cues.

Theoretical models of cue combination begin with a set of depth estimates provided by different cues, and assume that the visual system computes the optimal or most probable percept that is consistent with the different estimates. The weight attached to different cues takes account of their reliability in the particular viewing conditions, as well as the likelihood of various alternative percepts. Bayesian approaches (outlined in the tutorials section of the previous chapter) have been particularly successful. Perceptual learning has also been shown to influence cue combination (Haijiang et al., 2006; Backus & Haijaing, 2007).

Visual art forms such as representational painting and 3-D imagery rely on our ability to tolerate conflicts between depth cues during cue combination. Paintings exploit most of the monocular cues. Renaissance artists used converging lines and texture gradients to convey the three-dimensional shape of classical buildings; landscape artists use interposition and atmospheric perspective to indicate distance and depth ordering (as evident in the photograph of Figure 11.3; T-junctions can be seen where the contours of more distant mountains are occluded by nearer mountains); portrait artists use shading (*chiaroscuro*) to model the subtle three-dimensional contours of the human face and body (Mather, 2014). But the depth depicted in such pictorial scenes is contradicted by accommodation, vergence, and disparity cues which all indicate a flat, close-range support surface. Despite the contradiction, viewers are able to enjoy the convincing depiction of three-dimensional space in pictorial art.

Stereo 3-D cinema and television add binocular disparity to the traditional array of pictorial cues, but convey contradictory cues from accommodation and vergence (which are dictated by the viewer's distance from the cinema screen). The yolking mentioned earlier between the neural systems that control accommodation, vergence, and disparity reinforces the conflict. Furthermore misalignment during filming or presentation can introduce artifacts such as spurious vertical disparities, and filmmakers often magnify disparity by using unnaturally large interocular separations (to make stereo effects more impressive). Consequently the disparity information presented in a 3-D movie will contradict the observer's angle of convergence. Again, despite the contradictions many people experience no problems when viewing 3-D displays, but some people find the conflicts unpleasant and tiring. The TV and cinema industry is aware of the problems caused by cue conflicts in 3-D imagery, but there are at present no widely agreed guidelines for dealing with them (Banks et al., 2012).

Neurons at later levels of analysis may integrate information from different cues (Tsutsui, Taira, & Sakata, 2005). A coherent theoretical basis for variation in cue weight is provided by Bayesian approaches to vision (discussed in detail in the tutorials section of Chapter 10). The basic idea is that cues which are highly reliable in a given context (in other words, show low variability) are assigned more weight than cues which are relatively unreliable. Even when different cues are not ordinarily correlated, there is recent evidence that the visual system can learn new associations between them (Haijiang et al., 2006; Backus & Haijiang, 2007). New cues may be recruited into perceptual judgments after they have been associated with long-trusted cues during perceptual learning.

CHAPTER SUMMARY

The computational goals of depth processing include:

* Establishing the depth order of the visible surfaces
* Estimating the depth intervals between surfaces
* Estimating the absolute distance of surfaces and objects from the viewer
* Deriving estimates of three-dimensional surface geometry and object shape.

THE MULTIPLICITY OF DEPTH CUES

* A wide range of cues can provide information for depth processing.
* Monocular cues include:
  - Interposition
  - Height in the visual field
  - Atmospheric perspective
  - Retinal image size
  - Texture gradient (height, width, and density)
  - Image blur
  - Accommodation (a nonvisual cue)
  - Motion parallax
  - Shadows.
* Binocular cues include:
  - Vergence (a nonvisual cue)
  - Binocular disparity.
* All cues have limitations that constrain their support for depth computations.

CUE COMBINATION

- Most cues provide quantitative information about depth, but vary in their relevance to different depth computations.
- So the visual system combines information from different cues in a complex, flexible, and idiosyncratic way.
- Research indicates that the visual system takes the weighted average of the estimates provided by different cues. Cue weight varies according to stimulus conditions, task, and observer.

TUTORIALS

THE GEOMETRICAL BASIS OF STEREOPSIS

Stereopsis is the visual sense of depth based on binocular vision. When the eyes are converged on a given point in space, F in the top of Figure 11.17, an image of that point is projected onto corresponding retinal landmarks in the two eyes, namely the fovea. If a second point is present, it will also create a pair of images, one in each eye. The cue for stereopsis is based on the

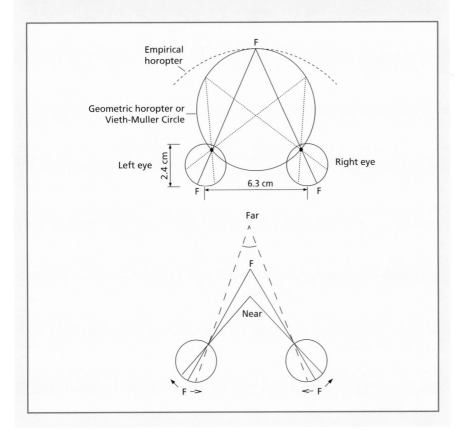

FIGURE 11.17
The geometrical basis of binocular disparity. Binocular fixation on point F produces images of F on the two foveas. Top: Corresponding retinal locations. The geometric horopter or Vieth–Muller circle is drawn through the set of points which project to geometrically corresponding retinal locations in the two eyes. Two such projected points are shown by dotted lines; their images are equally distant from the fovea in each eye. The empirically established horopter (dashed line; measured using judgments of visual direction) is actually slightly flatter than the geometric horopter. Bottom: Noncorresponding retinal locations. Points lying nearer or further away than the fixated point fall on noncorresponding retinal positions. For points lying directly in front of the observer, the images of a far point shift inwards or nasally in the two eyes (open arrows); the images of a nearer point shift outwards or temporally (filled arrows).

locations of these paired image points in the two eyes. If the pair of image points fall on corresponding positions (as in the top of Fig 11.17), then the second point is perceived to lie at the same depth as the fixated point F; if the paired images of the second point fall on noncorresponding, or disparate, retinal locations (as in the bottom of Fig 11.17) then that point is seen to lie at a different depth from the fixated point. The set of locations in space that project onto corresponding retinal positions is known as the horopter.

The Horopter

There are actually two ways to define the horopter, one based on geometry and the other based on empirical observation.

Geometric horopter

Geometric corresponding positions have the same retinal coordinates in the two eyes (in other words, they lie at the same retinal distance and in the same direction from the fovea in the two eyes). The geometric horopter is constructed by projecting rays out from pairs of retinal corresponding positions and finding where they intersect in space. Due to the way the eyes rotate in three dimensions to converge on specific fixation points, at any one eye position only a subset of the rays which could be drawn actually intersect. Essentially one can consider the horizontal geometric horopter to be a circle which passes through the fixation point and the nodal point of the two eyes, as shown in Figure 11.17, known as the Vieth–Muller circle.

Empirical horopter

Empirical corresponding retinal positions can be established by observation. At a given fixation position, the observer is presented with a stimulus element such as a point or line in one eye, and instructed to move another stimulus element presented to the other eye so that it appears to lie along the same direction in space as the first point. The empirical horopter is constructed from the intersection of rays projected out from pairs of empirical corresponding positions.

It is well established that the geometric and empirical horopters do not quite match. The empirical horopter is slightly flatter than the Vieth–Muller circle. Stereo vision is more precise near the empirical horopter, and it has been suggested that the shape of the empirical horopter optimizes visual performance for locations lying on the horizontal ground plane viewed at medium to far distances from a standing position (Schreiber et al., 2008).

Horizontal disparity

Figure 11.17 (bottom) shows two points which fall on noncorresponding retinal positions, one nearer than the fixated point (F) and one further away. The lack of correspondence in their image positions creates a binocular disparity. Two properties of binocular disparity are crucial for depth perception:

- The *sign* or direction of disparity depends on the sign of the depth difference between the fixated and nonfixated points. Notice in Figure 11.17 (bottom) that the images of the far point are displaced inward towards the nose (nasally) in each eye relative to the images of the fixated point (open arrows). The images of the near point are displaced outwards towards the temples (temporally) in each eye (filled arrows). Near disparities are also called crossed disparities, and far disparities are called uncrossed disparities. One way to remember this is to think of how vergence would change if you moved your eyes to the disparate point. To fixate on a more distant point you would have to uncross your eyes, while to fixate on a nearer point you would have to cross your eyes.
- The *magnitude* of the disparity depends on the magnitude of the depth difference between the fixated and nonfixated points. Imagine that the more distant point in Figure 11.17 (bottom) was positioned much further away than is shown here. Its image in each eye would swing around on the retina so that it was much further away from the image of the fixated point. Figure 11.14 earlier in the chapter shows how the magnitude of disparity varies with distance. Mathematically the magnitude of absolute binocular disparity actually corresponds to the difference in vergence angle between the fixated and nonfixated points.

Epipolarity

Figure 11.18 shows two eyes and a point (F) in the visual field. Each eye's nodal point is shown by the black dots (light rays pass through this point without being bent by the lens). A plane can be drawn so that it passes through point F and through the nodal point of each eye. This plane is called the epipolar plane (outlined with dashed lines in Figure 11.18). The projection of this plane on each eye's retina is a line, known as an epipolar line (blue lines in Figure 11.18). The images of point F in the left

FIGURE 11.18
Epipolar geometry. During binocular fixation on point F, a plane can be drawn so that it passes through point F and through the nodal point of each eye (epipolar plane). Light rays pass through the nodal point without changing direction. So the images of point F must lie somewhere along the lines where the epipolar plane intersects each retina (blue lines). This fact simplifies the solution to the correspondence problem, because it means that the search for correct matches can be restricted to epipolar lines.

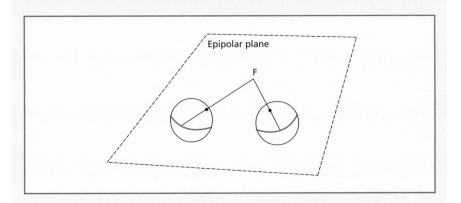

and right eyes must lie along these epipolar lines, a geometrical fact that is potentially very useful for solving the stereo correspondence problem. Recall from earlier in the chapter that in order to code depth from disparity accurately, the visual system must match a given image point in one eye with the image point in the other eye that arose from the same point out in the visual field. Epipolar geometry greatly simplifies the matching problem, because it means that searches for correspondence can disregard most of the image and be confined to epipolar lines. For a given image point in one eye, its correct partner in the other eye is guaranteed to lie along an epipolar line belonging to the same epipolar plane. The use of epipolar geometry in theories of stereo processing was discussed earlier in the chapter.

Stereograms and stereoscopes

Stereopsis is based on the slightly different images received by the two eyes when viewing a real three-dimensional scene. A number of techniques have been developed to create stereo images artificially. All involve a pair of images (**stereogram**) depicting the left- and right-eye views, that are usually delivered to the two eyes using an instrument called a *stereoscope*. Figure 11.19 shows a variety of stereograms.

Mirror stereoscope

Sir Charles Wheatstone (1802–1875) designed the first instrument, based on mirrors, which he called a stereoscope (published in 1838). Figure 11.20(a) illustrates its design. The left- and right-eye images (sometimes called half-images) are viewed through two mirrors. The angle of convergence of the eyes required to fuse the images into a single percept can be adjusted for accuracy.

Prism stereoscope

Sir David Brewster (1781–1868) studied Wheatstone's stereoscope and designed his own version of the instrument. In Brewster's stereoscope the half-images were placed side by side and viewed through lenses that created the angular convergence of the eyes and accommodation required to avoid the cue conflict described earlier in the chapter, in which convergence is not consistent with accommodation distance (Wade, 2012). Prism stereoscopes (shown in Figure 11.20(b)) aim to shift convergence so that it is more consistent with accommodation, while lenticular stereoscopes use lenses that shift accommodation distance rather than convergence angle. The glass in Brewster's device combined both of these techniques (Wade, 2012).

Wheatstone and Brewster entered into an acrimonious dispute about who first invented the stereoscope, but Wheatstone is now generally regarded as the creator of the first instrument (see Wade, 1983). Prism stereoscopes became a popular Victorian amusement, particularly after the enthusiasm shown by Queen Victoria at the Great Exhibition in 1851.

KEY TERM

Stereogram
An image designed to create an impression of depth when viewed binocularly; different parts of the image are seen by the two eyes.

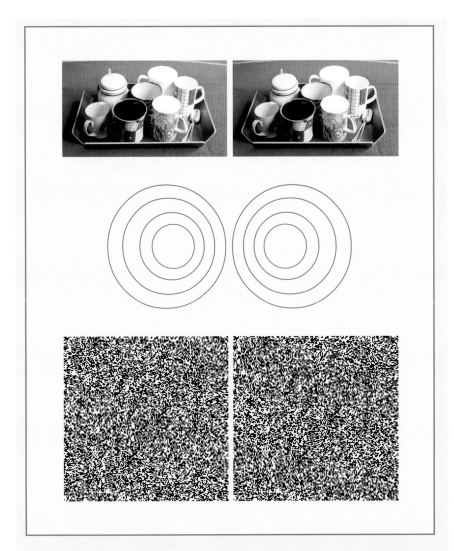

FIGURE 11.19
Examples of stereograms. When viewed through a stereoscope (shown in Figure 11.20) or with free fusion, a compelling impression of depth is perceived.

Anaglyphs

In this technique the left and right half-images are superimposed in a single image, but are printed or projected in different colors. For example, the left half-image may be rendered in red against a neutral light background, and the right half-image may be rendered in green against the same background. The observer views the stereogram through colored red and green filters (Figure 11.20(c)). If the left eye views the image through a green filter, the red parts of the image will not pass through the filter, so will appear dark. The green parts will be transmitted well, and will appear indistinguishable from the light background. In the right eye's view through the red filter, green parts of the image will appear dark and red parts will disappear into the background. The filters therefore deliver different images to the two eyes. This technique is simple and cheap, but suffers from cross-talk. Faint

FIGURE 11.20
A wide variety of methods have been devised for delivering stereo-pairs of images to the eyes.
(a) Mirror stereoscope;
(b) prism stereoscope;
(c) anaglyphs; (d) electro-optical shutters;
(e) free fusion;
(f) autostereograms.

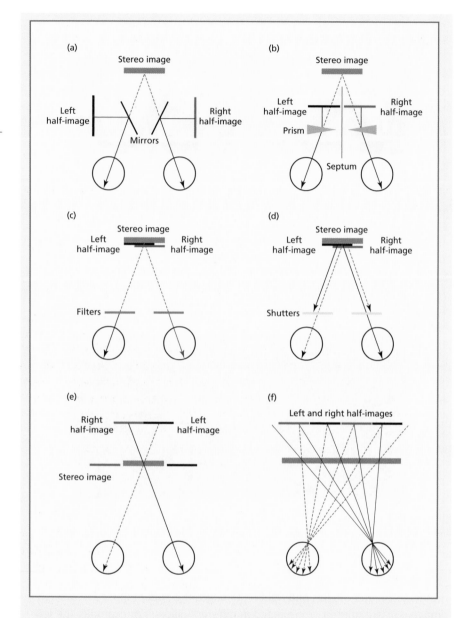

versions of one eye's image are often seen in the other eye, due to imperfect matching between the image colors and the filters. The color separation used in anaglyphs is a purely physical effect, and is not affected by any color deficiencies in the observer.

Modern 3-D movie theaters use a technique similar to the red–green anaglyph technique. As described in Chapter 6, light waves can be described as oscillating electrical and magnetic fields. Polarizing optical filters transmit light waves which oscillate only in a specific direction (such as up–down, or left–right). Most 3-D movies are transmitted as a series of frames which alternate rapidly between the left-eye view and the right-eye view (say, odd-numbered frames are intended for the left eye, and even-numbered frames are intended for the right eye) An optical polarizing filter placed in front of the cine-projector alternates between two different polarization planes in synchrony with the movie frame alternation. If the viewer wears spectacles in which two lenses also admit light polarized in the same two planes, then one eye will receive only the frames in one polarization plane and the other eye will receive only the frames in the alternate polarization plane.

Electro-optical shutters

In this modern computer-based technique, the left and right half-images are also presented in rapid alternation on a computer screen. The observer wears a pair of goggles containing electro-optical shutters. The shutters in the goggles allow the computer to occlude each eye's view completely and very rapidly (the goggles are connected to the computer via a lead or an infrared link). The computer is programmed to alternately occlude each eye's view in synchrony with the alternation between the images on the display, so that each eye only ever sees the appropriate stereo half-image. In Figure 11.20(d), the blue image is only seen by the left eye, and the black image is only seen by the right eye. If the alternation rate is sufficiently high, the observer sees apparently simultaneous and continuous images in the two eyes. Differences between the left and right half-images provide the usual stereoscopic depth cue. Modern electro-optical shutters can operate at very high alternation rates (exceeding 60 Hz), and are frequently used in research on stereopsis.

Free fusion

The simplest technique for delivering stereograms is to present the two eyes' images side by side and invite the observer to fuse them by freely crossing or uncrossing their eyes. As shown in Figure 11.20(e), if the eyes are crossed sufficiently, the two eyes' images superimpose to create a stereo image. The technique is difficult to master, partly because of the distraction of two unpaired half-images in the visual field (middle of Figure 11.20(e)), and partly because changes in vergence angle tend to produce concomitant changes in accommodation. A special kind of free fusion stereogram known as the *autostereogram* was developed by Tyler and Clarke (1990), and later inspired a large number of "magic eye" books and posters. The idea was to make free fusion easier by dividing the left and right half-images into thin vertical strips placed side by side (Figure 11.20(f)). Now the observer requires only a relatively small change in vergence to make each left-eye strip superimpose on the abutting right-eye strip, even when the stereo image is very wide. Left-eye views in Figure 11.20(f) are shown by blue dashed lines, and right-eye views are shown by continuous black lines (depth is actually created by varying the repetition width of the strips). Notice from the intersections of left- and right-eye sight lines that a given strip serves as the right-eye partner for the strip on its left, but the left-eye partner for the strip on its right. This results in the repetitive structure visible in *autostereograms*.

An abilty to free-fuse is very useful for viewing stereograms presented in books and journal articles. Although Figures 11.20(e) and 11.20(f) illustrate crossed free fusion, it is also possible to achieve uncrossed free fusion by uncrossing one's eyes (looking beyond the image) rather than crossing one's eyes to look in front of the image. Some observers prefer crossed free fusion, while others prefer uncrossed free fusion. As an aid to crossed free fusion it sometimes helps to fixate on an object such as a pencil held in front of the stereogram. If the object is moved back and forth while fixating on it, it should be possible to find a position at which the two halves of the stereogram superimpose to create a fused stereo image. As an aid to uncrossed free fusion, place a sheet of clear glass or rigid plastic on the stereogram, and view the reflection of a distant object in the surface of the glass. If an appropriate distance is selected, the two halves of the stereogram should fall into register to create a stereo image.

Stereograms often contain slight misalignments between the two eyes' views. One half-image may be vertically offset from the other or rotated slightly to introduce spurious binocular disparities. The visual system possesses self-correcting mechanisms which move the eyes to minimize such disparities. For example, rotation in one image can be corrected by rotating the eyes about the line of sight (cyclovergence, which normally occurs when we converge and look up or down at the same time). However such corrective movements can cause discomfort and fatigue (Banks et al., 2012).

Vertical disparity

This tutorial has concentrated on horizontal binocular disparity, but natural binocular images also contain vertical disparities, as described earlier in the chapter. Figures 11.12 and 11.13 show the left- and right-eye views of two vertical rectangles. Each eye has a slightly oblique view of each rectangle, which introduces vertical disparities between the eyes. Mayhew and Longuet-Higgins (1982) showed that the pattern of vertical disparity across the image depends on viewing distance. In the rectangles of Figure 11.12 and 11.13, for instance, vertical disparities increase progressively towards the edge of the scene. What Mayhew and Longuet-Higgins showed was that the rate of increase is determined by the absolute distance from which the rectangle is viewed.

Vertical disparities are therefore potentially very useful because they provide a visual measure of absolute viewing distance. Horizontal disparities reflect only relative distance, not absolute distance (see Figure 11.14). However, vertical disparities are actually very small, except at large retinal eccentricities, and there has been a long-running debate about whether and how the visual system makes use of them to estimate viewing distance (Rogers & Bradshaw, 1993; Banks et al., 2012; Duke & Howard, 2005).

Visual motion perception

12

Contents

INTRODUCTION

Movement of an object across your visual field, such as a person walking by, creates movement in the retinal image (provided that your eyes do not follow the moving person). Retinal movement carries a great deal of information, so even the simplest sighted animals have an ability to sense it. Information from retinal motion can be used for:

- *Figure–ground segregation* Shapes and objects that are camouflaged while static, and therefore invisible, can be segregated from their background as soon as they move on the basis of the relative motion. Prey animals such as small lizards and rodents move in short, rapid bursts of activity to minimize the time that they are visible to predators in this way.

- *Three-dimensional structure*   When any solid object moves, the retinal images of its various parts move relative to each other. For example, when you view a rotating globe, surface markings near the equator move across your field of view more rapidly than markings near the poles (see Figure 12.1). There is also highly structured variation in direction. The changes in speed and direction carry quite detailed information about the 3-D structure and distance of the shape, which is similar in certain respects to the depth information contained in static texture gradients (discussed in the previous chapters).
- *Social communication*   Movement is a significant component of human nonverbal communication in terms of gestures, dynamic facial expressions, and whole body movements. Lip movements are surprisingly important for verbal communication.
- *Visual guidance of action*   As we move about the world, image detail "flows" across the retina (see Chapter 11). The pattern of optic flow can be used to estimate the speed and direction of self-motion. For example, as you drive down a road, focusing on the horizon, image details from road markings, signposts, and pedestrians appear at the horizon and move through your field of view to create an expanding flow field. The rate of flow provides information on your speed, and the focus of expansion indicates your heading direction.

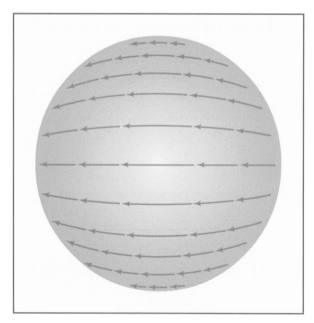

FIGURE 12.1
Arrows represent the speed and direction of surface markings on the sphere as it rotates. Markings near the poles move more slowly and follow a more curved path than those near the equator.

The importance of visual motion is dramatically illustrated by an unfortunate woman who lost the ability to sense motion following brain damage (Zihl, Von Cramon, & Mai, 1983). She had difficulty, for example, in pouring tea or coffee into a cup because the fluid appeared to be frozen, like a glacier. She found face-to-face conversations difficult because she could not see the movements of the speaker's face and mouth. Crowded rooms or streets made her feel unwell, because "people were suddenly here or there but I have not seen them moving." This problem was particularly acute when attempting to cross a road with moving traffic, although she had no difficulty in actually identifying the cars.

DETECTING MOVEMENT

Retinal motion detection requires some fairly sophisticated neural computations. Figure 12.2 illustrates why retinal motion detection is so difficult. The figure depicts the retinal image of a running figure seen in silhouette, at two slightly different times. The figure is darker than the background, so as it moves into previously empty retinal space the receptors in those regions will signal a decrease in retinal illumination; similarly receptors in regions vacated by the figure will signal an increase in retinal illumination as it returns to background level. The changes in illumination picked up by individual receptors tell us nothing about the movement of the figure. Movement in the opposite direction would also produce some increases and some decreases in illumination. Furthermore retinal illumination can change for

FIGURE 12.2
The left and middle images show the silhouette of a running figure at slightly different times. The right-hand image is a difference image, created by point-by-point subtraction of the light intensities in the first image from those in the second image. Increases in brightness from the left to the middle image appear as light areas in the difference image, decreases appear as dark areas, and unchanged areas appear as gray. Point-by-point intensity change cannot, by itself, specify movement direction.

a variety of other reasons; for example, a cloud may pass by, or the person may run through a shadow. The visual system uses a number of different computations to solve the problem of detecting the movement.

NEURAL MOTION DETECTORS

As an image moves across the retina a whole series of receptors will in turn register a transitory change in illumination. A simple neural circuit could detect retinal movement by comparing the change in response at any one receptor with the change in response at a neighboring receptor. Sequential activation of a series of receptors is a sure sign of retinal motion. A circuit for an elementary **motion detector** based on sequential activation is shown in the lower part of Figure 12.3. Two retinal receptor cells, A and B, transmit signals to a third comparator neuron, C. The comparator neuron performs motion detection as follows. The two receptors are positioned a short distance apart on the retina (Δs), and the transmission of the signal from receptor A to the comparator is slower than the transmission from B (by a time interval corresponding to Δt). The level of output at the comparator depends on the product of the signals arriving from A and B (in other words, their activities are multiplied together). So the comparator's output is very much higher when strong signals from the two receptors arrive together than when one or the other arrives alone. Motion-detecting circuits of the kind depicted in Figure 12.3 were first proposed in the late 1950s on the basis of observations of beetles and flies (Reichardt, 1961).

DIRECTION SELECTIVITY IN MOTION DETECTORS

We can examine the output of the comparator during the passage of the image of a car across the retina from left to right (see the right-hand side of Figure 12.3). At time 2 the car's image falls on receptor A, evoking a large response (10 units of activity) that begins traveling toward the comparator. The response will take one time interval to reach the comparator. By the next time interval (time 3) the image has reached the second receptor, B. Response at receptor A drops back to zero, but the high response at receptor B (10 units of activity) reaches the comparator immediately. Thus, at time 3 the two responses from A and B arrive together at the comparator, creating a very large response (100)—motion is detected.

Figure 12.4 shows the pattern of responses when the car moves in the opposite direction. In this case the two receptors' signals arrive at the comparator at different

KEY TERM

Motion detector
A neuron in the visual system that responds more strongly to retinal image motion in one direction than to motion in the opposite direction.

FIGURE 12.3
A simple neural circuit for detecting retinal motion from left to right. Numbers on the right refer to activity levels in the three cells A, B, and C. S and F refer to slow and fast transmission speed respectively. A detailed explanation can be found in the text.

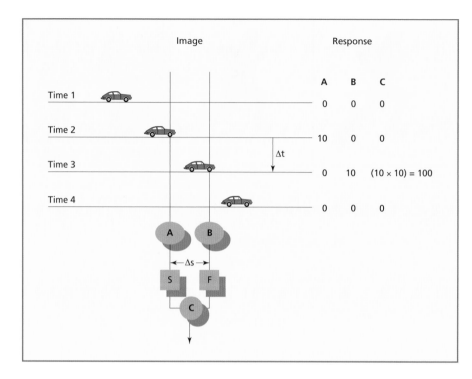

FIGURE 12.4
Response of the motion detector in Figure 12.3 to movement from right to left. The wiring of the circuit makes it selectively responsive to motion only in one direction.

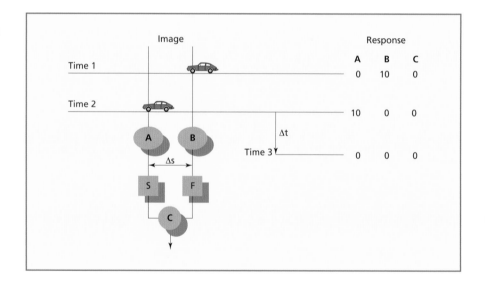

times. At time 1 receptor B's response travels immediately to the comparator C, provoking a low response. At time 2 the image of the car has passed on to receptor A. The resulting response does not arrive at the comparator until time 3, resulting in no response from the comparator. The neural circuit is thus selectively responsive to motion from left to right. A motion detector selectively responsive to motion from right to left can be made simply by rewiring the circuit so that the temporal delay is imposed on the line from receptor B to the comparator instead of on the line from receptor A.

ALIASING

Motion detectors of this kind are very sensitive to the properties of the motion stimulus. In particular, the velocity of the stimulus has to be such that the time taken for it to traverse the distance from A to B matches the difference in transmission speed in the two arms of the circuit. Only then will the signals from A and B arrive at C together, even for the preferred direction. If there is a mismatch because the stimulus moves too slowly or too rapidly, the detector may fail to signal motion at all—it is velocity sensitive. In certain conditions (e.g., if a succession of vehicles pass by at high speed) it may even respond to motion in the opposite direction, an effect known as "**aliasing**." An example is shown in Figure 12.5.

The motion detector is tuned to respond to rightward motion, as in Figures 12.3 and 12.4. Two vehicles pass the two receptors, moving rapidly from right to left. At time 1 the image of the first vehicle arrives at receptor A, having already passed receptor B. At time 2 the image of the second vehicle arrives at receptor B, and its response arrives at the comparator at the same time as the response from receptor A. As a result, the comparator erroneously signals the presence of rightward motion even though the vehicles are moving leftward.

The error arises because each receptor receives a rapid sequence of images as each vehicle passes, and responds to all of them. The comparator cannot pair up stimuli arriving at each receptor correctly. A simple way to avoid the confusion between different images would be to make each receptor selectively respond only to certain images. For example, if each receptor responded only to images having certain spatial structure (e.g., size, texture), or temporal structure (e.g., flicker rate) it is likely to respond only to the car, or only to the bus in the example.

As mentioned earlier, the detectors shown in Figure 12.3 are velocity sensitive. In order to deal with a range of image velocities, the visual system would require a population of detectors that vary in terms of the transmission speeds and/or spatial offsets built in to their circuits (for more details on velocity coding, see the tutorial at the end of the chapter).

? Why do spinning wheel spokes sometimes appear to rotate backwards in TV images?

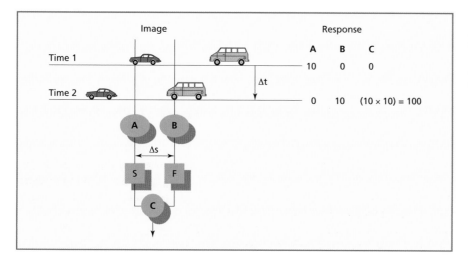

FIGURE 12.5
Aliasing. The motion detector is tuned to rightward motion, but in certain circumstances it also responds to leftward motion.

Adelson–Bergen or energy detector
A specific form of neural motion detector, which combines signals initiated at slightly different times from adjacent retinal locations.

Motion after-effect (MAE)
Following adaptation to movement in a given direction, a stationary pattern appears to move in the opposite direction.

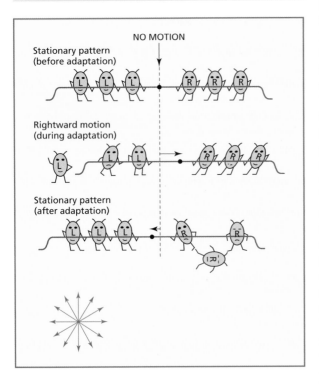

FIGURE 12.6
Explaining the motion after-effect. The classic opponent-process account assumes that the perceived direction of motion depends on a competition or tug-of-war between detectors selectively responsive to opposite motion directions. Adaptation reduces the responsiveness of one team, allowing the opposing team to signal motion even in the presence of a stationary pattern.

DIRECTION SELECTIVE CELLS IN PRIMATES

All the features of the motion-detecting circuit in Figure 12.3 are easy to implement in neural hardware. In insects, the inputs (A and B) correspond to photoreceptors in adjacent ommatidia of the compound eye, and are combined at the comparator by a multiplicative interaction (Reichardt, 1961). Similar circuits were found by Barlow and Hill (1963) in the retina of the rabbit. The primate visual system seems to possess neural motion detectors based on the same principles (Mikami, Newsome, & Wurtz, 1986), but located in the visual cortex. The most widely accepted theoretical model of these cortical motion detectors is known as the "**motion energy**" or "**Adelson–Bergen**" sensor (Adelson & Bergen, 1985): The inputs to the sensor (A and B) are not individual photoreceptors but intermediate neurons that collect information from a group of receptors, probably retinal ganglion cells (or cells in the LGN or cortex linked to ganglion cells; for example, cells with the receptive fields depicted in Figure 7.6). The fibers in the S branch of the circuit have more sluggish responses and lower conduction velocities than those in the F branch. Recall from Figure 7.18 that signals from parvo LGN cells arrive at the cortex slightly later than signals from magno cells, so this difference in transmission speed could be used in cortical motion-detecting circuits. The problem of aliasing depicted in Figure 12.5 can be avoided by making the spatial separation of the two input receptive fields small compared to the width of each field, and the temporal response of the circuit too sluggish to respond to problematic high velocities. Emerson, Bergen, and Adelson (1992) compared single-unit recordings from individual directionally selective cortical cells with responses predicted by the motion energy sensor, and found very good agreement.

PSYCHOPHYSICAL EVIDENCE FOR MOTION DETECTORS IN THE HUMAN VISUAL SYSTEM

The motion after-effect

Longstanding evidence for the existence of motion-detecting neurons in the human visual system comes from an illusion called the **motion after-effect (MAE)**, which was first reported by the ancient Greeks. After viewing a moving image such as a rapidly flowing stream for a short while (e.g., 60 seconds), subsequently viewed stationary images (such as the river bank) appear briefly to move in the opposite direction. The effect typically lasts about 15 seconds, but lengthy adaptation can produce effects that last many hours (reviews of the MAE can be found in Mather, Verstraten, & Anstis, 1998 and Mather et al., 2008). The MAE can be explained by adaptation in direction-selective neurons in the human visual system. Figure 12.6 illustrates the explanation in its simplest form.

The top of Figure 12.6 shows three neurons selective for leftward motion, and three selective for rightward motion. Perceived motion in the left–right dimension can be viewed as a tug-of-war between these two teams of cells. We see motion in the direction given by the team that wins the competition. In the presence of a stationary pattern there is only moderate activity (effort) from either team, so no motion is seen. During exposure to rightward motion (middle) the "right" team is highly active, but the "left" team is relatively weakly activated, so rightward motion is perceived. After a period of rightward adaptation and in the presence of a stationary pattern (bottom) the "right" team is fatigued, allowing the moderate activity of the "left" team to win the contest and signal leftward motion.

Figure 12.6 illustrates the classic opponent-process account of the MAE. A similar theory of opponent color coding was described in Chapter 8. It is important to appreciate that this account is too simple to offer a serious account of the MAE, because perceived direction of motion seems to involve a comparison of activity in cells tuned to a wide range of directions rather than just the opposites shown in Figure 12.6 (Mather's, 1980, "distribution-shift" account of the MAE; see also Snowden et al., 1991). One way to imagine this more complex explanation is in terms of many tug-of-war teams pulling on ropes joined together to create a radial pattern (inset of Figure 12.6). Each team pulls in its own direction, and the direction perceived is that given by the direction in which the center of the rope shifts relative to its neutral position. If one team is weakened by adaptation, then the center of rope will tend to move toward the opposite direction, if all other teams are equally active.

? *Compare the motion after-effect and its explanation with the tilt and size after-effects described in Chapter 9.*

Direction-specific threshold elevation

More evidence for motion detectors in the human visual system comes from another adaptation effect called **direction-specific threshold elevation**. Pantle and Sekuler (1968) measured the contrast threshold for detecting upward or downward moving bars, before and after observers were adapted to upward moving bars. Upward adaptation had no effect on observers' ability to detect downward bars, but elevated their threshold for detecting upward bars. In other words, adaptation made it harder to detect the presence of weak stimuli moving in the adapting direction. This effect is called *direction-specific threshold elevation*. It can be explained by changes in the responsiveness of direction-specific cells. Direct recordings from individual direction-selective neurons in cat and monkey cortex have confirmed that adaptation leads to a depression in responsiveness (Giaschi et al., 1993; Petersen, Baker, & Allman, 1985).

Motion adaptation effects show *interocular transfer*: an effect is still obtained when the subject views the adapting stimulus with one eye only, and is later tested using the other eye only (e.g., Moulden, 1980). Interocular transfer is clear evidence that the neurons involved in adaptation are located in the cortex, rather than earlier in the visual system, since only in the cortex are cells found that can be driven by stimulation from either eye. Neuroimaging studies of observers experiencing motion after-effects have found peaks of activity in an area of the human brain that is thought to be homologous to an area in monkey cortex that is known to be rich in motion-detecting cells (Tootell et al., 1995).

Motion-detecting receptive fields can be characterized in terms of their spatial frequency and temporal frequency tuning functions. See Chapter 9.

Compare random-dot kinematograms, and their theoretical significance, with random-dot stereograms described in Chapter 11

Random-dot kinematograms (RDKs)

Random-dot kinematograms (RDK) have been used in many psychophysical studies of motion detection. In a simple RDK two fields of randomly positioned black and white dots are presented sequentially at the same retinal location, separated in time by a brief interstimulus interval. The dots in the two frames are identical except that some or all of the dots in the second frame are shifted a certain distance relative to the first frame (see Figure 12.7). The observer's task is to report the direction of the shift. Using relatively small dots, direction can be reported reliably only for very short displacement distances (below approximately 0.25°) and interstimulus intervals or ISIs (below approximately 80 ms).

The two leftmost contour plots in Figure 12.8 show RDK direction discrimination data from Baker and Braddick (1985) for different combinations of displacement and ISI. RDK direction could be reported reliably (darkest regions) only for very short spatial intervals and temporal intervals. The upper

KEY TERM

Random-dot kinematogram (RDK)

A two-frame motion sequence containing pseudo-randomly arranged dots; some or all dots shift location in one frame relative to the other to offer a signal for motion detection.

FIGURE 12.7
A two-frame random-dot kinematogram. The arrangement of dots in the two frames is identical, except that all the dots in frame 2 are shifted leftward by two dot widths relative to frame 1 (indicated by the arrows identifying corresponding dots in the two frames). When presented as a two-frame animation, viewers perceive a leftward movement of the whole pattern.

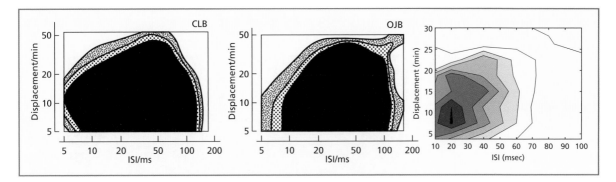

FIGURE 12.8
The left and middle panels show psychophysical data for two observers from Baker and Braddick (1985). The contour maps represent the percentage of correct motion direction judgments as function of RDK dot displacement and ISI. The right-hand panel shows the directional response of an Adelson-Bergen motion detector as a function of dot displacement and ISI. In all three plots darker areas correspond to better performance. Left and middle panels reproduced with permission from Pion Ltd, London www.pion.co.uk and www.perceptionweb.com.

spatial and temporal limits of motion detection using RDKs are thought to reflect the spatial and temporal tuning widths of the neural motion detectors described earlier (as originally suggested by Braddick, 1974). For example, if the two inputs to motion detectors in human visual system (A and B in Figure 12.3) are a short distance apart on the retina, then the system can only detect dot displacements over short distances; beyond a certain displacement in RDKs (known as Dmax) motion can no longer be detected reliably because the displacement exceeds the spacing of the receptor inputs. Figure 12.8 (right-hand graph) shows the computed output of a single motion energy sensor, for comparison against the psychophysical data (computations based on a computer implementation described at http://www.georgemather.com and reported in Challinor & Mather, 2010; darker areas indicate larger responses). The computed response of the detector is reliable only at short spatial and temporal intervals, consistent with Baker and Braddick's (1985) psychophysical data. The output of the model is also consistent with a number of other motion illusions (Adelson & Bergen, 1985; Challinor & Mather, 2010).

So the results of studies in human psychophysics, single-unit recording, and computational modeling have converged on the motion energy sensor as the most plausible model for motion-detecting neurons in the primate visual system. Many researchers use software implementations of Adelson and Bergen's detector model to explore the properties of low-level detectors, and compare their performance against the visual system's performance. The tutorials section at the end of the chapter introduces the conceptual framework which underpins the model, and computer code to implement it (in Matlab ©) can be downloaded from http://www.georgemather.com.

VARIETIES OF MOTION DETECTOR

All the motion displays described so far contain shapes that are defined by a difference in luminance, such as light bars, blocks, or spots against a dark background. Cavanagh and Mather (1989) called such displays **first-order**, because the moving shape is defined by a difference between the intensity values of individual image points inside the shape (e.g., light) and image points outside the shape (e.g., dark). Many experiments have employed displays in which the moving shape has no consistent point-by-point differences against the background, but differs instead in textural properties. Two examples are shown in Figure 12.9. In the upper two-frame stimulus, the dots in each frame have completely different spatial arrangements, but in both frames a central square region is distinguishable from the background. In the central square

KEY TERM

First-order motion display
A motion stimulus containing shapes defined by variations in luminance.

FIGURE 12.9
Two kinds of second-order motion stimulus. Top: A square shape defined by a difference in second-order texture shifts position from frame 1 to frame 2. Bottom: Traveling contrast reversal. In frame 2, the leftmost column of dots from frame 1 reverses in contrast; in frame 3 the second-left column from frame 2 reverses in contrast; in frame 4 the third-left column from frame 3 reverses in contrast; and so on.

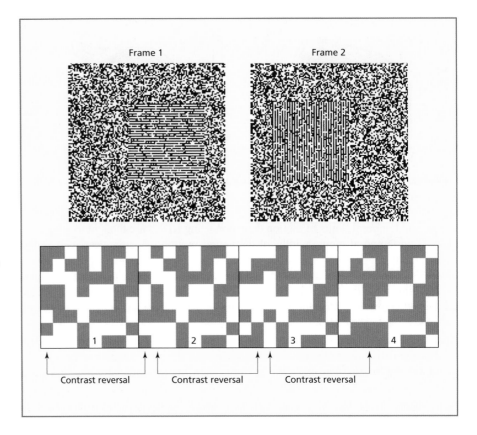

region of the first frame the dots tend to occur in horizontal runs. In the central region of the second frame, the dots tend to occur in vertical runs. Background dots are completely different (uncorrelated) across the two frames. The location of the square is shifted in one frame relative to the other to create a stimulus for apparent motion.

Notice that the central square of each frame at the top of Figure 12.9 contains the same black and white pixels as the background, but their pairwise arrangement is different. In the center of the first frame, for example, horizontally separated pairs of points are more likely to have the same intensity than pairs of points at other orientations. In the surrounding dots, the probability that any pair of points has the same intensity is the same at all orientations. Thus, the difference between the center and surround is defined by the properties of pairs of points, rather than the properties of single points. Cavanagh and Mather (1989) called such displays **second-order displays**. The lower stimulus in Figure 12.9 consists of four frames from a motion stimulus containing a field of random light and dark dots. From frame to frame, a single vertical column of dots (arrowed) reverses contrast (dark dots become light, and vice versa). The column selected for reversal advances across the pattern with each frame to create a stimulus for apparent motion. In this case the moving shape is defined by the properties of pairs of points separated in time rather than in space. Outside the column, luminance contrast does not change from frame to frame. Inside the column, contrast reverses from frame to frame.

Observers readily perceive apparent motion in second-order displays similar to those in Figure 12.9 (e.g., Ramachandran, Rao, & Vidyasagar, 1973; Lelkens & Koenderink, 1984; Chubb & Sperling, 1988). Yet neural motion detectors of the kind

KEY TERM

Second-order motion display
A motion stimulus containing shapes defined by variations in texture, with no corresponding variation in luminance.

described earlier, which respond to contours defined by intensity differences, would not be activated by second-order displays. The borders defining the moving shape in second-order displays are not defined by intensity differences but by textural differences. For example, there is no difference in intensity across the border of the square in the upper display in Figure 12.9, because there is an equal number of light and dark dots on each side of the border. The distribution of the dots (i.e., texture) varies across the border, but the dots themselves are uncorrelated.

One way to explain the apparent motion seen in second-order displays is to propose that motion detectors can be subdivided into two classes. One class encodes the motion of first-order patterns, and the other class encodes the motion of second-order patterns. Evidence consistent with the presence of second-order motion detectors includes the following:

- *Physiology* Several studies have reported that visual cells in cat and monkey cortex can respond to second-order motion. O'Keefe and Movshon (1998) compared responses to first-order motion (drifting intensity gratings) and to second-order motion (similar to the lower display in Figure 12.9). All cells responded to first-order motion; 25% of cells studied in area MT, and 9% of cells studied in V1 also responded to second-order motion. Albright (1992) reported a much higher proportion of MT cells (87%) responding to second-order motion. Second-order responses were usually weaker than first-order responses.
- *Neuroimaging* Ashida et al. (2007) used an fMRI adaptation technique to investigate order specificity. Successive presentation of two stimuli causes a reduction of the BOLD response in cortical regions containing cells responsive to both of them, but little or no reduction in regions containing cells activated by only one or the other. Ashida et al. (2007) found independent direction-specific adaptation to first-order and second-order motion in human MT.
- *Psychophysics* Ledgeway and Smith (1997) and Nishida and Sato (1995) reported adaptation to the motion of second-order patterns, and as you have seen in earlier chapters adaptation is a strong indicator of stimulus-tuned detectors. Apparent motion is seen in second-order RDKs, and is limited in the same way that first-order motion is (Mather & West, 1993).

The general consensus from these studies is that the visual system possesses two populations of neural motion detector (e.g., Nishida, Ledgeway, & Edwards, 1997; Sperling & Lu, 1998). One population contains first-order detectors, and corresponds to the motion energy sensors described earlier in the chapter. The other population contains detectors that respond to second-order motion. Sensitivity to second-order motion requires special texture coding processes prior to the motion detection circuit outlined earlier. The filter–rectify–filter or FRF scheme discussed in Chapter 9 offers a mechanism for detecting texture-defined borders.

Although the psychophysical evidence has been interpreted in terms of separate populations of first-order and second-order detectors, there are some puzzling details in the experimental data. The transfer of perceptual effects between first-order and second-order patterns is asymmetrical, with better transfer from first-order to second-order than from second- to first-order patterns (Schofield, Ledgeway, & Hutchinson, 2007; Petrov & Hayes, 2010). Also single-unit studies have not found evidence for cells that respond only to second-order stimuli. These results hint at partial overlap between the two populations, with some cells responding only to first-order patterns, and others responding to both kinds of pattern. Recent single-unit recording studies have identified a possible neural substrate for second-order responses, which may help to solve these puzzles (Tanaka & Ohzawa, 2009; Hallum & Movshon, 2014). As described in Chapter 7, many (though not all) neurons in V1 and V2 show surround suppression: The response to a preferred stimulus presented in the cell's classical receptive field is suppressed when stimuli are present in the surrounding extra-classical receptive field. Recordings have shown that cells without suppressive surrounds respond only to first-order patterns, but cells with suppressive surrounds respond both to first-order patterns and second-order patterns (provided that the stimulus matches the classical receptive field's tuning). One suggestion is that the latter cells do "double-duty" as detectors of both first-order and second-order contrast variation, so there are partially overlapping populations of neurons that deal with first-order and second-order patterns (Hallum & Movshon, 2014); some cells only respond to first-order stimuli (they do not have surround suppression), while others are able to respond to second-order patterns as well (they do have a suppressive surround).

INTEGRATING DETECTOR RESPONSES

Each neural motion detector can only respond to motion in a very small portion of the image, namely the area covered by its receptive field. In order to encode the motion of large, complex shapes and objects (e.g., moving cars, tumbling boulders, running animals, fluttering flags), the local detector responses have to be combined or integrated in some way. Available evidence points toward a number of different motion integration processes operating both in parallel and sequentially to solve specific problems of motion interpretation. One such process is located very early in the processing hierarchy, and operates directly on the outputs of motion detectors.

Figure 12.10(a) shows a rigid geometrical shape in two successive positions as it drifts horizontally across the visual field (central arrow). Local motion direction and speed vary around the shape, as shown by the arrows along each edge, demonstrating the need for integration in order to encode object motion; none of the local edge movements correspond to the global movement of the shape. The circles in Figure 12.10(b) represent the receptive fields of neural motion detectors in cortical area V1 which are maximally stimulated by each side of the shape (directions indicated by the arrows). Although the shape is moving horizontally, none of the local signals is actually in the horizontal direction. In fact each local motion signal is perpendicular to local contour orientation. The problem caused by the limited receptive field size of motion detectors is usually called the **aperture problem**. The visual system must somehow solve it and so unite the differing local signals to extract the horizontal movement of the shape.

? Motion integration theories exemplify the principle of population coding introduced in the first chapter.

KEY TERMS

Aperture problem
The ambiguity present in the response of an individual motion detector, caused by the limited spatial extent of its receptive field; true stimulus direction cannot be determined uniquely.

Velocity space
A graph in which arrows or vectors represent motion signals; the length of each vector specifies the speed of a signal, and angle specifies direction.

The velocity space model

The **velocity space** model of motion integration (also known as the *intersection-of-constraints* model; Adelson & Movshon, 1982; Simoncelli & Heeger, 1998) provides a mechanism for combining local detector responses to encode the motion of rigid shapes. In the model, neurons in visual area MT receive inputs from a range of neural detectors in area V1, as shown

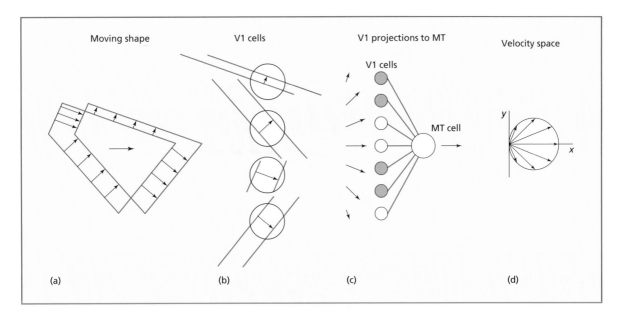

Moving shape | V1 cells | V1 projections to MT | Velocity space

(a)   (b)   (c)   (d)

in Figure 12.10(c). In the illustration a group of V1 detectors all project to a cell in MT which signals horizontal movement. Arrows represent their preferred direction and speed. With inputs from this particular set of V1 detectors, the MT cell will respond to rigid shapes moving horizontally rightward. A subset of the V1 cells is activated by the geometrical shape in Figure 12.10(a) (shaded cells in Figure 12.10(c)), resulting in a response from the MT cell.

To understand the logic behind this scheme, we need to plot the local signals in a velocity space diagram (see Figure 12.10(d)), which represents each detector's motion signal by an arrow (also called a vector). The angle of each arrow represents the direction of that signal, and the length of the arrow represents its speed. In Figure 12.10(a) and 12.10(b), notice that the speed associated with each signal depends on the angle between that signal and the motion of the shape. Signals in directions very close to the motion direction of the shape are relatively fast (long vectors). Signals in directions nearly at right-angles to the shape motion are relatively slow (short vectors). If vectors in different directions are plotted in a velocity space diagram, as in Figure 12.10(d), it becomes apparent that their end points lie around the circumference of a circle (assuming rigid motion). The circle passes through the origin (corresponding to zero velocity in a direction that is exactly perpendicular to the object motion) and through the point corresponding to the actual velocity of the object (maximum velocity in the direction of the object). If an integrative neuron is wired such that it receives inputs from a group of motion detectors having preferred directions and speeds that fall on this circle, as in Figure 12.10(c), then the neuron will encode horizontal motion of any rigid shape. Other directions of object motion can be encoded by integrator neurons that combine responses from other subsets of motion detectors.

Plaid patterns

There is a good deal of psychophysical and physiological evidence that motion integration does involve a velocity space computation. Much of this evidence has come from studies of **plaid** stimuli, made by superimposing two gratings drifting in different directions (see Figure 12.11). Adelson and Movshon (1982) found that

FIGURE 12.10
Integration of motion detector outputs. (a) A rigid shape moving rightward; (b) local responses from motion-sensitive neurons in V1; (c) connections to a motion-sensitive cell in MT that responds to global motion. Shaded cells are those activated by the shape; (d) "velocity space" representation of the local motion components in a horizontally moving shape.

FIGURE 12.11
A "plaid" pattern made by superimposing two drifting sine wave patterns. Although each sine wave alone drifts down to the right (arrows), the plaid pattern appears to drift horizontally. The velocity space representation (bottom) can explain this effect.

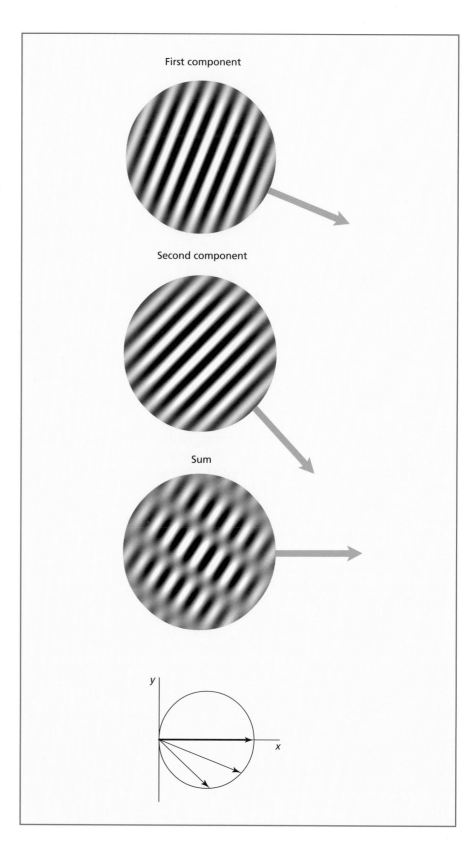

the two gratings often appear to lock together, moving as a single plaid pattern. The apparent direction of the plaid agreed with the direction predicted by the velocity space model of integration (bold arrow in the plot at the bottom of Figure 12.11). Single-unit recording data are also consistent with the model (e.g., Rust et al., 2006; Majaj, Carandini, & Movshon, 2007). However other evidence is not consistent.

Complex visual patterns tend to contain distinctive features such as line and edge terminations, corners and contour intersections. When the pattern moves, these features may not move in the same direction as that indicated by the velocity space computation, yet MT cells do seem to respond to the motion of feature terminators (Pack and Born, 2001; Pack, Gartland, & Born, 2004). Furthermore some psychophysical studies report that in certain conditions apparent plaid direction is intermediate between the predictions of the velocity space model and the motion of contour intersections (Yo & Wilson, 1992; Bowns, 1996), which has led some to propose that a process which tracks the movement of features in plaids also contributes to their apparent direction (for example, Wilson & Kim, 1994; Bowns, 2001; Bowns & Alais, 2006).

FEATURE TRACKING IN MOTION PERCEPTION

Although there is plentiful evidence that early visual areas contain motion selective neurons, as indicated in the previous paragraph many researchers argue that we can also detect motion independently of activity in neural detectors, by means of higher level processes that track visual features. A number of papers have reported motion perception effects that are very difficult to explain using neural detectors, of either the first- or second-order variety, but are consistent with feature tracking. Seiffert and Cavanagh (1998), for example, studied the perception of motion in two different kinds of slowly moving grating pattern. They found that observers' ability to detect the motion of luminance-defined (first-order) gratings depended on velocity, whereas their ability to detect the motion of various texture-defined (second-order) gratings depended on displacement distance. Seiffert and Cavanagh argued that velocity dependence is a property of motion detectors (as discussed at the beginning of the chapter), but position dependence reflects the operation of a feature-tracking mechanism. They concluded that, at least under the conditions they used, motion perception in the two kinds of pattern was mediated by qualitatively different processes: Neural detectors and **feature tracking**.

Several other studies adopted a different approach; rather than equating different kinds of stimuli with different kinds of process, they associated different perceptions of the same stimulus with the operation of different processes. Changes in apparent motion with changes in interstimulus interval, retinal location, pattern density luminance, or contrast were attributed to a shift from a system based on detectors to one based on feature tracking. The authors argue that the change in stimulus parameters took the pattern out of the range of one process and into the range of the other (Boulton & Baker, 1993; Smith, 1994; Sperling & Lu, 1998; Bex & Baker, 1999; Ukkonen & Derrington, 2000; Takeuchi & De Valois, 2009). These papers present a convincing case for a motion process based on feature tracking, in addition to one based on neural motion sensors. The feature-tracking process is likely to be part of a general-purpose attentional system rather than a specialized motion process, and may involve a network of neurons in the parietal and frontal cortices (Culham et al.,

1998): People with damage to the parietal cortex have deficits both in attention tasks and in high-level motion tasks, but not in low-level motion tasks (Battelli et al., 2001). Attentive tracking of stimulus motion is also discussed in Chapter 14.

The initial stages of motion analysis in the visual system thus seem to involve both neural motion sensors and feature-tracking mechanisms, which are likely to operate in tandem rather than in competition (Smith & Ledgeway, 2001), making for robust and reliable performance.

SPEED ESTIMATION

Perhaps surprisingly, it is still unclear how the visual system estimates the speed of moving stimuli. Most direction-selective neurons in primate cortical areas V1 and MT show some tuning for speed, though their response also varies with stimulus contrast (Priebe, Lisberger, & Movshon, 2006). Psychophysical adaptation studies also show that the human visual system has speed-tuned channels: Exposure to a high-speed stimulus reduces the apparent speed of all subsequent test stimuli, while exposure to a low-speed stimulus reduces the apparent speed of slow stimuli and raises the apparent speed of fast stimuli (Hammett et al., 2005). Other studies show that stimulus luminance and contrast can influence apparent speed (Hammett et al., 2007). Research on the MAE has found evidence for some speed tuning: After-effect duration depends jointly on adapting speed and test temporal frequency (Alais, Verstraten, & Burr, 2005).

The complex results of experiments on speed perception are open to different interpretations, so researchers have not been able to reach agreement on a theoretical model. Hammett et al. (2005) and Alais, Verstraten, and Burr (2005) proposed a relatively simple "ratio" model of speed estimation, in which apparent speed is given by the ratio of the outputs of two channels, one sensitive to slow flicker rates (low temporal frequencies) and the other sensitive to fast flicker rates (high temporal frequencies). Van Boxtel et al. (2006), on the other hand, advocate a more complex population-coding model with many more speed channels than two, which they claim is more consistent with neural tuning in MT. Others take a third approach based on Bayesian coding (Weiss, Simoncelli, & Adelson, 2002), in which the visual system has a bias (Bayesian prior) toward slow speeds. The debate about models is not resolved (see Hammett et al., 2007).

MOTION STREAKS

Motion processing is generally viewed as a prime function of the dorsal processing stream (see Chapter 7), separate from the form processing which occurs in the ventral stream. However several lines of research in recent years show that motion detectors in the ventral stream make use of the form information provided by motion streaks in order to encode direction (see Mather et al., 2013).

Due to the extended temporal response of the visual system (see Figure 7.4), briefly presented images remain visible for about one tenth of a second (e.g., Hogben & DiLollo, 1974). Fast-moving spots of light thus appear as streaks rather than as points (causing the attractive patterns seen in firework displays). As an example, a point moving at a moderate speed of 4 deg/sec across your field of view could produce a visible streak 0.4 degrees long, trailing behind it. The streak is necessarily aligned with axis of the point's motion, and thus offers information about its direction of travel. The orientation of the streak should be detectable by orientation-selective cells in the visual cortex, and several psychophysical studies provide evidence that orientation information does influence motion perception (Geisler, 1999; Burr & Ross, 2002). Geisler (1999) proposed that the outputs of motion-selective cortical neurons are combined with those of orientation-selective neurons to create "spatial motion-direction" sensors jointly tuned to motion direction and streak orientation. Motion detection threshold data are consistent with the proposal: masking patterns oriented parallel to the direction of a moving stimulus interfere with its detection more than patterns oriented at right-angles to the direction (Geisler, 1999; Burr & Ross, 2002). MAEs are also stronger when the adapting pattern contains stationary stripes parallel to the adapting direction rather than at right-angles to it (Mather et al., 2012).

So evidence from motion streaks (as well as from feature tracking in plaid patterns and other stimuli, described earlier) shows that motion and form information is tightly integrated in the visual cortex, rather than segregated as implied by the dorsal/ventral distinction.

INTERPRETING MOTION

Motion detection and integration constitute only the initial stages in a complex processing system which uses this information to draw inferences about self-motion, scene layout, object shape, and social intention.

DISTINGUISHING BETWEEN OBJECT AND SELF-MOVEMENT

Retinal motion can arise either from movement of an object in the world, or from movement of the observer's eyes or body (in the absence of object motion), or from a combination of both. It is obviously vital to make accurate attributions as to the source of retinal motion signals. The central nervous system has special-purpose processes which take account of retinal signals due to eye or body movements.

If you are at a roadside, glancing around at objects in the scene, your eyes will make rapid *saccadic eye movements* (see Table 6.2) which generate very high velocity retinal motion signals. The images of parked vehicles, for example, will move rapidly across your retina (lower half of Figure 12.12). If a moving vehicle passes through the scene and you keep your eyes still, the image of the moving vehicle will drift across your retina (top of Figure 12.12). If you visually track the vehicle as it passes by, your eyes will make smooth pursuit movements; the image of the moving vehicle will be stationary on the retina, but fixed elements in the scene (lampposts, parked vehicles, and so on) will drift across the retina in the opposite direction to the vehicle's motion. In order to cross the road safely you must correctly distinguish between retinal motion signals arising from moving objects in

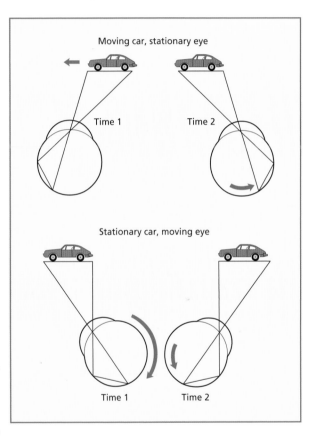

FIGURE 12.12
Two sources of retinal image motion. Object movement with a stationary eye (top): As a moving vehicle passes by a stationary eye, the image of the vehicle slides across the retina. Observer movement with a stationary object (bottom): As a moving eye passes by a stationary vehicle, the image of the vehicle again slides across the retina.

the scene and those arising from your own bodily movements. Separate processes deal with smooth pursuit eye movements and saccadic eye movements.

Dealing with pursuit eye movements

Komatsu and Wurtz (1988) found direction-selective neurons in macaque area MST which fired during smooth pursuit of a moving target in a dark room, and seemed to be driven by nonvisual signals; the cells continued to fire while the moving stimulus had disappeared from view. Two potential sources of nonvisual signals are (i) commands to move the eyes ("outflow") and (ii) feedback from stretch receptors in extraocular muscles which carry out the movements ("inflow"). The results of other studies indicate that MST cells are driven by outflow signals. For example, Ono and Mustari (2006) trained monkeys to track a moving visual target either while sitting still (and making volitional eye movements), or while being bodily rotated in a chair (and making involuntary vestibulo-ocular eye movements; see Table 6.2). The experimenters were careful to match the two conditions in terms of the retinal motion signals the monkey received, so that they differed only in the source of the eye movement signals (either voluntary or reflexive). MST cells responded only when the retinal motion was due to volitional movements. Other observations are consistent with the idea that volitional eye movement commands are used to cancel out retinal motion signals and thus avoid perception of movement. If you gently displace a stationary eye with your finger, introducing passively generated retinal motion, the world appears to move (Bridgeman & Delgado, 1984). Intrepid experimenters who administered a muscle relaxant (curare) to temporarily paralyze their own eye muscles reported that the world appeared to move whenever they tried (unsuccessfully) to move their eyes. The eye movement commands apparently canceled out nonexistent retinal motion, and so introduced spurious motion signals (Stevens et al., 1976). A more recent MAE study showed that these eye movement commands are adaptable (Freeman, Sumnall, & Snowden, 2003).

Haarmeier et al. (1997) described a clinical case history which confirms the importance of eye movement signals for the correct attribution of retinal motion due to smooth pursuit. R.W. was a 35-year-old male who was admitted to hospital presenting with symptoms of vertigo and nausea whenever he tracked moving objects. Psychophysical tests showed that R.W. was incapable of canceling out retinal motion signals caused by smooth pursuit eye movements, so he perceived movement in stationary scenes whenever he made smooth pursuit movements. Neuroimaging of his brain located a lesion in the human homologue of macaque area MST, the same area where Komatsu and Wurtz (1988) had found cells that fired during volitional eye movements.

Dealing with saccadic eye movements

Although the visual system should be responsive to the retinal movements created by saccades, we do not experience any visual motion while making saccades. Vision is blocked by two mechanisms (Wurtz, 2008). First, visual responses are suppressed by outflow commands. Psychophysical evidence for this suppression process comes from Kennard et al.'s (1970) report that after-images (imprints left by bright flashes of light) are not visible during saccades. Physiologically the suppression appears to be most marked in areas MT and MST (Ibbotson et al., 2007). Burr, Morgan, and Morrone (1999) argue that this saccadic suppression is driven by the responses of neurons at the lowest levels of the visual pathway, prior to the construction of motion-detecting receptive fields. The second mechanism for blocking vision during saccades involves masking (which was discussed in the context of audition in Chapter 5): The blurred image that would otherwise be visible during a saccade appears to be masked by the higher contrast images that precede and succeed the saccade (Campbell & Wurtz, 1978).

Dealing with self-motion

Self-generated actions such as walking and running create optic flow, a complex highly structured pattern of retinal motion which contains very useful information about the structure of the immediate environment and about the observer's movement through it (their heading and speed). The optic flow patterns created by self-motion can be decomposed mathematically into two components (e.g., Koenderink and van Doorn, 1976; Longuet-Higgins and Prazdny, 1980; see also Chapter 3):

* *Translation* of the eye forwards along a straight line path creates an expanding pattern of retinal motion, in which the focus of expansion corresponds to the heading direction.
* *Rotation* of the eye about an external center of rotation produces an internal complex pattern of retinal motion which may not have a focus of expansion.

The relative contributions of the two components depend on the particular movements executed. For example if you are traveling forward in a road vehicle while fixating on a point on one side, such as a traffic sign on the roadside, your self-motion involves a combination of forward translation and eye/head rotation. The resulting retinal flow pattern contains corresponding components of expansion and rotation which the visual system needs to disentangle in order to estimate your forward speed and heading direction.

Psychophysical and physiological data is consistent with the view that the visual system senses optic flow and does actually decompose it into its component movements and uses this information for navigation (e.g., Tanaka, Fukada, & Saito, 1989; Orban et al., 1992; Graziano, Andersen, & Snowden, 1994; Bex, Metha, & Makous, 1999; Meese & Harris, 2001). Bex et al. (1999) compared MAE magnitudes from adaptation to patterns which were closely matched for local motion but contained a global pattern of either radial, rotational, or simple translational motion. They found that the more complex movement patterns (radial or rotational motion) generated stronger MAEs, which they explained by proposing high-level motion selective mechanisms tuned to global optic flow patterns. Meese and Harris (2001) measured psychophysical sensitivity to large-scale rotation and/or expansion and found little or no interaction between the stimulus components, indicating that these motion components were processed by independent mechanisms. Physiological studies have found neurons in dorsal MST with very large receptive fields that seem to decompose optic flow into its components (Tanaka, Fukada, & Saito, 1989). Some neurons respond selectively to large-scale rotation while others respond to radial motion. These large MST receptive fields could be formed by converging inputs from neurons in MT with smaller receptive fields, each signaling local linear movement, laid out to create the appropriate flow pattern.

THREE-DIMENSIONAL STRUCTURE FROM MOTION

When you view a three-dimensional object, its different parts will be distributed at different distances from you (and some parts may be hidden from view by other parts). As a result, when the object moves the images of its parts will move relative to each other on your retina. In the rotating sphere described at the start of the chapter (Figure 12.1), points near the equator move across the field of view faster than points near the poles, and the latter follow curved paths while the former follow straight paths. Observers readily perceive coherent three-dimensional structure from this kind of motion stimulus. The percept is called "**kinetic depth.**" A sphere that is completely transparent and invisible except for many dots of light randomly scattered on its surface appears to be a flat, unstructured cloud of dots when stationary. When it moves its 3-D structure becomes clear despite the absence of shape cues. This shows that movement alone is sufficient to convey the 3-D structure of the object. Theories to explain kinetic depth fall into two categories: Position-based theories and velocity-based theories.

In principle it would be possible to infer the three-dimensional shape of a moving object from knowledge of the positions of a small number of points on its surface at different time instants. Ullman's (1984b) incremental-rigidity algorithm is an example of a process based on this principle. It was developed from his earlier (Ullman, 1979) proof that 3-D structure can be inferred from the positions of at least four points on the object at three different times. Alternatively, 3-D structure can be inferred from the retinal velocities of points in the image, rather than from their positions (Hildreth et al., 1995). The position-based and velocity-based theories of structure-from-motion map onto the feature-tracking and motion-detecting neural processes described in previous sections.

Psychophysical evidence on kinetic depth perception favors velocity-based theories rather than position-based theories. Several studies have used displays containing elements with very short lifetimes (e.g., Todd et al., 1988; Dosher, Landy, & Sperling, 1989; Mather, 1989; Dick, Ullman, & Sagi, 1991). In some studies the whole display was presented for a very short time. In other studies the display lasted much longer, but each dot in the display appeared only for a brief time before being replaced by a new dot elsewhere in the display. Subjects could perceive complex 3-D surfaces even in displays where each dot lasted only two frames, but only over temporal intervals below 80–100 ms and displacement distances of below 15′ arc. These limits are comparable to those found for the perception of simple apparent motion stimuli, as described earlier, which are consistent with neural motion detector properties (see Newsome et al., 1986). Andersen and Bradley (1998) argue that neurons in cortical area MT, and perhaps MST, are responsible for the computation of 3-D structure from the 2-D motion signals provided by V1 neurons. Neuroimaging research has implicated area V3 in the dorsal stream in the processing of 3-D structure from motion (Paradis et al., 2000).

SOCIAL INTENT AND AGENCY

Biological motion

Johansson (1973) created "point-light" displays of human actions by filming actors wearing patches of retroreflective material on their joints (shoulders, elbows, wrists, hips, knees, and ankles), in lighting conditions that ensured that only the patches were visible against a dark background (see Figure 12.13). When the displays were shown to naive observers, they spontaneously reported the perception of moving human figures. This effect has been replicated many times, and is also known as **biological motion**. An algorithm introduced by Cutting (1978) has also allowed researchers to create computer-generated point-light displays, which have been used in many experiments (e.g., Mather, Radford, & West, 1992; Neri, Morrone, & Burr, 1998). More recently, sophisticated 3-D motion capture technologies developed in the computer gaming and movie industries have been co-opted by researchers to create point-light displays from real human movements, recreating Johansson's original displays and many more (see Troje, 2002).

Observers can discriminate the actor's gender, mood, intention, skill, action type, and even identity from the pattern of dot movements in point-light biological motion displays (see a review in Blake & Shiffrar, 2007). Theories to explain the remarkable effectiveness of point-light biological motion displays have debated the relative importance of motion and form information. Some researchers have argued that the displays are processed by the motion analyzing dorsal stream. Motion signals certainly do seem to be important because spatiotemporal parameters which are critical for motion detectors are also important for the perception of biological motion displays (display duration, dot displacement distance, interframe interval; Johansson, 1976; Mather, Radford, & West, 1992; Thornton, 1998). It has also been proposed that the characteristic patterns of motion created by moving limbs stimulate a mechanism that selectively detects articulated terrestrial animals (a "life detector"; Troje & Westhoff, 2006).

However, other researchers point out the biological motion displays do contain form information, which could be processed by the form-analyzing ventral stream. If a point-light display is blurred, a very indistinct and fuzzy body-shaped form emerges which could serve as a stimulus for form processing. Beintema and Lappe (2002) used a manipulation in which dot locations were shifted around the body from frame to frame, and Beintema, Georg, and Lappe (2006) limited the display lifetime of individual dots. Both manipulations minimize the motion information available in the displays, yet some degree of biological motion perception is still possible. So Lange and Lappe (2006) proposed a model of biological motion perception that includes static posture-specific body shape cells which encode the pose adopted while walking.

Thus it seems that biological motion perception involves both dorsal (motion) and ventral (form) stream processing (Thirkettle, Benton, & Scott-Samuel, 2009;

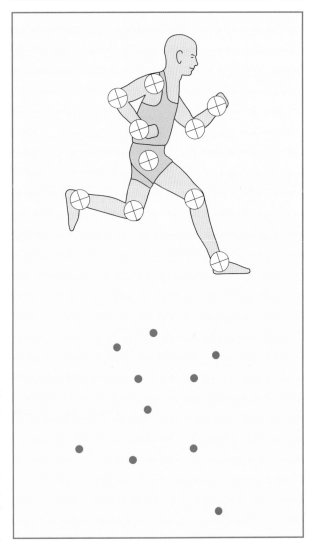

FIGURE 12.13
Biological motion. A moving figure (top) is represented by isolated points positioned at major joints (bottom). When the dots are animated, naive observers perceive a moving human figure.

recall from earlier that the two streams seem to interact during lower level motion detection as well). The superior temporal sulcus (STS) is a likely site where dorsal and ventral signals converge to create representations of biological motion (Ungerleider & Pasternak, 2004). Neuroimaging is consistent with this convergence, and also indicates that other areas are involved, including MT and the extrastriate body area (EBA); indeed these two areas probably overlap in the brain even though they are considered as part of dorsal and ventral streams respectively (Ferri et al., 2013).

Causality and agency

Michotte (1946, translated 1963) described a number of phenomenological observations in which collisions between elements in a dynamic display led to the impression that the elements "caused" each other to move. One's impression of causality depends on the spatial and temporal parameters of the display. In some cases the causality can appear as a simple mechanical interaction between the display elements that is consistent with Newtonian laws of motion that govern collisions and gravitational acceleration. For example, if the kinematics involve simple linear or curved trajectories, and accelerations/decelerations consistent with gravity or collision (balls on a pool table, projectiles launched at targets), then observers perceive mechanical causation. In cases involving unpredictable movements, perhaps lacking actual contact between moving elements, observers typically perceive the moving elements as intentional agents (Heider & Simmel, 1944; Scholl & Tremoulet, 2000). Even a single moving object can appear to be animate and intentional. Tremoulet and Feldman (2000) found that simultaneous changes in speed and direction were sufficient to give an impression of agency (imagine a spider fleeing across the room as you try to trap it in a glass).

Perception of causality in dynamic images seems to be fast, automatic, and tuned to the precise timing and distance relationships in the display, consistent with processing by networks of stimulus-tuned neurons. Neuroimaging studies of causality and agency perception have located these networks in the temporal and parietal lobes, in regions forming part of the dorsal stream (Blakemore et al., 2003).

Transformational apparent motion

Michotte (1950, see Thines, Costall, & Butterworth, 1991) also described the following phenomenon:

> One projects onto a screen any colored shape, such as a circle, and suddenly changes its color, size, or shape. . . . Under these conditions, one can have the impression that the object has undergone a change while remaining "itself." The same colored circle has become greenish, for example, or has dilated, or become oval.
>
> (p. 125)

> In fact, the change is so rapid that it always appears to be a partial evolution of the object, and it then occurs as a "growing into," and by virtue of this has its own anterior temporal limits.
>
> (p. 137)

Michotte believed that the phenomena he observed arose from visual processes that serve to make explicit the functional relations between real-world objects; how one object acts on another, for instance, or how an object changes its shape (see Tse, Cavanagh, and Nakayama, 1998). A neuroimaging study (Zhou et al., 2003) found that these shape-shifting displays activated areas in the anterior temporal lobe, part of the ventral "what" or form pathway, thus emphasizing again the interplay between the two processing streams during motion processing.

CONCLUSIONS

Our understanding of motion perception has made very significant advances over the last 30 or so years. At a neural level, there is a general consensus that the major processing stream for motion runs from cortical area V1 through area MT, and on to MST and STS; the dorsal route discussed in Chapter 7. Local motion is detected and encoded in V1 and MT. MST and STS appear to play important roles in the interpretation of complex motion patterns such as optic flow, 3-D motion, biological motion, and causality (e.g., Tanaka, 1998). There are extensive interactions with neurons that code spatial form.

Psychophysical and computational research has placed this neural processing in a functional context, emphasizing the use of image motion in computations of scene layout, object shape, and social intention.

CHAPTER SUMMARY

DETECTING MOVEMENT

- There is ample evidence that many organisms detect retinal motion using specialized neural circuits; motion detectors.
- Psychophysical evidence for neural motion detectors in the human visual system comes from studies of the motion after-effect, direction-specific threshold elevation, and random-dot kinematograms.
- Detector outputs are ambiguous due to the aperture problem, which can be solved by integrating across the outputs of motion detectors, and by tracking spatial features in moving patterns.
- We still do not know how speed is estimated by the visual system. Current explanations involve comparisons between channels sensitive to different speeds, but it is not clear how many channels are involved and how they are used.

INTERPRETING MOTION

- The "outflow" signals which drive eye movements are used to attribute retinal motion signals to eye movements rather than to external motion.
- Optic flow caused by self-motion provides information about heading direction and speed, and is analyzed by neurons in area MST, which

decompose flow into its component parts (translation, expansion/ contraction, and deformation).

- Motion detector responses can support the computation of 3-D object structure and kinetic depth.
- Point-light displays demonstrate that visual motion can support the perception of a human actor's gender, mood, and identity. Evidence indicates that this ability is based on integrating information from both the dorsal and ventral processing streams.
- Visual motion can also support the automatic perception of causality and agency in dynamic displays.
- Although motion analysis is considered to be part of the dorsal processing stream, several lines of evidence including motion streaks and biological motion show that there are extensive interactions with the ventral stream at all levels.

TUTORIALS

SPATIOTEMPORAL APPROACHES TO MOTION PROCESSING

Cortical motion-detecting neurons form the first stage of motion processing in the visual system. Several sections in this chapter invoke them to explain a wide range of perceptual phenomena. The best way to test the adequacy of these explanations is to implement a computational model of motion detector, supply it with the appropriate visual stimuli, and compare its output to the phenomena under test. This approach requires a conceptual framework within which stimuli, detectors, and responses can be defined. This tutorial describes the framework that is widely used in the scientific literature.

Motion as spatiotemporal orientation

Retinal images of shapes or objects obviously contain variations of intensity in two dimensions, x and y. When these shapes move, a third dimension of variation is added to the image—change over time, t. We can therefore represent motion in a space–time volume with dimensions x, y, and t. The top image in Figure 12.14 shows a car moving rightward. The mid-left image depicts this moving image in a three-dimensional x–y–t volume. As the car moves across the image, it sweeps out a volume in x–y–t space. We can slice through this volume horizontally at a particular y value to reveal a cross-section, shown on the mid-right, which reveals the image variation in two of the three dimensions, x and t. The two dimensions are plotted as x–t or space–time graphs in the bottom images of Figure 12.14. Note that

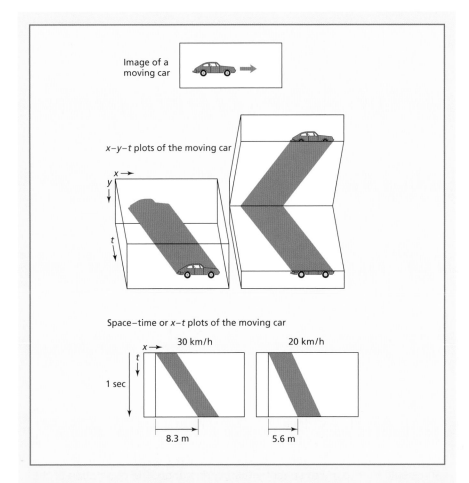

FIGURE 12.14
Representing a moving image in x–y–t and x–t plots.

rightward motion leads to an oriented structure in the space–time plot. Motion at a different velocity or in the opposite direction would alter the space–time orientation seen in the plot, because the slope of the pattern corresponds to velocity. For example, a car moving at 30 km/h (lower left) travels a distance of 8.3 meters in one second. A car moving at 20 km/h travels 5.6 meters in one second (lower right). Note the difference in slope between the two plots, corresponding to the difference in speed. Space–time plots provide a very convenient means of depicting the stimulus properties of moving images, and the response properties of motion detectors, as we shall see.

Motion detectors in space–time plots

How do neural motion detectors described earlier in the chapter fit into this form of representation? Motion detectors sample two different locations in the image at two different times, defined by their Δs and Δt constants, as shown at the top left of Figure 12.15.

FIGURE 12.15
Representing a motion-detecting receptive field in space–time plots.

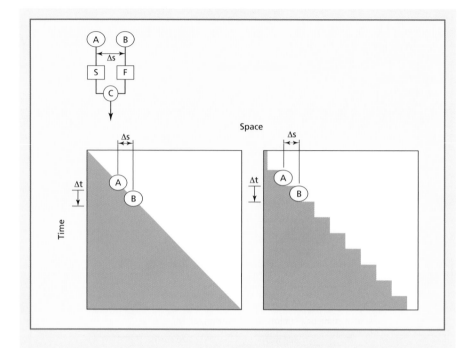

The two inputs to each detector can therefore be drawn in a space–time plot as two sampling points separated by a distance in space equal to Δs, and a difference in time equal to Δt, as shown in the left-hand space–time plot of Figure 12.15. Notice that the detector's input receptive fields fall along a tilted line in the space–time plot. For this reason, motion detectors can be said to respond to spatiotemporal orientation. The orientation of the receptive field defines its optimal velocity.

Adelson and Bergen (1985) proposed that cortical direction-selective simple cells were tuned to spatiotemporal orientation. The receptive field of the cells in Adelson and Bergen's model contain both excitatory and inhibitory regions, so that the response of each cell depends on how well a moving stimulus aligned with its receptive field structure. There is physiological evidence in support of this model. The upper space–time plot in Figure 12.16 illustrates the receptive field structure of a simple cell in V1 of the cat (McLean & Palmer, 1989). The white regions are responsive to bright stimuli, and the dark regions are responsive to dark stimuli. The cell clearly has a preference for rightward moving stimuli, as indicated by the tilted line at its preferred spatiotemporal orientation. Adelson and Bergen (1985) also proposed that complex cortical cells receive inputs from pairs of simple cells having different receptive field arrangements, so that complex cell responses would not depend on how the moving pattern aligns with receptive field structure. Adelson and Bergen (1985) called these complex cells "motion energy detectors." Data from complex cells in cat cortex (Emerson, Bergen, & Adelson, 1992) are consistent with this second

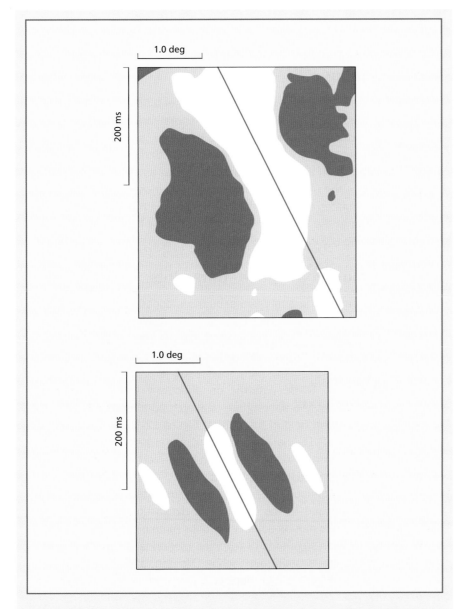

FIGURE 12.16
Space–time plots
of motion-sensitive
receptive fields. The
upper plot is based on
recordings from a simple
cell in cat V1 (redrawn
from McLean & Palmer,
1989, figure 1E). The
lower plot is based on
psychophysical masking
data (adapted from Burr,
Ross, & Morrone, 1986a,
figure 8).

stage of the model. A more detailed description of the motion energy model can be found in Bruce, Green, and Georgeson (2003) and at http://www. georgemather.com/.

There is good psychophysical evidence that the human visual system also contains motion detectors tuned to spatiotemporal orientation. Burr, Ross, and Morrone (1986a) estimated receptive field structure by measuring contrast sensitivity to movement in the presence of masking gratings at various spatial and temporal frequencies. The lower plot of Figure 12.16 illustrates their estimate of a human motion-sensitive receptive field. As in the case of the cat cell, it contains antagonistic subregions, and is optimally responsive at a particular velocity (shown by the tilted line).

Velocity tuning

Image velocity corresponds to spatiotemporal orientation, and each motion detector is tuned to a particular spatiotemporal orientation so in this sense motion detectors are velocity tuned. However, any single detector's response does not uniquely specify velocity, since its response depends on other parameters such as stimulus contrast as well as velocity. Even at the preferred velocity, the response to a particular stimulus will depend on how effectively it stimulates the antagonistic subregions of the receptive field. As discussed earlier in the chapter, we still do not know how motion detector responses are used to estimate velocity.

Apparent motion in space–time plots

Movement can be seen in animation sequences containing patterns which shift position discontinuously. The right-hand plot in Figure 12.17 shows a line moving discontinuously. At regular intervals the edge shifts rapidly to a new position (horizontal lines in the plot), but in between shifts it remains stationary (vertical lines in the plot). The result is a staircase pattern in the space–time plot. These patterns do effectively stimulate detectors with receptive fields at the appropriate spatiotemporal orientation, as the superimposed receptive field in the right of Figure 12.15 shows. It is easy to see from Figure 12.15 that responses in neural motion detectors can explain both perception of real motion (left-hand plot), and perception of discontinuous apparent motion (right-hand plot).

However, discontinuous motion weakly stimulates detectors tuned to the direction opposite to the direction of displacement. This happens because discontinuous motion actually contains motion components in both directions. If one adds segments of reversed motion to a smoothly drifting pattern, the result is discontinuous motion (Morgan, 1980). The left-hand space–time plot in Figure 12.17 depicts a line drifting continuously and

FIGURE 12.17
Space–time decomposition of discontinuous motion (right) into two components: A continuous forward component (left), and a reversed sawtooth component (middle). The velocity of reversed motion (middle) exactly cancels out the velocity of continuous forward motion (left) to create the discontinuous motion in the right. Only when the relatively high frequency sawtooth pattern is detectable can an observer tell the difference between continuous motion and discontinuous motion.

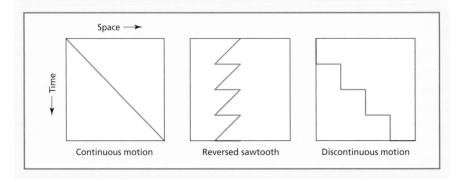

Continuous motion   Reversed sawtooth   Discontinuous motion

smoothly rightward. The middle plot depicts a line that repeatedly drifts leftward and then flicks rapidly back to its original position. The resulting pattern is known as a sawtooth wave. The right-hand plot is the motion that results when the continuous motion and sawtooth motion are combined in a single line. The line moves discontinuously rightward, because the reversed drift of the sawtooth component cancels out the forward drift of the continuous component, leaving only the rapid rightward flicks.

The presence of this sawtooth motion "hidden" in discontinuous motion helps us to explain some of the psychophysical differences between smooth motion and discontinuous motion. First, our ability to distinguish between the two (when the effectiveness of an animation begins to break down) probably depends on visual responses to the sawtooth component. When the sawtooth component is detectable by the visual system, observers perceive the discontinuity in the motion, but when it is too rapid to be detectable, all that is left is the continuous component, so the discontinuous motion is perceptually indistinguishable from real motion (Morgan, 1980; Burr, Ross, & Morrone, 1986b). Second, observers sometimes make errors in their reports of motion direction in apparent motion stimuli (Morgan & Cleary, 1992). This effect is probably due to motion responses to the reversed motion in the sawtooth component.

Second-order motion in space–time plots

Figure 12.18 shows a space–time plot of the contrast-reversing second-order motion stimulus illustrated in Figure 12.9 (lower). An array of randomly

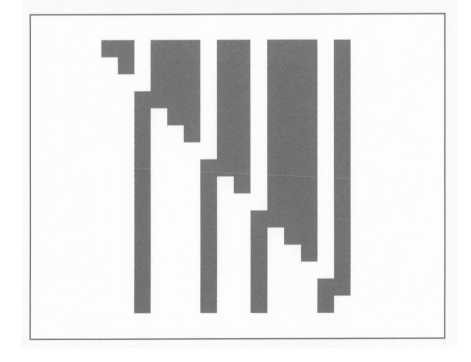

FIGURE 12.18
Space–time plot of the contrast-reversing second-order motion display shown in Figure 12.9.

bright and dark elements is shown on the x-axis of the plot (corresponding to one row in the 2-D pattern). Over a series of time intervals (y-axis), each element in turn reverses in contrast to create a spatiotemporally oriented texture border. Notice that the moving border contains no consistent intensity difference. At some positions it is defined by a decrease in intensity over time. For example, the blocks in the two leftmost columns are initially dark but become light. At other positions, the border is defined by an increase in intensity over time. For example, the block in the third column from the left is initially light, but becomes dark. A first-order motion-sensitive receptive field similar to those shown in Figure 12.16 would produce no consistent response to the border because there is no consistent pattern of intensity that can align with the receptive field subregions. The motion can be encoded by a detector that is selectively responsive only to decreases in luminance over time, or only to increases, as described earlier in the chapter.

Multisensory processing in perception

13

Contents

INTRODUCTION

Natural objects and events are usually multisensory. For example, during a face-to-face conversation with another human, or an encounter with an animal, both vocalizations and visual information (facial expression, lip movement, body attitude) are important. When a motorcyclist twists the throttle and the vehicle accelerates, there is an audible change in engine note, a change in visual movement seen through the helmet visor, and vestibular signals providing a sensation of bodily tilt and acceleration. It would be surprising if the sensory systems did not exploit such correlations between different modalities. Indeed the nausea experienced in virtual reality simulators (Nichols & Patel, 2002) suggests that the brain expects correlated signals to arrive, and is disturbed when they do not.

However the processing framework presented so far includes only limited scope for multisensory integration. Chapter 1 introduced a fundamental theoretical concept in sensory processing, the information processing device or module. By and large the intervening chapters have treated each sensory modality as an independent, autonomous information processing module. Figure 13.1 illustrates the general neural architecture of the system, for three senses. Separate modules process visual (brown), auditory (blue), and somatosensory (yellow) stimuli. Within each modality, dual processing streams specialize in "what" and "where" computations. Information

Why are modern flight simulators equipped with electric-pneumatic jacks?

FIGURE 13.1
The general cortical architecture of sensory processing, according to the modularity theory. Specialized processing systems are dedicated to different sensory modalities: Vision (brown), audition (light blue), and somatosensation (yellow). In each system information flow divides into two streams, one carrying "what" information and the other carrying "where" information. Multisensory processing occurs relatively late in the processing hierarchy, in the intraparietal sulcus (IP) and the superior temporal polysensory area (STP), both shown in multiple colors. Redrawn from Schroeder et al. (2003). Copyright © 2003 Elsevier. Reproduced with permission.

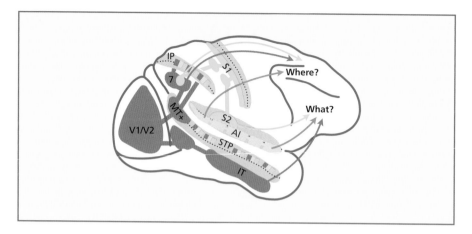

? *Analyse your experience of eating a particular kind of food, such as yoghurt or cheese, in terms of its multisensory components.*

KEY TERM

Modular processing
A theory of cognitive processing in which different functions such as vision, hearing, and memory are implemented in separate and independent processing modules.

from the different modalities is integrated only in later association or polysensory areas of the cortex (Driver & Noesselt, 2008), namely the intraparietal sulcus (IP) and the superior temporal polysensory area (STP).

The scheme in Figure 13.1 is consistent with Fodor's (1983) influential theory of cognition as a collection of independent information processing subsystems, often call "modules." **Modular processing** architecture has a number of virtues. Each subsystem can be optimized for its specific computational task, operating with maximum speed and efficiency rather than compromised to serve several functions at once. Any errors or inaccuracies remain confined to one task, rather than propagated widely. New sensory functions or modalities can be created by adding new subsystems as and when they are required. On the other hand completely independent sensory subsystems can pose problems. There is an issue about how time-sensitive processing can be coordinated across independent subsystems so that, for example, our visual perception of lip movements is synchronized with auditory perception of individual speech sounds. Furthermore independent subsystems cannot take advantage of correlated information in different sensory modalities, such as when we both see and hear someone speaking. Finally, as indicated at the beginning of Chapter 1 in Table 1.1, and in the intervening chapters, there is a great deal of overlap in the computational tasks performed in the different modalities, which independent subsystems cannot exploit:

Orienting Vision, audition and somatosensation all orient our attention to external events.

Object identification All the sensory systems supply information that can be used to identify objects, ultimately accessing the same stored representations.

Localization Both vision and audition have high-resolution processes for computing the location of objects and events.

Body motion Visual and vestibular responses contribute to estimates of body motion.

Flavor Information from olfaction, gustation and other senses is combined to mediate perception of food edibility and flavor.

A growing body of research demonstrates that, contrary to the notion that modality-specific subsystems are completely independent, information *is* shared across sensory modalities earlier in processing than previously thought. Integration of cues for body motion was discussed in Chapter 3, and flavor was discussed in Chapter 2, so the next section focuses on multisensory integration during orienting, object identification, and localization. A later section in this chapter will discuss how recent studies of synesthesia are also throwing new light on multisensory integration.

 How does your local supermarket exploit multisensory processing effects in perception?

MULTISENSORY PROCESSING

EVIDENCE FOR MULTISENSORY PROCESSING

Orienting

Orienting to novel or unpredictable stimuli is often studied by measuring reaction times (RTs) to their appearance. Diederich and Colonius (2004a) measured simple RTs to the presentation of stimuli in three different modalities in separate experimental sessions (unimodal stimulation): Flashes of light, auditory tones, or tactile vibrations applied to a toe. Auditory RTs were fastest (132 msec), followed by visual RTs (163 msec) and tactile RTs (177 msec). Using bimodal stimuli (two modalities presented at the same time) RTs speeded up by about 20–30 msec on average relative to unimodal RTs, and trimodal stimulation speeded up reactions by a further 10–20 msec. Cueing experiments produce similar results. In a typical experiment, the subject is required to respond as quickly as possible to a faint visual target stimulus presented either to the left or to the right of fixation, and an auditory or tactile cue is presented to one side of fixation or to the other side. The cue is "valid" when it appears on the same side as the target, and "invalid" when it appears on the opposite side to the target, as also described in the next chapter on attention. Reaction times are faster in valid trials than in invalid trials, indicating integration of information across the different modalities used for the cue and target stimuli (Butter, Buchtel, & Santucci, 1989; Spence et al., 1998).

The faster reaction times using multimodal stimuli may be due to changes in decision processing, such as reduced decision uncertainty, rather than changes in sensory response. Signal detection theory (SDT) offers tools that are used to distinguish between decision and sensory influences on cueing, because it provides separate measures of perceptual detectability (called d') and decision criterion (called bias or β; see the tutorials section at the end of Chapter 1). McDonald, Teder-Sälejärvi, and Hillyard (2000) and Frassinetti, Bolognini, and Ladavas (2002) used SDT measures in **cross-modal cueing** experiments. Subjects were required to detect weak visual stimuli in the presence of irrelevant auditory stimuli presented either on the same side or the opposite side of fixation, as described earlier. They found that detectability (d') was significantly higher when auditory stimuli were presented on the same side as visual targets than when they were presented on the opposite side. There were inconsistent effects on bias.

The graphs in Figure 13.2 show the improvement in reaction time and detectability when cue and target were presented on the same side (valid: Dark bars) rather than the opposite side (light bars). Reaction times were approximately 6% shorter, and detectability was 8% higher, when a valid cue was presented. These

> Modularity is a key principle in modern computer hardware and software system design, and offers the same advantages as it does for neural systems.

KEY TERM

Cross-modal cueing
Occurs when a cue stimulus presented in one sensory modality facilitates the detection or discrimination of a target stimulus presented in a different sensory modality.

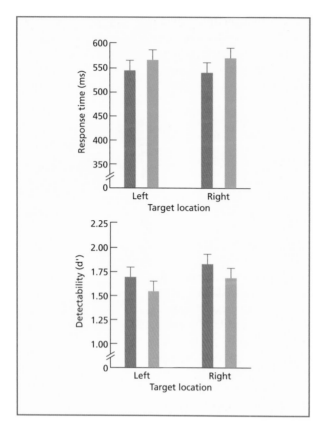

FIGURE 13.2
Reaction time (top) and detectability (bottom) in a cross-modal cueing experiment. Visual targets were presented to the left or right of fixation (horizontal axis). An auditory cue was presented either on the same side as the target (dark bars) or on the opposite side (light bars). Reaction times were faster, and detectability was higher, when the cue and target were presented on the same side. Adapted from McDonald, Teder-Sälejärvi, and Hillyard (2000), figure 3.

results indicate that cross-modal cueing does involve some modulation of relatively low-level sensory processes.

Two explanations have been proposed for enhanced performance using multimodal stimuli:

Parallel activation A bi- or trimodal stimulus generates activity in two or three modality-specific processing modules in parallel. Each is subject to some degree of random variation in its response (see "noise" in Chapter 1), but when activation level in any one module reaches its threshold level, the signal is detected. Processes in the different modalities are in a race to determine which one can reach threshold first. So RTs in response to multimodal stimulation should on average be faster than those to unimodal stimulation on statistical grounds, because there are multiple chances to detect the stimulus rather than just the one. This enhanced response is called "statistical facilitation."

Coactivation Modality-specific responses to multimodal stimuli come together at polysensory brain areas. The combined response is stronger and more reliable than responses generated by unimodal stimuli, so RTs and detectability are both better.

Diederich and Colonius (2004b) estimated the amount of statistical facilitation one would expect from parallel activation, under reasonable assumptions about how the different processes operate. They concluded that multimodal effects are too large to be explained by parallel activation, and must therefore be due to coactivation in polysensory neurons.

Object identification

We can identify a wide range of objects, including concrete entities such as animals and people, and abstract entities such as spoken words. Many objects provide multimodal information. For example, spoken words can be identified from a combination of sound and vision (lip movements). In a noisy environment, such as when holding a conversation or watching television in a crowded room, we have to understand what someone is saying against interfering background sounds. In this situation, visual cues from lip movements, facial expressions, and gestures have a significant impact on speech comprehension. The improvement in comprehension with visual cues is equivalent to an improvement in signal-to-noise ratio of up to 15–20 dB (Spence, 2002). In the **McGurk effect** (McGurk & MacDonald, 1976), the speech sound actually heard by a listener is altered by observation of the speaker's lip movements. For example, if the sound specifies /b/, but the lip movements are consistent with /g/, the subject may report hearing /d/. When the subject closes their eyes, /b/ is heard correctly. A number of other effects have been reported in which the different senses combine to alter perception of objects and their properties:

* *Sound and touch* Manipulating the sound made as the hands are rubbed together can alter the perception of skin texture (Jousmaki & Hari, 1998; Guest et al., 2002).
* *Smell and color* The strawberry smell of a liquid appears stronger when the liquid is colored red (Zellner & Kautz, 1990).
* *Sound and light* Auditory noise presented with light tends to be perceived as louder than noise presented alone (Odgaard, Arieh, & Marks, 2004).
* *Light and touch* Tactile discrimination thresholds are lower during visual observation (Kennett, Taylor-Clarke, and Haggard, 2001).

In all these experiments the researchers took steps to ensure that the change in stimulus quality reflected perceptual processes rather than response bias.

Localization

The apparent location of a sensory event in one modality can be influenced by information in other modalities. Ventriloquism is a long-established form of entertainment that relies on the audience localizing speech sounds at the moving lips of the ventriloquist's dummy rather than at the stationary lips of the ventriloquist. We experience this effect regularly when watching television, since the audio speaker is always located at the side or even at the rear of the television, yet we perceive the sounds to emanate from within the televisual scene. The illusion is actually due to biases introduced during multisensory interactions. Experimental evidence shows that the apparent location of a sound really is influenced by visual events: A flash of light influences the apparent location of a simultaneous sound (Radeau, 1994). Botvinick and Cohen (1998) describe a dramatic effect involving mislocalization of tactile stimulation. The experimental subject places an arm underneath a table, and a false arm fitted with a rubber glove is placed in view on the table directly above. The experimenter then strokes the subject's arm while simultaneously showing a brush stroking the false arm. Subjects report that the stroking sensation appears to be localized on the false arm—the arm appears to be their own arm despite obvious indications to the contrary.

THE NEURAL BASIS OF MULTISENSORY PROCESSING

Individual multisensory neurons respond to both unimodal and multimodal stimulation. The effect of the multimodal stimulus on a cell's response obeys three rules (Kayser & Logothetis, 2007):

Spatial coincidence A neuron sensitive to both visual and auditory stimuli may have receptive fields in both modalities; visual stimuli must fall in a specific region of space, and auditory stimuli must emanate for a restricted range of directions (these receptive fields were described in Chapters 7 and 4 respectively). The two receptive fields usually overlap in space. Multisensory response enhancement only occurs when the respective stimuli fall inside the area of overlap.

Temporal coincidence Response enhancement only occurs when stimuli in different modalities arrive at about the same time.

Inverse effectiveness If a neuron responds very strongly to a unimodal stimulus, its response changes relatively little when another stimulus is added. But if the unimodal response is weak, there are stronger interactions with other stimuli.

The importance of spatial and temporal coincidence suggests that strong multimodal responses are associated with stimuli that are likely to originate from the same object or event.

Turning to the question of where in the brain these multimodal neurons are found, the established view shown in Figure 13.1 is that multimodal processing occurs in high-level multisensory convergence zones in the brain (reviewed in Driver and Noesselt, 2008), but a number of different routes actually seem to be involved.

Superior colliculus

As mentioned in Chapter 7, this nucleus receives projections from multiple modalities, as well as the cortex, and is thought to be involved in multimodal orienting (Jiang, Jiang, & Stein, 2002). Some neurons in the superior colliculus, for example, show "**superadditive**" responses to multimodal stimulation; their response to stimulation from multiple senses is much greater than the sum of their response to each sense in isolation (see Alvarado et al., 2007).

Primary sensory cortex

Anatomical studies in primate cortex have found direct connections between early unimodal cortical areas, as well as connections between unimodal areas and polysensory cortex. Falchier et al. (2002) used an anatomical tracing technique to investigate connections between auditory cortex, visual cortex, and polysensory cortex (area STP). They found that primary visual cortex receives projections both from auditory cortex and from STP. Schroeder & Foxe (2002) found that auditory association cortex receives converging auditory, somatosensory, and visual inputs. Auditory and somatosensory inputs arrived in feedforward (bottom-up) layers of cortex, and visual input arrived in feedback layers (top-down). Rockland & Ojima's (2003) anatomical tracing study found that visual areas V1 and V2 receive projections both from auditory association cortex and from polysensory parietal cortex. It is also possible that projections from koniocellular neurons in the LGN provide feedforward cross-modal input to early unimodal processing areas (konicellular pathways were described in Chapter 7; Schroeder et al., 2003).

Research on the source of cross-modal effects in humans has relied on **event-related potentials (ERPs)**, which are minute but measurable fluctuations in electrical potential in the brain produced by changes in sensory stimulation. Specialized equipment can detect these fluctuations with millisecond accuracy. Several ERP studies have found short latency audiovisual interactions consistent with responses in early cortical areas (Giard & Peronnet, 1999; Foxe et al., 2000). Also, McDonald et al. (2003) claimed to find evidence for top-down feedback. They recorded ERPs

KEY TERMS

Superaddentive response
A response to a combined stimulus which is greater than the sum of the responses to each stimulus presented separately.

Event-related potentials (ERPs)
Minute fluctuations in electrical potential in the brain caused by changes in sensory stimulation.

during a standard cross-modal cueing experiment. When the auditory cue was presented at least 100 milliseconds before a visual target, ERP activity occurred in multimodal cortical areas slightly before activity in visual cortical areas. McDonald et al. (2003) state that the result "strongly suggests that feedback from multimodal to unimodal areas" is involved in cueing. Although the data are suggestive, they do not offer conclusive evidence for feedback. Care must be taken when interpreting ERP and fMRI activity, since they may be influenced by such factors as attention, arousal, and imagery (see Driver and Noesselt, 2008).

Secondary association cortex

Several regions of sensory association cortex are involved in multimodal processing. The orbitofrontal cortex in macaque monkeys contains multimodal neurons that respond to smell and taste, or smell and vision, or taste and vision (Rolls & Baylis, 1994), so this area is likely to mediate multimodal flavor perception.

Bimodal neurons in the superior temporal cortex (in the dorsal processing stream) may well play a role in the integration of visual and vestibular signals about body motion (Gu, Angelaki, & DeAngelis, 2008). Functional neuroimaging experiments show that the lateral area of temporal cortex integrates visual and auditory signals (Amedi et al., 2005).

Cross-modal integration of visual and tactile object processing takes place in an area of association cortex lying at the border between temporal and occipital cortex (in the ventral stream; Amedi et al., 2001). So multimodal processing occurs in both major cortical processing streams.

In summary, a range of psychophysical and neuroscientific experiments offers convincing evidence that multimodal processing is much more pervasive than it was once thought, embracing cortical areas that are traditionally viewed as modality specific. This evidence does not invalidate the prevailing modular theory of sensory processing (see Coltheart, 1999). The established view of the sensory cortex being divided up into several modality-specific subsystems still holds, given the overwhelming evidence for functionally specialized brain regions discussed in earlier chapters. However the evidence also indicates that the modality-specific systems are more sophisticated than we once thought, sharing information between them in order to modulate processing in each modality. Theories of information processing in the brain must accommodate such effects. An important theoretical question arises as to how the information from different modalities is combined. The tutorials section at the end of the chapter discusses one contemporary approach to answering this question.

SYNESTHESIA

WHAT IS SYNESTHESIA?

Synesthesia is an intriguing multisensory phenomenon in which stimulation in one sensory modality causes a sensory experience in another modality. For example, some people experience a color sensation not from visual stimulation, but from auditory stimulation. "Colored hearing" is most commonly associated with speech sounds. Different sounds evoke different colors. There are also reports of color sensations evoked by nonspeech sounds, by touch, and by smell. The most common type of synesthesia ("sensory union") involves ordered sequences such as numbers, letters, or days being perceived as sequences of colors. Ward (2008) reports that, for one subject with synesthesia, the letters A and E evoke shades of red, I, M, and N evoke white, D evokes yellow, and so on. Numbers are similarly distinct in terms of color, as are musical sounds and certain words such as days of the week or city names. This phenomenology is typical of synesthesia.

The phenomenon was once on the fringes of scientific research, considered not worthy of serious investigation, but recent research has moved it into the mainstream. The modern study of synesthesia is informed by and can in turn inform theories of multisensory processing.

SYNESTHESIA AS A SENSORY PHENOMENON

Early doubts about the scientific worth of synesthesia were fueled by those who questioned whether it is a genuinely sensory phenomenon rather than learned associative pairings of colors and sounds, perhaps created while learning to read. Several lines of evidence now argue convincingly against the learning account. Baron-Cohen et al. (1993) investigated the consistency of the pairings over time. Nine experimental subjects who reported synesthetic experiences were asked to report the colors evoked by 122 words, letters, and phrases. A matched group of control subjects were asked spontaneously to generate a color to associate with each stimulus, and encouraged to use a mnemonic to aid recall. Both groups were retested on 10% of the words, one year later in the case of the experimental group, and one week later in the case of the control. Ninety-three percent of the experimental group's color responses were identical on retesting after a year, but only 37.6% of the control group's responses were identical after one week. Baron-Cohen et al. (1993) concluded that the phenomenon is a genuinely sensory one. They found that the initial letter of the word tended to determine the color it evoked. Colors reported were generally idiosyncratic to different individuals, though the vowels "i," "o," and "u" were consistently associated with the same colors in different individuals: "I" was grey, "o" was white, and "u" was yellow.

Further evidence for the sensory nature of synesthesia comes from neuroimaging studies. Paulesu et al. (1995) used PET to study brain activation while blindfolded synesthetic subjects and controls were presented with spoken words or pure tones. Both groups showed activation of cortical language areas when words were presented as opposed to tones. In the case of synesthetic subjects, several secondary visual cortical areas were also activated during word stimulation. Nunn et al. (2002) used fMRI to locate the cortical regions activated by speech in subjects with synesthesia and in control subjects. Synesthetic subjects showed activation in area V4/V8 in the left hemisphere, a region normally activated by color. Control subjects showed no activation in V4/V8 when imagining colors in response to spoken words, despite extensive training on the association. Neuroimaging studies show that a wide range of cortical areas is involved in synesthetic experiences, including sensory and motor cortex and areas in the parietal and frontal cortex (Rouw, Scholte, & Colizoli, 2011).

Synesthesia tends to run in families, and population studies indicate a genetic contribution, though the genes involved have not been identified. For example, Baron-Cohen et al. (1996) found a prevalence of one case of synesthesia in every 2000 people. Many more women than men reported synesthesia; the female:male ratio was 6:1. One third of the cases identified by Baron-Cohen et al. (1996) reported familial aggregation. However genes cannot offer a complete account of the phenomenon, because synesthetic responses can be triggered by blindness. Rao et al. (2007) reported auditory ERPs in the visual cortex of subjects who were totally blind as a result of physical trauma.

THE NEURAL BASIS OF SYNESTHESIA

The most plausible account of synesthesia is that it involves direct neural connections between unimodal cortical areas, of the kind that were discussed in the previous section. These connections may be enhanced genetically in people with synesthesia, or strengthened in response to traumatic sensory deprivation. Recall that one explanation of the phantom limb phenomenon (Chapter 3) is cortical reorganization in response to altered sensory input. The prevalence of associations between colors and words in synesthesia is consistent with this account, because the cortical regions responsible for vision and speech are located near to each other. Wernicke's speech area lies sandwiched between auditory cortex and secondary visual cortex (see Figure 13.3). It is also intriguing to note that synesthetic experiences are particularly associated with ordered sequences (numbers, letters, days, months, etc.). Several researchers have proposed that visual processing involves the execution of *visual routines*, which are special self-contained cognitive processes, rather like computer programs, that perform certain tasks such as counting, indexing, and tracking, and are actively invoked by attention (Ullman, 1984a; Cavanagh, 2004; Roelfsema, 2005).

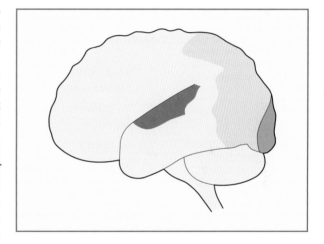

Perhaps the neural circuits mediating synesthetic experiences tend to be activated when counting or indexing routines are executed. Brain-imaging studies indicate that visual counting does involve a neural subsystem in secondary visual cortex, adjacent to speech and auditory areas (Piazza et al., 2002).

FIGURE 13.3
The dark brown area shows human striate visual cortex, and the light tan area shows extrastriate visual cortex. The dark gray area shows auditory cortex, and the yellow area shows Wernicke's speech area. Estimates of visual cortex were taken from Van Essen et al. (2001). The location of Wernicke's area is discussed in Wise et al. (2001).

THE UTILITY OF SYNESTHESIA

According to the theory of evolution, traits are transmitted to successive generations only when they confer an advantage on the host. What advantages might synesthesia provide? One suggestion is that people with synesthesia are more creative, and therefore more able to generate novel and adaptive ideas which promote survival and reproduction. This idea is contradicted by studies that find no conclusive evidence for differences in creativity between synesthetic and control subjects (Ward et al.,

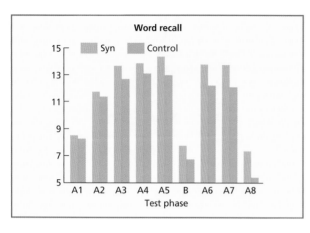

FIGURE 13.4

Word recall in synesthetic and control subjects. Each subject recalled 15 words that were read aloud by the experimenter. List A was read and recalled five times (A1 to A5), before list B was read and recalled (B). Finally list A was recalled three times (A6–A8) without being presented again. Synesthetic subjects consistently recalled more words than control subjects. Data taken from Yaro and Ward (2007), table 1.

2008). A more plausible account of the synesthetic advantage was offered by Yaro and Ward (2007), who compared memory in synesthetic and control subjects. The experiment required subjects to recall two lists of 15 words (A and B) read to them by the experimenter. List A was read and recalled five times, then list B was read and recalled. Finally list A was recalled on three occasions without it being presented again (the final recall test was two weeks later). Figure 13.4 shows the variation in word recall as this procedure progressed. Synesthetic subjects consistently recalled more words than control subjects. A small advantage in memory ability may be sufficient to sustain the synesthesia trait.

CHAPTER SUMMARY

EVIDENCE FOR MULTISENSORY PROCESSING

Multisensory stimulation aids processing in several ways:

- Orienting to novel stimuli is faster and more reliable with multimodal stimulation.
- The different senses combine to alter perception of objects and their properties.
- The apparent location of an event in one sensory modality is influenced by information in another modality.
- Visual and vestibular responses contribute to estimates of body motion.
- Information from several senses is combined to mediate perception of food edibility and flavor.

NEURAL SUBSTRATES OF MULTISENSORY PROCESSING

The responses of multimodal neurons obey three rules:

- Spatial coincidence
- Temporal coincidence
- Inverse effectiveness.

The established view is that multisensory neurons are found only in high-level convergence zones in temporal and parietal cortex, but recent research has found multimodal responses in other brain areas:

- Superior colliculus
- Primary sensory cortex
- Secondary association cortex.

SYNESTHESIA

Evidence for synesthesia as a genuine sensory phenomenon:

- Color-word pairings in synesthetes are too stable and idiosyncratic to reflect learned associations.
- Brain-imaging studies find differences between the brains of synesthetic and control subjects.
- Family and population studies indicate a genetic contribution.

Synesthesia is probably due to direct neural connections between unimodal cortical areas. The prevalence of color-word pairings may be due to the anatomical proximity of cortical areas encoding color and speech.

Synesthesia may have survived during evolution because it is accompanied by enhanced memory for words and colors.

TUTORIALS

BAYESIAN MODELS OF MULTISENSORY PROCESSING

Evidence for pervasive multisensory effects in perception indicates that object properties are often created by combining multiple sources of information. This begs the question as to how the information is combined. For example, if the brain receives both visual and auditory information as to the location of an object, such as a barking dog, it is unlikely that the location estimates in the two modalities will agree exactly because the two subsystems perform completely different computations on different information (for example, stereoscopic disparity in vision and interaural time differences in audition). So how does the brain compute a single estimate of location, which it must do in order to inform a decision on the best course of action (the dog can only have one location at any given moment)? The traditional view is that one sense, usually vision, tends to dominate over all others. More recently researchers have been using Bayesian inference in more sophisticated models of multisensory integration.

The basic principle in Bayesian inference theories (which were introduced in the tutorials section of Chapter 10) is to draw an inference about the world by combining different sources of evidence, while taking their reliability into account. Figure 13.5 shows a simple functional flow diagram of Bayesian inference in the context of multisensory processing. Each sensory modality (shown at the bottom of the diagram) supplies its own estimate of an object property such as location. Each estimate has a likelihood attached, which indicates its reliability. For example, acuity for position is much higher in vision than in audition, so the visual estimate should be

FIGURE 13.5

Flow diagram for Bayesian inference in multisensory processing. Each modality-specific module (bottom) supplies an estimate of a particular object property (likelihoods depend on the reliability of each estimate). The different estimates are combined with prior knowledge to produce a perceptual inference (posterior probability).

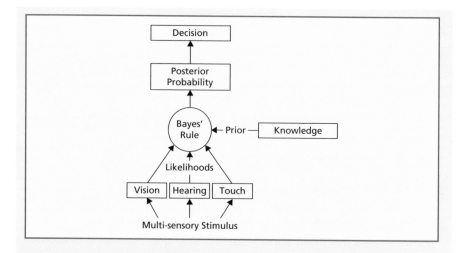

accurate and may therefore have a higher likelihood value. The different estimates are combined using Bayes' rule, which takes the average of the estimates but weights the contribution of each by that estimate's likelihood. Prior knowledge about the world also influences the final estimate, as described in Chapter 10. The result of the combination is a measure of the probability that a particular interpretation is correct (posterior probability); in the case of the earlier example, this would correspond to a particular location estimate.

This kind of model can be tested experimentally in studies of multimodal perceptual judgments. If the experimenter manipulates the relative reliability of different cues in the task, then according to Bayesian models the participants should alter the weight they attach to the cues when making their judgments. Alais & Burr (2004) asked participants to judge the location of a stimulus on the basis of combined visual and auditory cues (patches of light and brief audible clicks). They introduced small conflicts between the cues, displacing the position of one relative to the other, and also manipulated the reliability of the visual cue by blurring it so that it was spread over a wide area and consequently less precise. Results showed that unblurred light patches tended to dominate location judgments, but when blurred patches were used the auditory cue tended to dominate.

Ernst and Banks (2002) investigated the integration of visual and haptic (touch) cues in estimates of object size. They used virtual reality goggles to present images of small blocks, and a force feedback device to simulate the felt size of the blocks. Ernst and Banks (2002) manipulated the reliability of the visual cue. Similar to the effect reported later by Alais and Burr (2004), vision tended to dominate size judgments when it was a very reliable cue, but touch become more dominant when the visual cue was unreliable. The pattern of results in both experiments is consistent with a model of integration based on optimal Bayesian cue combination.

Attention and perception

14

Contents

INTRODUCTION

Everyday experience creates the illusion that our perceptual systems are omniscient: We see everything before us that is visible, hear everything within earshot, feel everything we touch, and so on. But research has revealed how inaccurate this view is. Our sensory systems do not automatically and continuously capture the entire sensory world in the same way that a video camera captures an entire visual scene, or a microphone records all audible sounds. While you are reading this text, for example, you are probably not aware of a multitude of sensory events; the touch of your elbow on the table, the distant rumble of traffic, other voices in the building, or the rustle of the wind outside a window. A moment's pause is needed to bring these other sensations into consciousness. In order to see, you must look; to hear, you must listen; to feel, you must touch; to smell, you must sniff.

What happens when you do not look, or listen, or touch, and so on? Most of the available information is lost; your opportunity to take it in has passed. Perception is a mental act which is initiated by a prompt either from the outside world (when a new stimulus, such as the bark of a dog, presents itself) or from inside the brain itself (when a task you are performing requires specific information from the outside world, such as a check for other road users when emerging from a road junction). We call this act of selection "paying attention."

FIGURE 14.1
Sustained visual attention is crucial for security monitoring tasks. Copyright © bibiphoto/Shutterstock.com.

Perception always involves selection or attention in some form or another, as will become clear in this chapter. It can involve selection over space, so that only sensory signals from a particular location or direction are subjected to analysis. If you are reading a text message on your phone while walking along the street, for instance, you may be oblivious to the person in full view right in front of you (perhaps also transfixed by their phone) who is on a collision course. Attention can also involve a focus on one sensory modality to the exclusion of others. You may be so engrossed in the latest text message from a friend that you do not hear the sound of the cyclist rapidly closing in on you from behind, even when they sound their bell. Finally, selection can occur over time, when you are expecting an event to occur in the near future. Imagine that you have stopped at a red traffic signal, waiting for the green light which signals you to proceed across a road junction. When the amber signal appears, you can focus attention ready for the imminent appearance of the green signal, and so proceed with minimal delay.

Given this diversity in the forms of attention it may not be surprising to learn that there is no single "thing" in the brain called attention, despite the subjective impression that it is a unitary mechanism. The act of attention relies on a number of distinct processes. Before we discuss some of those processes, it is worth spending some time considering *why* perception must be so selective. Why not simply process everything that impinges on the sensory systems, and decide afterwards what to do with it?

? *What are the implications of research on attention for people who use mobile phones while driving?*

THE NEED FOR SELECTIVITY IN PERCEPTION

There are two general explanations of the need for attention in perceptual processing, which are not mutually exclusive. One is based on physiological constraints and the other is based on processing constraints.

PHYSIOLOGICAL CONSTRAINTS

The brain places a high metabolic demand on the body. It typically amounts to about 5% of body mass, but accounts for 20% of the body's overall energy consumption in adult humans at rest. Electrical signaling in neurons accounts for a large proportion of the brain's energy consumption; the cortices consume 44% of the brain's energy supply (Lennie, 2003) and as you will know by now sensory processing occupies a large area of the cerebral cortex. Only a certain amount of energy can be supplied to the brain due to constraints in blood supply, and the amount available is sufficient to support high levels of activity in only a tiny fraction of all cortical neurons, perhaps as few as 1 in about every 60 neurons at any one time (Lennie, 2003). So the brain cannot afford to process all sensory inputs indiscriminately, and decide later which information is most useful. There simply is not enough energy available to do this. The brain's limited energy resource must be allocated flexibly among all the neurons in the cortex, according to moment-to-moment task demands. A fundamental property of cortical organization is regional specialization of function, which drives regional variations in energy consumption. So changes in neuronal activity are accompanied by changes in local cerebral blood flow, and this is the signal exploited in functional magnetic resonance imaging. In the cognitive domain, the switching of energy resources between specialized cortical regions translates into switching between different cognitive tasks, manifested as attention.

PROCESSING CONSTRAINTS

It can also be argued that due to processing limitations it is just not feasible to try to process everything at once, even if there was sufficient energy available. The notion that attention reflects some kind of processing limit in the brain has a relatively long history. As outlined in Chapter 1, we can consider the sensory systems as communication channels which transmit information from a source (the outside world) to a receiver (specialized neural populations in the brain). Mathematicians and telecommunications engineers know a great deal about the properties of electronic communications systems such as mobile telephone networks and Wi-Fi networks. All such systems have a channel capacity which places an upper limit on the amount of information that can be transmitted simultaneously (for instance, it is virtually impossible to make a mobile telephone call just as the clock strikes midnight on New Year's Eve, when everyone else is also trying to make a call, because the network cannot handle the volume of calls). In 1958 Donald Broadbent proposed that information processing systems in the human brain also have a limited capacity, which forces them to be selective about the inputs that are processed at any given moment. Broadbent (1958) described the selection process as "filtering." The sensory systems can be conceptualized in a traditional information flow diagram (Figure 14.2) as an array of parallel input channels, each simultaneously supplying the brain with information about the outside world. Central processes cannot handle such a large volume of information simultaneously, so a filter selects only a subset of these inputs at a time for transmission along a limited capacity channel to central processing systems. The filtering process corresponds to the thing we

FIGURE 14.2
The classic boxes-and-arrows model of information processing, first proposed by Broadbent (1958). The sensory systems provide a continuous stream of "messages" about the state of external world to a limited-capacity information processing channel. Messages are selected for processing by a filter. In Broadbent's model the messages were selected on the basis of their physical attributes.

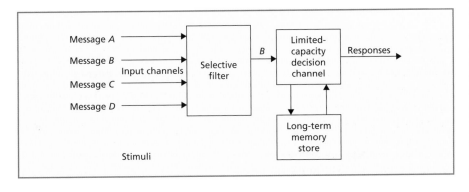

call "attention." Broadbent's original filter theory was succeeded by other theories of attention which implement the filter in different ways, but the basic process of filtering driven by the brain's limited processing capacity is still a core feature of modern theories of attention.

Sutherland (1989) described information flow diagrams such as the filter theory of attention depicted in Figure 14.2 as "boxology": "The construction and ostentatious display of meaningless flow charts by psychologists as a substitute for thought" (p. 58). Although this characterization is rather harsh because filter theories are consistent with a large body of empirical data (see Quinlan & Dyson, 2008), Sutherland did put his finger on a weakness of box-and-arrow approaches: A lack of rigorous detail on the constraints driving the architecture of the system. In the case of filter theories of attention, it would be preferable to justify the need for them using metrics that compare the complexity of the task to be performed against the resources available in the brain. Is sensory processing really too complex a task for the brain to perform "bottom-up," without some form of filtering?

Many tasks in perception can be characterized as matching problems: Visual objects, voices, written words, odors, and all manner of other sensory objects are recognized by comparing a specific input stimulus against an array of items stored in memory. When the degree of similarity between the stimulus and a stored item exceeds a threshold, a successful match is achieved. Recognition is an essential cognitive skill, and humans are very good at it. In the case of vision, for example, humans can identify tens of thousands of objects, typically within about 100 milliseconds after presentation of the stimulus. Given that neurons can fire no faster than 100 times per second, the brain appears to solve the visual matching problem in only 10 steps (synaptic relays) or so. Tsotsos (1990) presented a computational analysis of the complexity of the problem, in terms of the number of processing elements (neurons) and processing steps required for a solution (computational theories of perception are described in Chapter 1). He argued that in general matching problems involving a large set of stored items are too difficult to solve using algorithms (step-by-step procedures) based simply on "bottom-up" searches of a large memory store; they need too many processing elements, or too many steps (and therefore time), or both. A solution can only be achieved by incorporating "top-down" control of the search, which constrains the stimulus elements and memory items involved in the search. In other words, attention is essential for solving computationally complex matching problems.

MANIFESTATIONS OF ATTENTION

The functional goals of the sensory systems discussed in previous chapters center on the detection and recognition of perceptual features, objects, and events. So the different manifestations of attention serve to focus processing resources on specific features, objects, or events.

MODAL ATTENTION

The different sensory modalities are separable in terms of the underlying neural structures which serve them. Each modality has its own receptor array, afferent pathway, and cortical receiving area. The different modalities thus provide alternative routes for incoming information about features, objects, and events, and attentional processes allow the brain to enhance processing in selected routes. Psychophysical studies have found evidence for attentional enhancement of stimulus detection and discrimination in each modality. In vision, attention has been shown to influence motion detection (Alais & Blake, 1999; Raymond, 2000) and pattern discrimination (Lu & Dosher, 1998; Martinez et al., 1999). In hearing, attention allows listeners to eavesdrop on conversations in classic "cocktail party" situations (Cherry & Taylor, 1954; Fritz et al., 2007). In somatosensation, attention to a specific fingertip affects the tactile perception of texture (Sathian & Burton, 1991). In the chemical senses, attention affects the detectability of weak stimuli, though it is more difficult to attend to olfactory stimuli than to gustatory stimuli (Ashkenazi & Marks, 2004).

An important question concerns the interaction between different sensory modalities in demanding situations. Can people selectively attend to one modality to the exclusion of others? The answer seems to depend on the tasks employed. Tasks involving speeded responses (reaction times) show reliable attention effects (Spence & Driver, 1996; Spence, Nicholls, & Driver, 2001). Spence et al.'s (2001) participants responded to unpredictable visual, auditory, or tactile stimuli after having been instructed to expect a presentation either in one particular modality or in any modality. The results are summarized in Figure 14.3 (taken from data in table 4 of Spence et al., 2001). Results indicated that it is possible to selectively attend to one modality: reaction times were faster when stimuli appeared in the expected modality than when they appeared in an unexpected modality. However the effect is in the form of a cost for the unexpected modality, rather than a benefit to the expected modality, because reaction times to the expected modality are no faster than those when participants could not attend to an expected modality.

So reaction time tasks show cross-modal effects; responses in any one modality are slower when attention is directed towards another modality. Tasks measuring detection rates (sensitivity) rather than times show only intramodal effects (Larsen et al., 2003; Alais, Morrone, & Burr, 2006). For example, Alais, Morrone, and Burr (2006) measured auditory pitch and visual contrast thresholds while participants were performing a secondary task that was either intramodal or cross-modal. They found significant detrimental effects when the secondary task involved the same modality, but no effects when they involved a different modality. The difference between response time and sensitivity measures may relate to the cortical regions involved in two tasks. As discussed in the previous chapter, sensory cortex contains both modality-specific regions and supramodal regions. Perhaps those tasks that rely heavily on resources in early sensory cortex, such as basic detection tasks, show modality-specific effects, whereas those that load heavily on higher-level resources (time-limited decisions) show supramodal effects (Prinzmetal, McCool, & Park, 2005).

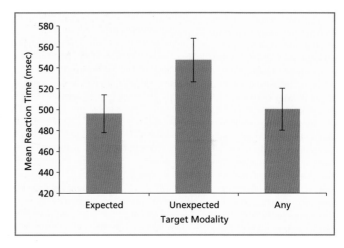

FIGURE 14.3
Results of an experiment to test whether it is possible to selectively attend to one sensory modality in a reaction time task. Responses were faster (left-hand bar) when the stimulus appeared in an expected sensory modality than when it appeared in an unexpected modality. The difference is due to a cost for the unexpected modality, not benefit in the expected modality. Responses in the latter were no faster than when there was no expectation at all (right-hand bar). Reprinted from Klein (2000). Copyright © 2000 Elsevier. Reproduced with permission.

FIGURE 14.4
Inhibition of return.
(a) Trial sequence: A spatial cue (S1) precedes the stimulus (S2) by a time interval called the cue-target onset asynchrony (CTOA).
(b) Results: The graph plots reaction time as a function of CTOA, for targets appearing at the same side as the cue (filled circles) or the uncued side. Responses are faster at the cued side only for short CTOAs; at long CTOAs responses are actually slower— inhibition of return to the cued location.

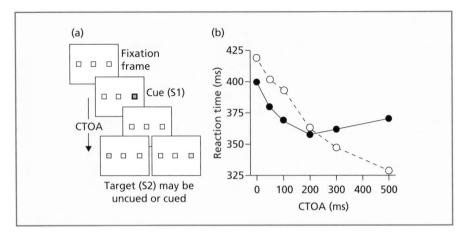

SPATIAL ATTENTION

Spatial attention is often likened to a spotlight which highlights a region of space (Cave & Bichot, 1999). If the goal of attention is to concentrate processing resources on objects relevant to the task at hand, then a spatial focus would make a great deal of sense: Objects in the natural world are mostly to be found at specific spatial locations in the environment. Spatial attention has been found to facilitate processing at the attended location and inhibit processing at other locations. Thus a **spatial attention cue** to the location of an impending stimulus improves detectability and reaction time, even when the cue and stimulus span different modalities. For example, an auditory cue can improve detection of a subsequent visual stimulus (e.g., McDonald, Teder-Sälejärvi, & Hillyard, 2000; see previous chapter). For optimal effect, the cue should precede the stimulus by 70–150 msec (Nakayama & Mackeben, 1989). Once attention is drawn away from one location to another, then processing at the original location is inhibited, an effect known as "**inhibition of return**" (IOR; Klein, 2000). Figure 14.4 shows a typical IOR effect.

The sequence of events in a typical trial is shown on the left. The trial begins with a spatial cue, a brief bright flash, at one of two peripheral boxes (left or right; S1), which triggers a shift of attention to the cued location. After a short interval known as cue-target onset asynchrony (CTOA) a target stimulus appears (S2) at one of the three boxes; targets are much more likely to appear in the center box than in either of the peripheral boxes (to discourage spatial attention from remaining at the cued location). As shown in the graph on the right, Posner and Cohen (1984) found that response times were faster to targets on the cued side (filled circles) relative to the uncued side (unfilled circles), but only at shorter presentation intervals.

IOR begins about 250 msec after attention is withdrawn from a location, and can last several seconds. Like sensory adaptation, IOR may reflect assumptions about the relatively stable structure of the sensory world. Adaptation represents a prediction that the world will remain fairly constant in the very near future. In the case of IOR, if a particular location is not of immediate interest it is unlikely suddenly to become interesting in the very near future. In this sense IOR can be viewed as facilitating foraging behavior; once a location has been checked during a search, there is no need to return to it in the near future.

Spatial attention has a resolution limit which is much worse than visual acuity as measured using standard Snellen charts or high-frequency gratings. It can be assessed by asking an observer to select out a target item such as a letter from an array of distractor items. As shown in Figure 10.6 and discussed in Chapter 10, a letter which is perfectly legible when presented by itself at a location away from fixation becomes unreadable when surrounded by other letters (He, Cavanagh, & Intriligator, 1997). The resolution limit seems to be imposed beyond primary visual cortex, because unresolved items can nevertheless yield orientation-specific after-effects (He, Cavanagh, & Intriligator, 1996).

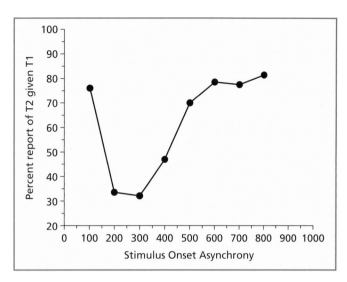

TIME-RELATED (TEMPORAL) ATTENTION

This form of attention involves the use of information to select a point in time when an event is expected. As described earlier, while you are waiting at a red traffic light, the change to amber gives you temporal information that a green signal is about to appear, speeding your response in the proverbial "traffic light Grand Prix" (Coull & Nobre, 1998). A standard task for studying temporal attention is known as **rapid serial visual presentation (RSVP)**. Lawrence (1971) presented a series of 12 words in rapid succession at the same location, all except one (the target) were the same (lower case, or belonging to the same semantic category), and the participant was required to name the odd target word (upper case or different category). Errors increased consistently as presentation rate increased, with substantial errors at rates above about 12 words per second. Later studies using RSVP tasks have found that when multiple targets are presented in the stimulus sequence, there is an interval of 200–500 msec after the appearance and detection of a target during which the probability of detecting a subsequently presented target is reduced. Figure 14.5 shows example data from Chun and Potter (1995). The participant was shown a rapid sequence of 16 single digits, one after the other at the same location. In amongst the stream of digits there were two upper case letters. The participant was required to report the two letters at the end of the trial. The figure shows the probability of reporting the second letter (T2) correctly, given that the first letter (T1) was reported, as a function of the interval between the two. There is a marked dip in accuracy at intervals between 200 and 400 msec.

Raymond, Shapiro, and Arnell (1992) labeled this phenomenon the **attentional blink**. The initial reports of the effect triggered many studies on the attentional blink, testing how much information is processed about the missed targets, and why. Recent findings indicate that multiple factors interact to produce the attentional blink, including competition between targets for processing resources (stimulus

FIGURE 14.5
The "attentional blink." Once the participant detects a target item in a rapidly presented sequence of digits, another target is unlikely to be detected if it occurs 200–400 msec later. From Chun and Potter (1995). Copyright © American Psychological Association. Reproduced with permission.

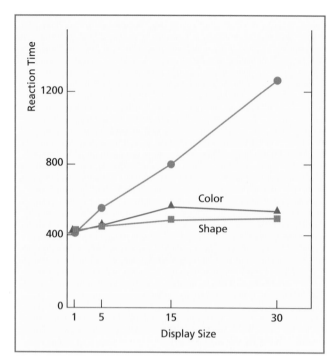

FIGURE 14.6
Feature and conjunction search. When target items were defined by a single feature (color or shape), reaction times were rapid and did not depend on the number of items to be searched (blue and purple lines). When targets were defined by a combination of features (color and shape), reaction times increased as the number of items to be searched increased (green line). Reprinted from Treisman and Gelade (1980). Copyright © 1980 Elsevier. Reproduced with permission.

registration, memory, response selection) as well as inhibitory processes that suppress responses to nontarget items (Dux & Marois, 2009).

FEATURE SEARCH

Attentional selection can involve individual features in a complex stimulus, such as a particular color or contour orientation, or whole objects (constellations of features). These features and objects can be distributed over time, space, and modality. Feature attention is often studied using visual search tasks. A simple task would require the participant to detect the presence of a target feature in the midst of an array of nontarget (distracter) features. The task is trivially easy and highly efficient when the feature is defined by a difference in a simple feature such as color, orientation, or size (**feature search**). The number of distracting elements makes little difference to the difficulty of the task. On the other hand, when target and distracters are defined by a combination of features (**conjunction search**), the number of distracters does affect performance; search time increases steadily with the size of the array to be searched. For example, in Treisman and Gelade's Experiment 1 (1980), the distracter items were a mixture of green Xs and brown Ts. In their feature search condition participants searched for targets defined by either a specific color (a blue letter) or shape (the letter S). In their conjunction search condition participants searched for targets defined by a conjunction of color and shape (a green T). The use of two targets in the feature search condition was to ensure that participants attended to both stimulus features (color and shape) in both conditions. Results (reproduced in Figure 14.6) showed that the feature search was much easier than the conjunction search. **Feature**-defined targets were found in about 400 msec, even when there were 30 items to search; in other words the whole stimulus array could be searched in parallel. On the other hand the search time for **conjunction**-defined targets increased linearly with the size of the search array; items were searched in series, one after the other. With an array of 30 items to search, it took about three times as long to find conjunctions compared to features. The difference between parallel feature search and serial conjunction search is often characterized in terms of the slope of the line relating reaction time to search array size. Parallel search is defined in terms of search slopes below 10 msec per item, while conjunction search is defined by search slopes exceeding 10 msec per item (Wolfe, 1998).

Initially these well-replicated results were characterized in terms of a contrast (dichotomy) between two alternative search strategies: Feature searches were said to be performed in *parallel* across the whole search array, while conjunction searches involved *serial* inspection of the array, element by element. Treisman and her colleagues proposed **Feature-Integration Theory (FIT)** to explain these results, which involved a corresponding dichotomous distinction between "preattentive" and "attentive" processing stages. In the preattentive stage, simple stimulus features are encoded early, automatically, and in parallel during visual processing, thus allowing parallel search. In the attentive stage, on the other hand, conjunctions of features—perceptual objects—require focal attention for encoding and are thus associated with serial search performance. The list of features in early preattentive vision should, one would expect, correspond to those extracted by neurons in the first two of three visual areas in occipital cortex (see Chapter 7). However, some features that are known to be encoded in early visual cortex do not seem to be available to guide searches; other features which have been found to guide searches, such as contour intersections, are not encoded early on. Indeed on the basis of data obtained using search tasks, preattentive processes seem to have some properties which are usually associated with later stages of processing (Wolfe, 2003). Another complication is that search data cannot definitively distinguish between the two search processes. There is no clear dichotomy in search slopes corresponding to the distinction between parallel preattentive search and serial attentive search (Wolfe, 1998). Moreover, estimates of how long it should take to process each item during serial search depend on a range of assumptions about the underlying process, such as the time required to segment each item from others, process its features, and then bind them together.

> **KEY TERMS**
>
> **Feature search**
> An experimental procedure in which the participant is shown an array of items (patterns such as letters, lines, gratings, and so on), which may or may not contain an "odd-one-out": A target item that is different from all others in terms of a simple feature such as color or orientation. The participant is required to report whether the target is present or absent.
>
> **Conjunction search**
> The same experimental procedure as for feature search, except that the target item is defined by a conjunction of features, such as a specific combination of color *and* orientation.
>
> **Feature-Integration Theory (FIT)**
> A theory proposed by Anne Treisman and colleagues to explain why conjunction searches are more difficult than feature searches; the former involves effortful attentive processing, while the latter involves automatic preattentive processing.

Thus, although FIT inspired a great deal of research on visual feature search, its simple dichotomy between serial and parallel searches has not been supported by the data. Two different kinds of model have been proposed to replace FIT. One kind preserves the serial versus parallel process distinction, but proposes a more nuanced interplay between them. Prominent in these theories is the "guided search" model, which proposes that very few items in the search array can be processed at one time, but the selection of candidate items for later identification is guided by preattentively acquired information. In early versions of the model a limited set of attributes such as orientation, size, and color were said to be processed preattentively. Recent updates of the model (see Wolfe et al., 2011) include global information about scene "gist" as another source of guidance. Gist was discussed in Chapter 9.

? *Think of some real-world examples in which scene gist can be a help, or a hindrance, during a search task.*

The second class of model abandons the serial versus parallel distinction altogether, arguing instead that all items in the search array are processed in parallel, but search efficiency (and therefore time) varies with the demands placed by the items on a limited processing resource (see, for example, Bundesen, Habekost, & Kyllingsbæk, 2005). As yet there is no definitive resolution between the two kinds of model.

OBJECT-BASED ATTENTION

Perceptual objects can be loosely defined as a collection of component parts that are treated by the brain as a single, coherent object. Although it is clear that attention can have a spatial focus, many studies have revealed the existence of a mode of attention that is based on the selection of a limited number of objects rather than a particular spatial location. The distinguishing feature of object-based attention as opposed to

KEY TERM

Multiple object tracking (MOT)
An experimental procedure to study object-based attention; the participant views an animation in which simple shapes move randomly around a computer screen, while trying to keep track of a small number of shapes. Results show that only four or fewer items can be tracked simultaneously.

Research has shown that magicians manipulate people's attention while performing their tricks. For example, people tend to look where the magician is looking, so the magician can direct people's attention towards the illusion and away from their sleight of hand.

Unlikely as it may seem, multiple object tracking tasks are currently used as part of the training regime in many professional sports, to keep athletes mentally alert.

FIGURE 14.7
Experimental paradigm to study multiple object tracking. Nine disks appear on-screen (left), and four of them flash briefly, identifying them as the disks to be tracked. All nine disks then move randomly around the screen (middle). After a short while all the disks stop, and the observer must select which four disks had flashed at the beginning (right). Performance deteriorates as the number of objects to be tracked increases.

feature attention is that all the component parts of the object are selected, even if they are not relevant to the task in hand (Schoenfeld et al., 2014).

Early evidence for object-based attention came from a study by Neisser and Becklen (1975). Their participants viewed two movies simultaneously, optically superimposed from two video screens, and were instructed to follow the action in one while ignoring the other in order to complete a simple task. For example, one movie contained a "handgame" and the other contained a "ballgame," and participants were required to count the number of times the hands in the former clapped each other. The task could be performed without difficulty, but participants failed to notice significant events which occurred in the other movie, even though they took place in the same part of the visual field. Later work on this kind of "inattentional blindness" has confirmed and extended these findings: Many studies have reported that experimental participants do not notice changes to stimuli when they take place outside of the current focus of attention (Ballard et al., 1997; Rensink, O'Regan, & Clark, 1997; Simons & Levin, 1997).

In another experiment involving superimposed shapes (Duncan, 1984), participants were briefly shown a box with a line struck through it, and asked to report two properties of the box (such as its size) or of the line (such as its orientation), or one property from each. Judgments that involved reporting two properties from the same object were performed more accurately than judgments that involved properties from different objects, consistent with the view that attentional selection was object-based.

A third paradigm that has been used to study object-based attention is **multiple object tracking (MOT)**. As shown in Figure 14.7, the participant views a computer display containing, say, nine disks (left panel). When the disks first appear, a few of them flash briefly. Then all the disks begin moving around the display randomly (middle panel). The observer must direct their attention to the disks that had flashed briefly at the start and keep track of their position. After a period of time the observer is asked to pick out which disks had flashed at the beginning (right panel). Observers can perform this task with over 85% accuracy when tracking up to five target disks

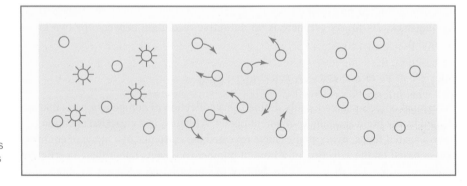

among ten identical items, but errors increase dramatically when observers are asked to track a larger number of items simultaneously (Pylyshyn & Storm, 1988).

Clinical evidence for object-based attention comes from cases of simultanagnosia, which is associated with bilateral lesions in parietal cortex. The disorder involves an inability to perceive more than one visual object at a time, even in relatively simple displays. For example, Luria (1959) reported the case of a soldier with a gunshot wound that included the occipitoparietal region of cortex. The patient was shown a variety of simple patterns in a large number of trials, and asked to report what he saw in each pattern: 25 of the trials contained a display consisting of just two shapes alongside each other, an outline circle and a cross. In only 3 trials towards the end of the sequence did the patient report seeing both shapes; most of the time he reported seeing just one shape or the other.

Examples of object-based attention can also be found in audition, as discussed in Chapter 5. Bregman (1990) argued that auditory streams play the same role in audition as visual objects do in vision. In auditory streaming, sequences of sounds are segregated perceptually into discrete perceptual objects on the basis of their physical characteristics (similarity in frequency, timing, and so on). As in the case of vision, primitive components (auditory tones) are brought together to form a complex perceptual object.

Daniel Kahneman and Anne Treisman proposed an explanation for object-based attention which involves "**object files**" (see Kahneman, Treisman, & Gibbs, 1992). According to this theory, attending to an object causes a temporary representation of the object to be created in the brain (an object file) which contains information about its physical properties and location. As the object moves or changes its features the file is updated by processes which track "objecthood" over time. For example, if one's attention is directed towards an object in a complex visual scene, possibly after it has appeared from behind an occluding surface, tracking processes assess whether it matches a currently active object file (attached to an object that had previously disappeared from view) or is a new object requiring its own file. Kahneman, Treisman, and Gibbs, (1992) sought evidence to support the theory by looking for priming effects in a simple letter naming task. When the letters had been previewed as part of the same perceptual object (a box which enclosed each letter) naming times were faster than when they had been previewed as parts of different objects.

Pylyshyn (1989) developed a related theory to understand how observers can keep track of items in MOT displays, which involves the notion of a "visual index" or "finger of instantiation" ("FINST"; by analogy with real physical fingers which can be used to point at and track moving objects). According to this theory, an identifying index is assigned to items in the visual field on the basis of salient cues. Each index is used by the attentional system to access information about the properties of the indexed object. Pylyshyn argued on the basis of MOT experiments that the system is able to assign only four indexes at a time.

As Pylyshyn (2000) acknowledged, the object-file and visual-index theories are based on the same idea: "The primary difference being that research into visual indexes concentrates on the pointer or link, whereas Kahneman et al. were concerned with what information is stored at the cognitive end of the link" (p. 203).

Research on object-based attention indicates that certain items or features in visual scenes are assigned index files from a small pool of available files, and the location assigned to each file travels about the scene as each item moves. Pylyshyn (2000) argues that these index files represent the visual system's first contact with the world of objects, prior to the encoding of object properties.

KEY TERM

Object files theory
A theory to explain object-based attention, which involves the creation in the brain of a notional file for each attended object, which is updated over time to keep track of changes in the object; it is similar to the *visual-index* theory of object-based attention.

NEURAL SUBSTRATES OF ATTENTION

A wide array of neuroscientific techniques has been brought to bear on the task of identifying the neural substrates of attention, from single-unit recording to neuroimaging. The standard experimental strategy is to compare neural responses in different attention conditions (attending to a particular stimulus versus attending to a different stimulus, or to no stimulus at all). In keeping with the diverse functional manifestations of attention outlined in earlier sections, the act of paying attention has been found to influence neural responses at many cortical levels, from low-level modality specific cortex to high-level association cortex, and in all modalities studied.

As is the case in other areas of neuroscience, more research has been conducted on vision than on any of the other modalities. A number of electrophysiological studies have recorded activity in single neurons in the primate visual system while at the same time manipulating the animal's attentional state using a visual discrimination task. Neural responses when the animal was attending to the stimulus falling inside the cell's receptive field were compared to responses when the animal was attending to a stimulus falling outside the receptive field. Results show that responses to stimuli at an attended location are enhanced relative to responses to stimuli at an unattended location (for example, Motter, 1993; Cook & Maunsell, 2002).

Figure 14.8 illustrates the effect of attention on single-cell responses in V1, V2, and V4. The graphs show orientation tuning curves obtained when the animal was attending to a visual field location either inside the receptive field or outside the receptive field. Responses are amplified during attention. Attentional modulation of this kind has been reported in several of the earliest visual cortical processing areas (e.g., Treue & Trujillo, 1999). The amount of response amplification is generally greater in higher-level cortical areas than in lower-level areas (Maunsell, 2004).

Consistent with the single-unit data, fMRI studies find that focal attention modulates activation in both extrastriate cortex and striate visual cortex (Tootell et al., 1998b). Attention boosts signals at attended locations and attenuates signals at unattended locations, in all visual areas. Striate cortex activation is relatively delayed, indicating that it is driven by feedback from higher cortical areas (Noesselt et al., 2002). Attention to features such as motion and faces modulates activity in areas of extrastriate visual cortex that specialize in those stimuli (O'Craven et al. 1997; Wojciulik, Kanwisher, & Driver, 1998).

Neuroimaging studies of other sensory modalities also report evidence for attentional modulation in early modality-specific cortical areas. Attention to taste

FIGURE 14.8
Orientation tuning curves derived from single-cell recordings in three areas of primate visual cortex, with and without attention. The solid lines show neural activity when the animal was attending to a location inside the receptive field of the cell; the broken lines show activity when the animal's attention was directed to a location outside the receptive field. Activity was higher when the animal was attending inside the receptive field. Data replotted from Motter (1993) figures 3, 4, and 5.

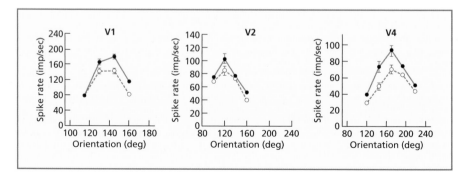

(Veldhuizen et al., 2007) or smell (Zelano et al., 2004) results in enhanced fMRI activation of early gustatory cortex (insula and operculum) or early olfactory cortex (piriform cortex) respectively.

What mechanism drives the modulation of activity in early sensory cortex? There are extensive reciprocal connections between many cortical areas, offering a route for descending signals from high-level attention networks to early sensory cortex. Imaging studies indicate that a distributed network of areas in frontal, parietal, and temporal cortex is involved in attentional control (for example, Corbetta et al., 1993; Hopfinger, Buonocore, & Mangun, 2000). Culham et al. (1998) used fMRI to investigate cortical regions activated during a multiple-object tracking task of the kind described earlier. Participants alternated between attentive tracking and passive viewing, so that the additional effect of tracking on activation could be inferred. Tracking produced bilateral activation in parietal cortex, frontal cortex, and area MT (though the latter was relatively weak).

Slotnik and Yantis (2005) studied the brain areas activated by perceptual reversals in an ambiguous display. Results showed transient increases in fMRI activation in the superior parietal lobule and intraparietal sulcus. Brouwer, van Ee, and Schwarzbach (2005) also reported activation in the intraparietal sulcus during perceptual reversals.

Thus it seems that circuits in parietal and frontal cortex control the shifting demands of stimulus-driven and goal-directed spatial attention. According to an influential proposal by Corbetta and Shulman (2002), goal-directed or top-down attention is controlled by a neural system located dorsally in the intraparietal cortex and superior frontal cortex, while stimulus-driven attentional shifts are controlled by a more ventral frontoparietal system, particularly in the right hemisphere. The latter system is said to act as a "circuit breaker" for sensory processing which draws attention to salient events. Neuroimaging data indicate that these frontoparietal networks are involved in several aspects of attention, including spatial attention (Silver, Ress, & Heeger, 2007), feature-based attention (Giesbrecht et al. 2003) and object-based attention (Yantis & Serences 2003).

CONCLUSIONS

Attention is multifaceted and intimately linked with sensory processing in all the modalities, guiding processes and influencing stimulus interpretation. The underlying neural modulation signals reach deep into the earliest levels of sensory analysis in the cortex from higher-order circuits in the frontal and parietal cortices. A key feature of attention is selectivity in processing. Modern research has been preoccupied with two major theoretical dichotomies, one involving early versus late selection models and the other involving serial versus parallel selection models. While dichotomies serve a very useful purpose in driving binary "A versus B" experimental predictions, results (and their interpretation) rarely allow just one unequivocal winner to be declared. Such is the case in attention research. Attentional processes are too diverse and complex to be explained by simple dichotomous distinctions. Recent models of attentional selectivity tend to incorporate elements from both sides of the earlier dichotomies, perhaps adding other distinctions, such as Wolfe's selective and nonselective pathways in his guided search theory (Wolfe et al., 2011).

Recent research has also begun to explore the way that emotion guides attentional selection of sensory stimuli. For example, Öhman, Flykt, and Esteves (2001) asked participants who were fearful of snakes but not spiders (or vice versa) to find feared objects in a visual search task. Search performance was better for feared targets than for nonfeared targets, suggesting enhanced attention to emotionally provocative stimuli. Neuroimaging research also supports the idea that "emotional attention" can modify perception (Vuilleumier, 2005). Another theme of recent work is to study attention "in real life" using complex natural stimuli rather than highly simplified laboratory stimuli, such as breast cancer screening and airport security scans (Evans, Birdwell, & Wolfe, 2013).

CHAPTER SUMMARY

The sensory systems do not automatically capture all the information that is available in the sensory world. Instead they select only the information that is most useful to the task at hand or potentially important for survival.

THE NEED FOR SELECTIVITY IN PERCEPTION

Perception is selective because:

- The brain is energy-starved, and cannot process all the sensory information it receives at once.
- The problem of interpreting incoming signals is too difficult to solve in bottom-up fashion, and requires top-down control to guide processing towards a solution.

VARIETIES OF ATTENTION

Processing resources can be focused on the basis of:

- Sensory modality
- Spatial location
- Time of occurrence
- Stimulus features
- Objects and events.

NEURAL SUBSTRATES OF ATTENTION

Two neural circuits in frontotemporal cortex are crucial for attentional control of processing. The dorsal system controls goal-directed or top-down attention, and the ventral system controls stimulus-driven or bottom-up attention. Signals from these systems can influence neural activity at the lowest levels of processing in the sensory cortex.

TUTORIALS

CONSCIOUSNESS AND PERCEPTION

To perceive is to be aware of the world. Conscious experiences of the mass of sensations, events, objects, and scenes that constantly bombard our sensory systems all our waking life are definitive aspects of perception. Some researchers have argued that attention is a requirement of conscious perception, as indicated at the start of the chapter. Certainly some of the research mentioned in this chapter points in that direction. For instance, the phenomenon of inattentional blindness indicates that if you do not attend to a stimulus, it is not consciously perceived and is not available for cognitive processing. There is an assumption, often left implicit, that attention and consciousness play a *causal* role in decision-making and behavior; in other words paying conscious attention causes behavior to occur as a direct consequence of that mental act. If we feel hungry, we attend to food: We find the reddest-looking apple in the fruit basket, then we pick it up and eat it. But there is a paradox hiding in this causal account of attention and consciousness.

The traditional philosophical view is that mind and brain are fundamentally different in kind, and that one cannot be reduced to the other. This account of consciousness is called Cartesian dualism, named after the French philosopher René Descartes. He believed that the dual spiritual and mental worlds communicated with each other through the pineal gland. However we now know that this small organ, which lies deep in the brain next to the thalamus, secretes melatonin in response to signals from the eye and so controls the body's diurnal rhythm. Most scientists believe that consciousness is inextricably connected to neural activity. The psychophysical methods described throughout the book are based on the assumption (psychophysical linking hypothesis) that changes in perception map onto changes in neural responses. So, in principle, for every change in attentional state or conscious awareness, one can define a parallel change in neural activity.

Large swathes of the brain are intimately linked with mental events in a highly specific manner. A neural correlate of consciousness (NCC) can be defined as "the minimal set of neuronal events that gives rise to a specific aspect of a conscious percept" (Crick & Koch, 2003). Neuroscientists have established a large number of NCCs, many of which are described in earlier chapters (consciousness research has tended to focus largely on sensory experiences or qualia, defined in the first chapter). For instance perception of motion is closely associated with activity in the midtemporal area of the cortex (MT), as indicated by the results of neuroimaging experiments (Tootell et al., 1995), single-unit recordings (Salzman et al., 1992), and clinical case studies of "motion blindness" or akinetopsia (Zihl, von Cramon, & Mai, 1983).

NCCs are inconsistent with Cartesian dualism but, as with all correlations, they cannot tell us about causation. Is consciousness *causal*, in the sense that it drives our decisions and behaviors? Mental causation implies that at least some decisions or behaviors would be impossible without consciousness. A number of theories have proposed causal functions for consciousness. For example, Tononi (2004) argued that consciousness functions as the "glue" that binds together disparate pieces of information in the brain. Maia and Cleeremans (2005) proposed that it serves to resolve the competition between alternative internal representations. Frith and Frith (2007) claimed that consciousness allows us to understand what other people are thinking. But here is the paradox: If consciousness is ultimately embodied in specific neural events, then any explanation of behavior that can be couched in terms of conscious causation can equally well be couched in terms of neural causation. Maia and Cleermans (2005) acknowledge as much regarding their proposed theory of consciousness, in stating: "It seems that it would be possible to have a system without qualia that would have the properties we outlined" (p. 402). The notion of consciousness becomes superfluous according to this view, and we should thus use terms such as "consciousness" and "attention" advisedly in scientific discussions.

The alternative view to mental causation, known as epiphenomenalism, is that consciousness is a by-product of decisions and behaviors. Mental causation implies that "when you feel an itch, you scratch it," whereas epiphenomenalism would argue that "when you scratch an irritant, you feel an itch." A number of experimental studies have produced evidence that is consistent with epiphenomenalism. Libet (1985) asked participants to make irregular, willed finger movements while he recorded electrical potentials from the scalp. Each finger movement was preceded by a brain activation spike called a "readiness potential" (RP), which is known to occur prior to voluntary actions. Libet's (1985) participants also viewed a rapidly rotating hand on a clock face, and were asked to report the position of the hand at the instant that they were aware of their intention to move their finger. When the timing of the reports was compared to RP times, Libet found that awareness actually followed the RP by about 350 msec. So participants only became aware of their intention to act one third of a second *after* the start of the neural events that triggered the action. In a different procedure, Castiello and Jeannerod (1991) asked participants to manually point to a visual target. Occasionally the target unexpectedly jumped to a new position after the action had been initiated. Participants could mostly make an appropriate correction to their action, but their awareness of the unexpected jump occurred more than 200 msec *after* the movement correction.

In many activities such as dowsing, divining, and Ouija board games, things happen apparently spontaneously without intentional effort on the part of the participants. The dowsing rod twitches, or the planchette slides across the Ouija board, apparently under its own volition. Wenger (2003) made careful measurements of the forces involved in a session of Ouija, and found that the participants did indeed initiate movements of the planchette despite their lack of awareness. Our experience of conscious free will is arguably a *post hoc* interpretation of the causes of our actions. However this epiphenomenalist view begs other questions. If conscious experiences serve no function, why do they exist at all? According to evolutionary theory, traits are retained only if they improve the prospects of survival and reproduction. Is consciousness adaptive, or is it a "spandrel," a by-product of an adaptation, like the umbilical cord (Gould & Lewontin, 1979)? Precisely *how* do neural events lead to conscious experiences? There is still no universal agreement on what kind of a thing consciousness is, how it can be measured empirically, and how neural events can give rise to it. These questions as well as the debate between mental causation and epiphenomenalism are unlikely to be resolved in the near future.

Individual differences in perception

15

Contents

INTRODUCTION

Experiments on sensation and perception are mostly conducted in university laboratories so participants tend to be university students who are, by and large, young, fit, well educated and highly motivated. Many of them are actually students of psychology or neuroscience. In the UK two thirds of university students are below the age of 24, with females in a slight majority. Despite using such a narrow sample of people, researchers assume that their conclusions generalize to the entire population. This assumption is open to question (see Henrich, Heine, & Norenzayan, 2010).

Conditions such as anosmia, deafness, scotoma, and agnosia (discussed in previous chapters) can have a profound effect on perception, so experimenters routinely exclude participants who have a condition that could adversely affect their performance. Even so, individual differences in the performance of "normal" subjects are often found and can be significant and highly stable across different testing sessions. But they are generally treated as "noise"—random fluctuations in response—and removed by averaging data across groups of subjects.

Several demographic factors are known to produce consistent individual differences in perception, and sometimes differences are found which cannot (or are not) attributed to demographics factors. This chapter will review evidence regarding the effects of all these factors on interindividual differences in perception.

AGE

CHANGES IN PERCEPTUAL CAPACITY OVER THE LIFESPAN

Many studies have measured perceptual capacities at different stages of the lifespan. The methodological problems of studying perception in infants are particularly demanding. Experimental procedures used to study adults are generally not suitable for research on infants, so a range of techniques has been developed specifically to cater for infants. The tutorial at the end of the chapter describes some of these techniques. When we compare data from infant studies against data collected from adults at various ages, a general pattern emerges of rapid early improvement followed by gradual decline. Figure 15.1 shows representative data from four sensory modalities. All of the graphs are plotted so that smaller y-axis values correspond to better task performance. Performance generally follows a U-shaped function, with optimal performance during the late teens and early twenties.

Vision

The two graphs in Figure 15.1(a) plot visual acuity over different age ranges, and are based on data in Atkinson (2000) and Owsley, Sekuler, and Siemsen (1983). They show that visual acuity (the ability to resolve fine spatial detail) improves dramatically over the first year of life but does not reach adult levels until the age of 4 or 5. There is a much more gradual decline in performance in the later decades of life (assuming that appropriate optical corrections are worn). Notice that even a 90-year-old's acuity is five times better than that of a 6-month-old infant.

Contrast sensitivity shows the same trend: Infant sensitivity is up to 10 times worse than an adult's, and peaks at a much lower spatial frequency (approximately 0.5 cpd, as opposed to 3 cpd in adults). Why does infant acuity improve so dramatically, and what underlies the decline in later life? We shall begin the search for possible causes in the peripheral visual system, namely in the optical and neural properties of the eye.

Developmental changes in the eye

The poor vision of newborn infants cannot be attributed to optical aberrations or accommodation defects. The newborn eye is relatively free of optical defects, though accommodation is relatively inaccurate (Atkinson, 2000). There are, however, marked structural changes in the retina over the first few months of life, which mirror the changes in acuity. The packing density of foveal cones does not reach adult levels until after the age of 4 years. Figure 15.2 (top) is an idealized representation of the cone mosaic of an infant (right) relative to an adult (left; based on Banks & Bennett, 1988).

Even within the same individual, perceptual functions are likely to vary as a result of such factors as diurnal rhythm, the menstrual cycle, life events, intake of psychoactive substances (nicotine, alcohol, caffeine), and so on.

[?] *Review the section on contrast sensitivity in Chapter 9.*

[?] *Why does cone packing density affect visual acuity?*

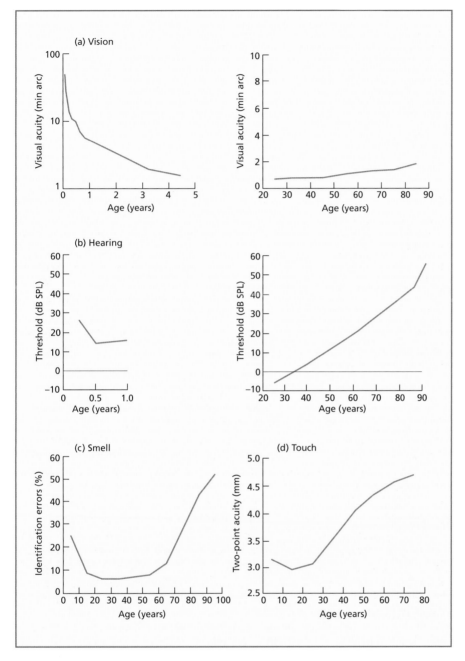

FIGURE 15.1
Perceptual capacity over the lifespan, in four sensory modalities. Data are plotted so that smaller values on the y-axis correspond to better performance. (a) Visual acuity (adapted from Atkinson, 2000, and Owsley, Sekuler, & Siemsen, 1983; note the different x- and y-axes in the two graphs); (b) hearing threshold (adapted from Olsho et al., 1988, and Morrell et al., 1996; note the different x-axis in the two graphs); (c) odor identification errors (adapted from Doty et al., 1984); (d) Touch discrimination (adapted from Louis et al., 1984).

Notice the markedly coarser sampling of the image in the infant retina. In addition, cone outer segment length increases by a factor of 10 or more during infancy (Youdelis & Hendrickson, 1986). Figure 15.2 (bottom) shows human foveal cones at different ages. Short receptors are much less sensitive to light than long receptors, as explained in Chapter 6 under "Photoreceptor length." A further limitation on the sensitivity of infant eyes is their small size (size matters as explained in Chapter 6). Overall, retinal factors certainly do limit the visual capabilities of infants. However, Banks and Bennett (1988) estimate that only about half of the difference between infant and

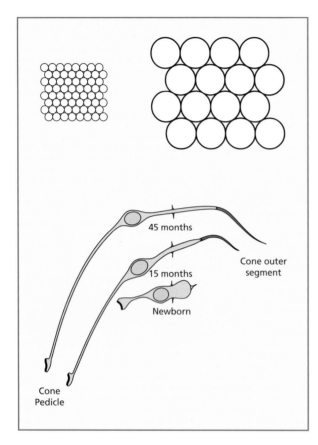

FIGURE 15.2
Developmental changes in the retina. Top: Idealized representation of the retinal receptor mosaic of a neonatal infant (right) and an adult (left, based on Banks & Bennett, 1988). Center-to-center separation is approximately 0.5′ arc in the adult receptor mosaic, and 2.3′ arc in the neonate. Bottom: Drawings of human foveal cones at different ages (newborn; 15 months old; 45 months old). Redrawn from Hendrickson & Youdelis, 1984.

adult acuity can be attributed to retinal factors. The remainder must reflect limitations in post-receptoral neural processing.

Biological aging of the eye

Some of the deterioration in vision during old age can be traced to the decreasing efficiency of the eye as an optical instrument:

- Reduced mobility of the pupil (*pupillary miosis*), which results in a tendency for the pupils in elderly observers to remain quite small even in dim illumination, with consequent reduction in retinal illumination.
- Reduced flexibility in the lens, leading to reduced accommodative range and long-sightedness (*presbyopia*).
- Increased light absorption by the lens (*senile cataract*), reducing retinal illumination and increasing light scatter.
- Degeneration of the central retina (*age-related macular degeneration*, or AMD).
- Photoreceptor loss due to the disappearance of the retinal pigment epithelium results in a progressive loss of central vision.

However, as in the case of early development, peripheral factors alone cannot account for all the effects of aging on visual acuity (Weale, 1991). Central factors will be discussed following a review of other sensory modalities.

Hearing

Data on hearing thresholds in Figure 15.1(b) are taken from Olsho et al. (1988) and Morrell et al. (1996), and represent the threshold for detecting a 4 kHz tone as a function of age. There are significant improvements in sensitivity over the first year, amounting to a change in threshold of 10 dB SPL between 3 months and 12 months of age. The deterioration later in life is much more dramatic, amounting to a 60 dB loss of sensitivity by the age of 90 (recall that a 3 dB change in threshold is equivalent to a halving of sensitivity). Age-related deafness is known as *presbycusis* (see Chapter 5). As in the case of vision, a number of peripheral factors are thought to be involved in age-related changes in hearing level.

Changes in the peripheral auditory system over the lifespan

Peripheral factors involved in developmental improvements in sensitivity include:

- Changes in the resonance of the outer ear.
- Middle ear effusions (buildup of fluid behind the eardrum) in very young infants.
- Immaturity in the cochlea.

Peripheral factors in presbycusis include:

- Decreased efficiency of sound transmission through the middle ear ossicles.
- Decreased flexibility in the basilar membrane.
- Deterioration in cochlear hair cells.

Lost hair cells are not replaced, so their number declines throughout life due to various factors including infections, ototoxic drugs, and exposure to loud sounds (Hudspeth & Konishi, 2000). Nozza (1995) and Frisina and Frisina (1997) argue that age-related changes in hearing are not entirely the result of peripheral effects, but also reflect changes in cortical auditory processing.

Smell and taste

Figure 15.1(c) plots errors in an odor identification task as a function of age, from Doty et al. (1984), based on a range of 40 odors. After developmental improvements up to the age of 10, presumably attributable to experience, performance remains relatively stable up to the sixties, when decline sets in. About two thirds of adults over the age of 80 have impaired olfaction (Murphy et al., 2002). Doty et al. (1984) argue that declining olfaction in the elderly is not due to deterioration in memory, since there is no significant correlation between scores in the odor identification task and scores in standard memory tests. On the other hand, there is evidence for deterioration in the peripheral olfactory system, including reductions in the efficiency and number of olfactory receptor neurons, perhaps caused by the cumulative effects of viruses and chronic inflammatory diseases (Doty et al., 1984). Rawson et al. (1998) compared the odor selectivity of olfactory receptors in young and old subjects, and found a marked decrease in selectivity in older subjects. Receptor losses seem to have consequences for secondary processes. Meisami et al. (1998) compared the number of glomeruli and mitral cells in young and old adults and found a significant decline with age. Young subjects had over three times the number of glomeruli and mitral cells found in elderly subjects, so one would expect them to have a better sense of smell. There is little evidence for significant taste receptor loss in the elderly. However taste detection thresholds increase with age (Methven et al., 2012), and older people have been found to require two or three times as much salt concentration to detect it in tomato soup (Stevens et al., 1991). Declining taste sensitivity may contribute to higher salt intake in the elderly, as well as loss of appetite (Schiffman & Graham, 2000).

> **?** *Why should the number of glomeruli affect odor identification?*

Touch

Figure 15.1(d) plots two-point discrimination of touch stimuli applied to the hand as a function of age, taken from Louis et al. (1984; see also Shimokata and Kuzuya, 1995); two point-discrimination was described in Chapter 3, and illustrated in Figure 3.6. Performance peaks in the late teens and early twenties, and declines monotonically thereafter. This steady decline can be partly attributed to changes in the mechanical properties of the skin (decreasing elasticity), and reductions in the number of touch receptors with age (Bolton, Winkelmann, & Dyck, 1966).

FIGURE 15.3
Brain weight in kilograms as a function of age (data from Dekaban & Sadowsky, 1978). Note the different x-axes in the two graphs.

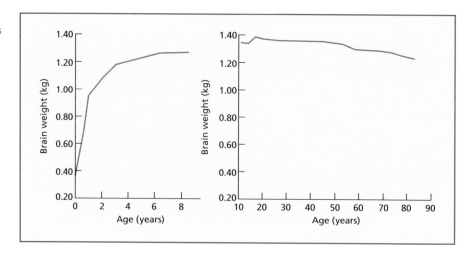

CHANGES IN THE BRAIN OVER THE LIFESPAN

It is clear from the preceding discussion that changes in peripheral sensory structures play a role in age-related changes in perceptual capacity. However, in many cases peripheral changes cannot entirely account for age-dependent effects. We must also consider the effects of age on the brain itself.

Figure 15.3 shows data on brain weight as a function of age, taken from Dekaban and Sadowsky (1978). Brain weight increases rapidly during the first few years of life, reaching a peak at the age of 20. Between the ages of 20 and 80 brain weight declines by 9%. The change in brain weight generally mirrors the change in perceptual capacity over the lifespan. In the next section we consider what changes in the brain may underlie the change in weight.

Developmental changes

Cortical development during the first years of life is characterized by growth in both dendrites and axons:

- Dendritic growth involves proliferation in the connections between neurons during infancy. In visual cortex, for example, synaptic density at birth is only 17% of the adult level (Huttenlocher & de Courten, 1987). This period of growth is followed by regression or pruning of connections back to adult levels during late childhood and adolescence (Webb, Monk, & Nelson, 2001).
- Cortical regions rich in axons are called **white matter**, whereas regions rich in neuronal cell bodies are called **gray matter**. **Myelin** is an insulating fatty sheath surrounding axons that promotes rapid and efficient neural transmission. Studies of white matter indicate that axon diameter and myelination continue to develop throughout childhood (Paus et al., 1999).

Developmental changes in the structure of the brain must play an important role in the improvements in sensory performance shown in Figure 15.1. They are likely to

KEY TERMS

White matter
Tissue in the brain and spinal cord containing cell axons.

Gray matter
Tissue in the brain and spinal cord containing neuronal cell bodies.

Myelin
A fatty sheath covering certain cell axons; it facilitates the transmission of neural impulses.

be regulated by sensory experience, so that the sensory systems attune themselves to the growing individual's environment. Classic experiments on selective rearing (e.g., Wiesel, 1982; Blakemore & Cooper, 1970) illustrate the degree to which sensory systems can mold themselves to their environment. Blakemore and Cooper (1970), for example, exposed kittens to patterns containing only vertical stripes for the first 15 months of life. Afterwards, the cats seemed blind to horizontal stripes. Electrophysiological recordings revealed that cats reared in a normal environment possessed orientation-selective cortical cells at all orientations. Selectively reared cats, on the other hand, possessed orientation-selective cells preferring only vertical orientations. Analogous effects have been found following selective exposure to stroboscopically flashed motion (Cynader, Berman, & Hein, 1973).

Biological aging

What does the brain lose as its weight declines in old age? For many years the dominant view was that brain aging involves progressive cortical cell death. Anatomical studies conducted in the 1950s had indicated that up to 40% of cortical neurons were lost during aging (senescence). However, recent research indicates that these early studies grossly overestimated cell loss (Morrison & Hof, 1997; Peters, 2002). Early estimates were based on cell counts in mounted brain sections, and were biased by shrinkage of brain preparations, and by the inadvertent inclusion of brains with neurodegenerative diseases. It now appears that there is no drastic loss of cells, or of synapses, in the elderly brain. On the other hand there is evidence for myelin breakdown and degeneration. A reduction in white matter by as much as 15% has been reported. This change may explain much of the decline in brain size shown in Figure 15.3. Myelin breakdown is likely to have important consequences for sensory and cognitive functioning. It will cause reductions in the conduction velocity of neural signals, and disrupt the timing of signals in neural circuits. Precise synchronization of neural firing is thought to be important during the construction of complex perceptual representations (Engel & Singer, 2001), so disrupted timing is likely to impede processing.

The preceding discussion assumes that a larger and heavier brain is generally an advantage in terms of greater computational efficacy and better task performance, but the issue is more complex than this: Big brains also have disadvantages. Larger brains could have larger neurons, or more neurons, or both. With larger neurons, signaling speeds may suffer and energy costs rise due to their longer axons and dendrites; with more neurons, it is more difficult to maintain the number of connections each neuron has with others in the brain (Kaas, 2000). Comparisons of brain size across species often do not give clear answers about the advantages of larger brains. For example, a lion has a much larger brain than a domestic cat, yet the brain functions of lions and cats appear to be quite similar (Kruska, 1988). Comparisons of brain size within a species such as humans are even more difficult to interpret in terms of performance benefits.

SEX

A huge number of experiments have been conducted to investigate differences in perceptual functions that can be linked to sex. Baker's (1987) extensive review found a female advantage in many functions, including tone sensitivity, taste sensitivity, odor recognition (see Figure 2.3 in Chapter 2), and touch acuity. Male

Scores tend to be normally distributed and the difference between mean male and female scores rarely exceeds 0.5 standard deviations. See Halpern (2000) for a detailed discussion of the statistics of gender differences.

subjects performed better in tests of spatial vision, and sensitivity to pain (Wiesenfeld-Hallin, 2005). It is very important to note that scores vary from one individual to the next even within each sex. Although the mean scores of male and female subjects may be different, this sex difference is usually small relative to the variability of scores within each sex.

To illustrate this point, Figure 15.4 shows mean performance in male and female subjects aged between 20 and 30 for several sensory modalities. The error bars mark the first and third quartiles in each distribution of scores: the lower error bar cuts off the lowest 25% of scores, and the upper error bar cuts off the highest 25% of scores. Mean female performance exceeds male performance in three of the four modalities, but there is extensive overlap in the distribution of scores, as indicated by the overlap in the error bars.

The largest sex difference in performance is usually found in variants of the **mental rotation** task (Voyer, Voyer, & Bryden, 1995). Two variants used by Collins and Kimura (1997) are shown in Figure 15.5. The test shape is shown on the left, and four comparison shapes are shown on the right, labeled (a) to (d). The subject's task is to select the comparison shape that matches the test shape, but viewed from

KEY TERM

Mental rotation
The manipulation of an internal mental image of a shape, so that it is visualized from a different viewing angle.

FIGURE 15.4
Male and female performance in four sensory modalities.
(a) Mental rotation (data from Collins & Kimura, 1997); (b) hearing (data from Morrell et al., 1996; dB SPL for 30 years at 4 kHz); (c) odor (data from Doty et al., 1984); (d) touch (data from Louis et al., 1984). Error bars indicate the first and third quartiles (25% and 75% of scores were lower than the values indicated by the bars, respectively). NB in the two left-hand plots, better performance gives higher scores in the graph, and in the right-hand two plots better performance gives lower scores in the graph.

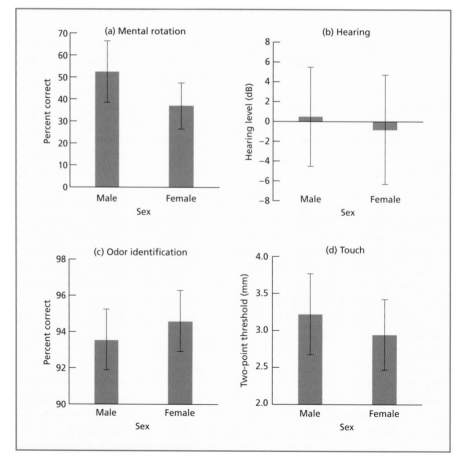

a different angle. The upper variant contains three-dimensional shapes similar to those used by Shepard and Metzler (1971). The correct shape (c) must be rotated in depth (about the *y*-axis) in order to create the same view as the test shape. The lower variant contains two-dimensional shapes. The correct shape (d) must be rotated in the picture plane (about the *z*-axis) to create the same view as the test shape (rotate the page by approximately 150°).

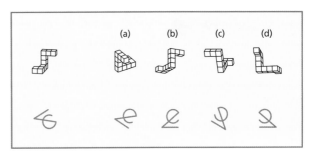

FIGURE 15.5
Typical stimuli in a mental rotation task. The test shape on the left is shown alongside four comparison shapes, labeled (a) to (d). The subject's task is to select the comparison shape that matches the test shape, viewed from a different angle. The version in the upper row contains line-drawn, three-dimensional shapes, as used by Shepard and Metzler (1971). The version in the lower row contains two-dimensional shapes, as used by Collins and Kimura (1997). Copyright © American Psychological Association. Reproduced with permission.

In common with many other studies, Collins and Kimura (1997) found that men performed better at this task than women. The data in Figure 15.4(a) show Collins and Kimura's results for the 3-D task in Figure 15.5 (calculated from Collins & Kimura, 1997, figure 3). On average, male subjects recorded over 15% more correct responses than female subjects. We can see from the error bars that 75% of male scores exceeded the average female score (compare the lower error bar in the male bar with the height of the female bar), but the top 25% of female scores were close to the average male score (compare the upper error bar in the female bar with the height of the male bar).

Sex differences have also been reported for many aspects of cognition. The largest female advantage occurs in tests of verbal ability, such as speed of articulation, fluency, and accuracy of speech production (Weiss et al., 2002). As in the case of the male advantage in spatial ability, the difference between the sexes is relatively small compared with the variability within gender.

THE ORIGINS OF SEX DIFFERENCES IN PERCEPTUAL FUNCTION

There has been a great deal of debate concerning the origin of sex differences in performance, no doubt partly fueled by sociopolitical issues. Some favor an explanation in terms of differences in experience and socialization between men and women. Others favor an explanation based on biological differences between male and female brains. Both factors are likely to be important, though their relative weight may vary with different aspects of performance. At least in the case of sex differences in spatial ability, evidence favors a biological explanation. Other mammalian species show gender differences in spatial behavior, including rats, mice, voles, and monkeys, and testosterone levels are known to influence performance in spatial tasks (Jones, Braithwaite, & Healy, 2003). Evolutionary pressure may have led to a gender difference in spatial ability. According to this argument, ancestral males who were best at navigation would have been the most successful hunters, and would have encountered more potential mates. On the other hand, female reproductive success would have been best served by reduced mobility, leading to greater energy conservation and reduced predation (Jones, Braithwaite, & Healy, 2003).

A fMRI study looked for differences between males and females in terms of brain activation during mental rotation and verbal fluency tasks (Halari et al., 2006). The study found the usual male performance advantage in mental rotation tasks, and female advantage in verbal fluency tasks. But there was no significant difference between men and women in the brain areas active while performing the tasks. The difference between male and female brains is apparently rather subtle.

CULTURE

Studies of cultural influences on perception have concentrated on two questions: (1) Do subjects from different cultures vary in **pictorial competence**? (2) Does the ecology of the visual environment influence perception?

PICTORIAL COMPETENCE

This issue focuses on the idea that subjects from cultures lacking pictorial representations find it difficult to interpret pictures. Scottish missionaries to Africa in the 19th century were the source of many anecdotal reports that "natives" were unable to recognize the content of pictures (Deregowski, 1989), and a view became established that "pictorial competence" is culturally transmitted. But there has been relatively little systematic research on the issue. Hudson (1960) developed an influential test of picture perception based on images of the kind shown in Figure 15.6.

Participants were asked three questions about each picture:

FIGURE 15.6
Typical line drawing from Hudson's test of picture perception, used in studies of cultural influences on perception. From Deregowski (1989). Copyright © 1989 Cambridge University Press. Reproduced with permission.

1. What do you see?
2. What is the man doing?
3. Which is nearer the man, the elephant or the antelope?

Responses were classified as "3-D" if the subject responded that the hunter was aiming at the antelope, and that the antelope was nearer than the elephant. Hudson (1960) administered his test to several groups of subjects in South Africa, classified as "schooled" or "unschooled," and as "white" or "black." The mean percentage of subjects in each group giving 3-D responses is shown in Table 15.1 (calculated from Hudson, 1960, table 2).

Schooled subjects gave many more 3-D responses than unschooled subjects, and Hudson concluded that:

> *formal schooling and informal training combined to supply an exposure threshold necessary for the development of the process [3-D perception]. Cultural isolation was effective in preventing or retarding the process.*
>
> (Hudson, 1960, p. 207)

However, there are serious reservations about the validity of Hudson's picture test. Jahoda and McGurk (1974) and Hagen and Jones (1978) argued that the results of

TABLE 15.1 Responses to Hudson's picture test in different culture groups

	Unschooled	Schooled
Black	8.56% (n = 204)	66.22% (n = 111)
White	15.33% (n = 60)	58.61% (n =187)

pictorial competence studies are heavily biased by the methodology. Hagen and Jones (1978) reviewed several picture perception studies in which results were significantly altered by the nature of the experimental instructions. Culture is likely to have influenced subjects' attitudes to instructions and test-taking, regardless of sensory effects. Furthermore, Hudson's pictures were relatively impoverished and geometrically inaccurate line-drawings, lacking textural detail and gray-level gradation. Notice from Table 15.1 that one in three responses of even "schooled" subjects was incorrect. Hagen and Jones (1978) argue that any test of picture perception that:

> *fails to generate nearly 100% three-dimensional responding in educated Western adults has faults of either design or procedure or both which leaves its validity open to serious question. It seems to us very unlikely that some 30% of educated Scots are **incapable** of seeing depth in pictures stylistically indigenous to their culture.*
>
> *(p. 191, their emphasis. Jahoda and McGurk, 1974, tested Scottish and Ghanaian subjects)*

ECOLOGY: THE "CARPENTERED WORLD" HYPOTHESIS

A number of studies have explored the idea that subjects living in highly industrialized environments perceive angles and straight edges differently from subjects living in environments lacking rectangular manufactured structures.

Illusion studies

The standard technique in early studies was to measure the magnitude of geometric illusions in groups of subjects from different cultures.

Ames Window

Allport and Pettigrew (1957) employed the rotating trapezoid illusion, or Ames Window. A sheet of metal is cut to form a trapezoidal window, and rotated about a vertical axis (see Figure 15.7(a)). Subjects generally report seeing the window oscillate from side to side rather than rotate, so that the longer vertical edge always appears closer to the viewer. Allport and Pettigrew (1957) used rural Bantu boys and urban African or European boys as subjects. They reported that in "optimal" conditions of distant, monocular viewing, both rural and urban subjects reported seeing the illusion (87.5% and 92.5% of reports, respectively). In "marginal" conditions of near, binocular viewing, fewer rural subjects saw the illusion than urban subjects (35% and 60% of reports, respectively).

Geometrical illusions

Segall, Campbell, and Herskovits (1963) measured the magnitude of the Müller–Lyer, Sander Parallelogram, and Vertical–Horizontal illusions in urban and tribal subjects in the USA, Africa, and the Philippines. Examples of these illusions are shown in Figure 15.7 (parts (b)–(d)). They reported that urban subjects showed larger illusion magnitudes than tribal subjects, for the Müller–Lyer and the Sander Parallelogram. Results for the Vertical–Horizontal illusion were mixed, with some

FIGURE 15.7
Examples of geometrical illusions used in studies of cultural influences on perception. (a) The Ames Window appears to oscillate back and forth when it is rotated about the vertical axis in only one direction. (b) The Müller–Lyer illusion. The line with outward-facing arrowheads appears longer than the line with inward-facing arrowheads. (c) Sander Parallelogram. The two diagonals appear unequal in length, but are actually equal. (d) The Vertical–Horizontal illusion. The vertical line is the same length as the horizontal line, but appears longer. (e) The Ponzo illusion. The two horizontal lines are equal in length, but the top line appears longer.

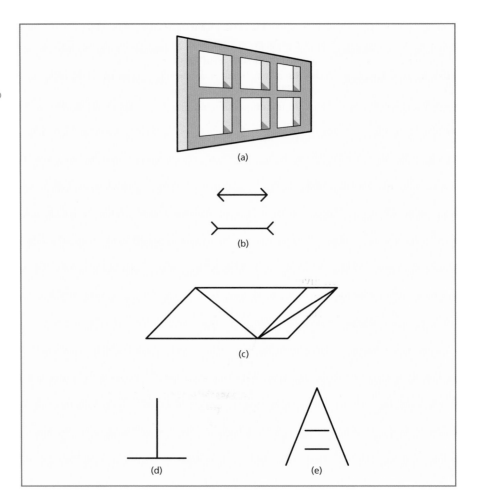

nonurban subject groups showing a larger effect, and others showing a smaller effect than urban subjects.

Leibowitz and Pick (1972) studied the magnitude of the Ponzo illusion (Figure 15.7(e)) in college students (both US and Ugandan) and in rural Ugandans. They reported that rural Ugandans saw no illusion at all, while college students (Ugandan and US) saw a relatively strong illusion.

The utility of illusion studies

It is unfortunate that geometrical illusions featured so prominently in early research on visual ecology. The classical psychophysical methods used in this research are notoriously vulnerable to bias effects introduced by instructions, or by observer attitudes, or even by experimenter attitudes (see the tutorial on psychophysical methods in Chapter 1). A further source of bias is the quality of the retinal image, which may have varied systematically between subject groups. The incidence of uncorrected refractive error was almost certainly higher in nonindustrialized, rural subjects, but was not measured in the studies reviewed above. In addition, different racial groups vary in terms of pigmentation of the lens, iris, and fundus. Such optical factors are claimed to produce significant variations in illusion magnitude and picture perception (e.g., Coren, 1989; Pollack, 1989).

So any obtained differences in measured illusion magnitude confound sensory effects and bias effects. Even if one sets aside issues of bias, data on illusion magnitude are of limited use because there is no universally agreed explanation for the illusions themselves, despite claims to the contrary in some of the cross-cultural literature. Indeed many illusions are likely to reflect the combined effect of several causes (Morgan, 1996). The lack of clarity on illusion causation makes it difficult to judge the significance of any differences in illusion magnitude.

The oblique effect

Annis and Frost (1973) approached the "carpentered world" hypothesis from a different angle. They investigated a well-known perceptual effect, known as the **oblique effect**. Many studies of subjects from industrialized cultures have shown that visual acuity is greater for lines oriented vertically or horizontally than it is for lines oriented obliquely. One explanation for the effect is that a "carpentered world" provides selective visual experience that favors vertically and horizontally oriented contours, which produces a bias in the orientation selectivity of cells in the visual cortex (recall the experiments on selective rearing by Blakemore and Cooper, 1970, mentioned earlier). Annis and Frost (1973) measured the oblique effect in urban Euro-Canadians and in nonurban Cree Indians. They found a larger oblique effect in the former than in the latter, which they interpret as supporting the "carpentered world" hypothesis. However, Timney and Muir (1976) took the same measurements from another two ethnic groups of subjects, one Caucasian and one Chinese, who were both raised in urban carpentered environments. Timney and Muir obtained effects similar in size to those found by Annis and Frost (1973). Chinese subjects showed a smaller oblique effect than Caucasian subjects. Timney and Muir (1976) argue that variations in the magnitude of the oblique effect may reflect genetic factors rather than environmental effects. Furthermore, Switkes, Mayer, and Sloan (1978), and Keil and Cristobal (2000) compared the spatial frequency content of images taken from carpentered and pastoral environments, and found no evidence for differences that would support the carpentered world hypothesis. Keil and Cristobal (2000) did report greater Fourier energy at vertical and horizontal orientations, but this was found in both manmade scenes and in natural scenes. Verticals occur in natural images due to vertical plant supports, and horizontals occur due to horizontal branches and leaves, and to the horizontal ground plane. Other studies support the view that inequalities in Fourier energy at different orientations are a general property of natural images, rather than a product of a carpentered world (Coppola et al., 1998; Girshick, Landy, & Simoncelli, 2011).

CULTURE EFFECTS

Data from cross-cultural studies are claimed by some to support the conclusion that perception is influenced by culture (e.g., Deregowski, 1989; Gregory, 1998). However, much of the evidence is either weak or subject to alternative interpretations, as discussed earlier. A rare piece of convincing evidence in favor of cultural effects comes from Werker and colleagues, who studied phoneme discrimination (phonemes are elementary units of speech, see Chapter 5 and Figure 5.10). They and others have found that infants younger than 12 months old are able to discriminate phonemes from all the world's languages, whereas older infants and adults cannot discriminate some phonemes not used in their native language (see Werker and Desjardins, 1995; Kuhl, 2004).

KEY TERM

Oblique effect
Reduced visual acuity for oblique lines and gratings, relative to vertical and horizontal orientations.

A few people possess
perfect pitch, which
means that they
can identify the
absolute pitch of
a sound without
aids, while most
people require a
reference pitch and/
or rehearsal in order
to identify absolute
pitch. Crummer
et al. (1994) found
that individuals with
perfect pitch had
the shortest ERP
latencies of all.

EXPERTISE

FORMAL TRAINING

There are several examples of perceptual differences linked to the level of expertise of the subject, as indicated by formal training.

Musicians

Crummer et al. (1994) studied the discrimination of timbre in notes produced by several musical instruments (cellos, violas, flutes, and tubas). Recall from Chapter 5 that different instruments produce different complex sounds even when playing the same note, giving each instrument its characteristic timbre. Crummer et al. (1994) found that all subjects could discriminate timbre reliably, but trained musicians had a slight advantage over nonmusicians. Musicians showed larger and faster event-related potentials (ERPs, brain waves) than nonmusicians.

Beauvois and Meddis (1997) studied auditory grouping. As described in Chapter 5 and illustrated in Figure 5.13, when two tones are presented in a repeated sequence, a higher frequency tone alternating with a lower frequency tone, two different groupings can be perceived. Rapid alternation leads to the perception of two streams, one high pitched and the other low pitched. Relatively slow alternation leads to perception of a single rhythmic form (a musical trill). Prolonged exposure (adaptation) to a streaming sequence biases subjects' perception of subsequent test sequences in favor of streaming, but this bias effect dissipates if a silent interval is interposed between adaptation and testing. Beauvois and Meddis (1997) found consistent differences in streaming responses between musicians and nonmusicians, as shown in Figure 15.8.

Musicians showed more perceptual segregation than nonmusicians, as is evident from the height of the curves in Figure 15.8 at short silent intervals. In addition, musicians required a longer silent interval to dissipate the bias than nonmusicians. Musicians apparently have a more finely tuned ability to perceive musical trills.

Visual artists

Thouless investigated shape and size constancy in a series of classic psychophysical experiments published in the 1930s. **Shape constancy** is the tendency for perceived

FIGURE 15.8
Strength of auditory
streaming as a function of
the duration of the interval
between adaptation and
testing (replotted from
Beauvois & Meddis,
1997). Musicians (left-
hand graph) showed
more streaming than
nonmusical subjects
(right-hand graph), and
the effect dissipated more
slowly. Reproduced from
Beauvois & Meddis, 1997,
with kind permission from
Springer Science and
Business Media.

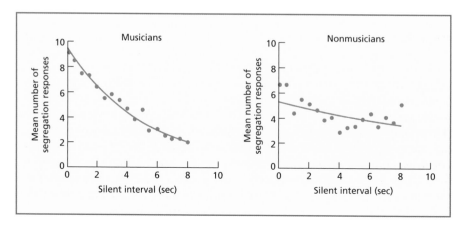

shape to remain relatively constant even when variations in viewing conditions produce marked changes in the retinal image. For example, if a flat circular disk is placed on a table top, and an observer views it from an oblique angle, the image of the disk on the retina will be elliptical due to foreshortening, as illustrated in Figure 15.9 (foreshortening was explained in Chapter 11, Figure 11.6). However, the observer tends to perceive the retinal projection of the disk as more circular than it really is.

In Thouless's experiments, observers were asked to match the shape of the disk as seen from their viewpoint with a series of alternative elliptical shapes varying in their degree of eccentricity. An observer showing perfect shape constancy would select the circle as the matching shape, since this is the actual shape of the disk. An observer showing no shape constancy would select the shape that matches the elliptical retinal image of the disk exactly. Most observers show partial shape constancy, selecting a shape intermediate between these two extremes. Thouless called this effect "phenomenal regression to the real object," and measured it in a large number of subjects. He expressed constancy scores on a scale from 0 (no constancy) to 1.0 (perfect constancy). Thouless (1931) compared the degree of constancy shown by trained artists and by nonartists, and Figure 15.10 shows his data (taken from Thouless, 1931, table 12).

Artists showed much less constancy than nonartists. Shape constancy is probably responsible for the difficulties most people experience when they attempt to create realistic life-drawings of three-dimensional scenes. It thwarts attempts to render viewed shapes accurately in a drawing, since it distorts perceptual impressions towards real object shapes. Trained artists counteract constancy more successfully than nonartists, but note that some constancy is present even in artists (their scores in Figure 15.10 are below 1.0). To overcome this residual tendency, artists have traditionally used aids such as Albrecht Dürer's device, a viewing window divided into squares using a wire grid. The three-dimensional scene is reproduced on paper divided up into a corresponding number of squares. Artists today generally use *sighting* to overcome constancy. Image proportions such as the projected width and height of the disk in Figure 15.9, are measured using a thumb positioned along a pencil or brush handle held at arm's length.

Kozbelt (2001) compared art students against novice artists in several visual tasks including mental rotation, identification of blurred photographs, embedded figures, and fragmented pictures. He found no difference between the groups in mental rotation scores. But art students performed markedly better than novices in the other three tasks involving degraded images, by as much as 52%. However, when Perdreau and Cavanagh (2013) recently compared artists against nonartists in three basic perceptual tasks—size matching, luminance matching, and visual search—they found that artists performed no better than untrained participants.

PRACTICE

At least some of the difference in performance between formally trained and untrained subjects must reflect a straightforward practice effect rather than innate ability as a musician or artist. Formally trained subjects spend a large proportion of their time, perhaps over many years, absorbed in relevant activities, such as artistic performance or observation and analysis of other artists' work. So there is plenty of scope for practice effects. Laboratory studies have shown that practice at even simple sensory tasks leads to consistent improvements in performance, as the following examples show.

FIGURE 15.9
Illustration of shape constancy. The mug tops in Figure 10.7 are elliptical, due to the oblique viewing angle. When an untrained observer is asked to select the ellipse in this figure that is the closest match to the mug tops in Figure 10.7, they tend to select an ellipse that is more circular than the image shape (phenomenal regression to the real object). The mug images in Figure 10.7 have aspect ratios corresponding to the two topmost ellipses in Figure 15.9.

? *Compare shape constancy with color constancy, described in Chapter 8.*

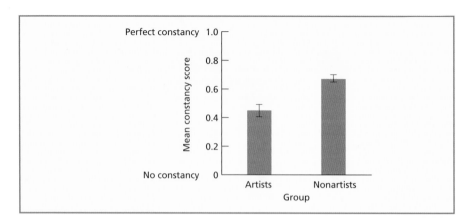

Odor

Rabin (1988) studied the ability of subjects to discriminate between unfamiliar odors. He found that a practice session in which subjects became familiar with the smells improved performance significantly relative to control subjects who were given no practice. Practiced subjects achieved 94% correct odor discrimination in the test phase, while control subjects achieved 81% correct discrimination. In a second experiment, Rabin (1988) found that detection rates for contaminants in familiar odors were higher than for contaminants in unfamiliar odors, especially when the contaminant itself was familiar. Detection was 20.5% better using familiar contaminants in familiar odors than when both were unfamiliar. This research bears out anecdotal claims that expert perfumiers and wine tasters can make finer discriminations than unpracticed subjects.

Vision

A number of studies have found that practice at simple visual discriminations improves performance significantly. The practice effects show a surprising degree of specificity. Fahle and Morgan (1996) employed two tasks that involved judging the relative positions of three small dots. One task involved judging the alignment of the dots, and the other involved judging the spacing between the dots. An hour of practice at either task improved discrimination performance by between 6% and 12%. When subjects switched from one task to another, the benefits of practice were eliminated and performance returned to a level similar to that shown in entirely unpracticed subjects. Beard, Levi, and Reich (1995) also used simple visual discrimination tasks. They found partial transfer of training between tasks, but no transfer to new retinal locations. When subjects were trained and tested using the same stimuli presented at the same location in the right eye, performance improved by 13.06%. When subjects were tested using the same stimuli but presented at a different location in the same eye, there was very little practice effect (2.34%). Such a high degree of specificity indicates that practice causes changes to occur in very early, retinally localized perceptual processes rather than in higher level cognitive processes. These results have led to a new view of the sensory cortex, in which the adult brain retains some degree of flexibility so that it can acquire new skills when the need arises (Sagi, 2011).

NEURAL CORRELATES OF EXPERTISE

We have already seen that subtle differences in perception resulting from age and sex can, to a large extent, be traced to physical differences in the brain. Can differences resulting from expertise be linked to differences in brain structure? Several studies have reported physical differences between the brains of trained and untrained subjects.

Schwartz, Maquet, and Frith (2002) conducted a fMRI experiment to investigate the neural substrate of learning a visual texture discrimination task. They found, as had previous studies, that intensive practice at the task using one eye improved performance using that eye but not using the other eye. Moreover, they found greater fMRI activation using the trained eye than using the untrained eye. The difference in activation level was restricted to early visual cortex (V1). Schwartz, Maquet, and Frith (2002) concluded that training induced neural changes in the earliest stage of cortical processing.

Elbert et al. (1995) used magnetic source imaging to compare the primary somatosensory cortex of experienced string musicians against a group of control subjects. They found evidence that the cortical representation of the fingers of the left hand is larger in string musicians than in control subjects. The magnitude of the difference between expert and control subjects was significantly correlated with the age at which the expert had begun to play their instrument, indicating a role for experience. A more recent study of musicians corroborates this finding. As discussed in the tutorials section of Chapter 5, Broca's area (BA 44) is well known to be associated with expressive language processing. Damage in this area leads to an inability to produce language, either spoken or written, which is known as Broca's aphasia. Broca's area is also important for several aspects of music processing. A recent neuroimaging study (Abdul-Kareem et al., 2011) found that the volume of Broca's area is positively correlated with the number of years of experience as a musical performer.

Bezzola et al. (2011) used MRI to investigate changes in the brain induced by extensive golf practice in novice golfers aged between 40 and 60 years. They found increases in gray matter in cortical areas associated with the task, namely sensorimotor cortex and areas forming part of the dorsal stream.

Maguire et al. (2000) took MRI scans of the brains of licensed London taxi drivers and of age-matched control subjects. They found that the posterior hippocampus was larger in taxi drivers than in control subjects. Hippocampal volume was correlated with the amount of time served as a taxi driver. Figure 15.11 shows hippocampal volume as a function of length of service.

The hippocampus is thought to play an important role in spatial tasks, and particularly in navigation. So Maguire et al. concluded that professional dependence on spatial navigation skills results in a redistribution of gray matter in the hippocampus. The correlation with experience supports their view that variations in hippocampal volume are acquired through experience (see also Woollett & Maguire, 2011).

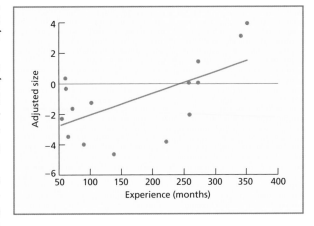

FIGURE 15.11
Volume of gray matter in the right hippocampus as a function of time spent as a London taxi driver (data from Maguire et al., 2000). The hippocampal volume was significantly correlated with experience ($r = 0.6$; $p < .05$).

IDIOSYNCRATIC INDIVIDUAL DIFFERENCES

A large number of papers have reported consistent interindividual differences in a range of perceptual and cognitive functions, which are not attributable to clinical or demographic factors and therefore are assumed to be idiosyncratic differences. For example:

- Ginsburg and colleagues found threefold variations in spatial contrast sensitivity in a large group of airforce pilots, but this variation could reflect differences in simple visual acuity, which was not measured (see Ginsburg, 1986).
- Halpern, Andrews, and Purves (1999) tested 20 subjects between 20 and 30 years of age (all members of Duke University, USA) using seven visual tasks ranging from orientation discrimination to form identification. They found large intersubject differences in performance. Scores in most tasks tended to co-vary, so if an individual scored highly in one task, he or she tended to score highly in other tasks. It is possible that at least some of the variation reported by Halpern, Andrews, and Purves (1999) reflected differences due to expertise and sex, since these factors were not controlled for in data analysis.
- Martens et al. (2006) studied the attentional blink (described in the previous chapter) in which detection of visual targets in a rapidly presented sequence of stimuli is impaired if they appear up to half a second after a previous target. Participants were drawn from the University of Groningen community, with no history of neurological problems. Martens et al. (2006) found that about 8% of participants show no attentional blink at all ("nonblinkers," as opposed to the majority of "blinkers" who show the effect).
- Kanai, Bahrami, and Rees (2010) measured spontaneous reversals in the apparent direction of ambiguous structure-from-motion stimuli (similar to the rotating spheres described in Chapter 12 and depicted in Figure 12.1) in 52 healthy volunteers and found consistent individual differences in reversal rates.

In some cases these differences can be related to structural differences in the participants' brains. For instance: Martens et al. (2006) found differences between "blinkers" and "nonblinkers" in the distribution and timing of EEG activity during task execution; Kanai, Bahrami, and Rees (2010) found structural differences in the parietal lobe that correlated with individual differences in perceptual reversal rates; other cases are described in Kanai and Rees (2011). A postmortem study also found significant individual differences in the size of the visual system. Andrews, Halpern, and Purves (1997) took postmortem measurements of the area and volume of several neural structures in the visual system in a sample of normal human brains (the optic tract, lateral geniculate nucleus, and primary visual cortex). Andrews, Halpern, and Purves (1997) reported a two- to threefold variation in the size of these components between individuals. They also found a high correlation between the size of the components, so brains with a large visual cortex also tended to have a large optic tract and lateral geniculate nucleus. The same research group later reported significant individual differences in performance on a range of visual tasks (Halpern, Andrews, & Purves, 1999, described above). The authors were tempted to conclude that: "interindividual variation in the amount of neural circuitry devoted to vision gives rise to differences in human visual ability" (p. 524).

At least some of the variability in brain structure reported in these studies may be due to uncontrolled differences in sex, age, or expertise. Andrews, Halpern, and Purves's (1997) donors, for example, ranged in age from 28 to 86 and their background (formal qualifications, occupation, pastimes, etc.) was not reported. As yet no study has attempted a direct correlation between individual task performance and brain structure with records of participant age, gender, and expertise. So the question of how idiosyncratic differences in perception arise is still unresolved.

CHAPTER SUMMARY

Although they are often ignored, there are significant interindividual differences in perception which relate to a number of factors that vary between experimental participants.

AGE

- Performance generally conforms to a U-shaped function, with rapid improvements in the first decade of life, followed by gradual decline after the fifth decade.
- These changes can be attributed to changes in the efficiency of the peripheral sense organs, and in the efficiency of signal transmission within the cortex.

SEX

- Sex differences are frequently reported in all sensory modalities, with female subjects generally outperforming male subjects except in tasks involving spatial vision.
- Male–female differences are usually small relative to the variability of scores within each sex.
- Physical differences between male and female brains, perhaps as a result of natural selection, could underlie some of the sex differences in performance.

CULTURE

- A number of studies claim to find differences in perception between subjects from nonindustrialized cultures and subjects from industrialized cultures.
- Early studies claimed that nonindustrialized subjects found pictures difficult to interpret, and were less prone to visual illusions involving judgments of straight lines and angles.
- Much of the evidence is not convincing, and subject to alternative interpretations.

EXPERTISE

- Formal training in music or art produces consistent differences in perception.
- Musicians can make finer discriminations of timbre and auditory streaming than nonmusicians.
- Artists show less shape constancy than nonartists, and do not perform better than nonartists in most of the visual tasks that have been studied.
- Practice at simple visual discriminations typically improves performance by more than 10%, but the effect does not transfer well between different tasks or between different retinal locations.
- Several neuroimaging studies have found physical differences between experts and nonexperts, indicating that plasticity in the cortex may be responsible for differences in performance.

IDIOSYNCRONY

- Marked individual differences in performance have been reported for a number of sensory tasks, with the corresponding variations in underlying neural structures. The origin of these differences is still unclear.

TUTORIALS

METHODOLOGY IN INFANT VISION

As we saw in the tutorials section of Chapter 1, a number of different techniques have been developed over the past 150 years for studying adult perception. These techniques cannot be employed in developmental studies because of the limitations of infants as experimental subjects. Young infants cannot understand instructions, and cannot tell the experimenter what they are perceiving. They have a limited behavioral repertoire, an inability to concentrate on a given task, and tend to fall asleep frequently. All in all, they present quite a challenge to the researcher.

Experimental psychologists have developed a range of special techniques that exploit the behavior of infants, particularly their inquisitiveness and inability to concentrate (see Atkinson, 2000). Psychophysical techniques have been developed to study an infant's ability to discriminate between two stimuli, which can be used to measure sensory thresholds and compare results against those obtained from adults.

Preferential attention

In this technique the experimenter presents the infant with two stimuli, and measures the relative amount of time the infant devotes to each. In early research the experimenter watched the infant's face and measured how long the child attended to each stimulus. In contemporary studies the experimenter bases measurements on videos of the infant, or on measures of eye fixation, to ensure objectivity. If the infant spends an equal amount of time attending to each stimulus, he or she may be unable to distinguish between them. If he or she attends more to one of the two stimuli, then the experimenter infers that the infant can discriminate between them and, for some reason, prefers one over the other. Fantz (1961) used this technique to show that infants have a spontaneous preference for more complex spatial patterns over simpler patterns. For example, when 2- to 3-month-old infants were shown a spatially uniform disk and a bull's-eye pattern, they spent over twice as long inspecting the bull's-eye. When shown a bull's-eye and a cartoon face, they looked towards the face for twice the time that they looked at the bull's-eye pattern.

Habituation

Infants generally become less attentive as they become more familiar with a stimulus, even an interesting one. If the stimulus is presented repeatedly, the infant will spend less and less time attending to it. This effect is called habituation. If the stimulus is changed the infant is likely to show renewed interest in the novel stimulus (dishabituation), provided that he or she can distinguish between the habituated stimulus and the novel stimulus. The change in looking time following a stimulus change provides a measure of stimulus discriminability. This technique can be used to measure the smallest change in stimulation necessary for the infant to detect the change, namely their discrimination threshold or just noticeable difference (JND).

Physiological measures

Some techniques do not rely on overt behavior at all, but instead take physiological measurements that indicate awareness of the stimulus. When an infant habituates, his or her heart rate decreases. An unexpected, and detectable, change in stimulation causes an increase in heart rate. Variation in heart rate thus offers a physiological measure of habituation.

Another commonly used technique involves recording event related potentials (ERPs) from 50 or 60 electrodes fixed to a skull cap. Fluctuations in sensory stimulation (the events) produce minute but measurable fluctuations in electrical potential in the brain. Specialized equipment can detect these fluctuations with millisecond accuracy. The timing, size, and location of ERP activity recorded on the scalp can be used to draw inferences about the time-course of processing in the brain and the location of the source of the activity.

THE IDIOSYNCRATIC VISION OF ARTISTS: VISUAL DYSFUNCTION?

The striking and original pictures created by celebrated artists indicate that they have a unique, idiosyncratic view of the world. However, it is possible that some artists suffered from a dysfunction of vision, and that this dysfunction played a significant role in shaping their work. A number of claims can be found in the literature regarding links between visual dysfunctions in certain individuals and the art they created.

Myopia and the Impressionists

Myopia or short-sightedness is a defect of accommodation that causes the retinal image of distant objects to appear blurred (see Chapter 6). It could be argued that myopia is an advantage to painters, since it preserves large shapes and blocks of colors, but removes otherwise distracting fine detail. Indeed the blurry images created by the Impressionists have been attributed to their myopia (e.g., Polland, 2004). There seems good evidence that at least some impressionists such as Cézanne and Renoir were myopic. Trevor-Roper (1988) reported a survey of 128 masters and pupils of the Ecole des Beaux-Arts in Paris in 1917, which found that 47% of those surveyed were myopic (short-sighted) and 27% were hyperopic (long-sighted). The opposite pattern is found in the general population; hyperopia is actually twice as common as myopia (see Wang et al., 1994). So Trevor-Roper (1988) suggested that the high incidence of myopia in the Impressionists could have had at least a limited effect on their artistic style. However the relative prevalence of myopia and hyperopia does vary dramatically with age (Wang et al., 1994), and if the majority of those surveyed in the Ecole des Beaux-Arts were below the age of 54, then the reported bias in favor of myopes is no more than would be expected in the general population.

Cataracts and Claude Monet

Cataracts create an opacity in the lens of the eye, which dims and clouds the image and alters the balance of wavelengths reaching the retina. It can be seen in the milky appearance of the pupil particularly in elderly individuals. An important causative factor is thought to be exposure to ultraviolet wavelengths in natural daylight (a good reason to wear sunglasses on very bright days; McCarty & Taylor, 1996). Claude Monet and Mary Cassatt both suffered from cataracts that almost certainly affected their paintings (Marmor & Ravin, 1997). Monet tended to paint the same scene repeatedly. A comparison of his paintings of the Japanese footbridge in the garden of his house at Giverny, executed early and late in the development of his cataracts, shows a clear change. The later paintings are much less distinct and more abstract, with a change in color balance from blue–greens to red–yellows. It is possible that these changes reflect a developing artistic style, or advancing age, but they are at least consistent with the changes that would be expected as a result of cataracts.

Macular degeneration and Edgar Degas

Degas suffered from myopia and a central blind spot that has been attributed to degeneration of his central retina, which meant that he could see nothing at the point he was actually fixating (Trevor-Roper, 1988). It has been suggested that Degas's preference for pastels, his habit of working from photographs, and his preoccupation with sculpting later in life can all be attributed to his failing sight (Elliot & Skaff, 1993).

Astigmatism and El Greco

The paintings of El Greco (Domenikos Theotokopoulos) show a characteristic vertical elongation, which has been attributed to astigmatism (Trevor-Roper, 1988). Astigmatism is an optical defect in the cornea of the eye. A normal cornea has spherical curvature, like the bowl of a soup spoon, whereas an astigmatic cornea has toric curvature (greater radius of curvature in one meridian than in the perpendicular meridian), rather like the bowl of a dessert spoon. Consequently images of points become lines in the astigmatic eye, and images of lines at some orientations are less distinct than those at other orientations. There are two objections to the claim that El Greco's style was influenced by astigmatism, one logical and the other empirical. The claim that El Greco painted elongated figures because he saw them as elongated has become known as the El Greco Fallacy (Firestone, 2013). Logically any distortion El Greco perceived would be applied both to the subject he painted and to the painting itself. The two distortions should cancel out, so his paintings would not be expected to show a distortion. It is possible, nevertheless, that El Greco's work could have exhibited distortion when he was working from memory rather than from life. Anstis (2002) tested the claim empirically by having a subject draw a freehand square from memory while wearing a lens designed to mimic astigmatism. The subject did indeed draw a distorted square. But when the exercise was repeated at regular intervals over a period of two days, the distortion gradually diminished, presumably due to perceptual adaptation. Anstis (2002) concluded that "[El Greco's] elongations were an artistic impression, not a visual symptom" (p. 208).

Stereoblindness and Rembrandt

Livingstone and Conway (2004) examined Rembrandt's series of self-portraits, most of which show one eye gazing directly at the viewer and the other deviating to one side. Such a deviation is consistent with a divergent strabismus or squint. An uncorrected squint normally causes stereoblindness, as discussed in Chapter 11. Livingstone and Conway (2004) suggest that stereoblindness may be an asset to artists, since it facilitates the process of transforming a three-dimensional real scene onto a two-dimensional canvas. Marmor and Shaikh (2005) urged caution in diagnosing Rembrandt's squint from his self-portraits.

It seems that evidence for the importance of visual defects in the work of famous artists is rather patchy. Some claims are plausible and seem well founded, while others are little more than speculation. More examples of the impact of eye and brain disorders on visual art can be found in Mather (2014).

Bibliography

Abdul-Kareem, I. A., Stancak, A., Parkes, L. M., & Sluming, V. (2011). Increased gray matter volume of left pars opercularis in male orchestral musicians correlate positively with years of musical performance. *Journal of Magnetic Resonance Imaging, 33*(1), 24–32.

Adelson, E., & Bergen, J. (1985). Spatiotemporal energy models for the detection of motion. *Journal of the Optical Society of America, A2,* 284–299.

Adelson, E., & Movshon, A. (1982). Phenomenal coherence of moving visual patterns. *Nature, 300,* 523–525.

Adrian, E. D., & Zotterman, Y. (1926). The impulses produced by sensory nerve-endings. Part 2. The responses of a single end-organ. *Journal of Physiology, 61,* 151–171.

Aggleton, J. (1992). *The Amygdala.* New York: Wiley-Liss.

Alais, D., & Blake, R. (1999). Neural strength of visual attention gauged by motion adaptation. *Nature Neuroscience, 2,* 1015–1018.

Alais, D., & Burr, D. (2004). The ventriloquist effect results from near-optimal bimodal integration. *Current Biology, 14*(3), 257–262.

Alais, D., Morrone, C., & Burr, D. (2006). Separate attentional resources for vision and audition. *Proceedings of the Royal Society of London B: Biological Sciences, 273*(1592), 1339–1345.

Alais, D., Verstraten, F. A., & Burr, D. C. (2005). The motion aftereffect of transparent motion: Two temporal channels account for perceived direction. *Vision Research, 45*(4), 403–412.

Albright, T. D. (1992). Form-cue invariant motion processing in primate visual cortex. *Science, 255,* 1141–1143.

Allport, G. W., & Pettigrew, T. F. (1957). Cultural influence on the perception of movement: The trapezoidal illusion among Zulus. *Journal of Abnormal and Social Psychology, 55,* 104–113.

Alvarado, J. C., Vaughan, J. W., Stanford, T. R., & Stein, B. E. (2007). Multisensory versus unisensory integration: Contrasting modes in the superior colliculus. *Journal of Neurophysiology, 97,* 3193–3205.

Amedi, A., Malach, R., Hendler, T., Peled, S., & Zohary, E. (2001). Visuo-haptic object-related activation in the ventral visual pathway. *Nature Neuroscience, 4*(3), 324–330.

Amedi, A., von Kriegstein, K., van Atteveldt, N. M., Beauchamp, M. S., & Naumer, M. J. (2005). Functional imaging of human crossmodal identification and object recognition. *Experimental Brain Research, 166*(3–4), 559–571.

Andersen, R. A., & Bradley, D. C. (1998). Perception of three-dimensional structure from motion. *Trends in Cognitive Sciences, 2,* 222–228.

Andrews, T. J., Halpern, S. D., & Purves, D. (1997). Correlated size variations in human visual cortex, lateral geniculate nucleus, and optic tract. *Journal of Neuroscience, 17,* 2859–2868.

Angelucci, A., & Bullier, J. (2003). Reaching beyond the classical receptive field of V1 neurons: Horizontal or feedback axons? *Journal of Physiology, 97,* 141–154.

Angelucci, A., Levitt, J. B., Walton, E. J., Hupe, J. M., Bullier, J., & Lund, J. S. (2002). Circuits for local and global signal integration in primary visual cortex. *Journal of Neuroscience, 22,* 8633–8646.

Annis, R. C., & Frost, B. (1973). Human visual ecology and orientation anisotropies in acuity. *Science, 182,* 729–731.

Anstis, S. M. (1974). A chart demonstrating variations in acuity with retinal position. *Vision Research, 14,* 589–592.

Anstis, S. M. (2002). Was El Greco astigmatic? *Leonardo, 35,* 208.

Anzai, A., & DeAngelis, G. C. (2010). Neural computations underlying depth perception. *Current Opinion in Neurobiology, 20*(3), 367–375.

Artal, P. (2014). Optics of the eye and its impact in vision: A tutorial. *Advances in Optics and Photonics, 6*(3), 340–367.

Ashida, H., Lingnau, A., Wall, M.B., & Smith, A.T. (2007). fMRI adaptation reveals separate mechanisms for first-order and second-order motion. *Journal of Neurophysiology, 97,* 1319–1325.

Ashkenazi, A., & Marks, L. E. (2004). Effect of endogenous attention on detection of weak gustatory and olfactory flavors. *Perception & Psychophysics, 66*(4), 596–608.

Atema, J. (1977). Functional separation of smell and taste in fish and crustacea. In J. Le Magnen & P. MacLeod (Eds.), *Olfaction and Taste VI* (pp. 165–174). London: Information Retrieval.

Atkinson, J. (2000). *The Developing Visual Brain.* Oxford: Oxford University Press.

Backus, B. T., & Haijiang, Q. (2007). Competition between newly recruited and pre-existing visual cues during construction of visual appearance. *Vision Research, 47,* 919–924.

Badcock, D., & Shor, C. (1985). Depth-increment detection function for individual spatial channels. *Journal of the Optical Society of America, A2,* 1211–1215.

Baker, C. L., & Braddick, O. J. (1985). Temporal properties of the short-range process in apparent motion. *Perception, 14,* 181–192.

Baker, M. A. (1987). Sensory functioning. In M. A. Baker (Ed.), *Sex Differences in Human Performance* (pp. 5–36). Chichester: Wiley.

Ballard, D., Hayhoe, M., Pook, P., & Rao, R. (1997). Deictic codes for the embodiment of cognition. *Behavioral and Brain Sciences, 20,* 723–767.

Banks, M. S., & Bennett, P. J. (1988). Optical and photoreceptor immaturities limit the spatial and chromatic vision of human neonates. *Journal of the Optical Society of America, A5*, 2059–2079.

Banks, M. S., Read, J. C., Allison, R. S., & Watt, S. J. (2012). Stereoscopy and the human visual system. *SMPTE Motion Imaging Journal, 121*(4), 24–43.

Bar, M. (2004). Visual objects in context. *Nature Reviews Neuroscience, 5*(8), 617–629.

Barker, D., Plack, C.J., and Hall, D.A. (2012). Re-examining the evidence for a pitch-sensitive region: A human fMRI study using iterated ripple noise. *Cerebral Cortex, 22*, 745–753.

Barlow, H. B. (1953). Summation and inhibition in the frog's retina. *Journal of Physiology, 119*, 69–88.

Barlow, H. B. (1972). Single units and sensation: A neuron doctrine for perceptual psychology? *Perception, 1*, 371–394.

Barlow, H. B. (1979). Reconstructing the visual image in space and time. *Nature, 279*, 189–190.

Barlow, H. B., & Hill, R. M. (1963). Selective sensitivity to direction of motion in ganglion cells of the rabbit's retina. *Science, 139*, 412–414.

Baron-Cohen, S., Burt, L., Smith-Laittan, F., Harrison, J., & Bolton, P. (1996). Synaesthesia: Prevalence and familiality. *Perception, 25*, 1073–1079.

Baron-Cohen, S., Harrison, J., Goldstein, L. H., & Wyke, M. (1993). Coloured speech perception: Is synaesthesia what happens when modularity breaks down? *Perception, 22*, 419–426.

Bartoshuk, L. M., & Beauchamp, G. K. (1994). Chemical senses. *Annual Review of Psychology, 45*, 419–449.

Battelli, L., Cavanagh, P., Intriligator, J., Tramo, M. J., Hénaff, M. A., Michèl, F., & Barton, J. J. (2001). Unilateral right parietal damage leads to bilateral deficit for high-level motion. *Neuron, 32*(6), 985–995.

Beard, B., Levi, D. M., & Reich, L. N. (1995). Perceptual learning in parafoveal vision. *Vision Research, 35*, 1679–1690.

Beauchamp, G. K., Bertino, M., Burke, D., & Engelman, K. (1990). Experimental sodium depletion and salt taste in normal human volunteers. *American Journal of Clinical Nutrition, 51*(5), 881–889.

Beauvois, M. W., & Meddis, R. (1997). Time decay of auditory stream biasing. *Perception and Psychophysics, 59*, 81–86.

Beintema, J. A., & Lappe, M. (2002). Perception of biological motion without local image motion. *Proceedings of the National Academy of Sciences USA, 99*, 5661–5663.

Beintema, J. A., Georg, K., & Lappe, M. (2006). Perception of biological motion from limited-lifetime stimuli. *Perception & Psychophysics, 68*(4), 613–624.

Benson, D. F., & Greenberg, J. P. (1969). Visual form agnosia. *Archives of Neurology, 20*, 82–89.

Berglund, B., & Engen, T. (1993). A comparison of self-adaptation and cross-adaptation to odorants presented singly and in mixtures. *Perception, 22*, 103–111.

Bergua, A., & Skrandies, W. (2000). An early antecedent to modern random dot stereograms—'The Secret Stereoscopic Writing'of Ramón y Cajal. *International Journal of Psychophysiology, 36*(1), 69–72.

Bernstein, I. L. (1978). Learned taste aversions in children receiving chemotherapy. *Science, 200*, 1302–1303.

Berson, D. M., Dunn, F. A., & Takao, M. (2002). Phototransduction by retinal ganglion cells that set the circadian clock. *Science, 295*, 1070–1072.

Bex, P. J., & Baker, C. L. (1999). Motion perception over long interstimulus intervals. *Perception and Psychophysics, 61*, 1066–1074.

Bex, P. J., Metha, A. B., & Makous, W. (1999). Enhanced motion aftereffect for complex motions. *Vision Research, 39*(13), 2229–2238.

Bezzola, L., Mérillat, S., Gaser, C., & Jäncke, L. (2011). Training-induced neural plasticity in golf novices. *Journal of Neuroscience, 31*(35), 12444–12448.

Biederman, I. (1987). Recognition-by-components: A theory of human image understanding. *Psychological Review, 94*, 115–147.

Biederman, I., & Cooper, E. E. (1991). Priming contour-deleted images: Evidence for intermediate representations in visual object priming. *Cognitive Psychology, 23*, 3930–4019.

Biederman, I., & Gerhardstein, P. C. (1993). Recognising depth-rotated objects: Evidence for three-dimensional viewpoint invariance. *Journal of Experimental Psychology: Human Perception and Performance, 19*, 1162–1182.

Biederman, I., Mezzanotte, R. J., & Rabinowitz, J. C. (1982). Scene perception: Detecting and judging objects undergoing relational violations. *Cognitive Psychology, 14*(2), 143–177.

Blake, R. (1993). Cats perceive biological motion. *Psychological Science, 4*, 54–57.

Blake, R., & Shiffrar, M. (2007). Perception of human motion. *Annual Review of Psychology, 58*, 47–73.

Blakemore, C. B., & Campbell, F. W. (1969). On the existence of neurones in the human visual system selectively sensitive to the size and orientation of retinal images. *Journal of Physiology, 203*, 237–260.

Blakemore, C., & Cooper, G. (1970). Development of the brain depends on the visual environment. *Nature, 228*, 477–478.

Blakemore, C., & Sutton, P. (1969). Size adaptation: A new after-effect. *Science, 166*, 245–247.

Blakemore, S. J., Boyer, P., Pachot-Clouard, M., Meltzoff, A., Segebarth, C., & Decety, J. (2003). The detection of contingency and animacy from simple animations in the human brain. *Cerebral Cortex, 13*(8), 837–844.

Bolanowski, S. J., Gescheider, G. A., Verrillo, R. T., & Checkosky, C. M. (1988). Four channels mediate the mechanical aspects of touch. *Journal of the Acoustical Society of America, 84*, 1680–1694.

Bolton, C. F., Winkelmann, R. K., & Dyck, P. J. (1966). Quantitative study of Meissner's corpuscles in man. *Neurology, 16*, 1–9.

Boring, E. (1942). *Sensation and Perception in the History of Experimental Psychology*. New York: Appleton-Century-Crofts.

Boring, E. (1950). *A History of Experimental Psychology*. Englewood Cliffs, NJ: Prentice Hall.

Bornstein, W. S. (1940). Cortical representation of taste in man and monkey. II. The localisation of the cortical taste area in man, a method of measuring impairment of taste in man. *Yale Journal of Biology and Medicine, 13,* 133–156.

Bosking, W. H., Zhang, Y., Schofield, B., & Fitzpatrick, D. (1997). Orientation selectivity and the arrangement of horizontal connections in tree shrew striate cortex. *Journal of Neuroscience, 17,* 2112–2127.

Botvinick, M., & Cohen, J. (1998). Rubber hands "feel" touch that eyes see. *Nature, 391,* 756.

Boulton, J. C., & Baker Jr., C. L. (1993). Different parameters control motion perception above and below a critical density. *Vision Research, 33*(13), 1803–1811.

Bouvier, S. E., & Engel, S. A. (2006). Behavioral deficits and cortical damage loci in cerebral achromatopsia. *Cerebral Cortex, 16,* 183–191.

Bowns, L. (1996). Evidence for a feature tracking explanation of why type II plaids move in the vector sum direction at short durations. *Vision Research, 36*(22), 3685–3694.

Bowns, L. (2001). IOC, vector sum, and squaring: Three different motion effects or one? *Vision Research, 41,* 965–972.

Bowns, L., & Alais, D. (2006). Large shifts in perceived motion direction reveal multiple global motion solutions. *Vision Research, 46*(8), 1170–1177.

Bracewell, R. N. (1978). *The Fourier Transform and its Applications.* London: McGraw-Hill.

Bracewell, R. N. (1989). The Fourier transform. *Scientific American, 260*(6), 62–69.

Braddick, O. J. (1974). A short-range process in apparent motion. *Vision Research, 14,* 519–527.

Braddick, O. J. (1980). Low-level and high-level processes in apparent motion. *Philosophical Transactions of the Royal Society of London, B209,* 137–151.

Bradley, M. M., Miccoli, L., Escrig, M. A., & Lang, P. J. (2008). The pupil as a measure of emotional arousal and autonomic activation. *Psychophysiology, 45*(4), 602–607.

Braitenberg, V., & Schuz, A. (1991). *Anatomy of the Cortex.* Berlin: Springer-Verlag.

Brandt, T., & Daroff, R. B. (1980). The multisensory physiological and pathological vertigo syndromes. *Annals of Neurology, 7,* 195–203.

Bregman, A. S. (1990). *Auditory Scene Analysis: The Perceptual Organization of Sound.* Cambridge, MA: MIT Press.

Bremmer, F., Klam, F., Duhamel, J-R., Hamed, S. B. & Graf, W. (2002). Visual-vestibular interactive responses in the macaque ventral intraparietal area (VIP). *European Journal of Neuroscience, 16,* 1569–1586.

Bridgeman, B., & Delgado, D. (1984). Sensory effects of eye press are due to efference. *Perception and Psychophysics, 36,* 482–484.

Briggman, K. L., Helmstaedter, M., & Denk, W. (2011). Wiring specificity in the direction-selectivity circuit of the retina. *Nature, 471*(7337), 183–188.

Brindley, G. S. (1960). *Physiology of the Retina and Visual Pathway.* London: Edward Arnold.

Broadbent, D. E. (1958). *Perception and Communication.* New York: Oxford University Press.

Brouwer, G. J., van Ee, R., & Schwarzbach, J. (2005). Activation in visual cortex correlates with the awareness of stereoscopic depth. *Journal of Neuroscience, 25,* 10403–10413.

Brown, P. K., & Wald, G. (1964). Visual pigments in single rods and cones of the human retina. *Science, 144,* 45–52.

Bruce, V., & Humphreys, G. W. (1994). Recognising objects and faces. *Visual Cognition, 1,* 141–180.

Bruce, V., Green, P. R., & Georgeson, M. A. (2003). *Visual Perception.* Hove: Psychology Press.

Brungart, D. S., & Rabinowitz, W. M. (1999). Auditory localization of nearby sources. Head-related transfer functions. *Journal of the Acoustical Society of America, 106,* 1465–1479.

Buckley, D., & Frisby, J. P. (1993). Interaction of stereo, texture and outline cues in the shape perception of three-dimensional ridges. *Vision Research, 33,* 919–933.

Bulthoff, H. H., & Edelman, S. (1992). Psychophysical support for a two-dimensional view interpolation theory of object recognition. *Proceedings of the National Academy of Sciences, 89,* 60–64.

Bulthoff, H. H., & Mallot, H. A. (1988). Integration of depth modules: Stereo and shading. *Journal of the Optical Society of America, A5,* 1749–1758.

Bundesen, C., Habekost, T., & Kyllingsbæk, S. (2005). A neural theory of visual attention: Bridging cognition and neurophysiology. *Psychological Review, 112*(2), 291.

Burr, D. C., & Morgan, M. J. (1997). Motion deblurring in human vision. *Proceedings of the Royal Society of London, B264,* 431–436.

Burr, D. C., & Ross, J. (2002). Direct evidence that "speedlines" influence motion mechanisms. *Journal of Neuroscience, 22*(19), 8661–8664.

Burr, D. C., Morgan, M. J., & Morrone, M. C. (1999). Saccadic suppression precedes visual motion analysis. *Current Biology, 9,* 1207–1209.

Burr, D. C., Ross, J., & Morrone, M. C. (1986a). Seeing objects in motion. *Proceedings of the Royal Society of London, B227,* 249–265.

Burr, D. C., Ross, J., & Morrone, M. C. (1986b). Smooth and sampled motion. *Vision Research, 26,* 643–652.

Burt, P., & Julesz, B. (1980). Modifications of the classical notion of Panum's fusional area. *Perception, 9,* 671–682.

Burt, P., & Sperling, G. (1981). Time, distance, and feature trade-offs in visual apparent motion. *Psychological Review, 88,* 171–195.

Butter, C. M., Buchtel, H. A., & Santucci, R. (1989). Spatial attentional shifts: Further evidence for the role of polysensory mechanisms using visual and tactile stimuli. *Neuropsychologia, 27,* 1231–1240.

Buzas, P., Blessing, E. M., Szmajda, B. A., & Martin, P. M. (2006). Specificity of M and L cone inputs to receptive fields in the Parvocellular pathway: Random wiring with functional bias. *Journal of Neuroscience, 26,* 11148–11161.

Cain, D. P., & Bindra, D. (1972). Responses of amygdala single units to odors in the rat. *Experimental Neurology, 35,* 98–110.

Cain, W. S. (1977). Differential sensitivity for smell: "Noise" at the nose. *Science, 195*(4280), 796–798.

Cain, W. S. (1982). Odor identification by males and females: Predictions versus performance. *Chemical Senses, 7,* 129–142.

Cain, W., & Johnson, F. (1978). Lability of odor pleasantness: Influence of mere exposure. *Perception, 7,* 459–465.

Campbell, F. W. (1957). The depth of field of the human eye. *Optica Acta, 4,* 157–164.

Campbell, F. W., & Green, D. G. (1965). Optical and retinal factors affecting visual resolution. *Journal of Physiology, 181,* 576–593.

Campbell, F. W., & Gubisch, R. W. (1966). Optical quality of the human eye. *Journal of Physiology, 186,* 558–578.

Campbell, F. W., & Robson, J. G. (1968). Application of Fourier analysis to the visibility of gratings. *Journal of Physiology, 197,* 551–556.

Campbell, F. W., & Wurtz, R. H. (1978). Saccadic omission: Why we do not see a grey-out during a saccadic eye movement. *Vision Research, 18,* 1297–1303.

Carandini, M., & Heeger, D. J. (2012). Normalization as a canonical neural computation. *Nature Reviews Neuroscience, 13*(1), 51–62.

Carey, D. P. (2001). Do action systems resist visual illusions? *Trends in Cognitive Sciences, 5,* 109–113.

Carlson, N. R. (2004). *Physiology of Behavior.* Boston, MA: Pearson.

Carlyon, R. (2004). How the brain separates sounds. *Trends in Cognitive Sciences, 8,* 465–471.

Carlyon, R. P., Plack, C. J., Fantini, D. A., & Cusack, R. (2003). Cross-modal and non-sensory influences on auditory streaming. *Perception, 32,* 1393–1402.

Carterette, E., & Kendall, R. (1999). Comparative music perception and cognition. In D. Deutsch (Ed.), *The Psychology of Music* (2nd ed., pp. 725–792). San Diego, CA: Academic Press.

Cass, J, & Alais, D. (2006). The mechanisms of collinear integration. *Journal of Vision, 6,* 915–922.

Castiello, U., & Jeannerod, M. (1991). Measuring time to awareness. *NeuroReport, 2,* 797–800.

Cavanagh, P. (1992). Attention-based motion perception. *Science, 257,* 1563–1565.

Cavanagh, P. (2004). Attention routines and the architecture of selection. In M. I. Posner (Ed.), *Cognitive Neuroscience of Attention* (pp. 13–28). New York: Guilford Press.

Cavanagh, P., & Mather, G. (1989). Motion: The long and short of it. *Spatial Vision, 4,* 103–129.

Cave, K. R., & Bichot, N. P. (1999). Visuospatial attention: Beyond a spotlight model. *Psychodynamic Bulletin & Review, 6*(2), 204–223.

Challinor, K. L., & Mather, G. (2010). A motion-energy model predicts the direction discrimination and MAE duration of two-stroke apparent motion at high and low retinal illuminance. *Vision Research, 50,* 1109–1116.

Changizi, M. A., Zhang, Q., & Shimojo, S. (2006). Bare skin, blood and the evolution of primate colour vision. *Biology Letters, 2,* 217–221.

Charman, W. (1991). The vertebrate dioptric apparatus. In J. Cronly-Dillon & R. Gregory (Eds.), *Vision and Visual Dysfunction Volume II: Evolution of the Eye and Visual System* (pp. 82–117). Basingstoke: Macmillan.

Chatterjee, S., & Callaway, E. M. (2003). Parallel colour-opponent pathways to primary visual cortex. *Nature, 426,* 668–671.

Chaudhari, N., Landin, A. M., & Roper, S. D. (2000). A metabotropic glutamate receptor variant functions as a taste receptor. *Nature Neuroscience, 3,* 113–119.

Chen, C. M., Lakatos, P., Shah, A. S., Mehta, A. D., Givre, S. J., Javitt, D. C., & Schroeder, C. E. (2007). Functional anatomy and interaction of fast and slow visual pathways in macaque monkeys. *Cerebral Cortex, 17,* 1561–1569.

Chen, X., Gabitto, M., Peng, Y., Ryba, N. J., & Zuker, C. S. (2011). A gustotopic map of taste qualities in the mammalian brain. *Science, 333,* 1262–1266.

Cherry, E. C. & Taylor, W. K. (1954). Some further experiments upon the recognition of speech, with one and with two ears. *Journal of the Acoustic Society of America, 26,* 554–559.

Chubb, C., & Sperling, G. (1988). Drift-balanced random stimuli: A general basis for studying non-Fourier motion perception. *Journal of the Optical Society of America, A5,* 1986–2006.

Chun, M. M., & Potter, M. C. (1995). A two-stage model for multiple target detection in rapid serial visual presentation. *Journal of Experimental Psychology: Human Perception and Performance, 21*(1), 109–127.

Churchland, P. S., & Sejnowski, T. (1992). *The Computational Brain.* Cambridge, MA: MIT Press.

Clarke, S., Thiran, A. B., Maeder, P., Adriani, M., Vernet, O., Regli, L., et al. (2002). What and where in human audition: Selective deficits following focal hemispheric lesions. *Experimental Brain Research, 147,* 8–15.

Cohen, M. M. (1973). Elevator illusion: Influences of otolith organ activity and neck proprioception. *Perception and Psychophysics, 14,* 401–406.

Cole, J., & Paillard, J. (1995). Living without touch and peripheral information about body position and movement: Studies with deafferented subjects. In J. Bermundez, A. Marcel, & N. Eilan (Eds.), *The Body and the Self.* London: MIT Press.

Collins, D. W., & Kimura, D. (1997). A large sex difference on a two-dimensional mental rotation task. *Behavioral Neuroscience, 111,* 845–849.

Coltheart, M. (1999). Modularity and cognition. *Trends in Cognitive Sciences, 3,* 115–120.

Cook, E. P. & Maunsell, J.H.R. (2002). Attentional modulation of behavioral performance and neuronal responses in middle temporal and ventral intraparietal areas of macaque monkey. *Journal of Neuroscience, 22*, 1994–2004.

Coppola, D. M., Purves, H. R., McCoy, A. N., & Purves, D. (1998). The distribution of oriented contours in the real world. *Proceedings of the National Academy of Sciences, 95*(7), 4002–4006.

Corbetta, M., & Shulman, G. L. (2002). Control of goal-directed and stimulus-driven attention in the brain. *Nature Reviews Neuroscience, 3*(3), 201–215.

Corbetta, M., Miezin, F. M., Shulman, G. L., & Petersen, S. E. (1993). A PET study of visuospatial attention. *Journal of Neuroscience, 13*, 1202–1226.

Coren, S. (1989). Cross-cultural studies of visual illusions: The physiological confound. *Behavioral and Brain Sciences, 12*, 76–77.

Coull, J. T., & Nobre, A. C. (1998). Where and when to pay attention: The neural systems for directing attention to spatial locations and to time intervals as revealed by both PET and fMRI. *Journal of Neuroscience, 18*(18), 7426–7435.

Crick, F., & Koch, C. (2003). A framework for consciousness. *Nature Neuroscience, 6*, 119–126.

Croner, L., & Kaplan, E. (1995). Receptive fields of P and M ganglion cells across the primate retina. *Vision Research, 35*, 7–24.

Cross, I. (2001). Music, cognition, culture and evolution. *Annals of the New York Academy of Sciences, 930*, 28–42.

Crummer, G., Walton, J., Wayman, J., Hantz, E., & Frisina, R. (1994). Neural processing of musical timbre by musicians, nonmusicians, and musicians possessing absolute pitch. *Journal of the Acoustical Society of America, 95*, 2720–2727.

Culham, J. C., Brandt, S. A, Cavanagh, P., Kanwisher, N. G., Dale, A. M., & Tootell, B. H. (1998). Cortical fMRI activation produced by attentive tracking of moving targets. *Journal of Neurophysiology, 80*, 2657–2670.

Culler, E., Coakley, J. D., Lowy, K., & Gross, N. (1943). A revised frequency-map of the guinea-pig cochlea. *American Journal of Psychology, 56*, 475–500.

Cumming, B. G., Johnston, E. B., & Parker, A. J. (1991). Vertical disparities and perception of three-dimensional shape. *Nature, 349*, 411–413.

Curcio, C. A., Sloan, K. R., Packer, O., Hendrickson, A. E., & Kalina, R. E. (1987). Distribution of cones in human and monkey retina—individual variability and radial symmetry. *Science, 236*, 579–582.

Cusack, R. (2005). The intraparietal sulcus and perceptual organization. *Journal of Cognitive Neuroscience, 17*, 641–651.

Cutting, J. E. (1978). Generation of synthetic male and female walkers through manipulation of a biomechanical invariant. *Perception, 7*, 393–405.

Cutting, J. E., & Proffitt, D. R. (1981). Gait perception as an example of how we may perceive events. In R. Walk & H. L. Pick (Eds.), *Intersensory Perception and Sensory Integration*. New York: Plenum.

Cynader, M., Berman, N., & Hein, A. (1973). Cats reared in stroboscopic illumination: Effects on receptive fields in visual cortex. *Proceedings of the National Academy of Sciences USA, 70*, 1353–1354.

Dacey, D.M. (2000). Parallel pathways for spectral coding in primate retina. *Annual Review of Neuroscience, 23*, 743–775.

Dacey, D. (2004). 20 Origins of Perception: Retinal Ganglion Cell Diversity and the Creation of Parallel Visual Pathways. In M. S. Gazzaniga (Ed.), *The Cognitive Neurosciences* (p. 281). Cambridge, MA: MIT Press.

Dacey, D.M., & Packer, O. S. (2003). Colour coding in the primate retina: Diverse cell types and cone-specific circuitry. *Current Opinion in Neurobiology, 13*, 421–427.

Dacey, D. M., Liao, H. W., Peterson, B. B., Robinson, F. R., Smith, V. C., Pokorny, J., et al. (2005). Melanopsin-expressing ganglion cells in primate retina signal colour and irradiance and project to the LGN. *Nature, 433*(7027), 749–754.

Darwin, C. J. (1997). Auditory grouping. *Trends in Cognitive Sciences, 1*, 327–333.

Darwin, C. J., & Ciocca, V. (1992). Grouping in pitch perception: Effects of onset asynchrony and ear of presentation of a mistuned component. *Journal of the Acoustical Society of America, 91*(6), 3381–3390.

Davenport, J. L., & Potter, M. C. (2004). Scene consistency in object and background perception. *Psychological Science, 15*(8), 559–564.

DeAngelis, G. C., & Newsome, W. T. (1999). Organization of disparity-selective neurons in macaque area MT. *Journal of Neuroscience, 19*, 1398–1415.

DeAngelis, G. C., Freeman, R. D., & Ohzawa, I. (1994). Length and width tuning of neurons in the cat's primary visual cortex. *Journal of Neurophysiology, 71*(1), 347–374.

de Lange, H. (1958). Research into the dynamic nature of the human fovea-cortex systems with intermittent and modulated light. I. Attenuation characteristics with white and colored light. *Journal of the Optical Society of America, 48*, 777–784.

de Monasterio, F. M., Gouras, P., & Tolhurst, D. J. (1976). Spatial summation, response pattern, and conduction velocity of ganglion cells of the rhesus monkey retina. *Vision Research, 16*, 674–678.

De Valois, R., Albrecht, D., & Thorell, L. (1982). Spatial frequency selectivity of cells in macaque visual cortex. *Vision Research, 22*, 545–559.

Dekaban, A.S., & Sadowsky, D. (1978). Changes in brain weights during the span of human life: Relation of brain weights to body heights and body weights. *Annals of Neurology, 4*, 345–356.

Delcomyn, F. (1998). *Foundations of Neurobiology*. New York: W. H. Freeman.

Delwiche, J. (2004). The impact of perceptual interactions on perceived flavor. *Food Quality and Preference, 15*, 137–146.

Deregowski, J. B. (1989). Real space and represented space: Cross-cultural perspectives. *Behavioral and Brain Sciences, 12,* 51–119.

Derrington, A. M., Krauskopf, J., & Lennie, P. (1984). Chromatic mechanisms in lateral geniculate nucleus of macaque. *Journal of Physiology, 357,* 241–265.

Derrington, A. M., & Lennie, P. (1984). Spatial and temporal contrast sensitivities of neurones in lateral geniculate nucleus of macaque. *Journal of Physiology, 357,* 219–240.

DeWitt, I., & Rauschecker, J. P. (2012). Phoneme and word recognition in the auditory ventral stream. *Proceedings of the National Academy of Sciences, 109*(8), E505–E514.

DiCarlo, J. J., Johnson, K. O., & Hsiao, S. S. (1998). Structure of receptive fields in area 3b of primary somatosensory cortex in the alert monkey. *Journal of Neuroscience, 18,* 2626–2645.

DiCarlo, J. J., Zoccolan, D., & Rust, N. C. (2012). How does the brain solve visual object recognition? *Neuron, 73*(3), 415–434.

Dichgans, J., & Brandt, T. (1973). Optokinetic motion sickness and pseudo-Coriolis effects induced by moving visual stimuli. *Acta Otolaryngologica, 76,* 339–348.

Dick, M., Ullman, S., & Sagi, D. (1991). Short- and long-range processes in structure-from-motion. *Vision Research, 31,* 2025–2028.

Diederich, A., & Colonius, H. (2004a). Bimodal and trimodal multisensory enhancement: Effects of stimulus onset and intensity on reaction time. *Perception & Psychophysics, 66*(8), 1388–1404.

Diederich, A., & Colonius, H. (2004b). Modelling the time course of multisensory interaction in manual and saccadic responses. In G. Calvert, C. Spence, & R. Stein (Eds.), *Handbook of Multisensory Processes.* Cambridge, MA: MIT Press.

Doetsch, G. S. (2000). Patterns in the brain: Neuronal population coding in the somatosensory system. *Physiology and Behaviour, 69,* 187–201.

Dosher, B. A., Landy, M. S., & Sperling, G. (1989). Kinetic depth effect and optic flow. I. 3D shape from Fourier motion. *Vision Research, 29,* 1789–1813.

Doty, R. L., Green, P., Ram, C., & Yankell, S. (1982). Communication of gender from human breath odor: Relationship to perceived intensity and pleasantness. *Hormones and Behavior, 16,* 13–22.

Doty, R. L., Shaman, P., Applebaum, S. L., Giberson, R., Siksorski, L., & Rosenberg, L. (1984). Smell identification ability: Changes with age. *Science, 226,* 1441–1443.

Dougherty, R. F., Koch, V. M., Brewer, A. A., Fischer, B., Modersitzki, J., & Wandell, B. A. (2003). Visual field representations and locations of visual areas V1/2/3 in human visual cortex. *Journal of Vision, 3,* 586–598.

Drewing, K., & Ernst, M. O. (2006). Integration of force and position cues for shape perception through active touch. *Brain Research, 1078*(1), 92–100.

Driver, J., & Noesselt, T. (2008). Multisensory interplay reveals crossmodal influences on "sensory-specific" brain regions, neural responses, and judgements. *Neuron, 57,* 11–23.

Duke, P. A., & Howard, I. P. (2005). Vertical-disparity gradients are processed independently in different depth planes. *Vision Research, 45*(15), 2025–2035.

Duncan, J. (1984). Selective attention and the organization of visual information. *Journal of Experimental Psychology: General, 113,* 501–517.

Duncan, R. O., & Boynton, G. M. (2003). Cortical magnification within human primary visual cortex correlates with acuity thresholds. *Neuron, 38,* 659–671.

Dux, P. E., & Marois, R. (2009). The attentional blink: A review of data and theory. *Attention, Perception, & Psychophysics, 71*(8), 1683–1700.

Edelman, S. (1995). Representation, similarity, and the chorus of prototypes. *Minds and Machines, 5,* 45–68.

Edelman, S. (1997). Computational theories of object recognition. *Trends in Cognitive Sciences, 1,* 296–304.

Edelman, S., & Duvdevani-Bar, S. (1997). A model of visual recognition and categorization. *Philosophical Transactions of the Royal Society of London, B352,* 1191–1202.

Ekman, G., Berglund, B., Berglund, U., & Lindvall, T. (1967). Perceived intensity of odor as a function of time of adaptation. *Scandinavian Journal of Psychology, 8,* 177–186.

Elbert, T., Pantev, C., Wienbruch, C., Rockstroh, B., & Taub, E. (1995). Increased cortical representation of the fingers of the left hand in string players. *Science, 270,* 305–307.

Elliott, D. B., & Skaff, A. (1993). Vision of the famous: The artist's eye. *Ophthalmic and Physiological Optics, 13,* 82–90.

Emerson, R. C., Bergen, J. R., & Adelson, E. H. (1992). Directionally selective complex cells and the computation of motion energy in the cat visual cortex. *Vision Research, 32,* 203–218.

Engel, A. K., & Singer, W. (2001). Temporal binding and the neural correlates of sensory awareness. *Trends in Cognitive Sciences, 5,* 16–25.

Engen, T. (1982). *The Perception of Odors.* New York: Academic Press.

Engen, T., & Ross, B. (1973). Long-term memory of odors with and without verbal descriptions. *Journal of Experimental Psychology, 100,* 221–227.

Enroth-Cugell, C., & Robson, J. G. (1966). The contrast sensitivity of retinal ganglion cells of the cat. *Journal of Physiology, 187,* 517–552.

Epstein, W. (1966). Perceived depth as a function of relative height under three background conditions. *Journal of Experimental Psychology, 72,* 335–338.

Erickson, R. (1982). The "across-fiber pattern" theory: An organizing principle for molar neural function. *Contributions to Sensory Physiology, 6,* 79–110.

Erickson, R. D., Doetsch, G. S., & Marshall, D. A. (1965). The gustatory neural response function. *Journal of General Physiology, 49,* 247–263.

Ernst, M. O., & Banks, M. S. (2002). Humans integrate visual and haptic information in a statistically optimal fashion. *Nature, 415*(6870), 429–433.

Eskew Jr., R. T. (2009). Higher order color mechanisms: A critical review. *Vision Research, 49,* 2686–2704.

Evans, E. F., Pratt, S. R., & Cooper, N. P. (1989). Correspondence between behavioural and physiological frequency selectivity in the guinea pig. *British Journal of Audiology, 23,* 151–152.

Evans, K. K., Birdwell, R. L., & Wolfe, J. M. (2013). If you don't find it often, you often don't find it: Why some cancers are missed in breast cancer screening. *PLOS ONE, 8*(5), e64366.

Fahle, M., & Morgan, M. J. (1996). No transfer of perceptual learning between similar stimuli in the same retinal position. *Current Biology, 6,* 292–297.

Falchier, A., Clavagnier, S., Barone, P., & Kennedy, H. (2002). Anatomical evidence of multimodal integration in primate striate cortex. *Journal of Neuroscience, 22,* 5749–5759.

Fantz, R. L. (1961). The origins of form perception. *Scientific American, 204*(5), 66–72.

Farah, M. J. (1999). *Visual Agnosia.* Cambridge, MA: MIT Press.

Farrell, J. E. (1984). Visible persistence of moving objects. *Journal of Experimental Psychology: Human Perception and Performance, 10,* 502–511.

Farrell, J. E., Pavel, M., & Sperling, G. (1990). The visible persistence of stimuli in stroboscopic motion. *Vision Research, 30,* 921–936.

Fasold, O., von Brevern, M., Kuhberg, M., Ploner, C. J., Villringer, A., Lempert, T., & Wenzel, R. (2002). Human vestibular cortex as identified with caloric stimulation in functional magnetic resonance imaging. *Neuroimage, 17*(3), 1384–1393.

Faurion, A., Cerf, B., Le Bihan, D., & Pilliasa, A. (1998). fMRI study of taste cortical areas. *Annals of the New York Academy of Sciences, 855,* 535–545.

Felleman, D. J., & van Essen, D. C. (1991). Distributed hierarchical processing in the primate cerebral cortex. *Cerebral Cortex, 1,* 1–47.

Ferri, S., Kolster, H., Jastorff, J., & Orban, G. A. (2013). The overlap of the EBA and the MT/V5 cluster. *Neuroimage, 66,* 412–425.

Ferrier, D. (1876). *The Functions of the Brain.* London: Smith Elder.

Fetter, M., Haslwanter, T., Bork, M., & Dichgans, J. (1999). New insights into positional alcohol nystagmus using three-dimensional eye-movement analysis. *Annals of Neurology, 45,* 216–223.

Field, D. J. (1987). Relations between the statistics of natural images and the response properties of cortical cells. *Journal of the Optical Society of America, A4,* 2379–2394.

Field, D. J., Hayes, A., & Hess, R. F. (1993). Contour integration by the human visual system: Evidence for a local "association field." *Vision Research, 33,* 173–193.

Firestein, S. (2001). How the olfactory system makes sense of scents. *Nature, 413,* 211–218.

Firestone, C. (2013). On the origin and status of the "El Greco fallacy." *Perception, 42*(6), 672–674.

Fisher, S. K., & Ciuffreda, K. J. (1988). Accommodation and apparent distance. *Perception, 17,* 609–621.

Fitzpatrick, D., Itoh, K., & Diamond, I. (1983). The laminar organization of the lateral geniculate body and the striate cortex in the squirrel monkey (saimiri sciureus). *Journal of Neuroscience, 3,* 673–702.

Fodor, J. A. (1983). *The Modularity of Mind.* Cambridge, MA: MIT Press.

Foster, D. H., & Gilson, S. J. (2002). Recognizing novel three-dimensional objects by summing signals from parts and views. *Proceedings of the Royal Society of London, B269,* 1939–1947.

Foster, D. H., & Nascimento, S.M.C. (1994). Relational colour constancy from invariant cone-excitation ratios. *Proceedings of the Royal Society of London, B257,* 115–121.

Fox, R., & McDaniel, C. (1982). The perception of biological motion by human infants. *Science, 218,* 486–487.

Foxe, J. J., Morocz, I. A., Murray, M. M., Higgins, B. A., Javitt, D. C., & Schroeder, C. E. (2000). Multisensory auditory-somatosensory interactions in early cortical processing revealed by high-density electrical mapping. *Cognitive Brain Research, 10,* 77–83.

Frassinetti, F., Bolognini, N., & Ladavas, E. (2002). Enhancement of visual perception by cross-modal visuo-auditory interaction. *Experimental Brain Research, 147,* 332–343.

Freeman, T. C., & Sumnall, J. H. (2005). Extra-retinal adaptation of cortical motion-processing areas during pursuit eye movements. *Proceedings of the Royal Society B: Biological Sciences, 272*(1577), 2127–2132.

Freeman, T.C., Sumnall, J. H., & Snowden, R. J. (2003). The extra-retinal motion aftereffect. *Journal of Vision, 3*(11), 771–779.

Frisina, D. R., & Frisina, R. D. (1997). Speech recognition in noise and presbycusis: Relations to possible neural mechanisms. *Hearing Research, 106,* 95–104.

Frith, C. D., & Frith, U. (2007). Social cognition in humans. *Current Biology, 17,* R724–R732.

Fritz, J. B., Elhilali, M., David, S. V., & Shamma, S. A. (2007). Auditory attention—focusing the searchlight on sound. *Current Opinion in Neurobiology, 17*(4), 437–455.

Fry, G., Bridgman, C., & Ellerbrock, V. (1949). The effects of atmospheric scattering on binocular depth perception. *American Journal of Optometry, 26,* 9–15.

Gagliardo, A. (2013). Forty years of olfactory navigation in birds. *Journal of Experimental Biology, 216*(12), 2165–2171.

Garcia, J., & Koelling, R. (1966). Relation of cue to consequence in avoidance learning. *Psychonomic Science, 4,* 123–124.

Gardner, M. B., & Gardner, R. S. (1973). Problem of localization in the median plane: Effect of pinnae cavity occlusion. *Journal of the Acoustical Society of America, 53,* 400–408.

Gegenfurtner, K., & Kiper, D. (2003). Color vision. *Annual Review of Neuroscience, 26,* 181–206.

Geisler, W. S. (1999). Motion streaks provide a spatial code for motion direction. *Nature, 400*(6739), 65–69.

Geisler, W. S., Perry, J. S., Super, B. J., & Gallogly, D. P. (2001). Edge co-occurrence in natural images predicts contour grouping performance. *Vision Research, 41,* 711–724.

Georgeson, M. A. (1992). Human vision combines oriented filters to compute edges. *Proceedings of the Royal Society of London, B249,* 235–245.

Georgeson, M. A., May, K. A., Freeman, T. C., & Hesse, G. S. (2007). From filters to features: Scale–space analysis of edge and blur coding in human vision. *Journal of Vision, 7*(13), 7.

Giard, M. H. & Peronnet, F. (1999). Auditory-visual integration during multimodal object recognition in humans: A behavioral and electrophysiological study. *Journal of Cognitive Neuroscience, 11,* 473–490.

Giaschi, D., Douglas, R., Marlin, S., & Cynader, M. (1993). The time course of direction-selective adaptation in simple and complex cells in cat striate cortex. *Journal of Neurophysiology, 70,* 2024–2034.

Gibson, J. J. (1950). *The Perception of the Visual World.* Boston, MA: Houghton Mifflin.

Gibson, J. J., & Radner, M. (1937). Adaptation, after-effect and contrast in the perception of tilted lines. I. Quantitative studies. *Journal of Experimental Psychology, 20,* 453–467.

Giesbrecht, B., Woldorff, M. G., Song, A. W., & Mangun, G. R. (2003). Neural mechanisms of top-down control during spatial and feature attention. *Neuroimage, 19*(3), 496–512.

Gilbert, A. N., & Firestein, S. (2002). Dollars and scents: Commercial opportunities in olfaction and taste. *Nature Neuroscience, 5,* 1043–1045.

Gilbert, C. D. (1995). Dynamic properties of adult visual cortex. In M. S. Gazzaniga (Ed.), *The Cognitive Neurosciences.* Cambridge, MA: MIT Press.

Gilbert, C. D., & Wiesel, T. N. (1985). Intrinsic connectivity and receptive field properties in visual cortex. *Vision Research, 25,* 365–374.

Gillam, B., & Borsting, E. (1988). The role of monocular regions in stereoscopic displays. *Perception, 17,* 603–608.

Ginsburg, A. P. (1986). Spatial filtering and visual form perception. In K. Boff, L. Kaufman, & J. Thomas (Eds.), *Handbook of Perception and Human Performance Volume II: Cognitive Processes and Performance.* New York: Wiley.

Girard, P., Salin, P., & Bullier, J. (1991). Visual activity in areas V3a and V3 during reversible inactivation of area V1 in the macaque monkey. *Journal of Neurophysiology, 66,* 1493–1503.

Girard, P., Salin, P., & Bullier, J. (1992). Response selectivity of neurons in area MT of the macaque monkey during reversible inactivation of area V1. *Journal of Neurophysiology, 67,* 1437–1446.

Girshick, A. R., & Banks, M. S. (2009). Probabilistic combination of slant information: Weighted averaging and robustness as optimal percepts. *Journal of Vision, 9*(9), 8.

Girshick, A. R., Landy, M. S., & Simoncelli, E. P. (2011). Cardinal rules: Visual orientation perception

reflects knowledge of environmental statistics. *Nature Neuroscience, 14*(7), 926–932.

Glasser, A., & Campbell, M.C.W. (1998). Presbyopia and the optical changes in the human crystalline lens with age. *Vision Research, 38,* 209–229.

Glennerster, A. (1998). Dmax for stereopsis and motion in random dot displays. *Vision Research, 38,* 925–935.

Glickstein, M. (1985). Ferrier's mistake. *Trends in Neurosciences, 8,* 341–344.

Glickstein, M., & Whitteridge, D. (1987). Tatsuji Inouye and the mapping of the visual fields on the human cerebral cortex. *Trends in Neurosciences, 10,* 350–353.

Goldstein, J. L. (1973). An optimum processor theory for the central formation of the pitch of complex tones. *Journal of the Acoustical Society of America, 54,* 1496–1516.

Goodale, M. A., & Milner, A. D. (1992). Separate visual pathways for perception and action. *Trends in Neurosciences, 15,* 20–25.

Gordon, I. E. (1997). *Theories of Visual Perception.* Chichester: Wiley.

Gould, S. J., & Lewontin, R. C. (1979). The spandrels of San Marco and the Panglossian paradigm: A critique of the adaptionist programme. *Proceedings of the Royal Society B, 205,* 581–598.

Gray, R., & Regan, D. (1997). Vernier step acuity and bisection acuity for texture-defined form. *Vision Research, 37,* 1713–1723.

Graybiel. A., & Hupp, E. D. (1946). The oculogyral illusion: A form of apparent motion which may be observed following stimulation of the semi-circular canals. *Journal of Aviation Medicine, 17,* 3–27.

Graziano, M. S., Andersen, R. A., & Snowden, R. J. (1994). Tuning of MST neurons to spiral motions. *Journal of Neuroscience, 14,* 54–67.

Green, D. M., & Swets, J. A. (1966). *Signal Detection Theory and Psychophysics.* Chichester: Wiley.

Gregory, R. L. (1980). Perceptions as hypotheses. *Philosophical Transactions of the Royal Society of London, B290,* 181–197.

Gregory, R. L. (1981). *Mind in Science.* Cambridge: Cambridge University Press.

Gregory, R. L. (1998). *Eye and Brain.* London: Weidenfeld & Nicolson.

Grill-Spector, K., Henson, R., & Martin, A. (2006). Repetition and the brain: Neural models of stimulus-specific effects. *Trends in Cognitive Sciences, 10,* 14–23.

Grimault, N., Micheyl, C., Carlyon, R. P. & Collet, L. (2002). Evidence for two pitch encoding mechanisms using a selective auditory training paradigm. *Perception and Psychophysics, 64,* 189–197.

Grossman, E. D., & Blake, R. (2002). Brain areas active during visual perception of biological motion. *Neuron, 35,* 1167–1175.

Gu, Y., Angelaki, D. E., & DeAngelis, G. C. (2008). Neural correlates of multisensory cue integration in macaque MSTd. *Nature Neuroscience, 11*(10), 1201–1210.

Guest, S., Catmur, C., Lloyd, D., & Spence, C. (2002). Audiotactile interactions in roughness perception. *Experimental Brain Research, 146,* 161–171.

Gurney, K. (2007). Neural networks for perceptual processing: From simulation tools to theories. *Philosophical Transactions of the Royal Society, B 362,* 339–353.

Haarmeier, T., Thier, P., Repnow, M., & Petersen, D. (1997). False perception of motion in a patient who cannot compensate for eye movements. *Nature, 389,* 849–852.

Haber, W. B. (1955). Effects of loss of limb on sensory functions. *Journal of Psychology, 40,* 115–123.

Hagen, M., & Jones, R. (1978). Cultural effects on pictorial perception: How many words is one picture really worth? In R. Walk & H. Pick (Eds.), *Perception and Experience.* New York: Plenum.

Haijiang, Q., Saunders, J. A., Stone, R. W., & Backus, B. T. (2006). Demonstration of cue recruitment: Change in visual appearance by means of Pavlovian conditioning. *Proceedings of the National Academy of Sciences, 103,* 483–488.

Halari, R., Sharma, T., Hines, M., Andrew, C., Simmons, A., & Kumari, V. (2006). Comparable fMRI activity with differential behavioural performance on mental rotation and overt verbal fluency tasks in healthy men and women. *Experimental Brain Research, 169,* 1–14.

Hallum, L. E., & Movshon, J. A. (2014). Surround suppression supports second-order feature encoding by macaque V1 and V2 neurons. *Vision Research, 104,* 24–35.

Halpern, D. F. (2000). *Sex Differences in Cognitive Abilities.* Mahwah, NJ: Lawrence Erlbaum.

Halpern, S. D., Andrews, T. J., & Purves, D. (1999). Interindividual variation in human visual performance. *Journal of Cognitive Neuroscience, 11,* 521–534.

Hammett, S. T., Champion, R. A., Morland, A. B., & Thompson, P. G. (2005). A ratio model of perceived speed in the human visual system. *Proceedings of the Royal Society of London B, 272,* 2351–2356.

Hammett, S. T., Champion, R. A., Thompson, P. G., & Morland, A. B. (2007). Perceptual distortions of speed at low luminance: Evidence inconsistent with a Bayesian account of speed encoding. *Vision Research, 47*(4), 564–568.

Harburn, G., Taylor, C., & Welberry, T. (1975). *Atlas of Optical Transforms.* London: Bell & Hyman.

Harmon, L. D., & Julesz, B. (1973). Masking in visual recognition: Effects of two-dimensional filtered noise. *Science, 180,* 1194–1197.

Harris, L. R. (1994). Visual motion caused by self motion. In A. T. Smith & R. J. Snowden (Eds.), *Visual Detection of Motion.* London: Academic Press.

Harris, M. G. (1994). Optic and retinal flow. In A. T. Smith & R. J. Snowden (Eds.), *Visual Detection of Motion.* London: Academic Press.

Hawley, M. L., Litovsky, R. Y., & Culling, J. F. (2004). The benefit of binaural hearing in a cocktail party: Effect of location and type of interferer. *Journal of the Acoustical Society of America, 115*(2), 833–843.

He, S., Cavanagh, P., & Intriligator, J. (1996). Attentional resolution and the locus of visual awareness. *Nature, 383,* 334–337.

He, S., Cavanagh, P., & Intriligator, J. (1997). Attentional resolution. *Trends in Cognitive Sciences, 1,* 115–120.

Hecht, E. (2002). *Optics.* Reading, MA: Addison-Wesley.

Heckenmueller, E. G. (1965). Stabilization of the retinal image: A review of method, effects, and theory. *Psychological Bulletin, 63,* 157–169.

Heider, F., & Simmel, M. (1944). An experimental study of apparent behavior. *American Journal of Psychology, 57*(2), 243–259.

Held, R. T., Cooper, E. A., O'Brien, J. F., & Banks, M. S. (2010). Using blur to affect perceived distance and size. *ACM Transactions on Graphics, 29*(2), Article 19.

Helmholtz, H. von (1877). *On the Sensations of Tone as a Physiological Basis for the Theory of Music* (A. J. Ellis Ed.) (1954). New York: Dover.

Helmholtz, H. von (1910). *Treatise on Physiological Optics Vol. III* (J.P.C. Southall Ed.) (1962). New York: Dover.

Helmholtz, H. von (1911). *Treatise on Physiological Optics Vol. II* (J.P.C. Southall Ed.) (1962). New York: Dover.

Hendrickson, A. E., & Yuodelis, C. (1984). The morphological development of the human fovea. *Ophthalmology, 91,* 603–612.

Henn, V., Young, L. R., & Finley, C. (1974). Vestibular nucleus units in alert monkeys are also influenced by moving visual fields. *Brain Research, 71,* 144–149.

Henrich, J., Heine, S. J., & Norenzayan, A. (2010). The weirdest people in the world? *Behavioral and Brain Sciences, 33*(2–3), 61–83.

Hering, E. (1964). *Outlines of a Theory of the Light Sense.* Cambridge, MA: Harvard University Press.

Hess, E. H. (1975). The role of pupil size in communication. *Scientific American, 233*(5), 110–119.

Hess, E. H., & Polt, J. M. (1960). Pupil size as related to interest value of visual stimuli. *Science, 132,* 349–350.

Hickok, G., & Poeppel, D. (2007). The cortical organization of speech processing. *Nature Reviews Neuroscience, 8*(5), 393–402.

Hildreth, E. C., Ando, H., Anderson, R. A., & Treue, S. (1995). Recovering three-dimensional structure from motion with surface reconstruction. *Vision Research, 35,* 117–137.

Hilgetag, C.-C., O'Neill, M. A., & Young, M. P. (1996). Indeterminate organization of the visual hierarchy. *Science, 271,* 776–777.

Hillis, J. M., Watt, S. J., Landy, M. S., & Banks, M. S. (2004). Slant from texture and disparity cues: Optimal cue combination. *Journal of Vision, 4*(12), 1.

Hogben, J. H., & DiLollo, V. (1974). Perceptual integration and perceptual segregation of brief visual stimuli. *Vision Research, 14,* 1059–1069.

Hollins, M., & Risner, S. R. (2000). Evidence for the duplex theory of tactile texture perception. *Perception and Psychophysics, 62,* 695–705.

Hollins, M., Bensmaia, S. J., & Roy, E. A. (2002). Vibrotaction and texture perception. *Behavioural Brain Research, 135,* 51–56.

Hopfinger, J. B., Buonocore, M. H., & Mangun, G. R. (2000). The neural mechanisms of top-down attentional control. *Nature Neuroscience, 3,* 284–291.

Horner, W. G. (1834). On the properties of the Daedaleum, a new instrument of optical illusion. *London and Edinburgh Philosophical Magazine and Journal of Science, 4,* 36–41.

Howard, I. (1982). *Human Visual Orientation.* New York: Wiley.

Howard, I., & Rogers, B. (1995). *Binocular Vision and Stereopsis.* New York: Oxford University Press.

Huang, T. (2005). Desert racers—drivers not included. *New Scientist, 2526,* November 19, 48.

Hubel, D. (1988). *Eye, Brain, and Vision.* New York: Scientific American Library.

Hubel, D., & Wiesel, T. (1959). Receptive fields of single neurones in the cat's striate cortex. *Journal of Physiology, 148,* 574–591.

Hubel, D., & Wiesel, T. (1962). Receptive fields, binocular interaction and functional architecture in the cat's visual cortex. *Journal of Physiology, 160,* 106–154.

Hubel, D., & Wiesel, T. (1968). Receptive fields and functional architecture of monkey striate cortex. *Journal of Physiology, 195,* 215–243.

Hubel, D., & Wiesel, T. (1974). Uniformity of monkey striate cortex: A parallel relationship between field size, scatter, and magnification factor. *Journal of Comparative Neurology, 158,* 295–306.

Hubel, D. H., & Wiesel, T. N. (1977). Ferrier lecture: Functional architecture of macaque monkey visual cortex. *Proceedings of the Royal Society of London, Series B, 198*(1130), 1–59.

Hudson, W. (1960). Pictorial depth perception in sub-cultural groups in Africa. *Journal of Social Psychology, 52,* 183–208.

Hudspeth, A. J. (1989). How the ear's works work. *Nature, 341,* 397–404.

Hudspeth, A. J., & Konishi, M. (2000). Auditory neuroscience: Development, transduction, and integration. *Proceedings of the National Academy of Sciences USA, 97,* 11690–11691.

Hurlbert, A. (1999). Colour vision: Is colour constancy real? *Current Biology, 9,* R558–R561.

Hurlbert, A. (2003). Colour vision: Primary visual cortex shows its influence. *Current Biology, 13,* R270–R272.

Hurvich, L. M., & Jameson, D. (1957). An opponent-process theory of color vision. *Psychological Review, 64,* 384–390.

Huttenlocher, P., & de Courten, C. (1987). The development of synapses in striate cortex of man. *Human Neurobiology, 6,* 1–9.

Hyvarinen, J., & Poranen, A. (1978). Movement-sensitive and direction and orientation-sensitive cutaneous receptive fields in the hand area of the post-central gyrus in monkeys. *Journal of Physiology, 283,* 523–537.

Ibbotson, M. R., Price, N.S.C., Crowder, N. A., Ono, S., & Mustari, M. J. (2007). Enhanced motion sensitivity follows saccadic suppression in the superior temporal sulcus of the macaque cortex. *Cerebral Cortex, 17*(5), 1129–1138.

Intraub, H. (1981). Rapid conceptual identification of sequentially presented pictures. *Journal of Experimental Psychology: Human Perception and Performance, 7,* 604–610.

Ittelson, W. (1951). Size as a cue to distance: Static localization. *American Journal of Psychology, 64,* 54–57.

Jacobs, R. A. (2002). What determines visual cue reliability? *Trends in Cognitive Sciences, 6,* 345–350.

Jaeger, W. (1972). Genetics of congenital colour deficiencies. In D. Jameson & L. Hurvich (Eds.), *Handbook of Sensory Physiology Volume VII/4: Visual Psychophysics.* Berlin: Springer-Verlag.

Jahoda, G., & McGurk, H. (1974). Pictorial depth perception in Scottish and Ghanaian children. *International Journal of Psychology, 9,* 255–267.

Jayakumar, J., Roy, S., Dreher, B., Martin, P. R., & Vidyasagar, T. R. (2013). Multiple pathways carry signals from short-wavelength-sensitive ("blue") cones to the middle temporal area of the macaque. *Journal of Physiology, 591*(1), 339–352.

Jeffress, L. A. (1948). A place theory of sound localization. *Journal of Comparative and Physiological Psychology, 41,* 35–49.

Jiang, W., Jiang, H., & Stein, B. E. (2002). Two corticotectal areas facilitate multisensory orientation behavior. *Journal of Cognitive Neuroscience, 14*(8), 1240–1255.

Johansson, G. (1973). Visual perception of biological motion and a model for its analysis. *Perception and Psychophysics, 14,* 201–211.

Johansson, G. (1976). Spatio-temporal differentiation and integration in visual motion perception. *Psychological Research, 38,* 379–393.

Johansson, R. S. (1978). Tactile sensibility in the human hand: Receptive field characteristics of mechanoreceptive units in the glabrous skin area. *Journal of Physiology, 281,* 101–125.

Johansson, R. S., & Vallbo, A. B. (1979). Tactile sensibility in the human hand: Relative and absolute densities of four types of mechanoreceptive units in glabrous skin. *Journal of Physiology, 286,* 283–300.

Johnson, E. N., Hawken, M., & Shapley, R. (2001). The spatial transformation of colour in the primary visual cortex of the macaque monkey. *Nature Neuroscience, 4,* 409–416.

Johnston, E. B., Cumming, B. G., & Landy, M. S. (1994). Integration of stereo and motion shape cues. *Vision Research, 34,* 2259–2275.

Jones, C. M., Braithwaite, V. A., & Healy, S. D. (2003). The evolution of sex differences in spatial ability. *Behavioral Neuroscience, 117,* 403–411.

Jonsson, F. U., Olsson, H., & Olsson, M. J. (2005). Odor emotionality affects the confidence in odor naming. *Chemical Senses, 30,* 29–35.

Jousmaki, V., & Hari, R. (1998). Parchment skin illusion: Sound-biased touch. *Current Biology, 8,* R190.

Kaas, J. H. (2000). Why is brain size so important: Design problems and solutions as neocortex gets bigger or smaller. *Brain and Mind, 1*(1), 7–23.

Kaas, J. H., & Hackett, T. A. (2000). Subdivisions of auditory cortex and processing streams in primates. *Proceedings of the National Academy of Sciences USA, 97,* 11793–11799.

Kahneman, D., Treisman, A., & Gibbs, B. J. (1992). The reviewing of object files: Object-specific integration of information. *Cognitive Psychology, 24,* 175–219.

Kanai, R., Bahrami, B., & Rees, G. (2010). Human parietal cortex structure predicts individual differences in perceptual rivalry. *Current Biology, 20*(18), 1626–1630.

Kanai, R., & Rees, G. (2011). The structural basis of inter-individual differences in human behaviour and cognition. *Nature Reviews Neuroscience, 12*(4), 231–242.

Karnath, H., Berger, M. F., Küker, W., & Rorden, C. (2004). The anatomy of spatial neglect based on voxelwise statistical analysis: A study of 140 patients. *Cerebral Cortex, 14,* 1164–1172.

Kayser, C., & Logothetis, N. K. (2007). Do early cortices integrate cross-modal information? *Brain Structure and Function, 212,* 121–132.

Keil, M. S., & Cristobal, G. (2000). Separating the chaff from the wheat: Possible origins of the oblique effect. *Journal of the Optical Society of America, A17,* 697–710.

Kelly, D. H. (1985). Visual processing of moving stimuli. *Journal of the Optical Society of America, A2,* 216–225.

Kennard, D. W., Hartmann, R. W., Kraft, D. P., & Boshes, B. (1970). Perceptual suppression of afterimages. *Vision Research, 10*(7), 575–585.

Kennett, S., Taylor-Clarke, M., & Haggard, P. (2001). Noninformative vision improves the spatial resolution of touch in humans. *Current Biology, 11,* 1188–1191.

Kersten, D., & Yuille, A. (2003). Bayesian models of object perception. *Current Opinion in Neurobiology, 13,* 150–158.

Kersten, D., Knill, D. C., Mamassian, P., & Bulthoff, I. (1996). Illusory motion from shadows. *Nature, 379,* 31.

Kersten, D., Mamassian, P., & Knill, D. C. (1997). Moving cast shadows induce apparent motion in depth. *Perception, 26,* 171–192.

Khan, R. M., Luk, C. H., Flinker, A., Aggarwal, A., Lapid, H., Haddad, R., & Sobel, N. (2007). Predicting odor pleasantness from odorant structure: Pleasantness as a reflection of the physical world. *Journal of Neuroscience, 27*(37), 10015–10023.

Kim, D. O., Molnar, C. E., & Matthews, J. W. (1980). Cochlear mechanics: Nonlinear behaviour in two-tone responses as reflected in cochlear-nerve-fibre responses and in ear-canal sound pressure. *Journal of the Acoustical Society of America, 67,* 1704–1721.

Kim, U. K., Jorgenson, E., Coon, H., Leppert, M., Risch, N., & Drayna, D. (2003). Positional cloning of the human quantitative trait locus underlying taste sensitivity to phenylthiocarbamide. *Science, 299,* 1221–1225.

Kingdom, F., & Moulden, B. P. (1992). A multi-channel approach to brightness coding. *Vision Research, 32,* 1565–1582.

Klatzky, R. L., Lederman, S. J., & Metzger, V. A. (1985). Identifying objects by touch: An expert system. *Perception and Psychophysics, 37,* 299–302.

Klein, R. M. (2000). Inhibition of return. *Trends in Cognitive Sciences, 4*(4), 138–147.

Knill, D. C. (1998). Discrimination of planar surface slant from texture: Human and ideal observers compared. *Vision Research, 38,* 1683–1711.

Knill, D. C., Kersten, D., & Yuille, A. (1996). Introduction: A Bayesian formulation of visual perception. In D.C. Knill & W. Richards (Eds.), *Perception as Bayesian Inference.* Cambridge: Cambridge University Press.

Knudsen, E. I., & Konishi, M. (1978). A neural map of auditory space in the owl. *Science, 200,* 795–797.

Koenderink, J. J., & van Doorn, A. J. (1976). Local structure of movement parallax of the plane. *Journal of the Optical Society of America, 66,* 717–723.

Koenderink, J. J., van Doorn, A. J., & Kappers, A.M.L. (1996). Pictorial surface attitude and local depth comparisons. *Perception and Psychophysics, 58,* 163–173.

Kolers, P. A. (1972). *Aspects of Motion Perception.* Oxford: Pergamon.

Komatsu, H., & Wurtz, R. H. (1988). Relation of cortical areas MT and MST to pursuit eye movements. I. Localization and visual properties of neurons. *Journal of Neurophysiology, 60*(2), 580–603.

Koshland, D. E. (1980). Bacterial chemotaxis in relation to neurobiology. *Annual Review of Neurosciences, 3,* 43–75.

Kozbelt, A. (2001). Artists as experts in visual cognition. *Visual Cognition, 8,* 705–723.

Kozlowski, L. T., & Cutting, J. E. (1977). Recognising the sex of a walker from a dynamic point-light display. *Perception and Psychophysics, 21,* 575–580.

Kraft, J. M., & Brainard, D. H. (1999). Mechanisms of color constancy under nearly natural viewing. *Proceedings of the National Academy of Sciences USA, 96,* 307–312.

Kratskin, I. L. (1995). Functional anatomy, central projections, and neurochemistry of the mammalian olfactory bulb. In R. L. Doty (Ed.), *Handbook of Olfaction and Gustation* (pp. 103–126). New York: Marcel Dekker.

Krauskopf, J., Williams, D. R., & Heeley, D. W. (1982). Cardinal directions of color space. *Vision Research, 22,* 1123–1131.

Krauskopf, J., Williams, D. R., Mandler, M. B., & Brown, A. M. (1986). Higher order color mechanisms. *Vision Research, 26,* 23–32.

Kravitz, D. J., Saleem, K. S., Baker, C. I., & Mishkin, M. (2011). A new neural framework for visuospatial processing. *Nature Reviews Neuroscience, 12*(4), 217–230.

Krubitzer, L. (1995). The organization of the neocortex in mammals: Are species differences really so different? *Trends in Neurosciences, 18,* 408–417.

Kruska, D. (1988). Mammalian domestication and its effect on brain structure and behavior. In H. J. Jerison & I. Jerison (Eds.), *Intelligence and Evolutionary Biology* (pp. 211–250). Berlin: Springer.

Kuffler, S. W. (1953). Discharge patterns and functional organization of mammalian retina. *Journal of Neurophysiology, 16,* 37–68.

Kuhl, P. K. (2004). Early language acquisition: Cracking the speech code. *Nature Reviews Neuroscience, 5,* 831–843.

Lackner, J. R., & DiZio, P. (2006). Space motion sickness. *Experimental Brain Research, 175,* 377–399.

Lamme, V.A.F., & Roelfsema, P. R. (2000). The distinct modes of vision offered by feedforward and recurrent processing. *Trends in Neurosciences, 23,* 571–579.

Land, M. F. (1999). Motion and vision: Why animals move their eyes. *Journal of Comparative Physiology A, 185*(4), 341–352.

Land, M. F., & Nilsson, D.-E. (2002). *Animal Eyes.* Oxford: Oxford University Press.

Landisman, C. E., & Ts'o, D. (2002). Color processing in macaque striate cortex: Relationships to ocular dominance, cytochrome oxidase, and orientation. *Journal of Neurophysiology, 87,* 3126–3137.

Landy, M. S., & Graham, N. (2004). Visual perception of texture. In L. M. Chalupa & J. S. Werner (Eds.), *The Visual Neurosciences* (pp. 1106–1118). Cambridge, MA: MIT Press.

Lange, J., & Lappe, M. (2006). A model of biological motion perception from configural form cues. *Journal of Neuroscience, 26*(11), 2894–2906.

Larsen, A., McIlhagga, W., Baert, J., & Bundesen, C. (2003). Seeing or hearing? Perceptual independence, modality confusions, and crossmodal congruity effects with focused and divided attention. *Perception & Psychophysics, 65*(4), 568–574.

Lashley, K. S., Chow, K.-L., & Semmes, J. (1951). An examination of the electrical field theory of cerebral integration. *Psychological Review, 58,* 123–136.

Laughlin, S. B., de Ruyter van Steveninck, R. R., & Anderson, J. C. (1998). The metabolic cost of neural information, *Nature Neuroscience, 1,* 36–41.

Lawless, H., & Engen, T. (1977). Associations to odors: Interference, mnemonics, and verbal labeling. *Journal of Experimental Psychology: Human Perception and Performance, 3,* 52–59.

Lawrence, D. H. (1971). Two studies of visual search for word targets with controlled rates of presentation. *Perception & Psychophysics, 10*(2), 85–89.

Ledgeway, T., & Smith, A. T. (1997). Changes in perceived speed following adaptation to first-order and second-order motion. *Vision Research, 37,* 215–224.

Lee, B. B. (2011). Visual pathways and psychophysical channels in the primate. *Journal of Physiology, 589*(1), 41–47.

Lee, B. B., Kremers, J., & Yeh, T. (1998). Receptive fields of primate retinal ganglion cells studied with a novel technique. *Visual Neuroscience, 15,* 161–175.

Lee, B. B., Martin, P. R., & Grünert, U. (2010). Retinal connectivity and primate vision. *Progress in Retinal and Eye Research, 29*(6), 622–639.

Lee, B. B., Smith, V. C., Pokorny, J., & Kremers, J. (1997). Rod inputs to macaque ganglion cells. *Vision Research, 37*(20), 2813–2828.

Lee, B. B., Wehrhahn, C., Westheimer, G., & Kremers, J. (1993). Macaque ganglion cell responses to stimuli that elicit hyperacuity in man: Detection of small displacements. *Journal of Neuroscience, 13,* 1001–1009.

Lee, T.-W., Wachtler, T., & Sejnowski, T. J. (2002). Color opponency is an efficient representation of spectral properties in natural scenes. *Vision Research, 42*(17), 2095–2103.

Leibowitz, H. W., & Pick, H. A. (1972). Cross-cultural and educational aspects of the Ponzo perspective illusion. *Perception and Psychophysics, 12,* 430–432.

Lelkens, A.M.M., & Koenderink, J. J. (1984). Illusory motion in visual displays. *Vision Research, 24,* 1083–1090.

Lennie, P. (1998). Single units and visual cortical organisation. *Perception, 27,* 889–935.

Lennie, P. (2000). Color vision: Putting it all together. *Current Biology, 10,* R589–R591.

Lennie, P. (2003). The cost of cortical computation. *Current Biology, 13*(6), 493–497.

Lennie, P., & D'Zmura, M. (1987). Mechanisms of color vision. *Critical Reviews in Neurobiology, 3*(4), 333–400.

Lennie, P., Haake, P. W., & Williams, D. R. (1991). The design of chromatically opponent receptive fields. In M. S. Landy & J. A. Movshon (Eds.), *Computational Models of Visual Processing* (pp. 71–82). Cambridge, MA: MIT Press.

Lerdahl, F., & Jackendoff, R. (1983). *A Generative Theory of Tonal Music.* Cambridge, MA: MIT Press.

Lettvin, J. Y., Maturana, H. R., McCulloch, W. S., & Pitts, W. H. (1959). What the frog's eye tells the frog's brain. *Proceedings of the Institute of Radio Engineers, 47,* 1940–1959. Reprinted in W. S. McCulloch (Ed.) (1965). *Embodiments of Mind.* Cambridge, MA: MIT Press.

Levine, J. (1983). Materialism and qualia: The explanatory gap. *Pacific Philosophical Quarterly, 64,* 354–361.

Levine, J. (1999). Explanatory gap. In R. A. Wilson & F. C. Keil (Eds.), *The MIT Encyclopedia of the Cognitive Sciences.* Cambridge, MA: MIT Press.

Lewis, G. (1926). The conservation of photons. *Nature, 118,* 874–875.

Liberman, A. M., Harris, K. S., Hoffman, H. S., & Griffith, B. C. (1957). The discrimination of speech sounds within and across phoneme boundaries. *Journal of Experimental Psychology, 54,* 358–368.

Libet, B. (1985). Unconscious cerebral initiative and the role of conscious will in voluntary action. *Behavioral and Brain Sciences, 8,* 529–566.

Lichenstein, R., Smith, D. C., Ambrose, J. L., & Moody, L. A. (2012). Headphone use and pedestrian injury and death in the United States: 2004–2011. *Injury Prevention, 18*(5), 287–290.

Linsenmeier, R., Frishman, L., Jakeila, H., & Enroth-Cugell, C. (1982). Receptive field properties of X and Y cells in the cat retina derived from contrast sensitivity measurements. *Vision Research, 22,* 1173–1183.

Lishman, J., & Lee, D. (1973). The autonomy of visual kinaesthesis. *Perception, 2,* 287–294.

Liu, J., & Newsome, W. T. (2003). Functional organization of speed tuned neurons in visual area MT. *Journal of Neurophysiology, 89,* 246–256.

Livingstone, M., & Conway, B. (2004). Was Rembrandt stereoblind? *New England Journal of Medicine, 351,* 1264–1265.

Livingstone, M., & Hubel, D. (1982). Thalamic inputs to cytochrome oxidase-rich regions in monkey visual cortex. *Proceedings of the National Academy of Sciences USA, 79,* 6098–6101.

Livingstone, M., & Hubel, D. (1988). Segregation of form, color, movement, and depth: Anatomy, physiology, and perception. *Science, 240*(4853), 740–749.

Locke, S., & Kellar, L. (1973). Categorical perception in a non-linguistic mode. *Cortex, 9,* 353–369.

Logothetis, N., & Sheinburg, D. (1996). Visual object recognition. *Annual Review of Neuroscience, 19,* 577–621.

Logothetis, N. K., Pauls, J., & Poggio, T. (1995). Shape representation in the inferior temporal cortex of monkeys. *Current Biology, 5*(5), 552–563.

Long, G. M., & Toppino, T. C. (2004). Enduring interest in perceptual ambiguity: Alternating views of reversible figures. *Psychological Bulletin, 130,* 748–768.

Longuet-Higgins, H. C. (1979). The perception of music. *Proceedings of the Royal Society of London, B205,* 307–322.

Longuet-Higgins, H. C., & Prazdny, K. (1980). The interpretation of a moving retinal image. *Proceedings of the Royal Society of London, B208,* 385–397.

Looy, H., Callaghan, S., & Weingarten, H. P. (1992). Hedonic response of sucrose likers and dislikers to other gustatory stimuli. *Physiology & Behavior, 52*(2), 219–225.

Lorig, T. (2002). The perception of smell. In D. Roberts (Ed.), *Signals and Perception* (pp. 309–318). Basingstoke: Palgrave Macmillan.

Louis, D. S., Greene, T. L., Jacobson, K. E., Rasmussen, C., Kolowich, P., & Goldstein, S. A. (1984). Evaluation of normal values for stationary and moving two-point discrimination in the hand. *Journal of Hand Surgery, 9,* 553–555.

Lu, Z.-L. & Dosher, B. A. (1998). External noise distinguishes attention mechanisms. *Vision Research, 38,* 1183–1198.

Luria, A. R. (1959.) Disorders of "simultaneous perception" in a case of bilateral occipito-parietal brain injury. *Brain, 82,* 437–449.

Macefield, G., Gandevia, S. C., & Burke, D. (1990). Perceptual responses to microstimulation of single afferents innervating joints, muscles and skin of the human hand. *Journal of Physiology, 429,* 113–129.

Machilsen, B., & Wagemans, J. (2011). Integration of contour and surface information in shape detection. *Vision Research, 51*(1), 179–186.

Maguire, E. A., Gadian, D. G., Johnsrude, I. S., Good, C. D., Ashburner, J., Frackowiak, R. S., & Frith, C. D. (2000). Navigation-related structural change in the hippocampi of taxi drivers. *Proceedings of the National Academy of Sciences USA, 97,* 4398–4403.

Maia, T. V., & Cleeremans, A. (2005). Consciousness: Converging insights from connectionist modeling and neuroscience. *Trends in Cognitive Sciences, 9,* 397–404.

Majaj, N. J., Carandini, M., & Movshon, J. A. (2007). Motion integration by neurons in macaque MT is local, not global. *Journal of Neuroscience, 27,* 366–370.

Makous, W. (1998). Optics and photometry. In R.H.S. Carpenter & J. Robson (Eds.), *Vision Research: A Practical Guide to Laboratory Methods.* Oxford: Oxford University Press.

Malnic, B., Hirono, J., Sato, T., & Buck, L. B. (1999). Combinatorial receptor codes for odors. *Cell, 96,* 713–723.

Malpeli, J. G., Schiller, P. H., & Colby, C. L. (1981). Response properties of single cells in monkey striate cortex during reversible inactivation of individual lateral geniculate laminae. *Journal of Neurophysiology, 46,* 1102–1119.

Manoussaki, D., Chadwick, R. S., Ketten, D. R., Arruda, J., Dimitriadis, E. K., & O'Malley, J. T. (2008). The influence of cochlear shape on low-frequency hearing. *Proceedings of the National Academy of Sciences, 105*(16), 6162–6166.

Marks, W. B., Dobelle, W. H., & MacNichol, E. F. (1964). Visual pigments of single primate cones. *Science, 143,* 1181–1182.

Marmor, M. F., & Ravin, J.G. (1997). *The Eye of the Artist.* Orlando: Mosby.

Marmor, M. F., & Shaikh, S. (2005). Was Rembrandt stereoblind? *New England Journal of Medicine, 352,* 631.

Marr, D. (1976). Early processing of visual information. *Philosophical Transactions of the Royal Society of London, B275,* 483–519.

Marr, D. (1977). Analysis of occluding contour. *Proceedings of the Royal Society of London, B197,* 441–475.

Marr, D. (1980). Visual information processing: The structure and creation of visual representations. *Philosophical Transactions of the Royal Society of London, B290,* 199–218.

Marr, D. (1982). *Vision.* San Francisco, CA: Freeman.

Marr, D., & Hildreth, E. C. (1980). Theory of edge detection. *Proceedings of the Royal Society of London, B207,* 187–217.

Marr, D., & Nishihara, H. K. (1978). Representation and recognition of the spatial organisation of three-dimensional shapes. *Proceedings of the Royal Society of London, B200,* 269–294.

Marr, D., & Poggio, T. (1976). Cooperative computation of stereo disparity. *Science, 194,* 283–287.

Marshall, J., Burbeck, C., Ariely, D., Rolland, J., & Martin, K. (1996). Occlusion edge blur: A cue to relative visual depth. *Journal of the Optical Society of America, A13,* 681–688.

Marslen-Wilson, W., & Tyler, L. K. (1980). The temporal structure of spoken language understanding. *Cognition, 8,* 1–71.

Martens, S., Munneke, J., Smid, H., & Johnson, A. (2006). Quick minds don't blink: Electrophysiological correlates of individual differences in attentional selection. *Journal of Cognitive Neuroscience, 18*(9), 1423–1438.

Martin, G. N. (1998). *Human Neuropsychology.* Hemel Hempstead: Prentice Hall.

Martinez, A., Anllo-Vento, L., Sereno, M. I., Frank, L. R., Buxton, R. B., Dubowitz, D. J., et al. (1999). Involvement of striate and extrastriate visual cortical areas in spatial attention. *Nature Neuroscience, 2*(4), 364–369.

Masland, R. H. (2001). The fundamental plan of the retina. *Nature Neuroscience, 4,* 877–886.

Masland, R. H. (2012). The tasks of amacrine cells. *Visual Neuroscience, 29*(01), 3–9.

Mather, G. (1980). The movement after-effect and a distribution shift model of direction coding. *Perception, 9,* 379–392.

Mather, G. (1989). Early motion processes and the Kinetic Depth Effect. *Quarterly Journal of Experimental Psychology, 41,* 183–198.

Mather, G. (1996). Image blur as a pictorial depth cue. *Proceedings of the Royal Society of London, B263,* 169–172.

Mather, G. (2006). Two-stroke: A new illusion of visual motion based on the time course of neural responses in the human visual system. *Vision Research, 46,* 2015–2018.

Mather, G. (2008). Perceptual uncertainty and line-call challenges in professional tennis. *Proceedings of the Royal Society B, 275,* 1645–1651.

Mather, G. (2014). *The Psychology of Visual Art: Eye, Brain and Art.* Cambridge: Cambridge University Press.

Mather, G., & Smith, D.R.R. (2000). Depth cue integration: Stereopsis and image blur. *Vision Research, 40,* 3501–3506.

Mather, G., & Smith, D.R.R. (2002). Blur discrimination and its relation to blur-mediated depth perception. *Perception, 31,* 1211–1219.

Mather, G., & Tunley, H. (1995). Temporal filtering enhances direction discrimination in random dot patterns. *Vision Research, 35,* 2105–2116.

Mather, G., & West, S. (1993). Evidence for second-order motion detectors. *Vision Research, 33,* 1109–1112.

Mather, G., Pavan, A., Bellacosa, R., Campana, G., & Casco, C. (2013). Interactions between motion and form processing in the human visual system. *Frontiers in Computational Neuroscience, 7,* 65.

Mather, G., Pavan, A., Bellacosa, R., & Casco, C. (2012). Psychophysical evidence for interactions between visual motion and form processing at the level of motion integrating receptive fields. *Neuropsychologia, 50*(1), 153–159.

Mather, G., Pavan, A., Campana, G., & Casco, C. (2008). The motion aftereffect reloaded. *Trends in Cognitive Sciences, 12*(12), 481–487.

Mather, G., Radford, K., & West, S. (1992). Low-level visual processing of biological motion. *Proceedings of the Royal Society of London, B249,* 149–155.

Mather, G., Verstraten, F., & Anstis, S. (Eds.) (1998). *The Motion Aftereffect: A Modern Perspective.* Cambridge, MA: MIT Press.

Matthews, N., Meng, X., Xu, P., & Qian, N. (2003). A physiological theory of depth perception from vertical disparity. *Vision Research, 43,* 85–99.

Maunsell, J.H.R. (2004). The role of attention in visual cerebral cortex. In L. M. Chalupa & J. S. Werner (Eds.), *The Visual Neurosciences Volume 2* (pp. 1538–1545). Cambridge MA: MIT Press.

Maurer, D., Lewis, T. L., Brent, H. P., Levin, A. V. (1999). Rapid improvement in the acuity of infants after visual input. *Science 286,* 108–110.

Maxwell, J. C. (1855). Experiments on colour, as seen by the eye, with remarks on colour blindness. *Transactions of the Royal Society of Edinburgh, 21,* 275–298.

May, K. A., Zhaoping, L., & Hibbard, P. B. (2012). Perceived direction of motion determined by adaptation to static binocular images. *Current Biology, 22*(1), 28–32.

Mayhew, J.E.W., & Frisby, J. P. (1981). Psychophysical and computational studies towards a theory of human stereopsis. *Artificial Intelligence, 17,* 349–385.

Mayhew, J.E.W., & Longuet-Higgins, H. C. (1982). A computational model of binocular depth perception. *Nature, 297,* 376–379.

McBurney, D. (1969). Effects of adaptation on human taste function. In C. Pfaffmann (Ed.), *Olfaction and Taste III.* New York: Rockerfeller University Press.

McCarty, C. A., & Taylor, H. R. (1996). Recent developments in vision research: Light damage in cataract. *Investigative Ophthalmology and Visual Science, 37,* 1720–1723.

McClelland, J. L., & Elman, J. L. (1986). The TRACE model of speech perception. *Cognitive Psychology, 18,* 1–86.

McClelland, J. L., Mirman, D., & Holt, L. L. (2006). Are there interactive processes in speech perception? *Trends in Cognitive Sciences, 10,* 363–369.

McDonald, J. J., Teder-Sälejärvi, A., & Hillyard, S. A. (2000). Involuntary orienting to sound improves visual perception. *Nature, 407,* 906–908.

McDonald, J. J., Teder-Sälejärvi, A., Di Russo, F., & Hillyard, S. A. (2003). Neural substrates of perceptual enhancement by cross-modal spatial attention. *Journal of Cognitive Neuroscience, 15,* 10–19.

McEvoy, S. P., Stevenson, M. R., McCartt, A. T., Woodward, M., Haworth, C., Palamara, P. & Cercarelli, R. (2005). Role of mobile phones in motor vehicle crashes resulting in hospital attendance: A case-crossover study. *British Medical Journal, 331,* 428–433.

McGurk, H., & MacDonald, T. (1976). Hearing lips and seeing voices. *Nature, 264,* 746–748.

McLean, J., & Palmer, L. A. (1989). Contribution of linear spatiotemporal receptive field structure to velocity selectivity of simple cells in area 17 of cat. *Vision Research, 29,* 675–679.

McQueen, J. M. (2005). Speech perception. In K. Lamberts & R. L. Goldstone (Eds.), *Handbook of Cognition* (pp. 255–275). London: Sage.

Meddis, R., & Hewitt, M. J. (1991). Virtual pitch and phase sensitivity of a computer model of the auditory periphery. I: Pitch identification. *Journal of the Acoustical Society of America, 89,* 2866–2882.

Meddis, R., & O'Mard, L. (1997). A unitary model of pitch perception. *Journal of the Acoustical Society of America, 102*(3), 1811–1820.

Meese, T. S., & Harris, M. G. (2001). Independent detectors for expansion and rotation, and for orthogonal components of deformation. *Perception, 30,* 1189–1202.

Meisami, E., Mikhail, L., Baim, D., & Bhatnagar, K. P. (1998). Human olfactory bulb: Aging of glomeruli and mitral cells and a search for the accessory olfactory bulb. *Annals of the New York Academy of Sciences, 855,* 708–715.

Melzack, R. (1990). Phantom limbs and the concept of a neuromatrix. *Trends in Neurosciences, 13,* 88–92.

Melzack, R., & Wall, P. D. (1965). Pain mechanisms: A new theory. *Science, 150,* 971–978.

Merigan, W. (1996). Basic visual capacities and shape discrimination after lesions of extrastriate area V4 in macaques. *Visual Neuroscience, 13,* 51–60.

Merigan, W. H., & Eskin, T. A. (1986). Spatiotemporal vision of macaques with severe loss of P_b retinal ganglion cells. *Vision Research, 26,* 1751–1761.

Merigan, W., Nealey, T., & Maunsell, J. (1993). Visual effects of lesions of cortical area V2 in macaques. *Journal of Neuroscience, 13,* 3180–3191.

Merzenich, M., Nelson, R. J., Stryker, M. P., Cynader, M. S., Schoppmann, A., & Zook, J. M. (1984). Somatosensory cortical map changes following digit amputation in adult monkeys. *Journal of Comparative Neurology, 224,* 591–605.

Methven, L., Allen, V. J., Withers, C. A., & Gosney, M. A. (2012). Ageing and taste. *Proceedings of the Nutrition Society, 71*(4), 556.

Michotte, A. (1963). *The Perception of Causality.* London: Methuen.

Mikami, A., Newsome, W. T., & Wurtz, R. H. (1986). Motion selectivity in macaque visual cortex. II. Spatiotemporal range of directional interactions in MT and V1. *Journal of Neurophysiology, 55,* 1328–1339.

Miller, G. (2000). Evolution of human music through sexual selection. In N. Wallin, B. Merker, & S. Brown (Eds.), *The Origins of Music* (pp. 329–360). Cambridge, MA: MIT Press.

Miller, I. J., & Reedy, F. E. (1990). Variations in human taste bud density and taste intensity perception. *Physiology and Behavior, 47,* 1213–1219.

Mollon, J. (1993). George Palmer (1740–1795). In C. Nicholls (Ed.), *The Dictionary of National Biography: Missing Persons* (pp. 509–510). Oxford: Oxford University Press.

Moncrieff, R. (1956). Olfactory adaptation and odour likeness. *Journal of Physiology, 133,* 301–316.

Monnier, P., & Shevell, S. K. (2003). Large shifts in color appearance from patterned chromatic backgrounds. *Nature Neuroscience, 6,* 801–802.

Mon-Williams, M., & Tresilian, J. R. (2000). An ordinal role for accommodation in distance perception. *Ergonomics, 43,* 391–404.

Moore, B.C.J. (1973). Frequency difference limens for short-duration tones. *Journal of the Acoustical Society of America, 54,* 610–619.

Moore, B.C.J. (1997). *An Introduction to the Psychology of Hearing.* San Diego, CA: Academic Press.

Moore, B.C.J., & Glasberg, B. R. (1986). The role of frequency selectivity in the perception of loudness, pitch, and time. In B.C.J. Moore (Ed.), *Frequency Selectivity in Hearing.* London: Academic Press.

Moore, B.C.J., Glasberg, B. R., & Shailer, M. J. (1984). Frequency and intensity difference limens for harmonics within complex tones. *Journal of the Acoustical Society of America, 75*(2), 550–561.

Morgan, M. (2003). *The Space between Our Ears.* London: Weidenfeld & Nicolson.

Morgan, M. J. (1980). Analogue models of motion perception. *Philosophical Transactions of the Royal Society of London, B290,* 117–135.

Morgan, M. J. (1986). Positional acuity without monocular cues. *Perception, 15,* 157–162.

Morgan, M. J. (1992). Spatial filtering precedes motion detection. *Nature, 355,* 344–346.

Morgan, M. J. (1996). Visual illusions. In V. Bruce (Ed.), *Unsolved Mysteries of the Mind.* Hove: Psychology Press.

Morgan, M. J. (2011). Features and the "primal sketch." *Vision Research, 51*(7), 738–753.

Morgan, M. J., & Cleary, R. (1992). Ambiguous motion in a two-frame sequence. *Vision Research, 32,* 2195–2198.

Morgan, M. J., & Hotopf, N. (1989). Perceived diagonals in grids and lattices. *Vision Research, 29,* 1005–1015.

Morgan, M. J., & Watt, R. J. (1982). Mechanisms of interpolation in human spatial vision. *Nature, 299,* 553–555.

Morgan, M. J., & Watt, R. J. (1997). The combination of filters in early spatial vision: A retrospective analysis of the MIRAGE model. *Perception, 26,* 1073–1088.

Morrell, C. H., Gordon-Salant, S., Pearson, J. D., Brant, L. J., & Fozard, J. L. (1996). Age- and gender-specific reference ranges for hearing level and longitudinal changes in hearing level. *Journal of the Acoustical Society of America, 100,* 1949–1967.

Morrison, J. H., & Hof, P. R. (1997). Changes in cortical circuits during aging. *Clinical Neuroscience Research, 2,* 294–304.

Morrone, M. C., & Burr, D. C. (1988). Feature detection in human vision: A phase-dependent energy model. *Proceedings of the Royal Society of London, B235,* 221–245.

Morrone, M. C., Burr, D. C., & Ross, J. (1994). Illusory brightness step in the Chevreul illusion. *Vision Research, 34,* 1567–1574.

Motter, B. C. (1993). Focal attention produces spatially selective processing in visual cortical areas V1, V2, and V4 in the presence of competing stimuli. *Journal of Neurophysiology, 70*, 909–919.

Moulden, B. (1980). After-effects and the integration of patterns of neural activity within a channel. *Philosophical Transactions of the Royal Society of London, B290*, 39–55.

Moulden, B. (1994). Collator units: Second-stage orientational filters. In G. R. Bock & J. A. Goode (Eds.), *Higher-order Processing in the Visual System. Ciba Foundation Symposium 184* (pp. 170–184). Chichester: Wiley.

Moulden, B., & Kingdom, F. (1987). Effect of the number of grey levels on the detectability of a simple line signal in visual noise. *Spatial Vision, 2*, 61–77.

Mountcastle, V. (1957). Modality and topographic properties of single neurons of cat's somatic sensory cortex. *Journal of Neurophysiology, 20*, 408–434.

Movshon, J. A., & Blakemore, C. B. (1973). Orientation specificity and spatial selectivity in human vision. *Perception, 2*, 53–60.

Mueller, C. G. (1951). Frequency of seeing functions for intensity discrimination at various levels of adapting intensity. *Journal of General Physiology, 34*, 463–474.

Murphy, C., Schubert, C. R., Cruickshanks, K. J., Klein, B. E., Klein, R., & Nondahl, D. M. (2002). Prevalence of olfactory impairment in older adults. *Journal of the American Medical Association, 288*(18), 2307–2312.

Myers, E. B., & Blumstein, S. E. (2007). The neural bases of the lexical effect: An fMRI investigation. *Cerebral Cortex, 18*(2), 278–288.

Nagasako, E. M., Oaklander, A. L., & Dworkin, R. H. (2003). Congenital insensitivity to pain: An update. *Pain, 101*(3), 213–219.

Naka, K. I., & Rushton, W.A.H. (1966). S-potentials from colour units in the retina of fish (Cyprinidae). *Journal of Physiology, 185*(3), 536–555.

Nakayama, K., & Mackeben, M. (1989). Sustained and transient components of focal visual attention. *Vision Research, 29*(11), 1631–1647.

Nakayama, K., He, Z. J., & Shimojo, S. (1995). Visual surface representation: A critical link between lower-level and higher-level vision. In S. Kosslyn & D. Osherson (Eds.), *Visual Cognition: An Invitation to Cognitive Science* (Vol. 2, 2nd ed.). Cambridge, MA: MIT Press.

Nakayama, K., Shimojo, S., & Silverman, G. H. (1989). Stereoscopic depth: Its relation to image segmentation, grouping and the recognition of occluded objects. *Perception, 18*, 55–68.

Nassi, J.J., & Callaway, E. M. (2006). The parvocellular LGN provides a robust disynaptic input to the visual motion area MT. *Neuron, 50*, 319–327.

Nathans, J. (1989). The genes for color vision. *Scientific American, 260*(1), 42–49.

Nealey, T. A., & Maunsell, J. H. (1994). Magnocellular and parvocellular contributions to the responses of neurons in macaque striate cortex. *Journal of Neuroscience, 14*, 2069–2079.

Neisser, U., & Becklen, R. (1975). Selective looking: Attending to visually specified events. *Cognitive Psychology, 7*(4), 480–494.

Nelson, G., Chandrashekar, J., Hoon, M. A., Feng, L., Zhao, G., Ryba, N.J.P., & Zuker, C. S. (2002). An amino-acid taste receptor. *Nature, 416*, 199–202.

Neri, P., Morrone, M. C., & Burr, D. C. (1998). Seeing biological motion. *Nature, 395*, 894–896.

Newell, A., & Simon, H. A. (1972). *Human Problem Solving.* Englewood Cliffs, NJ: Prentice Hall.

Newsome, W. T., Mikami, A., & Wurtz, R. H. (1986). Motion selectivity in macaque visual cortex. III. Psychophysics and physiology of apparent motion. *Journal of Neurophysiology, 55*, 1340–1351.

Newsome, W. T., Wurtz, R., Dursteler, M., & Mikami, A. (1985). Deficits in visual motion processing following ibotenic acid lesions of the middle temporal visual area. *Journal of Neuroscience, 5*, 825–840.

Nichols, S., & Patel, H. (2002). Health and safety implications of virtual reality: A review of empirical evidence. *Applied Ergonomics, 33*, 251–271.

Nishida, S., & Sato, T. (1995). Motion aftereffect with flickering test patterns reveals higher stages of motion processing. *Vision Research, 35*, 477–490.

Nishida, S., Ledgeway, T., & Edwards, M. (1997). Dual multiple-scale processing for motion in the human visual system. *Vision Research, 37*, 2685–2698.

Noesselt, T., Hillyard, S. A., Woldorff, M. G., Schoenfeld, A., Hagner, T., Jäncke, L., et al. (2002). Delayed striate cortical activation during spatial attention. *Neuron, 35*, 575–587.

Norris, D., McQueen, J. M., & Cutler, A. (2000). Merging information in speech recognition: Feedback is never necessary. *Behavioral and Brain Sciences, 23*, 299–370.

Nothdurft, H. C. (1993). The role of features in preattentive vision: Comparison of orientation, motion and colour cues. *Vision Research, 33*, 1937–1958.

Nowlis, G., & Frank, M. (1977). Qualities in hamster taste: Behavioral and neural evidence. In J. Le Magnen & P. MacLeod (Eds.), *Olfaction and Taste VI* (pp. 241–247). London: Information Retrieval.

Nozza, R. J. (1995). Estimating the contribution of non-sensory factors to infant–adult differences in behavioral thresholds. *Hearing Research, 91*, 72–78.

Nunn, J. A., Gregory, L. J., Brammer, M., Williams, S.C.R., Parslow, D. M., Morgan, M. J., et al. (2002). Functional magnetic resonance imaging of synesthesia: Activation of V4/V8 by spoken words. *Nature Neuroscience, 5*, 371–375.

O'Craven, K. M., Rosen, B. R., Kwong, K. K., Treisman, A., & Savoy, R. L. (1997). Voluntary attention modulates fMRI activity in human MT–MST. *Neuron, 18*(4), 591–598.

O'Keefe, L., & Movshon, J. A. (1998). Processing of first- and second-order motion signals by neurons in area Mt of the macaque monkey. *Visual Neuroscience, 15*, 305–317.

O'Shea, R., Blackburn, S. G., & Ono, H. (1994). Contrast as a depth cue. *Vision Research, 34*, 1595–1604.

Ochoa, J., & Torebjörk, E. (1983). Sensations evoked by intraneural microstimulation of single mechanoreceptor units innervating the human hand. *Journal of Physiology, 342,* 633–654.

Odgaard, E. C., Arieh, Y., & Marks, L. E. (2004). Brighter noise: Sensory enhancement of perceived loudness by concurrent visual stimulation. *Cognitive, Affective, and Behavioral Neuroscience, 4,* 127–132.

Öhman, A., Flykt, A., & Esteves, F. (2001). Emotion drives attention: Detecting the snake in the grass. *Journal of Experimental Psychology: General, 130*(3), 466.

Oliva, A. (2005). Gist of the scene. *Neurobiology of Attention, 696*(64), 251–258.

Olsho, L. W., Koch, E. G., Carter, E. A., Halpin, C. F., & Spetner, N. B. (1988). Pure-tone sensitivity of human infants. *Journal of the Acoustical Society of America, 84,* 1316–1324.

Ono, S., & Mustari, M. J. (2006). Extraretinal signals in MSTd neurons related to volitional smooth pursuit. *Journal of Neurophysiology, 96*(5), 2819–2825.

Ooi, T. L., Wu, B., & He, Z.J.J. (2001). Distance determined by the angular declination below the horizon. *Nature, 414,* 197–200.

Orban, G. A. (2008). Higher order visual processing in macaque extrastriate cortex. *Physiological Reviews, 88,* 59–89.

Orban, G. A., Lagae, L., Verri, A., Raiguel, S., Xiao, D., Maes, H., & Torre, V. (1992). First-order analysis of optic flow in the monkey brain. *Proceedings of the National Academy of Sciences USA, 89,* 2595–2599.

Osorio, D., & Vorobyev, M. (1996). Colour vision as an adaptation to frugivory in primates. *Proceedings of the Royal Society, B, 263*(1370), 593–599.

Osterberg, G. (1935). Topography of the layer of rods and cones in the human retina. *Acta Ophthalmologica, Supplement 6,* 1–103.

Overheim, R. D., & Wagner, D. L. (1982). *Light and Color.* New York: John.

Owsley, C., Sekuler, R., & Siemsen, D. (1983). Contrast sensitivity throughout adulthood. *Vision Research, 23,* 689–699.

Pack, C. C., & Born, R. T. (2001). Temporal dynamics of a neural solution to the aperture problem in visual area MT of macaque brain. *Nature, 409,* 1040–1042.

Pack, C. C., Gartland, A. J., & Born, R. T. (2004). Integration of contour and terminator signals in visual area MT of alert macaque. *Journal of Neuroscience, 24*(13), 3268–3280.

Palmer, A. R. (1995). Neural signal processing. In B.C.J. Moore (Ed.), *Hearing.* San Diego, CA: Academic Press.

Palmer, A. R., & Russell, I. J. (1986). Phase-locking in the cochlear nerve of the guinea-pig and its relation to the receptor potential of inner hair cells. *Hearing Research, 24,* 1–15.

Palmer, S. E., Rosch, E., & Chase, P. (1981). Canonical perspective and the perception of objects. In J. Long & A. D. Baddeley (Eds.), *Attention and Performance IX.* Hillsdale, NJ: Lawrence Erlbaum.

Pantle, A. J., & Sekuler, R. W. (1968). Velocity-sensitive elements in human vision: Initial psychophysical evidence. *Vision Research, 8,* 445–450.

Paradis, A. L., Cornilleau-Peres, V., Droulez, J., Van De Moortele, P. F., Lobel, E., Berthoz, A., et al. (2000). Visual perception of motion and 3-D structure from motion: An fMRI study. *Cerebral Cortex, 10*(8), 772–783.

Parker, A. J. (2007). Binocular depth perception and the cerebral cortex. *Nature Reviews Neuroscience, 8*(5), 379–391.

Parsons, R. D. (1970). Magnitude estimates of the oculogyral illusion during and following angular acceleration. *Journal of Experimental Psychology, 84,* 230–238.

Patel, A. (2003). Language, music, syntax and the brain. *Nature Neuroscience, 6,* 674–681.

Paul-Brown, D. (1996). Central auditory processing: Current status of research and implications for clinical practice. *American Journal of Audiology, 5,* 41–54.

Paulesu, E., Harrison, J., Baron-Cohen, S., Watson, J. D., Goldstein, L., Heather, J., et al. (1995). The physiology of coloured hearing. A PET activation study of colour-word synaesthesia. *Brain, 118,* 661–676.

Paus, T., Zijdenbos, A., Worsley, K., Collins, D. L., Blumenthal, J., Giedd, J. N., et al. (1999). Structural maturation of neural pathways in children and adolescents: In vivo study. *Science, 283,* 1908–1911.

Pelli, D. G., Palomares, M., & Majaj, N. J. (2004). Crowding is unlike ordinary masking: Distinguishing feature integration from detection. *Journal of Vision, 4*(12), 1136–1169.

Penagos, H., Melcher, J. R., & Oxenham, A. J. (2004). A neural representation of pitch salience in nonprimary human auditory cortex revealed with functional magnetic resonance imaging. *Journal of Neuroscience, 24*(30), 6810–6815.

Penfield, W., & Rasmussen, T. (1950). *The Cerebral Cortex of Man: A Clinical Study of Localization of Function.* New York: Macmillan.

Pentland, A. P. (1987). A new sense for depth of field. *IEEE Transactions on Pattern Analysis and Machine Intelligence, 9,* 523–531.

Perdreau, F., & Cavanagh, P. (2013). Is artists' perception more veridical? *Frontiers in Neuroscience, 7,* 6.

Peretz, I., & Coltheart, M. (2003). Modularity of music processing. *Nature Neuroscience, 6,* 688–691.

Perrett, D., Harries, M., Mistlin, A. J., & Chitty, A. J. (1990). Three stages in the classification of body movements by visual neurons. In H. B. Barlow, C. Blakemore, & M. Weston-Smith, (Eds.), *Images and Understanding* (pp. 94–107). Cambridge: Cambridge University Press.

Perrett, D. I., Rolls, E. T., & Caan, W. (1982). Visual neurones responsive to faces in the monkey temporal cortex. *Experimental Brain Research, 47,* 329–342.

Perry, V., Oehler, R., & Cowey, A. (1984). Retinal ganglion cells that project to the dorsal latergal geniculate nucleus in the macaque monkey. *Neuroscience, 12,* 1101–1123.

Peters, A. (2002). Structural changes that occur during normal aging of primate cerebral hemispheres. *Neuroscience and Behavioral Reviews, 26,* 733–741.

Petersen, S., Baker, J., & Allman, J. (1985). Direction-specific adaptation in area MT of the owl monkey. *Brain Research, 346,* 146–150.

Petrov, A. A., & Hayes, T. R. (2010). Asymmetric transfer of perceptual learning of luminance- and contrast-modulated motion. *Journal of Vision, 10*(14), 11.

Pettet, M. W., McKee, S. P., & Grzywacz, N. (1998). Constraints on long range interactions mediating contour detection. *Vision Research, 38,* 865–879.

Pfaffmann, C. (1955). Gustatory nerve impulses in the rat, cat, and rabbit. *Journal of Neurophysiology, 18,* 429–440.

Pfaffmann, C. (1959). The afferent code for sensory quality. *American Psychologist, 14,* 226–232.

Pfaffmann, C. (1974). Specificity of the sweet receptors of the squirrel monkey. *Chemical Senses and Flavor, 1,* 61–67.

Piantanida, T. (1991). Genetics of inherited colour vision deficiencies. In J. Cronly-Dillon & D. H. Foster (Eds.), *Vision and Visual Dysfunction Volume VII: Inherited and Acquired Colour Vision Deficiencies* (pp. 88–114). Basingstoke: Macmillan.

Piazza, M., Mechelli, A., Butterworth, B., & Price, C. J. (2002). Are subitizing and counting implemented as separate or functionally overlapping processes? *NeuroImage, 15,* 435–446.

Pierce, J. D., Wysocki, C. J., Aronov, E. V., Webb, J. B., & Boden, R. M. (1996). The role of perceptual and structural similarity in cross-adaptation. *Chemical Senses, 21,* 223–237.

Pinker, S. (1997). *How the Mind Works.* London: Allen Lane.

Pirenne, H. (1948). *Vision and the Eye.* London: Chapman & Hall.

Pirenne, M. (1962). Dark-adaptation and night vision. In H. Davson (Ed.), *The Eye* (Vol. 2, pp. 93–122). New York: Academic Press.

Pitcher, D., Charles, L., Devlin, J. T., Walsh, V., & Duchaine, B. (2009). Triple dissociation of faces, bodies, and objects in extrastriate cortex. *Current Biology, 19*(4), 319–324.

Plack, C. J., & Carlyon, R. P. (1995). Loudness perception and intensity coding. In B.C.J. Moore (Ed.), *Hearing.* San Diego, CA: Academic Press.

Plack, C. J., Barker, D., & Hall, D. A. (2014). Pitch coding and pitch processing in the human brain. *Hearing Research, 307,* 53–64.

Plant, G. T. (1991). Temporal properties of normal and abnormal spatial vision. In J. Cronly-Dillon & D. Regan (Eds.), *Vision and Visual Dysfunction Volume X: Spatial Vision* (pp. 43–63). Basingstoke: Macmillan.

Ploghaus, A., Becerra, L., Borras, C., & Borsook, D. (2003). Neural circuitry underlying pain modulation: Expectation, hypnosis, placebo. *Trends in Cognitive Sciences, 7,* 197–200.

Plomp, R. (1965). Detectability threshold for combination tones. *Journal of the Acoustic Society of America, 37,* 1110–1123.

Plomp, R. (1967). Pitch of complex tones. *Journal of the Acoustical Society of America, 41,* 1526–1533.

Poggio, G. F., & Talbot, W. H. (1981). Mechanisms of static and dynamic stereopsis in foveal cortex of the rhesus monkey. *Journal of Physiology, 315,* 469–492.

Pokorny, J., & Smith, V. C. (1986). Colorimetry and color discrimination. In K. R. Boff, L. Kaufman, & J. P. Thomas (Eds.), *Handbook of Perception and Human Performance Volume I: Sensory Processes and Perception.* New York: Wiley.

Polat, U., & Sagi, D. (1994). The architecture of perceptual spatial interactions. *Vision Research, 34,* 73–78.

Poldrack, R. A. (2012). The future of fMRI in cognitive neuroscience. *Neuroimage, 62*(2), 1216–1220.

Pollack, R. H. (1989). Pictures, maybe; illusions, no. *Behavioral and Brain Sciences, 12,* 92–93.

Polland, W. (2004). Myopic artists. *Acta Ophthalmologica Scandinavica, 82,* 325–326.

Pollard, S. B., Mayhew, J.E.W., & Frisby, J. P. (1985). PMF: A stereo correspondence algorithm using a disparity gradient limit. *Perception, 14,* 449–470.

Pons, T. P., Garraghty, P. E., Ommaya, A. K., Kaas, J. H., Taub, E., & Mishkin, M. (1991). Massive cortical reorganization after sensory deafferentation in adult macaques. *Science, 252,* 1857–1860.

Popper, K. (1963). *Conjectures and Refutations: The Growth of Scientific Knowledge.* London: Routledge.

Poremba, A., Saunders, R. C., Crane, A. M., Cook, M., Sokoloff, L., & Mishkin, M. (2003). Functional mapping of the primate auditory system. *Science, 299,* 568–572.

Posner, M. I. and Cohen, Y. (1984). Components of visual orienting. In H. Bouma & D. Bouwhuis (Eds.), *Attention and Performance Volume X* (pp. 531–556). Hillsdale, NJ: Lawrence Erlbaum.

Potter, M. C. (1976). Short-term conceptual memory for pictures. *Journal of Experimental Psychology: Human Learning and Memory, 2*(5), 509–522.

Pouget, A., Dayan, P., & Zemel, R. (2000). Information processing with population codes. *Nature Reviews Neuroscience, 1*(2), 125–132.

Priebe, N. J., Lisberger, S. G., & Movshon, J. A. (2006). Tuning for spatiotemporal frequency and speed in directionally selective neurons of macaque striate cortex. *Journal of Neuroscience, 26*(11), 2941–2950.

Prinzmetal, W., McCool, C., & Park, S. (2005). Attention: Reaction time and accuracy reveal different mechanisms. *Journal of Experimental Psychology: General, 134*(1), 73.

Pritchard, T. C., Hamilton, R. B., Morse, J. R., & Norgren, R. (1986). Projections of thalamic gustatory and lingual areas in the monkey, macaca fascicularis. *Journal of Comparative Neurology, 244,* 213–228.

Pugh, M. C., Ringach, D. L., Shapley, R., & Shelley, M. J. (2000). Computational modelling of orientation tuning dynamics in monkey primary visual cortex. *Journal of Computational Neuroscience, 8,* 143–159.

Purves, D., Augustine, G., Fitzpatrick, D., Katz, L., LaMantia, A., McNamara, J., & Williams, S. (Eds.)

(2001). *Neuroscience* (2nd ed.). Sunderland, MA: Sinauer.

Pylyshyn, Z. W. (1989). The role of location indexes in spatial perception: A sketch of the FINST spatial-index model. *Cognition, 32*(1), 65–97.

Pylyshyn, Z. W. (2000). Situating vision in the world. *Trends in Cognitive Sciences, 4*(5), 197–207.

Pylyshyn, Z. W., & Storm, R. W. (1988). Tracking multiple independent targets: Evidence for a parallel tracking mechanism. *Spatial Vision, 3,* 1–19.

Qiu, F. T., & von der Heydt, R. (2005). Figure and ground in the visual cortex: V2 combines stereoscopic cues with gestalt rules. *Neuron, 47,* 155–166.

Quinlan, P. T., & Dyson, B. J. (2008). *Cognitive Psychology*. Harlow: Pearson Education.

Quinlan, P. T., & Humphreys, G. W. (1993). Perceptual frames of reference and 2-dimensional shape recognition—further examination of internal axes. *Perception, 22,* 1343–1364.

Rabin, M. D. (1988). Experience facilitates olfactory quality discrimination. *Perception and Psychophysics, 44,* 532–540.

Radeau, M. (1994). Auditory-visual interaction and modularity. *Current Psychology of Cognition, 13,* 3–51.

Rafal, R. D. (1994). Neglect. *Current Opinion in Neurobiology, 4,* 231–236.

Ramachandran, V. S., & Blakesee, S. (1998). *Phantoms in the Brain: Probing the Mysteries of the Human Mind.* New York: William Morrow.

Ramachandran, V. S., Rao, V. M., & Vidyasagar, T. R. (1973). Apparent movement with subjective contours. *Vision Research, 13,* 1399–1401.

Rao, A., Nobre, A. C., Alexander, I., & Cowey, A. (2007). Auditory evoked visual awareness following sudden ocular blindness: An EEG and TMS investigation. *Experimental Brain Research, 176,* 288–298.

Rasch, R., & Plomp, R. (1999). The perception of musical tones. In D. Deutsch (Ed.), *The Psychology of Music* (2nd ed., pp. 89–112). San Diego, CA: Academic Press.

Rauschecker, J. P., & Tian, B. (2000). Mechanisms and streams for processing of "what" and "where" in auditory cortex. *Proceedings of the National Academy of Sciences USA, 97,* 11800–11806.

Rawson, N. E., Gomez, G., Cowart, B., & Restrepo, D. (1998). The use of olfactory receptor neurons (ORNs) from biopsies to study changes in aging and neurodegenerative diseases. *Annals of the New York Academy of Sciences, 855,* 701–707.

Raymond, J. E. (2000). Attentional modulation of visual motion perception. *Trends in Cognitive Science, 4,* 42–49.

Raymond, J. E., Shapiro, K. L., & Arnell, K. M. (1992). Temporary suppression of visual processing in an RSVP task: An attentional blink? *Journal of Experimental Psychology: Human Perception and Performance, 18*(3), 849.

Reed, C. L., Klatzky, R. L., & Halgren, E. (2005). What vs. where in touch: An fMRI study. *NeuroImage, 25,* 718–726.

Regan, B., Julliot, C., Simmen, F., Vienot, P., Charles-Dominique, P., & Mollon, J. (2001). Fruits, foliage and the evolution of primate colour vision. *Philosophical Transactions of the Royal Society of London, B356,* 229–283.

Reichardt, W. (1961). Autocorrelation, a principle for the evaluation of sensory information by the central nervous system. In W. Rosenblith (Ed.), *Sensory Communication* (pp. 303–317). New York: MIT Press.

Reid, R. C., & Shapley, R. M. (2002). Space and time maps of cone photoreceptor signals in macaque lateral geniculate nucleus. *Journal of Neuroscience, 22,* 6158–6175.

Rensink, R. A., O'Regan, J. K., & Clark, J. J. (1997). To see or not to see: The need for attention to perceive changes in scenes. *Psychological Science, 8,* 368–373.

Ressler, K., Sullivan, S., & Buck, L. (1994). A molecular dissection of spatial patterning in the olfactory system. *Current Opinion in Neurobiology, 4,* 588–596.

Riesenhuber, M., & Poggio, T. (2000). Models of object recognition. *Nature Neuroscience, 3,* 1199–1204.

Riesenhuber, M., & Poggio, T. (2002). Neural mechanisms of object recognition. *Current Opinion in Neurobiology, 12*(2), 162–168.

Robles, L., Ruggiero, M. A., & Rich, N. C. (1986). Basilar membrane mechanics at the base of the chinchilla cochlea. I. Input–output functions, tuning curves, and response phases. *Journal of the Acoustical Society of America, 80,* 1364–1374.

Robson, J. G. (1966). Spatial and temporal contrast sensitivity functions of the visual system. *Journal of the Optical Society of America, 8,* 1141–1142.

Rock, I. (1983). *The Logic of Perception.* Cambridge, MA: MIT Press.

Rock, I., & Palmer, S. (1990). The legacy of Gestalt psychology. *Scientific American, 263*(6), 48–61.

Rockland, K. S. & Ojima, H. (2003). Multisensory convergence in calcarine visual areas in macaque monkey. *International Journal of Psychophysiology, 50,* 19–26.

Rodieck, R. W. (1965). Quantitative analysis of cat retinal ganglion cell response to visual stimuli. *Vision Research, 5,* 583–601.

Rodieck, R. W. (1998). *The First Steps in Seeing.* Sunderland, MA: Sinauer.

Roelfsema, P. R. (2005). Elemental operations in vision. *Trends in Cognitive Sciences, 9,* 226–233.

Rogers, B. J., & Bradshaw, M. F. (1993). Vertical disparities, differential perspective and binocular stereopsis. *Nature, 361,* 253–255.

Rogers, B. J., & Graham, M. (1979). Motion parallax as an independent cue for depth perception. *Perception, 8,* 125–134.

Rolls, E. T. (2002). The cortical representation of taste and smell. In C. Rouby, B. Schaal, D. Dubois, R. Gervais, & A. Holley (Eds.), *Olfaction, Taste, and Cognition.* Cambridge: Cambridge University Press.

Rolls, E. T., & Baylis, L. L. (1994). Gustatory, olfactory, and visual convergence within the primate orbitofrontal cortex. *Journal of Neuroscience, 14,* 5437–5452.

Roorda, A., Metha, A., Lennie, P., & Williams, D. R. (2001). Packing arrangement of the three cone classes in the primate retina. *Vision Research, 41,* 1291–1306.

Rosner, B., & Meyer, L. (1982). Melodic processes and the perception of music. In D. Deutsch (Ed.), *The Psychology of Music* (1st ed.). New York: Academic Press.

Rousselet, G., Joubert, O., & Fabre-Thorpe, M. (2005). How long to get to the "gist" of real-world natural scenes? *Visual Cognition, 12*(6), 852–877.

Rouw, R., Scholte, H. S., & Colizoli, O. (2011). Brain areas involved in synaesthesia: A review. *Journal of Neuropsychology, 5*(2), 214–242.

Roy, E. A., & Hollins, M. (1998). A ratio code for vibrotactile pitch. *Somatosensory and Motor Research, 15,* 134–145.

Ruddock, K. (1991). Psychophysics of inherited colour vision deficiencies. In J. Cronly-Dillon & D. H. Foster (Eds.), *Vision and Visual Dysfunction Volume VII: Inherited and Acquired Colour Vision Deficiencies* (pp. 4–37). Basingstoke: Macmillan.

Rust, N., Mante, V., Simoncelli, E. P., & Movshon, J. A. (2006). How MT cells analyze the motion of visual patterns. *Nature Neuroscience, 9,* 1421–1431.

Sachs, M. B., & Kiang, N.Y.S. (1968). Two-tone inhibition in auditory nerve fibres. *Journal of the Acoustical Society of America, 43,* 1120–1128.

Sacks, O., & Wasserman, R. (1987). The case of the colorblind painter. *New York Review,* November, 25–33.

Saffran, J. R., Johnson, E. K., Aslin, R. N., & Newport, E. L. (1999). Statistical learning of tone sequences by human infants and adults. *Cognition, 70,* 27–52.

Sagi, D. (2011). Perceptual learning in vision research. *Vision Research, 51*(13), 1552–1566.

Salzman, C. D., Murasugi, C. M., Britten, K. H., & Newsome, W. T. (1992). Microstimulation in visual area MT: Effects on direction discrimination performance. *Journal of Neuroscience, 12,* 2331–2355.

Sathian, K., & Burton, H. (1991). The role of spatially selective attention in the tactile perception of texture. *Perception & Psychophysics, 50*(3), 237–248.

Sceniak, M., Hawken, M., & Shapley, R. (2001). Visual spatial characterization of macaque V1 neurons. *Journal of Neurophysiology, 85,* 1873–1887.

Schiffman, S. S. (1983). Taste and smell in disease. *New England Journal of Medicine, 308,* 1275–1279, 1337–1343.

Schiffman, S. S., & Graham, B. G. (2000). Taste and smell perception affect appetite and immunity in the elderly. *European Journal of Clinical Nutrition, 54*(3), S54–S63.

Schild, D., & Restrepo, D. (1998). Transduction mechanisms in vertebrate olfactory receptor cells. *Physiological Reviews, 78,* 429–466.

Schiller, P., Sandell, J., & Maunsell, J. (1986). Functions of the ON and OFF channels of the visual system. *Nature, 322,* 824–825.

Schleidt, M., Hold, B., & Attili, G. (1981). A cross-cultural study on the attitude towards personal odors. *Journal of Chemical Ecology, 7,* 19–31.

Schmidt, R. F. (Ed.) (1981). *Fundamentals of Sensory Physiology.* Berlin: Springer-Verlag.

Schmolesky, M. T., Wang, Y., Hanes, D. P., Thompson, K. G., Leutgeb, S., Schall, D., & Leventhal, A. G. (1998). Signal timing across the macaque visual system. *Journal of Neurophysiology, 79,* 3272–3278.

Schnapf, J., & Baylor, D. (1987). How photoreceptor cells respond to light. *Scientific American, 256*(4), 32–39.

Schoenfeld, M. A., Hopf, J. M., Merkel, C., Heinze, H. J., & Hillyard, S. A. (2014). Object-based attention involves the sequential activation of feature-specific cortical modules. *Nature Neuroscience, 17*(4), 619–624.

Schofield, A. J., Ledgeway, T., & Hutchinson, C. V. (2007). Asymmetric transfer of the dynamic motion aftereffect between first- and second-order cues and among different second-order cues. *Journal of Vision, 7*(8), 1.

Scholl, B. J., & Tremoulet, P. D. (2000). Perceptual causality and animacy. *Trends in Cognitive Sciences, 4*(8), 299–309.

Schooneveldt, G. P., & Moore, B.C.J. (1989). Comodulation masking release (CMR) as a function of masker bandwidth, modulator bandwidth and signal duration. *Journal of the Acoustical Society of America, 85,* 273–281.

Schreiber, K., Crawford, J. D., Fetter, M., & Tweed, D. (2001). The motor side of depth vision. *Nature, 410,* 819–822.

Schreiber, K. M., Hillis, J. M., Filippini, H. R., Schor, C. M., & Banks, M. S. (2008). The surface of the empirical horopter. *Journal of Vision, 8*(3), 7.

Schroeder, C. E. & Foxe, J. J. (2002). The timing and laminar profile of converging inputs to multisensory areas of the macaque neocortex. *Cognitive Brain Research, 14,* 187–198.

Schroeder, C. E., Smiley, J., Fu, K. G., McGinnis, T., O'Connell, M. N., & Hackett, T. A. (2003). Anatomical mechanisms and functional implications of multisensory convergence in early cortical processing. *International Journal of Psychophysiology, 50,* 5–17.

Schulkin, J., & Raglan, G. B. (2014). The evolution of music and human social capability. *Frontiers in Neuroscience, 8,* 292.

Schwartz, S., Maquet, P., & Frith, C. (2002). Neural correlates of perceptual learning: A functional MRI study of visual texture discrimination. *Proceedings of the National Academy of Sciences USA, 99,* 17137–17142.

Scott, S., Young, A., Calder, A., Hellawell, D., Aggleton. J., & Johnson, M. (1997). Impaired recognition of fear and anger following bilateral amygdala lesions. *Nature, 385,* 254–257.

Scott, S. K., Blank, C. C., Rosen, S., & Wise, R.J.S. (2000). Identification of a pathway for intelligible speech in the left temporal lobe. *Brain, 123,* 2400–2406.

Scott, T. R., & Giza, B. K. (2000). Issues of gustatory neural coding: Where they stand today. *Physiology and Behavior, 69,* 65–76.

Scott, T. R., & Plata-Salaman, C. R. (1999). Taste in the monkey cortex. *Physiology and Behavior, 67,* 489–511.

Segall, M., Campbell, D., & Herskovits, M. (1963). Cultural differences in the perception of geometrical illusions. *Science, 139,* 769–771.

Seiffert, A. E., & Cavanagh, P. (1998). Position displacement, not velocity, is the cue to motion detection of second-order stimuli. *Vision Research, 38,* 3569–3582.

Sek, A., & Moore, C. J. (1995). Frequency discrimination as a function of frequency, measured in several ways. *Journal of the Acoustical Society of America, 97,* 2479–2486.

Sela, L., & Sobel, N. (2010). Human olfaction: A constant state of change-blindness. *Experimental Brain Research, 205*(1), 13–29.

Shannon, C. E. (1948). A mathematical theory of communication. *Bell System Technical Journal, 27,* 379–423.

Shapley, R., & Hawken, M. J. (2011). Color in the cortex: Single-and double-opponent cells. *Vision Research, 51,* 701–717.

Sharpe, L. T., & Stockman, A. (1999). Rod pathways: The importance of seeing nothing. *Trends in Neurosciences, 22,* 497–504.

Shepard, R. N., & Metzler, J. (1971). Mental rotation of three-dimensional objects. *Science, 171,* 701–703.

Shepherd, G. (1988). *Neurobiology.* New York: Oxford University Press.

Shepherd, G. M. (1994). Discrimination of molecular signals by the olfactory receptor neuron. *Neuron, 13,* 771–790.

Sherman, P. D. (1981). *Colour Vision in the Nineteenth Century: The Young–Helmholtz–Maxwell Theory.* Bristol: Hilger.

Shimokata, H., & Kuzuya, F. (1995). Two-point discrimination test of the skin as an index of sensory aging. *Gerontology, 41,* 267–272.

Sicard, G., & Holley, A. (1984). Receptor cell responses to odorants: Similarities among odorants. *Brain Research, 292,* 283–296.

Sillito, A., & Jones, H. (2002). Corticothalamic interactions in the transfer of visual information. *Philosophical Transactions of the Royal Society of London, B357,* 1739–1752.

Silver, M. A., Ress, D., & Heeger, D. J. (2007). Neural correlates of sustained spatial attention in human early visual cortex. *Journal of Neurophysiology, 97*(1), 229–237.

Simoncelli, E., & Heeger, D. (1998). A model of neuronal responses in visual area MT. *Vision Research, 38,* 743–761.

Simons, D. J., & Levin, D. T. (1997). Change blindness. *Trends in Cognitive Science, 1,* 261–267.

Sincich, L. C., & Horton J. C. (2005). The circuitry of V1 and V2: Integration of color, form, and motion. *Annual Review of Neuroscience, 28,* 303–326.

Sincich, L. C., Park, K. F., Wohlgemuth, M. J., & Horton, J. C. (2004). Bypassing V1: A direct geniculate input to area MT. *Nature Neuroscience, 7,* 1123–1128.

Slotnik, S. D, & Yantis, S. (2005). Common neural substrates for the control and effects of visual attention and perceptual stability. *Cognitive Brain Research, 24,* 97–108.

Smith, A. T. (1994). Correspondence-based and energy-based detection of second-order motion in human vision. *Journal of the Optical Society of America, A11,* 1940–1948.

Smith, A. T., & Edgar, G. K. (1994). Antagonistic comparison of temporal frequency filter outputs as a basis for speed perception. *Vision Research, 34,* 253–265.

Smith, A. T., & Ledgeway, T. (2001). Motion detection in human vision: A unifying approach based on energy and features. *Proceedings of the Royal Society of London, B268,* 1889–1899.

Smith, C.U.M. (2000). *Biology of Sensory Systems.* Chichester: Wiley.

Smith, D. V., St. John, S. J., & Boughter, J. D. (2000). Neuronal cell types and taste quality coding. *Physiology and Behavior, 69,* 77–85.

Snowden, R. J., Treue, S., Erickson, R. G., & Andersen, R. A. (1991). The response of area MT neurons to transparent motion. *Journal of Neuroscience, 11,* 2768–2785.

Spence, C. (2002). Multisensory integration, attention, and perception. In D. Roberts (Ed.), *Signals and Perception* (pp. 345–354). Basingstoke: Palgrave Macmillan.

Spence, C., & Driver, J. (1996). Audiovisual links in endogenous covert spatial attention. *Journal of Experimental Psychology: Human Perception and Performance, 22*(4), 1005.

Spence, C., & Read, L. (2003). Speech shadowing while driving: On the difficulty of splitting attention between eye and ear. *Psychological Science, 14,* 251–256.

Spence, C., Nicholls, M. E., & Driver, J. (2001). The cost of expecting events in the wrong sensory modality. *Perception & Psychophysics, 63*(2), 330–336.

Spence, C., Nicholls, M. E., Gillespie, N., & Driver, J. (1998). Cross-modal links in exogenous covert spatial orienting between touch, audition, and vision. *Perception and Psychophysics, 60,* 544–557.

Sperling, G., & Lu, Z.-L. (1998). A systems analysis of visual motion perception. In T. Watanabe (Ed.), *High-level Motion Processing* (pp. 153–183). Cambridge, MA: MIT Press.

Spiridon, M., & Kanwisher, N. (2002). How distributed is visual category information in human occipito-temporal cortex? An fMRI study. *Neuron, 35*(6), 1157–1165.

Stanislaw, H., & Todorov, N. (1999). Calculation of signal detection theory measures. *Behavior Research Methods, Instruments and Computers, 31,* 137–149.

Stern, K. & McClintock, M. K. (1998). Regulation of ovulation by human pheromones. *Nature, 392,* 177–179.

Stettler, D. D., Das, A., Bennett, J., & Gilbert, C. D. (2002). Lateral connectivity and contextual interactions in macaque primary visual cortex. *Neuron, 36,* 739–750.

Stevens, J. C., Cain, W. S., Demarque, A., & Ruthruff, A. M. (1991). On the discrimination of missing ingredients: Aging and salt flavor. *Appetite, 16*(2), 129–140.

Stevens, J. K., Emerson, R. C., Gerstein, G. L., Kallos, T., Neufeld, G. R., Nichols, C. W., & Rosenquist,

A. C. (1976). Paralysis of the awake human: Visual perceptions. *Vision Research, 16*(1), 93–98.

Stevens, S. S. (1961). Psychophysics of sensory function. In W. A. Rosenblith (Ed.), *Sensory Communication.* Cambridge, MA: MIT Press.

Stevenson, S. B., & Schor, C. M. (1997). Human stereo matching is not restricted to epipolar lines. *Vision Research, 37*, 2717–2723.

Stockman, A., & Sharpe, L. (2000). The spectral sensitivities of the middle- and long-wavelength-sensitive cones derived from measurements in observers of known genotype. *Vision Research, 40*, 1711–1737.

Stoddart, D. (1990). *The Scented Ape.* Cambridge: Cambridge University Press.

Strauss, O. (2005). The retinal pigment epithelium in visual function. *Physiological Reviews, 85*(3), 845–881.

Sun, H., Smithson, H. E., Zaidi, Q., & Lee, B. B. (2006). Specificity of cone inputs to macaque retinal ganglion cells. *Journal of Neurophysiology, 95*, 837–849.

Surridge, A., Osorio, D., & Mundy, N. (2003). Evolution and selection of trichromatic vision in primates. *Trends in Ecology and Evolution, 18*, 198–205.

Sutherland, N. S. (1989). *A Dictionary of Psychology.* London: Macmillan.

Suzuki, Y., & Takeshima, H. (2004). Equal-loudness-level contours for pure tones. *Journal of the Acoustical Society of America, 116*(2), 918–933.

Switkes, E., Mayer, M. J., & Sloan, J. A. (1978). Spatial frequency analysis of the visual environment: Anisotropy and the carpentered environment hypothesis. *Vision Research, 18*, 1393–1399.

Takeuchi, T., & De Valois, K. K. (2009). Visual motion mechanisms under low retinal illuminance revealed by motion reversal. *Vision Research, 49*(8), 801–809.

Tanaka, H., & Ohzawa, I. (2009). Surround suppression of V1 neurons mediates orientation-based representation of high-order visual features. *Journal of Neurophysiology, 101*(3), 1444–1462.

Tanaka, K. (1993). Neural mechanisms of object recognition. *Science, 262*, 685–688.

Tanaka, K. (1998). Representation of visual motion in the extrastriate visual cortex. In T. Watanabe (Ed.), *High-Level Motion Processing.* Cambridge, MA: MIT Press.

Tanaka, K., & Saito, H. (1989). Analysis of motion of the visual field by direction, expansion/contraction and rotation cells clustered in the dorsal part of the medial superior temporal area of the macaque monkey. *Journal of Neurophysiology, 62*, 626–641.

Tanaka, K., Fukada, Y., & Saito, H. (1989). Underlying mechanisms of the response specificity of expansion/contraction and rotation cells in the dorsal part of the medial superior temporal area of the macaque monkey. *Journal of Neurophysiology, 62*, 642–656.

Tarr, M. J., & Bulthoff, H. H. (1995). Is human object recognition better described by geon structural descriptions or by multiple views? Comment on Biederman and Gerhardstein (1993). *Journal of Experimental Psychology: Human Perception and Performance, 21*, 1494–1505.

Tatler, B. W., Gilchrist, I. D., & Rusted, J. (2003). The time course of abstract visual representation. *Perception, 32*, 579–592.

Teller, D. (1984). Linking propositions. *Vision Research, 24*, 1233–1246.

Thines, G., Costall, A., & Butterworth, G. (Eds.) (1991). *Michotte's Experimental Phenomenology of Perception.* Hillsdale, NJ: Lawrence Erlbaum.

Thirkettle, M., Benton, C. P., & Scott-Samuel, N. E. (2009). Contributions of form, motion and task to biological motion perception. *Journal of Vision, 9*(3), 28.

Thornton, I. M. (1998). The visual perception of human locomotion. *Cognitive Neuropsychology, 15*(6–8), 535–552.

Thouless, R. (1931). Individual differences in phenomenal regression. *British Journal of Psychology, 22*, 216–241.

Timney, B. N., & Muir, D. W. (1976). Orientation anisotropy: Incidence and magnitude in Caucasian and Chinese subjects. *Science, 193*, 699–701.

Titchener, E. B. (1902). *An Outline of Psychology.* London: Macmillan.

Todd, J. T., Akerstrom, R. A., Reichel, F. D., & Hayes, W. (1988). Apparent rotation in 3-dimensional space: Effects of temporal, spatial and structural factors. *Perception and Psychophysics, 43*, 179–188.

Tolhurst, D. J. (1973). Separate channels for the analysis of the shape and the movement of a moving visual stimulus. *Journal of Physiology, 231*, 385–402.

Tononi, G. (2004). An information integration theory of consciousness. *BMC Neuroscience, 5*(1), 42.

Tootell, R.B.H., Hadjikhani, N. K., Hall, E. K., Marrett, S., Vanduffel, W., Vaughan, J.T., & Dale, A. M. (1998). The retinotopy of visual spatial attention. *Neuron, 21*, 1409–1422.

Tootell, R.B.H., Hadjikhani, N. K., Mendola, J. D., Marrett, S., & Dale, A. M. (1998). From retinotopy to recognition: fMRI in human visual cortex. *Trends in Cognitive Sciences, 2*, 174–183.

Tootell, R.B.H., Reppas, J. B., Dale, A. M., Look, R. B., Sereno, M. I., Malach, R., et al. (1995). Visual motion aftereffect in human cortical area MT revealed by functional magnetic resonance imaging. *Nature, 375*, 139–141.

Tootell, R.B.H., Silverman, M. S., De Valois, R. L., & Jacobs, G. H. (1983). Functional organization of the second cortical visual area of primates. *Science, 220*, 737–739.

Tootell, R.B.H., Silverman, M., Switkes, E., & De Valois, R. (1982). Deoxyglucose analysis of retinotopic organization in primate striate cortex. *Science, 218*, 902–904.

Torebjörk, H. E., & Ochoa, J. L. (1990). New method to identify nociceptor units innervating glabrous skin of the human hand. *Experimental Brain Research, 81*(3), 509–514.

Torralba, A., & Oliva, A. (2003). Statistics of natural image categories. *Network: Computation in Neural Systems, 14*(3), 391–412.

Treisman, A. M., & Gelade, G. (1980). A feature-integration theory of attention. *Cognitive Psychology, 12*(1), 97–136.

Tremoulet, P. D., & Feldman, J. (2000). Perception of animacy from the motion of a single object. *Perception, 29,* 943–951.

Treue, S., & Trujillo, M. (1999). Feature-based attention influences motion processing gain in macaque visual cortex. *Nature, 399,* 575–579.

Trevor-Roper, P. (1988). *The World Through Blunted Sight.* London: Penguin.

Triesch, J., Ballard, D. H., Hayhoe, M. M., & Sullivan, B. T. (2003). What you see is what you need. *Journal of Vision, 3,* 80–94.

Troje, N. F. (2002). Decomposing biological motion: A framework for analysis and synthesis of human gait patterns. *Journal of Vision, 2*(5), 2.

Troje, N. F., & Westhoff, C. (2006). The inversion effect in biological motion perception: Evidence for a "life detector"? *Current Biology, 16*(8), 821–824.

Tse, P., Cavanagh, P., & Nakayama, K. (1998). The role of parsing in high-level motion processing. In T. Watanabe (Ed.), *High-Level Motion Processing* (pp. 249–266). Cambridge, MA: MIT Press.

Tsotsos, J. K. (1990). Analyzing vision at the complexity level. *Behavioral and Brain Sciences, 13*(03), 423–445.

Tsutsui, K., Taira, M., & Sakata, H. (2005). Neural mechanisms of three-dimensional vision. *Neuroscience Research, 51,* 221–229.

Turnbull, H. W. (1959). *The Correspondence of Isaac Newton, Volume 1.* Cambridge: Cambridge University Press.

Tyler, C. W., & Clarke, M. B. (1990). The autostereogram. In J. O. Merritt & S. S. Fisher (Eds.), *Stereoscopic Displays and Applications. S.P.I.E. Proceedings, 1256,* 182–197.

Uchida, N., Takahashi, Y. K., Tanifuji, M., & Mori, K. (2000). Odor maps in the mammalian olfactory bulb: Domain organisation and odorant structural features. *Nature Neuroscience, 3,* 1035–1043.

Ukkonen, O. I., & Derrington, A. M. (2000). Motion of contrast-modulated gratings is analysed by different mechanisms at low and at high contrasts. *Vision Research, 40*(24), 3359–3371.

Ullman, S. (1979). *The Interpretation of Visual Motion.* Cambridge, MA: MIT Press.

Ullman, S. (1984a). Visual routines. *Cognition, 18,* 97–159.

Ullman, S. (1984b). Maximising rigidity: The incremental recovery of 3-D stucture from rigid and nonrigid motion. *Perception, 13,* 255–274.

Ullman, S. (1998). Three-dimensional object recognition based on the combination of views. *Cognition, 67,* 21–44.

Ungerleider, L. G., & Mishkin, M. (1982). Two cortical visual systems. In D. J. Ingle, M. A. Goodale, & R.J.W. Mansfield (Eds.), *Analysis of Visual Behavior* (pp. 549–586). Cambridge, MA: MIT Press.

Ungerleider, L. G., & Pasternak, T. (2004). Ventral and dorsal cortical processing streams. In L. M. Chalupa & J. S.Werner (Eds.), *The Visual Neurosciences* (pp. 541–562). Cambridge MA: MIT Press.

United States Naval Flight Surgeon's Manual, Third Edition (1991). Naval Aerospace Medical Institute. Available online at: www.vnh.org/FSManual/fsm91.html

Vallbo, A. B., Hagbarth, K.-E., & Wallin, B. G. (2004). Microneurography: How the technique developed and its role in the investigation of the sympathetic nervous system. *Journal of Applied Physiology, 96,* 1262–1269.

van Boxtel, J. J., van Ee, R., & Erkelens, C. J. (2006). A single system explains human speed perception. *Journal of Cognitive Neuroscience, 18*(11), 1808–1819.

Van Essen, D. C., & Gallant, J. L. (1994). Neural mechanisms of form and motion processing in the primate visual system. *Neuron, 13*(1), 1–10.

Van Essen, D. C., Lewis, J. W., Drury, H. A., Hadjikhani, N., Tootell, R.B.H., Bakircioglu, M., & Miller, M. I. (2001). Mapping visual cortex in monkeys and humans using surface-based atlases. *Vision Research, 41,* 1359–1378.

Vaney, D. I., Sivyer, B., & Taylor, W. R. (2012). Direction selectivity in the retina: Symmetry and asymmetry in structure and function. *Nature Reviews Neuroscience, 13*(3), 194–208.

Veldhuizen, M. G., Bender, G., Constable, R. T., & Small, D. M. (2007). Trying to detect taste in a tasteless solution: Modulation of early gustatory cortex by attention to taste. *Chemical Senses, 32*(6), 569–581.

Viemeister, N. F. (1983). Auditory intensity discrimination at high frequencies in the presence of noise. *Science, 221,* 1206–1208.

Viguier, A., Clement, G., & Trotter, Y. (2001). Distance perception within near visual space. *Perception, 30,* 115–124.

Vishwanath, D., & Blaser, E. (2010). Retinal blur and the perception of egocentric distance. *Journal of Vision, 10*(10), 26.

Vogten, L.L.M. (1974). Pre-tone masking: A new result from a new method. In E. Zwicker & E. Terhardt (Eds.), *Facts and Models in Hearing.* Berlin: Springer-Verlag.

Voyer, D., Voyer, S., & Bryden, M. P. (1995). Magnitude of sex differences in spatial abilities: A meta-analysis and consideration of critical variables. *Psychological Bulletin, 117,* 250–270.

Vuilleumier, P. (2005). How brains beware: Neural mechanisms of emotional attention. *Trends in Cognitive Sciences, 9*(12), 585–594.

Wachtler, T., Sejnowski, T. J., & Albright, T. D. (2003). Representation of color stimuli in awake macaque primary visual cortex. *Neuron, 37,* 681–691.

Wade, N. (1983). *Brewster and Wheatstone on Vision.* London: Academic Press.

Wade, N. (2000). William Charles Wells (1757–1817) and vestibular research before Purkinje and Flourens. *Journal of Vestibular Research, 10,* 127–137.

Wade, N. J. (2012). Wheatstone and the origins of moving stereoscopic images. *Perception, 41*(8), 908–924.

Wallace, W. P., Stewart, M. T., & Malone, C. P. (1995). Recognition memory errors produced by implicit activation of word candidates during the processing of spoken words. *Journal of Memory and Language, 34,* 417–439.

Wallach, H., & O'Leary, A. (1982). Slope of regard as a distance cue. *Perception and Psychophysics, 31,* 145–148.

Walls, G. (1963). *The Vertebrate Eye and its Adaptive Radiations.* New York: Hafner.

Wandell, B. (1995). *Foundations of Vision.* Sunderland, MA: Sinauer.

Wang, Q., Klein, E. K., Klein, R., & Moss, S. E. (1994). Refractive status in the Beaver Dam eye study. *Investigative Ophthalmology and Visual Science, 35,* 4344–4347.

Ward, J. (2008). *Synesthesia.* Hove: Psychology Press.

Ward, J., Thompson-Lake, D., Ely, R., & Kaminski, F. (2008). Synaesthesia, creativity and art: What is the link? *British Journal of Psychology, 99,* 127–141.

Warrant, E. J., & Nilsson, D.-E. (1998). Absorption of white light in photoreceptors. *Vision Research, 38,* 195–207.

Warren, R. M. (1970). Perceptual restoration of missing speech sounds. *Science, 167,* 392–393.

Warren, S., Hamalainen, H. A., & Gardner, E. P. (1986). Objective classification of motion- and direction-sensitive neurons in primary somatosensory cortex of awake monkeys. *Journal of Neurophysiology, 56,* 598–622.

Wässle, H. (2004). Parallel processing in the mammalian retina. *Nature Reviews Neuroscience, 5*(10), 747–757.

Watson, A. B. (2013). A formula for the mean human optical modulation transfer function as a function of pupil size. *Journal of Vision, 13*(6), 18.

Watt, R. J. (1988). *Visual Processing.* Hove: Psychology Press.

Watt, R. J., & Morgan, M. J. (1985). A theory of the primitive spatial code in human vision. *Vision Research, 25,* 1661–1674.

Weale, R. (1991). Effects of senescence. In J. Cronly-Dillon, J. J. Kulikowski, V. Walsh, & I. J. Murray (Eds.), *Vision and Visual Dysfunction Volume V: Limits of Vision.* Basingstoke: Macmillan.

Webb, S. J., Monk, C. S., & Nelson, C. A. (2001). Mechanisms of postnatal neurobiological development: Implications for human development. *Developmental Neuropsychology, 19,* 147–171.

Webster, M. A., Georgeson, M. A., & Webster, S. M. (2002). Neural adjustments to image blur. *Nature Neuroscience, 5*(9), 839–840.

Weinshall, D. (1989). Perception of multiple transparent planes in stereo vision. *Nature, 341,* 737–739.

Weiskrantz, L. (1986). *Blindsight.* Oxford: Clarendon Press.

Weiss, E. M., Kemmler, G., Deisenhammer, E. A., Fleischhacker, W. W., & Delazer, M. (2002). Sex differences in cognitive function. *Personality and Individual Differences, 35,* 863–875.

Weiss, Y., Simoncelli, E. P., & Adelson, E. H. (2002). Motion illusions as optimal percepts. *Nature Neuroscience, 5,* 598–604.

Wenger, D. M. (2003) The mind's best trick: How we experience conscious free will. *Trends in Cognitive Sciences, 7,* 65–69.

Werker, J., & Desjardins, R. (1995). Listening to speech in the 1st year of life: Experiential influences on phoneme perception. *Current Directions in Psychological Science, 4,* 76–81.

Westheimer, G. (1975). Visual acuity and hyperacuity. *Investigative Ophthalmology, 14,* 570–572.

Westheimer, G., & McKee, S. (1977). Spatial configurations for visual hyperacuity. *Vision Research, 17,* 941–947.

Wever, E. G. (1949). *Theory of Hearing.* New York: Wiley.

White, J. A., Rubinstein, J. T., & Kay, A. R. (2000). Channel noise in neurons. *Trends in Neurosciences, 23,* 131–137.

Whitfield, I. C., & Evans, E. F. (1965). Responses of auditory cortical neurons to stimuli of changing frequency. *Journal of Neurophysiology, 28,* 655–672.

Wiesel, T. N. (1982). Postnatal development of the visual cortex and the influence of environment. *Nature, 299,* 583–591.

Wiesenfeld-Hallin, Z. (2005). Sex differences in pain perception. *Gender Medicine, 2*(3), 137–145.

Wightman, F. L., & Kistler, D. J. (1992). The dominant role of low-frequency interaural time differences in sound localization. *Journal of the Acoustical Society of America, 91,* 1648–1661.

Wilcox, M., & Hess, R. (1995). Dmax for stereopsis depends on size, not spatial frequency content. *Vision Research, 35,* 1061–1069.

Williams, A. N., & Woessner, K. M. (2009). Monosodium glutamate "allergy": Menace or myth? *Clinical & Experimental Allergy, 39*(5), 640–646.

Williams, R. W. (1991). The human retina has a cone-enriched rim. *Visual Neuroscience, 6,* 403–406.

Wilson, H. C. (1992). A critical review of menstrual synchrony research. *Psychoneuroendocrinology, 17,* 565–591.

Wilson, H. R. (1978). Quantitative characterisation of two types of line-spread function near the fovea. *Vision Research, 18,* 971–981.

Wilson, H. R., & Kim, J. (1994). Perceived direction in the vector sum direction. *Vision Research, 34,* 1835–1842.

Wilson, H. R., Levi, D., Maffei, L., Rovamo, J., & De Valois, R. (1990). The perception of form: From retina to striate cortex. In L. Spillmann & J. Werner (Eds.), *Visual Perception: The Neurophysiological Foundations.* San Diego, CA: Academic Press.

Wilson, H. R., McFarlane, D., & Phillips, G. (1983). Spatial frequency tuning of orientation selective units estimated by oblique masking. *Vision Research, 23,* 873–882.

Wise, R.J.S., Scott, S. K., Blank, C., Mummery, C. J., Murphy, K., & Warburton, E. A. (2001). Separate neural subsystems within "Wernicke's area." *Brain, 124,* 83–95.

Witt, J. K., Taylor, J. E. T., Sugovic, M., & Wixted, J. T. (2015). Signal detection measures cannot distinguish perceptual biases from response biases. *Perception, 44,* 289–300.

Wojciulik, E., Kanwisher, N., & Driver, J. (1998). Covert visual attention modulates face-specific activity in the human fusiform gyrus: fMRI study. *Journal of Neurophysiology, 79*(3), 1574–1578.

Wolfe, J. M. (1998). What can 1 million trials tell us about visual search? *Psychological Science, 9*(1), 33–39.

Wolfe, J. M. (2003). Moving towards solutions to some enduring controversies in visual search. *Trends in Cognitive Sciences, 7,* 70–76.

Wolfe, J. M., Vo, M.L.H., Evans, K. K., & Greene, M. R. (2011). Visual search in scenes involves selective and nonselective pathways. *Trends in Cognitive Sciences, 15*(2), 77–84.

Wong-Riley, M., & Carroll, E. (1984). Effect of impulse blockage on cytochrome oxidase activity in monkey visual system. *Nature, 307,* 262–264.

Wood, R. W. (1895). The "haunted swing" illusion. *Psychological Review, 2,* 277–278.

Woollett, K., & Maguire, E. A. (2011). Acquiring "the Knowledge" of London's layout drives structural brain changes. *Current Biology, 21*(24), 2109–2114.

Wuerger, S. M., Atkinson, P., & Cropper, S. (2005). The cone inputs to the unique-hue mechanisms. *Vision Research, 45,* 3210–3223.

Wurtz, R. H. (2008). Neuronal mechanisms of visual stability. *Vision Research, 48*(20), 2070–2089.

Wyszecki, G., & Stiles, W. (1982). *Color Science* (2nd ed.). New York: Wiley.

Xiao, Y., & Felleman, D. J. (2004). Projections from primary visual cortex to cytochrome oxidase thin stripes and interstripes of macaque visual area 2. *Proceedings of the National Academy of Sciences USA, 101,* 7147–7151.

Xiao, Y., Wang, Y., & Felleman, D. J. (2003). A spatially organized representation of colour in macaque cortical area V2. *Nature, 421,* 535–539.

Xu, X., Bonds, A. B., & Casagrande, V. A. (2002). Modeling receptive-field structure of koniocellular, magnocellular, and parvocellular LGN cells in the owl monkey (*Aotus trivigatus*). *Visual Neuroscience, 19,* 703–711.

Yantis, S. (Ed.) (2001). *Visual Perception.* Hove: Psychology Press.

Yantis, S., & Serences, J. T. (2003). Cortical mechanisms of space-based and object-based attentional control. *Current Opinion in Neurobiology, 13*(2), 187–193.

Yaro, C., & Ward, J. (2007). Searching for shereshevskii: What is superior about the memory of synaesthetes? *Quarterly Journal of Experimental Psychology, 60,* 682–696.

Yeshurun, Y., & Sobel, N. (2010). An odor is not worth a thousand words: From multidimensional odors to unidimensional odor objects. *Annual Review of Psychology, 61,* 219–241.

Yin, T.C.T., & Chan, J.C.K. (1990). Interaural time sensitivity in medial superior olive of cat. *Journal of Neurophysiology, 64,* 465–488.

Yo, C., & Wilson, H. R. (1992). Perceived direction of moving two-dimensional patterns depends on duration, contrast and eccentricity. *Vision Research, 32,* 135–147.

Yost, W. A. (2000). *Fundamentals of Hearing.* San Diego, CA: Academic Press.

Youdelis, C., & Hendrickson, A. (1986). A qualitative and quantitative analysis of the human fovea during development. *Vision Research, 26,* 847–855.

Zachariou, V., Klatzky, R., & Behrmann, M. (2014). Ventral and dorsal visual stream contributions to the perception of object shape and object location. *Journal of Cognitive Neuroscience, 26*(1), 189–209.

Zahorik, P. (2002). Assessing auditory distance perception using virtual acoustics. *Journal of the Acoustical Society of America, 111,* 1832–1846.

Zald, D., & Pardo, J. (1997). Emotion, olfaction, and the human amygdala: Amygdala activation during aversive olfactory stimulation. *Proceedings of the National Academy of Sciences USA, 94,* 4119–4124.

Zarzo, M. (2008). Psychologic dimensions in the perception of everyday odors: Pleasantness and edibility. *Journal of Sensory Studies, 23*(3), 354–376.

Zeki, S. M. (1978). Functional specialisation in the visual cortex of the rhesus monkey. *Nature, 274*(5670), 423–428.

Zelano, C., Bensafi, M., Porter, J., Mainland, J., Johnson, B., Bremner, E., & Sobel, N. (2004). Attentional modulation in human primary olfactory cortex. *Nature Neuroscience, 8*(1), 114–120.

Zellner, D. A., & Kautz, M. A. (1990). Color affects perceived odor intensity. *Journal of Experimental Psychology: Human Perception and Performance, 16,* 391–397.

Zhang, Z., Deriche, R., Faugeras, O., & Luong, Q.-T. (1995). A robust technique for matching two uncalibrated images through the recovery of the unknown epipolar geometry. *Artificial Intelligence, 78,* 87–119.

Zhou, Y., Zhou, T. G., Rao, H. Y., Wang, J. J., Meng, M., Chen, M., et al. (2003). Contributions of the visual ventral pathway to long-range apparent motion. *Science, 299,* 417–420.

Zhou, Y.-X., & Baker, C. L. (1993). A processing stream in mammalian visual cortex neurons for non-Fourier responses. *Science, 261,* 98–101.

Zihl, J., von Cramon, D., & Mai, N. (1983). Selective disturbance of movement vision after bilateral brain damage. *Brain, 106,* 313–340.

Index

Note: italicized page numbers refer to figures and bold numbers refer to tables.